The History of Sligo: Town and County
Vol. I
By Terrence O'Rorke
First published in 1889

Clachan
Publishing

26 Rathlin Road, Ballycastle, BT54 6AQ,
Glens of Antrim.

Clachan Publishing
26 Rathlin Road, Ballycastle, BT54 6AQ,
Glens of Antrim.

Email: ClachanPublishing@outlook.com
Website: http://clachanpublishing-com.
ISBN—978-1-909906-07-5

This edition published 2013

Original edition DUBLIN:
James Duffy and Co., Ltd.,
14 & 15 Wellington Quay. 1889.
Source edition published 1890.

Copyright © of annotated and indexed edition, Clachan 2013

This book is sold under the condition that it is not sold, by way of trade or otherwise, be lent, resold, hired out or in otherwise circulated without the publisher's prior consent in any form of binding or cover other than that in which it is published and without similar condition, including this condition, being imposed on the subsequent purchaser.

THE
HISTORY OF SLIGO :

TOWN AND COUNTY

BY

T. O'ROURKE, D.D., M.R.I.A.

AUTHOR OF
"BALLYSADARE AND KILVARNET"

VOL. I.

A Clachan Republication

DUBLIN :
JAMES DUFFY AND CO., LIMITED
14 & 15 WELLINGTON QUAY

[All rights reserved.]

Content

Content i

ILLUSTRATIONS ix

Editorial x

PREFACE xii

CHAPTER I

THE DISTRICT OF SLIGO 1
Sligo made a separate county—Previously a part of the old county Roscommon—Areas comprised in the county: Tirerrill Corran and Leyney Coolavin Tireragh Carbury—The Erne the northern limit of the county in the 16th century—County irregular in outline; the Coast line—Mountain system—Geological formation of the ranges The Benbulben group—Minerals—Arigna mining companies—Silver and lead mines—Surface of the land—Woods and trees—Multiplication of birds—Pheasants and eagles—Rabbits and deer—Lakes and rivers—The Moy, and the Sligeach or Sligo—The Uncion, or Arrow, and the Owenmore—Lineage of the people—Invasions and immigrations—Consanguinity of present population.

CHAPTER II

BARONY OF CARBURY. 20
Migration of the Carbrians to the district of Sligo—Chiefs of Carbury—Aongus Bronbachall and Bishop Bronus—Chiefs of Carbury continued—Belong to Carbury Sligo, and not to Carbury Teffia, as O'Donovan thinks—O'Donovan's high-handedness—Carbury subject to the Kings of Connaught—Rivalry of the O'Connors and the Cinel Connell.

CHAPTER III

THE TOWN OF SLIGO 26
Beauty of the environs of Sligo—Mountain scenery; Benbulben—The stretch from Knocklane to Dromahair—Carlyle upon the scenery of Sligo—Town of Sligo comparatively modern—Proofs and illustrations—Allusion to the river Sligo in Colgan's *Vita Tripartita*—Battle of Sligo, and the Carrowmore cromlechs—Writer's views on the battle—The battle-field—Route from the north to Connaught Situation of "Grinder", mentioned in the poem on the battle Fearsats or strand passes—Shallowness of Sligo river—The cromlechs and circles of Carrowmore Dr. Petrie's and Mr. Roger C. Walker's views—Two different accounts of Battle of Sligo; Eoghan BelKnocknarea—meaning of name—O'Donovan's and Ven. Charles O'Connor's opinions—Writer's opinion—Confirmation of—

Everything makes for writer's view—Firbolg and Tuatha de Danaan theory utterly improbable—Sir James Ferguson on the Carrowmore Circles—Objections to writer's views answered—No proof of alleged cremation—New view confidently submitted to criticism—Ptolemy's *episemos polis* of Nagnata—This shadowy city unworthy of serious thought.

CHAPTER IV

THE FITZGERALDS AND SLIGO.. 49

No indication of a town in Sligo before the 12th century—Signs of population show themselves in the 13th century—River Sligeach, or Sligo; its shelliness—Puerilities on the subject—Maurice Fitzgerald the true founder of Sligo—He builds the castle—O'Donnell tries to take the castle, but fails—Battle of the Rosses; single combat between Fitzgerald and O'Donnell—Deaths of Fitzgerald and O'Donnell—Sligo in the conflict between the Fitzgeralds and De Burgos—Fitzgeralds and De Burgos reconciled—Fitzgerald and Clarus MacMailin, Archdeacon of Elphin—Foundation of the abbey or convent—Date of foundation; the Marquis of Kildare's mistake—Advantages enjoyed by the convent—Population of town English at this time—A view of the town as it looked under the Fitzgeralds—Sligo then a garrison rather than an ordinary town.

CHAPTER V

THE O'CONNORS AND SLIGO 62

The O'Connors come to the front—Battle of Magh Diughbha, or Crich Carbury—After the battle the O'Connors reside in Castletown—The battle of Crich Carbury disastrous to the O'Connors—Funeral of Donnell O'Connor—Wealth of the O'Connors—The time becomes favourable to them—Divisions in the O'Donnell family—High and commanding qualities of the O'Connors – Hugh O'Donnell's wife a furious Amazon—Cathal O'Connor single handed against all Connaught—Cathal's sons—Cathal Oge O'Connor's exploits—Four Masters unfair to Cathal Oge - *note*—Family feuds of the O'Donnells—Cathal Oge dies in Sligo of the Plague, or Black Death—Bridge of Ballysadare built by Cathal Oge—Heroism of Donnell O'Connor—An ugly blot on his memory—An able and valiant chief—O'Donnell burns Sligo—The town had greatly improved under the O'Connors—Time when the O'Connors became masters of Sligo—Cathal Oge moves from Castletown to Sligo—Proofs of this—Brian and Owen O'Connor—Dissensions in the O'Connor family The O'Donnells thrive on the disunion of the O'Connors—Capture of Sligo Castle in 1370—The castle the occasion of contention—Castle taken—O'Donnell pursues the O'Connors to Belladrehid—Teige Oge O'Connor's new style and title—Manus O'Donnell takes the castle—The English play again the leading part in Sligo—Their policy—Sir Henry Sydney and

Donnell O'Connor—Sydney takes O'Connor to England—Donnell O'Connor submits to Elizabeth—Royal letter in his favour—Sir Donnell evades engagements—Sir Donnell and Sir Nicholas Malby—Sir Donnell a match for the Queen and her Councillors—Had nothing heroic about him—Career of his brother Owen—Owen O'Connor and Bishop O'Hart—Sir Donnell's morality—Status of the O'Connor Sligo family—Perrott's Compositions with Sligo chiefs—Sir Donogh O'Connor—Sir Richard Bingham's efforts against—Commission to inquire concerning Sir Donogh O'Connor's claims—Celebration of marriages in those days—Hugh Roe O'Donnell and Sir Donogh—Rory O'Donnell and Sir Donogh—Submission of Sir Donogh to Mountjoy—Lady Desmond, Sir Donogh's wife—Lady Desmond's children—Her son at Kilmallock—Daniel O'Connor succeeds Sir Donogh—Sir Charles O'Connor—Sir Charles's brother, Donogh O'Connor—Teige O'Connor hanged in Boyle—Lady Desmond brought little luck to the O'Connors.

CHAPTER VI

SLIGO IN THE SEVENTEENTH CENTURY.. 109
Seventeenth century the most eventful in the history of Sligo—English and Scotch displacing the old Irish—Insurrection of 1641—Movements in Sligo—Massacre in the gaol—Explanation of the tragedy—The chiefs had no part in it—Savagery of Sir Frederick Hamilton—His principles—Irruption into Sligo—Burning of Sligo—Sir Frederick impervious to religious feeling—His treatment of Protestants—Sir Charles Coote captures Sligo—Ormonde blames the Confederates Sir R. Stewart Governor of the town.

CHAPTER VII

CONFEDERATE EFFORTS TO RECOVER SLIGO.......................... 121
Archbishop of Tuam tries to recover Sligo—Is defeated and slain—Lord Taaffe tries to recover the body—The Archbishop regarded as a martyr—Extraordinary career of Father Feenaghty—Tries to cure the sick with Dr. Queely's relics—Not certain that he possessed the genuine relics—The place of Dr. Queely's death hitherto unidentified—Most probably he fell in Cleveragh—Owen Roe O'Neill and Sligo—Sligo a thorn in the sides of Royalists and Confederates; recovered by Lord Clanrickarde—Disaffection and divisions among the Parliamentarians—Four independent armies, with different views—Sir Charles Coote summons Sir Garrett Moore to surrender Sligo—Sligo surrenders—Sufferings of Catholics—New Englanders invited to Sligo—County Sligo granted to the Cromwellians—Different classes of Cromwellians.

CHAPTER VIII

THE CROMWELLIAN SETTLEMENT OF SLIGO 136
A Commission to "sett out" the lands of Tireragh and Carbury—The Cromwellians a garrison—Cantoned through the county—They boycott the Irish—Spirit of Cromwellians—Disappearance of Cromwellian families—They erect a new fort in Sligo—People in the dark as to origin of this fort—Sir Albert Conyngham's report upon it—The Cromwellians keep a grip of their lands—Others claim their possessions—The O'Connor Sligo estate—Granted to the Earl of Strafford and Thomas Radcliff—The sons of the grantees—The estate divided—Particulars of the division—Money payments—Schedules annexed to the deed—Benjamin Burton Documents regarding the O'Connor Sligo estate—Report of the Solicitor-General—Clauses in the Acts of Settlement and Explanation—The name of O'Connor Sligo drops out of view—Peter O'Connor and nephews descendants of the old O'Connors Sligo—Character of Mr. O'Connor—A patriot of the best type—Other descendants of the old O'Connor stock.

CHAPTER IX

JACOBITES AND WILLIAMITES.. 156
Persecution in Sligo—Jeremy Jones at the bottom of it—Duke of Ormonde and Jeremy Jones—Movements of the Williamites—Sarsfield falls back on Sligo—Circumstances of Sarsfield's quitting Sligo—Sarsfield retakes the town—St- Sauveur and the Stone Fort—Henry Luttrell in Sligo—His tragic death—Sir Teige O'Regan made Governor of Sligo—Sir Albert Conyngham slain—Sir Teague and Lord Granard.

CHAPTER X

THE TREATMENT OF CATHOLICS 166
State of the country after the surrender of Limerick—Registration of the Clergy—Letters between Dublin Castle and the magistrates of Sligo—Courts of inquiry about nonjuring priests—Depositions of 28th Oct—Depositions of 4th Nov—Priests harboured in Morgan M'Carrick's house—Depositions of Owen Devanny, Matthew Fahy, and Bryan Hart—Depositions of Peter Kelly and Patrick Devanny—Depositions of Teige M'Donnagh and Bryan M'Donnagh—Depositions of William Bourke, Doonamurray—Depositions of Cormack M'Glone and Paul Cunigham, Drynaghan—Depositions of William Ward and Hugh Gallagher, Farrinacarny—Facts to be gathered from these Depositions—Magistrates apply for military aid—Letter of John De Butt, Provost of Sligo—Brigadier-General Owen Wynne examines witnesses—Jeremy Fury, discoverer under Anne's Penal Acts; Laurence Bettridge—Anecdote of the Nugents.

CHAPTER XI

THE ABBEY 178

The Abbey burned down in 1441—Local aid towards its restoration—Apostolic Letters of Pope John XXIII—Prior M'Donogh and Pierce O'Timony, chief local benefactors—The Abbey a singularly beautiful structure—Gabriel Beranger's description of it—Two sides of square nearly gone—Cloisters of great beauty—Sketch taken in 1776—Ambulatory, Pulpit, and Garth—Original portion and restored parts—Convent dedicated to Holy Cross—Curious epitaph—Sir Donogh O'Connor's Monument—Resembles the Earl of Cork's in St. Patrick's, Dublin—Lady Desmond buried with Sir Donogh—The Abbey cemetery, the chief one of the county—Distinguished persons interred therein—Records of the Abbey very meagre—Irish Provincials belonging to Abbey; Thadeus O'Devanny—He secures a convent at Louvain for the Irish Dominicans—Provincial Daniel O'Crean—Another Daniel O'Crean, Provincial; Sir Charles Coote—Provincial John O'Hart—Father O'Hart and Father Peter Walsh—Father O'Hart and popular education—Provincial Ambrose O'Connor—Ambrose O'Connor classed among Dominican writers—Dominicans fly from the Abbey during the scenes of the Popish Plot—Extreme distress of the Conventuals—Obliged to sell their chalices—A dishonest debtor—Prior pays debts with the proceeds of the chalices—Holy Cross bell—Priors of Holy Cross—Prior Andrew O'Crean—Prior O'Crean a special favourite in Sligo—He erects a market cross—Is buried in the Abbey—Fathers Dominick and Felix O'Connor—Father Felix, Prior of the Dominican Convent of Louvain—Dies in Sligo gaol, a victim of the Shaftesbury Plot—Priors M'Donogh, O'Connor (Michael) and Nellus—Very Rev. Dr. Goodman, Provincial and Prior—His eloquence—Builds the fine Church of Holy Cross—Father Boylan places a tablet over his grave—Conflict of claims to the mortuary offerings of the Abbey—A Board of Works restoration of Abbey desirable—Obstacles in the way imaginary—Abbey, the only historical structure now in Sligo—Advantages of restoration—The New Cemetery—Its monuments—Epitaphs—Father Casey's poetic epitaphs—Quaint epitaph in Templeboy graveyard.

CHAPTER XII

THE CHURCH OF ST. JOHN 220
A later church than those of Killaspugbrone and Killinacowen—The style gives no indication of its age—Rectory of Sligo between the Two Bridges—St. John's Church a foundation of Sir Roger Jones—Sir Roger's social standing—His monument—Churches in the rectory before Sir Roger's—Miler Magrath granted the Rectory *Intes Duos Ponyes*—A tergiversator like Talleyrand—King James on Miler's malpractices—Other State Church ministers—Catholic Church without freedom of action—Usurpers of Church property—Congenial work for the Usurpers—Sligo chiefs made Royal Wards—Except Thadeus O'Hara all remain true to the old religion—Succession of Protestant incumbents in St. John's—Rev. Eubule Ormsby—Curates of St. John's—Rev. Messrs. Armstrong and Montgomery—Strandhill Protestant Church.

CHAPTER XIII

THE BOROUGH OF SLIGO 236
Sligo created a borough in 1613—Names of burgesses—James the Second's burgesses—Device of Corporation seal—Sir Francis Leyster—Insignia of the Corporation—Alderman Colleary and the Mayoral chain—The Wynnes and the Corporation—Sligo gentry and the Council—Duties of the Council—The Council and elections—The town of Sligo small and shabby—Thomas Corkran gives an impetus to building—The streets and the scavenging staff—Nuisances in the streets—Public passes to the river—The bridge at the end of Thomas Street—Regulation of the market—Catholics, the helots of Sligo—Orthodoxy of the Council—Mr. Sexton and the Freedom of the Borough—Meetings of the Old and the New Council—Market people—Marketing in the streets—The goods exhibited—Convivialities of the time—Friendly relations of Catholics and Protestants—Change of relations—Dr. Petrie's opinion of Sligo people.

CHAPTER XIV

THE HARBOUR OF SLIGO 257
Sligo Bay—Hollinshed's estimate of the port—Intercourse between Sligo and the Continent—The quays of Sligo—Pier of Ballast quay—Nature deepening the bay—Efficiency of Harbour Commissioners—Merchants of Sligo—Merchandize—Butter merchants and market inspector—Sligo fisheries—Salmon fishery—Enhanced price of fish.

CHAPTER XV

STIRRING OCCURRENCES 267
The Volunteer movement—Meetings and Resolutions of Volunteers—Spirit of the Volunteers—Parliamentary elections—County elections—Wynne and Ormsby election—Incidents of the contest—King and Perceval election—Pasquin on the subject—Loss of life—Origin of the Clearance system—Battle of Carricknagat or Collooney—Tactics of the leaders—Bartholomew Teeling and Colonel Vereker—Heroism of Teeling—Suffering Loyalists—Interesting inquiry at Sligo Smuggling—Invasion of Cholera—Violence of the disease—Terrors of the situation—The Doctors and the Clergy—Right Rev Dr. Burke—Cases and deaths.

CHAPTER XVI 285

STREETS AND HOUSES 285
Look of the town as viewed from the Albert Road—Nomenclature of the streets modern—Explanation of the names—Public buildings; the Cathedral—Court-houses—Magisterial proceedings—Manor and Coroner's courts—Barony Constables—Barny McKeon and Tom M------ The Royal Irish Constabulary—Their concord and brotherhood—The Town-hall—Free library and reading room—Private bankers—Mullen, Black Ballantyne, and McCreery—Thomas McGowan, an interesting banker—Sligo National Bank shareholders—The Infirmary; Dr. McDowel and staff—The Fever hospital—The Famine of 1822—and the hospital Statistics of fever cases—Lunatic Asylum – Dr. Petit and staff Principles of management—Private houses—Water supply—Miss Colleary turns on the water—Hotels of the town—Handicrafts—Emigration – Messrs. Patrick and Peter O'Connor—Messrs. M'Neill and Sons' establishment—Messrs. O'Connor and Cullen's saw mills.

CHAPTER XVII 309

COOLERRA 309
Extent of the district—Its soil and surface—As seen from Rosses Point—Knocknarea—Misgan Meave—Prospect from Knocknarea—The Glen—The Granges—Cairns Hill—Nature of the Cairns—Writer's view on—Ecclesiastical divisions of Coolerra—Dependence of the Sligo district on Tireragh—A relic of Killaspugbrone church-—Dr. Petrie on the age of the church—Kilmacowen church; its patrons—The Cistercians of Boyle and Kilmacowen—Serious error of O'Donovan and his copyists—Captain John Baxter—Coolerra and the Ormsbys—Temple Bree—*recte, Tempul na brugh*—Parish Priest of Kilmacowen and Killaspugbrone—Curious old chapel of Kilmacowen.

CHAPTER XVIII

PARISH OF CALRY 326
The name of Calry—Mistake of O'Donovan—Beauty of the district and of the views from it—Hazelwood—Hazelwood house and demesne—Fine views from—Lough Gill—Archaeological and ecclesiastical memorials—Lake sometimes dangerous—Variations of depth—O'Connors, Creans, and Wynnes successive owners—The Wynne family as landlords and country gentlemen—Different estimates of—Brave act of present representative of the family—The Ormsbys—Willowbrook House—Burglary at Willowbrook—Illicit distillation in – Mrs. Ormsby Gore—A cadet of the Willowbrook family—Castledargan Ormsbys—The Parkes of Dunally—Sir William Parke—Dunally of Coolerra and Dunally of Calry—The Parkes not followers of Strafford as supposed—The Deerpark—Remarkable cashel—Druid's Altar—A singular monument—Opinions as to its nature—Perhaps the sepulchre of Eoghan Bel Aenachs or Fairs—Church theory of the Druid's altar—Writer would connect it with games; the district famous for games—Age of the structure—The Grianan of Calry—Mr. O'Connor and Major Wood-Martin's opinion—Writer's opinion—Description of Greenan Hill.

CHAPTER XIX

PARISH OF DRUMCLIFF 355
THE ROSSES, DRUMCLIFF, AND CASTLETOWN
The Rosses—Rosses Point as a watering place—Interior of the tract—Separation of the Rosses from Magherow—Saints Patrick and Columba in the Rosses—Cattle cures—"Striping" of the Rosses—The place improving under the Middletons—Drumcliffe name of—Glencar, charms of—The Waterfall and Sruth-an-ailan-ard Drumcliffe river and *Inis-na-lainne—Inis-na-lainne* identified—Major Wood-Martin's History would confound it with Inismurray—Writer's view—Glendallan, meaning of—Saints of Glencar or Glendallan—Saint Columba founder of Drumcliffe church—Importance of the place exaggerated—Proofs connecting Saint Columba with the church – Dr. Lanigan's opinion improbable—Annals of the monastery—Families of O'Beollain and O'Coineoil—Drumcliff particularly flourishing in the 13th century—Remains of the monastery—Castletown, a most interesting spot—The cradle of the O'Connors Sligo—Origin of the name Castletown—It is the Caisleu Conor of the Four Masters—Its populousness—Ravaged by Sir Frederick Hamilton—Lands of, pass to the Gores and the Parkes—Qualities of the soil—People comfortable—Botany of Benbulben—Geology of—Fantastic Boar hunt—Professor Hull on the formation of Benbulben.

Index 385

ILLUSTRATIONS

	PAGE	
Stone Circle and Cromlech of Carrowmore	Vol. I.	39
Knocknarea	Vol. I.	43
Sligo Abbey, With Specimen of Cloister	Vol. I.	198
St. John's Church In 1776	Vol. I.	225
Sir Roger Jones's Monument	Vol. I.	229
Old and New Seals of Corporation	Vol. I.	241
Plan of The Deerpark Cashel	Vol. I.	352
Druids' Altar and Triltthons	Vol. I.	353
Maps.		
Map of The Town Of Sligo	Vol. I.	xi
" of The Fearsats or Strand Passes	Vol. I.	35
" of The Carrowmore Circles And Cromlechs	Vol. I.	38

Editorial

A Sligo man by birth, Terence O'Rorke (b. 1819) was both born and had his early education in Collooney. On leaving school he determined to become a Roman Catholic priest and studied in Maynooth College where he was ordained in 1847.

With an aptitude for scholarship, he pursued post-graduate work in Maynooth and was appointed Professor of Theology in the Irish College in Paris.

However, he did not remain there long as pastoral needs in Ireland were urgent, and he was shortly transferred to the position of Parish Priest of Collooney when the position fell vacant on the appointment of Dean Durcan as bishop of Achonry.

He took up this position in 1853 and was to spend most of the rest of his life in Sligo.

Fr. O'Rorke was a very active Parish Priest both pastorally and administratively and saw to the completion of the church tower. Furthermore, he continued to follow his own scholarly interests, especially in the then uncharted area of local history.

In 1878 he published his history of the parish, The History and Antiquities and Present State of the Parishes of Ballysadare and Kilvarnet. He followed this with his two-volume History of Sligo County in 1889.

In writing these works he was very aware of the particular difficulties of a local historian in Ireland compared to the task of the local historian in England or Scotland where there was generally an abundance of local annals, official records, family papers, diocesan archives and a multitude of similar sourse material. However, in Ireland fires, family discontinuities and church suppression had hugely depleted the resources for the community historian, making archives at national level and in London all important.

Archdeacon O'Rorke is buried in the south transept of the Church of the Assumption. The only other person buried in the church is Father Dominic O'Connor C.C. who died of the Famine fever in 1848.

The present text has been derived from the Internet Archive, yet, we realise that the reader expects a much higher standard of presentation and accuracy from a book than does one who browses the web. We have therefore gone to great lengths to enhance and modernise the text to meet the highest standards of accuracy and scholarship.

The scanned text has been carefully proofread to ensure it is accurate and accessible. We have endeavoured to eliminate scanning errors. Some spellings have been modernised and standardised, however the original itself is not always consistent, a fact that probably reflects variable spellings in the source materials. We have done a little to standardize punctuation, but characteristic features of the author's style have been preserved.

We cannot take responsibility for errors that appeared in the original, and of course, the writer's knowledge and views reflect what was known at the time of writing. However, we do have to take responsibility for any errors that may have resulted from scanning and formatting.

All original footnotes have been retained and are unmarked. To make the text more accessible to the modern reader, additional footnotes have been added and these are marked as such. Any text in square brackets [..] has been added by Clachan editors. In addition, a comprehensive index has been created. These enhancements, we feel, make this edition worthy of the original.

Seán O'Halloran, BA, MA, EdD., Editor, November 2020

Acknowledgement

We are pleased to acknowedge and thank Internet Archive and Google books for making a scanned version of the book available on the web, and that the present text has been derived from:

https://openlibrary.org

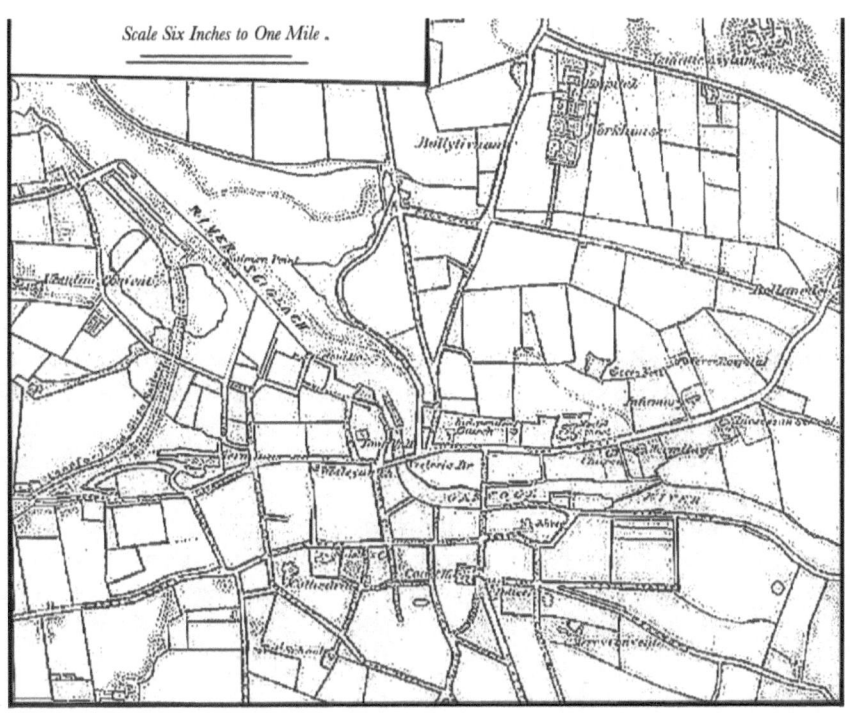

PREFACE

I HAVE tried to embody, in the following pages, the secular, the religious, the social, and, in some measure, the natural history of Sligo. I have spared no pains to collect and verify the facts which belong to the subject under each of these aspects. Knowing the great want of an original and authentic history of the county, and aiming at the supply of the desideratum, I have taken nothing at second-hand, but have gone in all cases for myself to the sources.

Though disposed at first to rely, more or less implicitly, on John O'Donovan[1] and the Ordnance Survey letter-writers[2], I had not proceeded far when, finding them generally unsafe, and frequently misleading guides, it became necessary to trust them, like others, only in proportion to the weight of the evidence which they bring to the support of their opinions. After demurring to the authority of O'Donovan, as to the matter in hand, it is almost superfluous to add that I set little store by his echoists and copyists—epithets which may with justice be applied to those who have written about Sligo since his day.

In saying so much of O'Donovan, there is no wish to question his right to rank, as he commonly does, as our leading modern authority on the topography of Ireland; and if I make bold to differ from him rather often, I do so without questioning the exceptional weight of his opinions in relation to those parts of Ireland, which he had opportunities of studying, an advantage which he never enjoyed in regard to Sligo.

As these pages are meant to be a record of facts, the reader will be little troubled with legends and "the prehistoric ages". It might be well for history, and particularly for Irish history, if there were no such word as pre-historic, the expression is so often employed as a cover for ignorance or indolence. Once the theory is set up that certain things are pre-historic, the student, instead of exhausting patiently and laboriously all the means within his reach, finds it more convenient, on meeting with troublesome difficulties, to fall back on this theory, and to class the object of his search as falling under it, little minding that what is pre-historic for him may be well within the province of history for a more intelligent or a more painstaking inquirer. The Round Towers were pre-historic for all the world till Dr. Petrie demonstrated their origin and uses.

---

[1] John O'Donovan (*Seán Ó Donnabháin*, 1806 –1861), from County Kilkenny, worked in the Ordnance Survey under George Petrie. His edition of *The Annals of the Four Masters*, has been called "the fount and origin from which most of Ireland's subsequent historical commentaries have been derived", [Clachan ed.].-

[2] The Ordnance Survey Letters contain the correspondence between fieldworkers and the Ordnance Survey Office in Dublin during the compilation of the first Irish Ordnance Survey Maps, [Clachan ed.].

It is the opposite presumption, namely, that all the remains of antiquity have their place in history if one could only find it out, that should hold the field. This principle would soon lead to valuable results. With such a rule and stimulus for inquirers, we should very probably have long since learned all about various County Sligo antiquities, which are now commonly consigned to the limbo of pre-historic times, as, for example, the circles and cromlechs of Carrowmore, the remains at Moytura, and that pre-historic relic, par excellence, the Druids' Altar of Calry Deerpark.

And the suggested method would have another precious result. It would stop or curtail the lucubrations[1] of some modern antiquaries who, as if they saw better in the dark than in the light, have little or nothing to tell while dealing with historic time, but positively luxuriate in description and detail once they enter on the fancied region of the pre-historic, where, they take it, no one can follow and check them.

Legends may have their use in the proper place, but history is hardly that place. The more esteemed, recent historians have acted on this principle. John Hill Burton, who is commonly spoken of as the latest and best historian of Scotland, shows, as has been observed by some of his critics, the frankest contempt for Scottish legend, and Dr. Momsen, in his "*Romische Geschichte*", not only ignores the legends of the first book of Livy, but ridicules the principle which induces antiquaries especially to inquire into "what is neither capable of being known or worth the knowing to inquire who was Hercules' mother, as the Emperor Tiberius is said to have done". While eschewing legends I have not thought it right to act in the same way in regard to antiquities. Taken in a wider and better sense than that implied in Momsen's sneer, antiquities comprehend the remains, as well material as moral, of ancient times; so that, in regard to the County Sligo, they comprise its raths, cairns, cromlechs, giants' graves, fortresses, old castles, religious houses; the names and associations of its rivers, lakes, hills, mountains, islands, and wells; and the religion, morals, manners, customs, and pastimes of its inhabitants. As much that belongs to these subjects is capable of being known and worth the knowing, I have studied them carefully; nor, it is hoped, without success, both with respect to themselves and to other matters, as it was in following up clues met with, while investigating them, I came upon the facts and arguments which support the many novel views now put forward in regard to the history both of the town and the county.

For I give a new and, it is believed, the true account of the rise of the town of Sligo; as also of some of its chief buildings, the origin of which has remained up to the present unknown: for instance, the Church of St. John, which is always referred, but erroneously, to pre-Reformation times; the

---

[1] A lengthy piece of learned writing, [Clachan ed.].

stone fort, which stood on the site of the new Town Hall, without anyone being able to tell how or when it got there; and the so-called "castles", which figure prominently in the Depositions of 1641, but which no one has attempted to trace further back. If the reader think it strange that these matters, which do not seem to be very recondite, should have lain so long in the dark, he will be still more surprised to find that the device on the arms of the town, which everybody in Sligo might be expected to understand, has been hitherto a mystery, and is now for the first time explained aright.

In reference to the rural districts of the county, I claim to have been equally fortunate in identifying historical places, which had eluded all previous efforts to identify them; such as, to name here only a few, *Bun Lainne*, misplaced by all our writers "off the coast" of Carbury; *Rath Ard Creeve*, ticketed by our antiquaries and historians as "obsolete;" *Ath Angaile*, of which O'Donovan, in one of the Ordnance Survey letters (Sept. 4th, 1836), writes to Mr. P. O'Keefe: "Do you find a place in the barony of Corran called *At Angaile*? By referring to the annals of Corran you will learn that it was the name of a castle. I have been on the look out for it these five years without success, and if you do not succeed in discovering it, I shall give it up as lost;" the *Dumecha nepotum Ailello* of Tirechan's Annotations in the Book of Armagh, supposed erroneously by commentators on Colgan and the Book of Armagh to be Shankhil], near Elphin; *Aenach Tiroilella*, referred to by the Four Masters under 1397, and mistaken by O'Donovan for Heapstown; *Srah an ferain*, mentioned in the same passage of the Four Masters as connected with *Aenach Tiroilella*; the Grianan of Calry; regarded formerly as the most beautiful spot in the province, but confounded recently with a very common-place little hill near the chapel of Calry; Claragh, the locality in which the Most Reverend Malachy O'Queely was slain by the Parliamentarians; the graveyard in which the kings and princes, who fell in the sanguinary battle of Ceis Corran in 971, were laid to rest; the Church of Bishop Lugid, in which the great Saint Kevin of Glendalough was ordained, and which the Saint's biographers, as well foreign as native, have all failed to find out; and many other places, equally unknown, though perhaps equally interesting.

And what most people will consider a matter of greater importance than the rectification of mistakes about local antiquities, I refute certain grave errors, advanced and popularized by two of the most eminent Irish archaeologists, Venerable Charles O'Conor and John O'Donovan, regarding the religious state of Ireland in the remote past, as I show that the reason on which the former founds his notions respecting Moon worship in the country is an idle fancy, and that the facts, from which O'Donovan tries to deduce the practice of Druidical worship among our ancestors, so late as the sixth century, are misunderstood by him, though if rightly understood, they lend themselves to no such conclusion.

As to the new view of the Carrowmore circles and cromlechs, and the suggested solution of the problem which they present, and at which O'Donovan, Petrie, Lord Dunraven, Sir James Ferguson, and a host of others, have tried the hand, the explanation now offered, if found to be the true one, of which there need be little doubt, must have an important bearing on megalithic remains in other parts of the country, and even in other countries; for if it be once admitted that the rude stone monuments of Carrowmore date from the sixth century of our era, antiquaries will have, what has been hitherto wanting, a term of comparison by which to judge analogous erections elsewhere.

The low date will appear to many an insuperable objection to the view now put forward. Two thousand four hundred and one years is a vast deduction from the age even of Irish antiquities, long-lived as they are supposed to be. Formidable, however, as looks the interval between A.M. 3330 and A.D. 537, there is no occasion to be frightened at it, as it is probably more imaginary than real. Modern archaeologists are fast abandoning General Vallancey and his school of antiquaries, with their antediluvian Irish history, their proofs of Celtic antiquities drawn from the Hindoo Puranas, and their Indo-Scythian monuments of Ireland, such as the so-called temple of Vishnu at Killeshandra in the County Cavan, and the temple of another pagan deity in Inismurray, in our own county, this latter being, according to the General, exactly similar to one in the island of Elephanta, called by the Gentoos, Mahoody! All this is now laughed at; and it is to be feared that a great deal of what still passes for Irish history deserves no better fate, being just as unsubstantial as the Inismurray "Mahoody".

Exaggeration has been the besetting sin of our historians, and this not only to the detriment of Irish history, but to the injury of the people's minds, by filling them with a credulity in regard to historical matters, which has been, and still is, in some cases, ready to swallow all kinds of impossibilities. In particular, everything has been so enormously antedated that, to approximate to correct times, one may strike off from traditional dates thousands of years with as little compunction as the bards and *seanachies* felt in piling them on. Instead of the science and arts and arms which those imaginative writers and their modern follower, Sylvester O'Halloran, love to dilate on as flourishing in pre-Christian times, intelligent students of our national history are now coming to admit, with Strabo, Pomponius Mela, Tacitus, Julius Solinus, Camden, Ware, Sir James Ferguson, and notably Father Innes in his exhaustive "Critical Essay on the Ancient Inhabitants of the Northern Parts of Britain or Scotland", that Ireland in those times was utterly unlettered and barbarous. If the opinions of the learned progress for some time further in the same direction, the outcome before long will probably be, to bring all or nearly all the existing antiquities of the county within the Christian era.

Fuller treatment would confirm the conclusions arrived at regarding the Carrowmore and other ancient monuments, but greater detail was impracticable in a book which is not a monograph on Sligo antiquities, or on any other single department of Sligo history, but a survey of the entire field, presented in a connected narrative—a narrative, too, which aims, within its limits, at completeness, and which, while furnishing special information for the student, contains a good deal to interest the general reader.

While giving antiquities ample room and verge enough, they were not allowed to encroach overmuch on space, which could be better occupied with the more recent and vital facts of our history. These facts, too little known, though full of interest, are given at considerable length. Such are, in regard to secular history, the rise, the rule, and the decline of our chief Celtic families the O'Connors Sligo, the O'Haras, the O'Garas, the MacDonoghs of Tirerrill and Corran, and the O'Dowds and Sweeneys, or MacSweeneys, of Tireragh. To the O'Connors Sligo alone are devoted more than a hundred pages, by no means an undue proportion, considering the preeminent place they occupied in the county from the beginning of the fourteenth to the middle of the seventeenth century; and as to the other families no one will grudge the space assigned them on finding that they produced men, some of whom, as, for instance, Brian MacDonogh of Collooney, and Counsellor Terence MacDonogh of Creevagh, deserve to live for ever in the grateful remembrance of their countrymen.

After the subjection and disappearance of the Celtic chiefs, their lands were parcelled out to Anglo-Irish, English, Welsh, and Scotch grantees the Taafes, Cootes, Coopers, Ormsbys, Joneses, Gores, Parkes, Straffords, and Radcliffs; of all of whom, memoirs, more or less detailed, are given; and as most of those families came in with Cromwell, or made common cause with Cromwell on his arrival, the occasion naturally arose of describing the Cromwellian settlement as it took form in the county, and of noting the principles and doings of the settlers and their descendants.

In regard to religious history: an account is given of the propagation over the county of the Christian religion first, by St. Patrick, St. Columba, St. Finian of Clonard, and other saints; next, by the primitive religious houses; and, later, by the larger, and more regular monasteries, notably those of Boyle and the islands of Loch Ce. In this connection an effort is made to ascertain the means of support possessed by monasteries and churches; and, coming down to more modern times, some light is shed on the State religion in the seventeenth century by examining the character and qualifications for office of those who served its ministry in the county.

As to social history: while the reader will be able to gather for himself, as he goes along, fair notions of the life led in the county at different periods, he will be helped more directly to correct ideas on the subject in the last chapter, which is specially designed to illustrate social conditions, and which, with this object, is arranged under the headings, Religion, Education, Dwellings, Tillage, Morals, The Bucks, Duelling, Local Worthies or Men of Mark, Sligo Newspapers, Roads, Music and Dancing, Holy Wells, Wakes, Popular Sports, The Seanachie, Contrasts, and Retrospect.

The account that is given of local antiquities follows the historical rather than the antiquarian method. The antiquary proceeds by examining the old world object in itself, studying its characteristics, comparing it with other objects of a similar kind, and thus, with the aid of comparison and induction, trying to determine its character and the purpose it was intended to serve. Such inquiries, however, in order to arrive at a trustworthy conclusion, must be exhaustive, and involve too dry and complicated a process for a general history like the present, being suited only for a special treatise. The historian, on the other hand, instead of considering the piece of antiquity in itself, and trying to make it tell its own story, relies rather on external evidence, and examines records to see whether they can cast any light on the object in question. It is in this way the Carrowmore circles and cromlechs are here treated. Thinking that an effort to gather from the dimensions in detail of each and all these structures, the personal circumstances of their builders was about as bootless as one to find out from the shape and sizes of a collection of hats, the history of the hatters, I have troubled myself comparatively little with mere measurements, but, turning away from the objects themselves, have sought their history rather in the annals and other old writings of the country.

For the sake of clearness in the narrative, the baronies are taken one after the other, instead of being carried on abreast; Carbury, as containing the county town, coming first, and receiving fuller treatment than the rest. As the districts, which came in the course of time, and under English law, to be incorporated in the county as baronies, were long unconnected and had separate histories, they could not, with any regard to perspicuity, be handled simultaneously as one whole; for the constant passing and repassing from one barony to another, which would then become necessary in order to maintain some degree of chronological sequence in the relation of events, must inevitably beget confusion. Such a process would only bring together a number of heterogeneous facts without affinity or connection of subject, or other principle of unity the operation resembling not a little that of making concrete, where measures of the different materials intended for the compound are tossed one over the other into the same heap, with the result that the original ingredients soon cease to be either separable or discernible. It might seem invidious to refer to an instance, for which, perhaps, one should not have far to go, of this confused and confusing manner of composing local history; but an example of the method attempted in these pages may be found in Dr. Charles Smith's well known and highly prized county histories, and more especially in that of Kerry, on which Macaulay bestows this extraordinary praise: "I do not know that I have ever met with a better book of the kind and of the size". The materials of this book are drawn for the most part from manuscripts, very little in it being taken from printed books, and nothing at all without independent inquiry. In treating of Sligo, and, indeed, of many other Irish localities, a writer finds his situation very different from what it would be, if he were dealing with places in England or Scotland or the principal countries of the Continent. In the latter cases he would generally have local annals, official records, family papers, memoires *pour servir*, and other such documents, to draw on for the facts of secular history; and, for those of ecclesiastical history, diocesan archives, registers of religious houses, chartularies, synodical acts, reports of episcopal visitations, and a hundred other like aids; but as to Sligo, if we name the meagre records of the Corporation, the Clerk of the Crown's books, and a few pages regarding the banishment of the Dominicans in 1698, written by Father Pat McDonough, the Prior of Holy Cross at that disastrous period, we exhaust the local manuscript sources of Sligo history.

    The destruction by fire in 1416 of the O'Curneen manuscripts of Church Island, Loughgill, occupied, as a matter of course, with the annals of Sligo and Leitrim; the disappearance, in some way not explained, of the records of the Connaught Presidency, which must have contained much of the official history of Sligo in the sixteenth and seventeenth centuries; and the burning, some sixty or seventy years back, by a servant, of a mass of valuable documents belonging to Holy Cross Convent, Sligo, which the stupid man took to be so much waste paper, are a loss to the history of the town and county which it would be hard to exaggerate. Among the Convent papers was, most probably, the Register, which Archdall, in his "*Monasticon*", article, "Cloonymeeghan", tells us existed in Sligo in his day. In the absence of these local helps the inquirer into Sligo history must betake himself to the British Museum, the Public Record Office, the Royal Irish Academy, Trinity College, and similar repositories; and, not finding in such places any connected, narratives of Sligo transactions, he has to wade through oceans of irrelevant matter to fish up here and there the facts that bear upon his subject. All this costs much time and labour; but of course it is only on that condition anything of value or interest can be put together. I have derived hardly any benefit from local traditions. Indeed, the opinions of the present inhabitants of Sligo regarding the antiquities or remote events of the neighbourhood are worth nothing. Whatever may be said of popular ideas on such a subject, as they exist in other parts of Ireland, where there has been no general disturbance of the Celtic population, they are untrustworthy in and round Sligo, owing to repeated removals of the native inhabitants and the substitution of English and Scotch—in their stead these changes destroying the continuity of local opinions.

In proof of this untrustworthiness, let me refer to two or three of the most popular and most firmly believed traditions connected with the town: One is, that the old building which stood on the site of the present Town Hall was an erection of the O'Connors, and that it got the name of "Lady O'Connor's Chair", by which it was popularly known, from a Lady O'Connor, who used to seat herself upon it when she wished to have a good view of the harbour; another is, that the tower, which figures in the arms of the town, represents the round tower of Drumcliff, and signifies that Drumcliff preceded Sligo as the chief town of Lower Connaught; and a third may be stated in the words of the Rev. John Wesley, as they are found in his "Journal" under date of A.B/19 May, 1778; —

> "I now received an intelligible account of the famous massacre at Sligo. A little before the Revolution, one Mr. Morris, a popish gentleman, invited all the chief Protestants to an entertainment, at the close of which, on a signal given, the men he had prepared fell upon them, and left not one of them alive. As soon as King William prevailed, he quitted Sligo. But returning thither about twenty years after, supposing no one then knew him, he was discovered and used according to his deserts".

Such are the most accredited beliefs of Sligo people and others regarding the past; and one may get a good idea of the value to be set on local views when one learns that these accounts, positive and circumstantial though they be, are one and all mere myths, without a particle of fact to rest on. Where a man of John Wesley's ability, and experience, and honesty, is led into error, it behoves others to be on their guard.

No county in Ireland has better claims to careful and painstaking treatment at the hand of writers than Sligo, for, in the whole island, there is no district that contains in a greater degree the elements which give interest to a locality scenery, antiquities, and association with important events. It would be easy, if need were, to bring forward a long catena of first-class authorities in proof of this statement; and, as it is, it may be useful to quote a few of them, if only to show tourists and other strangers the exceptional interest of all kinds possessed by the county:

"Altogether", writes Dr. Petrie in a letter dated Rathcarrick, August 16th, 1837, "this district I might say county is equally interesting to the geologist, the antiquary, and the lover of the picturesque". "County Sligo", says the eminent artist and antiquary, Mr. Wakeman, in an address to the Historical and Archaeological Association of Ireland, "is one of the most interesting localities in the British Isles, containing, as it does, a complete and unbroken series of monuments of all kinds military, ecclesiastical, and domestic from the earliest period known to British history down to the sixteenth century". "The town of Sligo", writes Fraser in his admirable "Hand-Book for Ireland", "is rather romantically situated. Perhaps no town in the kingdom enjoys a more diversified or more picturesque vicinage". "The environs of Sligo", says the Gazetteer of Ireland, "possess great diversity of character, most of the elements of first-rate landscape, several styles of scenic power and beauty, and a large aggregate amount of loveliness, brilliance, and magnificence". "County Sligo", observes Seaton F. Milligan, in a Lecture read before the Belfast Natural History and Philosophical Society, in the Museum, Belfast, on the 1st February, 1887, "is classic Irish soil. Its ancient history, if recorded by another Walter Scott, would lend a charm and an. interest to it, equal to any in Europe. It affords a field of study to the botanist, the painter, and the antiquarian".

Not to carry those references too far, I will cite only one more: John O'Donovan came to Sligo in 1836 to investigate and describe its antiquities for the Ordnance Survey Department, but finding preparations, which should have been made by others, incomplete, he begged Sir Thomas Larcom, the head of the department, to excuse him from going on at the time with the work, pleading the need of delay in these remarkable words: "I think it a pity to spoil so amazingly interesting a county by working in the dark". What, quite as much as these statements, proves the exceptional natural advantages of the county is the fact, that the highest English officials have often tried to acquire for themselves or their families as much of it as they could. Sir William Fitzwilliam procured for his brother, Brian Fitzwilliam, from Elizabeth, a grant of the Abbey of Ballysadare and all its possessions; Sir Richard Bingham plied English statesmen with repeated applications for the rich mensal lands of Ballymote Castle; Sir Charles Coote managed, under the Acts of Settlement and Explanation, to put his brother Richard, afterwards Lord Collooney, in possession of vast stretches of the county, which have since passed by purchase to the Coopers of Markrea; and Lord Strafford, Charles the First's Lord Lieutenant of Ireland, and Sir George Radcliffe, Stafford's relative and colleague in office, contrived, in some way that history has not sufficiently explained, to secure for their sons the great O'Connor Sligo estate, comprising the whole barony of Carbury, with large tracts and chiefries in each of the other baronies.

One will search in vain in any other part of Ireland for a district that can boast of such an array of witnesses to its merits, each witness, too, an expert in the matter on which he testifies. If some counties can compare with Sligo in particular points; if, for example, Wicklow and Antrim can rival it in picturesqueness; Kerry and Donegal though this is hardly the case in monuments of primitive times; the counties on the south and south-east coasts, in stirring events, mediaeval and modern; not one of them all, strong as the assertion may seem, can compare with it in the combination of these and the other attributes which impart to a region the interest which enlarges the mind and stirs the heart.

A Sligo man should be encouraged to investigate and study the past of the country by the great example of those county men who have preceded him in the pursuit. It is hardly going too far to say, that no county in Ireland has rendered such service as Sligo in this respect; for if you put away what was done by the MacFirbises of Tireragh from the thirteenth to the seventeenth century; by Tomultagh MacDonogh, Solomon O'Droma, and Manus O'Duigenan in compiling the Book of Ballymote; and by Ferral O'Gara, to whom Brother Michael O'Clery gives all the credit of the Annals of the Four Masters, you dry up, by the fact, the principal sources of ancient Irish history.

The invasion and usurpation of the Cromwellians, in the middle of the seventeenth century, put a stop to these studies in the County Sligo, so that nothing was done in them by any one from that period down to 1836, when members of the Ordnance Survey staff wrote the Sligo Letters (letters of no great value in themselves), and nothing at all, by a native of the county, down to 1878, when the writer published the "*History of Ballysadare and Kilvarnet*", a volume which, notwithstanding its limited scope and many imperfections, had the effect of turning people's thoughts to our local history.

In accordance with the usages of literary courtesy, though in opposition to his own ungenerous practice of ignoring other people's labours, it is right to mention here Major (now Colonel) Wood-Martin's "History of Sligo", as a local contribution to the history of the county; but having performed this act of duty, and while acknowledging, besides, that the Colonel, aided by his talented collaborateur, Mr. Jones, has done some good work for the neighbourhood by exploring, measuring, and mapping the rude stone monuments of Carrowmore and other places, it must in justice be added, however reluctantly, that the "History of Sligo" altogether fails to justify its title. It is the strong sense of this fact that has led to the present effort. I waited long to see would some more competent hand take up the subject, but finding none moving, I felt a call, in the absence of others, to make what attempt I could to clear away some of the fog in which the History in question has left our "amazingly interesting county." There is still work enough in the field for other labourers; and if what is now written should be superseded by something more worthy of the subject, nobody would be more pleased than the writer with the result. It is a case in which personal considerations should count for little with a Sligo man, when weighed in the balance against the fair fame of his county.

There may be people who will not like to find so many notes in the volumes. To some readers a page charged largely with references, whatever trouble it may have cost the writer, serves only to repel. For this reason the greater part of the quotations would have been omitted if that could be done consistently with the requirements of the case. Being, however, the first to traverse most of the ground gone over, and differing much as to the remainder, from those who had preceded me, I could not expect to have my witness accepted in such circumstances without corroboration from other quarters; and as many of the proofs adduced are drawn from manuscripts hitherto unpublished, and still inaccessible to ninety-nine out of a hundred readers, it became necessary, that people might be able to judge for themselves, to be precise in references, and, in many cases, to set under the eye the *ipsissima verba*[1] of the authorities. This may mar the look of the pages, but it must add in value much more than it takes away in appearance.

Treating of a county in which sectarian and party feelings have run perhaps higher than in any other county of Ireland, and in which people must still tread on the *ignes suppositos cineri doloso*[2], one may be allowed a reference to oneself, which in other circumstances would be justly condemned as egotistic; and, in this connection, I make bold to say, that I am as free, in what I write, from sectarian, party, or personal bias, as John Locke's new-born infant, with the mind clear as a sheet of white paper from impressions of any kind. If then anything here recorded bear hard on individuals or a class, it is from no ill will towards the one or the other, but solely from the obligation, which a writer on historical matters lies under, of telling the truth, irrespective of party or person, of creed or class. With private life I meddle never; but when instances of oppression or one-sidedness show themselves publicly in society, I would not be prevented from noticing and stigmatizing them, even though a friend should come in consequence to be counted the oppressor or the partizan.

Society must prevail over the individual, and truth over friendship *"Amicus Plato, amicus Socrates, sed magis arnica veritas"*[3]. It becomes now my pleasing duty, in concluding these remarks, to make my grateful acknowledgments to Colonel Cooper for obliging me with the use of his valuable MSS. relating to Sligo; and to my clerical friends through the county for the information kindly furnished regarding their respective parishes.

---

[1] Latin for "the very words", a legal term referring to an authority that a writer or speaker is quoting, [Clachan ed.]
[Unless otherwise indicated, as above, all footnotes are as in original [Clachan ed.]].
[2] A quotation from Horace You are treading on fire overlaid by treacherous ashes, [Clachan ed.].
[3] Plato is my friend, so is Socrates, but truth is a friend I prize above both

CHAPTER I

THE DISTRICT OF SLIGO

THE district of Sligo was formed into a separate county in the sixteenth century, at the time when the other existing counties of Connaught were constituted. About the middle of the thirteenth century, if not somewhat earlier, the province was divided into two counties—the county of Connaught and the county of Roscommon[1]—the former lying to the south, and the latter to the north, of a line which stretched from the Shannon to the Atlantic Ocean; and that this line was only ill-defined would appear from Harris's Hibernica[2] where we find the sheriff of Connaught and the sheriff of Roscommon maintaining, each that a certain specified district called Athruim O Many, belonged to his own county. The county of Connaught comprised the present counties of Clare, Galway, and Mayo; while the County of Roscommon took in the existing counties of Roscommon, Sligo, Leitrim, and Cavan, as well as the part of Donegal that lies between the Drowes and the Erne. Ware shows by abundant proofs, taken from the records of the country, that this dual arrangement continued in force down to the year 1565; and there is other evidence, which escaped his notice, that it lasted still longer; for we find Christopher Bodkin, the Archbishop of Tuam, signing, as Queen's Commissioner in Civil Causes, an injunction addressed to the sheriff of the county of Connaught", on the 2nd of October, 1567.[3]

Cox in his *Hibernia Anglicana* leans to the belief that the second division of Connaught into shire land into the shires of Clare, Roscommon, Galway, Sligo, Mayo, and Leitrim was effected by Thomas, Earl of Sussex, who was Lord Lieutenant from 1559 to 1565;[4] a more common opinion, held too by Sir James Ware,[5] is, that it was the work of Sir Henry Sidney, who entered on the office of Lord Deputy in 1565; while others, including O'Flaherty in his Ogygia, ascribe the change to Sir John Perrott, who

---

[1] " In the times of Edward I. and II. Conaught did not contain that whole province, as we now account it; but there was then the county of Conaught, which was but a part of that province, and the county of Roscommon, which is now accounted a part of the province of Conaught". Sergeant Mayart's Answer, etc., in Harris's Hibernica, Part I., p. 68.

[2] Part II., pp. 70-71.

[3] The Episcopal Succession in England, Scotland, and Ireland. By Fr. Maziere Brady, Vol. II., p. 135.

[4] In the time of Lord Lieutenant Sussex . . . Connaught was divided into six counties Clare, Galway, Sligo, Mayo, Leitrim, and Roscommon. . . .And yet some (not without probability) attribute this to Sir Henry Sydney". Hibernia Anglicana, Part I., p. 317.

[5] "Anno 1 565, Sir Henry Sydney divided Connaught into six counties." Harris's Ware, Vol. II., p. 34.

became Lord Deputy in 1584 the fact apparently being, that Lord Sussex originated the project, that Sir Henry Sydney executed it substantially, and that Sir John Perrott confirmed and completed it by his famous Compositions with the Connaught chieftains.[1]

Before the formation of the county Sligo, the areas, now comprised in it, were known as the countries or territories of Tirerrill, Corran, Leyney, Coolavin, Tireragh, and Carbury; names which now designate the baronies of the county. It will not be out of place to examine here for a moment what land these districts anciently contained as territories, and what they now contain as baronies; and, taking them in the order in which they lie in the preceding sentence, it would appear, in the first place, that Tirerrill has undergone little change in the coarse of time as to its contents. It was said of old to extend from the Yellow River of St. Patrick's Mountain to Tir Tuathail or Kilronan—*ab amne flavo Montis Sancti Patricii ad frontem de Tir Tuathail*—and these are the present limits of the barony; for the Yellow River of St. Patrick's Mountain, though not now known popularly by that name, can be no other than the stream which falls from the slopes of Slieve Gamh, and which, at its junction with the Owenmore, near Annaghmore, forms the western limit of Tirerrill. The mountain of Slieve Gamh was called St. Patrick's Mountain after St. Patrick, as he laboured much on it, raised churches on its slopes, and left his name to some of its wells, as, for instance, those of Dromard and Tullaghan. It is stated in an inquisition taken at Sligo on the 25th July, 1607,[2] that twenty quarters of the barony of Tirerrill were incorporated with the county Leitrim at the time of Perrott's Compositions, but with this exception Tirerrill, *recte* Tiroillill the land of Oilill is now in extent what it was in the early part of the sixteenth century, and what, most probably, it was before that time, and ever since it received

---

[1] "It was not until late in the reign of Elizabeth that the province of Connaught was brought under subjection to the Crown and laws of England. The proceedings by which that event was achieved were commenced by the Lord Deputy, Sir Henry Sydney, in A.D. 1575; and completed by a succeeding Deputy, Sir John Perrott, in A.D. 1585". O'Flaherty's West Connaught. By James Hardiman, p. 299.

Mr. Hardiman supports his assertion by a letter of Sir Henry Sydney, addressed to the Council of England, informing that body that he had "divided Connaught (besides the East Breanie or Oreilies and the Annalye or Offeralls countries; into fewer counties; namelye, Sligo, which was a part of Nether Connaught, and Maio, which was another part of the same; Galway, which was called Upper Connaught, and Rossecommon, which was called the Playnes of Connaught".—Ibid.

In the Ogygia O'Flaherty says: "There were six counties constituted in Connaught by Sir John Perrott, when Lord Lieutenant, viz.: Clare, Galway, Sligo, Maio, Roscommon, and Leitrim". Hely's Ogygia, Vol. I., p. 40.

[2] "There is twenty quarters of the barony of Tyre-Irrell in the possession of the countie of Leytrym, since the making of the Composition which the jurors finde by office, warrant, and other good proofes, to be of right parcell of the said county of Sligo". —Inquisition of 25 July, 1607, taken before Sir Anthony St. Leger, Knight, &c.

its present name from Oilill, the son of Eochy Moighmedhoin and Mongfmna.

On the other hand, Corran was much more extensive, as a territory, than it is, as a barony; for "the country called Corann", says O'Flaherty,[1] "formerly comprehended Galenga in the county of Mayo, Lugny and Corann, in the county of Sligo;" and Ware observes on the same point: "Coranna, a Territory, anciently comprehending Galenga (now the Barony of Galen, in the county of Mayo), Lugnia (now the Barony of Leny), in the county of Sligoe), and Coranna (now the Barony of Corrann), in the same county".[2] The contraction of the district is proved too by the old annals of the country; for places which now lie far outside the barony, belonged in ancient times to the territory, as Kilcoleman-Finn, now in Mayo, but of old in Corran,[3] and Cunghill, now in Leyney, but in Corran in the eleventh century.[4]

Leyney too has had its variations of extent. At first, when Cormac Galeng, the ancestor of the O'Haras and O'Garas, got possession of it, in the third century, the district of Corann or Coranna received the new name of Leyney or Luighne, in honour of Luigh, the son of this Cormac, and continued to retain the name, as an alias one, for several centuries. During this period places which certainly lay within the ancient territory of Coranna, as already defined, were said to be in Leyney. Under the year 1225 we read in the Four Masters that "Hugh O'Conor and the English pursued the sons of Roderic that night to Meelick, and for three nights afterwards continued plundering Leyney in all directions;" this plainly implying that Meelick and the neighbourhood of Meelick formed part of Leyney at the time. And under the year 1253 we are told by the same authority that "a monastery for Dominicans was founded at Ath-Leathan (Ballylahan), in Leyney"; and though John O'Donovan, in a note to this entry, ventures to affirm, that, "the Four Masters are wrong in placing this in the territory of Leyney, for it is certainly in the ancient territory of Gailenga, O'Gara's original country", still it is certain that it is O'Donovan himself who is tripping, and not the Four Masters; for not only in the Four Masters, but in all our old authorities, the diocese of Achonry, which included then, as it does now, the district of Galen, is styled the diocese of Leyney, and the

---

[1] O'Flaherty's Ogygia—Hely's translation—Vol. II., p. 236.
[2] Harris's Ware, Vol. II., p. 48.
[3] Dermot, the son of Roderic O'Conor, took the house of Hugh, the son of Manus O'Conor, at Kilcoleman-Finn, in Corran.—Four Masters, A.D. 1212.
[4] A battle was fought between Rory O'Conor, King of Connaught, and Hugh, son of Art O'Ruairc, at Conachaill, in Corann". Four Masters, 1087. On this entry O'Donovan remarks, in a note: "Now Cunghill, a townland in the parish of Achonry, barony of Leyney, and county of Sligo".

bishops of Achonry, the bishops of Leyney[1] nay, this very writer admits as much in another place; for, in a note in the Book of Rights,[2] he lays it down that the territory of Leyney and the territory of Achonry diocese are exactly identical.

Coolavin is not so old a denomination of territory as Tirerrill, Corran, or Leyney, and therefore the region, designated by it, has not been so liable to vary in extent. The ancient name of the district was Greagraidhe; but Coolavin did not, and does not, include as much land as Greagraidhe; for a considerable tract in the north of the present county Roscommon belonged to the latter district.[3] In other respects Coolavin has gained rather than lost, for it now includes part of Kilcoleman, which of old belonged to Corran.

Tireragh has lost much of its ancient extent. Always a most important portion of Hy Fiachrach, with which, however, it must not be confounded, as it was only a part of that extensive region.[4] Tireragh, or Hy Fiachrach of the Moy, stretched at one time from the Moy to the Erne. O'Donovan makes the Drumcliff river the oldest northern limit of this territory, but it is clear from the *Chronicon Scotorum* that it extended at one time all the way to the Erne, as this river is there set down as the boundary between the Fiachrach and Cinel Conaill.[5] Later, the Codnach, the river which discharges itself into the bay of Sligo at Drumcliff".6—became the extreme limit towards the north; and this river is set down in the

---

[1] Four Masters, A.D. 1213, 1218, 1226, 1236, &c. And Ware says: " In the ancient Annals of Ireland, the Prelates of this See for the most part are called Bishops of Luigny or Leny". Harris's Ware, Vol. II., p. 58.

[2] O'Donovan clearly contradicts himself on this subject; for while he writes in one place (Battle of Magh Rath, p. 252): "The ancient territory of Luighne is co-extensive with the present barony of Leyney, in the county of Sligo, in which the name is still preserved", he states in another: "The exact limits of their territory" (the Luigne) "are preserved in those of the diocese of Achadh Chonaire (Achonry), in the counties of Sligo and Mayo". Book of Rights, p. 103. According to this, then, the exact limits of the Luighne territory would be, at once, those of the present barony of Leyney, and those of the present diocese of Achonry, though the diocese is about three times the extent of the barony! Bonus aliquando dormilat! [sometimes even the good nod off – Clachan ed.].)

[3] Greagraidhe, now ridiculously called " The Gregories", a district in the south of the county of Sligo, supposed to be co-extensive with the barony of " Coolavin;" but it was originally much more extensive. O'Donovan 's note to "Book of Rights, "p. 99.

[4] Along with Tireragh, Hy Fiachrach included Tirawley, the district of Ceara, in the county of Mayo, the Hy Fiachrach Aidhne (co-extensive with the diocese of Kilmacduagh) the Cineal Aodha, na h-Echtghe (in the south-west of the county Galway) and Killovyergh, in the north western portion of the barony of Kiltartan, in Galway.—Tribes and Customs of the Hy-Fiachrach, p. 3.

[5] Chronicon Scotorum. By W. M. Hennessy, page 7. "Samoir between the Fiachrach and Cinel Conaill". Samoir was an old name of the river now called the Erne.

[6] O'Donovan's note in Tribes and Customs of Hy'Fiachrach, page 302.

Topographical poems of John O'Dugan,[1] and Giolla Iosa Mor McFirbis,[2] as the bound of the district in this direction. Even before the time of Giolla Iosa Mor McFirbis, Tireragh had shrunk up to Ballysadare river "the beauteous stream of salmons"[3] and on reaching that river, in his description of the territory, Giolla Iosa himself, notwithstanding his partiality as local bard, admits virtually that the land which lay beyond the "stream" does not belong to Hy Fiachrach, but belongs to Carbury:

> *"Let us pass into Carbury of the battles,
> Let us leave the soil of Hy Fiachrach".*[4]

By the pressure of the O'Rorkes and others the northern limit was forced still further back, on to the Beltra Strand; for the Four Masters tell us of Brian Ballagh O'Rourke, who died in 1562, that "his supporters, fosterers, adherents, and tributaries extended .... from Granard in Teffia to the Strand of Eothuile the Artificer, in Tireragh of the Moy".[5] And the Strand continued to be the bound of the territory, till baronies were formed, as it is, and has been all through, the bound of Tireragh as a barony.

The district of Carbury was of different dimensions at different times. In remote times it comprised Lough Melvin, for the Four Masters state that when the grave of Melghe Molbhthach was digging, "Lough Melghe burst forth over the land in Carbury;"[6] and we learn from the Tripartite Life of St. Patrick that Crich-Conaill, belonged at that time to Cairbre as far as Rath-Cunga,[7] a tract of about five miles in width. In O'Dugan's Topographical Poem there is mention of "the two Carburys", which shows the district was then divided; and though the writer supplies no means of knowing the extent or position of each division, we may with great probability conclude that "the two Carburys" of the poem coincide, or nearly coincide, with the Upper and Lower Carbury of recent times; the former stretching from Belladrehid to Kilsellagh river, and the latter from the Kilsellagh to the Duff river.

---

[1] "From the Codhnach of gentle flood,
The mark of the boundary
To the boundary of the Rodba, to be mentioned.
It is a beauteous perfect territory.
Of the illustrious race of Fiachrach".—Tribes and Customs of Hy Fiachrach, page 279.
　　"From the Rodba of prosperous course
I have bravely pursued my career
To the Codhnach of winding current". Ibid.
[2] Tribes and Customs of Hy Fiachrach, p. 275.
[3] Ibid.
[4] Ibid
[5] Annals of the Four Masters, A.D. 1562.
[6] Ibid., A.M. 4694.
[7] Tripartite Life of St. Patrick. Translated from the original Irish. By W. M. Hennessy, in M. F. Cusack's Life of St. Patrick, page 434.

The plain of the Moy or Magh Ene, on the south bank of the river Erne, was commonly regarded in the past, as part of Carbury, though there is respectable authority for considering it to have been a portion of Tirconnell or Donegal. As the northern limit of Carbury and the northern limit of Connaught coincided, there is the same diversity of opinion in regard to it under the one respect and the other, Connaught writers generally making the Erne the limit, and Ulster writers, the Drowes.[1] In forming the county Sligo, in the sixteenth century, the Erne was made the northern boundary, though, later, the Drowes was substituted as such: apparently with the object of allowing the counties of Fermanagh and Leitrim direct access to the seaboard, as may be inferred from a petition on the subject, which certain Undertakers, or would-be Undertakers, addressed during the Plantation proceedings of Ulster to the Commissioners of Plantation, and which opens as follows:—"Right Honourable—The 40 Undertakers whose names are hereunder written, are petitioners for a grant of that small part of the county Sligo, now in the King's hands, which lies between the end of Lough Erne and the sea; as they intend to have a market town on the south side thereof at Ballike, and from thence, three miles nearer the sea, to erect a strong corporation. This part of Sligo contains about three miles being a piece of ground very convenient adjoining the sea, for the necessary use of the inhabitants of that corporation for bringing in or transporting their commodities".[2] Whether it was this representation or some other consideration, that influenced the Government, the northern limit of the county Sligo, as well as of the barony of Carbury, was moved, soon after the receipt of the Undertakers' petition, from the Erne to the Drowes, and later to the Duff river, where it remains. The county then is bounded on the south-west by the county Mayo; on the north-west by the Atlantic ocean; on the north by the Atlantic and the river Duff; on the east by the county Leitrim; on the south-east by the county Roscommon; and on the south by the counties Roscommon and Mayo. As to latitude and longitude, the bay of Sligo lies 54°20' north latitude, and 8°40' west longitude; Sligo town 54°10' north latitude, and 8°25' west longitude; and the centre of the county 54°10' north latitude, and 8°35' west longitude.

---

1 For the Erne we have the *Chronicon Scotorum* (page 7). The Annals of Loch Ce agrees with the Chronicon Scotorum, and makes the northern and southern limits of Connaught to be, respectively, the Erne and Slieve Eichte.—Hennessy's Annals of Loch Ce, A.D. 1316.
For the Drowes on the other hand we have Colgan who writes, "*Magh Ene est campus Tirconnalliae ad australem ripam fluminis Ernei inter ipsum et Drobhais fluvium protensus*". —Trias Thaumaturga, page 180.
The Four Masters are at one time for the Drowes and at another for the Erne, according, probably, to the source from which they draw their information.—See years 1137 and 1597.
2 Calendar of State Papers of James I. Edited by Rev. C. W. Russell, D.D., and John P. Prendergast, Esq., vol. 2, page 315.

Though one would be inclined to infer from an inquisition taken at Sligo, in 1607, before Sir Anthony St. Leger, declaring the length of the county, from the Curlews to the river Erne, to be 40 miles, and the breadth from Ballifernan to Bellaghy, to be 40 miles, that the county is a square, the inference would be quite erroneous, for there is hardly a county in Ireland more irregular in outline. To reduce it to some symmetry it would be necessary to cut off, on the south, most of the barony of Coolavin, which runs in between Roscommon and Mayo; on the north, as much of the barony of Carbury as lies below a line running from Coney Island through Drumcliff, to the county Leitrim; on the east, the parishes of Shancoe and Kilmactrany in the barony of Tirerrill; and, on the west, the parishes of Easky, Kilglass, Castleconor, and Kilmoremoy, in the barony of Tireragh. Even with this adjustment there would still remain much zig-zag in the outline, not only along the sea coast, where the indentations are frequent and, sometimes, notable, but also inland, at some of the points where Sligo touches the adjoining counties.

The coast line, from the mouth of the Moy to that of the Duff, is sinuous and varied both in contour and elevation. The sea line is diversified not only by the three deep estuaries of Ballysadare, Sligo, and Drumcliff, but also by the mouths of several little rivers the Fined, Ballybeg, Easky, Dunneill, Skreen, Portavad, Kilsellagh, Carney by the headlands of Lenadoon, Aughriss, Raghley, Knocklane, and Mullaghmore; and by the minor points of Cloghagh, Leckacurry, Rathlee, Kinnasharnagh, Carrownrush, Carrickadda, Pollnagat, Carrownabinna, Lackaverna, Donagh, Lackmeeltaun, Rinnadoolish, Streedagh, and Rosskeeragh; while, as to elevation, the coast rises abruptly in some places at Aughriss, Knocklane and Mullaghmore; shelves off from the land, along a great part of the Tireragh shore, and, in Carbury, from Aghaphreghan to the mouth of the Drowes; sinks into flat strands at the mouth of the Moy, Dunmoran, Beltra, Coolerra, Bomore, Trawnavannoge, Trawativa, and Bunduff Strand; and slopes down gently and gradually to the water's edge in parts of Tireragh, at Beltra and Streamstown in Leyney, near Sligo on both the right and the left bank of the river, and at some other points in Carbury. This great variety in the sea line and the surface line of the coast, unlike the sameness, often met with elsewhere, is most pleasing to the eye, which, wherever it turns, finds new combinations of the picturesque.

Mountain scenery is so prevalent in the landscape, that almost wherever you happen to be, if you look about you, you will find yourself surrounded, or apparently surrounded, by mountains. The mountain system of the county forms to the eye, allowing for a few breaks, the figure of 8, or two connected circles, one superimposed on the other. The upper part of the figure is traced by the Ox Range, Slieve da En, Braulieve, the Curlews, Bockagh, and Mullaghnoe in the county Mayo, and contains the baronies of Corran, Leyney, Tirerrill, and the half barony of Coolavin; while the lower portion of the figure has its counterpart in Slieve da En and the Ox Range, as they are seen from the north, Knocknarea, Benbulben and the other hills of the Benbulben group together with the Donegal mountains, which, though belonging to another county, blend so naturally with those of Sligo, as to appear a continuation of them. This second circle encloses the baronies of Tireragh and Carbury. These elevations are of various altitudes the highest point of the Ox Range, above the level of the sea, being 1778 feet; of Slieve da En, 967 feet; of Braulieve, 1396; of the Curlews, 1062; of Cashelgal and Coologeaboy, 1430; of Knocknarea, 1078; of Benbulben, 1721; while the ridge of Slieve Lugha, including Bockagh (745 feet), and Mullaghnahoe (775 feet), is scarce bold enough to be dignified with the name of mountain.

The geological formation of these ranges varies. Slieve da En and the Ox Range are primitive, metamorphic, and volcanic rocks, composed of quartz, mica slate, gneiss, crystalline greenstone, but in different proportions and combinations, at different parts of the range; a narrow strip of old red sandstone runs along the sides of the range; while beyond this strip lies the floetz limestone, which permeates most of the county, running through the whole seaboard, from the Moy to the Duff, as well as through the baronies of Tirerrill, Leyney, and the greater part of Corran the stone, along the shore, in the parishes of Skreen and Ballysadare, being of prime quality, both as to the thickness of the strata and the texture of the grain, so as to supply material fit either for the blocks of a breakwater, or for articles of *vertu*; portions of it being susceptible of the finest carving and the richest polish. The Braulieve mountain, which forms the chief part of the Connaught Coal-field, contains the usual strata of the Coal Measures; millstone grit, limestone, and coal, etc. Mr. Kinaban[1] gives the following as the contents of a :—

---

[1] *Manual of the Geology of Ireland.* By G. Henry Kinahan, M.R.I. A. , etc. p. 121.

GENERAL SECTION OF THE CONNAUGHT COAL-FIELD

MIDDLE MEASURES		Upper Rocks	over	400 feet
	III	Kelve	about	1 foot.
		Intermediate Beds		50 feet.
	II	Coal		3 feet.
		Intermediate Beds		50 feet.
	II	Kelve		3 feet.
		Lower Beds		96 feet.
				603
	LOWER MEASURES			600
				1,203 feet

The Curlews and, more especially, the Sligo side of them, are supposed to consist of the Old Red Sandstone, which also passes down from the east end of them, for some distance, along the western shore of Loughs Ce and Arrow; but Mr. Kinahan in his *Geology of Ireland*[1] holds the formation is not true Old Red Sandstone, but limestone of the Burren type.

The same authority characterises Benbulben and the adjoining hills as Limestone Hills, and fixes the contents of a section as follows:
"4. Sandstones, the lowest beds of the coal measures.
3. Pale grey limestone, with magnesia limestone bands.
2. Thin bedded black shaly limestone, with magnesium limestone bands.
1. Olive, grey, and whitish sandstones, with black slate partings".[2]

Though Knocknarea lies to the south of the Sligo river, while the Benbulben hills are to the north, its geological formation seems to be the same, so that it may be set down as Burren limestone, or, as this formation is commonly called in England, mountain limestone.

It will come with surprise on many to be told that the Benbulben group of hills lay for ages at the bottom of the ocean, and that, vast as these ranges are, they are composed in large measure, like the Coral Islands of the South Sea, of fossil shells and shell-fish. And yet there is no room for doubt on the subject; for various specimens of the stone, when examined under the microscope by competent judges, exhibit unmistakably this composition. Professor Hull, an authority second to none on the geology of Ireland, bears witness after careful personal examination and study, that "the formation, notwithstanding its great thickness, must be considered as the work of marine animals, which lived in the waters of the clear ocean of the Carboniferous period, generally far removed from land, and uncontaminated by muddy or sandy sediment".[3]

---

[1] Ibid., p. 82.
[2] Ibid., p. 83.
[3] J Hull's Physical Geology of Ireland, p. 33.

It was long supposed that coal might be found in several parts of the Ox and Slieve da En mountains. This opinion, becoming generally known, brought scientific and practical coal miners to the place, who after making careful and extensive searches, and finding no trace or indication of coal, concluded there was no ground for the popular belief.

Iron stone exists in the mountains of Kilmacley; in a tract lying between Dromahair and Ballintogher; as well as on both banks of the Arigna river, and in other places. The Kilmacley mine was worked by a Mr. Rutledge "till all the woods of the country had been burned out and carried to Foxford, where he had iron works".[1]

In 1816, the well-known Jack Taaffe, who had recently purchased a large stretch of the Ox mountains, discovered what he took to be a valuable slate quarry on the property. The Reverend Mr. Neligan was then drawing up his *Statistical Account of Kilmactigue*, and sharing Mr. Taaffe's views of the quarry, reports it as capable of yielding slates six feet long, of any thickness required, of a close hard grain and blue colour, and so easily worked that "two intelligent hands could produce one thousand pounds' worth of slates in a month".[2] This promising find, which was to enrich its owner, and diffuse benefits of all kinds throughout the neighbourhood, ended, like so many others of the time and kind, in disappointment and loss.

An incomparably greater failure and loss resulted from the Arigna Collieries and Iron Works, about which, though belonging less to the county Sligo than to the neighbouring counties of Roscommon and Leitrim, a word or two may be said. The Iron Works were started in 1788 by three brothers of the name of O'Reilly, who soon incurred such losses that they had, first, to mortgage and, ultimately, to sell the property to the Messrs. Latouche, the famous bankers of Dublin, who had advanced to the O'Reillys large sums of money. One of the Latouches, thinking the concern a promising one, purchased from the bank the interest which the O'Reillys had parted with, and set to work single-handed with great energy and unstinted outlay, but with the result, which is well brought out in the following anecdote, as told by Isaac Weld, in his admirable Survey of the County Roscommon: "I well remember taking a ride with that excellent and kind-hearted man, Mr. Latouche, at a venerable period of his life, and on stopping before a large iron gate, in his beautiful park of Bellevue, being asked, whether I had ever before seen so costly a piece of workmanship? The gate was a spacious and goodly one, but there was nothing extraordinary in its appearance. 'I see you are hesitating, sir,' said the good old gentleman; 'and yet I can venture to assert that you never before saw a gate which cost the owner so much. That gate, sir, cost me £80,000, for it

---

[1] Doctor McFarlan's Statistical Survey of County Sligo, p. 10.
[2] Statistical Account of Ireland, Vol. II., p. 315.

is the only thing I ever got out of the Arigna Iron Works, in return for all my money expended there.'"[1]

It was in 1818, Sir Richard, or as he then was, Mr. Richard Griffith's report on the Connaught coal district was published, and as the paper spoke very favourably both of the coal and iron of the district, speculators were set in motion, so that in a year or two three different companies, the Arigna Coal and Iron Company, the Irish Mining Company, and the Hibernian Mining Company were in the field. The Hibernian Mining Company soon retired, having inferred from some experiments, which they prudently made, that they could not work with any prospect of remuneration; the Irish Mining Company continued raising and selling coal on a small scale for several years; while the Arigna Coal and Mining Company, after a series of fraudulent proceedings, hardly to be surpassed in the unsavoury history of joint-stock companies, after robbing their shareholders and demoralising the neighbourhood, collapsed disgracefully, pretending to suspend, but in reality, closing their operations.

There is little prospect of these coal fields being worked on any large scale with profit. It might be otherwise if Sir Richard Griffith's estimate, that the principal seam is three feet inches thick, were well founded, but instead of that, eighteen inches or thereabouts would seem to be much nearer the truth.

The expense of extracting the mineral from this thin seam is so great, that a ton of the large coal would cost perhaps as much at the pit's mouth, as a ton of Scotch coal at the quay of Sligo; and the consequence is, that the produce of the Arigna Collieries is rarely seen at present beyond the immediate neighbourhood, except in the shape of culm,[2] a cart of which may find its way occasionally to a lime-kiln at a considerable distance from the pits. Meantime, however, the mine is feebly worked to supply the demand of persons who live near it, but so remote from Sligo, where English and Scotch coals are sold, that the cartage would equal or exceed the price of the coal.

There is a silver and lead mine on the northern slope of the Ox Mountains, in the parish of Ballysadare, another at Abbeytown, in the same parish, and a third upon the very Harbour mouth of Sligo, "in a little demy-island commonly called Coney Island",[3] this last being the only one of the three mentioned by Boate, in his *Natural History of Ireland*, as if the others were unknown to him.

It does not appear that the Coney Island mine was ever worked, though the other two were, in the last century, the scenes of extensive operations, judging by the great quantity of debris which lies scattered upon

---

[1] Weld's Survey of County Roscommon, p. 38.
[2] coal dust; 1. slack. 2. anthracite, especially of inferior grade, [Clachan ed.].
[3] Thorn's Tracts and Treatises, Vol. I., p. 115.

them. In his *Tour in Ireland*, Arthur Young writes of the Abbeytown mine, "Near Ballysadare is a lead mine, but not worked with success, though very rich", People say that the works were carried on as long as there was timber in the neighbourhood for smelting, and that they were discontinued only when this fuel failed".

There is reason however to think that the poverty of the mine had a good deal to do with its abandonment. A few years ago, on Mr. Middleton purchasing Abbeytown, he sent over various specimens of the ore to England to have it tested, with a view to working the concern vigorously, in case the experiment warranted him, and on the trial leaving things doubtful, he sank a shaft of sixty or seventy feet, in search of a richer vein than any that showed itself near the surface, but failing to find it, he gave up the undertaking: a pretty satisfactory proof, when one takes into account his great intelligence and energy, that the mine under present circumstances is too poor to pay. It may still be hoped, considering the large tracts of the county in which the silver and lead appear, that veins will be one day found rich enough to warrant their working.

Minerals of other kinds are known to exist through the county: copper in the Ox Mountains, manganese in the Slieve da En range, garnets in the neighbourhood of Lough Esk, and asbestos on the confines of the county of Leitrim.

The surface of the county has quite changed in appearance within the last two centuries. The whole county was little better than a wilderness in the closing years of the 17th century. What the French Officers said of parts of Ulster in 1689, that a march through it was like "travelling through the deserts of Arabia", was quite true of the county Sligo, which had suffered more than most other places from the ravages which followed the insurrection of 1641. Since that time everything has been altered—Pestilential swamps have, by draining and cultivation, become rich tillage land, producing luxuriant root and cereal crops; extensive tracts which grew nothing but heath and furze are now covered with the sweetest and greenest of grasses; and from a county which struck the traveller, so late as the first years of the present century, as particularly destitute of trees and shrubs, Sligo has become perhaps the best timbered county in Ireland. If Wakefield who, in his *Account of Ireland*, writes, "On the 11th of September, 1809, I went to Nymphsfield through Sligo and Ballisodare, but I observed no trees during the whole course of the way", could now revisit the place, there is probably nothing, among all the great changes which have occurred, that would strike him so forcibly as the profusion of timber on all sides.

Woods are given, in writings of the seventeenth century, as then existing here and there on the skirts of the Ox Mountains, and of the Slieve da En range, round the Curlews, and along the northern shore of Lough Gara; but much of it is spoken of as "firewood;" and it is certain that the trees which grew in these places were small in number and size, as compared with those which may be now seen in Union Wood, and Slish Wood; the demesnes of Markrea, Annaghmore, Templehouse, Hollybrook, Hazelwood, and Lissadell; and in other places, where the gnarled oak, the spreading beech, and the stately ash, reach their fullest perfection.

Trees in vast numbers have been cut down of late in those places and removed. For about twenty years, carts have been constantly on the roads of the county, carrying off timber from woods and demesnes to the Bobbin Mill of Messrs. McNeill in Sligo, to Mr. Glynn's Chemical Works at Collooney, to Mr. Anderson's Saw Mill, Sligo; to Messrs. Manly's Saw Mill at Collooney, and to other places; and still this enormous consumption has not diminished the supply very sensibly, at least to the eye of the casual observer. Except in one or two cases, planting, to supply the place of the timber removed, is not practised to the extent it ought. Colonel Cooper has planted large tracts on the south side of Slieve da En, on the Ox Mountain, at Derreens, the Sessus in the parish of Cloonacool, and the neighbourhood of Lough Esk, and here and there in Union Wood, Ballygawley Wood, and the demesne of Markrea; the number of trees planted in these places within the last twenty years, reaching at least a million and a half. Mr. O'Hara, too, has planted a good deal in his demesne of Annaghmore.[1]

---

[1] The following are the dimensions of some of the largest existing trees in the county:

MARKREE DEMESNE.

Species.	Girth at surface of Ground. feet.	Girth at four feet high. feet.
1. Ash	25¼	15¾
2. Ash	21	14
3. Ash	18	12
1. Beech	23	15½
2. Beech	22	14
1. Elm	19½	13½

The following are the dimensions of some of the largest existing trees in the county:

TEMPLEHOUSE DEMESNE.

Species.	Girth at surface of ground. feet.	Girth at four feet high. feet.
Flowering Ash	16	10
Common Ash	15	9
Copper Coloured Beech	10	8
Cedar of Libanus	13	7

CLOONEMAHON DEMESNE.

Ash	19½	12-5½ in.

ANNAGHMORE DEMESNE.

Beech	18	15
Fir	15	12
Ash	14	10
Oak	12	9

As a matter of course, the security and shelter of plantations have led to the multiplication of such singing birds as blackbirds, thrushes, linnets, finches, &c.; and it is hard to tell whether the student of nature is more struck by the sights or by the sounds which he meets with in his rambles through the groves of the county. The scenery in some of these tracts is varied and beautiful hills and shady dells, crags covered with coppice wood or enamelled with wild flowers, alternating with stretches of full grown forest trees.

The eagles which used, a couple of centuries ago, to frequent the peaks of Benbulben and the Ox Mountain have nearly disappeared. Mr. Sibery, junior, has shot three of them in his time; and last year (1887), another was seen, which must be still at large. Hawks are diminishing greatly in numbers, and abandoning their haunts, though some of them still retain possession of *Carrig-na-shouk* the hawk's rock near Coolany; and if man or boy comes near the rock, they are sure to sally forth from their eyrie on the face of the precipice, and to keep whirling round high up in the air, screaming and clattering till the intruder has taken himself away out of their sight, and left them again in quiet occupation of this their immemorial retreat.

While these formidable and hardy birds are dying out, pheasants, introduced in the county about a dozen years ago, are multiplying in our woods and demesnes. When Wakefield wrote his *Account of Ireland* in 1812, there were no pheasants in the country except a few "in a coop at the seat of Lord Bantry, and some in Lord Roden's park, county Down", though, at present, owing to the great care that is taken of them, they are found, in constantly increasing numbers, in all the parks of the county Sligo, where their exquisite plumage so bright, so glossy, so beautifully blended and varied, offers the most charming object conceivable to the eye. The famous Greek philosopher, Solon, is said to have been so struck by the dazzling beauty of this bird, that when Croesus, the fabulously rich king of Lydia, showed him all the gorgeous adornments of the Lydian throne and palace, and asked him had he ever conceived anything so fine, the philosopher replied, that he could think of nothing finer except the plumage of the pheasant. The following figures, marking the proceeds of a day or two's shooting in a county Sligo demesne, of an average size, give an idea of the proportion of pheasants to other species of game in the county: 335 pheasants, 45 woodcocks, and 53 hares.

An authentic anecdote or two, current till lately about Sligo, show that eagles were numerous in the neighbourhood in the early years of the century. First: a well-known rope manufacturer, named Billy Black, was tricked rather cleverly by a country woman who passed on him, at a high price, an old plucked eagle for a turkey. It is told that Billy's cook found the cooking of the bird rather tough work, and Billy himself, the eating of it still tougher. Second: eagles were to be had so near the town as Cairns Hill, and one of them, that was shot there on a moonlight night, but not killed outright, though blinded, flew into the town and down through Market Street, putting out the candles of the shops by the flapping of its wings, to the consternation of the people, who, at first, regarded the occurrence as a supernatural visitation.

Rabbits are more numerous just now than at any former time, on account of the greatly enhanced price, and the daily increasing demand that is for them: For these reasons, they are better preserved than in the past—owners of land finding them, in many instances, more profitable than cattle or sheep. In some pasture tracts, on which cattle are taken in to be depastured for the six months from May to November at a given rent, as much profit is sometimes made by sale of the rabbits trapped, as by the rent of the cattle. Thus, in a large stretch near Knocklane, in Carbury, where the rent of the grazing cattle brought in 300, the sale of the rabbits is said to have realized 330. If the demand for the small quadruped continues to increase, it is not unlikely, that, as some landlords found it their pecuniary interest to substitute on their estates cattle for human beings, so these, or other landlords, may soon come to count it more profitable to have rabbits than to have cattle on their lands.

The leading gentry of the county keep deer either in parks, walled in for the purpose, as in the case of Colonel Cooper, Mr. O'Hara, and Mr. Wynne, or more at large in their demesnes as in the case of others. Sir John Davis, who wrote in 1613, his celebrated *Discoverie of the True Causes why Ireland was never entirely subdued*, tells, that in his time, there was "but one Parke stored with Deere in all this Kingdom, which is a Parke of the Earl of Ormond's, near Kilkenny", but since that day deer parks have become sufficiently common in Ireland with a good proportion in the county Sligo. Colonel Cooper's park is stocked with about fifty deer, chiefly of the fallow kind, with a few red deer; and Mr. O'Hara, Mr. Perceval, Mr. Wynne, and Sir Henry Gore Booth's parks or demesnes contain equally large numbers.

Sligo is one of the most favourably circumstanced counties of Ireland in respect of water, containing the three great lakes of Gill, Arrow, and Gara, with scores of minor lakes and lakelets; the four great rivers of Moy, Uncion or Arrow, Owenmore, and the Sligeach or Gara vogue; with many rivers and rivulets, and quite a number of spring-wells one at least on an average to the townland the water of several of them, being so pure, limpid, and palatable, that nothing, it is said, like it can be had elsewhere.

Lough Gill deserves the first place among the lakes of the county. Reserving for another place some remarks on its appearance and surroundings, it will be enough to state here that it is about eight miles long and two and a-half broad; and that it is of very varying depths, the changes of bottom level being frequent and abrupt, resembling in this respect the surface of the adjoining townlands of Corrownamodow and Aghamore, which is a series of sharp hills and hollows. The greater part of Lough Gill belongs to the county Sligo, lying between the barony of Carbury on the north, and that of Tirerrill on the south, but a considerable stretch lies in the County Leitrim.

Like Lough Gill, Lough Arrow belongs to two different counties, a part of it being in Roscommon, but much the larger part in Sligo. It is 102 feet above sea level, is about eight miles square, though owing to the high banks, it hardly looks that size. It is famous for its gilleroo trout, which brings fishermen from all quarters in the month of May.

Lough Gara called, anciently, Lough Techet, lies partly in each of the three counties of Sligo, Roscommon and Mayo. Its surface elevation above the sea is 222 feet, and its area seven miles square.

The minor lakes are Esk, which stretches between Lsyney and Tireragh, is a mile and a quarter long, and 607 feet above sea level; Talt in Leyney, about a mile long, and 455 feet above sea level; Templehouse, between Corran and Leyney, which is an expansion of the Owenmore river, and is about two miles long, and 386 feet above sea level; a little to the south of Templehouse, Cloonacleigha, three-fourths of a mile long, and 400 feet above sea level; Tubberscanavan, called in Down Survey Knockmullen Lough, greatly reduced in area by recent drainage; Ballygawley, or Ballydawley, a charming little lake about a mile square, lying in the valley between Slieve da En and the Ox Mountains; Skean, more than half of which is in Roscommon; Colgagh, in the parish of Calry; Glencar, partly in Sligo and partly in Leitrim; Cloonty, near Cliffony, in the parish of Ahamlish, part in that parish and part in the county Leitrim; and some scores of lakelets here and there through the county, but more especially on the northern slopes of Slieve Gamh and Slieve da En, where they often take a deep bowl shape.

The Moy, which holds the first place among Sligo rivers, is popularly supposed to rise in a well in the townland of Cloondrihara, but its source is more correctly placed, on the Ordnance Survey maps, in the interior of the Ox Mountains, where its infantine movements escape the gaze of the vulgar, like the infant Nile, which, as Lucan tells, is similarly privileged:

"Nec licuit populis parvum te, Nile, videre".[1]

Even when the mountain stream has descended into the valley, it is still so tiny that little boys can easily jump across it. By degrees as the Mad river, the Owenaher, the Talt, and the Owen Garrough, pay their tributes, it swells and expands, and is already a fine river when it winds around the quiet, sacred groves of Benada Convent, in measured, noiseless movement,

---

[1] 'Nor can the small people see the Nile', [Clachan ed.].

as if guarding against disturbing the religious meditations of that holy retreat. At Rathmagurry, it enters the county Mayo, and after a detour of several miles in that county, comes back from its excursion, and joins again the county Sligo at a point about two miles above Ballina, from which point it forms the boundary between the two counties.

The Sligeach has been always reckoned one of the chief rivers of Ireland, and is numbered by Eochy O'Flynn[1] among those which Partholan is said to have found before him on coming to the country:

"Muadius, Sligachus Samerius dictus—Buasuis perennis per rura amaena, Modornus, Finnus velde limpidus—Banna inter Lee et Eile".

It is about two miles long from where it issues from the lake to the Victoria Bridge, and it is this part of the river which received the name of Garavogue, the part below the bridge being known from time immemorial, as *Sligeach*. Garavogue or Awen Garrough signifies Rough River, and the name was applied to the Sligo river, when the stream was shallow and impeded by rough stones in the bed. As it will be necessary to recur to this subject, there is no need to dwell further on it here.

The Arrow, or Uncion, rises in Lough Arrow, runs for ten miles in a north-north-westerly direction, passing by Riverstown, Cooperhill, and Markrea, and joining the Owenmore at Collooney, flows on in a broad and rapid stream to the sea at Ballysadare.

The Owenmore takes its rise in Tubber-na-neeve well, in the parish of Kilfree; forms for some distance the mutual boundary of Corran and Coolavin; acquires such increase near Buninadden that some would count that place its source; passes through, or touches on, the parishes of Kilshahy, Drumrat, Cloonoghill, and Emlaghfad in Corran; expands at Templehouse into a lake, which lies partly in Corran and partly in Leyney; winds in loops through the flat lands adjoining the so-called Island near the village of Ballinacarrow; turns, or used to turn, the machinery of two or three mills at Thornhill; moves slowly through the demesne of Annaghmore; receives, as it quits the demesne, the tributary waters of the Owenbeg, or Owen na Leave; unites with the Uncion at Collooney; and, greatly increased in width and volume, hastens over the intervening slopes and ledges to the bay of Ballysadare. As this river, in length of run, body of water, and picturesqueness of course and surroundings, is greatly superior to the Arrow or Uncion, it is strange that it should pass, as it commonly does, as a tributary of the Uncion, instead of the latter being counted the tributary, and the Owenmore the principal river. The small rivers through

---

[1] Eochaidh Ua Floinn in Irish—'Eochy O'Flynn, was a poet, and author of historical and dinnseanchus (lore of places) poems, [Clachan ed.].

the baronies, though benefiting greatly their respective districts, call for no special notice in this place.

The passage of the Owenmore through Collooney offers some charming views, of which the following description by the writer (*Ballysadare and Kilvarnet*, p. 50) will give some idea, though a very imperfect one. "Coming slowly and gravely into the town, passing demurely by the beautiful glebe of Ardcotton, leaping playfully, after it gets from under the rector's eye, over two or three hundred yards of fantastic ledges, till it makes a splendid plunge of twenty feet at the fall, and throws up a cloud of glittering globules to hide its antics; then darting rapidly away to the east in a bold and graceful curve, to pay its respects to McDonogh's Castle; and, after receiving the waters of its tributary, the Arrow or Uncion, moving with a sense of new dignity majestically along under the overhanging trees of Union Wood, and, like Galatea in the eclogue,

'Et fugit ad salices et se cupit ante videri,'[1]

coming out now and again from under the shade to show itself to admirers before disappearing finally from view at Ballysadare, our river discloses, in a run of two miles, as many beauties as any other river in Ireland in the same length".

A word or two regarding the lineage of the people will not be out of place before passing on to the separate consideration of the baronies. While it may be assumed that the main element in the population of Sligo is Celtic, there is good ground for thinking that the Anglo-Saxon element is much more considerable than is commonly supposed. This would seem to follow clearly from the crowds of people that came over to this county from time to time from England or the Lowlands of Scotland, and settled in it. As will be seen hereafter, the town of Sligo, when first founded by Maurice Fitzgerald, was stocked with English inhabitants, and the place continued English while the Fitzgeralds and Burkes held sway in Lower Connaught, that is, for about a hundred years. During these years not only the town but most of the county, notably the baronies of Leyney and Tireragh, was in the possession of the foreigners, and so remained from 1237, when the Barons of England began to build castles in Connaught, down to about 1333, when they were defeated and expelled by the O'Haras, O'Dowds, and other native chieftains.

In the earlier years of the seventeenth century streams of immigrants were constantly coming across the channel to this part of Ireland, and settling themselves here and there through it; and after the ill-starred Insurrection of 1641, the Cromwellians invaded the county *en masse*, spread themselves over its different districts, and occupied the town of Sligo so

---

[1] "And he fled to the willows, and hopes to be seen", {Clachan ed.].

exclusively, that it may be doubted, whether at one time a single Catholic Celt could be found within its limits. Nor did these accessions cease with the seventeenth century. They have been since kept up, through importations, by our gentry, of batch after batch of domestics and others, who, when their term of service expires, and one batch is succeeded in office by another, instead of going back to their native place in England or elsewhere, are generally located, after the manner of an overflow meeting, on such valuable farms as may be vacant or available.

These invasions and immigrations could not fail to affect largely the natural descent of the inhabitants. The masses that came over, on the occasion of wars or insurrections, like the individuals who came over for domestic service, did not in general return, but settled down in the county, and became gradually absorbed in the population. The English and Scotch names so often met with in all the baronies, indicate the descendants of the immigrants, though it should be borne in mind that the foreign blood is much more common in the neighbourhood than the foreign names. The old maxim that the prefix of Mac or O makes known the genuine Irishman, is not now as generally true, at least in the county Sligo, as it used to be in the past, or as it may still be in other counties; for many an O'Connor, O'Hara, O'Dowd, or MacDonogh, notwithstanding the O or Mac, has, perhaps, as much Saxon as Celtic blood in his veins. Let any man who demurs to this statement, start inquiries with regard to particular families in his neighbourhood, and he will probably find, while examining the genealogical tree of any Celtic family he may select, that he will not have to go far back to discover more than one Saxon graft on the Celtic trunk. And, conversely, if he make the experiment on a family with a Saxon name, he is likely to arrive at a similar result. It is well to be acquainted with this state of things, both for the sake of having correct knowledge on the subject, and in the interest of social peace and harmony; for if the inhabitants of the county recollected this relationship, and had often in the mind the mollifying consideration, that they are not only living side by side in the same district, but that the same blood is flowing in their veins, they would hardly be so prone, as they have too often shown themselves, to look on one another as aliens and enemies.

So much having been said regarding the county at large, we shall now take up the baronies that compose it, beginning with Carbury.

CHAPTER II

BARONY OF CARBURY

CARBURY takes its name from Cairbre, third son of Niall of the Nine Hostages. This Niall had eight sons, Loegaire, Conal Crimthan, Fiach, Manius, Conal Gulban, Owen, Cairbre, and Ennius; and as the first four remained in the southern parts of Ireland, their descendants were called the Southern Hy-Nialls; while the descendants of the last four, who took possession of the north, got the name of the Northern Hy-Nialls. John, O'Donovan, in a note to the Four Masters, under the year 669, supposes the migration of the Carbrians to the neighbourhood of Sligo, to be subsequent to that year;[1] but in this he is not only in error, but in contradiction with himself, for in a note, under the year 598, he writes, "The Cinel Cairbre were at this period seated in the barony of Carbury, and county of Sligo", to which barony they gave name. Anyhow the entry of the Four Masters at 598, is so clear as to leave no room for doubt, for the Annalists state expressly that a battle was fought that year at Aughriss, in Tireragh, between the descendants of Cairbre and the descendants of Fiacra,[2] which, of course, supposes the former to be in the neighbourhood at the time; and from their being there at that time, and being then so settled and organized, as to be able to cope successfully with the powerful people of Tireragh, we may reasonably infer that they were in the district from the days of Cairbre himself, who, in his own day, to use the words of Colgan, "possessed in Connaught the district called after him, Carbury".[3] Unlike his brothers who, between the time of Saint Patrick and the year 1000, furnished in their descendants forty-five monarchs to the throne of Ireland the Southern Hy-Nialls, 19, and the Northern, 26 Cairbre supplied only one, his grandson, Tuathal Maelgarb; and old writers ascribe the difference to a curse of St. Patrick on the family, for having been repeatedly outraged by Cairbre, who seems to have been a particularly ill-conditioned and brutal person.[4] Though Cairbre's descendants had so little to do with the throne

---

[1] "The race of Cairbre were at this period seated in the barony of Carbury, in the county of Longford, but their descendants afterwards settled in, and gave their name to, the present barony of Carbury, in the county of Kildare, and the barony of Carbury, in the county of Sligo".

[2] "The battle of Eachros, in Muirisc, by Colman, chief of Cinel Cairbre, against Maelcothaigh, chief of Cinel Fiachra, of Muirisc; and the battle was gained over Maelcothaigh"

[3] Trias Thaumaturga, p. 544.

[4] Tunc S. Patricius perrexit ad locum agonis regalis, qui dicitur Tailtin, ad alterum filium Neill Corpre . . . Sed Corpre noluit credere; voluit vero jugulare Patricium, ideo appellavit Patricius eum inimicum Dei, et dixit, ei; Semen tuum serviet seminibus fratrum tuorum; et de semine tuo rex non erit in aeternum.—*Trias Thaumaturga*, p. 25. To account for the

of Ireland, they ruled for several centuries over the district of Carbury; and a diligent search in the Four Masters, and other authorities, has enabled the writer to discover the names of the following chiefs of that district, who were all descendants of Cairbre, through one or other of his two sons, Garban and Coman or Coeman: —

1. Colman He was the chief of Cinel Cairbre, who defeated the people of Tireragh in 598.
2. Sgandal. Mac Firbis, in his Genealogical writings,1 thus mentions this ruler, "Tuathal Maolgarbh, king of Ireland, had two sons, namely, Garban (of whom was Sgandal, who succeeded to the sovereignty; Ui Duibhduin, and Ui Duibhne of Cillespuig-Brone); and Coman or Coeman, father of Hugh, father of Aongus Bronbachall, the religious". Sgandal is mentioned in the Four Masters, also.
3. Maelduin, Sgandal's son, was chief of Cinel Cairbre in 665.2
4. Dubhduin, another son of Sgandal,3 succeeded Maelduin, and was chief of Cinel Cairbre in 669, when he slew Seachnasach, monarch of Ireland. 4
5. Aongus Bronbachall, called the Religious, who was grandson of Coman, ruled as chief of Cinel Cairbre, though we cannot fix his exact place in the succession. He died, according to the Annals of Ulster, in 6485. He is the person spoken of in the 13th chapter of the First Book of Adamnan's Saint Columba,6 which runs thus, "This man, having been banished with his two brothers from Ireland, came to Columba, who was then living in Britain; and the saint, after blessing him, thus foretold what was to happen him: 'This youth, surviving all his brothers, will bear rule, a long time in his country; nor will he ever fall into the hands of his enemies, but will die in old age, a tranquil death among his friends.' All this happened as Columba predicted". This epithet Bronbachall, Dr. O'Conor renders baculi dolorosi, in his translation of the Annals of Ulster; in the term Dr. Reeves thinks, there is reference to the "pilgrim's staff;" and the writer takes leave to conjecture, that Aongus must have taken the "staff" in honour of Bishop Bronus, or Brone, a conjecture which derives no little support from the prefix Broil, and also from the fact that some, at least of Aongus' family, lived at Killaspugbrone.7

---

reign of Tuathal Maelgarb, notwithstanding this prophecy, Colgan adds in a note (p. 45), Ubi hic legitur Rex non *erit*, legendum est *Reges non erunt*; nam juxta omnesnostros historicos fuit unus rex Hiberniae de semine Corprei, nempe Tuathalius cognomento Maelgarbh .... Unde exactius Auctor Op. Trip. par. 2., cap. 4 and 27, sic refert maledictionem, De tua stirpe nec reges nec regni exurgent piguora.

1 Geneal. MS., p. 167. Quoted by Dr. Reeves in his Adamnan, p. 41.
2 Ibid. -
3 Andaman's Life of St. Columba, by Dr. Reeves, p. 41.
4 Four Masters, 669.
5 A.C. 648, Mors Oengusa, Bron-bachlae regis Ceinuil Coirpri.
6 Page 41 of Dr. Reeves' edition, the Latin words are: "Hic namque de patria cum aliis duobus fratribus effugatus, ad Sanctum in Britannia peregrinantem exul venit; cuique benedicens hoc de eo prophetizans sancto promit de pectore verba; Hic juvenis defunctis ejus ceteris fratribus superstes remanens, multo est regnaturus in patria tempore; et inimici ejus coram ipso cadent; nec tamen ipse unquam in manus tradetur inimicorum, sed morte placide senex, inter amicos morietur. Que omnia juxta Sancti verbum simt adempleta. Hic est Oingusius cujus cognomentum Bronbachal".
7 His cousin, Ui Duibhne, is set down, by Mac Firbis, as of Cill-esping-Brone—Reeves' Adamnan, p. 41.

5.1 [sic] Fergus, son of Maelduin, and chief of Cinel Cairbre, fell in the battle of Corann, 681.2

6. Muirghes, another son of Maelduin, and chief of Cinel Cairbre, died, according to the Annals of the Four Masters, in 696, and according to the Annals of Ulster, in 697. He is the "Muirghes, son of Maelduin, son of Scannal, an illustrious king of Cairbre's race", mentioned in Colgan's Vita Tripartita.3

7. Conor, who was also a son of Maelduin, and chief of Cinel Cairbre, died in 704.4

8. Conall Mean succeeded Conor as chief of Cinel Cairbre, and was slain in 718, in the great battle of Allen.5

9. Flaherty, son of Conall Mean, and chief of Cinel Cairbre, died in 747 6

10. Cathal, son of Conall Mean, and Lord of Carbury Mor, died in 766.7

11. Cathmugh, son of Flaherty, and Lord of Carbury, was slain in the battle of Ard-mic-Rime in 787.8

12. Dunadhach, son of Raghallach, Lord of Cinel Cairbre Mor, died in 871. Of him was said: -

"Dunadhach, a noble protection, a famous man by whom hostages were held, A pious soldier of the race of Conn (lies interred) under hazel crosses at Drumcliff.9

13. Fearghal, son of Foghartach, Lord of Cairbre Mor, died on an expedition in 974.10

14. Donnchadh, Lord of Cairbre, was killed by the Hy-Fiachrach-Muirisc, in the doorway of the church of Serin Adamnan in 1030.11

15. Murchadh, son of Searrach, Lord of Cairbre Mor, died in 1032.12

There can be little doubt that all these were chiefs of the county Sligo Carbury, though O'Donovan regards such of them, as he notices, as belonging to Carbury Teffia, in the present barony of Granard, county of Longford.

It would be tedious to go over the whole list, but one or two cases may be noticed, to give a sample of Mr. O'Donovan's *modus agendi*. In a note to the entry, "Cathal, son of Conall, lord of Cairbre-Mor, died", he observes: "The addition of *mor* to Cairbre here is probably a mistake by the Four Masters;" and to confirm this conjecture he refers to the entry, as it is given in the *Annals of Ulster*, where it reads thus: "A.D. 770—Cathal, Mac Conall Minn, ri Coirpri, *moritur*; "but this reference, instead of making for him, tells rather against him, for it shows that the Conall of the Four Masters is the Conall Meann who fell in the battle of Allen,[13] and who was

---

[1] Original numbering. All square brackets signify Clachan edits, [Clachan ed.].

[2] Annals of the Four Masters, *sub anno*.

[3] A.D. 697, Mors Muirgisa, Mic Maelduin, regis Generis Corpri.—Hennessy's Translation, p. 439.

[4] Four Masters, *sub anno*, 704.

[5] Ibid., 718.

[6] Ibid., 747.

[7] Ibid., 766.

[8] Ibid., 787.

[9] Ibid., 871.

[10] Ibid., 974.

[11] Ibid., 1030

[12] Ibid., 1032.

[13] Annals of the Four Masters, 718.

certainly chief of the Sligo Carbury, as he is set down both in the Four Masters[1] (and in the *Chronicon Scotorum*[2] among "the chieftains and leaders of Leath-Chuinn", who fought the battle of Allen against the Leinster-men, including, of course, those of Carbury Teffia or Granard. At the entry, "Dunadhach, son of Raghallach, Lord of Cinel Cairbre Mor", he remarks: "The Cinel Cairbre Mor was seated in the barony of Granard", though the juxtaposition of Drumcliff and Cairbre Mor should have made it clear to him that there was question of the Carbury of Sligo, even if he forgot that Colgan, our greatest authority on the topography of Ireland, regards Cairbre Mor and Cairbre Drumcliff as one and the same place.[3] Whenever indeed the phrase "Cinel Cairbre" occurs in the first thousand years of the Annals of the Four Masters, O'Donovan takes it to mean the Carbrians of Longford, though invariably it designates the inhabitants of our Sligo Carbury, "Cairbre" simply,[4] or "Cairbre-Teffia",[5] being employed as the name of the Longford Carbury; and as the same distinction is observed in the Chronicon Scotorum, it is the more strange that O'Donovan and some other writers should miss it.

The following is another characteristic example of the high-handedness with which O'Donovan brushes out of his way the authorities from which he thinks fit to differ. After quoting from the Annals of Ulster the entry, "Battle of Taidbig, in which the Luigni were overthrown, Cinel Cairbre gained the victory", and remarking thereupon –"the old translator in *Cod. Clarend.* 49, has mistaken the meaning of this in the following version: 'Battle of the wood called Taidbig, where Luigni of Connaught were overthrowne, and *Generatio* Cairbre, conquerors, *victoriam accepit*,'" he thus settles the matter of his own mere motion, and without alleging a particle of either reason or authority: "It should be— 'The battle of the wood called Caille-Taidbig, where the Luighni [of Meath] were overthrown, and *Generatio* Cairbre, *victoriam accepit*.'[6] Such dogmatism, *pace tanti viri*,[7] is *un peu trop*[8]; for not even his recognised pre-eminence among modern labourers in the field of Irish language, literature, and topography, entitled him to the privilege, whenever the Four Masters or approved translators of

---

[1] Ibid.
[2] *Chronicon Scotorum*. Edited with a translation. By William M. Hennessy, M.R.I.A., *sub anno*, 718.
[3] Regio quae nunc Carbre-mhor, nunc Carbre Droma-cliabh dicitur.—Acta Sanctorum, p. 141.
[4] Four Masters, 731; and Chronicon Scotorum, 235, 249, 277.
[5] Four Masters, 747. Two obits under this year—one, "Flaherty, chief of Cinel Cairbre died; "the other, "Conaing Ui Duibhduin, Lord of Cairbre Teffia, died"—would alone show the error of O'Donovan.
[6] Note in O'Donovan's Four Masters, under the year 757.
  [7] "if so great a man will forgive me", Lat., [Clachan ed.].
  [8] "a little too much", Fr., [Clachan ed.].

our annals stood in the way of some peculiar opinion of his, to dispose of them by averring, without a shred of proof, on his mere *ipse dixit*,[1] that the Four Masters had mistaken their facts, and the translators had mistaken their originals. At all events, it is patent from the slips just mentioned, and from many others noticed elsewhere in these pages, that O'Donovan bestowed comparatively little thought on the county Sligo, and that, in consequence, he is by no means a safe guide to its history and antiquities.

Dwelling in Connaught, the Cinel Cairbre were subject to the Kings of the province; first, to the fourteen Kings of the Hy Fiachrach race who ruled over it,[2] and, next to the Hy-Bruin Kings, who belonged, mainly, to the O'Conor family. As, however, the Carbrians were of the same stock as the Cinel Owen and Cinel Connell, they had a greater leaning to the inhabitants of Ulster[3] than to those of Connaught, with whom they were often at variance. After the sovereignty of the province had passed from the Hy-Fiachrach to the Hy-Bruin, the O'Dowds still claimed to rule over Lower Connaught, which included Carbury, at least the portion of it to the south of Drumcliff, and they are given in O'Dugan's Typographical Poem, as "Lords of North Hy-Fiachrach from the Robe to the Codhnach;"[4] but their authority over Carbury was merely nominal; for we know that the Cinel Cairbre were strong enough to carry hostilities to the very heart of the Hy-Fiachrach territory, and to defeat its people even on their own ground.

From the time the O'Connors settled in Carbury, in the twelfth century, to the abolition of Irish tenures in the seventeenth century, there was a perpetual contest between them and the Cinel Connell for the chief authority in Carbury. In the battle of Crich Cairbre[5] the Cinel Connell asserted their claim, and were the undoubted chiefs of the territory for near

---

[1] 'Say-so" or allegation, [Clachan ed.].
[2] "Fourteen Kings of the race of Fiachra", &c. Tribes and Customs of Hy-Fiachrach, p. 93.
[3] "Of the dividend of the Hy-Fiachrach themselves
Is the land of Cairbre of the level plains,
But of the Hy-Neill is the lineage of the men,
. . . .
The Clann Cairbre of the flowery white mountains,
Are under the mansions of the western people". Ibid., p. 277-279.
"Ard-Macha belongs to Eoghan's race,
And Derry to the race of Connell; The seed of mild Cairbre have Drumcliabh,
Though the Connacians like it not.
  May their thanks and their blessings
  Conduce unto my soul's quiet,
  But I grieve for my good people,
  How Cairbre upon them pressed."—Book of Fenagh.
[4] Cambrensis Eversus—Edited by Rev. Matthew Kelly, Vol. I., p. 255.
[5] Four Masters, 1181.

two centuries, as appears, first, from their defending the territory against all invaders;[1] second, from their taking up the chieftain's rents;[2] third, from their alienating a portion of the territory;[3] and, fourth, from their enemies regarding any injury inflicted on the district as an injury inflicted on the Cinel Connell.[4] The O'Connor family did not submit to this supremacy, and, in the middle of the fourteenth century, not only vindicated the right to be paramount themselves in Carbury, but invaded Tyrconnell, and acquired there, for a short time, authority over the O'Donnells. The latter, however, maintained, all through, their pretensions to Carbury and Lower Connaught; and, so late as the middle of the sixteenth century, we find Manus O'Donnell taking up the rents of Lower Connaught, and even petitioning Henry VIII. to be made Earl of Sligo, where, the petition alleged, "his ancestors had held the castle for a thousand years;" an allegation, by the way, egregiously at variance with the fact, for at the date of the petition (April 22, 1542), the castle was only completing the three hundredth year of its existence. No English monarch gave any countenance to this extravagant ambition of the O'Donnells, and in 1603, when Rory O'Donnell, on the death of Hugh Roe, in Spain, was about to be created Earl of Tyrconnell, James I. ordered that he should first "renounce all claim upon O'Connor Sligo's country", which Rory accordingly did.

Having premised these remarks on the old Irish Chiefs of Carbury, we will now consider the district in detail, and, as far as possible, parish by parish, beginning with the town of Sligo, which is the capital of the barony, as well as of the county, and which is situated in the ecclesiastical union of Sligo, partly on the left bank of the river, and partly on the right. The parochial union of Sligo consists at present of the parishes of St. John, Kilmacowen, and Killaspugbrone.

---

[1] Four Masters, 1187.
[2] Ibid, 1213.
[3] Ibid, 1230.
[4] Ibid, 1235.

CHAPTER III

THE TOWN OF SLIGO

THE scenery around Sligo is admitted to be at least equal to that of any other town or city in Ireland. So much is allowed by all who visit the place; but those, who try to discriminate more nicely, will come probably to the conclusion, that the environs of Sligo are decidedly superior in beauty to anything of the kind in the country. If the elements of first-rate landscape mountain and valley, wood and water, picturesqueness of outline and softness of colouring are to be had in other places, it will be found on comparison, that they do not exist in such perfect combination in those places as upon the banks of the Garvogue. Be the stand-point where it will in the neighbourhood north, south, east, or west and the prospect is exceptionally fine, though that to the north, extending from Knocklane, in the west, to the head of Loughgill in the east, is, perhaps, the finest.

Of this beautiful region the background is all mountain, and the foreground a sweep of rich, gently swelling, or gently sloping land, every perch of which is under the eye, all the way from the sea to Benbo, which hill, though not belonging to Sligo county, contributes not a little to its embellishment.

The mountain part of this view can hardly be surpassed, Though the ranges are only about 1000 feet high, you find they could not be higher without marring the beauty of the scene, by imparting to it a gloom, of which there is now no trace, and also by shutting out the view of the Donegal mountains, which at present serve to perfect and complete the landscape. Towards Dromahair the crest of the range is a good deal broken, the blocks or masses taking various shapes, the prevailing one being circular, like that of a truncated cone. A beautiful example of this formation is the cone called O'Rorke's Table, from its resemblance to a round table; but local tradition has not yet decided, whether it was here, or in the hospitable Hall of Dromahair, came off –

> "---- *O'Rorke's noble feast, that shall ne'er be forgot*
> *Or by those who were there, or by those who were not".*

Not far from the table is another and a higher block, to which the country folk give the name of O'Rorke's Chair doubtless some chair of state, if not the inauguration chair; for if intended to supply the chief with a seat at the banqueting table aforesaid, he must have been put to a great disadvantage, by the distance, in the management of his knife and fork.

Further on is another section of the mountain called Cooleageboy, a kind of circle too in form, but in itself rougher and more massive than either the Table or the Chair. Looking at it from near its base, a man of lively imagination would soon come to trace some resemblance between its shaggy sides and the shako[1] of a grenadier. Between Coologeboy and Benbulben intervenes Cashel Gal or Slieve-gan-baiste mountain, a fine bold range, which would be more thought of if found elsewhere, but which suffers from its neighbourhood with the beautiful Benbulben. Go where you will through Ireland; pass in review whatever is excellent and most admired in the mountain scenery of Kerry, Connemara, Down, Donegal and Antrim; and if you have taste, and are without prejudice, you will admit that, both as to outline and colouring, there is nothing equal to, nothing almost second to, the graceful, the stately, the incomparable Benbulben. Straight as an arrow, symmetrical through its length in all its proportions, sleek and glossy as a well-groomed horse, it gives the idea of flesh rather than of stone; and there are certain points in Tireragh and Leyney, from which, if you look, you bring Benbulben and Knocknarea into exact line, and get inclined to fancy that they are things of life, engaged in a race westward, but just brought to a stand by the sea appearing suddenly in front.

Another object which Benbulben, or, rather, the more northern portion of it, resembles, is the forepart of a ship, but of a ship in an inverted position; for the straight crest is like the upturned keel, the curved face like the prow, and the sloping sides like the hull, with deck underneath.

A gentleman familiar with the form of the modern war ship, called the ram, says that the "keel" of the mountain just as it stands, in its natural position, looks like the sub-aqueous beak with which that ship pierces the man-of-war against which it is propelled.

The region in front of those mountains is not unworthy of the beautiful back-ground. The stretch from Knocklane to near Dromahair is some twelve or fourteen miles long, while the average depth between the mountains and the sea, for one part of the length, and between the mountains and the lake, for the remainder, is about four or five miles. The lie of the land is a gentle slope down to the water's edge, with here and there little knolls and swells, which give variety to the scene, without hiding any of it from the eye.

Man's taste and industry have co-operated with the bounty of nature in enriching and embellishing this favoured tract; for cultivation has developed all the fine properties of the soil, so that such tillage fields, as the district contains, are models of tasteful, skillful, and fruitful husbandry; while the green sward which covers nineteen-twentieths of the whole area is greener and glossier, more especially in the immediate neighbourhood of Lough Gill, than can be seen in any other part, even of "Our own Green Isle". If travellers often complain of the bleak, bare, and treeless condition of many other parts of Ireland, they can find no such drawback here; for

---

[1] a tall, cylindrical military cap, [Clachan ed.].

timber abounds, not only in the fine demesne of Lissadell, at one end of the stretch, and in that of Hazelwood, at the other, but in the intermediate sweep too, where trees are numerous, and occur sometimes in single line, sometimes in belts of several lines deep, and again in symmetrical clumps, which not infrequently embosom imposing mansions or cosy cottages.

A fact which shows the superiority of this region in natural beauty is, that it extorted the admiration of so able and prejudiced a judge as Carlyle. Though he had hardly a good word for any other part of Ireland, when he visited the country in 1849; though his judgments of the districts through which he passed are brimful of contempt, such as "an ugly hare, moory country", "a dingy, desolate looking country", "a scrubby ill cultivated country", "ragged avenues of wood not quite so ugly as nothing", "troublous hugger-mugger aspect of stony fields and frequent, nearly all, bad houses;" though he damns even Killarney with such faint praise as "rather beautiful, by contrast especially; well enough but don't bother me with audibly admiring it", still, the moment he comes in view of the environs of Sligo, even at such a distance as Dromore, on the road from Ballina, a change comes suddenly over him, as appears from those words of his diary, "Country alters here . . . beautiful view of the sea, of Sligo bay, with notable mountains beyond . . . much indented coast . . . decidedly a pleasant region, with marks of cultivation everywhere, tho' still too treeless;" but when he reaches the high ground over the town, and the full panorama of the region lies expanded before him the stately heights of Benbulben, Cashelgal, and Knocknarea the wide undulating plain of Magherow diversified with wood, and coppice, and tillage fields, and sweeps of pasture lands, that seem instinct with the life of the flocks and herds which move over them the soft emerald slopes of Hazel wood and Holy well, lined into avenues, or diapered into geometrical figures, with trees as flourishing and stately as the cedars of Libanus the winding bay on the one hand, the sweet shining lake on the other the fine public buildings of the town, and the attractive residences of all kinds, scattered in conspicuous positions, over the country when all this breaks at once upon the view, the evil spirit is at last exorcised outright; and as Balaam, who came to curse, cried out, "How beautiful are thy tabernacles, Jacob, and thy tents, O Israel! As woody valleys, as watered gardens near the rivers, as tabernacles which the Lord hath pitched, as cedars by the waterside;" so the cynical, hostile, prejudiced, spiteful Carlyle, softened and warmed by the scene before him, and carried, as it were, out of himself, exclaims, "Sligo at last; beautiful descent into it; *beautiful town and region altogether.*"

The town of Sligo is modern when compared with many other towns in Ireland. While the history of these may be traced back with ease to the earlier centuries of our era, there is no evidence to show that Sligo existed, either under its present name, or under a different one, at any time anterior to the thirteenth century. Though this assertion will come with surprise on minds which have got their notions of Sligo from certain silly stories, which would connect the town with "prehistoric ages", it is not the less true on that account, as those stories themselves have not a particle of proof to support them.

Not only is there no proof, but there is not even any probability, internal or other, in favour of this alleged antiquity. On the contrary, probability of the one kind and the other, points unmistakably to the modern origin of the town.

For, first, the situation of the place lying at the bottom of the deep basin formed by the overhanging hills of Rathvritoge (the Green Fort) and Cairns, and the high ridge of land to the south-west, would prevent people from congregating or settling there in times of such lawlessness and rapaciousness that men needed to be always on the watch against enemies and freebooters. In such a state of things, the chief recommendation of places of habitation or resort was, that they should afford an extensive prospect, so as to enable one to descry at a distance the approach of marauders; and it was under the influence of this consideration that the earlier inhabitants of Ireland constructed raths the residences of remote times in high situations, held assemblies on the tops of hills, ran roads across mountains eschewing everywhere the valleys and raised the round tower to such a height as to command a view of all the circumjacent country. So potent was this principle of action that it operated beyond the grave; for the dying man took care that his body after death should repose on some one of those hills which he frequented during life, as if he felt that what survived of him could not be otherwise sufficiently secure from outrage.

Proofs and illustrations of these remarks lie scattered abundantly over Ireland in all the remains of antiquity; and we shall find that, nowhere, are they in greater number than throughout the county Sligo, if we only call to mind the cairns which surmount Knocknarea, Cairns-Hill, Slieve da En, the Ox Mountains, Keash, and Knocknashee, as well as the raths and cashels which line the coast from the Moy to the Drowes, and lie thick through all the inland districts from the north of Carbury to the south of the barony of Leyney; this latter territory, from the great number it contains of those conspicuous raths or forts, being formerly called Leyney of the Fortifications.[1] Those various structures, situated always on eminences or other commanding positions, and hardly ever in hollows, serve to prove that a low-lying, secluded situation, like that of Sligo, whatever might be its advantages in other respects, would never have been chosen in those times for a centre of population. To select such a site for such a purpose would

---

[1] The Battle of Magh Rath, with a translation and notes, by John O'Donovan. Page 253.

look like bringing people into a *cul de sa*c, only to deliver them up to their enemies without means of defence or chance of escape.

And external probability leads to the same conclusion as internal. In the two or three allusions to Sligo, which are found in our earliest authorities, the reference is, in each case, to the river of the place and not to a town. Tirechan, in his Annotations in the Book of Armagh, after recording the foundation of a church at Killaspugbrone by Saint Patrick, represents the saint telling the monks of the new house, that the sea would encroach on them in the latter days, and that they would be forced to remove to the river Sligo, "hard by the wood:" from which observation, it would appear, that it was a wood and not a town that stood, in the time of Saint Patrick, on the banks of the Sligo river.[1]

The next allusion to Sligo, which we meet with, is connected also with the history of St. Patrick, and, like the one we have been considering, relates to the river. It occurs in the *Vita Tripartita*, where we are told that the saint, having reached the river Sligech, and having been treated very kindly and obligingly by some fishermen, whom he met there, blessed the river in requital of their kindness, and made it exceptionally fruitful. There is one other early mention of the river. It is contained in the old life, printed by Colgan, of Saint Farannan, in the interesting passage which enumerates the saints who had assembled at Easdara (Ballysadare), to meet and honour Saint Columba after the Convention of Drumceat, "Ita of Sligech or the Sligech" being there given among those who were present on the occasion. The absence of any indication of a town in those three references goes far to show that no town existed in the times to which they relate; but the omission, coupled with the internal probability derived from the nature of the place, and the character of the period, is so conclusive as to leave no room for doubt upon the subject in the mind of any reasonable man.

Passing now from those incidental notices of Sligo, which appear to be the only early notices of the kind in existence, as the "Book of Armagh contains perhaps all the old fragments of Irish literature now remaining to us", and coming to the direct references to the place, which are contained in the historical annals of the country, we shall look there too in vain for any sign of a town existing prior to the date already set down.

The first mention of Sligo which we find in the regular history of the country occurs, in the *Annals of the Four Masters*, under the year A.D. 537; in

---

[1] "Et dixit ecce mare jeciet nos de hoc loco in novissimis temporibus et exibitis ad flumen Sliachae ad sylvam".—Irish Antiquarian Researches, by Sir William Betham. Part ii. Appendix, page xxxii. Betham misses the meaning of this passage and gives it the following absurd translation: "And he said, behold the sea lays before us, from this place, and ye will return by the river Sligo to the wood". Ibid. p. 880. The correct rendering of the passage is, "And he said, Behold the sea will cast us forth out of this place in the latter times, and you will go away to the river Sligo, hard by the wood".

the *Annals of Tighernack* under the year A.D. 543; and in the *Chronicon Scotorum* at the same date. The entry opens with the words, "The Battle of Sligo;" and that Sligo here means the river of Sligo we have the unimpeachable authority of O'Donovan, who expressly says so in a note to the passage, in his edition of the Four Masters.

But this entry and the battle it records, are too important in their bearing on Sligo history to be dismissed in a sentence; and the more especially, as the writer cannot help thinking that this battle is connected with the extraordinary sepulchral monuments of Carrowmore, "the largest collection of monuments of the kind in the British islands, and, probably, with the exception of that of Carnac, in Brittany, the most remarkable in the world".[1] Hitherto these structures have been supposed to date from the time of the Firbolgs and Tuatha de Danaans, and to mark the site of a great conflict between their contending armies, but the advocates of this opinion have to face the objection that there is neither written record nor oral tradition in support of such a battle in the locality. To meet this difficulty they give out that the defeated Firbolgs, when retreating from the bloody field of the southern Moytura, according to some, of the northern Moytura, according to others, were overtaken in the Peninsula of Cuil Irra, by the victorious enemy, and cut to pieces, so that the place was covered with the dead. They add, that the bodies were buried where they lay, and that the circles and cromlechs which we now see, and numerous others, which have disappeared, were erected over the slain by their surviving comrades.[2] This explanation looks plausible enough at the first view, but the drawback is, that it is all assumption, pure and simple, without a shred of proof. And there are on the contrary one or two objections which serve to discredit it; as, first, that the unfortunate Firbolgs, in the hurry to get away from their victors, had no time to engage in such works; and, second, that no similar memorials are to be found at Moytura, where the main, battle is assumed to have been fought, and where it is natural to suppose that still greater slaughter prevailed. Had the Firbolgs at any time subsequent to the date of the battle been able to set monuments over the remains of their brethren in Cuil Irra, they would not have neglected to pay a like tribute of respect to those who had fallen at Moytura.

---

[1] Proceedings of Royal Irish Academy, Vol. I., p. 140, In a letter addressed from Rath Carrick to Sir Thomas Larcom, Mr. Petrie writes, "I have now completed the list of this remarkable series of ancient monuments which, excepting the monuments of Carnac, in Brittany, is, even in its present state of ruin, the largest assemblage of the kind hitherto discovered in the world". The Life of George Petrie, &c., by William Stokes, &c., p. 253.

[2] "I have no doubt", says Petrie, "but I shall hereafter be able to prove that these are the tombs of the Belgse, who, after the battle of the southern Moytuira, in Mayo, retreated into this peninsula of Cuil Irra, having been again defeated and their King slain in crossing the strand of Ballysadare Bay,—Life of George Petrie, &c., p. 254.

Turning now to the writer's views regarding the Battle of Sligo, it will be convenient, first of all, to set under the eye of the reader the entry of the Four Masters on the subject. It runs thus: "The battle of Sligeach by Fergus and Domhnall, the two sons of Muircheartach Mac Earca; by Ainmire, son of Sedna; and Ainnidh, son of Duach, against Eoghan Bel, King of Connaught. They routed the forces before them, and Eoghan Bel was slain, of which was said,

> The battle of the Ui-Fiachrach was fought
> With fury of edged weapons against Bel,
> The kine of the enemy roared with the javelins,
> The battle was spread out at Grinder.
> The Sligeach bore to the great sea
> The blood of men with their flesh,
> They carried many trophies across Eabha,
> Together with the head of Eoghan Bel".

The magnitude of this battle may be inferred from the rank of those engaged in it. On one side Fergus and Domhnall, sons of the late monarch, the renowned Muircheartach Mac Earca, who has been styled the "Hector of the O'Neills", marched at the head of the Cinel Eoghan; while on the same side Ainmire and Ainnidh, or Ninnidh, the grandsons of Conal Gulban, led the troops of Cinel Conaill, the two contingents comprising all the forces of Ulster. On the other side, Eoghan Bel, the King of Connaught, led in person the men of Connaught. The scene of the conflict stretched from the estuary of Sligo to the estuary of Ballysadare, and was "spread out" at Grinder, a place which, though hitherto unidentified,[1] may be Carrow Crin,[2] a spot situated on the edge of the right bank of the Ballysadare river or channel. Within these limits the battle mainly raged, but as it is stated in the lines quoted, that some of those engaged were drowned in the Sligeach, and that their bodies were carried out to sea, we might perhaps conclude that the Connaught-men, either before, or during the battle, had reached the north side of the river, and suffered heavy loss while driven back across it by the victorious enemy to the south side, where the defeat of the Connaught forces would have been consummated with great slaughter.

To enable us still more to realize the lie of the battle-field, as well as to throw light on much that shall be said later on, it will be well to indicate here the route usually pursued by the Northmen in their invasions of Connaught, and by the Connaughtmen in their inroads on Ulster; and this we cannot well do without first divesting ourselves of all associations connected with the present town of Sligo, with its approaching roads, its

---

[1] This might be read 'at Hinder,' but neither form of the name is now extant".—O'Donovan's note, A.T.M.

[2] Commonly called Kelly's Town at present; and in the past it sometimes got the name of Belfersdy, i.e. Mouth of the Ford.

bridges, streets, and adventitious surroundings, and carrying the thoughts back to a time when these roads, bridges, streets and surroundings did not exist, and the site was a wild wood. Such was the state of things at the date of the battle of Sligo, and for several centuries later. In those early times the Ulster men, after crossing the Erne at Ballyshannon or Belleek, moved on through Bundoran, Bunduff, Bundrowes, Cliffoney, Grange, keeping all along as close to the sea as they could,[1] till they reached Breaffy, when they turned towards Lissadell, and passed on through Ballygilgan and Carney, to Fined. Here, if necessary, they halted till the tide was out, when they passed the strand to Doonierin road. From Doonierin they moved through Gregg and Ballincar to the point called in the *Annals of the Four Masters*, Reanna-an-Liagain,[2] and known at present to the pilots of the Rosses as Stand-alone-point, but given correctly in Nimmo's map as "Stone-Alone-Point;" and now, instead of going up to the site of Sligo town, where there was no means of passing the river, they crossed the channel and strand to the Finisklin side.

Leaving Finisklin or Gibraltar, they soon reached Carrowcrin, the next stage in their journey, and from Carrowcrin passed easily the Fiontragh strand, when the tide was off it, to Streamstown, in the parish of Ballysadare, over a *fearsat* or ford in the channel, marked in the *Down Survey* map and much frequented down to half a century ago.[3] At Streamstown the whole of Connaught lay before them to the right, Tireragh and Tirawley; to the left, Tirerrill and Breffney; and in front, Corran, Roscommon, and all South Connaught. So late as the year 1536,[4] we find the forces of Hugh O'Donnell following this line of march passing between the Duff and the Drowes, the night of the day on which they had set out from Ballyshannon; encamping, the next night, at Finfir or Fined; proceeding the following day, by Doonierin, to Fearsat-Reanna-an-Liagair, and crossing the *Fearsat* to Coolerra; and after ravaging Coolerra for three days and three nights, "marching westwards across the strand into Tireragh of the Moy".

And that, in the primitive ages, this *Fearsat* formed the great passage from Calrigia or Carly, to Coolerra, we may learn from the legend, according to which "this place was called Rinn-Liagain from Liagain, a heroic warrior of the Fomorians, who was slain there as he was on his way to the battle of Moytura".[5] Though it may be probable, as it is apparently in keeping

---

[1] Ordnance Survey Letter Book of County Sligo.
[2] A.D. 1536.
[3] This was a common passage from Streamstown to Coolirra in the past; but became disused in consequence of a man named O'Donoghue having been drowned near it, having missed the exact spot for crossing. He was driving a cow before him at the time.
[4] Annals of the Four Masters, 1536.
[5] Annals of the Four Masters, 1536.

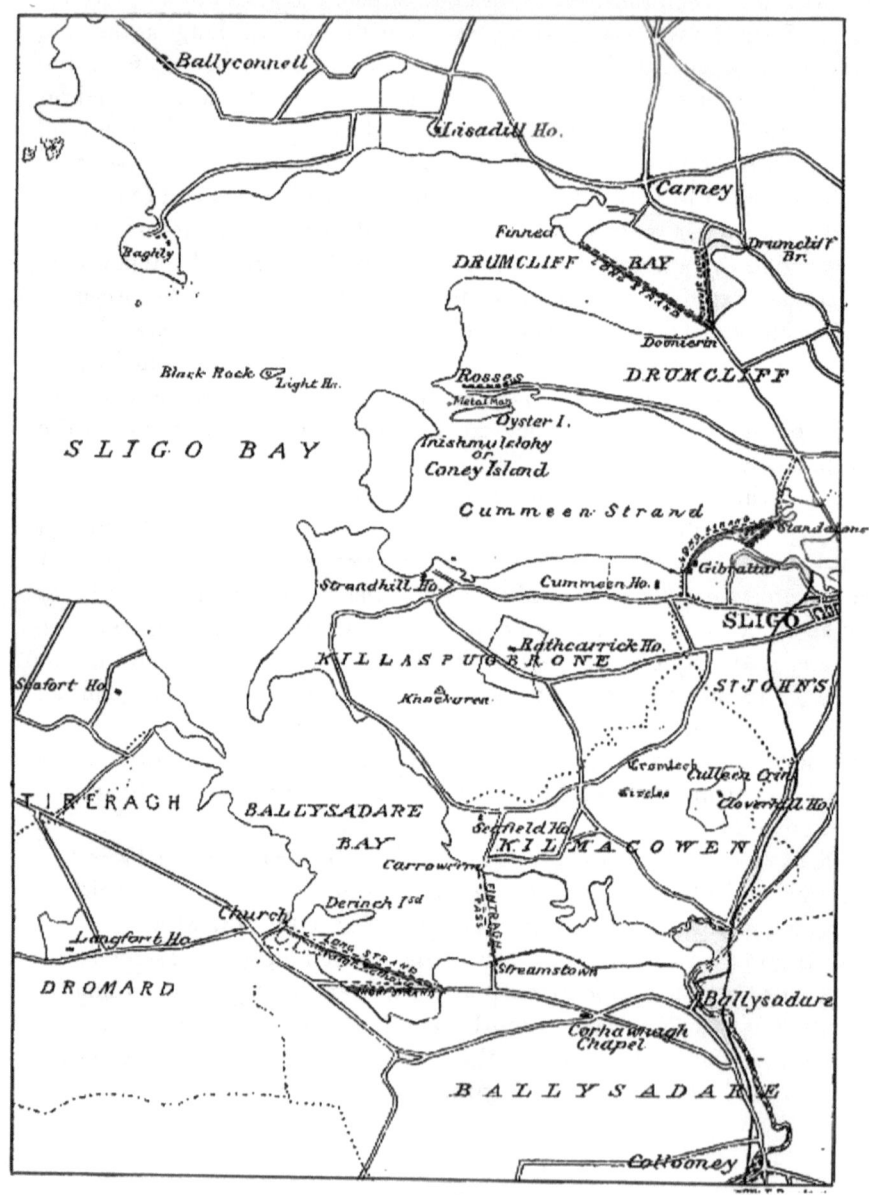

Scale 1½ Inch to one Mile.
PARISHES thus ------ TOWNLANDS thus ......

with Dr. Petrie's views on the extent of the battle-field, that the Crinder of the burial place of a man whom they name McGlanaghan, and who lived the poem is Carrowcrin, it seems much more probable that it is the "Culleen Grin", given in Petty's printed map of Sligo, and marked in *Down Survey*, as a denomination of 25 acres, 1 rood, and 18 perches, the property of Mr. Dodwell, and lying in that part of Cloverhill, which contains the well-known open grave with the inscribed stones. The country people tell at that this grave has never had any connection with the cromlechs, and that it is a comparatively recent date; and, that this is so is clear enough not only from an inspection of the district which is covered, or has been covered, with circles and cromlechs to within a short distance of the grave and *no farther*, but also from the ornamentation of the stones round this particular grave, no trace of ornament having ever been discovered in any of the numerous circles or cromlechs of Carrowmore. Indeed the observation of the old poem that "the battle spread out at Crinder", is so entirely in accord with the state of the field even at present, assuming Crinder to be Culleen Grin, that any intelligent person, seeing from the Seafield road circles or remains of circles, scattered here and there in the direction of Culleen Grin, or Cloverhill, *but not beyond*, and hearing of the bones constantly dug up in the spots from which circles have disappeared, would at once conclude that the battle raged mainly in that direction and region.

That other remarkable line of the poem, "The Sligeach bore to the great sea, the blood of men with their flesh", would, of itself, establish the writer's opinion that the battle occurred at the lower river, for had the slaughter happened on the site of the town, as others suppose, the dead bodies would have lain where they fell as they could not be touched by the tidal waters, which alone could carry them out to sea. But it is evident that they fell on the strand, or in the fearsat of the channel, where part of the battle took place, so that when the tide rose it swept them beyond the bar.

For it must not be lost sight of, that the *fearsats* of the neighbourhood were the public passes of early times, and often of times even not very remote from our own. Before coast roads were made the *fearsat* from Fined to Doonierin across the Drumcliffe estuary; the *fearsat* from Stone-Alone-Point to the Coolirra side of the channel, across the Sligo river, and that from Carrowcrin to Streamstown, across the Ballysadare river, formed the great highway for large bodies of men such as armies, and for heavy vehicles. The line of march of O'Donnell's army in 1536, shows this to have been the case in the sixteenth century. Those who crossed the Sligo river from the north side, passed down from Ballincar, by a lane which still exists, to the level ridge of shore, that stretches from the Bathing House to Stone-Alone-Point, where they entered the *fearsat* which led them to the Coolirra side. Here there were three passes before them: one at Finisklin, one at

Gibraltar, and one at Scardan, and there is reason to think that the one at Gibraltar was the leading pass, as the strand leading to it was as firm as a macadamized roadway.

In connection with the Sligo *fearsat*, it is important to remember that the river was much shallower in the past than it is at present, or has been recently. Even so late as 1821, when Mr. Nimmo drew up his map of Sligo Port, the depth of water at the pass of Stone-Alone-Point was only one-sixth of a fathom or one foot. It is well known to those who have examined the matter that in former times—far less water came up the river from the sea, and that far less came down the river from Loughgill the present surface level of the lake being at least four feet over the level of a hundred years ago—so that the channel must have been fordable at several points, and the ford at Stone-Alone-Point must have been so shallow, that people could pass it nearly dry-shod. As to the upper river, that above the bridge, the dam at the bridge, by keeping back the water, has entirely altered the appearance as well as the depth of the stream, so that, what was formerly both narrow and shallow is now a broad and deep river. Even still, if the water coming from Loughgill were allowed free flow, the river between the distillery and the Victoria Bridge would be one of the shallowest in the province. In an inquiry held by the Commissioners of Fisheries in Sligo, on the 18th October, 1845, Mr. Abraham Martin, as reported in the Sligo Journal of October 24, observed, "Were I to leave the sluice open for 24 hours in each week in summer it would drain off all the water". Coming back to the battle of Sligo, it is easier now than it was before to understand how Coolirra became the scene of the conflict, the place lying straight in the way of the hostile armies. And it may be remarked, in passing, that a more suitable place for a battle, if any place can be suited to deeds of slaughter, it would be very hard to find. Looking at the lofty mountains of Benbulben, Castlegal, and Leitrim, the rugged ranges of Slieve da En and Slieve Gamh, and the towering hill of Knocknarea, set round in a seeming circle, one would be led to fancy that nature herself had drawn the lists around the combatants; while the combatants themselves, in seeing those almost insuperable obstacles to escape on all sides, with the exception of one or two gaps, where the still more formidable obstacle of the sea barred the way, could not help plucking resolution from the situation, and feeling that their only hope of safety lay in valour and victory. This feeling must have contributed much to the obstinateness of the battle, and to the great loss of life, which we are warranted, even according to the meagre account of the Annals, in believing to have taken place, but still more warranted, if we may connect, as the writer thinks we should, the numerous circles and cromlechs of the district with this particular engagement. All seem now agreed in repudiating the opinion which held them to be Druids' Altars, and

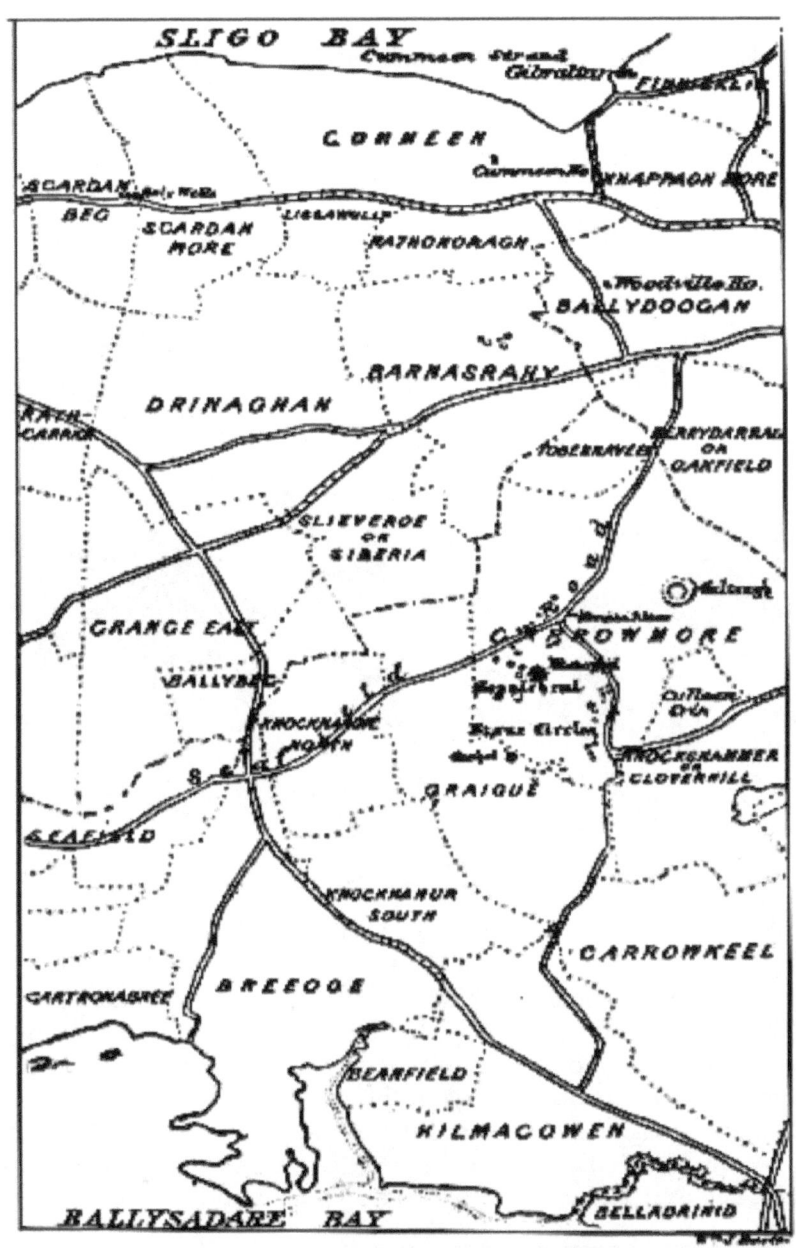

MAP SHOWING STONE CIRCLES &C.
PARISHES thus - - -   TOWNLANDS thus ......
Scale 1½ Inch to One Mile.

in regarding them as sepulchral monuments, raised over men who had fallen in some great battle.

These structures were all on the same plan—a circle and, in a few instances, two or three concentric circles of large stones, the diameter of the enclosure being generally about forty feet, but sometimes more, and the stones varying in size from one foot to four or five feet high.

STONE CIECLE AND CROMLECH AT CARROWMORE, NEAR SLIGO.[1]

Thirty or forty of these, on an average, were set, at regular intervals, generally within a foot or two of each other, round a centre, so that they formed so many points of the circumference. As cromlechs, or the remains of cromlechs, are found as centres in the circles which survive, we may conclude that originally they formed the centres of all the circles, which, according to Mr. Petrie, must have been at one time more than two hundred, and were at the date of his visit[2] sixty-four, though now reduced

---

[1] Drawn from a sketch by Petrie, for the Very Rev. Doctor O'Rorke, P.P., by W. F. Wakeman, August 2nd, 1888. VOL. I.
VOL. I.

[2] In a letter of Mr. Petrie to Sir Thomas Larcom, we read, "I merely write you a line to say that, after yesterday's investigation of the sepulchral circles at Carrowmore, I am far from done, though I brought up my notes to forty circles. I now verily believe there could not originally have been less than two hundred". Life of George Petrie, LL.D., by William

to less than a fourth of that number. Mr. Petrie regarded it as probable that the circles "had been carried on originally from one extremity of the peninsula to the other", that is, from the estuary of Ballysadare to that of Sligo; and, in searching for evidence of this opinion, he found remains of some of those monuments to the north, in the townland of Barnesrahy, though he failed to make any similar discovery to the south.[1] Considering, however, the many centuries that have elapsed since the original erection of these structures, at a time when there was hardly a single stone fence or house in the entire peninsula; and considering that the district is now intersected in all directions with such fences and covered with such houses, the absence of the circles, or even of their recognizable remains, is no disproof of their past existence, as the materials must have been used in building houses and field walls. But whatever may be thought of the prolongation of the line of circles towards the north and south, it would appear to be pretty certain that a second line, starting at right angles from the first, and stretching in a westerly direction, extended all the way to Misgan Meave, on the top of Knocknarea. This was the opinion of Petrie as also of the late Mr. Walker, whose acquaintance with the district was more minute and accurate than that even of Petrie; and anyone who to-day ascends Misgan Meave, and looks in the direction indicated, will see enough, in the clusters of large stones under view, to convince him of the soundness of that opinion.

The condition of things then, in Carrowmore and the neighbouring townlands, is just what one should expect, supposing the place to have been the scene of the battle of Sligo, and *supposing the history of the battle, as given in the old Life of St. Ceallach, to be the true one.*

There are two accounts then of this engagement, which may be designated, respectively, the account of Ulster and the account of Connaught; the former, that given in the Annals, and the latter, that contained in the Life of Saint Ceallach. According to the version of the Annals the conflict would have been "short, sharp, and decisive", resulting in a complete victory for the Ulstermen, who returned home bringing with them the trophies of the conquered, and, among those trophies, the head of Eoghan Bel. But according to the Connaught story, the Connaughtmen, even though their king was mortally wounded, were the victors, as they encamped after the battle on the field, and *continued there several days.*

Stokes, M.D., D.C.L., Oxon, p. 242. In the detailed list of the circles, given by Dr. Stokes, from Petrie's manuscript, the number is brought up to 64.—Life of George Petrie, &c., pp. 242-254.

[1] "It occurred to me as probable that a careful examination of the townlands, lying to the north and south, might furnish evidences that the series had been carried on originally from one extremity of the peninsula of Cuil Irra to the other; and though my anticipations were not realized towards the south, the investigation was rewarded by the discovery of several monuments to the north, as in the townland of Barnesrahy, &c". Ibid., p. 252.

During these days the dying King gave orders about his interment, directing that he should be buried in Rath O'Fiachrach, in a standing posture, and with his red javelin in his hand. Though this rath has not been identified, it cannot be any other than that on which the so-called Misgan Meave now stands on the summit of Knocknarea, the whole of this part of the present barony of Carbury belonging, in the olden time, to the O'Fiachrachs, as part of Tireragh.[1] This position would correspond exactly with that described in Saint Ceallach's life,[2] as being "on that side" of the "hill", which overlooks the route from Connaught to the north; that route corresponding closely with the present Seafield road to Sligo, and passing from Carrowcrin, or Kellys-town, through Carrowmore, on to Barnesrahy. And some aid to this conjecture may be derived from the word "hill" which could hardly apply to any other spot in the peninsula, Knocknarea being the only hill in it.

---

[1] Tireragh extended formerly from the river Robe to the river Codhnach of Drumcliffe;
"From the Rodha of prosperous course,
   To the Codhnach of winding current".—Tribes and Customs of Hy-Fiachrach, p. 279.

[2] The following account of the burial of Eoghan Bel is taken from the Irish Life of Saint Ceallach. The translation is by O'Donovan:—
"Eoghan also told them to bury himself with his red javelin in his hand in the grave. Place my face towards the north, on the side of the hill by which the northerns pass when flying before the army of Connaught; let my grave face them, and place myself in it, after this manner. And this order was strictly complied with; and in every place where the Clanna Neill and the Connacians met in conflict, the Clanna Neill and the northerns were routed, being panic-stricken by the countenances of their foes, so that the Clanna Neill and the people of the North of Ireland therefore resolved to come with a numerous host to Rath O'Fiachrach, and raise the body of Eoghan from the grave, and carry his remains northwards across the Sligo. This was done, and the body was buried at the other side of the river at Aenach Locha Gile, with the mouth down, that it might not be the means of causing them to fly before the Connacians".—Tribes and Customs of Hy-Fiachrach, p. 472.

King Laery was buried in a similar position, and with similar surroundings.
We read in Aubrey de Vere's Insfail: -
"They buried the King upon Tara's Hill,
In his grave upright, there stands he still.
"Upright there stands he, as men that wade
By night through a castle, undismay'd;
On his head is the gold crown, the spear in his hand,
And he looks to the hated Lagenian band".
And Eoghan Bel's thoughts, like Laery's, were warlike and vengeful;
"But we are as men, through dark floods that wade;
We stand in our black graves undismay'd;
Our faces are turn'd to the race abhorr'd,
And ready beside us stand spear and sword,
Ready to strike at the last great day,
Ready to trample them back into clay".—Inisfail.

Additional confirmation of the writer's view may be drawn from the usual acceptation of the word Knocknarea, by the people living in the neighbourhood; for though eminent antiquaries and Irish scholars take Knocknarea to mean either the Hill of the Moon, or the Hill of Executions, the people in and near Coolerra generally understand, by the name, the Hill of the King, no doubt King Eoghan Bel, no other being in any way associated with it, and, in particular, not Eochy, King of the Firbolgs, as he, according to all our authorities, was slain on the strand of Beltra, and there buried under the famous cairn, formerly counted among the wonders of Ireland.

But it is right to state, before proceeding further, that the writer cannot accept any of the three foregoing explanations of the word Knocknarea, certain, though their respective authors profess to be about them. The Venerable Charles O'Conor, takes it to be a mere matter of course that the name, Knocknarea, means Hill of the Moon;[1] O'Donovan, while blaming O'Conor for this opinion, and expressing surprise "that so acute a critic should commit such a blunder", affirms positively that it signifies Hill of the Executions;[2] and the inhabitants of Coolerra are equally convinced that it is Hill of the King.

While the opinions of O'Conor and O'Donovan have little in their favour except the *ipse dixits* of those distinguished men which, of course, is no inconsiderable support, it is easy to understand how the local view originated. Finding a tradition in the neighbourhood that a king was buried in Misgan Maeve, and knowing the Irish word "righ" sometimes appearing in English under the form "rea" to signify a king, the people with a precipitancy, not unusual in such circumstances, jumped to the conclusion that Knocknarea was in name, as well as in fact, the Hill of the King.

The true etymology, however, will, no doubt, be found by following a clue supplied in the Life of Saint Cormac, as given in Colgan's *Acta Sanctorum*, at the 26th of March. It is there expressly stated that *Rosredheadh* was the ancient name of the Knocknarea district; and as *Rosredheadh*, or its equivalent *Ros na Reidh*, means the promontory of the smooth, level, mountain top, it seems to follow that Knocknarea otherwise *Knoc na Eeidhis*—the Hill of the smooth, level top, a designation which describes perfectly the peculiar outlines and character of the hill.[3]

---

[1] By-the-by, Knock na Rea signifies literally the Mountain of the moon, very probably from the ancients celebrating their Neomenia on that hill"

[2] Letter written from Sligo on July the 2nd, 1836, and given in the Ordnance Survey Letter Book of the County Sligo. In this communication, he writes Knocknarea as Cnoc na riagh, and affirms that it is always so spelled in old documents. Ha states too, that a legend in the Dinnseanchus proves the correctness of this spelling. He does not give the legend.

[3] "Reidh (ray) is usually applied to a mountain flat, or a coarse, moory, level piece of land among hills. "- Irish Names of Places, first series, p. 387. The learned and accurate author adds, "There is a well-known mountain over the Killeries in Connemara, called Muilrea,

KNOCKNAREA, CO. SLIGO.[1]

The smooth and level contour of Knocknarea comes out strikingly when the hill is contrasted with the surrounding mountains. If the traveller by the coach road from Ballysadare to Sligo look around him on reaching the top of the long bray at Tawnafortis, and after observing, to the southeast, Slieve da Eu—a maze of knobs, bosses, and ravines; to the southwest, the Ox Mountains, looking from this point exactly like the petrified breakers of a raging sea; and to the north, Castlegal range with its breaks, its geological faults, and rugged crest; and then turn the eye to Knocknarea, rounded off and smoothed as if by machinery, he cannot fail to be forcibly struck by the singular appropriateness of the name, Smooth Hill, given by our ancestors to this elevation. In this respect they are in full agreement with Mr. Frazer, who in his Handbook for Ireland hits off so felicitously the physical features and scenery of the country; for he describes Knocknarea as "a singularly formed, solitary, *flat-topped*, verdant hill, crowned with a large sepulchral tumulus". "Flat topped hill " is not a bad English equivalent for Knocknarea, that is, Cnoc-na-reidh. It is really strange that eminent Irish, scholars, like Charles O'Conor and John

---

and this name characterizes its outline compared with that of the surrounding hills, when seen from a moderate distance; Mael-reidh, smooth flat mountain". This very apposite example would suffice itself to fix the genuine import of Knocknarea.

[1] Drawn on the wood by Mr. Wakeman, from a sketch by Miss O'Connor of Ballyglass.

O'Donovan, did not think of this natural and obvious explanation instead of excogitating arbitrarily their far-fetched "Neomenia " and "Execution " theories. It must not be forgotten, as it has an important bearing on the age and character of the Carrowmore antiquities, that the flat top of Knocknarea comprises a considerable area apparently several hundred acres and that the cairn or Misgan stands on the eastern, that is, the *Sligo edge* or side, while the plain itself stretches faraway to the west thus verifying to the letter those words of the Life of St. Celleach *"on the side of the hill* by which the northerns pass when flying before the army of Connaught".

If any confirmation of the writer's opinion as to the etymology of Knocknarea were needed, it would be found in the popular pronunciation of the last syllable of the name, which, however affected speakers may sound it, is always pronounced by the people like the English word "ray" the exact sound of *reidh* according to Dr. Joyce, who writes, in his Irish Names of Places (First Series, p. 387), "Reidh (ray) is usually applied to a mountain flat or a coarse, moory, level piece of land among hills". The sound comes out well in a street ballad on "Sligo Town", composed by a Sligo man in New York, sung through the different cities and towns of the United States, and purchased on the Niagara Suspension Bridge, from the ballad singer by Professor Judge of Maynooth College. Take the following stanza or two:—

"I love old Ireland all around, the north, south, east and west,
But who can blame me if I love that dear old town the best?
'Twas there that first my infant eyes beheld the light of day,
Near Sligo town that lies so snug at the foot of Knocknarea.

I love my dear adopted land, I love it as my life,
I love it dearly as I love my children and my wife;
But who can blame me if I love old Ireland far away,
And Sligo town that lies so snug at the foot of Knocknarea?"

This pronunciation alone would upset the analogy which O'Donovan tries to establish between Adnarea and Knocknarea, as the last syllable of the former word is invariably pronounced throughout the counties of Mayo and Sligo, as if written *ree*. It is hoped then that this explanation of the name of Knocknarea, though put forth now for the first time, will be recognised as the true one; and it must be the more acceptable, as it takes away, from the most beautiful hill in the province, the reproach of having once been a vile place of executions, while, at the same time, it keeps us all at a safe distance from the moon, with which archaeologists and antiquaries are sometimes in closer proximity than is desirable. Had Charles O'Conor and John O'Donovan fallen in with the *rosredheadlh* of St.

Cormac's Life, they would, pretty certainly, have been saved from their respective mistakes.

Everything then makes for the writer's view of the battle of Sligo:—first, the situation of the Carrowmore monuments, lying, as they do, just between the Sligo river and Carrowcrin, the exact position indicated in the lines quoted by the Four Masters;—second, the fact that the cromlechs stand on, or along, the highway which led, in primitive and early times, from the estuary of Ballysadare to the estuary of Sligo;—third, the cairn on Knocknarea, which is taken by Petrie to be the burying place of the chief or leader of the warriors in whose honour the cromlechs were raised, and which, standing, as it does, *on the Sligo side of the hill*, corresponds precisely with the description, in the Life of St. Ceallach, of Eoghan Bel's grave, "placed on the side of the hill by which the northerns pass when flying from the armies of Connaught;"—fourth, the antecedent probability that the Connaught army, after honouring their leader and king, by raising the great cairn over his remains, would discharge a similar duty towards their subordinate leaders and comrades, a duty so easily performed, owing to the blocks of Ox Mountain stone which then strewed the spot, as they still strew various other stretches in the neighbourhood; and, lastly, the stay of several days made by the troops on the battle-field, during which time there was hardly anything else to occupy them or detain them except the erection of those monuments.

The solution now offered of the puzzle, presented by the Carrowmore circles and cromlechs, is so natural as to make it a matter of surprise that it did not occur to somebody earlier. The chief cause of this, no doubt, was the phrase, the "Battle of Sligo", which people, with modern associations in the head, took to mean the battle of the town of Sligo, instead of the battle of the river of Sligo, which the words certainly signify. If men remembered this, and reflected at the same time that the stream below the bridge is rightly called the River of Sligo, and was exclusively so called in the past, they would have identified long before this the scene of the famous battle, which cost Eoghan Bel his life.

There may, perhaps, be found some who will not still admit that the arguments just adduced establish conclusively the connection of the Carrowmore monuments with the Battle of Sligo, but no one who considers attentively and impartially what has been said, can deny that the connection has got probability, if not absolute certainty, in its favour, unlike, in this respect, to the Firbolg and Tuatha de Danaan theory, for which nothing intelligible is alleged, which is unsupported by a shred of historical writing, or a syllable of respectable tradition, and which at bottom is only a wild guess at the origin of those hitherto mysterious structures, either by sciolists[1], whose opinions are worthless, or by persons who, however eminent in other respects, lacked the local knowledge which might lead them to the true solution of the problem.

Assuming then the connection, a point of great importance to the archaeologist is gained by his learning the exact age of those monuments. Sir James Ferguson, in his Rude Stone Monuments, rejecting the ideas of the Four Masters, who date the monuments of Cong or the southern Moytura, and of Carrowmore, which Sir James supposed to be the northern Moytura, to the respective years of 1896 and 1869, B.C., refers them to the Christian era, and shows, in several passages, a desire to bring them as far down in that era as he can. "I should", he says in one place, page 197, "from their internal evidence, be much more inclined to assume that the battles must have taken place one or two centuries after the birth of Christ", and, not satisfied with an origin so early, though two thousand years later than that assigned by the Four Masters, he observes on the next page, "But after the most earnest attention I have been able to give to all that has been written and said on the subject, and a careful comparison of the monuments on these fields with those of other countries, I would, on the whole, be inclined to bring them forward a century or two, if I could find a gap to throw them into, rather than date them earlier. They look older and more tentative than the English circles described in the last chapter, but not so much as to lead us to expect a difference of four or five centuries. On the other hand, they are so like those on the Bravalla field, and other monuments in Scandinavia, to be described hereafter, that it is puzzling to think that seven or ten centuries elapsed between them".

If Sir James Ferguson lived now, and learned that the "gap", he was so anxious to find, was discovered, and that, according to the discovery, the Carrowmore circles would date from the sixth century, it is certain from everything he has written, that he would endorse heartily the opinion of the writer, and hold the solution, now offered, to satisfy perfectly all the conditions of the problem.

Before passing on, it may be remarked that the construction, called Rath O'Fiachrach in Saint Ceallach's life, is plainly identical with that named Rath Righbaird in the Four Masters, and Fossa Riabairt in the Book of Armagh, near which St. Patrick is said to have founded the church of Killaspugbrone; the situation assigned to each being precisely the same.

Just one word regarding objections which, on examining this new view of the Battle of Sligo, may rise in the minds of some. The absence of bronze and iron implements, or arms, from finds in the battle-field; the marks of fire on objects connected with the cromlechs; and the bones of mammalia and small rodents, as well as the shells of shell-fish, met with in

---

[1] A pretended expert, [Clachan ed.].

excavations of Carrowmore, seem to some persons to militate against the modern date of the engagement. But there is really nothing in these objections. As to the absence of bronze and iron objects, it is rather late in the day to found an argument on this fact, or alleged fact; for even if we suppose the field to have been strewn with such objects, there was time and occasion enough to pick them up in the thirteen centuries which have elapsed since the conflict took place more especially as they would lie on the chief highway of the county, and under the eyes of the passersby. The objection too would carry its authors further than they might wish, for it would lead them to deny the well authenticated date of the battle of Cuildreimhne (Cooldroman), as no one has heard of iron or bronze objects having been found on that spot. And the "three days", or "week", or longer time, the troops of Eoghan Bel remained on the field gave them plenty of opportunity to recover dropped arms in case such were lying about. Besides, the absence of bronze or iron is assumed without warrant, and even against evidence; for Dr. Petrie, in his lucid description of the Carrowmore circles and cromlechs, observes, in paragraph 63, "Within the central enclosure, as stated by the people of the neighbourhood, a bronze sword was found about forty years ago". One swallow, it is true, does not make a summer, but when we see one, we can hardly be wrong in thinking that others are hardly far off, so that this bronze sword suggests the presence of others.

The "marks of fire" are just as inconclusive. When we recollect that the victors encamped for several days on the battlefield, and that during those days they had their camp fires for cooking and heating purposes in all directions, we have, in the fact, explanation enough of all the fire marks that appear.

Nor do the bones of the mammalia, we hear of, tell in any way against the new view. They make for it rather; for the Four Masters, and other annalists, expressly tell us that there were kine on the-battle field; and as to the bones of rodents and to shells, they are merely the remains of the rabbits and oysters on which the Connaughtmen regaled themselves during their stay in Coolerra, where both rabbits and oysters have always existed in great plenty. From the line –

"The kine of the enemy roared with the javelins",

we learn the curious fact that the stratagem of the insurgents of 1798, of driving cattle before them at the battle of New Ross, to receive the first onset of the battle, was made use of, thirteen hundred years earlier, by the Connaughtmen in the battle of Sligo. Efforts have been recently made to show that cremation was practised at the interments of Carrowmore, but there is no proof whatever of that contention. In Dr. Petrie's sober and masterly analysis of the monuments and their contents, he never thought of cremation, in connection with the human remains, though he mentions such finds fourteen times,[1] but always without the slightest hint of a belief that they had been burned or, as the phrase is, cremated. "Human bones have been discovered within this circle;" "human bones were found within this circle by Mr. Walker;" "as usual human bones were found within this tomb;" "in all these circles bones were found beneath the cromleacs;" such are the phrases he always employs when recording finds of the bones of men. It is very different, however, when there is question of the remains of animals; as, for instance, in paragraph 51, where he writes: "The half-calcined bones of horses and other animals were, and are still, found in the cairn in great quantity". And in the same context he says: "The persons who first opened this monument assert that they found nothing within it but burnt wood and human bones", where certainly, had these bones been subjected to fire, he would have noted the circumstance, as he notes it in regard to the wood. So far, then, from the remains of the battle, as they exist or have existed, being an objection, they supply additional proof of the correctness of the opinion, which is now respectfully but confidently submitted to the judgment of antiquaries, historians, and the general public.

From the absence, in the foregoing remarks, of all reference to Ptolemy's so called "eminent city"—*episemos polis*—of Nagnata, it will be seen that the writer has no faith in the alleged identity of that mysterious city with the town of Sligo. Indeed he does not see that anything tangible

---

[1] For a quietus of this foolish cremation theory it may be well to quote in detail the words of Dr. Petrie:
Paragraph 1. "Bones were found beneath the cromleac".
" 2. "Human bones have also been discovered within this circle".
" 3. "Mr. Walker had this cromleac searched and found an interment within it".
" 10. "An interment was found within the cromleac".
" 15. "Human bones were found within the cromleac by Mr. Walker".
" 17. "Within the enclosure Mr. Walker found human bones and the fragments of an urn".
" 22. "Within the cromleac an interment was found by Mr. Walker".
" 23. "Human bones found within the cromleac".
" 29. "As usual, human bones were found within this tomb".
" 31. "Human bones were found within this cromleac".
" 40. "As usual, human bones were found in the tombs".
" 46. "In all these circles bones were found beneath the cromleacs".
" 51. "The persons who first opened this, the most important monument of the entire series, assert that they found nothing within it but burnt wood and human bones. The half-calcined bones of horses and other animals were, and are still, found in the cairn in great quantity".
" 63. "Human bones have been found within the central enclosure, and, as stated by the people of the neighbourhood, a bronze sword was found about forty years ago".—Life of George Petrie. By William Stokes, M.D., D.C.L., Oxon., &c., pages 243-4-5-6-7-8-9,

can be quoted in favour of the allegation, except, perhaps, Ptolemy's mention of such a place as lying *somewhere* in Connaught, which, considering that geographer's inacquaintance with this country, does not amount to much. "It is well to know", says the Rev. Dr. O'Conor, in the first volume of his *Rerum Hibernicarum Scriptores* (p. xliv.), "that the geography of Ptolemy is full of errors, especially in regard to northern Britain, which he makes to run towards the east, whereas it actually runs towards the north; and if he cannot be relied on with regard to Britain, for which, as a Roman province, good sources of information were open to him, he must be much more untrustworthy in respect to Ireland, on which the conquering Romans had never set foot. "When Tacitus, who had peculiar opportunities of acquiring correct notions of Ireland, while writing the life of Agricola, blunders so egregiously as to place the island midway between Spain and Britain—*medio inter Brittaniam et Hispaniam*—it is clear that the map of Ptolemy, who lived much about the same time, should be received with great caution and under correction. And unless the learned biographer of Agricola was as deceived in regard to the other circumstances of the country as he was about its geographical position, his evidence would go far to disprove the existence in it of great cities, for he tells us he had heard that a single legion would have been sufficient to subdue the whole island, which would show that the population was both small and sparse".

But granting even that this *episemos polis* rose somewhere on the Connaught coast, there is no ground for placing it on the site of Sligo. Of those who, assuming it had a real being, try to fix its situation, some would set it at Drumcliff; Dr. O'Conor, *near* Sligo (*prope Sligoam*); Sir James Ware, "not far from Sligo;" Mr. Harris, in the village of Mayo, in the county of that name; Baxter and Hardiman, at the town of Galway; and the present writer, for reasons given in his *Ballysadare and Kilvarnet*, at Ballysadare. When, then, there is so much uncertainty with regard to the whole subject; when this "eminent city" may be a mere invention of some lying or imaginative traveller, who served as Ptolemy's informant, it would be rash to accept its existence on such doubtful evidence, but still more rash and unreasonable, in the absence of the slightest trace or tradition of it in the neighbourhood, to locate it at Sligo the most unlikely, of a hundred sites, lying between Bunduff and Galway; for any of the successive colonies, which inhabited the country in the remote past, would sooner perch a town on the summit of Benbulben, or range it round the cairn on Knocknarea, than sink it in the deep hollow in which the town of Sligo lies. It would be mere waste of time then, in an historical inquiry, to bestow serious thought on this shadowy city of Nagnata.

CHAPTER IV

THE FITZGERALDS AND SLIGO

BETWEEN the date of the battle, we have been considering, and the twelfth century there is nothing to indicate the existence of a town in Sligo, the name not being once mentioned in the annals of the country during all that time. Nor is it found in St. Bernard's *Life of St. Malachy*, though that interesting biography contains the names of all the places of note in Ireland, towards the middle of the twelfth century, the time at which the piece was composed. We miss it in like manner from Giraldus Cambrensis' *Topography of Ireland*, which, being written professedly and by order of the English King, as a description of Ireland, at the period of the Anglo-Norman Invasion, would certainly contain some reference to Sligo if the town then existed, or, at all events, if it had emerged from obscurity. And a third work, though a much more modern composition, but founded on old documents, *The Wars of the Gaels*, which is occupied with the doings of the Danes in this country, is as silent about Sligo as the *Life of St. Malachy*, or the *Topography of Ireland*. To these authorities may be added those publications of the Celtic and Archaeological Societies the Book of Rights, and the Topographical Poems of O'Dugan and O'Heerin which describe and illustrate the condition of Ireland at the arrival of the English, in whose pages, as in those already quoted, one will look in vain for the name of Sligo. But it is useless to pursue those quotations further, as it is clear, if the town existed and flourished in the earlier ages of our era, as some people believe, or, perhaps, affect to believe, that mention of it could hardly fail to be found in one or more of the writings already referred to, which, for the most part, were composed for the express purpose of commemorating such persons and things as were deemed worthy of public notice.

It is only in the thirteenth century we begin to find at last signs of the district of Sligo being, or becoming, populous. An entry under the year 1227, in the *Annals of Loch Ce* tells us: "A depredation was committed in Sligech by the Justiciary, and by Brian, son of Turlough when they took many women prisoners". The same annals relate a similar occurrence under the year 1236, "The Foreigners of Erinn pursued Felim to Roscommon, and pursued him from thence to the bridge of Sligech; and as they did not overtake him they committed great depredations on Tadhg O'Conor; and they then seized a great number of noble women, whom they carried away with them in captivity". But it may be doubted whether these women, who no doubt were carried away by the English, as the Sabine women of old were carried away by the Romans, to be taken as wives, came from the present site of Sligo, or from the adjoining districts. It is likely, for the reasons already indicated, that they came from the more elevated tracts of the neighbourhood, such as the Green Fort and Cairns, where from the earliest times there must have been some population, considering the fame and fruitfulness of the Sligo river.

The Sligech is one of the longest known, and best known, rivers in Ireland, being counted among the nine or ten rivers which Partholan, the alleged first inhabitant of the country after the flood, is said to have found before him on his arrival in the island.[1] It has also been fruitful to a degree surpassing other Irish rivers; yielding salmon, both above and below the waterfall, all the year round, unlike the other rivers which fail to give the fish at certain times; and before dredging and quay building began, this river, below the fall and on both its banks, contained shell-fish in such abundance as to earn for it the name of Sligech, that is, the shelly river. To bring this shelliness better home to the mind, it is necessary to carry one's thoughts back to those early times when the part of the river below the fall was the chief, or the only, part of it traversed; when the common passage from the northern bank to the southern, and *vice versa*, was over the fearsat or "flat" which lay between Stand-Alone-Point and Finisklin or Gibraltar; and when the traveller must have been ankle deep in shells and shell-fish almost every step he took.

At the beginning of this century, and for several years later, plenty of shell-fish might be had on or near the spot on which Lyons's Terrace now stands; and even at present, once you go outside the range of the harbour works, turn where you will along the channel, you come upon mussels, in one place, and cockles in another, in such abundance as is not to be met with in any other estuary of the country. And if the harbour works, by ejecting the fish from their old *habitat*, have somewhat obscured the proofs which went to show the character of the Sligo river, they have, on the other hand, disclosed to us a fact which lets in a flood of light on the subject; for about the year 1867, as the dredging cans had reached a greater depth than usual, they touched on what at first was taken to be a new stratum of earth, but what proved to be an oyster bed, which, after long discussion, and even legal investigation, was admitted to have been there from a time, of which there existed neither memory nor record: all the circumstances of the case going far to show, what some had already suspected, that the channel and the whole region of the river's mouth, were formerly a vast oyster bed. This abundance of oysters in the river was so characteristic of the place in the past that reference to it occurs in the arms of the town; for the hare, that is there seen scampering across the strand from the direction of Ballincar, is

---

[1] O'Flaherty's Ogygia, translated by Rev. J. Hely, Vol. I., p. 5.—Eochy O'Flann, in Rerum Hibernicarum Scriptores.—Auctore Carolo O'Conor, S.T.D., Tom. I., p. lvii.

represented carrying on one of its hind feet a fine oyster, on which it had stepped, and which closed upon the foot, as if to signify, that the fish were so numerous, that even the light-footed hare could not cross the scene without bringing with it evidence of the fact. If some people, who have tried to account for the name of Sligo by rummaging for shells in the boggy site of the present town, had been able to realize the state of things we have been describing, we should have been spared pages of puerilities which it is no small penance to read.[1]

Such teeming subsistence then in salmon and shell-fish, as this river supplied, could not fail at any time to attract people to its neighbourhood. And the same cause that attracted them would also retain them, so far, at least, as they could feel secure against the violence of the times. As this security, however, could hardly be expected on the very banks of the river, where hostile troops were frequently passing and repassing, and where individuals had no shelter or defence against numbers, it is likely that the inhabitants of the place resided habitually some little distance up the hills, where they would be in great measure out of harm's way, and where, at the same time, they would be within easy distance of the river, so as to be able to go to it, from time to time, for their supplies of food. This state of things

---

[1] "The river Sligo is not remarkable for shells if we credit the inhabitants who say they never saw shells in it, and that the town has not taken its name by reason thereof, for they never call it Sligo river, it always goes by the name of Garvog in Irish, and Gitly in English, but by reason of cartloads of shells having been found under ground in many places within the town, where houses stand now". Letter of T. O'Connor to Sir T. Larcom, dated Sligo, September 12th, 1836.

Whatever apology may be offered for O'Connor, who was a stranger and a bird of passage, none can plead a similar excuse for Major Wood-Martin, who, adopting O'Connor's theory, writes thus: "In the Four Masters, the appellation of Sligo is apparently derived from Sligeach, signifying shelly river, from slig, a shell. Although such is not now a characteristic of the river, yet, shortly previous to 1836, on sinking foundations for the erection of houses, a quantity of white shells was discovered in various localities within the area now occupied by the town; and in 1881, a similar result followed excavations for the reception of pipes for an intercepting sewer along the river bank within the town. The occupants of a range of cottages not far from the Sligo strand, employ themselves during the summer season in gathering cockles and mussels.

The shells are thrown out in a heap near the cottages; the white mass thus formed is remarkable, and would accumulate to an immense pile were not the shells removed for spreading on walks instead of gravel, or for adding to compost heaps, when becoming disintegrated, the shells act as lime in fertilizing the soil. Now if we suppose the ancient inhabitants of Sligo, with whom fish formed a staple article of diet, untrammelled by police regulations forbidding refuse to be thrown out in front of their dwellings, it is certain that in the course of a very few years the accumulation of shells would form a deposit such as is often found in digging deeply on the site of the ancient town{?) and the white glittering heaps seen from a distance may not improbably have given rise to the distinctive appellation of Sligo, i.e. shelly". —History of Sligo, p. 50.

If this were the genesis of the name, there would be no end of Sligos round the coast of Ireland, as there is no end of cockle cadgers' villages and their "glittering heaps" of shells.

probably lasted for a considerable period, the river daily becoming better known, and daily attracting greater numbers, till, in the course of time, they became so numerous as to invite the raids recorded in the *Annals of Loch Ce.* And it might have lasted much longer, only that Maurice Fitzgerald saw the great capabilities of the present site of Sligo, and resolved to turn them to due account.

The name of Maurice Fitzgerald should be always held in honoured remembrance by the inhabitants of Sligo, he being the real founder of their town. Grandson of the Maurice Fitzgerald who came to Ireland in 1169 to aid Dermot McMurrough, and son of Gerald Fitz Maurice, first baron of Offaly, styled by Sir Bernard Burke, "Patriarch of the house of Kildare", he increased largely the honours and possessions derived from father and grandfather, having been twice Lord Justice of Ireland, and having, in addition to the lands inherited in Leinster, acquired estates in Munster, Connaught, and Ulster. Passing through Sligo during his second viceroyalty, while in conflict with the O'Conors of Connaught and the O'Donnells of Tyrconnell, his experienced eye saw the fitness of the place for a castle, to serve at once as a garrison for English troops, and as a bar to the co-operation of his Connaught and northern enemies. The want of such a fortress he had experienced more than once himself in his warfare with the native chiefs; as, for instance, in 1236, when he sought to capture Felim, King of Connaught, and when the king escaped to O'Donnell, though the English troops pursued him in hot haste to the bridge of Sligo.

The castle was built in the year 1245, according to the *Annals of the Four Masters*; but, according to *Grace's Annals*, in 1242, a date which the Duke of Leinster adopts.[1] King Felim, in the first instance, was directed by the Lord Justice to erect it, and received for the purpose, as a gift from Fitzgerald, the lime, and stone, and other materials which had been designed for a religious hospital in Sligo;[2] but Felim did not proceed with

---

[1] "In 1242 he built the castle of Sligo. "Earls of Kildare. By the Marquis of Kildare, p. 13. Grace, who is his lordship's authority, writes: "1242 Arx de Sligagh construitur per Mauritium FitzGerald Justiciarium Hiberniae". Dowling, in his Annals, does not specify the date, but, before the entries under the year 1227, states: "Circa haec tempora Mauritius FitzGerald Justiciarius Hiberniae edificavit castrum de Sligagh in Conatia, vivente Philimo O'Conchur rege ibidem".—Dowling's Annals, p. 14.

[2] We read in the Four Masters, under the year 1245, as follows: "The castle of Sligo was erected by Maurice FitzGerald, Lord Justice of Ireland, and by the Sil Murray; for Felim was ordered to erect it at his own expense, and to convey the stones, lime, and houses of Trinity Hospital thither, after the Lord Justice had granted that place to Clarus MacMailin in honour of the Holy Trinity". In the Annals of Loch Ce, under the year 1245, the entry runs thus: "The castle of Sligech was built by MacMaurice FitzGerald, Justiciary of Erinn, and by the Sil-Muiredhaigh; for Fedhlim was told to erect it at his own expense, and to convey thereto the stones and lime of the hospital house of the Trinity, after this place had been previously given by the Justiciary, i.e., Maurice FitzGerald, to Clarus MacMailin

the work, for some reason not recorded, but most probably from the abomination in which Irish chieftains held castles, as the chief means employed to despoil themselves and subjugate their country, a motive which must have weighed all the more with the king, on recollecting how he profited himself by the absence of such a structure in his escape from the English in 1236.

But Fitzgerald was not to be diverted from an undertaking so calculated to further his designs on Lower Connaught and Tyrconnell, and, taking the matter into his own hands, he erected the castle; adroitly, however, associating the O'Conors with himself in the erection, for the purpose, no doubt, of securing their interest in a structure, which they had so much to do with themselves.

Having incurred the displeasure of Henry III. by some dilatoriness, real or imagined, in executing an order of the king, calling him to Wales, Fitzgerald was deprived of the viceroyalty in 1245, but he did not, on that account, desist from a main object he had in view in building the castle, which was, to take Sligo to himself from both the northern Irish and those of Lower Connaught. Accordingly, in 1246, he raised an army at his private expense, and, invading Tyrconnell, divided that territory into two parts, giving one part to a creature of his, Cormac, the grandson of King Roderick O'Conor, and leaving the other to Melaghlin O'Donnell, requiring from him, in guarantee of good faith, hostages which the English took with them to Sligo, and left there in the new castle. O'Donnell chafed under this indignity and injury; and making a dash, in 1246, at Sligo to recover the hostages, he failed to penetrate into the castle, though he had forced his way into the bawn or fortified area that surrounded the structure. To complete his discomfiture and humiliation the English hanged the hostages before his eyes from the battlements of the castle, just as he was beginning his retreat. Nor did his misfortunes end here; for FitzGerald, having made elaborate preparations to punish the attack on Sligo, and to strike a decisive blow against the Irish, proceeded in 1247, accompanied by his henchman, Cormac O'Conor, to the north, crossed the Erne, after a long and gallant resistance on the part of the Cinel Connell and the Cinel Owen, slew O'Donnell, scattered his forces, devastated his territory, seized vast herds of his cattle, and set up, in the room of the fallen chief, a new ruler, Rory O'Canannain, a member of the family that ruled Tyrconnell, before Melaghlin O'Donnell got to the head of affairs. FitzGerald had hardly

---

in honour of the Holy Trinity".—Annals of Loch Ce. Edited, with a translation, by William M. Hennessy, M.R.I. A. In a note the learned editor refers the reader to the year 1242, where the grant of the hospital is recorded: "The Hospital of Sligech was presented by the Justiciary to Clarus MacMailin in honour of the Trinity". The meaning of these somewhat obscure entries must be that given to them in the text.

turned his back when O'Canannain renounced the English connection, feeling that his tenure of office, and even of life, would be very short among the Cinel Connell if he adhered to his foreign patrons. To punish this backsliding, the son of FitzGerald, at the instigation of Godfrey O'Donnell, a son of Donnell, led an army to the north, but O'Canannain, at the head of the Cinel Connell, took his stand on the banks of the Erne, and stopped the advance of the invaders. On the failure of the son, the father, Maurice FitzGerald, took the field in person, and defeated the Cinel Connell, making Godfrey chief, and banishing O'Canannain, who soon fell fighting in an attempt to regain his lost position.

If O'Canannain cost FitzGerald trouble and treasure, Godfrey O'Donnell in the end cost him his life. At first the new ruler of Tyrconnell practised great self-restraint in regard to the English, and confined his forays to the Irish of Tyrone and Fermanagh; but, alarmed at the continued advance of FitzGerald, and maddened by the castle of Cael Uisce, which that able man had erected, or rather re-erected for it was first built in 1211. O'Donnell, to break through the net being drawn around him, having found a favourable opportunity, demolished the castle of Cael Uisce, and burned and plundered the town of Sligo, slaying great numbers of the English there. Pursued, as they were carrying off the booty, by a large army of English, collected from all sides, and led by Maurice Fitzgerald, the Northerns halted to give battle in Roscede or the Rosses, at a place called, in the Four Masters, Creadran Cille, and, in the *Annals of Loch Ce*, Credran-Columb-Cille.[1]

Both leaders and men behaved themselves with great spirit. While the battle was in progress O'Donnell and Fitzgerald sought each other out, and, engaging in a single hand to hand encounter, they fought with such resolution, that both of them were mortally wounded. After desperate fighting the English were beaten and routed, and nothing, says the chronicler, but the wounds of Godfrey prevented him from chasing the flying enemy beyond the Moy. Maurice was the first to succumb to his wounds. Sick in body, and sore in mind, seeing his power in Connaught so shaken, he was carried to Youghal to a monastery which he had himself founded; and there this renowned statesman and warrior died, in the habit of a Friar Minor.

---

[1] Four Masters, 1257—Annals of Loch Ce, 1257 Credran Cille or Credran Columcille has hitherto eluded identification. The writer is of opinion that Credran is a colloquial contraction for Cor-eder-da-abain, i.e., the Round hill between the two rivers, an exact description of the surface and position of the spot, as it lies between the Sligo and Drumcliffe rivers. And that the place was known topographically as the spot "between the two rivers", we may infer from a phrase of McFirbis, who thus writes of it Verum Murchertus O'Connor cum Carbriis *eos inter duos fluvios assecuti, &c.* (In O'Donovan's Four Masters, sub anno, 1396.)

O'Donnell's end was still more sensational and dramatic. Having been carried back to the north and having, for greater quietness and security, been placed in an island of Loch Beathach, in the barony of Kilmacrenan, county of Donegal, his enemy, Brian O'Neil, of Tyrone, on hearing of his helpless and hopeless condition, demanded hostages, in token of the submission of the Cinel Connell. Roused by the danger which threatened his people, Godfrey called them to arms, ordered at once the bier in which he was to be buried, and directing his followers to lift him out of the bed in which he lay, and place him in the bier, had himself thus carried, in the midst of his troops, to meet the enemy. The battle took place on the banks of the Swilly, near Letterkenny, where the Cinel Connell, fired by the example and exhortations of their dying chief, rushed against the Cinel Owen, bore them down on all points, and compelled them to fly, leaving "on the field many men, horses, and a great quantity of valuable property". The battle over, his faithful people took the victorious chief again on their shoulders for the return journey, but they had not gone far, when, finding that his end was just at hand, they laid him down in the open street of a village, called then Congbhail, now Conwal, to die a death, which, for devotedness to country and sacrifice of self, was as glorious as any ever chronicled in history, or imagined in romance.

After describing the battle of Creadran Cille, the *Annals of the Four Masters* add the observation, "In consequence of the success of this battle the English and the Geraldines were driven out of Lower Connaught;" but, that this assertion is true only in a very modified sense, and that the Geraldines, though much weakened, and residing generally elsewhere, still kept a grip of their possessions in Lower Connaught, there is ample evidence to show. In 1260 "a depredation was committed by MacMaurice on O'Donnell. A party of O'Donnell's men overtook them (*i.e.* the plunderers) at Beannan Breacmhoighe and burned and killed some of them. A great depredation was committed on Fitzmaurice by O'Donnell, who plundered the whole of Carbury". O'Donnell would not have plundered Carbury if he did not regard it as a possession of his enemies, the Geraldines, nor would the latter have defended it against him if they did not still hold it as their own. But the Geraldines were so occupied about this time with the O'Briens and MacCarthys in the South, and the Burkes in the west, that they were fain let Carbury shift, in great part, for itself. In their conflict with the Burkes, then represented by Walter, Earl of Ulster, they proceeded so far as to seize, and imprison, in the castles of Lea and Dunamase, Richard de Burgh, the Earl's heir, together with the Lord Justice Richard de Rupella, or Capella, John Cogan, and Theobald Butler; an act which threw the whole country into commotion, and which the Earl of Ulster avenged by carrying a desolating war into the Connaught possessions of the Geraldines, and taking to himself their Connaught Castles, that of Sligo being of course among them; but whoever held this castle in 1265, it was demolished, that year, by Hugh, son of Felim O'Conor and Donnell Oge O'Donnell, as well as the castles of Benada and Rath-ard-creeve, the former place being a well-known village in the county Sligo, and the latter, though hitherto not identified, being undoubtedly the townland of Ardcree, in the parish of Kilvarnet, barony of Leyney, and county of Sligo.

Again, in 1269, we find the Geraldines asserting their ownership of Sligo, by re-erecting the castle, which Hugh O'Conor and Donnell Oge O'Donnell had destroyed four years before. But still they had so much on hand in other places, that they were not able to hinder O'Donnell and the Cinel Connell from burning the town of Sligo in 1270, nor Hugh O'Conor from demolishing the castle in 1271. And, owing to the same cause, they let the castle lie in ruins from 1271 to 1293, when, as the Annals of Ulster have it, "The Castle of Sligo was made by John FitzThomas, and he went over to the King of England's house;" though the structure was hardly erected when Hugh, son of Owen O'Conor, King of Connaught, apparently during the absence of John FitzThomas in England, came and levelled it again with the ground. Engrossed, however, with weightier cares, John FitzThomas was unable, this time, to see to the rebuilding of it; for that characteristic spirit of the Geraldines, which would brook no man as superior, whether the man was in a private, or in an official station, involved him in a protracted quarrel with William de Vesci, Lord Justice of Ireland; and though FitzGerald's immense influence in England and Ireland, not only averted evil consequences, but turned the contest to his credit and advantage, still he had no sooner triumphed over De Vesci, than, in an evil hour, he laid hands on Richard de Burgh, the famous Red Earl, the first subject of the realm, confined him for three months, from the 6th December to the 12th March, 1295, in the Castle of Ley, and thus, if we are to credit Grace's *Annals of Ireland*, brought on himself the royal displeasure, with the loss of Sligo and all his other possessions in Connaught. If he lost his Sligo estate on this occasion, he soon recovered possession of it, for we find him pledging it for his liabilities in 1298, when the Lord Justice, Sir John Wogan, brought about a reconciliation and family alliance between the two houses of De Burgh and FitzGerald, There is nothing in the annals or records of the country to show that, after this date, the Geraldines exercised any act of authority or ownership in Sligo, though it seems certain they never relinquished their pretensions, for so late as the sixteenth century, when the O'Connors and O'Donnells were contending for the lordship or captaincy of the territory, we find the Earl of Kildare of the day laying his own claims to the dignity before the Lord Deputy and the Queen.

As the secular history of the town of Sligo may be said to begin with Maurice FitzGerald, so also may the ecclesiastical. It is true, there is mention in old authors of a St. Mofrisius, "son of Fachtna of Sliged", called in the *Martyrology of Tallaght*, "Midu mac Fachtna OSligid", who must have lived long before FitzGerald's day, but this would merely show that a certain religious person dwelt, in very early times, somewhere on the banks of the river, but not that he resided in the site of the present town, which, for reasons already stated, would have been a very unsuitable place to occupy. Unfortunately there is nothing known of this saint beyond the mere fact that he existed, and that he was one of the "saints", or religious persons, who came to honour Columba at Ballysadare, when that saint was passing through the place after the famous convention of Dromceat.

Even before Maurice FitzGerald built the castle, he had endeavoured to have a religious house erected in Sligo, as it were for the purpose of consecrating the soil of the place for the secular structures he meant to raise. In this pious undertaking he was associated with the famous Clarus McMailin, Archdeacon of Elphin, and head of the Premonstratensian Monastery of the Trinity, in Trinity Island, Loch Ce, the most distinguished ecclesiastic of that time in Ireland. This remarkable man devoted himself to the introduction and propagation of the Premonstratensian Order in Ireland, a work in which he was singularly successful, having established houses of the order in Loch Ce, Lough Outer, Ardcarne, Kilross, and other places. Being respected for his zeal and other virtues by the English as much as the Irish, he had little difficulty, wherever he applied, in procuring sites for his establishments, as also aid towards their erection, and suitable endowments. Maurice FitzGerald, when Lord Justice, was a great admirer of Clarus, and among other marks of confidence and esteem, presented him with a plot of ground in Sligo for a religious house, and with the means to build it. For some cause not mentioned, the work was not proceeded with, though costly preparations were made for it, and all the building materials collected. From the words of the *Annals of Loch Ce*, and those of the Four Masters, it would appear that a different kind of foundation was intended for Sligo, from those which Clarus McMailin had established elsewhere, as that of Sligo is designated an hospital-house—in Irish, *tige spidel*—while the others are called monasteries for Canons—in Irish, *mainisdrech cananach*;—and the reason why the hospital-house was not eventually built may perhaps be found in this difference, as the Archdeacon would naturally have no great desire to go on with an undertaking that he must have found to be alien to his favourite institute, which had not for aim, at least not for direct aim, to occupy itself with laymen, but to form ecclesiastics of high attainments, combining at once the virtues of the monk and those of the secular priest.

If the project of a religious house came to nothing on this occasion, it was taken up again, ten years later, and carried into effect when Maurice FitzGerald founded the monastery of the Dominicans, and had an adjoining cemetery consecrated. Maurice was the first to introduce the Franciscans and Dominicans into Ireland; and having founded a house of the Franciscans at Youghal, in or about 1232, it was natural that he should, next time, confer a like distinction on the Dominicans. Under any circumstances his great piety would lead him to extend religious foundations; but in founding the Sligo house, he was moved not only by his general dispositions, but also, it is said, by a special desire to make reparation for the part which he had, whether unintentionally, as himself alleged, and swore, or by design, as many others asserted, in the tragic end of Richard Earl Marshall, an occurrence which created a more profound sensation, in both England and Ireland, than perhaps any other event of the period. If the original records of the monastery still existed, we should doubtless find that FitzGerald had provided for a perpetual Mass for the deceased Earl's soul, and had probably endowed a chantry for the purpose.

Though the erection of the monastery of Sligo is recorded both in the *Annals of the Four Masters* and the *Annals of Loch Ce*, the name of the founder is mentioned in neither. In this silence, as also in the similar silence of Clyn, Dowling, and Grace, a Dominican writer of the last century, John O'Heyne, took on himself, without authority or proof of any kind, to credit one of the O'Connors with the erection; but, in so doing, he differs from all the writers who preceded him and followed him on the subject, for Ware, Lodge, Harris, De Burgo, as well as recent writers, like the Marquis of Kildare, are unanimous in referring the work to Maurice FitzGerald. And all these authorities, with the apparent exception of the Marquis of Kildare, who by a misprint, gives 1236, are agreed in assigning 1252 or 1253, as the date of the building.[1]

To anyone who has realized the condition of things in Sligo about the year 1252, there is no room for doubt on the subject, as Maurice FitzGerald was at that period sole owner and arbiter of the place; nor could even a cabin be put up there at the time without his authority. It was,

---

[1] Seeing a different date given in the Earls of Kildare for the foundation of the monastery from that assigned by other authorities, the writer took the liberty of bringing the matter under the notice of the late Duke of Leinster, and of requesting to be informed whether there was any mistake in the date of 1236. His Grace kindly replied as follows by return of post:

"Carton, Maynooth, 9th January,—

"VERY REV. SIR I have received your letter of yesterday, and beg to say, in reply, that I have no doubt the date 1236, in my book is a misprint.

"I am your obedient Servant, " LEINSTER.

"The Very Rev. T. O'Rorke, D.D., P.P.", &c.

besides, long after this the O'Connors obtained any footing in the town. Considering the means, and taste, and experience of FitzGerald, the new structure, in its style and proportions, must have been worthy of its destination; but it would be difficult now to discriminate between the parts of the original building and those of later erection; nor is this the place to make the attempt, which may be tried hereafter. Anyhow, the site, from whatever point of view it is considered, was most suitable for a religious establishment in the thirteenth century. Defended in front and rere by the hills of Rathavritoge (Green Fort) and Cairns, which no doubt were well fortified by so experienced a soldier as Maurice FitzGerald; with the grassy slopes of Cleveragh and Cairns for their flocks and herds; with an unlimited supply, from the lake, on one side, and from the sea, on the other, of excellent fish so essential an article of food, when half the days of the year were *maigre*[1] days; and with the prestige of having the first man in the country for their founder and patron; the Dominicans of Sligo were held in greater consideration, and enjoyed more of the securities, conveniences, and comforts of life than the religious of most other places. And in other important respects they were equally fortunate. On the border of one of the most picturesque lakes of Europe; over the banks of a fine river; in full view of the noble mountain scenery which stretches from Dromahair to near the sea coast of Carbury; reminded by the running river and the everlasting hills respectively of the fleeting life of the world, which they had abandoned, and the "eternal weight of glory", for which they now lived and laboured; they had always around them objects admirably fitted to gratify their taste and nurture their devotion.

At no time since the invasion had the Anglo-Normans such sway in Ireland as in the middle of the thirteenth century. At that date Maurice FitzGerald, the Justiciary, Hugh de Lacy, Earl of Ulster, Richard Burke, "Great Lord of Connaught", and Walter de Ridelsford, High Baron of Leinster, led an army from east to west and from north to south of Ireland, trampling down all opposition before them, The state in which they left the places through which they had passed, may be gathered from what the *Annals of Loch Ce* tell respecting Connaught: "The Foreigners left Connaught without food, clothes, or cattle; and they did not carry off with them either pledges or hostages on this journey; and they left neither peace, nor quietness, nor tranquility, nor happiness, in the country; but the Gael themselves were robbing and killing one another regarding the residue which the Foreigners left in it on this occasion". A few years later, when the Lord Justice, Theobald Butler, was leading an army to the north, the Cinel Owen were so cowed as to adopt the resolution, "that since the power

---

[1] prescribed for abstinence from meat, [Clachan ed.].

of the Foreigners was over the Gael of Erinn, to give hostages to the Foreigners, and to make peace with them for the sake of their country".

At this time the population of Sligo was exclusively, or almost exclusively, English. The two establishments, which employed most of the inhabitants, the castle and the monastery, were English in their origin and inmates. They would therefore employ only fellow-countrymen, and, at a moment when feelings of nationality were exceptionally strong, would have as little as possible to do with the Irish. Of the nationality of those who occupied the castle there can be no doubt, they being the English troops of Maurice FitzGerald; while the inmates of the monastery must also have come from England, there being no Irish Friars Preachers in the county at that time. The frequent resort of English to the town would also go to show they were numerous there. In 1249, a party of young men, with Pierce Poer, and Daniel Trew at their head, were on the way to the castle of Sligo, when they were encountered and defeated by Hugh O'Conor. In the same year, after a campaign, in which the Lord Justice and FitzGerald acted in concert, and plundered and wasted Roscommon and Breffney, when the Justiciary returned to Meath, FitzGerald proceeded with the English of Connaught and Munster to Sligo, to rest himself and his forces in the town. The *Annals of the Four Masters* (1269), record that Brian, son of Donnell Duv O'Hara, was slain by the English of Sligo, probably in some raid which they made from the town to Leyney. As Tireragh too, at this period, from the Moy to Ballysadare, was in the hands of the Berminghams and the English, there must have been frequent and friendly intercourse between Bermingham's people and their fellow-countrymen of Sligo. With so many proofs of English life and action in and around Sligo, and without anything to show the presence of Irishmen in the place, there is good ground for thinking, that the native element was rigidly excluded, as far as possible, from the Sligo of the FitzGeralds; though in spite of every effort to shut them out, Irishmen, from time to time, as we have seen, paid flying visits, which would have been gladly declined, as on All Saints' Day, 1247, when the Cinel Connell made their way into the bawn; in 1257, when Godfrey O'Donnell burned the town, and took away its valuables; in 1271, when Donnell Oge O'Donnell laid it again in ashes; and in the same year, when Hugh, the son of Felim O'Conor, demolished-the castle, which it had failed the two O'Donnells to reach.

Unfortunately there are hardly any data which would enable one to draw out a view, however imperfect, of Sligo, as it appeared under the Geraldines, in the thirteenth century. From what is said in the *Annals of Loch Ce*, under the year 1246, of "the bawn of the town", we may conclude that the place was protected by some kind of fortification. The word "bawn" is derived by some from the German verb "bauen", to build, and by others from the Irish word "badhun", sometimes written "bodun", a cowfort; but whatever may be the derivation and the second seems the correct one the Irish term for "bawn" came in the course of time to mean a fortified enclosure for men, or horses, or cows, or other valuables, though, earlier, it signified only a cow-fort, cows or cattle being then the only wealth people possessed. Those bawns were constructed of different materials at different times; at first, of sods and stakes, and, later, of lime and stone. "The earlier kind of bawn", says a well-informed writer in the Ulster Journal of Archaeology, "seems to have been an enclosure, square or circular, surrounded by a thick embankment of earth, impaled with wooden stakes or branches of trees, and surrounded with a deep trench;" but as time progressed, and mechanical knowledge advanced, some bawns became substantial, and even massive structures of solid masonry, flanked in several instances with towers thirty or forty feet high, the curtain walls being twenty feet or more high, and four, five, or six feet thick. The bawn of Sligo was, no doubt, of the more primitive kind, something like that which we read of in the *Annals of Loch Ce,* and the *Annals of the Four Masters,* as existing at Rindown, and consisting of "ramparts and ditches". Within this enclosure stood the castle and the monastery; within it, in small, rude huts of timber, covered with strips of sod, dwelled the retainers of the castle and the servants or labourers of the monastery; within it was held the market in which the residents purchased such commodities as they needed, and could find; and into it were driven at night, and, not infrequently, when forays were apprehended, for the day, or for several days, the cattle and horses belonging to the castle and the monks. Without probably any sensible departure from historical truth and accuracy, we may then figure to ourselves the bawn stretching from near the old distillery to Knappagh Road, and from the river up to the rising ground, which runs from the Convent of Mercy to the Dominican Church; this space being fenced in, on the north, chiefly by the river, and, on the other three sides, by a rampart, fosse, and palisades. And if we stand, in thought, on the rising ground that overlooks the bawn, and observe for a little what falls under the eye in the enclosure the area all astir with military manoeuvres, some repairing or strengthening the fortifications, several engaged here and there with their horses or armour, and numbers receiving training and instructions for contemplated nestings—we shall gain a fair idea of the Sligo of Maurice FitzGerald and the thirteenth century, and learn that it had the look and character of a garrison far more than of an ordinary town.

CHAPTER V

THE O'CONNORS AND SLIGO

IT was just as the Geraldines were losing their hold on Sligo that members of that branch of the O'Conor family which received, in the sixteenth century, the name of O'Connor Sligo, were coming to the front in the transactions of the district. These O'Connors led a singularly quiet and retired life for more than a century before the time at which we are now arrived, that is, from the death, in 1181, of their ancestor, Brian Luighnech, the son of Turlough More, King of Connaught. At the date mentioned, when Brian was slain in the battle of Crich Carbury, they disappear from view, and do not reappear till the fourth quarter of the thirteenth century. In the interval between those two dates, the *Annals of the Four Masters* are filled with the doings of the other sons of Turlough More, especially with those of Roderic, of Cathal Croderg, of Hugh Brefneach, and of Murtough Muimneach; but one would search in vain through all our Annals for the movements of the sons of Brian Luighnech, a fact which of itself suffices to show the decisiveness of the battle of Crich Carbury.

This battle was fought at a place called Magh-Diughbha,[1] which has not been hitherto identified, but which can be no other than the plain or valley of the river Duff, as the name imports, Magh-Diughbha signifying literally the plain of the Duff. The combatants were, on the one side, the troops of the north, under the leadership of Flaherty O'Muldory, the chief of Tirconnell, and on the other, the forces of Connaught, under the command, no doubt, of Brian Luighnech, though this is not expressly stated. The subject of dispute was the rule of Carbury, or perhaps the rule of all Lower Connaught, from the Curlew Mountains to the river Erne. This subject was, often before, the occasion of military or diplomatic meetings between the rulers of the north and those of Connaught; as, for instance, in 1151, when "an army was led by the son of Nial O'Lochlan, with the Cinel Connell, Cinel Owen, and Airghialla, across Eas Roe, until they reached the Curlews, in Coran. Thither hostages were brought to them by Turlough O'Conor, and they returned to their houses;"[2] and in the year 1152, when "a meeting took place between O'Lochlan and Turlough

---

[1] Annals of Lough Ce, 1181.
[2] Annals of the Four Masters, 1151.

O'Conor at Magh-Ene, where they made friendship under the Staff of Jesus, and under the relics of Colum-Cille".[1]

But the battle of Magh-Diughbha was an event of transcendent importance, a great pitched battle, which both sides felt to be decisive of their pretensions to the disputed territory, and in which, accordingly, they put forth all their strength. The result was disastrous to the Connaught men, who not only lost sixteen[2] chiefs of the O'Conor family, including Brian Luighnech and Manus, two sons of Turlough More; three grandsons, Melaghlin, Murray, and Murtough; and very many others, high-born and humble-born *"nobiles et ignobiles;"* but sustained all round so crushing a defeat that, in the words of the Four Masters, "the Cinel Connell held the Connacians for a long time after this battle under subjection".[3] It is true the

---

[1] Ibid., 1152.
[2] Ibid., 1181.
[3] Annals of the Four Masters, 1181. This battle being so important, the reader will like to have before him the very words in which our annalists describe it: "Flaherty O'Muldory", says the Four Masters, "Lord of Tirconnell, defeated the sons of the King of Connaught on the Saturday before Whitsuntide. Sixteen of the sons of the lords and chieftains of Connaught were slain by the Cinel Connell, as well as many others, both of the nobles and plebeians. They held the Connacians under subjection for a long time after this battle, which was known by the name of Cath Criche Carbury [i.e., the Battle of the Territory of Carbury]".

The words of the Annals of Loch Ce are: "The battle of Magh-Diughbha was gained over the sons of Turlough More O'Conor by Flaherty O'Muldory, King of Cinel Connell (and of, it is said, 'the battle of the royal heirs'), in which were slain Brian Luighnech and Maghnus; and the three sons of Hugh, son of Turlough O'Conor, viz.: Melaghlin, Murray, and Murtough; and Hugh, grandson of Hugh, son of Rory, King of the West of Connaught; and Donough, son of Brian O'Fallon, *et alii nobiles et ignobiles cum eis* (Donough, son of Donnell Midhech O'Conor, it was that brought Flaherty O'Muldory to defend the territory of Carbury for himself). And the bodies of those nobles were conveyed, after their deaths, to Cloonmacnoise, and interred in the sepulchre of the nobles of their ancestors".

In the Annals of Boyle we have only this short entry on the subject: 1181—"Battle of the kings' presumptive".

In commenting on this passage, in his History of Ireland and Annals of Boyle (Vol. II., p. 306), Mr. D'Alton says: "The sons of King Roderic were defeated in this bloody battle;" but it was not the sons of Roderic, but the sons of Turlough More, Roderic's father, who sustained the defeat.

It is to this battle the Book of Fenagh refers in the lines:
"Greater than Mughron's death will be
The battle of the kings in Cairbre,
The host of Conall will triumphant be,
After inflicting slaughter upon us".
—The Book of Fenagh. By W. M. Hennessy and D. H. Kelly, p. 279.
The right application of these lines has not been pointed out before.

King Turlogh O'Conor was married at least three times; first, to Tailtin, daughter of Murrough O'Melaghlin, who died in 1128; secondly, to Deryorgilla, daughter of Donel O'Lochlan, who died at Armagh, while on a pilgrimage there, in 1151; and thirdly, to

Annals of Kilronan and the *Annals of Boyle* record a victory *"ubi multi occciderunt"*[1]—the next following year, gained by Roderic O'Conor and his son, Conor Maenmoi, over Donough, son of Donnell Midhech O'Conor and O'Muldory; but this could be only an insignificant affair, if it happened at all, as the Annals of the Four Masters are altogether silent upon it.

Anyhow, it did not reverse or undo the result of Oath Criche for O'Muldory continued to dominate Carbury,[2] and the O'Connors (Sligo) to live on in obscurity just as before. The place where those O'Connors lived after the defeat of Cath Criche Carbury is nowhere stated; but the writer, after the most diligent investigation, is quite satisfied that it was in the district of Castletown, on the slopes of Benbulben, where we find them when they emerge again into notice.[3] Here they retired after the battle, and here they remained.

Of Andrias, the son of Brian Luighnech, nothing is told in our annals; but Teige, the son, or the grandson,[4] of Andrias, is represented as a prominent figure in the movements of the times. In the conflict for the kingship of Connaught between Cathal and Manus, the sons of Conor Roe and grandsons of Murtough Muimnech, Teige sided with the latter, and fought against Cathal in the battle of Collooney, and lost in that engagement his son, slain by Neal Gealbuy O'Conor,[5] who, in turn, fell, the following year, at the hand of the enraged father.[6] This Teige, who had for wife Sabia, daughter of Hugh Buy O'Neil, lived to an advanced age, and died a Gray Friar, in the abbey of Boyle, where he had retired and assumed the religious habit a short time before his death.[7]

The only male issue of Teige O'Connor and Sabia O'Neil was Donnell, who, though a very bold and brave man, is still more remarkable for the exploits of his sons than for his own. His death, as was the usual fate of Irish chiefs at that period, came from the sword, and, another circumstance characteristic of the times, by the hand of a relation. The

---

Dubhchoblach, daughter of O'Mulrony, of Moylurg, ancestor of the MacDermots. His sons were Maelisa, Abbot of Roscommon; Hugh Dall, Teige Aluin, Hugh, Cathal, Donal, Roderick, King of Ireland; Brian Luighnech, ancestor of the O'Connors Sligo; Brian Brefnech, Manus, Lochlaun, Murtough Muimnecb, Donough, Maelseachlaiun, Teige Fidnacha, Cathal Migaran, two Conors, Dermod, Donal, Maurice, Teige Dairen, and Murchadh Finn.

[1] Annals of Loch Ce, 1182. "A victory was gained by Rory O'Conor over O'Muldory, *ubi multi occiderunt*"

[2] Annals of the Four Masters, 1187, 1188.

[3] See account of Castletown, in Parish of Drumcliff.

[4] Called Teige, son of Andrias, in Annals of Loch Ce, 1301; but in the same Annals, under the year 1308, the genealogy is, Donnell, son of Teige, son of Brian, son of Andrias.

[5] Annals of the Four Masters, 1291.

[6] Ibid., 1292.

[7] Annals of Loch Ce, 1307.

Annals of Loch Ce contains the following lively account of his death and burial, which casts a flood of light on the ideas and manners of the opening years of the thirteenth century: "Donal (son of Teige), son of Brian, son of Andrias, son of Brian Luighnech, son of Turlough More O'Conor, Tanist of all Connaught, and the royal heir of greatest property and wealth, of greatest hospitality and prowess, of greatest sovereignty and possessions, that was in Connaught (for the extent of his land was from Corr-sliabh-na-Seghsa to Cael-uisce), was slain in an encounter with Hugh Brefnech, son of Cathal Roe O'Conor. And the person who wounded him was Dermod, son of Simon-na-Tragha. And God was merciful to him, for he lived that night, and until he saw the priest and received the Body of Christ and unction, on the morrow; after which he died. And his body was then taken to Corrsliabh (the Curlews), and there was not taken with a dead body, in later times, such a quantity of droves, and garments, and cattle, of cavalry, and of kernes, as were taken in this procession with him to his sepulchre; and his remains were nobly and honourably interred in the monastery of the Buill (Boyle)".[1]

It may seem strange to find "droves, and garments, and cattle", figuring in a funeral procession, but they were intended as offerings for the monks of Boyle, and the poor depending on the monastery; for it was usual, from the earliest times, with chieftains and princes to give such alms for the good of the soul. The *Chronicon Scotorum* supplies us with an early and remarkable example of this liberality in its obituary, under the year 1065, of "Hugh O'Conor, the champion of the west of the world, the Cuchulain of the Gael, the flood of dignity and nobility of Erinn, and the man who was wont to give the most of food and clothing, of gold and cows for his soul in Erinn"; and *the Annals of the Four Masters* has another striking instance of it, under the year 1214, where, after recording the death of Manus O'Conor, it adds, "He was buried outside the door of the church of Fenagh; and three times the full of Clogna-Biogh, together with thirty horses, were given as an offering for his soul". Princes sometimes made similar presents to learned men and poets, as we see in *Annals of Four Masters*, under the year 1338.

After making full allowance for any exaggeration that might be found in the language of the passage quoted from the *Annals of Loch Ce*, it is still clear from it, that Donnell O'Connor was a chief of great possessions and power for his time; and, it may well excite surprise, how his family were

---

[1] Annals of Loch Ce, 1307. The obituary of the Four Masters omits all reference to the funeral, and runs thus: "Donnell, son of Teige, son of Brian, son of Andrias, son of Brian Luighnech, who was son of Turlough Mor O'Conor, Tanist of Connaught, a man of great prowess and hospitality, who was universally esteemed, was slain by Hugh Brefnech, the son of Cathal Roe O'Conor".

able to acquire such wealth and position, considering the comparatively retired life which they had led. But their flourishing condition may perhaps be traced to the neutral attitude they took after Cath-Criche-Carbury; for while other branches of the great Sil-Murray family (the O'Conors of Connaught), threw themselves into all the warlike movements around them, and lost generally more than they gained by incursions and conflicts, the descendants of Brian Luighnech, cured of all present ambition by the disaster of Magh Duibha, and acquiescing wisely in their defeat, devoted themselves to the acquiring and multiplying of flocks and herds, and in due time reaped, in the acquisition of immense wealth, the reward for which they laboured. Wealth generally brings with it power and the consciousness of power; and the descendants of Brian Luighnech, now feeling themselves well able to play a leading part in the country, threw themselves into the contests of the day with an energy all the greater for their former inaction. Nor would they have been able to continue the pacific life they had been leading, even if they were disposed to do so; for their innumerable cattle naturally excited the cupidity and predatory attacks of powerful neighbours, at a time when men felt little scruple in appropriating everything they could seize and secure with the strong hand. And, as a matter of fact, it was to rescue their cattle, and punish the marauders, that Teige, and his son Donnell, first reappear after their temporary effacement.[1]

The time at which the O'Connors re-entered public life was very favourable for them; for it was much easier then to rise to power in Carbury than it had been at any moment since the death of Brian Luighnech. The two powerful English families that had been successively masters of it — the MacCostellos and the Geraldines — were no longer in the way. Gilbert MacCostello, to secure the territory for himself, had erected, in 1211,[2] a castle at Cael Uisge or Belleek, with the sanction and co-operation of John de Gray, the excommunicated bishop of Norwich, who was King John's Lord Justice of Ireland at the time. But MacCostello was slain in the castle, the following year, and the building itself was burned to the ground.[3] Gilbert's inheritance passed on to Philip MacCostello, for the *Annals of the*

---

[1] "A great depredation was committed by Hugh, the son of Cathal O'Conor, and the Clann Murtough, upon Teige, the son of Andrias, in Magh Ene". Annals of the Four Masters, 1301.
"Dermot O'Flanagan, chief of Tuathratha, his two sons, and many others, along with them, were slain at Bunduff, by some of the household of Donnell, son of Teige O'Conor, who had pursued them, to deprive them of a prey which they were carrying off from Magh Ene". Ibid., 1303.
[2] "An army was led by the Connacians, at the summons of the English bishop and Gilbert MacCostello to Assaroe; and they erected a castle at Cael Uisge"
[3] "Gilbert MacCostello was slain in the castle of Cael Uisge; and the castle itself was burned by O'Hegny".

Four Masters, under the year 1214, state that "Carbury was then the possession of Philip MacCostello"; but being unable, without castle or stronghold, to maintain his footing against the attacks of the O'Rorkes and neighbouring chiefs, he abandoned Carbury about this time.

The Geraldines kept their hold much longer than the MacCostellos had done, and might, perhaps, have held on in Carbury to the present day, as in Kildare, if they had not come into collision with the all-powerful Red Earl, and the authority of England which supported his cause.

The movements of the O'Connors were facilitated also by the state of ruin, in which the castle of Sligo lay, and which lasted from 1294 to 1310, when, as the Four Masters and the *Annals of Loch Ce* state, "the castle of Sligo was erected", or, as the *Annals of Clonmacnoise* have it, "was repeared (repaired) and made", by the Red Earl. Another factor, in their rise or revival, was the feud which arose in 1295, between the two sons of Donnell Oge O'Donnell—Hugh and Turlough and which, lasting through the first quarter of the fourteenth century, wasted the strength of that powerful family in a fratricidal contest.

Nowhere can one learn better the truth of the maxim, that union is strength, than in the annals of Ireland; for the reader of those annals sees in every page, that the rise or fall of native chieftains depends almost exclusively on the union or the division of the members of their families. If the members are united with one another, and with the chief, he is able to hold his own, whatever other enemies he may have to contend against; but if the members turn on each other, or on him, he is sure to sink, whatever may be his talents or resources. It is thus the *Annals of the Four Masters* supplies a most suggestive commentary to such scripture texts as "Every kingdom divided against itself shall be made desolate; and every city or house divided against itself shall not stand". "And a man's enemies shall be they of his own household". And this union or division reacts on rivals, who wax in strength as the opposing chief wanes in domestic or family support, and wane as he waxes. The English turned this condition of things to account so effectually that they gained more by it than by their own prowess. Strongbow owed less to his knights than to Dermod McMurrough; the Fitzgeralds, de Burgos, Berminghams, and Costellos, were equally indebted to native aid for their successes in Connaught; and if we may anticipate, Lord Mountjoy, who did more to make Ireland amenable to English rule, than any Englishman who had preceded him from the invasion, would never have gathered such laurels but for the co-operation, covert or open, of the Queen's O'Donnell, the Queen's O'Neil, the Queen's Maguire, and the Queen's other Irish chieftains.

The occasion being thus opportune for the O'Connors Sligo, the men were not wanting. For years that family had produced a succession of chiefs endowed with all those high and commanding qualities which go to form the hero; and though enemies multiplied, and difficulties and dangers thickened[1] as time advanced, those chiefs triumphed over all dangers and difficulties, and were more than a match for their multitudinous enemies. In a united but constantly diminishing body, as one or other of the brothers came to a violent end, the seven sons of Donnell O'Connor—Rory, Manus, Cathal, Murtough, Donough, John, and Teige sometimes by themselves, and sometimes in alliance with others, took an active and leading part in all the public transactions of the time in Connaught.

After dealing by themselves with their less powerful enemies, inflicting, near Ballysadare, a severe defeat on the English of Tireragh and Leyney, and avenging the death of their father in the blood of its perpetrators,[2] they joined Felim O'Connor, the king of Connaught, MacDermot, and the English; and their united forces proceeded through Corran and Leyney, and thus brought unspeakable evils on the latter district; for their enemies, Rory O'Conor, and Teige O'Kelly—went to borrow the language of the *Annals of Loch Ce*—"in pursuit of Felim and MacDermot, and the tribes that were with them, to Leter-Leyney, and the slopes of Slieve Gamh, and to Glen-Fathroimh (1315) in particular, where they killed many thousand cows, and sheep, and horses; and they stripped gentlewomen, and destroyed small children, and little ones, on this journey; and never during the memory of the people, was so much cattle uselessly destroyed in one spot". Later on we shall identify this spot.

While the sons of Donnell O'Connor were engaged in those forays, Hugh O'Donnell, chief of Tirconnell, at the instigation of his wife, who was daughter of Manus O'Conor, against whom the sons of Donnell were then in conflict, invaded Carbury, and "threw down" the castle of Sligo, in which, according to the annalists, "great spoils were found".[3] The injury inflicted by her husband on the territory of the sons of Donnell not being enough to satisfy this furious Amazon, she called together her relatives, and other forces, and at their head attacked the churches of Drumcliff, and plundered

---

[1] A great depredation was committed by Mulrony McDermot, on the sons of Donnell O'Connor, in the territory of Carbury. Another great depredation was committed upon them by the Clann Murtough, who had concluded a peace with them, and given them hostages, but afterwards acted treacherously towards them. Another great depredation was committed by Brian O'Dowd, and Foreigners of Leyney, and the Ui-Fiachrach, on the same sons of Donnell O'Connor". Annals of the Four Masters and Annals of Loch Ce, 1308. These entries are in immediate succession in the Annals.

[2] "Hugh Ballad, son of Cathal, son of Conor Roe, son of Murtough Muinnech, was slain in treachery by Cathal, son of Donnell O'Connor, and Hugh, son of Art, and Diarmaid, son of Simon-na-tragha were also slain by them in revenge for their father having been killed by Diarmaid".—Annals of Loch Ce.—An. 1315.

[3] Annals of Loch Ce An. 1315.

their "Comarbs and clerics".[1] Adding murder to sacrilege, this wicked woman compassed the death of Rory, the eldest of the seven brothers, by paying assassins to "remove" him, though he had, unlike his brothers, renounced his claims to Carbury, and recognized O'Donnell as the Lord paramount of the district.[2]

But the death of Rory, and of the next in age, Manus, who fell in the disastrous battle of Athenry, rather helped than harmed the O'Connor family, as it brought to the front Cathal, the third eldest, who was probably the ablest and bravest man in all Ireland at the time. With his brothers he lived at Fasachoille—the waste of the wood,—now Castletown, in Carbury, and watched over that territory, a lion in vigilance and daring.

Encouraged, probably, by the death, of Rory and Manus, Meyler de Exeter and some of the descendants of Murtough Muimhnech made an incursion into Carbury; but the lion sprang from his lair, pounced on the invaders, and strewed the banks of the Methenagh, or Drumcliff river, with the dead bodies of De Exeter, Donnell O'Conor Muimnech, and several of their followers.[3] He was next attacked by all the chiefs of Connaught, including Turlogh, King of Connaught, Mulrony MacDermot, Prince of Moylurg, Ualgarg O'Rorke, Lord of Breffney, O'Kelly, chief of Hy Many, and Tomultagh MacDonogh, Lord of Tirerrill. Finding they had no ordinary person to deal with, the chiefs formed this vast coalition, to make sure of crushing their formidable adversary. In this crisis Cathal played the part of a statesman as well as of a hero. On his enemies reaching his neighbourhood, he offered them liberal terms if they desisted from their undertaking, and retired in peace; but these terms they disdainfully rejected, convinced that they had him completely in their power.

Thrown back thus on himself, he faltered not, nor shut himself up in his fortress, but, making little of the overwhelming numbers of the enemy, came forth from his entrenchments, delivered battle in the open, and inflicted a disastrous defeat, slaying numbers both of leaders and followers, and putting the rest to a disgraceful rout. [4]

---

[1] Annals of Loch Ce An. 1315. The Annals of Clonmacnoise relate thus these occurrences. "Hugh O'Donnell, Prince of Tirconnell, came to the lands of Carbrey, in Connaught, and destroyed all that country by the advice of his wife, the daughter of Manus O'Conor, and came herself with a great route of gallowglasses, and took all the spoyles of the churches of Drumkleiw, without respect to church or churchman of that place".

[2] And Dervorgil, daughter of Manus O'Conor, retained a band of gallowglasses, and gave them a reward for the killing of Rory, son of Dounell O'Conor, who was subsequently slain by them in violation of the relics of Tirconnell. —Annals of Loch Ce, 1316.

[3] Annals of Loch Ce, 1317.

[4] A great army was assembled by Mulrony McDermot, King of Moylurg, and the noblest who were in this army were Turlough O'Conor, King of Connaught, and Ualgarg O'Rorke, King of Breffney and Conmaicne, and Conor O'Kelly, King of Hy-Maine, and Tomultagh McDonogh, Lord of Tirerrill. And they all proceeded to attack Cathal, son of Donnell

Carbury being now secure, Cathal assumed the offensive; and, sallying forth from Fasa-coille, with his victorious army, first, harried Moylurg, to punish McDermot, and next, deposing Turlogh, King of Connaught, seated himself in the vacant throne, and ruled the province as King, from 1318 to 1324, when he was slain by Turlogh O'Conor, the deposed prince. All Cathal's actions prove him to have been a man of commanding talents and indomitable courage; and if he sometimes practised deceit and guile against his enemies, as cannot be gainsayed, this only proves, that be was no better, in this respect, than his contemporaries, at a time when Irish chiefs are constantly represented by our annalists as acting "*per dolum*" or treacherously.

Two, at least, of the sons of Cathal, King of Connaught, Rory and Cathal Oge, inherited their father's warlike qualities, and abilities. Rory resided at Fasa-coille, and knew how, like his father, to defend that fortress; for, being attacked by Ualgarg O'Rorke, he not only repelled the attack, but overtaking O'Rorke at Calry, defeated him in battle, slew all his gallowglasses, and put himself to death, by burning over his head the church of Killery, in which he had taken sanctuary.[1] Opposed by a formidable coalition of enemies, the ClanMurtough, Nial O'Donnell, the MacDermots, and all the English and Irish they could get to aid them, Rory gave as much trouble as he received; and though defeated on one occasion with great slaughter at Collooney, and driven, on another occasion, into his fortress of Ballymote, he was still able to burn MacDermot's stronghold, and to hold his own against all his enemies, till he was treacherously slain in 1350, at Bricklieve, by the sons of Farrel McDonogh, at the instigation of Hugh O'Conor, King of Connaught, who no doubt felt ill at ease, as long as so formidable a competitor for his throne as Rory lived.

Cathal Oge, another son of King Cathal, was still more conspicuous than Rory for abilities and exploits. Coming into notice for the first time in 1355, when he joined Mac William Burke who was then at enmity with the English of West Connaught, his career till his death in 1362, was a

---

O'Connor, to Fasacoille. And Cathal offered them liberal terms on condition that they would not go to him; but they did not accept them from him. And these nobles advanced to the very middle of his fortress; but this occurred not through flight or timidity on his part. And Cathal advanced furiously, bravely, against them from out of the houses, and encountered them. And Conor O'Kelly, King of Hy-Maine, was slain, and Brian, son of Turlough O'Conor, heir to the sovereignty of Connaught, and Brian, son of Manus, and Cathal, son of GillaChrist MacDermot, *et alia multi nobiles et ignobiles*, were either wounded or killed.—Annals of Loch Ce—An. 1316

[1] *Odo O'Roirk Rodei icum filius (recte filium) Cathaldi O'Conor apud Fasacoillead depredatus, in templum Cille-hoires confugit, et templo incenso occiditur.*—Book of Lecan, in O'Donovan's Four Masters—An. 1346. The Four Masters say, "O'Rourke was afterwards pursued by Rory O'Conor and the Clann Donogh, and was killed by Mulrony MacDonogh. This was a lamentable deed".

continued series of brilliant victories without a single defeat or check. In 1355, he burned the town of Tuam in spite of the English; in 1360, he slew Dermot, son of Donogh Reagh McDermot, and overran Tyrawley with an army, "destroying many of its houses and churches;"[1] in 1361, having been set upon by MacWilliam, MacFeorais, and the English of all Connaught, who "ravaged and wasted Leyney and Tireragh", he led an army into the enemy's territories, "plundered McFeorais' and MacHubert Burke's people, and spoiled and destroyed the whole country;"[2] and in 1362, he and the King of Connaught captured the castle of Ballintuber, and, invading Meath, which belonged to the English, "desolated it by fire, burned the church of Kilkenny, and fourteen other churches in which the English had garrison",:[3] and did the English many other injuries, after which they returned in safety and triumph to their homes.

But the most remarkable perhaps of his victories was that which he acquired in 1356, over the Cinel Connell or O'Donnells. Cathal Oge was the first of the family, since the battle of Criche Carbury, that dared to measure swords with the Cinel Connell; and his victory over them at Ballyshannon was so decisive, that he became by it chief of Tirconnell, as is recorded in the *Annals of Ulster*: a fact which the Four Masters, with less regard for the claims of history than for the vanity of the O'Donnells, have the weakness to suppress.[4] The omission is the more reprehensible, as the Four Masters should have little sympathy with those chiefs of Tirconnell who brought the defeat and humiliation on themselves and on their country by their selfish internecine quarrels. Had they been less selfish and more patriotic, so as to unite in defence of Tirconnell, they might have defied Cathal Oge and all Connaught, but instead of union, dissensions existed among them to such an extent, in the time of Cathal Oge, and for more than half a century previous, that all the chiefs, who ruled Tirconnell during

---

[1] An army was led by Cathal Oge to Sir Edmond Burke, by which he plundered Mac William's country as far as the castle of Lehinch. – O'Flaherty in O'Donovan's Four Masters, 1360. Note.

[2] Annals of the Four Masters, 1361.

[3] Annals of the Four Masters, 1362. The Annals of Clonmacnoise give the following version of these events: "A.D. 1362, Hugh MacFelym O'Connor, King of Connaught, and Cahal Oge O'Connor, marched with their forces to Meath, burnt and destroyed all places where they came, to (as far as) the hill of Cnock-Aysde in Kynaleagh. Of that journey they burnt fourteen churches, and the church of Kilkenny in Machaire Kwyorchnie, and committed many outrages upon the English of Meath, and were so many that it were hard to recount them; returned at last to their houses in safety".

[4] O'Donovan in his edition of the Four Masters, anno 1369, writes in a note, "Cathal Oge, the son of O'Conor Sligo, made great efforts to conquer Tirconnell at this period; and it is stated in the Dublin copy of the Annals of Ulster under the year 1356 (recte 1359) that he became prince of Tirconnell. The Four Masters, however, who had the Annals of Ulster before them, have suppressed this passage, thinking that it would derogate from the glory of the O'Donnells. This passage is given from the Annals of Lecan.

that period, either obtained the chief power, or maintained it when reached, by the murder of a brother or other near relative. In 1303, Hugh, the son of Donnell Oge O'Donnell, became chief by slaying Turlough, of Cnoc-an-Madhma. At the close of Hugh's long rule in 1333, his two sons, Conor and Art, were rivals for his position, and Conor secured the place for himself by dispatching Art. Conor, in turn, fell in 1342, by the hand of another brother, Nial, who, himself, was treacherously and murderously slain by "Manus Meabhlach (the deceitful) O'Donnell, his kinsman",[1] most probably in the interest of Aengus (the son of Conor) O'Donnell, who assumed the chieftaincy. In due time Aengus met the fate of his predecessors, being killed *per dolum* by Manus O'Donnell,[2] apparently a different person from Manus the Deceitful, the murderer of Nial. Notwithstanding the tragic end of all those O'Donnells, Aengus's succession was as eagerly sought, and as fiercely contested, as if it were the presage of a long and happy life, and not the sure precursor of a speedy and ignoble death. Felim, the son of Hugh O'Donnell, and John, the son of Conor, were the rivals this time; and though Felim became the O'Donnell, John continued in opposition till he slew him, and obtained the coveted prize in 1356.[3] John, too, had to pay the penalty of his ambition, but, more fortunate than his predecessors, who lost their lives in family feuds, he had the honour of falling in the battle-field, while trying to repel the invasion of Cathal Oge O'Connor. It was well for the O'Donnells that Cathal Oge had so much on hands in other places during the remainder of his life; for whether he could, or could not, subject Tirconnell permanently to the O'Connors, he would, at all events, have dealt a blow to the family of O'Donnell, from which, in their divided condition, they might never have been able to recover.

Cathal Oge, on his return from Meath, had to encounter an enemy at Sligo far more formidable than any he had met with, north or south, in his various expeditions. This was the terrible plague,[4] called *Cluithe an Rìgh*

---

[1] Annals of the Four Masters, 1348.
[2] Annals of Loch Ce, 1352.
[3] Felim, the son of Hugh, son of Donnell Oge O'Donnell, Lord of Tirconnell, was slain by the son of his own brother, viz., John, son of Conor O'Donnell, and John then assumed the lordship of Tirconnell without opposition.—Four Masters, 1356.

[4] The pestilential period of the 14th century, writes Sir William Wilde, in his Table of Cosmical Phenomena, &c., published in Vol. I. of the Census of Ireland for the year 1851, was both in duration and intensity, the most remarkably calamitous in these annals. It dates from 1315, and lasted almost without interruption for 85 years. It commenced with the foreign invasion of the Scots, under Edward Bruce, at a time when the country was labouring under the double scourge of famine and partial civil war, and its effects were to increase the one and render the other general. Epizootics succeeded, followed by smallpox, then dearth again with unusual severity of the seasons and intense frosts, accompanied by the first appearance of influenza, and an outbreak of the Barking Mania. Subsequently appeared the

(the King's Game), apparently, a return of the Black Death, which appeared first in Europe, towards the middle of the fourteenth century, and lasted at intervals to the middle of the seventeenth, and is graphically described, as to the former period, in the contemporaneous pages of Boccaccio's *Il Decameron*, and, as to the latter, in Pepys' and Evelyn's Diaries. Though this pestilence raged in all parts of Ireland in 1362, and great numbers fell by it, our annalists make particular mention of Cathal Oge, as its principal victim—a circumstance that shows the high estimation in which he was everywhere held. His obit is given by the national annalists as follows: by the Four Masters, "Cathal Oge O'Conor, a Roydamna of more fame, renown, strength, heroism, hospitality, and prowess, than any in his time, died of the plague at Sligo;" by the *Annals of Clonmacnoise*, "Cahall Oge O'Conor, the hardiest man, of greatest valour, of any nobleman in his time, died of the plague at Sligiagh, the 3rd of November;" and by the *Annals of Loch Ce*, "Cathal Oge O'Conor, the king's son of greatest fame, and generosity, and renown, and politeness, strength, and heroism in his own time, died of the plague in Sligech, the third day after All hallows tide".

While Cathal Oge's recorded achievements were almost exclusively in war, or what was then called war, still his erection of a stone and mortar bridge across the river of Ballysadare, one of the first structures of the kind in Connaught, if not in Ireland, proves that his civil and political talents

---

Black Death, the King's Game, and the third pestilence The Black Death appeared in Ireland in 1348, and was described as "a very great pestilence in Ireland, which had before gone through other countries". This was styled the first pestilence; the second raged thirteen years afterwards, i.e. in 1361 or 1362; the third about 1373; the fourth in 1382; and the fifth in 1391. The most succinct account of this pestilence given is that of Friar Clyn, who says, "This year, and chiefly in the months of September and October, great numbers of bishops and prelates, ecclesiastics and religious, peers and others, and in general people of both sexes, flocked together by troops in pilgrimage to Tachmoling, insomuch that many thousands of souls might be seen there together for many days. Some came on the score of devotion, but the greatest part for fear of the pestilence. It first broke out near Dublin, at Howth and Dalkey; it almost destroyed and laid waste the cities of Dublin and Drogheda, insomuch, that in Dublin alone, from the beginning of August to Christmas, 1400 souls perished. The author himself, it seems, died of this plague the year following, of which he had a foresight, for he closes his Annals in 1348, thus, "And lest the writing should perish with the writer, and the work fail with the workman, I leave behind me parchment for continuing it; if any man should have the good fortune to survive this calamity, or any one of the race of Adam should escape this pestilence, to continue what I have begun". The second great plague in King Edward's reign commenced in 1361 or 1362, and continued during the remainder of that decade . . . Cluithe an Righ, or the King's Game, was the name of some epidemic .... O'Flaherty in a gloss upon the words, Cluithe an Righ, calls it, The Plague, "*an plaigh*," but it may also have been a return of the Black Death, which was especially epidemic in Europe at the time, and has been described by Boccacio, and many other eye-witnesses of its effects. "The first time", says Hecker, writing of its progress and mortality in Europe, "it raged chiefly among the poor, but in the year 1360, more among the higher classes. It also destroyed a great many children, whom it had previously spared, and but few women".

were on a par with his military abilities, and as much in advance of those of his contemporaries.[1]

It may perhaps be doubted whether he was the official head of the O'Connors of Carbury or Sligo in his day, though it is far more likely he was not. If the prominence and brilliancy of his career would lead us to think that he occupied that place, the silence of our annalists on the subject is a stronger argument on the other side; for had he been chief, they would hardly have failed to note so important a fact, in his obituary. Anyhow the O'Connors Sligo do not descend from Cathal Oge, but from his uncle, Murtough, who died in 1329, "Lord of Carbury, and a good materies of a King of Connaught".[2]

Murtough is the first of the O'Connors, who is styled in our annals Lord of Carbury; and the head of the family continued to be called Lord of Carbury, or Lord of Carbury and Sligo, up to 1536, when Teige, the chief of that day, took the style and title of The O'Connor Sligo. Donnell, Murtough's son, and, apparently, his immediate successor in the lordship of Carbury, must have been very young—little more than an infant at the father's death, in 1329, as he survived until 1395. There is nothing known of him during the lifetime of Cathal Oge, but his career from the decease of Cathal Oge was a series of brilliant achievements on all sides against the O'Donnells (1389-1390-1392), against the MacDermots of Moydurg (1385), against the Burkes of Tyrawley (1385-1395), against the Barretts of Mayo (1386), and against some of the O'Conors of Machaire Connacht (1388). In his enterprises he was supported generally by the O'Rorkes, with whom he was connected through his wife, and by the MacDonoghs, to whom he was related by his mother, who was Fefalgia McDonogh; and with the forces of Breffney, Tirerrill, and Carbury, at his back, he feared no enemy or combination of enemies. *Nemo me impune lacessit*[3] seemed to be his motto; and when Carbury was invaded on one side by O'Donnell, and on the other by Mac William Burke, Donnell was not slow to retaliate, and to give back as good as he got. On one occasion indeed in 1388 when Turlough an Fhina O'Donnell, arriving at Sligo at the head of an army, plundered Carbury, Donnell, to save the territory from further mischief, submitted to the victor, but in less than a year he returned Turlough's visit, demolished the castle of Kilbarron, and carried off the spoils of Tirconnell.

One ugly blot, however, the murder of his cousin Teige, son of Manus, rests on the memory of Donnell. This Teige was a brave and

---

[1] A bridge of lime and stone was built by Cathal O'Conor across the river of Easdara. —Annals of the Four Masters, 1360.
[2] Murtough, the son of Donnell O'Conor, Lord of Carbury, and a good materies of a King of Connaught, died. —Annals of the Four Masters, 1329.
[3] "No one attacks me with impunity", Clachan ed.].

ambitious man, and contested with Donnell the chieftaincy of Carbury. Two battles at least took place between the rivals; one in Lower Carbury in 1365, in which Teige defeated Donnell, and the other in 1367, at Beltra Strand, in the parish of Ballysadare,[1] in which Donnell got the better of Teige. As however neither engagement was decisive enough to settle the contest between the cousins, the territory in dispute was divided, North Carbury being given to Teige, and South Carbury, including Sligo, to Donnell. Both parties, probably, were dissatisfied with this arrangement, but it was the friends of Donnell, and, no doubt, at Donnell's instigation, who set themselves to undo it. In execution of this design, Teige had been induced to go on business to Rory, King of Connaught, which however he did not do without receiving a solemn guarantee of security; but still the unfortunate man had no sooner appeared before the king than he was treacherously seized, and passed on to the "tender mercies" of his mortal enemy, Donnell, by whom he was at once thrown into chains in the Castle of Sligo. The moment Teige was imprisoned Donnell resumed sway in all Carbury; but feeling insecure in his ill-gotten possessions, so long as the right owner lived, even in captivity, Donnell in 1372, butchered the defenseless cousin in prison with his own hands: not being able, perhaps, to find anyone else to do the nefarious deed.[2] The fate of Teige called forth the deepest horror throughout Ireland, so that the whole transaction passed into a proverb, and people, when they wished to signify a crime of transcendent enormity, used to say, "The treatment of Teige, the son of Manus was not worse" as if this was the *ne plus ultra* of evil doing.[3]

---

[1] The affair at Beltra was a rather important engagement. "A victory was gained by Donnell, the son of Murtough O'Conor, the O'Rourkes, and the Clann-Doaough, with their retained kerns, over Teige, the son of Manus, on Traigh-Eothuile an t-Saoir. The gallowglasses of the son of Manus, one hundred and fifty in number, were slain, as were also Donnell, son of Sorley, Donnell Oge, his son, the two MacSweenys, the son of the Bishop O'Dowda, and William MacSheehy.—Annals of the Four Masters, 1367.

[2] O'Donovan observes in a note under the year 1372 in his edition of the Four Masters: "It is stated in the Dublin copy of the Annals of Ulster, that Donnell killed Teige with his own hand while in confinement, and that the act was the most repulsive and abominable deed ever committed in Ireland". To this passage O'Flaherty adds the following clause, from O'Mulconry: "Ipsius Donaldi manu confossus, postquam ab anno 1368 detentus ab eo in vinculis"—stabbed by the hand of Donnell himself.

[3] The Annals of Clonmacnoise, as translated by Magheoghagan, records thus this occurrence, under the year 1368: "Teig MacMagnus mac Cahall was deceitfully taken by the King of Connaught, in his house of Ard-an-Killin, being brought thither to the king's house by Cormack MacDonogh upon his security, of which villainous dealing that old Irish proverb grew, by comparing thereof to any wicked act – 'The taking of MacManus was no worse.' He was within a little while after worse used; for he was given over to Donnell MacMurtagh O'Connor, who vilely did put him to death in the castle of Sligeach; whereof ensued great contentions and general discords throughout all Connaught, especially between O'Connor, MacWilliam, and MacDermoda."

But however we may condemn Donnell for this shocking and unnatural affair, we must admit that he was a singularly able and valiant chief, and that he greatly increased the authority, and enlarged the territory, of the O'Connors Sligo. If his predecessors extended the rule of the family from Ballyshannon to Sligo, he stretched it on from Sligo to the Curlews; and if his father died Lord of Carbury,[1] Donnell died "Lord of Carbury and Sligo, and Lord also of the tract of country from the mountain (Curlews) downwards".[2]—(Four Masters.)

Donnell's death, which occurred in 1395, was a signal for attacks from all sides on Carbury and Sligo. Though Murtough Baccagh, his eldest son, succeeded on his death, to the lordship, the sons of Cathal Oge[3] left nothing untried against him to secure the territory for themselves. With this object they allied themselves with the enemies of Murtough, with O'Donnell (1397), and Sir William Burke (1398), and brought them several times to Lower Connaught. To say nothing of a foray early in the year 1396[4], an invasion of Carbury and Sligo took place, towards the close of that year, which must have inflicted great damage on the territory, judging from the strong language of the Four Masters: "An army was led by O'Donnell (Turlough, son of Nial Garv) and Teige, son of Cathal O'Conor, to Sligo; and they burned the whole town, both its edifices of wood and stone; and the son of Conor Moinmoy, with many others, was slain by them on this occasion. It was grievous that this town should have been burnt, for its buildings of stone and wood were splendid," and two years later, the town had to bear another attack, which was hardly less disastrous than that of 1396, and which is thus recorded in the *Annals of Clonmacnoise*, "MacWilliam Burke and the sons of Cathall (Cathal Oge O'Connor), assaulted the castle

---

[1] Murtough, the son of Donnell O'Conor, Lord of Carbury, and a good materies of a king of Connaught.—Annals of the Four Masters, 1329.
Donnell's pedigree is thus given in Duald McFirbis' genealogical work: "Donnell, son of Murtough, son of Donnell, son of Teige, son of Brian, son of Andreas, who was son of Brian Luighnech, who was the son of Turlough More O'Conor, monarch of Ireland".

[2] "Donnell, the son of Murtough O'Conor, Lord of Carbury and Sligo, and lord also of that tract of country from the mountain downwards, died in the castle of Sligo a week before Christmas".—Four Masters, 1395.

[3] According to the pedigree of the O'Conors, preserved in the Book of Lecan, fol. 72-74, Cathal Oge had three sons, Rory, Manus, and Teige, by Graine, the daughter of O'Donnell; two, Cathal and Rory, by Honora, the daughter of Sir Redmond Burke; two, Donnell and Felimy, by the daughter of the archbishop; and Dermot, who died in 1370.—Note to Four Masters, 1385.

[4] O'Donnell marched an army into Carbury, and a part of this army came up with the sons of Melaghlin Caech MacMurtough, who were watching and guarding the country for the Connacians, with a great body of cavalry. They were defeated by O'Donnell, and they left the most of their horses behind them. Carbury was afterwards plundered by O'Donnell, who returned home with preys.—Note of O'Donovan in his edition of the Four Masters, anno, 1396.

of Sligeagh, burnt the whole towne, tooke the spoyles thereof, and ransacked it altogether". Between the sons of Cathal Oge O'Connor, O'Donnell, and Mac William Burke, unfortunate Sligo at this time was like the kingdom of Judea, as described by the prophet Joel: "That which the palmer worm hath left, the locust hath eaten; and that which the locust hath left, the bruchus hath eaten; and that which the bruchus hath left, the mildew hath destroyed".[1] But however these calamities may have injured the town of Sligo, they did not damp the courage, or lessen the power of its ruler, who continued to keep his enemies at bay, and, sometimes, to invade their territories, up to 1403, when, in the words of the *Annals of Loch Ce,* "Murtough Baccagh, son of Donnell, son of Murtough O'Conor, Lord of Lower Connaught, died" (in "the Castle of Sligo", Four Masters), "after triumphing over his enemies in every part of all Erinn, the Friday after the festival of Michael", 29th of September.

It is clear, from the entry of 1396, that the Sligo of the O'Connors in the fourteenth century was very different from the Sligo of the FitzGeralds in the thirteenth. The town, as the latter family left it, was, with the exception of the castle and monastery, little else than a collection of rude and fragile huts; and it reflects great credit on the O'Connors, that, under their fostering care, the place had improved so much as to warrant the flattering description of the Four Masters, that "its buildings of wood and stone were splendid". In the fourteenth century private houses of stone must have been very few in these kingdoms. If, as Macaulay tells us,[2] most of the houses of London, at the time of the Restoration, were of lath and plaster, it is but reasonable to think, that people had not taken much to building in stone, three centuries earlier, in the provincial towns of England and Ireland.

There can be little doubt that Sligo was a good deal indebted to Cathal Oge for its stone houses; for the intelligent and enterprising mind, which conceived and executed the project of replacing, with a stone and mortar bridge, the rickety contrivance of intertwined boughs of trees, which, according to local tradition, led across the broad and turbulent river of Ballysadare, was also the man to feel the necessity of substituting stone buildings for the wattle and wickerwork constructions that then existed in Sligo. In any case, the famous bridge of Ballysadare could hardly fail to give an impulse to building in and near Sligo; for, that undertaking once completed, the disengaged masons would naturally try to turn the hand to other works; and, as supply begets demand, they would thus bring about

---

[1] Joel, chap, i., v. 4.
[2] Macaulay's *History of England*, third edition, Vol. I., p. 350. "At the time of the Restoration the city had been built, for the most part, of wood and plaster. ... A few specimens of this architecture may still be seen in these districts which were not reached by the great fire".

the desired employment. Moreover, the noble quarry, brought to light during the excavations for the bridge, must have supplied an additional motive for constructing in stone, as the people of Sligo thus found, within easy reach, the best building material in Ireland. The fashion of building new houses, whether in stone or wood, having once set in, would be encouraged and forwarded by Donnell, who, on the death of Cathal Oge, succeeded to all that chief's influence, and who, during his long and prosperous tenure of office, was in the best condition to render effective aid; and he would be the more eager to turn people's thoughts to material improvement of this kind, in order to divert the attention of his ambitious cousins and others from plots against himself, just as the late Napoleon is said to have taken to the adornment of Paris, for the purpose of giving his enemies something else, to think and talk of, than his own political acts and movements. Such would seem to be the course of the progress, which took place in the material condition of Sligo during the fourteenth century; but whether these were, or were not, the exact stages of the improvement, there can be no doubt whatever of the improvement itself, considering the emphatic testimony of the Four Masters. From the statement of the annalists we may, perhaps, be justified in concluding that the houses of Sligo, towards the close of the fourteenth, century, were as neat and handsome as at any moment between that period and the beginning of the present century, since which time all, or nearly all, the houses, that are now standing, have been erected, as we shall see hereafter.

The exact time at which the O'Connors became masters of Sligo is not known, nor is the particular member of the family who first took possession of the town. It is sufficiently certain that they had nothing to do with the place as long as the Geraldines owned it; for the O'Connors, during all this time, were living quietly and contentedly at Castletown, and had no desire to provoke a quarrel with any one, much less with the powerful family of the Fitzgeralds. Nor, for the same reason, would they meddle with it while the formidable Red Earl was connected with it, which was from 1310, when he built or repaired the castle, to 1326, when he died.

Judging by probabilities, in the absence of positive proofs, Cathal Oge would seem to have been the first of the O'Connors to lay hold of Sligo, at least the first to reside in the town. The time in which he flourished was very favourable to the enterprise, the murder of William, Earl of Ulster, in 1333,[1] having unsettled the rights of property in Connaught, and bred confusion throughout the kingdom. By repeated grants of the province of

---

[1] William Burke, Earl of Ulster, was killed by the English of Ulster. The Englishmen who committed this deed were put to death, in divers ways, by the people of the King of England; some were hanged, others killed, and others torn asunder, in revenge of his death.—Annals of the Four Masters, anno 1333.

Connaught from the English crown to her ancestors,[1] Elizabeth, the heiress and only child of the murdered earl, was sole legal owner of the province on her father's death. Fearing, if she were married to some personage of exalted station and power, as she was sure to be, that they would themselves be humbled, the junior branch of the de Burgos, in avoidance of this fate, usurped her possessions, renounced their allegiance, abjured English law, from which indeed they had nothing but punishment to expect; and, to secure for their usurpations the support of the Irish, assumed Irish names and dress, and, in their mode of life, conformed in all things to Irish laws, manners, and customs. In this way they acquired the sympathy and aid of the Irish, and in this way too they encouraged, by their example, Irish chieftains to encroach on possessions which had been previously in the occupation of the English. Such being the circumstances of the country in Cathal Oge's day, he, no doubt, was induced by them to move into Sligo.

But we are not left altogether to inference in fixing on him as the first O'Connor who took possession of Sligo; for all the annals of the country expressly tell us that Cathal Oge died in Sligo, which would signify, in the absence of any indication to the contrary, that Sligo was his habitual residence. When we add to this, that the chief who immediately preceded his day is styled Lord of Carbury,[2] while those who immediately followed are called Lords of Carbury and Sligo, the proof is nearly complete, that it was Cathal Oge who first put the family in possession of the town, and commenced those marked improvements in its buildings which we have been noticing.

Besides Murtough Baccagh, who died, as has been said, in 1403, and whose mother was Meave O'Rorke, Donnell had at least four other sons, Brian, Owen, Turlough Carrach, and Donough; and of them Brian, Owen, and Turlough Carrach became successively Lords of Carbury and Sligo. Brian's lordship lasted thirty-seven years, from 1403 to 1440, during which time he took a leading, indeed the foremost part, in all the public transactions of Connaught,[3] and conducted several successful expeditions

---

[1] Henry II. granted the province to William Fitz-Andelm de Burgo in the year 1179. Hardiman's History of Galway, p. 45. On the 12th of September, 1215, King John granted the entire of Connaught to Richard de Burgo, the Red Earl. This grant was confirmed in 1218 by Henry III. to the Red Earl and his heirs. On the 12th June, 1225, a mandate arrived from England, directing William Earl Marshal, the Lord Justice, to seize on the whole country of Connaught (stated to have been forfeited by O'Conor), and to deliver it to Richard de Burgo, at the yearly rent of 300 marks for the first five years, and after that period 500 marks for ever, excepting, however, five choice cantreds of land near Athlone, which were supposed to have been reserved for the use of that garrison.—Hardiman's History of Galway, p. 47.
[2] Annals of the Four Masters, 1329.
[3] Annals of the Four Masters, 1409, 1412, 1413, 1418, 1430, &c.

against his enemies.[1] Though his mother was, according to O'Donovan, "Raghnailt O'Donnell, daughter of Turlough, Lord of Tirconnell, he was generally at war with the grandfather, sometimes in aggression, and, sometimes in defence;[2] and if O'Donnell burned and plundered the territory of Carbury, as far as Sligo (1422), Brian, on his side, spoiled all Tirhugh, from Ath-na-Gall to Ballyshannon, including its grass, corn, and buildings, and burned Murvagh, O'Donnell's fortress.[3] And the castle of Bundrowes which he erected in 1420, in spite of all the efforts of the Kinel-Connell to stop the work, supplies a still more signal proof of Brian's great power.[4]

On the death of Brian[5], in 1440, his brother Owen succeeded to his place; but though this Owen, who is the ancestor of the O'Connors Sligo, had given, before attaining the lordship,[6] abundant proof of military talent and courage, he had no opportunity of distinguishing himself in the field, during the short time that he held the lordship, having been slain three or

---

[1] Take those specimens of his expedition. A great army was mustered by Brian, the son of Donnell, son of Murtough O'Conor (of Sligo), by MacDonough of Tirerrill, and by the sons of Tiernan O'Rourke; and they placed provisions and stores in the castle of Roscommon, in despite of the men of Connaught from the mountain upwards, all of whom, both horse and foot, had assembled together to oppose them. On the same night they returned to Airm, and on the next day to their own houses.—Four Masters, 1409.

A great army was led by Brian, son of Donnell, son of Murtough O'Conor (of Sligo), about Lammas, first into Gaileanga, and thence into Clann-Cuain, Ceara, and Conmaicne Guile Toladh, into which latter territory he brought the Clann Maurice na-m-Brigh, and their creaghts. The Clann-William Burke, the O'Flahertys, the O'Malleys, the Barretts, the inhabitants of the barony of Gaileanga, and the Costelloes, assembled to oppose them; but all these (numerous as they were), did not venture to give them either skirmish or battle, although Brian, in despite of them, burned their territories, destroyed their corn-fields, and burned their fortresses, viz., Caislen-an-Bharraigh (Castlebar) of Leth-inis, and Baile-Loch-Measca (Loughmask Castle.) He then left the Clann-Maurice with their creaghts in their own territory; and he obtained peace from the English and Irish on this expedition, and returned home in safety.—Four Masters, anno 1412.

[2] Annals of the Four Masters, 1420-1422.

[3] Ibid., 1419.

[4] The castle of Bundrowes was commenced by Brian, the son of Donnell, son of Murtough O'Conor; but the Kinel-Connell, with their forces, came to prevent the work. Brian assembled another army to assist them, namely, his own kinsmen, i.e., Teige O'Rourke, and MacDonough, with their forces, so that the KinelConnell did not dare to proceed eastwards across the Urscatha on that occasion, but remained encamped in the Bay of Assaroe . . . After that victory, Brian returned home. Four Masters, 1420.

[5] Brian, the son of Donnell, son of Murtough O'Conor, Lord of Lower Connaught, and star of the valour and bravery of the Irish of his time, died, two days before the festival of St. John, after having been thirty-seven years in the lordship. Four Masters, 1440. —The Annals of Loch Ce, sub anno 1440, style him Lord of Sligo.

[6] Annala of the Four Masters, 1420-1422.

four years after his elevation to that station, by one of the MacDonoughs in a private quarrel.[1]

The place vacated by Owen, Turlough Carrach secured for himself, but secured it, at the cost of dissensions in the O'Connor Sligo family, and of division in the O'Connor Sligo territory. For the first forty-four years of the fifteenth century, that family was singularly united. The language which the Four Masters often employ, such as, the "sons of Donnell" led such and such an expedition; the "sons of Donnell" repelled such and such an attack; shows that the sons of Donnell always acted in concert, and that cordial union prevailed between the members of the family. During this time, too, the territory was united and prosperous, and the Lord of Carbury was also Lord of Sligo. But this state of things entirely changed on the decease of Owen; for when Turlough Carrach assumed authority in Sligo, Owen's sons, in revenge, joined O'Donnell and Philip Maguire, and with them invaded Sligo, burned the town, and slew many of Turlough Carrach's friends, including Tomultagh McDonough, Lord of Tirerrill (1445).

About the same time the sons of Murtough Baccach and the sons of Brian had a quarrel of their own,[2] so that the grandsons of Donnell had now become as noted for dissensions as their fathers had been for union. Family strife, as usual, produced weakness and humiliation, with the result that the O'Connors Sligo[3] were of little or no account, in the affairs of the province during the second half of the fifteenth century. During this period their names are hardly mentioned in our annals, except in connection with their fratricidal quarrels, as, for example, in the *Annals of Dudley Firbis*, where we read under the year 1446,[4] "Daniel fitz Murcharty O'Connor, Lord of

---

[1] Owen, the son of Donnell, son of Murtough O'Conor, Lord of Sligo, and of the territory of Carbury, was slain with a cast of a javelin, by one of the sons of Cormac McDonough; for the son of Melaghlin, who was son of Cormac McDonough, had been previously slain in a quarrel by the grandson of John O'Hart, and it was on this account that Owen, the son of Donnell, was slain.—Annals of the Four Masters, 1444.

[2] Dudley Ferbis writes thus: Warr betwixt the sons of Morty backagh O'Connor, and the sons of Brien FitzDaniel O'Connor, so that Manus FitzBrien's son was taken prisoner in that warr, and another of his sonnes was wounded, so that they did much harm to each other.

[3] The style and title of O'Connor Sligo, did not come in vogue until 1536, and the phrase is used here, as it has been in other places, by anticipation, as a convenient one for designating the descendants of Brian Luignech, in contradistinction to other branches of the O'Conors of Connaught.

[4] One or two other instances of these unfortunate dissensions will not be amiss here. The Annals of the Four Masters says, under the year 1494: "Donnell, the son of Owen O'Connor, Lord of Sligo, a prosperous and warlike man, who possessed that tract of country from the Curlieu Mountains to Bunduff, being at the summit of his affluence, was treacherously slain and burned, in an attack by night, in the bawn of the castle at Bunfuine, by the sons of Rory, son of Turlough Carrach, namely, John and Brian; and Rory, the son of Turlough Carrach, took his place". And under the year 1495: "Rory, the son of

Carbery-of-Drumclaw, with the most part of his kinsmen, or brothers, were killed by Eogan O'Connor's sons, in the Benden, and Ruairy fitz Brian O'Connor was made Lord in his place", and in the *Annals of the Four Masters*, where it is stated, under the year 1489, that "Owen, the son of Felim, son of the Lord of Carbury, and the two sons of Murtough, son of Owen, i.e. Murtough Oge and John, were treacherously slain by Calvach Caech, the son of Donnell, son of Owen; and O'Donnell, who was the guarantee between them, plundered and ravaged Carbury, in revenge of their misconduct, and the violation of his surety and guarantee". Meantime the O'Donnells, through these dissensions of the O'Connors, acquired great authority over Carbury and all Lower Connaught; for in 1458, we find them receiving the hostages of Lower Connaught; in 1469, disposing of the forces of Lower Connaught; and in 1470, taking the castle of Sligo and receiving the submission of Lower Connaught.[1]

It will not be out of place to dwell a moment on one or two of the occurrences just mentioned. The capture of Sligo castle in 1370, which was the outcome of a long and methodical siege, was the heaviest and most humiliating blow received by the O'Connors Sligo, in the fifteenth century. It left them, for the time, completely at the mercy of their enemies. So long as the castle was safe, and in their hands, they could not be wholly defeated; for when O'Donnell, or Mac William Burke, invaded their territory, and they were unable, as sometimes happened, to cope with him in the field, they had only to retire to this fortress, and remain there till the enemy withdrew, when they could come forth again, and recover, in a short time, much of the ground they had lost. But, deprived of the castle, every defeat was decisive for them, as they had no place in which to rally, and to retrieve their position. Indeed, from this time forward, the main object of most of the conflicts between the O'Connors Sligo, and their enemies, and between

---

Turlough Carragh O'Conor, Lord of Carbury of Drumcliff, died. A contest arose among the descendants of Donnell concerning the lordship of the country, namely, among Felim, the son of Manus, son of Brian, Rory Oge, the son of Rory Ballagh, and Murtough Caech, the son of Manua O'Conor. Rory Oge and Turlough, son of Rory, son of Brian, fell by each other in a combat at Drumcliff, in consequence of which the country was left to Felim".

[1] "The castle of Sligo was taken by O'Donnell from Donnell, son of Owen O'Conor, after having besieged it for a long time, and O'Donnell obtained on this occasion his own demands of gifts, besides (receiving) submission and tribute from Lower Connaught. It was on this occasion that he obtained the book called Leabhar-Gearr, and another called Leabhar-na-h-Uidhri, and the chairs of Donnell Oge, which had been brought westward in the time of John, the son of Conor, son of Hugh, son of Donnell Oge O'Donnell".— Four Masters, 1470. John O'Donnell ruled over Tirconnell from 1356 to 1380. During this time the O'Connors obtained several victories over him in 1365-1366—1359; but it was probably in that of 1359, gained by the heroic Cathal Oge O'Connor, that the chairs were carried away.

different individuals of the O'Connors themselves, was to possess the castle; and during the remainder of the fifteenth century, and much of the sixteenth, this structure and its immediate surroundings, were the scene of almost perpetual hostilities.

In 1478 the castle was taken from O'Donnell by MacWilliam Burke, and handed over to the family of Brian, the second eldest son of Donnell O'Connor; in 1494 the descendants of Owen, another son of Donnell, took forcible possession of it, on which occasion Hugh Roe O'Donnell came and besieged it, but failed to make himself master of it, though he continued his efforts for many months, and suffered during the time very heavy losses;[1] and in 1495, Con O'Donnell, in the absence of his father, Hugh Roe, at the Court of King James, of Scotland, renewed the siege, in which his father had failed, and in which himself would have failed still more egregiously, only that Hugh Roe returned, in the meantime, from Scotland, and hearing of Con's critical position, hastened to his assistance, and defeated their common enemies at Belladrehid, in a hard-fought battle, attended with great loss of life.[2] Though O'Donnell gained the castle this time, he had hardly taken it, when he was dislodged, by Mac William of Clanricard,[3] who reinstated Calvach Caech, the son of Owen, in possession; an act to which O'Donnell, making a virtue of necessity, gave his adhesion the following year, when, having by his influence secured the lordship of Carbury for Felim, grandson of Brian, he agreed that the castle of Sligo should remain in possession of Calvach Caech; an arrangement which, no doubt, he sanctioned, the more readily, as it weakened the O'Connors by dividing their territory.

---

[1] O'Donnell, i.e., Hugh Roe, went with his forces to the castle of Sligo, and remained a great part of this year encamped around it On this occasion many of his people were slain, among them the son of MacWilliam Burke. Many others were also slain by the warders of the castle, i.e. by Brian Caech, the son of Teige, son of Owen; Calvach Caech, son of Donnell, son of Owen; and by Muintir Airt. These transactions occurred in summer.—Four Masters, 1494.

[2] Con, son of Hugh Roe, and his forces, surrounded the town of Sligo, and continued to besiege it for some time. The descendants of Owen O'Conor mustered a very great force to relieve Sligo And now when both armies had their weapons of valour ready for action, O'Donnell came up with them, for he had arrived from Scotland, and having heard, at his own fortress of Donegal, of the danger that his son was in, he had stopped there only one night, and was now come to relieve him. Upon O'Donnell's arrival in the centre of his people, both armies gave each other a fierce and vigorous battle, in which the army of Lower Connaught was defeated by O'Donnell, and in which, besides the Lord of Tirerrill, the Lord of Tireragh, and two grandsons of Owen O'Conor, many others were slain, drowned, or taken prisoners.—Four Masters, 1495.

[3] This fact is slurred over by the Four Masters, who are always too tender in regard to the O'Donnells, but it is given in the Annals of Ulster, sub anno 1495: "Mac William of Clanrickard, proceeded with an army, at the instance of Calvach Caech, to drive O'Donnell from the castle of Sligo, and O'Donnell left the castle".

The castle continued in the sixteenth century to be the bone of contention, that it had been in the fifteenth. In 1501 the grandsons of Turlough Carrach, who were very powerful and active about this time, surprised it, and made themselves masters of it, after a sanguinary struggle, in which John, grandson of Turlough, fell by the hand of Calvach Caech, who in turn was slain by the invaders. The O'Donnells, meantime, left nothing undone to recover possession. Hugh Oge O'Donnell besieged it in vain in 1512, and again in 1513, though in the latter year he sat before it from the 1st of February to June; but three or four years later, in 1516, he had better success, for which he was indebted mainly to a pilgrim of high rank, who had come from France to perform his devotions at St. Patrick's Purgatory, in Lough derg, and to whom, during his stay in the country, O'Donnell was unremitting in according the honours and hospitalities of Tirconnell. To requite this courtesy, the French Knight, on reaching home, dispatched to Killybegs for his friend, a vessel carrying heavy ordnance, to aid in capturing the castle of Sligo. On the arrival of the ship, O'Donnell ordered it to the harbour of Sligo; and, proceeding himself to the town by land, at the head of an army, he attacked the place at once by sea and land. Even thus it was only after meeting so obstinate and spirited a resistance from the townsfolk, as to be obliged to batter the whole town, that he was able to make his way into the castle. The following is the account of this transaction contained in the *Annals of the Four Masters*: "The castle of Sligo was taken by O'Donnell (Hugh Oge, the son of Hugh Roe), after it had been a long time out of his possession. It was thus he succeeded in taking it. A French Knight came upon his pilgrimage to St. Patrick's Purgatory, on Lough Gerg; and, on his arrival, and at his departure, he visited O'Donnell, from whom he received great honours, gifts, and presents; and they formed a great intimacy and friendship with each other; and the knight, upon learning that the castle of Sligo was defended against O'Donnell, promised to send him a ship with great guns; and the knight, too, performed that promise, for the ship arrived in the harbour of Killybegs. She was steered directly westwards to Sligo; and O'Donnell and his army marched by land, so that they met from sea and land at the town. They battered the town very much before they obtained possession of it, and O'Donnell gave protection to the warders".

For eleven years he now maintained his hold of the place, but had to encounter two formidable sieges of it in the meantime. The first was in 1522, when the troops of Munster, under the O'Briens, and the troops of Connaught, under MacWilliam of Clanrickard, O'Conor Roe, O'Conor Don, MacWilliam Burke, and MacDermot of Moylurg, being on their way to join O'Neil in his conflict with the O'Donnells, stopped to take the town of Sligo, unwilling to leave so important a place in their rear; but this danger did not in the event prove as formidable as it looked at first; for the besiegers, on hearing that the O'Donnells had defeated their adversaries in the great battle of Cnoc-Buidhe (Knockavoe), and were already at Carrownamodow, at the foot of Benbulben, in victorious march to Sligo, decamped and retreated in haste across the Curlews.[1]

The second attempt on Sligo was made by the O'Connors. Being now fairly united among themselves, and being supported by the MacDonoughs, they surrounded Sligo, and sought to take the castle, to which, no doubt, they thought they had better claims themselves than the distant chiefs of Tirconnell; but O'Donnell, learning their designs and efforts, hastened to the relief of the place, and, on the enemies retiring before him, pursued them to Belladrehid, inflicted on them there a most serious defeat,[2] and compelled them to accept such conditions of peace as he thought well to dictate. Sometime after, in the year 1533, Teige Oge O'Connor got possession of the castle, having obtained it in a nocturnal attack, which he made in collusion with O'Donnell's warders, who had arranged to betray it.

This chief was an able and ambitious man, and, wishing to excel all the O'Connors who had gone before him, he assumed, in 1536, the style and title of The O'Connor, the distinguishing name of preceding lords being MacDonnell mic Murtough, that is, descendant of Donnell, son of Murtough.[3] In order to prove himself not unworthy of the new distinction, he made two incursions in the year he obtained it: one against the Clann Costello of Kilcoleman, from which he brought back a famous coat of mail, given him, in token of submission, by Rory Costello, and, as a hostage, Rory himself; and the other against O'Conor Roe and his allies, from which he carried home hostages, and, a prize he seemed to set a still higher value

---

[1] The great victory of Cnoc-Buidhe added greatly to the fame of Hugh Duv O'Donnell, which was still more enhanced by the precipitate retreat of the Munster and Connaught armies. "Scarcely did the defeat of Cnoc-Buidhbh, in which many men had been slaughtered, and vast spoils obtained, procure greater renown or victory for O'Donnell throughout Ireland than this bloodless retreat".—Annals of the Four Masters, 1522.

[2] The Connacian army left great spoils of horses, arms, and armour, to the Cinel-Connell on that occasion, and from the time that Hugh Roe, the son of Nial Garv, had gained the battle of Ceideach-droighnech over the Connacians, where many of them were slain, the Cinel-Connell had not given a defeat to the Connacians, which redounded more to their triumph, or by which they obtained more spoils, than this defeat of Bel-an-droichit".—Annals of the Four Masters, 1526.

[3] Teige Oge, son of Teige, son of Hugh, son of Turlough Carragh O'Conor, was proclaimed the O'Conor. And this was not the usual name of the person who was lord of Sil Conor in Lower Connaught, but whosoever of them was lord of Lower Connaught, was usually called MacDonnell Mic Murtough. Nevertheless, it was to exalt his family, and to excel the kings preceding him, that he was proclaimed by this change of name.—Annals of Loch Ce, an. 1536.

upon, the ornamental door of the castle of Turrock, which was thenceforth set up, as a trophy, in the gateway of Sligo Castle.[1]

Nor was Teige, this same year, without attack himself; for O'Donnell invaded Lower Connaught, passed through, and ravaged Carbury and Tireragh; and though O'Conor on this occasion made some pretense of giving battle, he fought rather shy of the enemy, retiring to Belladrehid, and allowed the Tirconnell chief to return home with little loss, after destroying much property, but "without obtaining rent or tribute, submission or homage, from the chiefs of Lower Connaught on that occasion, which was unusual with him", as the Four Masters have it.[2] Though this O'Donnell, Hugh Duv, died some months later,[3] O'Connor Sligo had to encounter a still more formidable enemy in the late chieftain's son, Manus, who was hardly installed in authority when he invaded O'Connor's territory; burning and ravaging Carbury, Tirerrill, Corran, Leyney, and Tireragh. This happened in 1537, but in 1538 Manus dealt a still deadlier blow, when he captured the castle of Sligo, which had foiled all the efforts of his father, and which was well defended by brave warders with powerful ordnance.[4] With this stronghold in his hands Minus was able, in 1539, to obtain the hostages of Lower Connaught; in 1542, to exact rent or tribute from the chiefs of Lower Connaught; and, in general, to act as Lord Paramount of the territory.

As to Teige Oge O'Connor, he disappears from view at the capture of the castle in 1538, and is no more heard of till it is related under the year 1545, that he was slain at Ath-chinn-Locha[5] by Cormac McDermot, who was himself slain soon after, and of whose death the *Annals of Loch Ce*

---

[1] These troops returned, having accomplished their expedition, as was pleasing to them; and they took with them to Sligo those hostages, namely, the son of O'Kelly, and the son of O'Hanly; and they also carried with them the variegated door of the castle which they had taken, in order to place it as a door in the castle of Sligo.—Four Masters, 1536.

[2] Annals of the Four Masters, 1536.

[3] This is a portion of the long and elaborate eulogium of the Four Masters on Hugh Duv O'Donnell: "O'Donnell (Hugh, the son of Hugh Roe, son of Niall Garv, son of Turlough of the Wine, Lord of Tirconnell, Inishowen, Kinel-Owen, Fermanagh, and Lower Connaught) [died; he was] a man to whom rents and tributes were paid by other territories over which he had extended his jurisdiction and power, such as Moylurg, Machaire Connaught, Clann-Conway, Costello, Galleanga, Tirawley, and Comnaicne Cuile to the west; and to the east, Oireacht-Ui-Chathain, the Route, and Clannaboy; for of these there was not one territory that had not given him presents, besides his tribute of protection", &c.—Annals of the Four Masters, 1537.

[4] An army was led by O'Donnell (Manus) into Lower Connaught, and triumphantly took the castle of Sligo, which was well defended by warders and cannon, after it had been for some time out of his possession, and it could not be taken until then.—Four Masters, 1538

[5] O'Connor Sligo, i.e. Teige Oge, was slain at Ath-chinn-locha—Annals of Loch Ce, 1545.

remarks: "It was right of God that he should fall, for he acted badly in killing O'Conor Sligo, in treachery, at Ath-chinn-locha or Loch Teched".[1]

Teige, son of Cathal Oge, succeeded Teige Oge, and ruled as chief from the latter's death in 1545 to his own death in 1552, if he did not begin to rule earlier, which would seem probable from Teige Oge's obscure condition since 1538; from Teige having the disposal of the Connaught hostages so early as 1542;[2] and from his entering into a treaty or compact in 1539, regarding the castle of Sligo, with Manus O'Donnell. On Teige's death there was a dispute about the succession, in which all the O'Conors and the MacDermots took action, either on one side or the other; but Donnell, the second son of the late chief, by his own energy and by the devoted co-operation of his elder brother, Cathal Oge, succeeded, after a protracted contest, to the lordship, which, with the aid of the English, he retained to the end of his life.

From this time forward the English play an important part in the affairs of Sligo. Disappearing from view, with the De Burgos and Geraldines, in the early part of the fourteenth century, they now reappear on the scene, and reassert themselves, after an absence of three centuries. Between the fourteenth century and the reign of Henry VIII. the monarchs of England rarely interfered in Irish affairs outside the Pale, but from the year 1541, when Henry received the title of King of Ireland, the great aim of British rulers and statesmen, in regard to this country, was to make all its parts, as well without as within the Pale, amenable to English authority and law. In pursuance of this policy, they induced Irish chiefs, by profuse gifts of dignities, of money, and even of dress,[3] to renounce their Irish captaincies, and accept English lordships or other titles instead; to

---

[1] Annals of Loch Ce, 1545.

[2] Mac William brought with him the hostages of Teige Oge, son of Teige, son of Hugh; and the hostages of Teige, son of Cathal Oge, and of Lower Connaught.—Annals of Loch Ce, A.D. 1542.

[3] Henry VIII., in writing of the Earl of Tyrone to the Lord Deputy and Council, observes, "And for his reward we gave unto him a chayne of threescore poundes and odde, We pay'd for his robes, and the charges of his creation, threescore and five poundes tenue shillinges two pens, and We gave him in redy money oon hundreth poundes sterling".— State Paper ccclxxxi, quoted in Moore's History of Ireland, Vol. III., p. 322. And again, "We have granted unto every of them, and their heires masles, summe house and pece of lande nere Dublyn, for the keeping of their horses and traynes, at their repayre to our parlyaments and counsailles". – Ibid.

O'Neill, who was the first of the Irish chiefs to surrender, covenanted:—1. To renounce the name of O'Neal; 2. That he and his followers should use English habits, language and manners; 3. That their children should learn English; 4. -That they should obey English laws, and not cess their tenants, nor keep more gallowglasses than the Lord Deputy allows; 5. That they should build houses and husband their land in English manner; and 6. That they should answer all general hostings, as those of the Pale do, and shall not succour any of the King's enemies. Cox's Hibernia Anglicana, p. 275.

surrender their Brehon tenures and customs, and take back their lands as grants from the king on the usual conditions of English landed estate; and, in general, to exchange their Irish status, with its dependence on their septs, for an English status, resting on, and supported by, the authority of the Crown. The advantages which were thus offered, and which tended to make the chiefs independent of their septs, were eagerly embraced both by the Anglo-Irish and the Irish lords; and, in no very long time the Butlers, the Fitzgeralds, and the Burkes, as well as the O'Briens, the O'Neils, the O'Donnells, and the O'Connors Sligo, had exchanged their old position for the new one. A change, however, of such moment was not affected in a day, nor in some places as readily as in others, local circumstances prejudicing or predisposing the mind in regard to it. The nearer people lived to the seat of government the more they were drawn to the new order of things; and when the chief was Anglo-Irish there was more sympathy for it than when he was Irish *pur sang*. For the causes indicated, the new system was enforced in some places under Henry VIII, whereas in others it was not introduced before the reign of Elizabeth, or even the reign of James.

The adhesion or submission of the O'Connors Sligo to this policy of England dates from the first Lord Deputyship of Sir. Henry Sydney, which began in the year 1565.[1] It is true Sir Henry's predecessor in office, Lord Sussex, passed through Sligo with an army in 1561, but, owing to a stratagem of Calvagh O'Donnell, which is mentioned by the Four Masters, and by which that cunning chief outwitted both the O'Connors and the Deputy,[2] Sussex was prevented from having any communication with the O'Connors on that occasion.

Sir Henry Sydney on assuming office, lost no time in "making warre" on the "Arch-rebell, Shane O'Neill;" and it was on reaching Sligo, after marching in triumph through Ulster, that he received the homage of Donnell O'Connor. When leaving the town, the Deputy took Donnell with him to Boyle, where they entered into a formal treaty or indenture with one another, by which O'Connor –

> First.—Acknowledges Elizabeth to be his liege Lady and Queen, and to be sole and supreme in both ecclesiastical and temporal causes.
> Second.—Promises not to adhere to any rebel or enemy of the Queen, but to act against them all, and, especially, against John (Shane) O'Neill.

---

[1] Three times her Majestic hath sent me her Deputie into Ireland—MS. Memoir of his government in Ireland, by Sir H. Sydney.

[2] Sussex then proceeded, across the Erne, into the territory of Carbury, to lay siege to the castle of Sligo. Calvagh, noticing this, bethought him of a stratagem; he sent his own standard to the town, and displayed it on the battlements of the tower. The Lord Justice asked whose standard it was that he saw. Calvagh made answer and said that it was his own standard; and that the town was his own, and had belonged always to his family; upon which the Lord Justice delivered up the keys of the town to Calvagh.—Four Masters, 1561.

Third.—Agrees that, whereas the Lord Deputy, on the Queen's behalf, has entered into the castle of Sligo, and demanded a certain annual rent, and the Earl of Kildare has claimed the castle and rent by right of inheritance, and Lord Calvagh O'Donnell has demanded the same, he (O'Connor) will pay half a year's rent to O'Donnell; while the Lord Deputy promises "to discuss and adjudicate touching the rights of the Queen, and the said Earl, after the feast of the Purification".

Fourth.—Engages to aid O'Donnell against O'Neill with his horsemen and kerne, and this not of any right, but in compliance with the mandate of the Lord Deputy for the Queen's service.[1]

On Sydney's return to England in 1567, he was accompanied by O'Connor Sligo and several other chieftains;[2] and Sir Donald, if we are to rely on John O'Donovan and Cox, was confined, for some time after his arrival, in the tower of London, though other authorities are silent on this imprisonment, which, indeed, seems quite inconsistent with the friendly relations between Sir Henry Sydney and the Sligo chief. But however, this may be, O'Connor soon gained the esteem and confidence of the Queen, and a new indenture was entered into between him and Elizabeth, fixing their relations. The preamble of this interesting instrument says, "The said O'Connor Sligo came to the Queen at Hampton Court, the 8th November, in the 9th year of her reign, and there, in his Irish tongue, by an interpreter, declared to her Majesty that the chief cause of his coming was to see and speak to the powerful and illustrious princess, whom he recognized to be his sovereign Lady, acknowledging that both he and his ancestors had long lived in an uncivil, rude, and barbarous fashion, destitute of the true knowledge of God, and ignorant of their duty to the imperial crown of England; he asserted that he had continually resisted that odious traitor and rebel, Shane O'Neill. At the same time he made his humble submission to the Queen, and now he does the same in the following manner:—

First.—He acknowledges the Queen to be his natural princess and sovereign lady.
Second.—He not only submits his life, land, and goods, to the Queen's mercy, but also surrenders and resigns his office of Captain of O'Connor Sligo, into her hands, with all the castles, manors, &c., which he holds as O'Connor Sligo in the countries

---

[1] This treaty is styled "Indenture between O'Connor Sligo and Sir Henry Sydney, K.G., Deputy General in Ireland, with the Council of that Kingdom on the one part, and Donald O'Connour, commonly called O'Connour Sligo of the other part". It was "Signed at the monastery of Aboile (Boyle), 24th October, 8" (1566.)

[2] The Lord Deputy, soon after this capture, went over to England, taking with him the Earl of Desmond, the Baron of Dungannon, O'Conor Sligo, and others. The Earl of Desmond and O'Conor Sligo were confined in the tower of London, but O'Conor, by indenture, made his submission to the Queen, and was, therefore, set at liberty.—Note of O'Donovan in his edition of the Four Masters, sub anno 1567.

Sydney at length prevailed to get licence to go for England; he carried with him the Earl of Desmond, the Baron of Dungannon, O'Conor Sligo, O'Carol, and others. . . . Being come in to Hampton Court, he was well received for the present by the Queen. . . . However, the Earl of Desmond and O'Connor were clapt up in the tower, and Sir John of Desmond was sent for, and imprisoned in the same place.—Hibernia Anglicana, Vol. I., p. 326.

of Carbury, Tireragh, Moay Layen (Maghera Leyney) Cowlavin, Cormer (Corran), and Tirerrill, in Connaught, imploring the Queen's pardon and grace, and that he may henceforth be reputed as an Englishman, and praying her to grant him his said country and lands to be held of her Majesty, and to be exempted from subjection and servitude, and all burdens imposed by O'Donnell, or any other, but the imperial crown of England.

Third.—The Queen receives him into her grace and protection, and, accepting the said surrenders and resignation, promises, after due inquiries, "to grant him, by letters patent, all his lawful possessions in tail-male, at a certain rent, which is not to exceed 100 Irish, and which may be paid either in money or kind of the same value".

Fourth.—He binds himself in 10,000 to observe the conditions of this indenture.

Witnesses: Nicholas Bacon, Lord-Keeper of the Great Seal.
Francis, Count of Bixford.
Robert, Count of Leicester.
William Howard of Effingham.
Edmund Rogers.
Francis Knollys.
William Cecyl.
Ambrose Caique, Duchy of Lancaster.
Walter Mildmaye.
Henry Sydney, Lord Deputy of Ireland.
James Dior.
John Southcote.
Richard Onslow.
Luke Dillon.
Nicholas White.
Owen O'Conchur, Cleric, brother of the aforesaid Donald, and others;" whose names are not given.

In pursuance of this Indenture Donnell received, as he was setting out for Ireland, the following royal letter:—

Eliz. R. "Whereas, Sir Donald O'Connor Sligo, Knyght of the partes of Conagh, cummyng with our right trustie Sir Henry Sydney, Knyght, our Deputie of that our realme, hither to our Courte, to acknowledge his loyal dutie to us his soveraigne Lady, hayth very humbly and voluntaryly submytted himself to our grace, and freelie surrendered to us all his possessions; whereupon wee have receyved hym into our protection, and have farther accorded to make unto hym and the heyres males of his father, certayne Estates of Inheritaunce, as more at lardge may appeare by our letters patent, which he will showe youe; Wee have thought mete to recommend hym unto youe, as one whom wee certaynly trust will prove and continue a faythful subject; and, therefor, wee will and chardge you readily to hear sondre complaynts as he hayth to make unto youe, for the deteyning certain his castles from hym, as he sayth, that is to say, the castells of Bondrowys by O'Donnell, and Ballintogher by O'Rourke, and Ardnaree by Olyver Burghes' sons, and that you cause the sayd parties to appear and make answere before yourselfs or souch other as you shall think mete, to hear the complaynts of the sayd O'Conor Slego, and to give direction for restitution to the sayd Sir Donald O'Conor, of that which shall be found due to hym by order of justice. And furthermore wee will, that if there hayth bene any spoyles made of any his goods during his absence, in comrnyn hither and retourne thither, that upon his complaynt, order be gyven for the trial thereof, and restitution to be made to hym, as the case shall requyre; Lastly, we let you to understand that upon his humble and reasonable request, wee are well contented that the howse of the Fryerie of Slego, wherein, he sayth, the sepulture of his auncestors hayth bene, shall be so preserved, as the Friars thear, being converted to secular priestes, the same howse may remayne and contynue as well for the sepulture of his posteritie, as for the mayntenance of prayer and service of God. And yf in any onther reasonable thinge the said Sir Donald O'Conor Siego shall for the mayntenance of hymself, his tenants and possessions in our realm, as shall belong to a good and faythful subject, requyre your ayde, wee will and chardge youe to ayde and assist hym, in our name, to the best of your power, for so wee are disposed to showe all favour to so good a servant and subject, as wee take hym to be; and by the experience wee have sene of his behaviour here, we think assuredly he will contynue j And where he hayth requyred that he might have the true copie of this our letter, wee are contented that youe shall delyver unto hym a copie of the same, in souche sorte as in lyke cases youe are accustomed, under our seale theare. Given under our signet at our Palais of Westminster, the xxvth daie of January, 1567, the tenth year of our reign."

Sir Donnell, on his return to Sligo, was in no haste to perform the engagements of the Indenture. Having compassed his main object, in securing the protection and patronage of the Queen, he neglected to sue out the regrant of his lands, which could not be done without expense, and which, besides, might bring him the ill-will of some of his people. Whatever may have been the motive of his conduct, he allowed twelve years to pass without moving at all in the matter, and, what must have been still more vexatious to the thrifty Queen, without paying a penny of the stipulated rent. To increase her displeasure, she was told that O'Connor Sligo, whom she had taken to be a paragon of simplicity and candour, had outwitted herself and all her renowned statesmen, and had palmed off on the royal Council, as a correct statement, a cooked account of his lands and circumstances, putting the value of the lands so low as to lead to the fixing of an entirely inadequate rent. The Queen was nettled by all this; and in the Instructions[1] which she addressed to Sir Nicholas Malbie, on his taking office as President of Connaught, she urges him, in a strong-worded paragraph, to bring the slippery Sligo chief to his duty.[2] But O'Donnell, who

---

[1] Orders to be observed by Sir Nicholas Maltby, for the better government of the Province of Connaught.

[2] Whereas O'Conor Sligo, upon a wrong suggestion made unto us of the small circuit and dishability of his countrie, obtained of us a warrant for a grant to pass in Ireland for the freedom of his lands, in consideration of £100 Irish per annum, to be paid by him; which grant he hath neither passed there or observed the conditions to be performed on his part; Wee think it meet that ye treat with him to yield to such composition as the rest of the captains of countries within that province have consented unto rateably, according to the quantity of his country, which we think reasonable, as well in respect of our charge and expences in settling a government there for defence of him and others of his quality, as also that the conditions to be observed by him have not been kept according to the words and meaning of our former grant.

"On the 26th December", writes Cox, in the Hibernia Anglicana, Vol. I., p.385, "O'Conner Sligo, who had formerly taken a Patent for the county Sligo, at the yearly rent of £100 per annum, did covenant that in lieu of cess he would pay every year a fine horse, and 100

could over-reach much abler men than Sir Nicholas Malbie, would not be brought to book by him. While always ready to *pay* his *respects* either to the Governor of Connaught,[1] or to the Lord Deputy, he[2] maintained, to the last, an insuperable objection to *paying* one or other of them *rent*; and, whatever efforts the Governor may have made—and he left nothing unattempted—[3] to carry out the instructions of the Queen, in regard to O'Connor Sligo; these efforts were in vain; for it was only on occasion of Sir John Perrot's famous Composition with the magnates of Sligo, in the year 1585, when Sir Nicholas was a year dead, that Sir Donnell accepted the letters patent, which conveyed the grant, and regulated the tenure of his possessions. He survived the Composition only three years, and passed them in attending to local affairs, improving his territory, and building a new bridge across the Owenmore at Ballysadare, which was one of the chief works in which he was engaged. This politic chief died on Little Christmas night at Sligo, the 1st of January, and was buried with his ancestors in the abbey.[4]

Judging by the period in which he lived, and the persons he had to deal with, in England and Ireland, Sir Donnell must have been a man of great ability, to pass through life so successfully. To get all he desired from Elizabeth and her Council, while giving little else in return than smooth words; to gain and retain the favour of the English, without forfeiting the good opinion, or good will, of the Irish;[5] to benefit religion in Sligo by

---

large fat beeves per annum, at Michaelmas at the castle of Athlone, and also that he would at all hostings bring 20 Horse and 60 Foot, and maintain them 40 days, and would pay in money £25 per annum, and that in cases of necessity he should assist the Queen with all his Forces, and that he should make legal estates to the Freeholders, they paying their proportion of the foregoing Contribution; and the Queen granted O'Conner all Forfeitures for Felony, or by Outlawry, or Recognisance, and all Waifs, Strays, and Penalties for Bloudshed".—Cox—Hibernia Anglicana, Vol. I., p. 385.

[1] Annals of Loch Ce, 1577. Letter of Malbie to Earl of Leicester, written from Athlone, July 20, 1582

[2] Annals of Loch Ce, 1578. O'Connor Sligo and Brian McDermot went to Dublin to the great council, and they were five weeks at that court, and received great honour from the Council of Erin.

[3] It was to bring him to compliance that English troops were quartered on him, and that the castle of Bundrowes was taken from him and sold to O'Donnell. Of the latter transaction the Annals of Loch Ce says: Bundrowes was given to O'Donnell by the Justiciary, who exacted twelve hundred marks from him for it, *vel amplius*; and we would say that it was wrong to sell the residence of Brian Luighnech's descendants (the O'Connors) to O'Donnell, if fear allowed us to say it.

[4] O'Connor Sligo, i.e., Donnell, son of Teige, son of Cathal Oge, the choice of the Gael of Erinn, died on Little Christmas night in Sligo, and was buried in it.—Annals of Loch Ce, 1588.

[5] The words of the Four Masters, in announcing the death of his son, show this: Calvagh, the only son of O'Conor Sligo, died. He was the more lamented in the territories, because the noble couple Donnell O'Connor and Mor O'Rorke from whom this free-born shoot

adroitly saving the monastery from suppression, without incurring the imputation, or suspicion, of thwarting the wishes of the Queen, in the matter of the Reformation, on which she had set her heart; and to keep his country quiet, and the members of the O'Connor family united among themselves, and united to him, at a time, when the neighbouring families of the O'Donnells and the O'Rorkes were ruining themselves by fratricidal contests; all this bespeaks great gifts of intellect and will, great powers of persuasion and command, great knowledge of the motives which influence human action, and great mastery of the means by which one brings over others to one's views and interests. In saying so much, we have given Sir Donnell O'Connor all the praise which can be claimed for him; for, that there was anything heroic about him; that he did, or would, make extraordinary sacrifices for faith, morality, or honour; that he was ever actuated by chivalrous principles of any kind, is what no one, acquainted with his career, can maintain.

It will be of use to refer to a transaction or two in the life of Sir Donnell in confirmation of this view of his character; and the reference is likely to be the more acceptable to the reader, as it will make him acquainted with one of the O'Connor family, who has hitherto "slept in the shade", though playing a rather remarkable part in all the public movements of his day. This is Owen or Eugene O'Connor, the youngest brother of Sir Donnell.

When a youth he was sent by Sir Donnell to Christ Church, Oxford, where he had an exhibition; and while he was at the University, we find Sir Donnell writing to Cecil, to thank him for past kindness to the young man, and to solicit a continuance of the patronage.

The next time we meet with Owen, is at the execution of the Indenture between the Queen and O'Connor Sligo, when he signed the instrument as a witness in Westminster Palace. After this he proceeded to Ireland in quest of ecclesiastical preferment, and succeeded in his object to the "top of his bent". While waiting for a bishoprick, he passed the time in traversing the country, and spying out such benefices or dignities as might be "concealed" from the Queen, of which he unearthed a goodly number, receiving them all from the authorities for his pains as a "discoverer". The rectories of Skreen and Castleconnor, with the priory of Aughriss, and the vicarages of Dromard, Kilmacshalgan, and Corcagh, or Templeboy, in Tireragh; the island of Innismurry, in the high seas; the rectory between the

---

sprang had no hope or expectation of any other child after him. That tract of territory from Magh Ceidne to Ceis-Coraum, and from the river Moy to the boundary of Breifny, was awaiting him as its only inheritor and comarb, if he should survive his father. The Annals of Loch Ce say: This loss has grieved the heart of Connaught.

two bridges, and the vicarage of Ahamlish, in Carbury; the rectory of Drumcliff; the rectories of Aghanagh, Kilmacallan, and Coolea, with four quarters of land and tithes in Killery, two quarters in Kilmacroy, half a quarter and tithes in Drumdonay all in Tirerrill; the deanery of Achonry, in Leyney; and, in fine, the bishopric of Killala, which came in good time, afforded some salve to his wounded conscience for what it may have suffered, when he renounced, or pretended to renounce, the religion of his fathers.

Though Owen O'Connor had a custodian of the see of Killala in 1585, and signed the Composition of Perrot, that year, as Bishop Elect, he was not consecrated, if consecrated at all, until 1591, when he became the first Protestant bishop of that ancient see. At the same date he was appointed, by the Queen, Administrator of Achonry, the bishop of that diocese being the celebrated Eugene O'Hart; and as O'Connor and O'Hart were great personal friends, as well as members, respectively, of two families, which had been always singularly devoted and loyal to one another, O'Connor allowed the Achonry bishop to manage the diocese as he pleased, stipulating only that himself should receive the larger share of the revenues,[1] which seem to have been the only incident of the episcopal office, for which he cared.

Owen O'Connor died in 1607, three or four years after the death of Eugene O'Hart. There is a tradition, in the diocese of Achonry, of a promise

---

[1] According to Lynch's History of the Prelates of Ireland (Bodleian MSS.) the bishop of Killala, Eugene O'Connor was appointed by the Queen, on the 1st December, 1591, Administrator of Achonry, and, being an old friend of O'Harte, bishop of Achonry, "allowed him quiet possession of the see for the sum of 180 marks annually".—The Irish Reformation by W. Maziere Brady, p. 159.

If the whole truth were known, it might appear that O'Connor made this arrangement as much for the sake of his old religion, as of his "old friend". Being still a Catholic in heart he may have never pocketed a farthing of the 180 marks; the alleged contract with Bishop Hart being probably a blind to keep the eyes of the Government off that zealous and able prelate while labouring for the maintenance of the persecuted religion.

It is right to observe that there is no sufficient proof of Owen O'Connor having been ever either ordained priest or consecrated bishop. The addition of "cleric", which he appended to his name, when signing, as a witness, the indenture between the Queen and his brother, Sir Donnell, does not imply ordination, but only the ceremony of tonsure; nor does the title of Dean of Achonry, as Robert Weston, about the same time, though not an ecclesiastic, was styled Dean of St. Patrick's (Mason's History of St. Patrick's, p. 170); while he might also be called Bishop of Killala, though a layman like Dr. Nehemias O'Donnellan, of whom Teige O'Dugan, the family genealogist, writes in his pedigree of the O'Donellans: "Queen Elizabeth granted him the living of Tuam, and though he never was in holy orders he was called Archbishop of Tuam" (Tribes and Customs of Hy Many, p. 171). As we never hear of Eugene O'Connor having attempted the performance of any clerical function, he seems to have regarded his deaconship and episcopate as mere civil concerns, and sources of income: his whole object, says Archdeacon Lynch, "being to enjoy riches and pleasures", "*ut se divitiis et voluptatibus expleret.*"

which he exacted, from Doctor O'Hart, to the effect that, if his death sickness should come in the bishop's lifetime, the latter, on receiving a concerted message, should hasten to administer to him the last rites of the Catholic Church.[1] If this was so, the promise was secured in vain, the bishop being dead in the time of O'Connor's need. Considering now the career of Eugene O'Connor, and the part which Sir Donnell had in starting him in that career, it would he hard to credit the latter with much loyalty to the Catholic faith. And his morality was of a piece with his faith, if we are to judge by his conduct, on the death of his eldest brother, Cathal Oge, who was slain in open warfare, by a party of Scots, who were then in the pay of Sir Nicholas Malbie, Governor of Connaught. Unlike many sons of Irish chieftains, Donnell and Cathal Oge O'Connor were fraternally attached and true to each other, all through life. In the circumstances, it was only to be expected, that Donnell should feel deeply the tragic end of a brother whom he loved ardently, and no one could blame him for showing his feelings in every legitimate way. But instead of this, he avenged Cathal Oge's death in a manner opposed, apparently, to the laws of nature, religion, and honour.

Sir Nicholas Malbie, deciding about this time to invade the territories of O'Rorke, who was very hostile and troublesome to the English, sent some of the English troops, that were to take part in the expedition, and, with them, the party of Scotch that slew Cathal Oge, to the county of Sligo to remain for a little, under the care and protection of Sir Donnell, with whom the Governor was then at peace and in alliance. Dissembling his feelings and intentions, Sir Donnell distributed those troops in cantonments through the county, that he might be the more able, when they were thus divided, to carry out his design; and having gained over to the plot the English officers, his troops and theirs fell on the unfortunate Scots, "while sleeping in their beds and couches" and "slew Alexander and a great number of his people". It is evident that Malbie connived at the massacre, if he was not its chief instigator, in order to get rid of the Scots", who were very obnoxious to the English authorities in Ireland.[2] Anyhow

---

[1] This tradition has nearly died out, though very rife, some thirty years ago, when the writer heard it in all its particulars from Rev. John Flynn, Parish Priest of Curry. The date of Eugene O'Connor's death is fixed by a letter written in 1607 by Sir Arthur Chichester to the Earl of Salisbury, in which we read, "There is another bishoprick fallen void in Connaught by the death of Owen O'Connor, uncle to Sir Donough O'Connor Sligo".

[2] John O'Donovan mistakes the nature of this transaction, and suggests an emendation of the text to bear him out. "There must be some error here", says he, "as Alexander and his people were in the service of Sir Nicholas Malbie on this occasion, It should evidently be, when O'Connor Sligo had received intelligence that the people of Sir Nicholas were thus situated", &c.—Note in Four Masters, 1581. Had O'Donovan thought better of the matter, and read the version of the Annals of Loch Ce, he would have seen that there was no "error" in the statement of the Four Masters, and that the people of Sir Nicholas had treacherously employed their swords against their own comrades. The words of Loch Ce

this treacherous proceeding places the morality of Sir Donnell O'Connor in a very unamiable light. Sir Donnell, it may be stated, received his knighthood on the 4th April, 1567, from the Lord Deputy, Sir Henry Sydney, at Loughrea, Hugh O'Donnell receiving a similar honour at the same time and place (Carew MS. Vol. 15751588, p. 149).

In passing away from Sir Donnell, who ruled Sligo, first as a Celtic chief, and afterwards by authority of English law, we should try to carry with us a correct idea of the status of the O'Connor Sligo family, as well under the old, as under the new regime. Before conforming to English laws and customs in the sixteenth century, the O'Connor family consisted of several branches, all the male members of which were eligible for the position of chief. The branches at this time were the descendants of the Donnell O'Connor, who died in 1395; the O'Connors, who preceded him, including the families of Cathal King of Connaught, and of his heroic son, Cathal Oge, having disappeared from Lower Connaught and from history. This Donnell had four sons who were successively Lords of Sligo Murtough Baccagh, Brian, Owen, and Turlough Carrach and whose respective families settled in different parts of Carbury—the head-quarters of Murtough Baccach's being Dunally; of Brian's, Grange of Coolerra; of Owen's, Castletown and Grange of Lower Carbury; and of Turlough Carrach's, Askelly. All these shared alike the blood and dignity of the O'Connor Sligo family, and stood in these respects on the same level, till one of them furnished the Chief, who by his election became paramount as

---

are, "A great army was sent to Lower Connaught by the Governor of the Province .... And there were five or six hundred Scots with the sons of Donal Ballagh McDonnell. And all the Saxons that were along with the Captains went into the county Sligo . . . Soon after that O'Conor Sligo entreated all the Saxon captains that were there to join him. The chieftains of Lower Connaught, along with O'Conor Sligo and those Saxons attacked the Scots", &c.—Annals of Loch Ce, 1581.

In Major Wood Martin's History of Sligo it is said, "In the Chronicle of Lough Key shame is expressed for Conor's part in the crime". The direct opposite is the fact; for while blaming others the annalists excuse O'Connor. Their words are, "It cannot be said that O'Conor was not justified in his own share of it". We read in Major Wood Martin's History of Sligo, "Sir Donald O'Conor died at the close of 1587" (*recte* 31 December). "His uncle Donough assumed the title, considering himself to be the heir by Brehon law, but Bingham would not listen to his claim, and expelled him from the country; Donough crossed the channel to present his claims to Elizabeth in person, and the commission sent into the county after the death of O'Conor "to enquire his heir against the title of the Crown, found in favour of Donough Mac Cale Oge O'Conor, nephew of the deceased. This "uncle Donough", and his "Brehon law title", and his "expulsion" from the country are all myths. Donough O'Connor was not the uncle but the nephew of Sir Donnell; he was not "expelled" the county by Bingham, but left of his own accord, for the Court of Elizabeth; nor did he invoke the "Brehon law", but the law of the land which, in this matter, was the law of England.

well over the O'Connors, as over the other chiefs of Lower Connaught, and had added to his patrimonial possessions the lands and revenues provided for the maintenance of the chief. The O'Connor Sligo, once elected, or in office, had authority over the entire of Carbury and over Leyney, Tirerrill, Corran, Coolavin and Tireragh; and received tribute not only from the local chiefs of Carbury, but also from the chiefs of the other territories, from the O'Haras of Leyney, the McDonoghs of Tirerrill and Corran, the O'Garas of Coolavin, and the O'Dowds and McSweenys of Tireragh. And he possessed, besides, castles and lands in these territories in Leyney, Meemlough; in Tirerrill, Collooney; in Corran, Ballymote; in Coolavin, Knocknaskeagh; and in Tireragh Buninna.

To compensate for all those rights and revenues, and to meet the equities of the case, Perrott in his Composition, passed by letters patent to Sir Donnell O'Connor, and to "the heirs male of the body of his father, the castell or manor of Slego in the barony of Carbry; and Meynlaghe (Meemlough) in the barony of Magherylenye (Leyney); and all the lands appertayning as well to the name and calling of O'Connor Sligo, as also which, belong or appertayneth to Sleight Owine O'Connor from whom the said Sir Donnell is said to be descended; also a yearly rentcharge of 13s. 4d. going out of every quarter of the residue of the said quarters of the lands of Sleight Muryertaghe, Sleight Briene, and Sleight Tirlaghe Carragh O'Connor; and also 8s. out of every quarter of 154 quarters in the barony of Tireragh; 10s. out of every quarter of 20 quarters in the barony of Coolavin; 6s. 10d. out of every quarter of 156 quarters in the barony of Magheryleynie; 6s. 6d. out of every quarter of 166 quarters in the barony of Tirreryelle; and 9s. 3d. out of every quarter of 110 quarters in the barony of Corren".[1]

This assessment, considering the value of money at the time, secured to Sir Donnell an immense revenue; and with this princely income and his proud pre-eminence over everybody in the county before our mind, we can understand why he declined an earldom proffered by the Government, feeling that the title would be rather a diminution than an increase of his dignity in the eyes of the people.[2]

---

[1] These arrangements are set out at length in the Indenture of Composition between Sir John Perrott and the magnates of Sligo. Hardiman, in his edition of O'Flaherty's West Connaught, professes to give a copy of the document, but the writer, fancying he saw gaps in the enumeration of the lands of the county, examined the original roll, and found sundry denominations entirely omitted, so that the printed copy in West Connaught is quite untrustworthy.

[2] "Daniel More O'Connor was regarded with such favour by the Queen, that when he refused the diploma of Earl, she granted to him the title of O'Connor Sligo".—Archdeacon Lynch.—*De Praesulibus Hiberniae* (Bodleian manuscript.)

It is clear that the O'Connors Sligo rose in the sixteenth century above the other O'Connors of the country, as much as they had risen in the fourteenth, when Cathal became King of Connaught. Moore, speaking of Sir Donnell's father, Teige, calls him "the great O'Connor of Connaught", and adds, "This chief, called the great O'Connor of Connaught, was the most powerful of the five chieftains of that name; the four others being O'Connor of Offaley, O'Connor Roe, O'Connor Don, and O'Connor Corcomroe" (History of Ireland, Vol. III, p. 276).

The next O'Connor Sligo was Donough, nephew of the deceased Sir Donnell, and son of Cathal Oge, Sir Donnell's eldest brother. The succession was not effected without great opposition, on the part of Sir Richard Bingham, who maintained, in divers official documents, that Donough was base-born, and without right to the inheritance. In a letter of Sir Richard's, dated Athlone, May 21, 1588, and addressed to the Earl of Leicester, he says,

> "The Commission sent down into Sligo for the inquiry of Sir Donnell O'Connor Sligo, after his death, proceeded in favour of Donnogh McCale Oge against the title of her Majesty in these lands. The heir is base-born and illegitimate, and the land, especially Sligo itself, by descent and lawful inheritance, is now thrown into the lap of her Majesty. As the haven and castle are of so great importance, lying in the only strait through which the Scots accustom to annoy the province, I hope you will not suffer it to be conveyed from her Highness.
>
> It may be some will inform thither, I mean such as have received rewards, that the taking of this from Donnogh O'Connor may breed stirs among the Irishry. But the people of this province are dejected and made subject to the sword. Yet, I wish the young man should have part or all of his uncle's lands, the castle and town of Sligo only excepted, and hold the same as a free gift in respect of his uncle's loyalty".

Bingham wrote additional letters on the subject, some addressed to Burghley alone, and some to him and the other Lords of the Council in England; and in all he advances the same arguments against Donough's suit; that he was illegitimate, that he could not claim under Sir Donnell's patent, and, above all, that Sligo being "the key and door of Connaught", "the entrance and passage of that province", "set in the fore-front of the ill-affected", was too important a place to be allowed out of the Queen's possession, in which, "by the providence of God" it was now placed.

Fortunately, Donough O'Connor had a "friend in court", who was able and willing to stand by him, even against so powerful a man as Sir Richard Bingham. This was the Lord Deputy, Sir John Perrott, whose generous nature led him, during his administration, to hold the balance fair between all classes under his authority, and to protect the old Irish from injustice and oppression at the hands of the English and Anglo-Irish, whether these were in a private or in an official station. It was he who formed the Commission to which Bingham, in the letter to Lord Leicester, refers, and which throws most important light on the family history of the O'Connors Sligo. The members of this Commission were all that could be desired, in order to place its acts and decisions beyond the reach of cavil or suspicion, the commissioners being the Bishops of Meath and Kilmore; the Chief Justice of the Common Bench; the Chief Baron of the Exchequer; the Second Justice of the Common Bench; the Sergeant-at-Law; the Attorney General; and a lay gentleman, named John Elliot, probably the secretary. This Commission, which opened at Sligo on the 4th March, 1588, after hearing witnesses, finds, in direct contradiction to the assertions of Sir Richard Bingham, Cathal Oge O'Connor and his son, Donough, to be legitimate; Donough to be the next male heir of his grandfather, Teige; and, consequently, to inherit, by law and right, under the patent of Elizabeth.

Notwithstanding this finding, Bingham still maintained the illegitimacy of both father and son. And even an Exchequer Inquisition, sped in Sligo under John Crofton, but controlled by Bingham, arrived at the same conclusion. Without imputing corrupt motives to Bingham and Crofton—which it is hard to avoid doing—they may, perhaps, be absolved from the charge of deliberate wrong-doing in consideration of their ignorance of law, and particularly of Canon Law, on which the case in question mainly depended.

As the impediment of clandestinity, for want of promulgation, or, at all events, of sufficient promulgation, was hardly in force at the time in the province, marriage would rest for its validity on the consent of the parties marrying, and not on its celebration *in facie ecclesiæ*, or before the person appointed by the State to officiate. If two qualified persons pledged their mutual consent, that consent, whether given in public or in private,—with or without solemnities, in the presence or in the absence of the minister of religion, formed the marriage contract, and constituted the parties man and wife. Laymen, unacquainted with this principle, and accustomed to solemnization of marriage in churches, might not recognize marriages devoid of this solemnity, and resting on consent alone; whereas jurists and canonists, able to distinguish between what is essential and what is accidental, would feel themselves bound to admit their validity. It is in this way, no doubt, we are to account for the different opinions in regard to the legitimacy of Cathal Oge and his son. To avoid what might be taken for an act of apostacy, he would not have his marriage celebrated in one of the Elizabethan churches, and had it performed privately, in the presence, probably, of a priest, which, with Catholics, was the usual way of marrying at the time;[1] and the Commissioners, having the facts established before

---

[1] Middleton (Marmaduke), the Protestant Bishop of Waterford, writes to Walsingham in 1580:—"No marriage agreeing with God's law and her Majesty's proceedings, for either they marry in houses, with Masses, or else before two or three laymen without any minister taking of hands, and so they live as man and wife".—Brady's State Church in Ireland, p. 74.

them in evidence, pronounced in accordance with the Canon Law, for the validity of the contract; while others, either ignorant of the facts, or unable to make the necessary distinction between substance and form, regarded the proceedings as null and void.

But as Sir John Perrott left Ireland soon after the decision of the Commission, Bingham was able to carry out his wishes against O'Connor, who betook himself for redress to England, where, it would appear, he remained till the year 1596, when, on Sir Richard being disgraced and recalled, O'Connor came back in triumph, and accompanied by a great number of Englishmen. Whether it was that long residence in England had made Sir Donough thoroughly English in his views and wishes, or that he knew his honours and possessions to depend on the services he should now render to the Queen, he devoted himself, from his arrival in Ireland, with the greatest zeal, to promote her interests throughout the country. In the prosecution of this design, he co-operated in all things with the new Governor of Connaught, Sir Conyers Clifford; brought over, through his brother-in-law, Theobald-na-Long, many of the Burkes of Tyrawley to the side of the English; and formed of them, the McDonoughs, O'Harts, and MacDermotts, a powerful party, against Hugh Roe O'Donnell, who was the most active and troublesome antagonist the English had in the province.

Having thus proved his loyalty, and having received a severe wound, while fighting against Red Hugh on the banks of the Erne, he went over, about the Christmas of 1597, to England, where his wife lived, but returned to Ireland in the spring of the following year, and served under Essex for some time in Munster, in the campaign against Desmond. After a few months, he came to the county Sligo; and, Collooney being the only castle at his service in the district, he took up his residence in it.

Finding O'Connor thus within reach, O'Donnell lost no time in attacking him. Supported by his sturdy ally and cousin, Brian Oge O'Rorke, he besieged the castle of Collooney, defeated and slew Sir Conyers Clifford, who was hastening, with considerable forces, to raise the siege, and, sending Clifford's head into the castle, in witness of the defeat of the English, forced O'Connor to join the confederacy of the Ulster and Connaught chiefs.

This alliance, which O'Donnell spared no pains to cultivate, and to which O'Connor, very probably, was never over-much attached at heart, lasted for about two years, during which the Sligo chief co-operated with the Irish, accompanied, at the head of the troops of Lower Connaught, Red Hugh in an expedition to Thomond, and rendered him other important services, more especially in securing and covering the passage of the Northern forces through Sligo. In 1601, however, when Mountjoy was drawing the net round the Irish chiefs, O'Donnell suddenly arrested Donough O'Connor, and confined him in an island of Lough Esk, near

Donegal, alleging that he was betraying the Irish, and acting as a spy for the English authorities; but, though this disgraceful charge may derive some appearance of probability from the well-known practices of the English authorities at the time, it is only fair to add, that there is no proof whatever of Donough's criminality except the allegation of O'Donnell, who might have been easily deceived in such a matter. On the contrary, it would appear from the following statement of Lord Mountjoy and the Council, that O'Connor had not done anything to help the English, though they were trying to frighten him into compliance with their wishes: "We resolve to threaten O'Connor Sligo, who had often showed himself desirous to submit himself, upon any appearance of his defence, that if he do not presently declare himself against O'Donnell before the plantation of Ballishannon, he shall despair for ever to be received to mercy". It was probably the letter which conveyed this threat to O'Connor that led to his arrest, for, in a communication of Mountjoy's to Sir Oliver Lambert, Governor of Connaught, we read: "O'Connor Sligo was restrained of his liberty upon a letter I sent to him, so that he hath a just pretext for standing out". The Sligo chief was rather unfortunate in his correspondence, for, while the letter of Mountjoy led to his captivity, a letter of O'Neill, written in reply to O'Connor, and intercepted by the English authorities, brought the edge of the Government upon him.

Whether guilty or innocent of the complicity with which O'Donnell charged him, he was kept in durance, on Lough Esk, so cruelly fettered that his legs were nearly rotted by the irons—the imprisonment lasting about two years, two eventful years; for the battle of Kinsale and the departure of Red Hugh to Spain took place while he was in captivity. In the absence of Red Hugh, his brother, Rory, who occupied his place, liberated O'Connor Sligo, when the two chiefs agreed and engaged to co-operate with one another in their public proceedings in future. To this engagement they were faithful, and, as allies, fought against, and defeated the English in a battle on the Curlews, as well as in some smaller affairs in the neighbourhood of Ballysadare; but learning, after some months, that Red Hugh had died in Spain, and receiving at the same time favourable offers from Mountjoy, on condition that they relinquished hostilities and came in, they proceeded together to Athlone, where the Lord Deputy then was, and made their submission to the Queen; O'Connor, on the occasion, receiving his lands by an English patent, dated 1602, the 44th year of Elizabeth.[1]

---

[1] The following is the form of submission sworn to and subscribed by O'Connor Sligo, Rory O'Donnell, the Flahertys, MacDermotts of the Curlews, Conor Roe, and others, on the 4th of December, and some subsequent days (Anno 45 Elizabeth):—

"That I doo acknowledge Elizabeth by the grace of God Queen of England, France, and Ireland, to be the only true, absolute, and sovereign Lady of the realme of Ireland, and of every part, and of all the people thereof, unto whose gracious mercy I doo submit myself,

From Athlone, when the weighty business on hand was completed, he returned to Sligo, and set himself to the work of re-establishing his broken fortunes. Considering that his possessions in the country were so long deprived of supervision and care, that in the absence of the owner they were exposed to injury from friends and enemies, and that a devastating war raged over the country for several years, it is easy to understand that the task was a most arduous one; and though people may think that the life he had led, conversant only with war and politics, unfitted him for the duty of retrieving and rearranging a vast landed estate, where everything was in disorder, there is evidence to show that he performed his part with all the tact and skill of a lawyer or land agent. Finding considerable scopes of his inheritance in the hands of Sir William Taaffe, who received them by royal grant or other legal transfer, Sir Donough bought them back; and being short of money to pay for all he purchased, he raised the necessary funds by mortgaging other lands to friends and relatives, who were disposed to allow exceptional facilities for redeeming the mortgage.

While engaged in these transactions, he learned that Sir James Fullerton had received a royal grant of Ballymote, and the extensive mensal lands of its castle, which Sir Donough regarded as an injury done to himself; but though he complained through Viscount Cranbourne, and claimed the lands in question as belonging to O'Connor Sligo's inheritance, he complained and claimed in vain. Nor could he be much surprised at this, for Ballymote was excepted out of the lands passed in Sir Donnell O'Connor's patent, as Ballyshannon, quite recently, was reserved, when Rory O'Donnell was receiving back Tirconnell from the Crown. Indeed it was the practice of English statesmen at this time, in regranting lands to Irish chiefs, to reserve one or more strong places, to be committed to some

---

my lands, and goods, and with all faithful repentance for my unnatural disobedience unto her royal Majesty doo most earnestly implore her mercy and pardon for myself, and such of my fellows as with me have been reduced to this wicked rebellion.

"Further I doo renounce all and any manner of obedience unto any other power or potentate, which I owe only to my said dread sovereign Elizabeth, and utterly abjure any dependency and adherence to any of her enemies whatsoever, or disloyal subjects, and doo promise, swear, and vow from henceforth to live in her subjection, in all dutie and obedience, and to use my best endeavours to the uttermost of my power, to withstand and confound any enemy either foreign or domestic, that shall attempt anything against the sacred person or estate of her Majesty, or the hurt of her faithful and obedient subjects, and especially and namely I do renounce (as before) and promise my endeavours against the King of Spain, and the arch-traitor, the Earl of Tyrone.

"All this as I doo upon my salvation swear, so if I do herein break my oath, I doo acknowledge myself not only to be worthy of all infamy and extreme punishment, but to be ever after accounted unworthy of the name of a Christian, or the society of men; to the which as I have unfainedly sworn, so I doo now in witness whereof set to my hand".—Harris's *Collectanea de Rebus Hibernicis*, Vol. V., p. 426. (Manuscript in the Dublin City Library.)

official or other trusted person, on whom, under all circumstances, they could rely.

Sir Donough was married to Lady Eleanor Butler, the Countess of Desmond, the second wife and the relict[1] of the unfortunate Earl Gerald, "*ingens rebellibus exemplar*".[2] There is reason to believe that the Countess was a clever, intriguing, ambitious woman, and rather ill affected to the Government, which seems natural enough, when one calls to mind the fate of her late husband. A circumstance that gives colour to this view of her character is, that she wrote private letters herself, and induced Sir Donough to write ones, urging her daughter, Lady Joan, to accept O'Donnell for her husband, and sent a confidential waiting woman of hers to convey the daughter away; and when Sir George Carew spoiled her game by lodging the messenger in gaol and committing Lady Joan to the custody of a Limerick Alderman for safe-keeping, the Countess, on being taxed with the proceeding, averred that her sole object was to make a good and loyal subject of O'Donnell.

But Carew was not such a simpleton as to believe this version of the affair, and divined the true motive of the proceeding,—

"This marriage", says he, "with O'Donnell, the messenger pretends was contracted by the Countess to the end to reduce him to subjection .... but as I suppose, and the rest of the council, it can be to no other end intended than to kindle new fire in this province".

The author of *Pacata Hibernia*, after detailing the means employed by Carew to find out the true nature of this intrigue, goes on to say: —

"The old craftie Countesse understanding that this complot was discovered, pretended that her indeavours in seeking to effect this Marriage, tended to no other end but to reduce O'Donnell to be a Subject, although indeede there was nothing lesse meant; The President and Councell upon the discovery (for preventing such further mischiefe as they foresawe might arise by this marriage) committed the Lady Joane to an Alderman's House, and *Marie ny Shye* (the said Countesse servant) close prisoner in the Gaoll, till time and occasion should minister further opportunitie to deale in that affaire of so great importance". [3]

The Countess had several children by her first husband. O'Donovan seems to think there were only two daughters, but this is a mistake, for there were five; Margaret, married to Dermod O'Conor Don; Joan, of whom we have been speaking, to Dermod O'Sullevan; Catherine, to Sir Daniel O'Brien; Ellen, first to Donnell O'Connor Sligo, secondly to Sir Robert

---

[1] widow, [Clachan ed.].
[2] 'the model of a great rebel'. [Clachan ed.].
[3] *Pacata Hibernia*. Reprinted in Dublin, 1810, from the original edition of 1633, pp. 194, 195. Judging by Father Mooney's sketch of Red Hugh, he would make an eligible husband. "He was of middle stature", says the Father, "ruddy, of comely grace, and beautiful to behold. His voice was like the clarion of a silver trumpet, and his morals unimpeachable".—Father Meehan's Earls of Tyrone and Tyrconnell.

Cressy, and thirdly, to Lord Dunboyne; and Ellice, to Sir Valentine Browne. There was an only son, James FitzGerald, an incident in whose life throws a flood of light on religious feeling in Ireland in his day. Taken to England by the government on his father's death, and brought up a Protestant, Elizabeth meant, all along, to use him, in due time, for decoying the inhabitants of Munster to her views in religion and politics; and when what she thought the right moment had arrived, she sent the young man over to Sir George Carew, the President of the province, authorizing that official to introduce him to the people as heir of their favourite Desmonds. It was on a Saturday evening he arrived at Kilmallock, and the people who, ignorant of his religion, had flocked from all sides to welcome him, received him as an angel from heaven; but, when they found him attending Protestant service the following day, they became so enraged, that they loaded him with all kinds of indignities and outrages, not only yelling at him, whenever he appeared in public, but carrying their contempt and hate so far as to spit upon him in the streets. Elizabeth finding her trump card go for nothing, had the youth recalled to England, where he soon died and not without exciting suspicion of foul play.

Though the Countess received a large annual income or pension from England, Donough O'Connor was excessively liberal to her in the marriage settlements, making over to her even some possessions which he had no legal power to give, so that it became necessary after his death to institute a suit at law for the recovery of some of the lands thus transferred.

It was only in 1604, Donough was knighted; for in a list, drawn up in 1618, of "Knights made in Ireland since the King's first coming to the Crown", we find, under the year 1604, "Sir Teig O'Rorke, and Sir Donnogh O'Connore Sligo". He died in August, 1609, after a life, so chequered by reverses and successes, as to contain no bad index of the eventful times in which he lived. His death occurred rather suddenly, and quite unexpectedly, while a "session or assize for the county was being held at Sligo;"[1] and, what is somewhat strange, O'Conor Roe * died in Sligo on the same occasion. It is stated in an inquisition that Tomultagh MacDermot was Sir Donough's

---

[1] Sir Arthur Chichester in a letter to Salisbury, writes: "Sir Donogh O'Connor is dead. A letter from his brother, who is his heir, has just arrived. He is an unstaid man, and in the late Queen's days served the Spaniards".

Sir Robert Jacob, Judge of Assize in Connaught, writes on the same occasion to Salisbury: "O'Connor Roe and O'Connor Sligo, two of the greatest Irish Lords in Connaught, died while they were holding sessions in Sligo. O'Connor Sligo died without issue, and his lands descended to his brother, Donnell O'Connor, who is a widower of the age of 4 or 5 and 30 years. He is to marry with one of the Earl of Desmond's daughters; he speaks English well; he was bred up in the wars in France, the people have a great opinion of him, and he is like to prove an honest man, if his grafting upon a crabbed stock do not alter his proper nature".—Dublin, 19 Oct., 1609.

blood relation and next heir, but the latter, the day before he died, made a will, leaving all his possessions to his brother Donnell or Daniel. Sir Donough was buried with his ancestors, in the Abbey of Sligo, on the epistle side of the sanctuary, in the spot over which now stands the mural monument erected in memory of him and his wife, the Countess of Desmond, who survived him near half a century, and died in 1656.

To Sir Donough then succeeded Donnell or Daniel his brother, or, to speak more accurately, his half-brother, for they had not the same mother, though Cathal Oge was the father of both. The new chief of Sligo had passed his life on the Continent, and served in the armies of France and Spain. For this his people esteemed him the more, and were proud to have him at their head. For this, however, the Lord Deputy and others looked on him with suspicion, but, as his title to Sligo was clear, it would have been of no use to dispute it, and he was allowed to enter into quiet possession the moment he arrived from abroad. Little more than thirty years of age at his accession to the estate, and a widower, his career was very short and unmarked by any event calling for mention, except his marriage to Lady Ellen FitzGerald, the daughter of Sir Donough's wife, the Countess of Desmond, which having been arranged before he came to the country, was celebrated soon after his arrival. His death took place on the 20th June, 1611, and he was buried, no doubt, with his brother in the abbey, though this is not expressly stated.

The next Lord of Sligo was Charles O'Connor, a son of Daniel's by a former marriage, for Daniel was a widower when he married Lady Ellen FitzGerald. Being only ten years old at his father's death, Charles became a King's ward, and the wardship was granted to Sir Faithful Fortescue, who proved himself a faithful guardian of the minor's interests in temporal matters. Finding the Countess of Desmond in possession of large scopes of the O'Connor Sligo country, to which she had no legal right, and which she obtained by claiming them as part of her jointure, he called Chichester's attention to the injustice by letter, and instituted a successful suit at law against the Countess for the lands in question. In the letter to the Lord Deputy, he says, "The late Queen, in the 44th year of her reign, under an English patent, granted the lands in question to Sir Donogh O'Connor for life, and to his issue in tail male remainder to Daniel O'Connor, his brother, by a second venter for life, and to his issue in tail male, and divers remainders over. As for the lands she claims there were passed in the recovery 13 castles, 100 messuages, 10 gardens, 4000 acres of moor, 1000 acres of pasture, 1000 acres of wood, and 3000 acres of heath in Sligo, Ballymohary, Court, Bradcullon, Lyssedoyle, Bunnina, Dirretchane, Carrick, Ballydrehot, Buninna, Moylagh, and Downcibre".

After complaining that the Countess and her daughter had nearly all the estate, Fortescue adds, "But for your lordship's care and foresight to preserve the estate of the boy, all the lands had reverted back to Sir William Taaffe, which was purchased for him, and for which your lordship paid £500. The suit was tried in Sligo at Trinity Term, 1613, and resulted in an order of Court for taking the possessions in dispute out of the Countess' hands. This improved Charles O'Connor's estate, though much of it was still away from him; but, whatever it was, he did not enjoy it long, as he died on the 21st July, 1625. Like his uncle, Sir Donough, and his granduncle Sir Donnell, Charles was a knight; but he was besides a baronet, a dignity which Donough or Donnell could not enjoy, as it did not exist in their time, the order of baronets having been created by James I. in 1611, and having been introduced into Ireland only in 1619, when Sir Charles Blundell was created the first Irish baronet.

It was on May the 11th, 1622 (20 Jac. I), that "Charles Connor, Esq., of Sligo, County Sligo", was created a baronet (*Liber Munerum*, Vol. I, Part I., p. 73.)

Lodge and Archdall's Peerage of Ireland[1] states that Sir Charles died in 1634, but in this these writers are in error, as the inquisition quoted is decisive on the subject. And they state too, that Sir Charles was married to Lady Sarah McDonnell, daughter of the Earl of Antrim, in which statement they are also mistaken; for though negotiations for the marriage were in progress in 1625, the year of his death, nothing came of them, owing partly to Sir Charles' declining health, and partly to the intervention of the Lord Deputy Falkland who, on hearing of the proceeding, wrote thus to the authorities in England: "The young gentleman's father was a person of extraordinary consequence here, and himself hitherto well trained up, both in that kingdom and this, in religion, the consideration whereof and the doubt how this match may change him, cause me to write". No doubt it was the religion of Lady Sarah that chiefly attracted Sir Charles towards her, for it is pretty certain, whatever Falkland and others might have thought of the matter, that he was a Catholic in his heart.

Sir Charles' heir was his brother Donogh. It was he and not Sir Charles, as Lodge and Archdall thought, that married Lady Sarah McDonnell. Donogh was twenty years and six months old at the death of his brother, and died himself in 1634, as the following Funeral entry in a manuscript Pedigree Book of Sir Bernard Burke informs us: —

"Donogh O'Connor Sligo of Sligo, in the county of Sligo, Esq., departed this mortal life at Sligo, the xiii th day of the month of May, anno 1634. He had to wife

---

[1] Vol. I., p. 207. Article, MacDonnell, Earl of Antrim. D'Alton in King James's Irish Army List, Vol. I., p. 533, falls into the same mistake, as does Rev. George Hill in his MacDonnells of Antrim, p. 250. The two latter erred, no doubt, from relying implicitly on the Peerage of Ireland, instead of going themselves to the original authorities.

Lady Sarah, daughter of the Right Honble. Randall McDonnell, Earl of Antrim, by whom he had no issue. Teige O'Connor Sligo, uncle and heir of said Donogh, does under his hand testifie the truth of this certificate being taken by me, Thomas Preston, Esq., Ulster King of Arms, to be recorded in my office the xxvi th of Aprill, 1635".

The Sligo estate now reverted to Teige O'Connor, who, like Sir Donogh and Daniel, was a son of Cathal Oge, and therefore uncle of Donogh and his heir in tail male. This Teige's son, Teige also by name, who was the next O'Connor Sligo, lived in the trying days of 1641, and though he cast in his lot with the Old Irish in the fatal conflict of the times, he never ceased inculcating humanity and moderation on those around him. Such conduct should have saved his life, and would probably have saved it, only that he had the ill luck to be the heir of a great estate, which his enemies coveted, and which they could not, with any decency, appropriate till he was put out of the way. The ownership of a landed estate by a Catholic was the "irremissible sin" in the eyes of the Cromwellian victors, and Teige O'Connor had to pay the penalty. For this he suffered at Boyle, as we learn from Morison, who thus writes in his Threnodia Hiberno-Catholica: —

"Illustrissimus Dom Thadaeus O'Connor Sligo, ex ultimorum, ac potentissimorum, Hiberniae monarchum prosapia satus, vir mirae innocentiae ac bonitatis, post amnestiam cum toto regno factam, in oppido de *Boyle* in Conacia, suspendio necatur, anno 1652" (Thaddaeus O'Connor Sligo, descended from the royal race of the last and most powerful monarchs of Ireland; a man of great goodness and innocence; was hung in the town of Boyle in Connaught, A.D. 1652, after the general amnesty had been granted.)

Teige's son, Martin, who is the first burgess named in the list of James the Second's burgesses of Sligo, lost, by the fall of James, all chance of recovering the great inheritance of his family, and seeing the lowly condition to which he was reduced, and the exaltation of his enemies, might well say with Job: "But now the younger in time scorn me, whose fathers I would not have set with the dogs of my flock".

Eleanor Butler, wife of Sir Donogh, brought as little luck to the O'Connors Sligo family as she had brought to the Earls of Desmond, of whom her unfortunate husband was the last. Though she was an honourable match for Sir Donogh, it may be doubted whether his family did not lose much more than they gained by the marriage. If she brought them some accession of dignity, belonging as she did by blood and alliance to the first of the great Anglo-Norman houses, she was also the occasion of a great diminution of their estate. Not long before she joined them, the head of the family, according to the *Annals of the Four Masters*, ruled all the territory stretching from Magh Ene to Keshcorran, and from the river Moy to Breffney, while at her death, in 1656, there was hardly a foot of all this which he could call his own.

In comparison of Sir Donogh, the succeeding heads of the family were poor men. With more than one third of the chieftain's lands in the hands of the Countess of Desmond; with great scopes in the possession of her daughter, Lady Cressy; and, after the death of Donogh O'Connor, with considerable stretches encumbered for the jointure of Lady Sarah McDonnell, very little of the property was available for the O'Connors; and with such crippled resources the family were ill able to play an effective part in the trying scenes of the seventeenth century, when money counted for more than the sword, so that one may be warranted in holding the clever but selfish Countess to be a telling factor in the decline and fall of the O'Connors Sligo.

CHAPTER VI

SLIGO IN THE SEVENTEENTH CENTURY

STIRRING as has been the history of Ireland at all times, the seventeenth century was the most eventful period through which the country has passed. Opening with the battle of Kinsale; closing, virtually, with the battle of Aughrim the intermediate occurrences being in keeping with these weighty events the axe was then, if ever, laid to the root, when the whole fabric of society was overhauled and rearranged. And while previous disturbances were always of a local character, those of that time took in the whole country, Sligo, as might be expected from its situation, coming in for more than a full share of the trouble.

A sense of insecurity and danger created throughout the county feelings of discontent and unrest, and, in many instances, of disloyalty. Sir Donough O'Connor, the first man in the county, felt sore for the wrong done him in depriving him of Ballymote, and handing it over, with 22½ quarters of the adjoining lands, to Sir James Fullerton. And the feeling was embittered when the same foreigner was granted the governorship of the castle of Sligo.

In other parts of the county too, the English and Scotch, on one title or another as grantees, as mortgagees, as trustees, or as purchasers were displacing the Old Irish, so that the constant transference of lands from the natives to foreigners, became the most marked feature of the times. Sir John King got from the Crown large tracts of land in all the baronies of the county; Sir William Taaffe received similar grants in Corran, Carbury, and Tirerrill; John Taaffe, son of Sir William, held several quarters of land in Tireragh; John Crofton of Roscommon had large scopes of church lands in Tirerrill and Leyney; William Crofton of Templehouse like scopes in Leyney, Tirerrill, and Carbury; Richard Lord Boyle, the lands of Court Abbey, Ardnaree Abbey, and other lands in Leyney, Corran, and Tireragh; Sir Oliver St. John, Christopher Delahide, Thomas Greene, John Baxter, Roger Jones, his son-in-law, John Ridge of Roscommon and several others, foreign either by birth or blood, including the Blakes, Frenches, Lynches, and Nolans of Galway, obtained the old, immemorial possessions of the O'Connors, McDonoughs, O'Haras, and O'Garas.

The Irish gentry were more troubled on the score of religion even than on the score of property. Incapacitated by their faith from preferment of any kind in the districts over which they had lately ruled as masters; crushed by ruinous fines under Elizabeth's Act of Uniformity for non-attendance at Protestant worship; deprived of the ministry and consolations of religion by the King's Proclamation of 1605, banishing "all Jesuits, missionary priests, and other priests whatsoever, that derived authority from the See of Rome;" the only alternative allowed them was disloyalty to God or disloyalty to the civil power. To fret them still more, reports were in constant circulation that the Puritans of England and Scotland were coming over to extirpate Catholics and Catholicity, root and branch, out of the land.

Strafford's administration aggravated all these evils. His proceedings, in finding the king's title to the county Sligo, as well as to the other counties of Connaught, and thus annulling all the existing titles of owners and occupiers throughout the province, was commonly regarded as a preliminary to the banishing of the Irish, and the planting of English and Scotch on the land in their stead. And he was counted as great an enemy to the religion, as to the property of the Irish; for people credited him with the intention of forcing, by pains and penalties, Catholics, and, indeed, all who lived in the country, to join one great comprehensive State Church, which he meant to establish the moment his hands were clear of the business of defective titles. Such were some of the disabilities, the troubles, and the fears of all Irish Catholics on the eve of the terrible outbreak of 1641.

Though the insurrection began on the 23rd of October, and had overrun, in about a week, the counties of Donegal, Tyrone, Derry, Fermanagh, and Cavan, that is, all Ulster, except the towns of Enniskillen, Derry, and Coleraine, it was only in the beginning of December it showed itself in Sligo. Here, as elsewhere, the first care of the insurgents was to seize the strong places. For this purpose men flocked from all parts of the county, and from portions of the county Leitrim into Sligo, to secure the town and the two castles, or so-called castles, which it contained. The first batch of insurgents, that arrived, came from Lower Carbury, which comprised the parishes of Drumcliff, Ahamlish and the county Sligo portion of Rossinver, and were led by Teige Buy O'Connor, and Captains Bryan, Charles, and Hugh O'Connor, the three last being brothers of O'Connor Sligo; this body was followed by the men of Upper Carbury, those who lived between the Kilsellagh stream and Belladrehid, under the command of Donnell McBrian Darrough O'Connor, who quartered them in the houses adjoining St. John's Church; the men of Tirerrill marched under Brian McDonongh of Collooney, and Patrick Plunket of Markrea; while the Leitrim contingent had for leader Owen O'Rorke of Dromahair, chief of his name.[1]

---

[1] The full list of leaders, according to the deposition of William Walsh, a deposition by no means trustworthy, was as follows: "Teige O'Connor Sligo, reputed Generall of the Rebels in these parts, Mr. Bryan O'Connor, Captain Charles O'Connor, a fryar, Captain Hugh O'Connor, all brothers to O'Connor Sligo, Captain Bryan McDonogh, Captain Luke Taaffe, Captain Francis Taaffe, Captain Patrick Plunket, Captain Donell McBryan Darrough O'Connor, Captain John O'Crean, Captain Bryan McSwine, Captain Roger McOwen McSwine, Captain Phelim O'Connor, Captain Teige, MacRory O'Connor,

Having quartered their men through the town, the leaders met in the Abbey, to deliberate on their future proceedings, and, especially, to appoint a commander-in-chief. It would appear, from the deposition of Colonel Owen O'Rorke, that there was no great competition for the dangerous honour; for being offered to Teige O'Connor Sligo, it was declined by him; when, without further discussion or ceremony, it was assumed, rather than received, by Brian McDonough of Collooney, a man not unfitted for the post, being possessed of indomitable courage, and being connected, by blood or marriage, with all the old Irish and Anglo Irish families of the county.

The task now before the insurgents, which was to capture two castles but indifferently defended, was an easy one. One of these fortresses belonged to Lady Jones, the relict of Sir Roger Jones. This structure, being attacked, in front, by the troops of Captain Robert McConmy of Tireragh, and, in the rear, by those of Captain Patrick Plunket, of Markrea, was the first to give in; and seeing it in the possession of the Irish, Ensign Cotton, who commanded the other castle, called O'Crean's Castle, opened a parley with the besiegers. Disliking, however, the terms offered, he informed those under him that "if they did not like this quarter, he would live and die with them;" but it would appear that neither he, nor those with him, had any real wish to prolong the defence, for he immediately accepted the proffered conditions, which were, that the besieged "should have their lives and as much of their goods as they could carry on their backs, with a convoy to pass whither they pleased", if they did not elect, as they were free to do, to remain in Sligo.

The two so-called castles were strongly built stone houses, for it was usual at the time to call such houses, though private residences, castles. One of those structures was built by the Creans or O'Creans, and the other by Sir Roger Jones. They stood at the east end of Castle Street, and near to one another.

The old castle, dismantled in 1595, by O'Donnell, must have become a mere mass of ruins long before this, as we may infer from the design of Essex in 1599, as recorded in the Four Masters, to build a new "impregnable fortress in Sligo" a design frustrated by the battle of the Curlews, and never resumed afterwards.

Captain Teige O'Connor of the Glen, Captain Con O'Connor, of the same, Colonel Owen O'Royrke, Captain McOwen Oge O'Royrke, Captain Bryan Ballagh O'Royrke, Captain Teige McBryan Ballagh O'Royrke, Captain Hugh McDonogh, Captain Robert McNamee, Captain William Oge McPhelim McGlannagh (Clancy), of the Dartry, in the county of Leitrim. Captain Teige McPhelim McGlannagh of the same, Captain William McGlannagh of the same, Mr. Kedagh O'Bannaghan, Mr. James French, and Jeffry French, his sonne, and Edmond McBryan McSwine, Guardian of the Dominicans of the Abbey of Sligo".

In compliance with the terms of the surrender, a considerable number were convoyed to Boyle, one batch by Captain Brian McDonogh, and another under the charge of Captain Patrick Plunket; and if any of the latter party were maltreated by roughs on the road, as is alleged, there is no evidence, at least no evidence amounting to proof, that this was done with the connivance or consent of Plunket. Bryan McDonogh left all his party safe in Boyle.

One foul blot, however, stains the record of Sligo at this time the massacre which took place in the gaol. That a massacre of some kind happened is sure; that about a score of defenseless persons probably less than more—including at least one woman, were sacrificed, can hardly be denied; but that the tragedy was planned and commanded by the officers, at a formal meeting in the Abbey, as is alleged in the deposition of James Martin, (while William Walsh deposes that this meeting took place in Lady Jones' house or castle,) or that the horrors with which Jane Steward's deposition is full, had any existence outside her own inventive brain and wicked tongue, passes all belief.

In any case these two witnesses put themselves out of court; Jane Steward by admitting she was so sick, in her own house, all this time, that she could not stir, and that she only had her information "from those that escaped, and from her Irish servants, and others of the town;" and James Martin, son of Arthur Martin, by declaring "that he *heard from his mother* there was a meeting of officers in the Abbey, that *a poor beggar seeing it entered, and was listening to the deliberations*, when they resolved to put those in gaol to death".[1] According even to Jane Steward's own deposition, four at least of the victims, or intended victims, of the massacre, who were in the gaol and eye-witnesses of what occurred, Robert Gumble, ex-provost of Sligo, Edward Newsham, Edward Mercer, and Jane Steward's own son, Joseph Steward, escaped and survived the scene; and is it not clear that these, or some of them, would have been produced as witnesses, if they were able to back up her ghastly deposition? But they were kept out of the way, and the swearing was left to this Jane Steward, who had £1,200, the value of her alleged losses, to gain by her performance, if she swore well up to the mark!

As it is nowhere stated why the British were put into the gaol, we may conjecture that it was to save them from the violence of the mob, to which they were exposed if they remained in their houses. This is what commonly occurs even at present during insurrectionary or revolutionary movements, though it sometimes happens, when there is not an adequate, or well organized protecting force, that what is intended for an ark of safety is converted by the malice of evil men into a trap of destruction, as might be illustrated by scenes of the French Revolution, or even of the Irish

---

[1] Deposition of James Martin.

rebellion of '98. Indeed, the prison is always one of the first places attacked by insurgents, in order to reach those confined, with the purpose either of sacrificing or of saving them, according as they are obnoxious or acceptable to the assailants. In some such way as this the "labourers" and "butchers' boys" of the Depositions, knowing the British to be in the gaol, found their way into the prison, and gratified their brutal instincts by an act which was a great crime, but which was also a great blunder, as calculated to bring odium and disgrace on their cause.

A still more probable explanation of the tragedy is, that it was the sudden and unpremeditated outcome of a drunken orgy. It is admitted that the persons who were most concerned in the crime, either as instigators or perpetrators, including the O'Connor Sligo's brothers, passed the early hours of the night in question in drinking heavily; for Jane Steward herself deposed that she went "into the room of Helen Trimble", where they were assembled, and stayed there, while they were drinking five quarts of aqua vitae" With such evidence before us there is no need to seek further for the cause or motive of the gaol massacre—the *aqua vitae* being in this, as in most Irish cases, at the bottom of the crime.

Before they were put into the gaol, the victims of the massacre had been for some time in the custody of Captains Hugh and Charles O'Connor, who, as we learn from the depositions of Brian Ballagh O'Rorke and Colonel Owen O'Rorke, "had committed the English that were then in the town upon suspition of surprysing the castles", and to prevent them from co-operating with the English of Roscommon, who were said to be in full march upon Sligo.

While thus acquitting the chief leaders O'Connor Sligo, the Taaffes, Brian McDonough, Owen O'Rorke, and Patrick Plunket of all complicity with the authors of the massacre, it must be admitted that O'Connor's two brothers, Charles (who seems to have been a friar) and Hugh, may fairly be suspected of some participation in the crime, either in the way of direct co-operation, or of connivance, or of cowardly toleration of what they were bound to prevent, if possible. The offence, though never proved, was charged upon them in their own day; and that the charge was not altogether a trumped up one, may be inferred from the fact deposed to by Sir Francis Taaffe, that himself and his brother, with a large military force, arrested the O'Connors, and lodged them in the castle of Ballinafad, there to await trial for their alleged conduct—a circumstance, if tending to justify suspicions against the O'Connors, serving to clear the heads of the insurrection at Sligo from hand or part in the detestable doings of the gaol. The captives were released or escaped from confinement before trial; but in the year 1652 Hugh O'Connor—Charles may have been then dead or out of the country—came to Lord Clanrickard, near Ballyshannon, and asked his lordship to question him regarding the massacre—a proceeding which would indicate innocence, though it failed to convince Clanrickard, who threatened to hang him on getting to Ballyshannon. The sudden approach of the enemy against Clanrickard's troops, put an end to the parley with Hugh O'Connor, and stopped all ulterior proceedings.[1]

If Charles and Hugh O'Connor were guilty, which is, at worst, doubtful, they acted very differently from Owen O'Rorke, Teige O'Connor Sligo, and other leaders, who not only protected the persons of the British, but took charge of their money and goods, which they kept safe for the owners, and delivered back when all danger was passed. Owen O'Rorke being examined on the 17th May, 1653, testified that "being in Lady Jones' house, and asked for protection, he protected several, and among the rest William Browne, the minister, taking charge of bundles for them, and also of money, which he delivered up afterwards". Teige O'Connor Sligo, too, protected John Braxton, Provost of Sligo,[2] and all others that he could; and, seeing the disorders of the place, complained bitterly that he was unable to stop outrages.[3]

The gaol massacre supplied the notorious Sir Frederick Hamilton with a pretext for one of those raids in which that brutal man was in the habit of ravaging, like a wild beast, whatever places he fell upon. You would search in vain the annals of the seventeenth century, prolific as it was in cruel men, for a more ruthless monster than this Sir Frederick. We are shocked while thinking on the savageries of certain human tigers of the East, like Genghis Khan or Tamerlane; but give Hamilton their opportunities, and he would equal or eclipse their performances. Only let him have "line and scope" enough, and he would burn cities—more populous than Delhi or Bagdad, would raise an obelisk of human heads to overtop that of Tamerlane with its ninety thousand.

Should the reader feel inclined to turn away from this juxtaposition of Sir Frederick Hamilton and Tamerlane as an extravagance, let him read and study a tract or pamphlet, written or inspired by Sir Frederick, and he will probably admit, that the author of the sayings and doings there recorded, possessed a natural inborn cruelty, which if it had free play, was equal to the perpetration of any and every enormity. The man who gloats over human suffering; who hunts men and women, young and old, with horse and foot, and kills them "like vermin;" who counts indiscriminate massacre "good sport;" and whose great principle of action is to "destroy with fire and sword, all that can be come at;" that man is already a

---

[1] Deposition of Sir Francis Taaffe, before Sir Charles Coote and Walter Carwardine, at Galway, 23rd May, 1653.
[2] Deposition of John Braxton, Provost of Sligo.
[3] Deposition of Peter O'Crean.

Tamerlane in heart, and will be a Tamerlane in act, whenever he can. And such a one, even on his own showing, was Sir Frederick Hamilton.
[The following is an extended footnote in the original, Clachan ed.].

The pamphlet is entitled, "A true Relation of the manner of our Collonel Sir Frederick Hamilton's returne from Londonderry, in Ireland, being sixty miles from his Castle and Garrison, where he was at the beginning and breaking out of this Rebellion, with the particular services performed by the Horse and Foote companies which he commandes, garrisoned at Manorhamilton, in the county of Leitrim, in the province of Connaught".—Thorpe Collection in Dublin Library.

A few items, copied from this production, will give some idea of its contents:—

"A party sent towards Sligo, where we met with a number of rogues" (his usual name for the Irish) "hurt divers, killed 3, brought home their heads to our Collonel, with a lusty prisoner who was hanged next day",

"Killed about 30 in 3 cabbins, and hanged our guide, who died a most obdurate villain". "Killed and stript many of their best men".

"Marched towards the Rosse, where we killed 60 of their ablest men with 2 of their famous priests".

"Lying in ambush till noon within two miles of Sligo, and those we expected not appearing, as our orders that day were to burn and prey what we could, we burned several villages as Donoly (Doonally), Formorley (Formoyle), Collrey (Calry) and Lisscluff, with many other straggling houses. . . . when county gathered we killed above 40 of their best men, stript them all, divers of their best gentry as the O'Connors, and the O'Harts being thus killed". "Sent a party of horse and foot upon them, where we had good sport in killing near 60 of them with all their three Captains, and Captain Teige O'Connor's wife. . . . and burned the town of Broadcullin, with divers small villages".

"Took prisoner Charles Maguire after breaking his leg; to cure him had him carried on a barrow to the gallows, where he rayled at us for not getting a souldier's death after serving in France and Spain".

"We killed over three score of their best men, with divers other gentlemen whom our boys stript ... to God's holy name be the praise and honour".

"Burned and killed in the houses upwards of three score persons".

"Chased the people like dogs with horse and foote from hill to hill, killing a number " . . . "and our souldiers boyes stripped near 30 of their best men of the counties Sligo and Leitrim, including Mulmury McTernan, ex-sheriff, Bryan O'Rorke, and John O'Crean, all being prime gentlemen of the two counties, cutting off on that day about 60 of them".

The following is what the pamphlet says of the raid on Sligo:—"Our Collonel after taking Parke prisoner and putting on an officer of his own, marches straight to Sligoe .... Coming near the towne he commanded a halt, and the party to be drawn up in a body, using some comfortable encouraging speeches, asking if our stomachs did serve as his did to attempt the burning of the towne now so neere it which maintained so many rebellious enemies, who had joyned in the burning our poor garrison, and so many times encamped about us and sought our destruction. This motion was no sooner made by our Collonel than cheerfully embraced by us all, so recommending us to his divine mercy, who had many times delivered and assisted us, we marched towards the dawning of the day. Our Collonel coming to the bridge gives orders to the foote cheerfully to follow their sergeant with what silence and speede they were able, and once entring the towne no man presume on pain of death to enter any house for plunder, but with fire and sword to destroy all we could come at, calling all the streete if any British prisoners were among them,

they should draw to us, as divers did. Our Collonel with his horse falling on many good houses full of people upon this side of the bridge, where he burned and destroyed all, appointing his rendezvous with the foote at the south-west end of the Towne, when he crossed a fooard which brought him close to the friary, when the foote met and fired their brave mass and fryery, where, it is said, we burnt many good things which people had given for safety to the friars and all their superstitious trumperies belonging to the mass. It was thought some of the friars themselves were burnt; two of them running out were killed in their habits. As we finished this work and giving God the praise for the success . . . our Collonel held it fit to haste homewards . . . notwithstanding our wearisome march and hot service that night in burning the Toune of Sligo where it is confest by themselves was destroyed that night neere 300 soules by fire, sword, and drowning, to GOD'S EVERLASTING GREAT HONOUR AND GLORY AND OUR COMFORT".
It is hard to conceive that any human being should be capable of these unspeakable brutalities and blasphemies.

It is said that this monster has even to-day his admirers, but no man with a particle of either faith or feeling would be found among them. Reverend John Wesley, in his Journal under date, 5th May, 1769, writes: "Rode to Manorhamilton; so-called from a poor wretch, who settled here in the last century, and was famous for nothing else but hanging up all the Irish who fell into his hands."

The irruption of Hamilton into Sligo took place on the night of the 1st July, 1642. Learning from his spies that the garrison, and all the armed men of the town, would be engaged in a distant expedition that night, he made arrangements to fall on the place in their absence. Setting out from Manorhamilton soon after dark, and stopping for a little at Newtown, where he took Mr. Parke prisoner, and put a creature of his own in command, he resumed his journey, and arrived at Sligo between one and two o'clock. Having reached the spot where the Ulster Bank now stands, and spoken a few burning words to his followers, calling on them to have "stomachs" like his own for the work before them, he divided his force into two parties, a party of horse and a party of foot, and, directing the horse to remain with himself, he ordered the foot to cross the bridge, and proceeding as silently and swiftly as they were able, "to destroy with fire and sword all they could come at". The work of destruction began at once, and, in a very short time, a circle of raging flames surrounded the town, and lines of flames ran along the various streets, the houses, which were for the most part framed with timber and covered with thatch, igniting, in that dry and warm season of the year, like tinder.

On the north side of the river, comprising the district of the present Holborn Street, Stephen Street, and the Mall, where there were a good many houses "full of people", all were "burned and destroyed" by the horse under the immediate orders of Hamilton himself; while in the region stretching from the west side of the bridge along the present Knox's St., John St., Batcliffe St., Market St., Castle St., and through the other inhabited spaces to the south of the river, the houses were all given to the flames by the foot soldiers. By the time the foot had accomplished their part of the havoc, they were joined by the horse, who had, with their commander, already crossed the river at Buckley's ford; and both parties now uniting, fell upon the Abbey, set fire to everything they could, within and without the church and conventual buildings, and burned altars, altar ornaments, vestments, and various articles of value committed by the towns people for safe keeping to the friars. Some of the religious must have perished in the flames, and two of them, who ran out into the street in their habit, to see what was the matter, were killed the moment they appeared; this sacrilege serving as a not inappropriate finish to the horrors of the most memorable night through which Sligo has ever passed.

If a single house on fire, filled suddenly with smoke and flames, so as to render egress extremely difficult and hazardous, and to drive the inmates frantically about in search of some door or window through which to escape, while they rend the air with their shrieks and cries for help, is a spectacle which, when once witnessed, haunts the mind ever after, what must one think of a gigantic conflagration, which enwraps in its burning embrace a whole town, when all the avenues of escape are carefully barred and stopped, and when fugitives from the flames are driven back into them, and wretches, jumping for safety from windows into the street, are received on pikes and sword points.

The unnatural orgy being now ended; the whole town being one vast charnel house; the majority, three hundred probably, of the inhabitants, who went to bed a few hours before in health and security, being now corpses many burned to death in their houses, some dispatched with the cold steel in the streets, as they tried to avoid the raging fire, and others, while seeking to hide themselves in back yards and gardens, driven into the river and there knocked on the head the actors in this terrible tragedy, after congratulating one another on having thus given "everlasting great honour and glory to God", as well as "comfort " to themselves, retraced their steps to Manorhamilton, there to prepare for new enterprises in incendiarism and murder.

Let nobody try to excuse Sir Frederick Hamilton's excesses on the score of strong religious feeling, a plea sometimes put forward to extenuate the conduct of other fiery spirits of the seventeenth century. Religious feeling is respectable and, to a great extent, extenuating, even when it is abused, or perverted; but there is nothing to show that Sir Frederick was ever much moved either by religious feeling, or religious conviction. As far as evidence of any kind goes, religion as well as politics consisted for him in self-aggrandisement; and whoever thwarted him in this, be he Catholic or Protestant, Celt or Saxon, became his enemy. It was thus with "all the

Protestant gentlemen and officers in the North"[1], who were disgusted by the mean and low arts with which he endeavoured to raise himself by depreciating men of the greatest merit and worth.

And he acted on the same principle at Manorhamilton towards those Protestants whose lands he coveted, or who stood otherwise in the way of his greed or ambition; representing one neighbour, Sir W. Cole, as disaffected to the English Parliament; charging another, Mr. Parke, of Newtown, with being in collusion with the O'Rorkes; and giving out that the Very Rev. Dean Berkley, who disobliged him in some way "carried himself more like a devil than a dean". Except courage, which he certainly had in no ordinary degree, he possessed no other high or estimable quality. Touch him where you will, and you find him all over an unmitigated brute; as impervious to sentiments of humanity or courtesy as an African savage. When he receives a civil letter from Teige O'Connor Sligo, full of civilities, and reminding him of the friendship that formerly existed between their families, he sends back a grossly insulting answer, concluding, "Yours with scorn;" and when he communicates himself with the Irish army, he addresses his letter, "To the most unworthy, cowardly Colonels, Captains, and such like ragged Regiment now gazing for our Colonel's Easter provisions neere Dromahair and Crewly".—Compliments and regards are sent by him in this polite fashion, "Commend me to that lowsie lord's sonne, Luke Taaffe, and his base brother-in-law, Bryan MacDonnaghy". Unprincipled then, malignant, self-seeking, false hearted, cruel, brutal, scurrilous, a liar, a whisperer, a calumniator with the conscience of a Tamerlane, and the manners of a Hottentot; such are some leading features in the character of Sir Frederick Hamilton, the arch enemy of Sligo in his day.

For three years from the date of the burning, Sligo was left free to rise as best it could, from the ashes to which Hamilton had reduced it. Meantime, Teige O'Connor Sligo, held the castle, and governed the town, without having any troops to defend it, except a local regiment, of which he was colonel by commission from the Confederation of Kilkenny. Ormonde, struck with the importance of the place, and its weak defence, had offered the Confederation to send a military force to it if they consented to contribute towards their maintenance, and to recognise him as commander-in-chief; but they refused to accept these terms; and, being in no condition themselves to furnish a fitting garrison, the town had to

---

[1] Carte's Ormonde, Vol. I., p. 533. This able writer says, "Sir Frederick was now grown universally odious to all the Protestant gentlemen and officers in the North. His violence, rapines, cruelties, and insupportable insolencies, which few of them had escaped, was the first occasion of that aversion to him; but it was much increased by the use he made of his credit with the Parliament to lessen their services in order to exalt his own, and to supplant them in their commands".

depend for safety on the absence or forbearance of an enemy. *"Quidquid delirant reges plectuntur Achivi,"*[1] and Sligo had to pay the penalty of the dissensions between the Confederates and Ormonde.

Well aware of the state of things in the town, Sir Charles Coote, who had been just appointed President of Connaught by the Parliament of England, resolved to signalize his appointment by the capture of the place. For this purpose he organized an army of 4,000 foot and 500 horse,[2] others say 8,000 foot and 500 horse,[3] composed of English and Scotch Protestants, and commanded by Sir Robert Stewart, an officer of ability, who had shown himself able to hold his own even when opposed to Owen Roe O'Neill. He was ancestor to the much-lamented Sir R. Stewart, who lost his life in the Soudan. This force rendezvoused at Augher, in Tyrone, and marching from that town, in the middle of summer, 1645—the artillery having been sent on by sea—they reached Sligo in a few days, and opened fire without delay.

An open town, without walls or forts, and lying in the bottom of a deep valley, could not hold out long against so formidable a force, though O'Connor Sligo, who commanded,[4] did not yield till the enemy had lost 500 men, as well as a Lieutenant Colonel, a Sergeant Major, a Captain, and other officers, and failing to take Crean's castle to which the Irish had retired, had promised fair and honourable quarter. The terms thus offered were accepted, but the faith given was disgracefully broken, for the moment the Irish issued from the castle, all including 200 men of the garrison, and a vast number of women and children, were disarmed, stripped, and massacred, two men and two women being the only persons that escaped slaughter.

The fall of Sligo was known in a few days all over the kingdom. A dispatch of Garret Dillon, one of the officers engaged, to Sir Ulick Bourke, being forwarded by him to Lord Dillon, Ormonde's President of Connaught, was sent on, in hot haste, to Ormonde himself, who, while admitting the gravity of the crisis, threw all the blame of it on the refusal of the Confederation to accept the conditions he had offered. Carte seems to regard the defence of Sligo on this occasion, as merely formal, but it is plain from the letter of Garret Dillon and from another of Monsignor Scarampi[5]

---

[1] "for any madness of their kings, it is the Greeks who take the beating" (Horace), [Clachan ed.].
[2] Carte's Ormonde, Vol. I, p. 545.
[3] Spicilegium Ossoriense, Vol. I., p. 293.
[4] Carte's Ormonde, Vol. L, p. 535.
[5] "The forces for Sligo were composed of detachments out of the old Scotch and English regiments; and having, with their artillery, which was sent by sea, battered down one or two houses in the place, O'Connor surrendered the castle".
Garret Dillon's letter has not been published, but runs thus: "Lough (Glynn), July, 1645.

that it was a very grave affair. The town being taken, Sir R. Stewart was constituted its governor, but the state of things in the North requiring his presence there, he left his Lieutenant-Colonel in Sligo with a garrison of 500 men.

Sir,—I must now be the author of a woful tragedy, for yesterday morning after the battering of two houses in Sligo the enemy made a hott and furious assault upon the rest of the town, where they have lost 500 men—a Lieutenant Collonal, one Sergeant-Major, a Captain with other officers; nothwithstanding all their loss, and not regarding their men's lives, they attempted Crean's house, where our men betook themselves, who behaved themselves so gallant as they bett them from it; upon which the enemy sounded a parley; and promised a fair and honorable quarter; whereupon our men came away, and after coming into the streete were disarmed, stript, and foully murthered; soe as never a man escaped but 2 men and 2 women; Major Rouck (Rorke?) is come hither this night, who lost three score and six of his own company, with his officers in the service: Major Generall with greefe hereof keeps his bed; all the Scotch marched from Bellahy this morninge to Sligo with 4 or 5000 cowes. I make no question but now the province will be their owne drumaheir (Dromahaire) morere (?) Coulloony, and the rest of the garisons in that county are forsaken, and burned; Ballimote and titemple (Templehouse) excepted, all the castles in Tireragh payes contribution allready to the enemy; my father (Sir Lucas Dillon) is expected at Dunmore this night. I pray, Sir, look well to yourself, for I am sure you will be very much aimed at; and be sure to store yourself with provisions; thus with my humble service to my aunte, I remain

"Your owne servant,
" GER. DILLON.

"To Sir Ullick Bourke, Knight and Baronet these.
- (Carte Papers, Vol. xv., p. 146.)
"I pray despatch this to my Lord President and bid him be careful of himself there."
Monsignor Scarampi's letter (from the Rinuccini Papers, Florence) is dated 14th July, 1645, and contains the following reference to Sligo:—"In Conacia incendia rerum omnium, praedae animantium, caedes puerorum et mulierum ab 8,000 peditibus, et 500 equitibus Scotis et Anglis. Obsederunt et ceperunt, amissis plusquam quingentis ex his, Sligoam, opportunissimam nostro malo et eorum securiati munitionem, in qua posteaquam se pactis dediderant, occiderunt barbare praesidium nostrum circa ducentorum militum necnon omnes pueros et mulieres. Remedium aut nullum aut tardum, deficientibus mediis utinam non animis".
Spicilegium Ossoriense—By Right Rev. Patrick Francis Moran—First Series, p. 293.

CHAPTER VII

CONFEDERATE EFFORTS TO RECOVER SLIGO

THE Confederates, when it was too late, realized the value of Sligo as the key of Connaught, and did their best to retrieve a loss which they should have exerted themselves more to prevent. Ordering the Archbishop of Tuam, Malachy Queely, whom they had just made their President of Connaught,[1] to recover Sligo, that martial prelate, who judged it right, in the terrible times in which he lived, to wield the sword as well as the crosier, led about 2,000 men against the place, and was, in the beginning of the attack, so successful as to make himself master of St. John's Church, at one end of the town, and of the Abbey at the other. This success, however, was short lived; for Sir C. Coote, who, no doubt, was kept well informed of the Archbishop's movements, arriving from the North, in the nick of time, at the head of an army of English and Scotch troops, the Confederates retired immediately from their positions, and, being overtaken by the enemy's horse, broke ranks, and took to flight, when they were cut down by the Northerners, who pursued them, sword in hand, for several miles.

The victory was an important one; for Coote took "several standards and colours", "two waggons with rich spoile and money," "150 horses with pistols", all "the luggage, tents, and ammunition", "four and twenty drums", and "28 officers of note".[2] But what crowned the event, both as a disaster

---

[1] There were now three different Presidents of Connaught Dr. Queely, the President of the Confederation; Sir C. Coote, the President of the English Parliament; and Lord Dillon, Ormonde's President.

[2] The Covenanters' account of the conflict is as follows: "A true relation of the late success at Sligo against the Irish rebels, performed by Sir Charles Coote, Sir William Cole, and Sir Francis Hamilton, with the particulars hereafter expressed.

"On Sunday the 17th October, 1645, the Irish rebels having surrounded the towne with 1,000 foot and 300 horse, the garrison seeing little hope of the advance of the Ulster forces (who were then neere them at Bundoran), though unknowne to them, conceived it absolutely necessary to hazard the fighting with the rebels with their own strength and Sir William Cole's troops, rather than to starve themselves and lose their out garrisons which were blocked up, the enemy lying between them; Captain Richard Coot and Captain Richard Cole commanded our horse, being 200, who charged the rebels horse very resolutely, and fell to the sword pell mell, and beat them amongst the divisions of their own foot, and routed them. And Lieut. Col. Sanderson sallying out of the town with his foot, and Sir Francis Hamilton coming in the nick of time with his troops, they had all execution upon the rebels for miles. In the pursuit their commander and President of that province was slaine (the Titular Archbishop of Tuam). Our men took 105 of their horses with pistols, all their baggage, tents and ammunition, there were two waggons with rich spoile and money in them, they took several of their standards and colours, four and twenty drums, and officers of note in number 43 (another copy 28) who are now prisoners in Sligo, about 200 of their men being killed in the place, two or three and twenty drowned.

for the Irish, and a triumph for the Covenanters, was the death of the Archbishop. While others saved themselves by flight he remained on the ground, either because he disdained to fly, or because "being obese and of great stature"[1] he was ill able to do so. Before he fell, several priests, who stood by him to the last, were slain around him, after which he was, first, shot with a pistol ball in the reins, and next, mangled and despatched with swords. The author of *An Aphorismical Discovery* states that the Archbishop was first hanged and then decapitated;[2] but there is as little authority for this statement, as there is for the horrid allegation of the same writer, that he was lured on to destruction and betrayed by Sir James Dillon,[3] There is, however, good reason to think that the prelate was treated with great barbarity by the enemy; for Bruodin, his near relative, who was well acquainted with the facts, narrates[4] that he was slain after quarter given, that his right arm was first cut off, and that he was then hackedd to pieces.

We had but 1 killed of Sir W. Cole's troop and 6 horsemen hurt and some horse. The Archbishop was a principal agent in their wars, and one of their supreme Councell; divers letters and papers of importance were found upon him. Prisoners at Sligo:—Morogh ne Do O'Flaherty, Lieut. Colonel to Richard Bourk, cousin german to Earl of Clanrickard, and his next heir; John Gardy, Lieut. Colonel to Sir Tibbot Bourk, eldest son to Lord Mayo; Richard Bourk, Major to Richard Bourk; Captain William O'Shaghnasie, brother to Sir Roger O'Shaghnasie; Captain Garret Dillon, son to Sir Lucas Dillon; Captain Costolagh, with divers other inferior officers. Killed: The titular Archbishop of Tuam, the rebels' President of Connaught, a great incendiary Captain Brown brother of Geffory Brown the lawyer."—The above account taken for the most part from a pamphlet called "The Irish Cabinet", and contained in box 41 of the Haliday collection, Royal Irish Academy. Among the papers found on this occasion was the Instructions of the King to Glamorgan, which was at once ordered to be printed and published by the Parliament, in order to excite odium against the King.

[1] The Irish Hierarchy in the Seventeenth Century. By Rev. C. P. Meehan, M.R.I. A., etc., p. 118, fifth edition.

[2] "Now assured that their prisoner was that great prelate, they suffered all others to go at pleasure, hanged and beheaded this eminent prelate". —Gilbert's History of Affairs in Ireland, 1641-1652. Part 1., p. 94.

[3] "Sir James Dillon, a prime pillar in Ormond's buildinge, taking to heart the displacing of Taaffe, never made scruple of his oathe to the contrary, but thought now to avenge on the innocent that suposed wronge, though it fell on God's minister .... Such is the fruite of faction in these our daies, as of adulterie in Herod's, that seeinge we have not got a Baptiste to beheade him, will pay it in the execrable betraying of a most worthy archbishop, whose like in godlinesse, liberalitie and zeal was not to be had in Ireland". —Idem.

After reading what the "Aphorismical Discovery" has about the circumstances of Dr. Queely's death, it is hard to avoid the conclusion, that the writer was at once ill informed and ill intentioned, in what he says about occurrences in Sligo.

[4] "Non procul a castro oppidi de Sligo in manus Scotorum rebellium, incidifc patrise pater, ac verus gregis sibi commissi pastor, illustrissimus Dominus Malachias Queleus Tuamensis Archiepiscopus, Generalis Taaffe in bello coadjutor. Presulem hunc diguissimum, barbari Calvanistas, post datam fidem, abscissa prius dextera, AN. 1645, in minutas secuerunt partes".

Lord Taaffe, the day after the disaster, sent a trumpeter to Sligo to demand the body, but the enemy would not part with it without a ransom of £30; and we learn from Father Meehan[1] though he does not give the authority on which he bases the statement, that "the money was paid by Walter Lynch (apparently, the Bishop of Clonfert,) who had the remains conveyed to Tuam, where fitting obsequies were performed before the interment". It is strange that no account has come down of the place where the Archbishop was buried—a circumstance tending to create a suspicion that the ransom was not paid, nor the body recovered; so that, after all, the mutilated remains may rest somewhere in or near Sligo.

As was natural enough, the death of Dr. Queely at the hands of furious Covenanters, who hated his faith still more than his person, caused him to be regarded by many as a martyr. And this opinion was spread abroad and fostered by one of the most remarkable and influential men of the period, Father Finaghty, commonly known, in his day, and long after, as the "wonder-working priest of Elphin", about whom a word or two will not be out of place: This extraordinary man was, perhaps, not a very unnatural phenomenon of the sensational times in which he lived.

Originally a native and priest of the diocese of Tuam, he devoted himself during the persecution of Cromwell, to the care of the people of that diocese, and ministered to them in their places of refuge and concealment. Numbers of other priests did the same; but whether it was from superior zeal, greater eloquence, or some other peculiar gifts, he was

---

[1] "Irish Hierarchy in the Seventeenth Century", p. 118, fifth edition. The following version of the disaster at Sligo was forwarded to the warden of Galway: "Here is a true tragedy of the unhappy expedition to Sligoe, viz., last Saturday, in the afternoon, our forces, after taking the Abbie of Sligoe, and hearing of the approach of Coote with strong relief from the North, begun to march back from Sligoe; and though they beate the enemy that day and the day before, yet then, a few horse of the same enemie put them most shamefully to flight, in which flight (proh dolor.) my lord archbishop, Father Teige Conel, Father Augustine Higen, with other clergymen, were killed and pittifullie mangled, and soe left in the way near Sligoe. General Taffe sent a trumpet to Sligoe, and got newes, on the 27th instant, that the Scots will not part with my lord archbishop's body without getting out of it 30 sterling. The trumpetter brought with him two letters from the commander of Sligoe, offering to exchange prisoners; ours write that they are kindly used by them, and desire relief and ransome. John Garvey is prisoner in Newtown with Mr. Jackson, and the rest at Sligoe; their names are as followeth: Lieut. Colonels Morogh Flaherty and John Garvey. Majors Richard Bourke and Wm. Shaughnessy. Captains Gerald Dillon and Roger Costelo. Lieutenants Christopher Ryan, Conor O'Hayne, and Tiege Flaherty. Cornets, John Barnewell and Wm. Ferel. Ensigns, John Bedlow, Bryan Kelly, Hugh McGillecooly, and James Linch. Troopers, Richard Bedlow, Edward Fitzgerald, Garret Dillon, Richard Bourk, John Boyle, John FitzGarret, Francis Cadell, Christopher Kent, Richard Bourk and John Higgin. Drummers, Thomas Walsh and Connor Quinn. Two footmen with a cornet and seven troopers formerly taken in the skirmish at Ballimote". The writer of above was John Dowly, Vicar-General of Tuam.

soon singled out by the people from his fellow labourers, so that he was follwed often by crowds of a thousand, fifteen hundred, two thousand persons, through woods, and bogs, and mountains, wherever he turned from the troops that scoured the country in pursuit.

Sharing to the full the dangers and privations of his followers; sleeping like them on the bare ground in the open air; subsisting like them on coarse and scanty food; exposed like them, and even more than them, to the vengeance of the persecutor; he gained daily more and more on their affections, until at last he was regarded by them rather as a prophet of the type of Ellas or Eliseus, than as an ordinary priest. Nor was this very surprising; for, substitute Cromwell for Jezabel; the wilds of Connemara for the "desert of Damascus;" the mountain stream for the "torrent Carith;" and a sleep under the hazel or holly, for the "sleep under the shadow of the juniper tree" and the parallel between these prophets and the priest, is so striking, as to suggest naturally the idea of the people.

One can understand too, how, in his peculiar circumstances, seeing himself constantly surrounded by persons who credited him with supernatural powers, Father Finaghty came ultimately to regard himself in the same light, and to exercise those powers with which he believed himself invested, as we find him doing even under the Commonwealth, but more freely and regularly, under the Restoration. In the year 1662 he procured, we are told, a pass from some one high in the State, authorizing him to travel where he liked through Ireland, and to meet the people—a privilege which he made use of, by traversing much of the country "praying, touching, crossing (exorcising), blessing wells, and imparting to their waters his own virtue". Wherever he turned the sick came to him, or were brought to him, in great numbers; and—as to use his own words – "he never denied the gracious gift of curing all diseases", he ministered to everyone that applied. In time his fame reached England, and the royal circle, and he was even introduced or smuggled into the palace of Charles II. to touch the eyes of one of the Queen's ladies in waiting, who had lost her sight.

There is no need to say that Father Finaghty and his proceedings became a subject of absorbing interest throughout the country. To the mass of the people, and to a few men of station and abilities, as Geoffrey Browne, the famous lawyer, and Mr. Beling, the Father was a saint, pure and simple, with his credentials in his works; while some scientists and thinkers, including Sir W. Petty, Sir R. Southwell, Dr. Yarner, and Father Peter Walsh, who took a more human view of the subject, did not show the less interest, on that account, in his doings; observing him in public and in private, attending his meetings, studying his movements, submitting themselves to his operations, and leaving no stone unturned to get at the secret of his success, whatever it was. Even Ormonde himself, either for some reason of State, or from curiosity, desired a conference with him, but the priest, after the time and place of the meeting were fixed, falling ill, and needing change of air, or pretending to need it, left Dublin for the west of Ireland, before the appointed day, so that the interview with the Lord Lieutenant never came off.

This remarkable man seems to have believed that Dr. Queely's death was a genuine martyrdom; for, in dealing with the diseased, he usually touched them with relics, or supposed relics of the archbishop; and he gave out that he had cured more than 500 sick persons by the application, with the repetition, during the process, of the words: "If Almighty God wills that the soul of him whose relics are now present, should be worshipped here on earth with the honour due to a saint and martyr, let this infirmity depart".[1]

The words, "or supposed relics", are introduced advisedly in the preceding sentence; for though the opinion was pretty general, in the middle of the seventeenth century, that Father Finaghty employed in his proceedings the real relics of Dr. Queely, the matter was not regarded as certain by the Tuam Synod or Congregation of 1660, as, after examining the subject, they decide or decree as follows: "Different accounts having been laid before us regarding those bones and relics of the Most Reverend Malachy, the last archbishop of Tuam, slain in the late Catholic war by the heretics, which the Reverend James Feenaghty, priest and exorcist of the diocese of Elphin, makes use of for expelling demons and curing other infirmities, as well as for other purposes, the Synod having inquired into their genuineness, although it finds that they appear by the divine power to

---

[1] Collections on Irish Church History. By L. F. Renehan, D.D., Vol. I., p. 405. In a letter of Rinuccini to Cardinal Panfilio, dated Kilkenny, Nov. 20, 1645, the Nuncio writes of Dr. Queely, "During the few days I was at Limerick, very sad news for the Kingdom reached me, namely, the unfortunate death of the archbishop of Tuam. He died before I had an opportunity of knowing him, not to speak of having dealings with him, as was suggested to me by the instructions of your Eminence. This worthy prelate, after the loss of Sligo, returned from Kilkenny to Connaught to repair the disorders of that province; and I have been informed that when departing from Kilkenny he took away his things, and bade farewell to many persons, as if he were never to return, mentioning certain prophecies concerning bishops of his Church, to which vain sorts of predictions I perceive this people to be much inclined. When he returned to the siege of the beforenamed castle, he heard that the enemy in their turn were becoming increased in number, and not at once taking the necessary precautions, either from disbelief of the intelligence, or for some other reason, he suffered the enemy to fall upon him and was put to flight. At first two Religious, whom together with some other captains he had with him, were slain near him, and at last he himself had his life suddenly ended by a pistol shot in his reins. They give out that he was heard to say before expiring, that up to that time he had given all his strength to defend the Catholic religion, and that he then willingly gave his life for the same cause. And truly he worthily closed the period of his earthly career with acquiring in heaven a reward corresponding to his great merits.—*Brady's Episcopal Succession*, Vol. xi. p. 141.

effect some signs and cures, still, for just causes, it has deferred till further proof is offered, to recognize them as the true and undoubted relics of the holy man *(Delatis ad hanc congregationem diversis rationibus de ossibus et reliquiis bonae memoriae Reverendissimi Domini Malachiae ultimi Tuamensis Archiepiscopi in nupero Catholicorum bello interfecti, ab Haereticis, quibus utitur Reverendus D. Jacobus Finachty sacerdos et Exorcista Dicecesis Elphinensis inter alia expellendis Daemonibus et aliis infirmitatibus curandis; facta inquisitione de veritate eorum quamvis nonnulla signa et curationes Divina virtute videntur operari, justas tamen ob causas in ulteriorem probationem distulit Synodus easdem pro veris et indubitatis viri sancti reliquiis admittere.)*

The place of Dr. Queely's death seems to be as great a mystery as the place of his burial.[1] According to all he fell "near Sligo", or "under Sligo", or, "not far from the castle of Sligo", but the exact spot, which was called "Clare", "Clara", or "Claragh", has not been hitherto pointed out or discovered. Besides the Claragh in question there were two Claras in the county of Sligo, one in Carbury and the other in Leyney; but neither of these could be the scene of the tragedy—not the former, which lies in the parish of Ahamlish and far below the Sligo river, which the archbishop did not cross; nor the latter, which is distant some fifteen miles to the south of Sligo far beyond the range of the action in which he lost his life. The writer is satisfied that the spot in question is that now called Cleveragh, or "Cleveragh Demesne;" for, in the first place, Claragh and Cleveragh are so like, as words, that one might easily be confounded with the other; secondly, Claragh is actually given as an alias for "Cleveragh or Cleuragh" in the Tripartite Deed of the Division of Sligo between Strafford, Wilson, and Lesley; thirdly, Cleveragh is "near Sligo", or "under Sligo; " fourthly, it is *"not far from the castle of the town of Sligo*: 1 (Non procul a *castro* oppidi de Sligo. *Bruodin*); and lastly, adjoining, as it does, the river Sligo and Lough Gill, it is almost the only place, in the neighbourhood of Sligo, where the "Two or Three and twenty drowned", mentioned in the bulletin, could have met with their fate. These reasons seem to establish satisfactorily the identification of Claragh and Cleveragh; and they are greatly strengthened

---

The following epitaph was intended for his tomb, should the resting place of the remains be ever discovered:—

"Praesulis hic multo laniatum vulnere corpus
Canitiesque sacro sanguine sparsa jacet
Pro rege non renuit vitam profundere pastor
Quam bene pastorem mors ista decet bonum.
Purpurei fulgete Patres in murice sanguis
Pulchrius hic vestri muricis igne rubet".

—Father Meehan's—*The Irish Hierarchy*, p. 119. The word "rege" in the third line is probably a misprint for "grege".

by the proximity of Cleveragh to the Abbey, which the archbishop had just taken, and from which he must have begun his retreat.

Had Dr. Queely known more of the art of war, he would have conducted his attack on Sligo with more caution, or, perhaps, would have declined the attempt altogether, as Lord Taaffe, General Preston, and Owen Roe O'Neil deliberately did.

Taaffe having received a commission from Ormonde to reduce and punish such Connaught garrisons as had violated the articles of the Cessation, levied an army of about 3,000 men for the purpose; and with these troops took Tulsk by storm, and Castle Coote by siege, received the surrender of Elphin and Jamestown on conditions, and, getting the governors of Boyle to engage on oath to observe the Cessation, reappointed them in charge of the place. But finding the capture of Sligo a rather perilous undertaking, the road near Boyle being impracticable for the carriage of ordnance, and the country waste and destitute of provisions,[1] he deferred the enterprise to some more suitable occasion.

Similar considerations prevented General Preston from measuring his strength with the Parliamentarians of Sligo, though the Confederation was most anxious to see them dislodged from the place. It was hoped and expected that Preston would march from Boyle on Sligo; and the *Aphorismical Discovery* goes so far as to state that "General Preston and his armie marched forwarde to Sligo (after taking castle of Roscommon) where all the enemie garrisons were, all which were surrendered upon demande, on sight of the armie and ordinance;" but this positive and circumstantial statement is belied by the General's own letter, explaining why he did not even attempt the service expected from him.[2] Preston's letter from Boyle is

---

[1] In a letter to Ormonde (August 27, 1645) he writes, "My not advancing from the Boile to Sligoe was occasioned through want of provisions, it being impossible to subsist in so depopulated a country, and withal there being many impediments to the carriage of artilery, without which nothing of advantage could there be performed, so I now only imploy thither partys of hors and foot, to comfort the few inhabitants and preserve the harvest".

[2] This letter is written from Boile Campe, addressed to Lord Muskery and others, and dated July 27, 1646. Preston writes, "We hold it may not stand with the safetie of the armie to advance towards Sligoe, until the General of Ulster be with his armie in the field . . . Moreover our artilerie cannot be carried over the Curlews, unless we draw small pieces with much difficulty. Neither have we any match but 1,000 weight, which will not suffice for two days in a siege . . . We have intelligence of the enemy marching to Sligoe, to whom we must give battle if we goe so far. We shall remain heere for further orders, as going further will certainly engage us in a battle, for which we fynd not ourselves in fighting equipage. If it shall be thought fit that we advance, we must have a month's means at least, without which we cannot move, without the hazard of losing the whole army, for all the way before us is so destroyed and waste that nothing is to be had for monie or otherwise, soe that every soldier must have forth with him at least a month's provisions". Peace being proclaimed on the 30th July, Preston had nothing more to do in regard to Sligo.

dated 27th July; and as peace was proclaimed on the 30th of that month, there was no need for further action on his part.

Owen Roe O'Neil in turn was directed by the Confederates to wrest Sligo from those who held it for the Parliament of England. Undeterred by the difficulties of the enterprise, and the obstacles in the way, this cool headed and able general accepted the duty laid on him, and, as a first step towards its accomplishment, engaged his troops in making a suitable military road across the Curlews. But they were not left long at the work; for the Supreme Council of the Confederation, with an inconstancy of purpose, which was not peculiar to this occasion, suddenly ordered O'Neil and his army to Leinster, so that Owen Roe had no opportunity of performing anything noteworthy in regard to Sligo, though there is abundant proof that no one appreciated better than he did, the vast importance of the place, as a cardinal point in the strategy of the war.

Sligo, thus held for the Parliament, was a thorn in the side of Ormonde, as well as in that of the Confederates. Not being in a state to secure it by force, he set on foot secret negotiations with two of the Parliament's officers, Colonel Henry Gore and his brother, Sergeant Major Francis Gore (direct ancestor of the Lissadell family), which he hoped would bring him to the possession of the town. These officers, like some others in the North, either sick of the excesses of the Parliament, or convinced that the royal cause would triumph in the end, and wishing to be on the winning side, were not indisposed to treat with him. His proposals were made through Sergeant Major General, Sir George Monro, whom Ormonde instructed to offer himself to the Gores as a person authorized by the Lord Lieutenant to treat with them; to assure them that in case they brought over with them 300 armed men, these men should be constituted regiments, should be placed under the command of the two brothers, and should have provision made for them as for the rest of the royal army; and to inform Lieutenant Colonel Henry, the elder brother, that if Sligo was reduced by his means, he should be appointed its governor.[1]

These *pourparlers* did not gain their object, at least, at the time, no doubt, for some cause beyond the control of the negotiators; for Sir Francis Gore's good will, on this and other occasions, was rewarded under the Act of Settlement, by a grant of lands in Kilkenny, Sligo and Galway. Henry died in 1651, long before he could receive a similar reward.

The honour of recovering Sligo was reserved for Lord Clanrickarde. His army came before the place on the 3rd of July (1649), and after a week's negotiation and the threat of an assault, the town was surrendered to his lordship, the besieged receiving liberal conditions. On the same occasion

---

[1] These particulars are contained in a letter of Ormonde to Clanrickarde, and dated May 11, 1649. This letter is in the *Carte Collection*.

the neighbouring garrison of Newtown was surrendered, a place, according to Clanrickarde, little inferior, if inferior at all, to Sligo.

The forts would hardly have been given up so tamely only that there were divisions and disaffection among those who held them. Ormonde's negotiations, after all, bore fruit, so that his friends were inside as well as outside Sligo, and when the more fiery spirits of the garrison would resist *a toute outrance* the cooler and more calculating heads, which he had gained over the Gores, and Sir R. Stewart, who was still Governor counselled, and brought about, compliance with Clanrickarde's demands.[1] The Parliamentarians charged a Scotch officer named Henderson, with betraying the town to Clanrickarde.

There is reason to think that the O'Connors were as little inclined as the Parliamentarians to submit to Lord Clanrickarde, if left to themselves; but they were restrained from opposing him, by a letter of Major-General Lucas Taaffe, on the part of the Confederation of Kilkenny, calling on them to submit to his Lordship, or to take the alternative of being "branded as traitors". Had they opposed, it would have been in the interest of the Nuntio's party in the Supreme Council. Taaffe's letter is dated, April 29, 1649, and is addressed to Captain Donough O'Connor and Captain Roger O'Connor, or either of them.[2]

At no time since the beginning of hostilities in 1641, was the importance of Sligo, as a place of garrison, more appreciated than at the time we have now reached. Complicated as the drama of the war was all through, the plot thickened as things were coming towards a close. In the North there were four independent armies, each, with different views and interests: Owen Roe's; Sir Charles Coote's.; that of the Scotch; and that of Sir R Stewart and the Lord of Ards; while in the South there was Ormonde's, or, the royal army; Preston's; and that of Inchiquin, who was

---

[1] The Parliamentarians gave out that Colonel Henderson, a Scotchman, betrayed the place to the Irish. "Sligo", writes one of them, "sold to Clanrickarde by Henderson, whereby Connaught is lost".—Gilbert's History of Affairs in Ireland, Part ii., pp. 335 & 443. Clanrickarde reported the capture of Sligo to Ormonde in a letter dated 9th July, 1649, and written from Sligo Campe—"Upon the 3d of this present month I sat down before the forte of Sligo, and sent a summons to it which procured a treaty—and that broken, and preparations for an assault, upon a second treaty, occasioned by a despatch of Sir R. Stewart, we came to a seasonable agreement, and the 7th of this month it was surrendered to me, upon, I must confess, somewhat large conditions, if the importance of the place, and the danger so far from assistance did not render it necessary. I was attacked the same night suddenly by a powerful party of enemys horse and dragoons under Richard Coote, but seeing we had the forte, and were ready to receive them, they retired. I gained 7 pieces of ordnance, two drakes, and above 100 barrels of powder, and match proportionable. Tomorrow I expect surrender of Newtown, a place, though not so famous in print, yet of equal strength to this forte, which in the opinion of others of better judgment, is a very strong and regular work, &c".

[2] This letter is in the Carte Collection.

acting now in concert with, and in subordination to, Ormonde, but who could not be relied on to persevere in such sentiments and action. And in nearly each of those armies there were sections little less hostile to each other, than to the enemy or enemies, these differences affecting even the English and Scotch, who had lately come over, as if there was something in the air or soil of unfortunate Ireland, which served to disintegrate and divide everything it touched, native or foreign.

In this muddle or jungle, the leaders of the armies were more than ordinarily anxious to take advantage of their rivals, and without due regard, apparently, to either principle or decency. Even Owen Roe showed a somewhat strange disposition to ally himself with the enemies of the country, and engaged in transactions which had an equivocal look, such as his dealings with Monk, and more especially, his raising the siege of Derry in the interest of Sir Charles Coote. *An Aphorismical Discovery* of Treasonable Faction (Part iii., p. 211), excuses Owen Roe on the plea of necessity: "In the beginning of May, O'Neil, finding himself destitute of all possibility of doing good, and having no means left him under God's providence, but a few poor creaghts[1] of his own country to maintain himself and the few men he kept on foot still, nor no ammunition, nor means left to get anything unless by taking some desperate course, on which, he settled his thoughts, and off-hand summoned a provincial council to meet at Belturbet, when it was concluded (upon a former invitation sent by Sir Charles Coote), to treat with him for ammunition, and commissioners appointed immediately to meet him for that purpose, or his commissioners at Newtown, near Drumahaire (Dromahair), where Colonel Richard Coote and Major Ormsby met, and agreed to give thirty barrels of powder, ball and match proportionately, three hundred beeves, or 400 in money conditionally, O'Neill should march with his army to relieve Derry".

Both O'Neil and Coote were eager to obtain a footing in Sligo. O'Neil applied to have two hundred men of his own received into the place for the purpose, as he alleged, of strengthening and guarding it against the Parliamentarians, and promised, on his honour, to withdraw this contingent when asked by the Governor to do so; and to induce Sir Garret Moore to accede to the request, Owen Roe assured him that, to his own knowledge, Sir Charles Coote had offered a bribe of £1000 to somebody in the garrison to betray it, and had declared that "money would not keep the place from him". What opened Moore's eyes still more to the dangers that threatened was, that he was informed of an offer made to O'Neil, apparently by a

---

[1] From the Irish word *caoraigheacht*, and signified a herd and its attendants passing through other people's lands. It included members of the aristocracy displaced in time of war, moving as a train of refugees -- landless nobles, poets or mercenary soldiers, [Clachan ed.]

person in the town, whom Moore did not know, to surrender[1] it secretly to that general. The arrival of Cromwell put a stop to these negotiations.

Sligo was not troubled from this time to May, 1651, when Sir Charles Coote summoned the Governor, Sir Garret Moore, to surrender. It is probable that this summons was only a ruse on the part of Coote,to throw Moore off his guard while the northern army was passing the place. However this may be, Moore returned a spirited and defiant answer to the summons, which must have convinced Sir Charles that he could not get Sligo without fighting for it, and thus losing time that might be more profitably employed elsewhere.

[Clachan ed.—The following is a lengthy footnote in the original.]
The following are the summons and answer: "Sir, Being come hither with the army under my command, I thought fitt before any attempt against that place under you, to desire to speake with you for prevention of effusion of Christian blood, which if you accept of, this shall be your conducte on my reputation for the freeing of you from any prejudice or violence from any under my command, either in your coming hither, or returne at your owne pleasure, which being all, I rest your servant, "CHARLES COOTE".

(Answer.) "Sir, I have receaved your letter whear you desire to speake with me before you make any attempt on this place to prevent the effusion of Christian blood. In answer to you, I make this returne, that had I found by any assurance from you an inclination in you to become a good subject, and to fall from those rebellious spirits who had a hand in the unparalleled murder of our late soveraine Charles the first, and to repent making yourself guilty thereof, in having joyned in the actors. Upon that score you may probably speake with me, with assurance that any proposal made by you shall have a safe conveyance to his Excellency the Lord Marquesse of Clanrickarde, Lord Deputy Generall of Ireland.

Without such a resolution in you, you may not expect, though tender of Christian blood as any man, any personall conference with me. As for your attempts you pretend to make, or any of your partie against this place, rest assured, by the grace of God, you shall meete an entertainment suitable to your attempt, and becoming me to give you as a person to whom is intrusted the maintaining and preserving this place by the sayd Lord Deputy for his Majesty and my countrey's use, and soe conclude,

"Sligo Fort, the 19th May, 1651,
"Your servant,
"GARRETT MOORE".
"For Sir Charles Coote, Knight and Baronett".

---

[1] These particulars are contained in a letter of Sir Garret Moore to Ormonde dated Sligo, Sept. 29, 1639 (Carte Collection, Vol. 25), in which Moore says: "Gen. O'Neil was telling me that Sir Charles Coote sent him for great newes that this place was taken by Terlagh McCafferie, and does assure me that money will not keep it from him, and that to his knowledge he offered £1000 to get it. And I am also informed that another undertook to get it for Gen. O'Neil himself, but who the betrayer should be I am ignorant of—Gen. O'Neil advised me to be very careful of this place, being of consequence. He sent an offer to Col. Acheson to send unto the town 200 men, and that upon his honour and parole he would draw them out when Col. Acheson pleased"

Coote's movements on this important occasion are thus described in a Diary of the day given in Mr. Gilbert's History of Affairs in Ireland, Part iii., p. 232: "The 17th (June), the Lord President's troops marched from Ballyshannon, within 6 miles of Sligoe, where they continued 2 daies. The 20th they passed the river of Sligoe, where they rested 5 daies, expecting the coming upp of Colonel Russell's regiment; the 26th they marched from within 2 miles of Sligoe, on the Connaught side, 2 miles further to the bridge of Killone (Collooney), . . . They found that Clanrickarde, with a considerable part of his army, had possessed the passages of the Curlews, a place of exceeding great advantage to them and disadvantage to ours; and accordingly leaving the Curlews to the left hand, they turned toward the sea, and by strange and unexpected waies by Ballaghy passe, got undiscovered into the county of Mayo".

If Sligo escaped on this occasion the tender mercies of Coote, the respite did not last long. Having gained his main object, in securing a passage for his troops into the heart of Connaught, Sir Charles kept the Irish of the province engaged, while Ireton was prosecuting the siege of Limerick, which city was surrendered to him on the 27th October, 1651, under circumstances which reflect little credit on the inhabitants. Ireton being removed by death, Coote laid siege to Galway, and obtained possession of the place on the 12th May, 1652, an event which practically closed the war. Soon after this the garrisons around Sligo gave in: Ballyshannon surrendering on the 26th May; Newtown, at the head of Lough Gill, on the 3rd June; and Ballymote, on the 24th June; and, on the 14th July, articles for the surrender of all the Connaught forces, including those of Sligo, were agreed on between Colonel Richard Coote, Major Robert Ormsby, Captain Henry Sankey, and Adjutant Charles Holcroft, by authority of Right Honorable Charles Coote, Lord President of Connaught; and Commissary John Reynolds, on the behalf of the Commonwealth of England, on the one part; and Lord Viscount Mayo, Major-General Lucas Taaffe, Colonel Garrett Moore, Colonel Hugh O'Connor, and Colonel Hugh O'Kelly, for and behalf of themselves, and behalf and by authority of Sir Ulick Bourke, Baronett, Colonel Richard Burke, Colonel William Bourke, Colonel Francis Taaffe, Colonel Donough Kelly, Captain Thomas Bourke, Captain John Bourke, Colonel Terence McDermott, Lieutenant-Colonel Donnell O'Connor, Captain John Burke, Lieutenant-Colonel Bryan O'Kelly, Colonel Teigue O'Connor Sligo, Colonel Ulick Bourke, Lieutenant-Colonel Teigue Bourke, Colonel Teige O'Kelly, Lieutenant-Colonel, Dermot O'Daly, Captain Cormuck O'Hara, Captain William Donnellan, and Captain Carbery McEgan, and in the behalf of all others comprised in these articles, and now in arms in the province of Connaught against the Parliament, of the other part.[1]

Order upon order was now issued by the Parliamentary authorities for clearing the Irish out of the towns and cities of the country; and the spirit in which those orders were carried out may be inferred from the fact that the chief actors under them regarded it as a duty of religion, no less than of self-interest, to exterminate or banish the natives, and to treat them as the Hebrews formerly treated the Hethite and the Gergezite, and the Amorrhite, and the Chanaanite, and the Pherezite, and the Hevite, and the Jebusite, taking as addressed to themselves the commands laid on the Israelites in the Book of Deuteronomy—"When the Lord shall have delivered them to thee, thou shalt utterly destroy them—. Thou shalt make no league with them, nor shew mercy to them . . . Destroy their altars, and break their statues, and cut down their groves, and burn their graven things . . . Thou shalt consume all the people, which the Lord thy God will deliver to thee".[2]

There is nothing in the Lamentations of Jeremias more touching than the accounts that have come down to us of the sufferings, at this time, of the Irish Catholics. Mr. Prendergast, who has made the subject his own, and who must continue to be the one great authority on all that relates to the Cromwellian settlement of Ireland, thus sums up these accounts, many of which are contained in official documents: "Ireland, in the language of Scripture, now lay void as a wilderness. Five-sixths of her people had perished. Women and children were found daily perishing in ditches, starved. The bodies of many wandering orphans, whose fathers had embarked for Spain, and whose mothers had died of famine, were preyed upon by wolves. In the years 1652 and 1653, the plague and famine had swept away whole countries, that a man might travel twenty or thirty miles and not see a living creature. Man, beast, and bird were all dead, or had quit those desolate places. The troopers would tell stories of the place where they saw a smoke, it was so rare to see either smoke by day, or fire or candle by night".[3] As an illustration of the thoroughness with which the work of extermination was accomplished in the towns, take the statement of Colonel Hewson, Governor of Dublin: "Though Dublin hath formerly swarmed with Papists, I know none now there, but one who is a chirurgeon[4] and a peaceable man". The example of Dublin was followed in the

---

[1] The forces of the county Roscommon, to deliver up their arms and horses at Roscommon, those of the county Sligo, at Ballymote, and those of county Galway, at Loughrea.
[2] Deuteronomy vii. 1.
[3] Cromwellian Settlement of Ireland—By John P. Prendergast, Esq., p. 139.
[4] An alchemist who studies anatomy and uses this knowledge to heal, [Clachan ed.].

provincial towns, and it is doubtful whether even one Papist, after the clearance, could be found in Sligo.

After emptying the hive —to use the metaphor of Mr. Prendergast— the authorities cast about for a new swarm; and failing to find, nearer home, people who would come and settle in Sligo, they sent invitations across the Atlantic, and, enlarging on the natural advantages of the place, prayed the sons of the Pilgrim Fathers to come and possess this commodious seaport, with considerable scopes of the neighbouring rich land. To leave them ample time to make up their mind, and to supply an additional inducement for their return, it was arranged that about two thousand acres round Sligo, including Coney and Oyster Islands, should be given to them, and should await their acceptance for twelve months; but tempting as these offers were, they were declined by the New Englanders who, no doubt, had land enough in America, and besides, like other people, thought a bird in the hand worth two in the bush. The reader will be glad to see the Order in Council regarding this matter. It is as follows: -

"Edmund Leech to be admitted tenant to the lands about Sligo.

"Upon consideration had of the petition and proposalls of Mr. Edmund Leech and others for the plantation of the towne of Sligo, and some lands thereabouts, with families out of New England:—It is ordered that the Commissioners General of the Revenue do lett unto the said Edmund Leech the lands about Sligo, commonly called the Statute Mile, and the two little islands, viz. Oyster Island and Coney Island (containing by estimation two thousand acres or thereabouts) for the use and behoof and interest of such English families as shall come from New England in America, in order to the said Transplantation for the tenure of one year from May next, upon such terms and conditions as they shall consider reasonable for the encouragement of said planters. Dublin, 10th April, 1655.—THOMAS HERBERT, Clerk to ye Council".

By the Ordinance for the Satisfaction of the Adventurers for Lands in Ireland, and the Arrears due to the Soldiery, passed on the 26th September, 1653, and declaring the war at an end, Connaught was assigned to the Irish, who were to be removed, bag and baggage, from the other provinces. At first the only part of the province reserved from the Irish was a belt of ground, four miles wide, beginning at Sligo, and stretching round the coast to Limerick, this border being intended for soldiers who should keep the transplanted to their quarters, and shut out relief by sea; but as the disbanded troops of the Commonwealth, though well provided for already, were still pressing for more land, they received, first, three miles wide of the coast belt, and, next, the whole county Sligo, with the exception, apparently, of Coolavin, of which, being in general heath and rocks, they probably would not take a present.[1]

---

[1] "The baronies of Tirera and Carbury, in Sligo, then Tirerril, Corran, and Leyney were first taken away, and set out to satisfy the disbanded. And the transplanters, who had received

In this way the population of the county was entirely changed; and while the old inhabitants the O'Connors, the MacDonoghs, some of the O'Haras, the O'Garas, the O'Harts, the O'Dowds had to fly across the sea as wild geese—the name given to those who took service in Continental armies or were shipped to Barbadoes for the sugar plantations, or were knocked on the head like wild beasts, or hid themselves in the mountains in hope of a change in the times, their lands and places were occupied by the Cootes, the Coopers, the Kings,[1] the Ormsbys, the Jones, the Griffiths, the Irwins, &c., whose descendants have since played so important a part in the affairs of the district.

---

assignments there had to gather up their flocks and herds, and with their weary and heart-broken wives and children, to begin their wanderings again". Ibid,, p, 188.

[1] Some of these would take it for an indignity to be classed with the *Omnium-gatherum* "crew", to borrow Lord Clare's word that came over with Oliver Cromwell, or followed in his wake. Even while joining against the old Irish, they had a fierce aversion to one another, the Cromwellians, *pur sang* calling the others "Tame Tories", and these retorting with the wellknown nickname of "Roundheads". A very interesting contemporary report of the "State of Ireland in 1652", given in Gilbert's History of Affairs in Ireland, Part III., pp. 354-5, tells that "the officers of Coote's armye were for the most part natives of Connaught, and estated formerly in that province". On this account they would not allow their lands to be disposed of by public auction like other lands; and when the Commissioners of the Public Revenue attempted to do so, Major King, son and heir of Sir Robert King, stepped up to them and said, "Gentlemen, I doubt it will pussle you to find a tennant for my land, for if this be a hand (holding up his hand), whoever attempts to enter on any foot that's myne, I'le send his soul to Heaven or Hell, and you shall know that having fought for liberty, and gained my freedom, I scorne to be enslaved by any mechannick amongst you; and so farewell". Major Ormsby was not less outspoken, for he cried out, "Gentlemen, if this be the justice we may expect at your hands before you be well seated in security, I'll not this year become your tenant, nor shall my sword turn plowshare".

The term "mechannick" was a flout at the low origin of Cromwell's officers and soldiers often thrown in their faces. In a paper on the "State of Ireland in 1654", among the Rinuccini MSS., and published in the 2nd volume of Spicilegium Ossoriense, p. 132, they are described as "Nec nobiles, nec honesto loco natos veleducates, sed sutores, sartores, mangones, textores, palliones, lanios, lanarios, coriarios, tabernarios, et ejusmodi sordidissimos quosque e plebis Anglicaniee foece opifices et artifices eorumque filios a Parlamento et Cromwello indutos in milites, centuriones, chi liarchos, atque alios militise duces pedestres, equestresque, deindeque urbium atque oppidorum gubernatores aliosque magistratus etiam civiles".

CHAPTER VIII

THE CROMWELLIAN SETTLEMENT OF SLIGO

THOUGH ultimately the four baronies of Carbury, Tireragh, Corran, and Tirerrill, were given up to the usurpers, it was at first intended to assign them only Carbury and Tireragh; and accordingly a commission bearing date the 10th day of January, 1655, issued forth from the Commonwealth authorities empowering Major "William Shepherd, Major John King, Captain Robert Morgan, Captain Robert Oliver, Major John Folliott, Captain Charles Holcroft, Captain Jo. Eyre, Captain John Hollshaw, Edward Crofton, and William Webb, Esq., or any three of them,

> "to sett out by lott the number of sixty-three thousand one hundred and thirty acres, thirty two perches, according to the measure of 21 feet to the perch, and 160 perches to the acre, of the lands belonging to the Commonwealth within the baronies of Tirera and Carbury in the county of Sligo, in satisfaction of thirty-one thousand five hundred sixty-four pounds two shillings arrears due to the disbanded officers and souldiers and other persons, in a schedule to the said commission annexed mentioned,[1] which commission is the same in tearms and instructions, *mutatis mutandis*, with the commission issued unto the county of Corke, for setting out of lands to the disbanded officers there, which bears date with those presents. The commission by which the said baronies were surveyed bears date the 20th September last. The barony of Carbery is the first that is to be drawn lotts for, the lotts to be published by the above-named persons 7 days before the lotts are drawn. The said William Sheaperd, John King, John Folliott, Robert Morgan, after they have taken the oath, are to administer the same to the rest".[2]

Before the introduction of the Cromwellians the Protestant population of the county Sligo was only one hundred and forty souls,[3] but after the settlement of the new comers through the county the proportion of Protestants to Catholics was considerable, 481 individuals coming in under the above commission. The Cromwellians have been often styled a Garrison; nor without reason; for any one that thinks a little on how the Tituladoes—leading Cromwellian landholders—were placed through the county Sligo, must see that the dominant idea, in the minds of those who placed them, was to secure the possession of the county, and to keep the Irish in subjection. With this object, the Tituladoes were set down on points of vantage, near the chief roads or passes, opposite fords and bridges, and in the county town. Richard Coote by the bridge of Collooney; Cornet Cooper at Markrea; William Mortimer at Lisconny; Charles Cartwright at

---

[1] The writer failed after a diligent search to find this schedule.
[2] The Commonwealth Book marked $^A/_{81}$ These Commonwealth Books are now in the Public Record Office, Dublin, having been removed there some time ago from the Bermingham Tower of Dublin Castle.
[3] John P. Prendergast in the Kilkenny Archaeological Journal, Vol. 1., p. 398.—Carte's Ormond, Vol. 1., p. 212.

Riverstown; Ralph Carter at Knockanarrow; Morgan Farrell at Carrickbanaghan; Henry Ellis at Geevagh; Henry Hughes at Ballinafad; and Edward Nicholson at Bricklieve; they commanded the fords and bridges of the Owenmore and the Uncion, and the chief places and passes of Tirerrill.

In Tireragh, with several Tituladoes in each of the parishes in Kilmackhalgan—John Bourke, Robert Hillas, William Edwards and John Irwin; in Castleconor John Nicholson and Lewis Wingfield; in Killglasse Robert Morgan, Thomas Wood, and John Moore; in Easky William Ormsby, James Ormsby, George Ormsby, and William Boswell; in Skreen Lewis Jones and Jeremy Jones; in Dromard Henry Craston (Crofton), John Irwin, and Edward Irwin; in such a situation hardly a Papist mouse could show itself without being observed by some Cromwellian eye, and immediately "squelched". Corran was similarly guarded, having John Duke, Robert Duke, John Geale, Donnell Conallan, John Clifford, Edward Hill, Henry Bierast, and John Houlder, in Kilmorgan; Francis King, and William Webb in Emlaghfad; Timothy House in Cloonoghill; Richard Meredith in Kilshalvey; and Robert King in Tumour.

In Carbury Humphrey Booth, Roland Thomas, and Henry Crawford held Sligo Town; Thomas Soden and Philip Sulevan the parish of Ahamlish; Charles Collis, Roger Parke, Thomas Griffith, Anthony Ormsby, and Thomas Osborne, Drumcliff; and William Tod, Henry Nicholson, Thomas Ormsby, and Manus Lenehan, the parish of Calry, then called Annagh.

In Leyney, owing, no doubt, to the Croftons and the chief of the O'Haras making common cause with the usurpers, there were only three Tituladoes—Edmund Wood, living at Moineagh, Edmund Pole at Magherenoir, and Thomas Rosevill at Tullyhugh.

And in the half Barony of Coolavin, most of which was already held by the Kings of Boyle, there was fixed only one Titulado, Henry Tifford of Kilfree.

Cantoned thus through the length and breadth of the county; occupying all the castles and strong strategic positions; placed within easy reach of each other, so as to be able, in case of need, to afford mutual assistance; with arms in their hands; and with all the forces of the Government at their back; the Cromwellians, in order to enjoy and improve their good fortune, had only to keep down the natives, a service for which they felt a peculiar relish.

Most of the usurpers came over with Cromwell in 1649, and were the Cromwellians *pur sang*, but some of them lived in the country before Oliver landed, as the Cootes and Coopers, Kings and Croftons, and bear the name of Cromwellians only inasmuch as they took service or office under the Protector. There must have been some variety of character in individual Cromwellians, as there, is in every other collection of human beings, but the body or species, at least of Cromwell's own troopers, had certain well marked characteristics, more especially contempt of the Irish people and hatred of the Catholic religion, peculiarities which many of them have transmitted, little changed, to those that came after them, so that while the families of the English who came over in the days of Elizabeth and James, or earlier, have generally fraternized with the Irish around them, some of them becoming "more Irish than the Irish themselves", the descendants of the Tituladoes have commonly shown themselves as anti-Irish and anti-Catholic as their forefathers could have been at the time they first settled in the country. Of course they cannot now act, and, to do them justice, show no inclination to act, towards an Irish Catholic after the fashion of two centuries ago, when their ancestors might horsewhip him or even shoot him with impunity; but it is to be feared, that some of them still regard the poor Papist as little better than a pariah or a leper, and shun him accordingly.

Long before Captain Boycott's name furnished a new designation for certain unsocial proceedings, the proceedings themselves were invented and practised by the descendants of Cromwell's soldiers and officers against the descendants of the old Irish. To isolate, to exclude from benefits open to others, to set the mark of Cain upon the brow, and to treat as an alien or an enemy; this is boycotting, and this is what many of the Cromwellians have been doing, as far as they could, in regard to the Catholic Irish, and what some of them continue, openly, or underhand, still to do. If they have lands to let, if they have employment to give, if they have patronage to bestow, if they have distinctions or benefits of any kind to confer, no Catholic has any business to apply so long as there are any of their own co-religionists within reach. Proofs of these assertions are everywhere under the eye: on their estates, where every farm or house worth having is in the possession of non-Catholics; in their mansions, where all the situations, from that of steward to that of scullery maid, are similarly filled; in their demesnes, where land stewards, foresters, game keepers, gate keepers, are all of the favoured religion; and in public offices, such as those of Dispensary doctors, County cess collectors, Petty Sessions clerks, and others, of which they have the patronage, and which they seldom or never help a Catholic to obtain, except in the absence of other applicants. To such lengths is this unsocial exclusiveness carried, that some landlords and agents scruple not to violate Acts of Parliament, in the spirit, if not in the letter, in order to exclude Catholics from the benefits which the laws of the land have opened to them. To give an instance: the Land Act of 1881 gives the tenant a right to sell his interest in his holding, but the landlord overrules the provision of the law, and practically annuls the legal right of the tenant, by compelling him to pass the farm to some Protestant nominee, as might be shown by several recent occurrences through the county.

In truth the spirit of some of them is that which Adam Loftus expresses in a famous letter, where he writes: "I have indited of treason all the noblemen, gentlemen, and freeholders, in the counties of Dublin, Meath, Kildare and Wicklow, which, I hope, will be a great advantage to the Crown, and good to this poor Kingdom, when these rascals shall be confounded and honest Protestants planted in their places".

It is unpleasant to have to animadvert on such doings, but to pass them over in silence would be to suppress interesting facts which not only throw important light on the actual state of the country, but must influence its political and social condition for some time to come, as the Irish people are now in a mood to resent these proceedings as long as they last, and, if things be carried too far, to engage, by way of retaliation, in a struggle *a outrance*,[1] in which either they or the landlords must go to the wall. And the writer can hardly be blamed for noticing the exceptional hostility of Cromwellians to everything Catholic and Irish, as a recent writer, who in religion, political principles, and feelings, is one of themselves, thus refers to the subject:—"Colony after colony of Englishmen have come over to this country from time to time, but we have had no body of settlers possessed of such hostility to the native Irish as the Parliamentary soldiery. From whatever cause this may have arisen, it has existed *and exists still*".[2]

Most of the Cromwellian families have disappeared from the county, and, among them, those that had the name of being particularly hostile to the people and to the people's religion. The first Lord Collooney, Richard Coote, who is said in Gilbert's *Aphorismical Discovery of Treasonable Faction*, to have burned at Trim a venerated religious relic of the place, the famous statue of the Blessed Virgin, has now no descendant in the county.[3] Charles Collis of Castlegal, whom local tradition or gossip represents as having a gallows at Collisford, erroneously called Collinsford, on the Drumcliff river, for hanging the political suspects of the neighbourhood, is no longer

---

[1] To the limit, [Clachan ed.].
[2] History of Bandon By George Bennett, Esq., B.L., pp. 189-190.
[3] "Sir Charles Coote, Blond-sucker, having reached Trim, and the weather being very cold, his son Richard, afterwards Lord Collooney, cut up a wooden statue of the Blessed Virgin, and made a fire of it for his father, which Sir Charles never enjoyed, for before he could place himself before it, word was brought that the Irish had already entered the town. On receiving the news he called his men to arms, and sallied forth to meet the enemy, but a ball either of a friend or a foe—for it is not known of which put an end to his stormy career. The body was conveyed to Dublin amid the execrations of the Irish, and there interred with the epitaph, "England's honour, Scotland's wonder, Ireland's terror, here lies under".

represented in the place by any one of his name or lineage.[1] The Joneses of Tireragh, so numerous once in the barony that you met them at every turn of the road; so powerful that they could do in the district just as they liked; and so anti-Catholic that they tried to get up a little Popish Plot of their own in the county in 1678, when Titus Gates and his coadjutors were operating in England, are now so extinct, that a Jones is as much a *rara avis* in Tireragh, as the eagle which, a couple of hundred years ago, used to haunt the Ox Mountains there, and swoop down occasionally on the lands and barn door fowl of the neighbourhood. It is much the same in the other baronies, so that of the sixty Titulado families, quartered on the county Sligo under the Commonwealth, there remain only four or five, these being, it is to be believed, of the better or milder type of the species, and therefore coming down to us, probably, in accordance with Darwin's law of the "survival of the fittest".

The chief work the Cromwellians undertook in the town of Sligo was the erection of a new fort. The old castle of Sligo which Hugh Roe O'Donnell demolished in 1595 (under circumstances described graphically by the Four Masters at that date, lest it should fall into the hands of the English) was never repaired, though Elizabeth desired its restoration; for, in articles propounded through Commissioners by the Queen to O'Donnell, it was proposed that "he should re-edify the castle;" but he excused himself by submitting that, what he did, he did from necessity, and that, as the castle was his own, the loss of it fell upon himself, adding, however, that in any case, he was not able to undertake so expensive a work.[2] One of the duties too laid on Essex, when in Ireland, was to erect an impregnable castle at Sligo "as a constant defence against the Ulstermen;"[3] but the result of the battle of the Curlews prevented the execution of this project, and the matter was not resumed from that time to the time of Cromwell.

Seeing then there was no strong place to retire to, in case of an attack, which there was still ground for apprehending, the Cromwellians set about providing such a fortress. The rising ground, through which Quay Street now passes, was the site selected, which was a very suitable one, as it commanded the town sufficiently, and adjoined the sea, on which they relied for succour in case danger arose. It is supposed that the town-hall stands on the exact spot formerly occupied by the fort; but this is not quite

---

[1] The last of them, Farrel Collis, was living at Knockroe, near Collooney, towards the end of the last century. Doctor Collis, of Stephen's Green, descends from William Collis, elder brother of Charles.—Information acquired in Sir Bernard Burke's office.

Charles Collis died in 1685, and Robert, his fourth son, married Jane, daughter of Thomas Jones of Cargin. Charles Collis resided at Magheramore, in Drumcliff.

[2] Carew MSS., Vol. 1589-1605, p. 162.

[3] Annals of the Four Masters, 1599.

so; for it occupied as well a part of the grounds of the college on the west side of the street. If Cromwell's troopers know anything now of what passes in Sligo, it is enough to make them gnash their teeth in the grave, to think that those Popish priests, whom they thought they had exterminated, are now their successors in the occupation of the hill, and that the Mass, which was not to be allowed wherever the Parliament of England had power, is now practised more frequently in the heart of their stronghold than in any other spot of the county.[1] The plan of the fort, which was a small one, was a square with four bulwarks or bastions, one at each angle. The bulwarks were carried to their full height, whatever that may have been, which is not recorded, but as they were built hollow, and were not filled with earth, they could afford little accommodation to either men or cannon; but the curtain walls connecting the bastions were only about 10 feet high when the works were stopped. The interior was left in a still more unfinished state than the outer walls, as it contained nothing but the foundations of some buildings which were intended to serve as lodgings for the men, and stables for the horses, of the garrison. Such was the state in which its builders left the New Fort of Sligo.

Without claiming great credit for the discovery, it may be mentioned that this is the first time the origin of the fortress has been given in print. Major Wood Martin, finding mention of it in books, and fancying, apparently, that it dropped down from the clouds, ready made, like the Palladium, talks of it as "old", as "old and crumbling", as "in utter ruin", though he might have learned, even from his Harris, that it was "finished" for the first time only in 1689, and from other quarters, that the body of the work was built only about thirty years previous.

The royalists after the Restoration, regarded this legacy of the Ironsides as the proverbial white elephant, and were at a loss to know what to do with it. From a letter of Lord Kingston to the Duke of Ormonde, it would appear that his Grace was for demolishing it, and it was probably this letter of Lord Kingston that saved it from destruction.[2] A report of Sir Albert Conyngham, drawn up some months before Kingston wrote,

---

[1] "If by liberty of conscience you mean a liberty to exercise the Mass, I judge it best to use plain dealing, and let you know, where the Parliament of England have power, that will not be allowed of". Letter from Oliver Cromwell to the Governor of Ross.—Cromwell in Ireland (page 186), by the Reverend Denis Murphy, S.J. With Map, Plans, and Illustrations. Whoever would acquire a full and correct knowledge of Cromwell's movements and proceedings in Ireland must read and re-read this sober and scholarly volume.

[2] "I should not desire this from your Grace, if I durst adventure upon demolishing either of the two forts of Belamoe or Sligo, until I had attended your Grace and discoursed more particularly on them than 'tis possible for me to do by letter, and perhaps your Grace will think fit to advise with others before you admit the pulling down of 2 forts which (though very imperfect), cost, at least, 4000 the erecting. Boyle, June 15, 1666".

contributed, no doubt, to this result; for, being appointed by the Master of the Ordnance, Sir Robert Byron, to visit the forts of Sligo and Athlone, and to report upon them, he suggested, rather than recommended, that this fort should be preserved and completed, as well because it had already cost a large sum, as also because the situation, so far from the garrisons of Boyle on the one side, and of Londonderry and Enniskillen on the other, needed such a fortress. This report, being the writer's chief authority for what is here stated, and being, besides, very interesting in itself, is given below.

[Clachan ed.—The following is the content of the extensive footnote that follows.]

The first part of report regards Athlone. The writer next goes on to say:—"This day I reviewed this fort very diligently. It is a small square fort erected by the Usurpers. It hath foure small bulwarks regular enough. The bulwarks were finished to their full height, but not filled up with earth, soe that men cannot stand to doe any service in them, neither can any gunns be placed uppon them untill the bulwarks be made fitt for service. As for the 4 curtains, they were never brought to any competent height, but remain unfinished, so that it may be scaled everywhere uppon the curtains with ladders no longer than 8 or 10 feet.

"As for the lodgings within, there are only some foundations, and all that is at present is only a little hutt or shade intended for a stable, which is their guardhouse, and another little cabin where the store is, which is all undone with wett, which has come in upon it. I have made choice of place most convenient to place the 4 guns which are appointed o be mounted there. The situation of this fort is upon a river, which is navigable to the fort and no further, for under the fort is a bridge, which is the usual thoroughfare from Ulster to Connaught. This river comes out of a logh, which boarders upon the county of Leitrim, and is not fordable but in summer, neere this bridge, so that Dudley Costello with his party passed at this foorde neere the bridge about a fortnight since to goe into the county Mayo from Leitrim. The situation of this place makes it very considerable, for on the Ulster side there are no garrisons nearer to it than Inniskillen and Londonderry, which are very remote, and on the Connaught side none nearer that the Boile, which is only a horse quarter, and hath nothing of a strength. This place had an old castle in the time of warre, which proved of great consequence to any party that had it, for whosoever hath Sligo in likelyhood will have the whole country under obedience. If it should be thought fitt to finish this fort, there is a good quantity of oake timber ready, which was provided for it, and would be a great helpe for to build lodgings for a governor and garrison. There was 2500 employed in the work already by the Usurpers, and in my judgment it would require 1000 yet to finish and complete it as intended. The sending of thig is committed to Capt. Montgomerie, Lieutenant of the Ordnance to the Master". "Sligo, Sept. 6, 1666".

Probably the most striking immediate effect produced in Sligo by the Restoration was the stoppage of the works at the New Fort; for, in other respects, things were allowed to go on much as they had been going, under the recent regime. As the disbanded officers and soldiers held a firm grip of their possessions in the town and county, and as they had, besides, arms in their hands, which they were no way loth to use upon occasion; the public authorities of that day entertained no desire to meddle in any way with them, and, the more especially, as those authorities themselves were

Cromwellian in all their antecedents and sympathies. Lord Mountrath (late Sir Charles Coote), and Lord Orrery (late Lord Broghill), were Lords Justices of Ireland; two men as hostile to the old Catholics of the country, and as friendly to the new inhabitants, as any other two men in existence; and Mountrath's brother, Lord Collooney, whose personal status and fortune were wound up with the continuance of the existing state of things, exercised, under the central government, the chief power and command in the county Sligo. With such "friends in court" the Usurpers of Sligo seemed as secure in their estates and lands as the king was on his throne. And if the issue lay exclusively between them and the old Irish, they would not be incommoded; but claims were soon put forth by others, who had better backing at court than even the Cootes and their confederates; and these claims were decided in a way which affected seriously the interests of not a few of the newcomers.

The claimants on this occasion were William Earl of Strafford, and Thomas Radcliffe, Esq., sons and heirs, respectively, of Thomas Earl of Strafford, and Sir George Radcliffe. We learn from the Act of Explanation, if we can rely entirely upon that authority, that Teige O'Connor Sligo, in or about the year 1636, sold the O'Connor Sligo estate, extending, even then, over most of the county, to Thomas Earl of Strafford and Sir George Radcliffe, through Sir Philip Percival, who represented the purchasers on the occasion. At this time Strafford had the country in a welter by his violent efforts to establish the King's title to Connaught; and it throws new light on that statesman's character to learn that, while thus occupied, he could find time and means to secure a good slice of the province for himself.

As he and Sir George got Sir Philip Percival to act for them, it would appear they wanted to avoid figuring themselves in the transaction, through fear, apparently, that their personal intervention would bring some doubt on that single-minded devotion to the royal interests, which each of them professed to feel.

The whole matter must have been managed with remarkable secrecy, for there is not a word about it in any of the publications of the time; neither is there the slightest reference to it in the two folio volumes of Strafford's Letters, nor in the Life and Original Correspondence of Sir George Radcliffe.

If other authorities are silent on the transaction, the Act of Parliament devotes several clauses to it, one of which runs thus: "Whereas Sir Philip Percival, Knight, deceased, for and on behalf of Thomas, late Earl of Strafford, and Sir George Radcliffe, Knight, deceased, and their heirs, in or about the year 1636, did contract and agree with Teige O'Connor Sligoe, uncle and heir in taile to Donogh O'Connor Sligoe, then lately deceased, and also with Edmond MacJordan and Dorothy, his wife, sole sister and heir-general to the said Donogh, for divers lordships, manors, castles, lands, tenements, and hereditaments, in the county of Sligoe, being formerly the estate of the said Douogh O'Connor Sligoe .... be it therefore enacted that all and singular the said lordships formerly belonging to the said Donogh O'Connor Sligoe, and the said Teige O'Connor Sligoe, or to either of them, shall and are hereby settled upon William Earl of Strafford, son and heir of the said Thomas Earl of Strafford, and Thomas Radcliffe, Esq., son and heir of the said Sir George Radcliffe; and that they be forthwith settled in possession by the Commissioners appointed to the execution of this Act". Only that the Statute Book is so clear and express, there would be ground for doubting the reality of the sale; for one would think, if Teige O'Connor Sligoe sold the estate, as alleged, that it should have passed soon after into the possession of the buyers; whereas it had not changed hands so late as 1641, as O'Connor Sligo is given in the Down Survey Book of Distributions as owner, at that date, of the lands concerned in the sale.

And it must look somewhat strange and suspicious that the purchasers and their representatives waited for Teige O'Connor's death before trying to make good their claim; though the explanation of the delay may probably be found in the weighty and engrossing public occupations of Strafford and Radcliffe up to 1641, and the troubles and changes of Government from that time to the Restoration in 1660. Anyhow, more light is needed to satisfy the mind on the particulars of the negotiations between Teige O'Connor Sligo and Sir Philip Percival.

As it was, neither the O'Connors nor the Cromwellians relinquished their pretensions without a struggle; for we learn from the Act of Explanation, that William Earl of Strafford, Thomas Radcliffe, Esq., and Sir John Percival, had to institute a suit for possession before the Lord Lieutenant and Council of Ireland against Martin O'Connor, grandson and heir of Teige O'Connor Sligoe, deceased, Richard Lord Baron of Collooney, and others: Lord Collooney and the "others", representing the Usurpers, settled on the estate by the Commonwealth. The decision was in favour of the plaintiffs, and, in conformity with it, the estate was settled on William Earl of Strafford, and Thomas Radcliffe.

The O'Connors and Cromwellians being thus disposed of and the way being now quite clear, Charles II. made a formal grant of the lands in question to William Earl of Strafford, and Thomas Radcliffe, Esq., who had procured a certificate of their claims from the Commissioners appointed for executing the Acts of Settlement and Explanation, namely, Sir Edward Smith, Chief Justice of the Common Pleas, Sir Edward Denny, Baronet, Sir Allen Broderick, Sir Winston Churchill, and Edward Cooke, Esq., so that now the grantees held the estate by Act of Parliament, by royal grant, and, supposing their own story true, by lawful purchase. It was a matter of course that the King should be glad to help these two men, as their fathers had laboured and suffered so much for the royal cause. Strafford lost his head for Charles I.; and Radcliffe, after narrowly escaping the same fate, spent the remaining years of his life in the service, on the Continent, of Charles' two sons—afterwards Charles II. and James II. —and devoted himself so zealously, even in sickness, to that service, that his biographer writes of him, "With one side torpid and half dead, this faithful exile continued to the last actively employed in providing for his master's present wants, and promoting his Restoration".[1] Sir George died in 1657, and the straits to which he was reduced before death may be seen in those touching lines, written by him in 1656, "I am now labouring to get credit for a suit of clothes, which is more than I have made these five years, and now my old frippery grows thin".

To understand how Strafford and Sir George came to be so united in friendship, we must recollect that they were family connections, Radcliffe being married to the Earl of Stratford's cousin, Anne Trappes, daughter of Sir Francis Trappes; and the union was probably strengthened by their pursuing the same devious course in politics; for both began public life as "advanced" patriots, but soon turning the back on the popular party, ended as devoted courtiers. When Strafford came to Ireland in 1633, as Lord Lieutenant, resolved to bend everybody and everything to the royal will, he felt the need of able and trusted co-operators, and induced the King to appoint Sir George Radcliffe Chief Secretary, and Christopher Wandesford, another relation, Master of the Rolls. While Strafford was the head that devised the bold measures of the Government, these two officials were the hands that carried the measures into effect.

His private affairs, too, Strafford left, all through life, to their management; and at his death he made them the executors of his will, and the guardians of his son; the words of the will being,—"I make my beloved friends, Christopher Wandesford and Sir George Radcliffe, Knight, mine Executors of this will .... I commend the care of the education and government of my son to my said Executors". The sons of the Lord Lieutenant and Chief Secretary were very different men from their fathers. While Stafford's genius towered above that of all his contemporaries, and Sir George Radcliffe was little, if at all, inferior, to the chief statesmen around him, Lord William Strafford and Thomas Radcliffe were as commonplace persons as could be easily found in any class, and had little to boast of, except that they were the sons of their distinguished fathers, and the inheritors of large estates and possessions. This is more especially true of Radcliffe, who was so good-for-nothing and weak-minded that he

---

[1] The Life and Original Correspondence of Sir George Radcliffe, Knight, LL.D.; the Friend of the Earl of Strafford. By Thomas Dunham Whitaker, LL.D., F.S.A., p. 288.

put himself very much in the hands of a cunning servant named Wilson, to whom he even bequeathed by will the half of the Sligo estate, leaving the other half to an aunt, Margaret Trappes.[1] It may be mentioned, in passing, that Mary Trappes, sister of Margaret, was married to Charles Townly of Townly Hall, Lancashire, a name not unknown in connection with the modern politics of Sligo.

[Clachan ed.—The following is the content of the extensive footnote that follows.]

> It throws light on the character of monuments and epitaphs that, while the eminent Sir George Radcliffe has neither the one nor the other to perpetuate his memory, his worthless son is honoured to this day with a monument in the parish church of Thornhill, England, to which his remains were removed from Dublin for interment, and with the following eulogistic epitaph:—"M.S.his memory, his worthless son is honoured to this day with a monument in the parish church of Thornhill, England, to which his remains were removed from Dublin for interment, and with the following eulogistic epitaph:
> "M.S.
> Thomae Radcliffe, Arm.
> Qui ex illustri Radcliviorum familia ortus,
> Georgii Militis et Annae Traps filius,
> Candida mente et felicissima indole imbutus,
> Variis artibus et scientiis ornatus,
> Et mirabili morum suavitate praeditus,
> Postquam per plurimos annos exul,
> Exulis Regis sui causa,
> Regiones exteras peragraverat;
> Tandem post reducem Regem
> In Hiberniam se contulit;
> Regique ibidem a sacris conciliis inserviens,
> Secundis rebus non magis elatus
> Quam antehac adversis depressus
> Pietate, temperantia, probitate, caeterisque virtutibus
> Adeo inclaruit,
> Ut non eget fucosis laudibus,
> Nec hoc monumento,
> Ad famam ejus perpetuandam:
> Memoria quippe justi manet in aeternum,
> XIII. Kal. Julii MDCXXIII. in agro Eboracensi natus,
> III. Kal. Nov. MDCLXXIX. Dublinii denatus,
> Unica familes suae spes improles et coelebs
> Hic et in mille amicorum pectoribus
> Reconditus jacet;
> Cui Margareta Traps matertera et Joshua Wilson domesticus
> Haeredes ex asse instituti,
> Hoc qualecunque gratitudinis
> Quam memoriae monumentum,
> Suis sumptibus erigi curarunt".

The death of Thomas Radcliffe in 1679 led to radical changes in the conditions of holding the estate. Up to that event the property was held in common by Lord Strafford and Radcliffe, and they received each an equal share of the rents and revenues of the whole; but now the estate was divided so as to give a separate share to each of the present owners, Lord William Strafford, Joshua Wilson, and John Leslie, Esq., D.D., to the last of whom Margaret Trappes had sold her share and interest. The division or partition was effected by a tripartite deed made on the 21st July, 1687, between the Right Honourable William Earl of Strafford, of the first part; the Rev. John Leslie, Doctor of Divinity, of the second part; and Joshua Wilson, of the city of Dublin, gentleman, of the third part. As Lord Strafford was entitled to half of the whole estate, and Dr. Leslie and Joshua Wilson to a fourth part each, the indenture, after reciting all the lands, tenements, and hereditaments, to be disposed of the manor, town, and lands of Sligo; various scopes of land in Carbury, Tirerrill, Corran, Leyney, Tireragh, and Coolavin; the rectories of Ahamlish, Aughriss, Dromard, Templeboy, and Kilmacshalgan; yearly rents and chiefries coming and payable out of several quarters of land lying, up and down, through the county; the abbey, abbey quarter, and abbey lands of Sligo, as held by Lord Taaffe on the 27th June, 1638; the yearly fairs and weekly markets of Sligo, and the tolls, profits and customs thereof proceeds thus:—"And whereas the said William, Earl of Strafford, the said Doctor John Leslie, and Joshua Wilson, have come by agreement to a full and perfect partition and division of the said lands into two moieties, the one moiety thereof to be enjoyed by the said William Earl of Strafford and his heirs, and the other moiety thereof to be enjoyed by the said Doctor John Leslie, Joshua Wilson, and their respective heirs. And whereas the said Doctor John Leslie and Joshua Wilson have also, by agreement, come to a full and perfect partition and division of their moieties of the said lands, the one half of the said moiety, that is to say, one-fourth part of the said whole lands and premises to be enjoyed by the said Doctor John Leslie and his heirs, and the other half of the said moiety, that is to say, one-fourth part of the said whole lands and premises, to be enjoyed by the said Joshua Wilson and his heirs, by which said partition and agreement all the lands, tenements, and hereditaments mentioned in the first schedule hereunto annexed, are come and fallen to the share of said William Earl of Strafford, to be held and enjoyed by him and his heirs, as his and their full moiety of all and singular the premises, and by the said partition and agreement all the lands, tenements, and hereditaments mentioned in the second schedule hereunto annexed, are come and fallen to the said Doctor John Leslie, to be held by him and his heirs, as his and their full fourth part of all and singular the premises; and by the said partition and agreement all the lands, tenements, and hereditaments, in the third schedule hereunto annexed are come and fallen to the said Joshua Wilson to be held and enjoyed by him and his heirs as his and their full fourth part of all and singular the premises. Now this indenture witnesseth, that it is hereby concluded and agreed on by and between the said parties . . . that the said partition and division made of the said lands, tenements, and hereditaments and premises, shall for ever hereafter stand good, firm, and effectual, and shall be binding to all the said parties, their heirs and assigns respectively".

The indenture next arranges for certain money payments by the parties between themselves, so as to conform still better the shares to the respective claims, it being impossible to distribute the lands, tenements, and hereditaments, so nicely as to meet the exact requirements of the case. Any inequality found to exist was adjusted by him, who had more than his right, making up for it in money to him who had less.

A monopoly in milling was left and secured to Lord Strafford:—
"And the said John Leslie and Joshua Wilson, severally and respectively for them and their several heirs and assigns . . . do hereby covenant and grant to and with the said William Earl of Strafford, his heirs and assigns, that no mills of any kind shall hereafter at any time be built on the north or south side of River Garvagh, and that all persons whatever on their respective lands in the parishes of St. John's, Kilmacowen, and Killaspickbrone, called Cullurin, and in the town of Sligo, and the quarter of Rath, shall be obliged to grind all their corn at Sligo mills, that are now built, or shall hereafter be built, and also to tuck all their cloth at such tuck mill or mills as shall hereafter be built by the said William Earl of Strafford, his heirs, tenant or tenants, or assigns, except those who are already obliged to the mills of Rathbroghan, they having their corn and cloath as well ground and tucked at the said mills, and at as reasonable rates as in any other mills near adjacent thereunto, provided the said mill or mills be in repair, and do not want water, and that each person have his turn as is usually accustomed".

And, in conclusion, the contracting parties thus provide for any omissions which may be found in the indenture: "And it is lastly agreed by and between the said parties that all lands, tenements, hereditaments, houses, gardens, waste plots, profits, chiefries[1], franchises, privileges, and advantages belonging to the said William Earl of Strafford, Doctor John Leslie, and Joshua Wilson, as tenants in common, that are omitted out of the schedules hereunto annexed, and whereof no partition or division is hereby made between the said parties, shall be still held and enjoyed by them as tenants in common, according to their several and respective interests therein, that is to say, one moiety thereof by William Earl of Strafford, his heirs and assigns, and one-fourth part thereof by the said John Leslie, his heirs and assigns, until a further partition and division shall be made of all such omitted parcels between the said parties. In witness thereof the parties to these presents interchangeably have set their hands and seals, the day and year first above written."—(21st July, 3 Jacobi II.)

---

[1] A small rent paid to the lord paramount, [Clachan ed.].

To this deed are annexed three schedules, one for each of the portions unto which the estate was divided; and as these schedules record all the denominations of lands then on the estate, the extent in acres, roods, and perches, of these denominations, and the names of the persons possessing them, they throw a flood of light on the state of the county, at the period to which they refer, and will therefore, if possible, be given in the Appendix[1].

To complete what has been said regarding the connection of the Straffords with Sligo, it will be convenient to state here that upon the death of Earl William, his estate in Sligo passed by sale out of the family. As in the partition we have been considering, so also in the transaction under consideration the transfer was effected by a tripartite indenture, the parties to the present deed being three trustees under the Earl's will, namely, Doctor William Spenser, Rector of Thurnscoe, in England, James Grenelagh, of Wentworth Woodhouse, and Abraham Nixon, of Coolattin, in county Wicklow, of the first part; the Honourable Thomas Wentworth alias Watson, of the second part; and Benjamin Burton, of the city of Dublin, merchant, of the third part. The will of the late Earl, under which the sale was effected, is dated 9th September, 1695, and the deed of sale itself the 24th day of August, 1697. The deed was confirmed by a decree of the courts issued 10th February, 1697,[2] and running thus: "That the agreement made between the plaintiff Wentworth, and the plaintiff Burton, for sale of the Manor of Sligoe, in the county Sligoe, part of the estate of the late Earl of Strafford is according to the true intent and meaning of the said Earl's will, and that the deed perfected by the defendants, Spenser, &c., trustees under said will, pursuant to such agreement, be confirmed to all intents and purposes. It is likewise ordered that the sum of £10,780, which was paid by the plaintiff Burton, upon the perfection of said deed, be applied towards the discharge of the legacies bequeathed by the said Earl's will, and the incumbrances on said estate". The Thomas Wentworth, or Watson, I mentioned in these documents, was the son of Lady Anne Wentworth, eldest daughter of the Earl of Strafford. She married Edward Watson, Lord Buckingham, and, in this way, the unsettled Strafford estates in England and Ireland passed, first, to the Earls of Rockingham, and next, to the Earls Fitzwilliam, to whom they belong at present. Benjamin Burton, the purchaser of the property, was the third son of Samuel Burton, high

---

[1] Appendices appear in Vol. II, [Clachan ed.

[2] Repertory to Decrees in Record Office, Dublin: The following receipt was given for the money paid, "Received from Benjamin Burton, merchant, the sum of 10,780 sterling, being the full consideration for the within-mentioned purchase. In witness whereof we have hereunto put our hands this 24th day of August, 1697.

"WILLIAM SPENCER, JAMES GRENELAGH, ABRAHAM NIXON".

sheriff of Clare, and grandson of Thomas Burton, who, with a brother, Francis, settled in Ireland in 1610, at Buncraggy, in the county of Clare. Benjamin, being the youngest son of Samuel, devoted himself to commercial pursuits, amassed a large fortune as merchant and banker in Dublin, became Lord Mayor of the city, and served for several years as its representative in Parliament. His family is now represented by the Burtons of Burton Hall, Carlow, the Burtons of Carrigaholt Castle, county Clare, and the noble house of Conyngham, Mount Charles, county Donegal. The estate he bought from the representatives of Lord Strafford, and, particularly, the Sligotown portion of it, is still known and spoken of as the "Burton Property".

The writer, not satisfied with the references to the transfer of the O'Connor Sligo estate, which are contained in the Acts of Settlement and Explanation, set himself to search for further information, and, after searching in vain, in the Public Record Office, Trinity College, and the Dublin Library, had the good fortune to fall in at last with documents which throw great light on the matter in hand. These documents he found, with a vast number of others, in seven folio volumes, which are concerned with the Acts of Settlement and Explanation, and which still remain in the Birmingham Tower of Dublin Castle, though nearly all the other ancient muniments[1] of that famous depository have been transferred within the last few years to the Public Record Office in the Four Courts. The papers that regard the Sligo property are voluminous, extending over more than a score of *closely written folio pages*, so that a summary of their contents is all that can be given here.

Wheresoever the body shall be, there shall the eagles also be gathered together, says the Gospel, and the fallen inheritance of the O'Connors Sligo attracted various birds of prey from all sides.

> First. —The so-called "Forty-nine officers" prayed the king not to grant away the estate till they were allowed an opportunity of stating their own claims upon it.
> Second. —Lord Collooney, Sir Francis Gore, and Erasmus Smith, on behalf of themselves, and of "100 Protestant families of Adventurers and Souldiers", that got possession of it from the Commonwealth authorities in 1659, petitioned the King not to accede to the application of Lord William Strafford and Thomas Radcliffe for a clause in the Act of Settlement to ratify the purchase or pretended purchase of their fathers.
> Third. —The Countess of Mountrath and her children appeared by attorney, and alleged rights derived from the late Earl of Mountrath.
> Fourth. —Patrick French, as a mortgagee, petitioned the King to safeguard his rights.

These petitions gave rise to counter petitions, and the conflict continued while the Bills of Settlement and Explanation were in preparation.

---

[1] Supporting documents, [Clachan ed.].

The King referred all the documents to the Solicitor General, who drew up a long and detailed Report of the whole case, and from this document it appears: first, that Donogh O'Connor, at his death in 1634 without issue, left the property encumbered with the jointures of Lady Sarah McDonnell, Lady Desmond, and Lady Cressy, and with several mortgages; second, that Teige O'Connor, the uncle and heir of Donogh, sold the estate to Sir Philip Perceval in trust for Lord Thomas Strafford and Sir George Radcliffe, who obtained actual possession of some of it; third, that, according to the conditions of the sale, the purchasers should pay off all the incumbrances, and that Teige should receive back 3,000 acres free and unencumbered; fourth, that the case gave rise to litigation before the Lord Lieutenant and Privy Council, which lasted for three days; and fifth, that Teige O'Connor, the seller, died before 1641, and that Teige his son, owing to the part he took in the insurrection of that year, forfeited all claim to the 3,000 acres, which, in effect, were divided between Sir Francis Gore and Captain Robert Parke, according to the proportions of the adjoining lands that each already held.

Martin O'Connor is mentioned in these proceedings as "a petitioner", but it would appear that the name was used without his consent, for he did not appear or "put in an answer;" though "the heirs and assigns "of Teige O'Connor were ordered by the Council on the 6th October, 1662, to make answer. When he found his claims prejudged, owing to the rebellion imputed to his father and the consequent forfeiture, he declined to interfere, feeling that the proceedings, as far as he was concerned, were only a farce. It is a pity there is no record of his view of the case; for, seeing the iniquity of the times, one cannot help thinking that the unfortunate O'Connors Sligo were swindled out of their immense estates. The outcome of these transactions was the insertion of one clause in the Act of Settlement, and of six clauses in the Act of Explanation, bearing upon the O'Connor Sligo estate. The clause in Act of Settlement (ccxxiii.) enacts that the lands in Sligo, purchased in trust for Lord Thomas Strafford and Sir George Radcliffe, shall be vested in the King, until the Chief Governor and Council adjudge to whom they belong, upon hearing of the persons concerned, and that the judgment shall have the force of law.

The clauses of the Act of Explanation, which refer to this matter, are those marked ccix., ccx., ccxi., ccxii., ccxiii., ccxiv. The clause ccix. recites that Sir Philip Perceval, on behalf of Lord Strafford and Sir George Radcliffe, purchased lands about the year 1636, from Teige O'Connor Sligo.

Clause ccx.   provides, that all depositions taken in a case lately before the Lord Deputy and Council may be made use of as proofs in this matter.

Clause ccxi.   orders Strafford and Radcliffe to pay within six months the money due to incumbrancers by Teige O'Connor.

Clause ccxii.   enacts, that the Adventurers and the Commissioned Officers who served the King in Ireland before the 5th June, 1649, now in possession and to be removed, shall have so much of other forfeited lands set out to them as may be sufficient to reprise and satisfy them for two full third parts of the lands whence they are to be removed.

Clause ccxiii.   provides, that the lands of Bradcullen (Castletown) and other lands, which were to be settled on Teige O'Connor, shall not be settled on Lord Strafford and Thomas Radcliffe, but shall be disposed of to Sir F. Gore and Captain Robt. Parke according to the several proportions which they possess.

Clause ccxiv. runs thus: Whereas, Sir Philip Perceval and Sir George Radcliffe, or one of them, did, in like manner, purchase some other parcels of lands, tenements, and hereditaments in the said county Sligo from several other persons, Lord William Strafford and Thomas Radcliffe shall be restored to all the rights in law and equity of their fathers to the said lands, tenements, and hereditaments the adventurers, soldiers, and commissioned officers now in possession to be reprised.

These enactments, and the consequent transfer of the estate, caused several adventurers, soldiers, and commissioned officers, to remove from the county Sligo, but there is good reason to believe that a majority of them held their ground, and, acting on Mr. Parnell's principle, long before Mr. Parnell's time, "kept a grip" of their lands, and found possession to be more than the proverbial "nine parts of the law". At this date the proud name of O'Connor Sligo drops out of view; nor is there henceforth any written evidence to attest the condition of the family or its genealogical succession, so that history, strictly so called, can give no help towards identifying its present representative. Pedigrees are generally traced by means of public, or of family documents, or of both; but neither are forthcoming in the present instance; for, the O'Connors Sligo, having fallen from their social status, public documents took no notice of them; and as they had lost all their property, there could be no occasion for wills or deeds, even if the law allowed Catholics to be parties to such instruments, which, as everyone knows, it did not.

Nor could it be expected that the O'Connors themselves would show an interest in such a subject amidst their sufferings and dangers, when domiciliary visits of the authorities were common, and when the preservation of a pedigree would be regarded as a standing claim to confiscated estates, and therefore as a species of high treason. While Sligo was full of their co-religionists, and a relative of their own was dying there the death of a martyr, their great desire would naturally be, not to assert, but to efface themselves.

In the absence of written records, we must recur to local tradition for guidance, and this guide points unmistakably to Mr. Peter O'Connor of Cairnsfoot, and his nephews, as the genuine descendants, and present representatives, of the old O'Connors Sligo. On this point there seems to be no difference of opinion among such of the old inhabitants of the town and county as still love to talk of the days that are gone. Sixty or seventy years ago the tradition was still more precise and emphatic, for the neighbours of Connell O'Connor, who was Peter O'Connor's grandfather, and who had some peculiarity of walk, used to say of him, that the step of Martin Backagh a distinguished member of the O'Connor Sligo family was breaking through him: thus voicing the popular belief and tradition, that he and his belonged to the genuine old stock.

Mr. Peter O'Connor reflects back as much honour on his ancestors as he derives from them. There never lived in Sligo a more deeply respected man; for all classes admire him, as the Athenians admired Aristides, whom they surnamed The Just. As a magistrate and grand juror, he is the very personification of justice, incapable of being moved a hair's breadth to the right or to the left by any earthly consideration except the merits of the case for adjudication. As a landlord in four of the five baronies of the county, he is swayed solely by a desire to promote the public good and the welfare of his tenants; in proof of which, one has only to call to mind the schoolhouses and teachers' residences which he has erected and endowed at Carrowroe in Carbury, Dunflin in Tireragh, and Crossboy in Tirerrill; the improvements, both as regards neatness and comfort, which he has effected in the farmhouses on his estates; and the solicitude with which he watches over his tenants—in all their concerns and interests in their difficulties helping them with loans and gifts; in their illness feeing doctors to attend them; and in all their troubles sustaining them by his sympathy, his advice, and his purse.

While thus attentive to special claims, he is not the less responsive "to every note of complaint within the wide scale of human woe". Though he takes all the care he cannot to let the left hand know what the right hand doeth, enough still comes to light to fill one with wonder at the extent of his benefactions.

It would hardly be going too far to say that he gives more than all the other inhabitants of the county put together. Memorials of his charity are everywhere around you through the town of Sligo in respectable houses where, unknown to the world, he relieves the genteel indigent; in the cabins of the lanes and suburbs, where we may find as many old men and women, pensioners of his bounty, as would stock a good sized hospital of the Little Sisters of the Poor; in the new schools on the Albert Road, at the Lungy, in Quay-street, and on Gallows Hill, in connection with which he reserves to himself the little ambitioned and modest function of defraying all the expenses, while he leaves to others the much coveted credit of being counted the builders; and in the Cathedral, where the high altar, the fine Gothic benches, the noble turret clock, and the charming chime of bells must serve as lasting monuments, both of his munificence and his piety.

The county is little less indebted to him than the town; for there is hardly a place of worship or a schoolhouse in it that does not count him among its benefactors; and so far-reaching is his charity, that it sometimes passes beyond town, and county, and province, and fills the needy with good things even in the metropolis. The writer will not easily forget, how the late John O'Daly, the well-known bookseller of Anglesea Street, used to declare that, in the embarrassment which overtook him towards the close of his career, his best friend was Mr. O'Connor of Sligo, whom he had never seen.

Next to charity, personal independence is the leading feature of Mr. O'Connor's character. Like the perfect man of the Stoics, he is self-sufficing; and unlike too many who place their happiness in the plaudits of others, and in the possession of some public honour or office, he is content with a private station and the approval of his own conscience and judgment. Except the Grand Jury, the Board of Guardians, and the Dispensary Committee, which he attends sedulously in the interests respectively of the burdened tax-payer, the destitute, and the sick, he leaves to those who ambition them, other public distinctions, including that of member of parliament for the borough or the county of Sligo, which, as everyone knows, was always within his reach and at his acceptance.

Though no party man, he is a patriot of the best type, ready to sacrifice everything for the country; and those who know him best will tell you, that in some of the crises through which Ireland has passed, thousands of Mr. O'Connor's money, unknown to the world, were expended in her service. With his benevolence, his independence of character, and his hundred other noble qualities, he will bear comparison in many respects with the most distinguished of his ancestors; for though they held the rank of chiefs and princes, enjoyed almost sovereign power, and rarely acknowledged any temporal superior in their territory, still, it maybe doubted, whether any of them, with all those prerogatives, did so much good in his lifetime as has been done already by Mr. Peter O'Connor, the latest O'Connor Sligo.

The nephews of Mr. O'Connor are worthy, in every respect, of the head of the family. They are Mr. James O'Connor, of Ballyglass, so well known for his talents, accomplishments, and high principles; Mr. Simon Cullen, as upright a merchant and as just a magistrate as there is in the province; Mr. John Mulhall, the able and universally esteemed Private Secretary to the Lord Lieutenant; and Mr. George Kelly, a distinguished member of the Connaught bar.

Mr. Peter O'Connor, late of Minnesota, and now of California, is another nephew, as well as a full namesake of Mr. O'Connor, of Cairnsfoot, and may be described as a counterpart, in the United States, of his uncle in Ireland, exemplifying in his life all the uncle's peculiar virtues and talents, and held, in consequence, by everybody in similar esteem and respect. People who have been to America speak in terms of the highest praise of this gentleman and his admirable family, two of whom are nuns, and one a priest a trait in which Mr. O'Connor resembles the old O'Connors Sligo, who were rarely without priests and nuns in their families. It is gratifying to Sligo men to find this scion of the old stock command by his native qualities, even in a strange land, the homage of all who know him.

No doubt there are still connected with the county other descendants of different branches of the old O'Connor stock; and among them may be named Reverend Patrick O'Connor, the respected Parish Priest of Cloontuskert and Kilgefen, and his brothers, they being, there is good reason to believe, descendants of the Owen O'Connor mentioned in the Tripartite Deed between Strafford, Leslie, and Wilson.

CHAPTER IX

JACOBITES AND WILLIAMITES

WHILE these changes in the ownership of the lands of Sligo were taking place, the county in other respects, too, was in an unsettled state. The persecution raised in England by the hideous imposture of Titus Gates[1] and Lord Shaftesbury, soon passing to Ireland, reached the county Sligo in a couple of months, and created a ferment in the district, as was natural enough, considering the mixed character of the population. The Usurpers, though now twenty years in possession, were not free from apprehension of disturbance; and some of them, perhaps, believed the wild stories in circulation of intended massacres, while others affected to believe them, in order to bring new odium on the old Irish. The result was that the Catholics of the neighbourhood had not the life of a dog, and were obliged, in self-preservation, to keep out of sight, while any priest or layman of position, that could be reached, was arrested and thrown into Sligo gaol, where Father Felix O'Connor, the Prior of the Dominicans of Holy Cross, died the death of a confessor, if not of a martyr, in 1678, when the persecution was at its worst.[2] This bad spirit was stirred up by a proceeding of Jeremy Jones, of Tireragh, which he relates in an interesting letter, found in the Carte Collection, and addressed to the Duke of Ormonde. The proceeding in question was the arrest of some stroller or traveller on pretence of his being a Jesuit, and the sending of him publicly to Sligo to be committed there to goal. An occurrence of the kind, coupled with the startling stories then coming from England, could not fail to throw the whole county into alarm, which, no doubt, was the very thing Jeremy Jones intended and desired. For, that the capture of the so-called Jesuit was an episode of the Popish Plot, must be clear enough to any person that considers the respective averments of Gates and Jones. "The Pope", says Macaulay,[3] in detailing Gates' allegations, "had entrusted the government of England to the Jesuits. The Jesuits had, by commissions, appointed Catholic clergymen, noblemen, and gentlemen, to all the highest offices in Church and State. A French army was to land in Ireland".

In the same way, Jones' Jesuit "was one of the twelve Jesuits sent into the country by the Pope and French King .... several other Jesuits had

---

[1] Titus Gates made a sworn statement to the effect that a Catholic plot existed for the murder of Charles II. This created a frenzy of anti-Catholic feeling, resulting in the hanging, drawing and quartering of the greatly respected Archbishop of Drogheda, Oliver Plunkett. Two years later Gates was found guilty of perjury, and sentenced to be pilloried, flogged, and imprisoned for life.

[2] Narrative of Father Patrick McDonogh.

[3] History of England, Vol. I., p. 233.

in their keeping and trunks several commissions under the great seal of France and the Pope .... their designs, if not obstructed before the fourth of March next, will redound to the ruin of this nation". Such coincidences are too remarkable to be the result of accident; and they go very far to show that Jones, Thornton, and Fitzgerald, were bearing a part, on a small scale, at Sligo, in the "hideous romance",[1] in which Gates and his confederates were figuring so conspicuously in London, and that the sensational statements on both sides of the channel were *ejusdem farrago libelli*.[2] The Duke of Ormonde saw through the imposture, and took no notice of Jones or his protégé, Fitzgerald, knowing well they were accomplices of Shaftesbury.

It is very likely they were set in motion by Jones, the bishop of Meath, for "nobody", says Carte,[3] "was more active in procuring these witnesses than the Bishop of Meath, who had been Scout-master General to Oliver Cromwell's army, and who now exerted himself to the utmost to serve that great and worthy patriot, his very good friend (as he styles him), the Earl of Shaftesbury". Ormonde's estimate of the Popish Plot witnesses appears in several of his letters, as, for instance, in one to his son, the Earl of Arran, in which he writes, "All these witnesses (I doubt), forswear themselves. Those that went out of Ireland with bad English and worse clothes, are returned well-bred gentlemen, well caronated, periwigged, and clothed. Brogues and leather straps are converted to fashionable shoes and glittering buckles; which, next to the zeal Tories, thieves, and friars have for the Protestant religion, is a main inducement to bring in a shoal of informers. They feel it more honourable and safe to be the King's evidence, than a cow stealer, though that be their natural profession".[4] The extraordinary letter addressed to the Duke of Ormonde by Jeremy Jones is given in the notes.

[Clachan ed.—The following is the content of the extensive footnote that follows.]

"In Sligoe, Nov. 12, 1678.

"May it please your Grace,

"There was taken in my neighbourhood the last week by one Henry Thornton (an officer in the militia troope under my command), a Jesuite, by name John Fitzgerald, borne in the County of Kerry, and, as he saith, not above 7 weeks in Ireland. He took shipping in August last at Nants in ffrance and came for England, and staid in London some time, and from thence took shipping at Bristoll and landed at Belfast the beginning of September following, and soe forwards. After apprehending of him I had him before me as justice of the peace, and some

---

[1] Idem.
[2] Books of the same composition, (lat.), [Clachan ed.].
[3] Carte's Life of Ormonde, Vol. II., p. 498.
[4] Carte's Life of Ormonde. Vol. 2, p. 109. Appendix.

examinations taken of the said Thornton and others that were by when he was soe apprehended, and heard him utter some words that discovered that he was sent over a one of the twelve Jesuites sent into the country by the Pope and ffrench King to seduce the people by their service.

After taking which examinations I had the justice's Mittimus with him to Gaole, but taking him that night to my own house, and telling him of the danger he was of death, and likewise promising him to intercede with your Grace for him, if he would doe good service and discover the rest of his confederates in this Kingdom, whereupon after he had sworn both myself and Thornton to his secrecy and not to reveale what he should tell us but to your Grace and one Booth, a justice of the peace in this county, and a brother-in-law of mine, he immediately then did disclose unto us where there were eight or nine of his society dispersed, according to the enclosed note of their names and several others which had in their keeping and Trunckes severall Commissions under the great seal of ffrance and the Pope with several other things of consequence he ommits until he comes before your Grace, which if not obstructed before the 4th of March next, will redound to the ruin of this nation. On this I brought him to the towne of Sligo and have him secured in the Town Martiall's house with a soldier of the army attending him night and day at my charge, being loath to cast him into the common dungeon or to discourage him from doing his intended service before your Grace, which both he and I humbly desire may be speedily done for fear of the Rabble and the fear of sudaine absenting of the said Jesuites out of this Kingdom, soe humbly craving your Grace's speedy orders what shall be further done with him",

"In all submission, I subscribe your Grace's most obedient servant,
"JERE JONES".

This trouble was hardly over when Sligo was involved in the contest between King James and William of Orange. This conflict took neither side by surprise; for both parties had regarded it for some time as inevitable, and were busy in their respective preparations. The Williamites were the first to move in Sligo. On the 4th January, 1688, they held a public meeting in the town, constituted themselves a military "association", and appointed as their commanders-in-chief, Lord Kingston and Chidley Coote, the former being the son of the first Lord Kingston, and the latter the son of the first Lord Collooney; two lords who owed both titles and fortunes to their revolutionary principles and proceedings. The interval between the 4th January and the 22nd March, was passed by the officers and men of the association in furthering the objects of their organization, in procuring horses, arms, and ammunition, in acquiring military discipline, in finishing the stone fort, erected by the Cromwellians, in re-modelling the Green Fort, and in settling outpost garrisons at Newtown, Ballintogher, Markree, Collooney, and Cottlestown, in Tireragh.[1] While thus engaged they intended to remain at Sligo, and hold the town for the Prince of Orange, but after keeping possession of it from the 4th January to the 22nd March, they left the place much against their will, at the latter date, in compliance

---

[1] Lord Kingston's "Relation" in Mackenzie's Narrative of the Siege of Londonderry, pp. 15, 16, 17, 18.

with an order or invitation of Colonel Lundy, who directed them to move to the North, and quit Sligo, observing that this town would be untenable in case mishap befel Derry and Enniskillen, an advice for which Lundy has been much blamed, though perhaps the best that he or any military man could give in the circumstances. Having remained for about a month on the banks of the Erne, Lord Kingston went to England, and his troops, on the approach of the enemy, retired to Enniskillen, and were thus able to take part in those conflicts of Belleek,[1] Belturbet,[2] Bundroose,[3] Newtown Butler,[4] Boyle,[5] and elsewhere, which have surrounded the name of Enniskilliniers with a halo of well-earned renown.

One result of the important action of Newtown Butler was the falling back of Sarsfield upon Sligo, a position, however, which he was obliged to quit in a few days under circumstances disgraceful in the extreme to all under his command, *if we are to rely on the account of the occurrence* which is found in Hamilton's Actions of the Enniskillen-men, and which is to this effect:— Colonel Tiffan having been stationed at Ballyshannon by the Enniskilliners, sent his lieutenant-colonel and son-in-law, Francis Gore, in the direction of Sligo to reconnoitre, and get intelligence of the enemy. Gore, being the son of Sir Francis Gore, of Ardtermon, had an acquaintance with the district, which fitted him well for the service laid on him; and recognizing in a Jacobite prisoner, brought in near Ardtermon, his own foster brother, he promised the captive liberty, and substantial reward if he carried privately to Sligo a friendly message to four or five officers of the Irish army, whom Gore affected to be very desirous to serve. The message was, that they should save themselves at once, as twenty thousand Williamites were marching in hot haste to Sligo, resolved to put everything there to fire and sword on their arrival. The foster brother engaged to do as desired to put the officers named on their guard, and to leave all others to their fate; but on getting beyond the reach of Gore's troops, he warned, as Gore intended and wished, every man, woman, and child, met with on the road, of the danger they were in, and on entering Sligo spread the alarm on all sides through the town and camp.

The stratagem deceived everybody; and troops of soldiers and civilians were already well on their way to Athlone before Sarsfield heard anything of the panic. He lost not a moment in calling the troops before him by beat of drum, but no one came at the call, so that this gallant soldier was under the humiliating necessity of following the fugitives, which,

---

[1] Harris's Life of William III., p. 218. t Ibid., p. 219. Ibid., p. 221.
[2] Ibid., p. 219
[3] Ibid., p. 221
[4] Ibid., p. 224
[5] Ibid., p. 246

however, he did not do till he broke up with his own hands the carnages of the cannon. Whether these are or are not the exact circumstances of Sarsfield's leaving Sligo which is, to say the least, extremely improbable,[1] it is certain that he had to abandon the town on this occasion, and that the place was immediately occupied by the Williamites.[2]

While the armies of James and Schomberg were lying idle at Dundalk, Sligo became the centre of some stirring events. The Enniskilliners, bearing ill the inaction of the camp, sought Schomberg's leave to proceed to Sligo in quest of employment, and the Duke not only complied with their request, but sent with them strong cavalry patrols, under the command of Colonel Russell, to keep the passes clear between Connaught and Dundalk. The dashing Lloyd now felt himself strong enough to deal a blow to the enemy. Hearing that large numbers of the Irish, some said 5000, but Lloyd himself, in a letter to Schomberg, reported them as about 900 were assembled at Boyle, ready to fall on Sligo, he resolved to be beforehand with them, as was his wont.

Putting himself at the head of 1000 men,[3] he marched at night towards them, hoping to take them by surprise. They were, however, on the alert; but this did not prevent or delay Lloyd's attack; and falling on them with his characteristic vigour, he gained a complete victory, slew about 700 on the field, and in the pursuit, took more than forty officers prisoners, including the Colonel in command, and two other Colonels, and between Boyle, Jamestown, and Drumsna, secured the enormous prey of 10,000 cattle.

This victory afforded Schomberg's army the only pleasant moments they enjoyed while detained in the pestilential camp at Dundalk; for when the dispatch, which was sent to announce the good news, reached the Duke, his Grace, not only rode slowly, with head uncovered, along the Enniskillen horse and foot, drawn up in line to receive the compliment, but he caused

---

[1] This account rests entirely on the authority of Hamilton, who thus introduces it: "And here I would have ended, having been no longer an eye-witness to any of their actions at Enniskillen, but I cannot omit the manner of our taking Sligo, and driving Colonel Sarsfield and his party from thence. *And although I was not present at the action as at most of the rest*, yet I had the account of it from a person of good credit, and so may with confidence relate it here; and thus it was." This hearsay evidence is an utterly insufficient voucher for transactions so improbable in themselves. Story has no reference to this gossiping narrative; nor has Harris; nor Macaulay, who collected every scrap of evidence that bore upon the struggle between William and James, and who would hardly have failed to give us a picturesque paragraph or two on the dramatic occurrences at Sligo, if he regarded them as founded in fact. We may regard the whole story then as a fabrication; though adopted and paraphrased, with additions, by Major Wood Martin in *Sligo and the Enniskittiners*.

[2] Macaulay's History of England, Vol. III., p. 245, first edition

[3] J Harris' Life of William III., p. 246.

the triumph to be proclaimed by all the ordnance of the camp, and of the ships in the harbour, thus making land and sea to join in glorifying the event.

The triumph, however, was short-lived. James, acting on the principle *Fas est et ab hoste doceri*,[1] detached from the royal army five[2] regiments for service in and around Sligo, as Schomberg had done. This small force was put under the command of Sarsfield, who did not allow the grass to grow under his feet. Impatient to retrieve the discredit of the hasty evacuation of Sligo, he seized Jamestown, which Lloyd's garrison relinquished without striking a blow, and on the evening of the next day entered the town of Sligo after an extraordinary march, and after sweeping, at the end of it, out of his way the enemy who, having taken up an advantageous position, tried hard to bar his entry into the town. As Sarsfield entered by the south side, Russell with his horse left by the north in retreat to Ballyshannon; but Lloyd and a French captain, named St. Sauveur, instead of following the example and advice of Russell, though chief in command, resolved to make a stand, and with this object threw themselves, the former into the Green Fort, and St. Sauveur into the old castle. On thinking better of the situation, Lloyd withdrew his men during the night, and marched after Colonel Russell, but St. Sauveur, with the characteristic vanity of the Frenchman, would not give in so readily; and finding the old castle untenable, he led his party into the Stone Fort.[3] There was no electric light in those days; and St. Sauveur, to guard against an attack in the dark on his quarters, having smeared some fir poles with tar, set fire to them, and thus lighted up the fort and the approaches to it. The precaution was a wise one; for it enabled him to see a battering engine, called the Sow,[4] which the Irish, after nightfall, began to move towards the fort, but which he destroyed before it could be got into position. Finding, however, the place untenable, the Frenchman surrendered it, but on highly honourable terms; and Sarsfield was so pleased with the gallant conduct of the foreigner and his little force, that he did all he could, but in vain, to bring them over to the side of James.

These events raised Sarsfield greatly in the estimation of friends and enemies. In any case the surprising march in one day of so many miles over the rugged road which lay between Jamestown and Sligo, and which included the passage of the Curlews, the Alps of Connaught, would add to

---

[1] It is right to learn even from an enemy, [Clachan ed.].
[2] Macaulay's History of England, vol. 3, p. 429
[3] As Colonel Wood Martin confounds the "fort" and the "castle", it is well to note the distinction. The Williamites first entered the "castle", but finding it "crasie", passed out of it to the Stone Fort. "The castle being crasie", says a letter in the 11th volume of the Thorpe collection, "our men quitted it and got into the fort".
[4] For a detailed account of this engine, see Harris' Life of William III., pp. 246-247.

the fame of the most distinguished commanders; and the magnitude of the feat in this instance was greatly enhanced by the character of the adversaries that blocked the way—Lloyd, who never before turned the back on any enemy, and St. Sauveur, conspicuous for bravery, even among the bravest captains, in Schomberg's army. Sarsfield's capture of Sligo on this occasion may not have been as fruitful in results as his famous surprise of Williams' siege train, but in itself one exploit was hardly less brilliant than the other.

One of the regiments under Sarsfield's command during this episode of the war, was that of Colonel Henry Luttrell; and it was, apparently, now for the first time, that this unprincipled man was brought into official connection with Sligo, though Major Wood Martin, without quoting any authority, and apparently without any authority to quote, tells us that "one of James' first acts was the appointment of Colonel Henry Luttrell to the Governorship of Sligo".[1] While Sarsfield moved about in the neighbourhood, he left Luttrell in Sligo palisading the town, to make up, as far as might be, for the absence of a wall. The line of palisades started from the Green Fort, crossed the river near the present old distillery building, ran up the Chapel Hill, passed westward through Old Market Street, High Street, on to Prince's Street, turned down towards George's Street, and, wheeling back through Cadger's Field and along the quay, completed a zig-zag circle, which enclosed within its ambit the Green Fort and the Stone Fort, the Abbey and St. John's Church, and the greater part of the area of the present town. In this work, as well as in the strengthening of the Green Fort, Colonel Luttrell was aided by R. Burton, "his Majesty's engineer", whose presence shows the great value set at this time, by his Majesty and his Majesty's advisers, on the town of Sligo.

Henry Luttrell was the James Carey of the Williamite war, quite as notorious and odious, and, considering his military profession, rank and obligations, still more guilty than the wretched Invincible. A man of undaunted courage, and brilliant talents, and member of a family second to none in the country, his baseness and guilt were aggravated by his personal gifts and family honours. And, as if he communicated a taint to the blood of the family, the Luttrells that came after him were so infamous for his and their own crimes, that Junius, in his day, considered it impossible to degrade further "the name of Luttrell".[2]

The exact time at which Satan entered into this Judas is not known, but it is probable enough that the evil spirit took possession of him when he was recalled from Sligo to make room for Sir Teague O'Regan. For his conduct soon after, at the battle of the Boyne, was equivocal, and in evident contrast with the gallantry which carried everything before it in the attack

---

[1] Sligo and the Enniskilliners, p. 63.
[2] Quoted in Macaulay's History of England, Vol. 4, p. 109.

on the Williamites at Sligo. Anyhow, he was detected in correspondence with Ginkell during the siege of Limerick, and tried by a court-martial for the proceeding. And when the capitulation of that city left him more free to show his hand, he laboured, by word and example, to keep the Irish at home, as Ginkell desired, and to prevent them from accompanying Sarsfield and other leaders into the service of France and Spain.

For the service rendered on this occasion, and "perhaps," says Macaulay, "for other services, he was rewarded with a grant of the large estate of his elder brother, Simon, who firmly adhered to the cause of James, with a pension of five hundred pounds a year from the Crown, and with the abhorrence of the Roman Catholic population". Though Henry Luttrell lived up to the year 1717, he was pursued by the unrelenting hatred of his fellow countrymen to the last, and on the night of the 2nd of November in that year, as he was going, in a sedan chair, from one street to another in Dublin, he was shot and mortally wounded, surviving only to the next day, the hand that slew him being, says Matthew O'Conor, "probably that of an enthusiast who sought to avenge the wrongs of his country in the blood of the traitor". Even the blood of the wretched man did not assuage the feelings of his enemies, and the kind of Requiescat commonly pronounced over his grave may be inferred from the bitterness of the following popular epigram of the time:

> *"If Heav'n be pleas'd, when mortals cease to sin*
> *And Hell be pleas'd, when villains enter in*
> *If earth be pleas'd, when it entombs a knave*
> *All must be pleas'd now Luttrell's in the grave!"*

After remaining for more than six months at Sligo, Luttrell, with his regiment was called away,[1] partly, to lend a hand in the impending battle between James and William, and partly to make room for Sir Teague O'Regan, who, after his admirable defence of Charlemont, was judged the fittest person to be made governor of Sligo, at a crisis when the town had become more than ever, what it has been often called, "the Key of Connaught". Appointed in June 1690, O'Regan continued in authority till the 15th of September, 1691, and during all that time took his measures so adroitly, that he never gave the enemy, though bold and experienced, and always on the watch, the smallest advantage. Setting comparatively little store by the stone fort, he relied chiefly on the Green Fort, which is often called Sir Teague O'Regan's Fort, as well because he resided so long in it, as because he added greatly to its strength by new works. Art, combining thus with nature, rendered this great earthwork impregnable by any open or sudden assault.

---

[1] Harris's Life of William III., p. 266.

And Sir Teague took care to be well informed of what was going on in the neighbourhood, and, as far as possible, to prevent any mischief, which might be brewing, from coming to a head. Hearing, in June, 1691, that a large force of Williamites, 500 foot and 200 horse, had passed round through Leitrim, from the north to Tireragh, he hastened in person with 200 foot and 80 horse to the bridge of Ballysadare, to observe and check their movements; and when they tried to force the bridge, he drove them back with great loss, and was on the point of chasing them off the field, when, in the nick of time, they received large reinforcements, upon which, though pursued for some distance, he moved his men in good order to Sligo, himself being among the last to enter the town.

Another sally, which took place, at the dawn of day, on the 5th of September, 1691, was still more successful. This time the number of men led out was three times as great as in the preceding instance, and the leader was Colonel Edward Scott. The object of the movement was to fall on Sir Albert Conyngham, who with his regiment of dragoons was under canvas at Knockbeg, beside Collooney. The guard that morning was ill-kept at Knockbeg; for, before the alarm was sounded, Scott's men were among the tents; and, before any resistance could be offered, Sir Albert was transpierced with a halbert as he was trying to get into the saddle, and several of his men were put to the sword, while the rest of the regiment, abandoning their commander and their comrades, and flying off in a disgraceful panic, never drew rein till they arrived at Boyle, reaching that place in a plight which, even by their own official account,[1] was sorry in the extreme.

Notwithstanding these successes, the superior numbers and resources of the enemy were soon to prevail. As Athlone and Galway had been just taken from the partizans of James, the Williamites were now able to send overwhelming forces to Sligo. Between the troops dispatched from Galway under Balldearg O'Donnell, and a well-equipped body of 5,000 militia, levied in Dublin and other places, and led by Lord Granard, who was appointed commander-in-chief of all the troops employed in the reduction of Sligo, there must have been about 10,000 men on the south side of the town, when his Lordship appeared before it on the 12th of September. Confronted by this irresistible force; invested, on one side, by the sea, and, on the other sides, by a chain of posts stretching from Killybegs, in the north, to Tireragh, in the west; without hope of relief from any quarter; with no good object to serve by prolonging the resistance; and with a prospect of being of use in Limerick, where the followers of James were making their final effort to retrieve the royal cause; O'Regan, after satisfying to the full the claims of honour and duty, felt bound, as a practical,

---

[1] Ballysadare and Kilvarnet, p. 69.

conscientious man, entrusted with the fate of all serving under him, to accept the honourable terms granted to the garrison, of proceeding to Limerick with their baggage and arms, and of taking with them ample provisions for the journey, these terms to extend to all the military adherents of James in the neighbourhood. Till he received these liberal terms, Sir Teague held out unflinchingly; and even the night of the day, on which Granard arrived, was passed in an ordnance duel between his Lordship and the sturdy governor, in which an English ensign had his head whipped off by a cannon from the Green Fort. Whatever may be thought of Mitchelburn, who conducted the siege, and who was taxed at the time with self-seeking, it seems admitted on all hands that O'Regan, throughout the entire defence, bore himself disinterestedly and even chivalrously.

Mitchelburn gave out that the place had been surrendered to himself before Lord Granard appeared on the scene, but it is plain from the official correspondence, from Harris,[1] and from the actual conflict between his Lordship and the town, that the statement is untrue.

There is nothing, at least nothing that the writer has seen, to show that the garrison reached Limerick before the capitulation of that city. That, on the contrary, they stopped or were detained somewhere on the way, would seem to follow from the 13th of the Military Articles, which runs thus, "Those of the garrison of Sligo that are joined to the Irish army, shall have the benefit of this capitulation; and orders shall be sent to them that are to convey them up, to bring them hither to Limerick the shortest way". By this article, and the preamble to the Civil Articles, which declares the Treaty of Limerick to be "in the behalf of the Irish Inhabitants of the city and county of Limerick, and the counties of Clare, Kerry, Cork, Sligo, and Mayo" it is seen that the Irish inhabitants of the county Sligo are expressly guaranteed the benefits of the treaty.

The following unpublished letter of Colonel Mitchelburn, taken from Clarke's Correspondence (MS. in Trinity College), contains so many interesting details in connection with the siege and surrender of Sligo that it is given here entire. It is addressed to the Lords Justices.[2]

---

[1] Page 322.

[2] Owing to pressure on space the letter is omitted here, but will, if possible, be given in the Appendix. [The appendices appear at the end of Vol. II, [Clachan ed.]]

CHAPTER X

THE TREATMENT OF CATHOLICS

THE treaty of Limerick not only put an end to the conflict between James and William, but closed that long series of wars in which the Irish had been opposed to the English from the invasion of Ireland in the twelfth century. From 1691 there was no uprising of the Irish against the English for more than a century, when the partial outbreak of 1798 took place. But the times which followed the treaty of Limerick, if free from the evil of war, suffered from other evils, hardly less grievous; and certainly more humiliating; for war is at all events evidence of life and spirit, whereas the dumbness, the dejection, the stagnation, which prevailed all over the country in the eighteenth century indicated only disease or death. Whatever spirit survived in the country at the conclusion of the war was soon crushed out by the Penal laws and the tyranny of those who administered them.

In the year 1691, a couple of months after the Articles of Limerick were signed, an Act of Parliament excluded Catholics from Parliament, from municipal corporations, from civil and military offices, and for the most part, from the exercise of the liberal professions; in 1695, another act banished all Papists, exercising ecclesiastical jurisdiction under the penalty of high treason if they returned; in 1703, under Queen Anne, was passed the first Act to Prevent the further Growth of Popery, which, along with renewing the prohibitions and penalties of 1695, ordered all Popish priests to be registered at the Quarter Sessions to be held after St. John the Baptist Day in 1704; and in 1709 the second Act to Prevent the further Growth of Popery, imposing the oath of abjuration on the Priests whose names, residences, and parishes, they had already ascertained. In these Acts the laity were not forgotten, for they were disabled from purchasing land; from renting lands on beneficial terms: from holding place or office; and from educating their children either at home or abroad.

Bad as these laws were in themselves, the evil was greatly aggravated by the way in which they were administered. "The corruption at the source", says Macpherson, "extended itself to every channel of Government; the subordinate magistrates, the justices of the peace, as if all law was at an end, made their own will and pleasure the rule of their conduct depriving many of their effects, and dispossessing many of their lands". The registration of the clergy, which took place in compliance with the law of 1703, casts considerable light on the conduct of the county Sligo in the beginning of the eighteenth century, as it gives the names of the Catholic Parish Priests of the county at the time, the parishes which they served, their age, their residences, the dates of their ordination, the names of the ordaining bishops, and the names of two sureties, bound each in the penal sum of 50 sterling, to guarantee "that every such Popish priest shall be of peaceable behaviour, and not remove out of such county where his or their place of abode lies, into any other part of the kingdom." In Dr. Renehan's *Collections on Irish Church History*, it is stated that the two securities should be Protestant, but this seems to be an error, for the act speaks only of "sufficient sureties" without any reference to their religion, and some of the county Sligo bail belonged to well-known Catholic families, as the Creans, the Harts, the MacDonoghs, and must have been Catholics themselves.

The execution of those acts, and of the instructions constantly issuing from Dublin Castle regarding them, formed for a long time the chief occupation of the local authorities throughout the country. The Justices of the Peace, though bigoted and desirous to execute the Penal Laws, found themselves perfectly unable to carry their wishes into effect. *Quid leges sine moribus?*[1] and as the principles, the faith, and the feelings of the people were in direct antagonism to these persecuting enactments, the magistrates were constantly crossed and balked in their projects and proceedings.

Such was the state of things in Sligo as well as in other places. Several letters which passed between the central authorities in Dublin and the Sligo magistrates are preserved in the Record Office, Dublin, and the correspondence shows the great pressure of the Castle authorities on the one side, and the zeal and efforts of the magistrates on the other, as well as the obstacles which rendered those efforts ineffectual. Under the date of December 12th, 1712, we find Percy Gethin, W. Ormsby, and Richard Lindsay, writing to the Castle, that they had summoned the priests to come in and take the oath of abjuration, that none of those summoned appeared, and that in consequence warrants were issued against the defaulters, but without effect. Another letter of the same time, signed by Edward Wingfield, W. Ormsby, William Smith, George Wood, and Robert Lindsay, informs the Supreme Council that they had again issued warrants for the "apprehending of all such Popish priests as had not taken the oath of abjuration". On the 16th April, 1714, the High Sheriff, William Smith, reports that he had distributed the last Proclamation relating to Papists, to the following Justices of the Peace—William Ormsby, Percy Gethin, Robert Lindsay, Richard Crofton, Lewis Jones, Edward Wingfield, Kean O'Hara, Theobald Caulfield, Francis King, and John De Butt. Two months later (8th June), in answer to a communication from Dublin Castle requiring the magistrates to "put the laws in execution against all Popish Regulars and Seculars", seven of the Sligo Justices of the Peace—E. Crofton, R. Lindsay, H. King, W. Ormsby, Percy Gethin, Toby Caulfield, and Lewis Jones writes to Secretary Dawson, "We doe assure you her Majesty has not subjects in

---

[1] What are laws without morals, [Clachan ed.].

any of her dominions who would more faithfully obey her commands, and would sooner put them in execution than those in the magistracy of this county. We are obliged to let you know that we have made use of all expedients we could think of by issuing warrants and otherwise, and found no benefit of it, and it is all our opinion that if the Government will please to give orders to the soldiery to give us their assistance on due application, we question not of giving a good account of our duty; and without which the Papists are so numerous and so insolent, and in a more particular manner at this time, that without them we cannot pretend to do any considerable service".

The magistrates stated only their genuine sentiments in these communications with the Castle, for they left no stone unturned to give effect to the instructions sent down by the high officials of the government. With the view of discovering the "dignitaries", "regulars", "non-juring priests", and other papists obnoxious to the law, they summoned before them some of the leading Catholic laymen of the town and county, and examined them regarding their knowledge of such persons. The inquiries were conducted with the aim of applying the recent penal laws, more especially the 9th of William III. (1697), for banishing all papists exercising ecclesiastical jurisdiction, and all regulars of the popish clergy; the 2nd of Anne (1703), chap, vi., for preventing the further growth of popery; and the 8th of Anne (1709), chap, iii., for "explaining and amending an act intituled: An act for preventing the further growth of popery". By this last act the oath of abjuration was made compulsory, and thus, according to the graphic language of Mr. Froude (English in Ireland, Vol. I., p. 333), "the last rivet was driven into the chain of the penal code". As there was no question of this oath at the general registration of the clergy in 1704, the parish priests came freely forward and complied with the requirements of the law; but their names and residences being thus ascertained and registered, the authorities now issued proclamation after proclamation calling on the registered parish priests to come in again and take the oath of abjuration. The clergy shrank with horror from the sacrilegious act prescribed, and the magistrates made it their chief business to force compliance, and to punish the refractory. It was with this object that Sligo Justices of the Peace now held several courts of inquiry, the proceedings of which were duly reported to the Castle. In his searches at the Record Office, Dublin, the writer was fortunate enough to fall in with these documents; and they are given here, *in extenso*, as they are singularly interesting and furnish a truer idea than any narrative account could, of what took place at the time almost enabling us to see with our own eyes, and to hear with our own ears the actual working of the Penal Laws. The first court of inquiry was held on the 28th October, 1712, and the following is the record:—

Depositions as to non-juring Popish Priests celebrating mass in town or county, 1712. Before Percy Gethin, Wm. Ormsby, Robt. Lindsay, and Wm. Smith.

The Depositions of Mr. Thos. Corkaran, of Sligoe, and other of the Popish inhabitants of the town of Sligoe, taken before Percy Gethin, Wm. Ormsby, and Robt. Lindsay, Esqrs., three e rof her Majesty's Justices of the Peace for the said county, this 28th day of October, 1712.

Thomas Corkaran, of Sligoe, Merchant, being duly sworne upon the Holy Evangelists and examined, saith that the last time he heard mass was about 15 days agoe, about the 13th inst., and that the said mass was celebrated by one Peter Feighny, and that after the manner used in the church of Rome, and that the said Peter Feighny was *Registered, but is a non-juring Popish Priest* of the parish of Killadoone in this county, and that *he does not know where he resides*, and that he knows of no *Popish dignitarys or Regulars* in the said county, and further this examinant saith not.

John Mayly, of Sligoe, being duly sworne upon the Holy Evangelists, and examined saith, that the last time he heard mass was about 15 days agoe, the 13th inst., and that the same was celebrated by Peter Feighny, and that after the manner used in the church of Rome, and that the said Peter Feighny was Registered Popish Priest of the Parish of Killadoon, in this county, but is a *non-juror;* he saith also that he did hear one Molass O'Mioghan, who is a priest in the County of Leitrim, say mass in Sligoe after the usual manner in the house of Patrick French, about three weeks agoe, and further, this examinant saith not.

Patrick Lynch, of Sligoe, being duly sworne upon the Holy Evangelists, and examined saith, that the last time he heard mass was about the 13th inst., at the chappel or mass-house in Slygoe, and that it was Peter Feighny, who is a Registered Popish Priest of the Parish of Killadoon, in this county, who did celebrate the same after the usual manner, but that the said Peter Feighny *is a non-juror,* and he also saith he did heare one Molass O'Mioghan, who is a Parish Priest in the county of Leitrim, say Mass at widdow French's house in Sligoe, about three weeks agoe, and further this deponent saith not.

Richard Brewin, of Sligoe, being duly sworne upon the Holy Evangelists, and examined saith, that the last time he heard mass was about the 13th inst., at the chappell or mass-house in Sligoe, and that it was Peter Feighny, *who is Registered, but a non-juring Popish Priest* of the parish of Killadoon in this county, who did celebrate the same, and that he also saith that he heard one Molass O'Mioghan, who is a priest in the county of Leitrim, neare adjoining, say mass about, three weeks agoe in widdow French's house in Sligoe, and that he knows of *no dignitary* of the church of Rome, or *any Regulars* in the county, nor of any *Popish schoolmasters, tutors, or ushers,* and further, deponent saith not.

Other depositions before us, Novr. 4th, 1712.

James Fahy, of Sligoe, Apothecary, being duly sworne upon the Holy Evangelists, and examined saith, that the last time he heard mass was at the mass-house or chappel neare Sligoe, about the 15th October last, and that it was Peter Feighny who was *Registered Popish Priest* of the parish of Killadoon, in this county, but is *a non-juror,* who did then celebrate the same, and that there were then present, James Jolly, and severall other Popish inhabitants of the towne of Sligoe at the said mass, and that he did not see any strangers present at it, neither priest nor fryar, but that Denis Kerrigan, who is *Registered non-juring* Popish Priest of the parishes of St. John's and Calry, in this county, was then present being his parish; he further saith that he heard mass severall times within these six months last past 228 from the said Denis Kerrigan and Peter Feighny in the chappell aforesaid, and at Patrick Devany's house, and at his own house in Sligoe, and he also saith that he did hear mass celebrated at Ballyshanny, in the county of Donegall, by one Turlough McSwine, a reputed Fryar of the order of Saint Francis, and of the abby of Donegall; he further saith that he did see another Fryar in Sligoe, by the name of John McGwyr, and another called Feighney, and another called Garret Cullicin, all itynerant, and that *he knoweth not where any of the said fryars or regulars doe either reside or abide*; he further saith, that in the north of the kingdom he knows of several regulars, viz., John Paddeene, and one Father James Patten, and one Father John Gallagher, and *he knows not their residence,* although he had frequently seen them there, and he saith he hath seen *no Dignitary of the church* of Rome that he knows off, but saith that *he has heard of severally as of a bishop,* one *McDermott,* in the county of Roscommon, who is Titular Bishop of Elphin, *and of one Rourke,* who is Titular Bishop of Killala, and saith that he believes that the said bishops doe ordaine severall young priests, but that *he has seen none of them,* and further this examinant saith not.

Charles Fallon, of Sligoe, being duly sworne upon the Holy Evangelists, and examined, saith, that the last time he heard Mass was about the 15th October last past, and that severall Popish inhabitants of the towne of Sligoe were then present, and that it was Dennis Kerrigan, the Parish Priest, that did then celebrate same, and this examinant further saith that he heard no Mass within these six months last past, but from the said Dennis Kerrigan and Peter Feighney, and that they did usually celebrate the same at the Chappell or Mass House; he further *saith that the said priests did use to be at one Morgan McCarric's house in Sligoe before the Government Proclamation, but where they resided since he knoweth not, neither does he know of any Popish Dignitary or Regular in this kingdom, nor of any Popish school-masters, tutors, or ushers, and farther* this Deponent saith not.

Owen Devanny, of Sligoe, merchant, being duly sworne upon the Holy Evangelists, and examined, saith, that some time within a month he heard Mass at the Chappell or Mass-house of Sligoe, celebrated by Peter Feighney, Registered Popish Priest, of the Parish of Killadoone, in this county, *who is a non-juror,* and this examinant saith that within these six months past he heard Mass from Dennis Kerrigan, his registered Parish Priest, *who is also a non-juror,* and this examinant saith also that he knoweth one Father James Feighney, a Regular of the Order of St. Dominick, whom he heareth is or is to be Prior of the Convent of Sligoe, and he saith that he knows of no other Regulars or Dignitarys of the Church of Roome, neither does he know of any popish schoolmasters, tutors, or ushers in this county, and further this Deponent saith not.

Matthew Fahy, of Sligoe, apothecary, being duly sworne upon the Holy Evangelists, and examined, saith, that about a fortnight agoe, he did see Mass celebrated at the Chappell or Mass-house near Sligoe, by Peter Feighney, *non-juror, registered Popish Priest,* of the parish of Killadoon, in this county, and that Owen Devanny and several other of the Popish inhabitants of the town of Sligo were then present, and he further saith he knows of one Father James Feighney, a Regular, who did lately celebrate Mass at the Mass house, or Chappell, neare Sligoe, after the usual manner, and he saith that he knows of no other Regular or Dignitary of the Church of Roome, *neither does he know of any Popish schoolmasters, tutors, or ushers, and farther this Deponent saith not.*

Bryan Hart, of Sligo, merchant, being duly sworne upon the Holy Evangelists, and examined, saith, that he heard Mass at the Mass house, neare Sligoe, about agoe (sic) from Peter Feighney, and that he heard Mass several times within six months last past, from Dennis Kerrigan, the Parish Priest, and from one James Feighney, a Regular, and this examinant also saith that being at the funerall of one Mr. Conmy, about twelve miles from Sligoe, in the said county, about the beginning of August last, that he heard several Masses from three or four priests that he knows not, and farther saith, that he heard and saw at the funerall one McDermott, reputed to be Titular Bishop of Elphin, and this examinant saith that he has heard that the said Bishop has been in this kingdom five years, but that he knows not his place of abode, and farther this Deponent saith not.

Peter Kelly, of Sligoe, hatter, being duly sworne upon the Holy Evangelists, and examined, saith, that the last Mass he heard was at Bundrowes, in the county of Donegall, neare adjoining to this county, and that the same was celebrated by Father Patrick Sweeney, Priest of the Parish of , in the said county, and he also saith he heard Mass about a fortnight ago at the Mass-house from Peter Feighney, and he further saith, that he heard Mass from one James Feighney, a Regular, lately in the Mass-house of Sligoe, and he believes the said James to be a Fryar, because he begged of him, and farther this Deponent saith not.

Patrick Devanny, of Sligoe, being duly sworne upon the Holy Evangelists, and examined, saith, that the last Mass he heard was at Widdow French's house, in Sligoe, from one Molass O'Mioghan, a Parish Priest, in the county of Leitrim, neare adjacent, and that he heard Mass severall times within these six months from Dennis Kerrigan, *the non-juring Parish Priest*, and from Peter Feighney, the *non-juring* Popish Priest of the Parish of Killadoone, in this county, and also from James Feighney, a Regular, and farther this Deponent saith not.

Ju co. nobis, PERCY GETHIN.
W. ORMSBY.
ROBERT LINDSAY.

The foregoing depositions did not advance much the chief object of the magistrates, which was to obtain such information as would lead to the arrest and punishment of the incriminated persons. It will be observed that the witnesses are clear and explicit enough as to the saying of Masses, though they know nothing of the address of the *non-juring priest*s, the dignitaries, the regulars, the popish schoolmasters, or ushers. If they can tell that, for instance, the Rev. Denis Kerrigan, the registered popish priest of St. John's and Calry, and Reverend Peter Feighney, resided "at Morgan McCarrick's house in Sligo", the information is found to be of no use, as it refers to a period prior to the issue of the Government Proclamation, while the deponents know nothing of the residence of the priests since that time, having, of course, taken good care to remain ignorant of the dangerous secret. In this way the witnesses might, with a clear conscience, give a rather wide berth to the myrmidons of the law.

The preceding depositions, which came all from townspeople, were taken on the 28th of October, and the 4th November; and on the 29th October and 11th November country witnesses were examined and deposed as follows:—

The Depositions of Teig McDonnagh, of Ballyraghahoe, and others, taken before us, William Ormsby and William Smith, Esq., two of her Majesty's Justices of the Peace for the county, this 29th day of October, 1712.

Teige HcDonnagh being duly sworne upon the Holy Evangelists, and examined, saith, that he heard Mass last Sunday, was sennight, at Castle Corragh, in the parish of Shancough, in this county, and that the same was celebrated by one Bryan

McDermott Roe, alias John Smith, a priest lately come into the county, in the place of Peter Feighney (as this Deponent is informed) who was registered popish priest, of the parish of Killadoon, in this county, and since removed to Sligoe, and further this Deponent saith, that the said Bryan McDermott Roe lives near *Slievegurmoyle*, in the barony of Tyrerrill, and further this Deponent saith, that the said Peter Feighney celebrated Mass in the parish of Shancough yesterday, being the 28th inst., and farther he also saith that he did see one Thomas Rutledge, a reputed fryar, and knows no place of residence he has, and this Deponent also saith that he did see one Rourke whom he hears is Titular Bishop of Killala.

Bryan McDonnagh, of Behy, being duly sworn upon the Holy Evangelists, and examined, saith, that he did hear Mass celebrated on Sunday last at Tawnagh, in the parish of KillMcAllen, by Matthew Brehun, registered (*non-juring*) popish priest of the parish of Tawnah, in this county, and that this Deponent did also heare Teige Davey celebrate Mass in the parish of Ballysadare, in this county, at Carrickbanaghar, the said Teige Davey being registered *non-juring* popish priest cf Kittashalva in the said county, and this examinant farther saith that he heard there are several fryars in the country, but that he neither knows them nor their place of abode.

William Bourke of Doonamurray being duly sworne upon the Holy Evangelists, and examined, saith, that on Sunday last was sennight he heard Mass at Castlecarragh, in the parish of Kill McTrany, by one Bryan McDermott Roe, alias Smith, and saith that the said McDermott Roe disguises his name to cloake his Power in the church; this Deponent also saith that he heard one Bryan Higgins say Mass within the space of two months in the parish of Killross; and that the said Bryan Higgins dwells at Dunmore in the parish of Ballysummahan, being Registered *non-juring* Popish Priest of the said parish, in this county; this Deponent also saith he heard one Denis McDermott celebrate Mass in the parish of Kill McTrany, in this county, the said Denis McDermott being registered *non-juring Popish Priest* of the parishes of Kill McTrany and Shancough, in the said county, and this Deponent also saith that he saw one Garrett Cullican, a fryar, proceed at Guievagh, in said parish of Kill McTrany aforesaid, and this Deponent saith also that he did see one Gallagher, an Ittenerant fryar, at Longa, in the parish of Ballysummahan aforesaid, and this Deponent saith also he did see one Thomas Rutledge, a fryar, and heard him say mass at Longa aforesaid, in the parish aforesaid, and this Deponent saith he did see one Rourke, who is reputed to be Bishop of Killala, travelling on the roads in the barony of Corran, and this Deponent further saith, he heard that there was one McDermott, Bishop of Elphin, some time ago in the upper part of the Barony of Tirerrill, in this county.

Ju co. nobis.
W. ORMSBY.
WM. SMITH.

Commitatus Sligoe.	The Depositions of severall persons taken before us Percy Gethin and Robert Lindsay, Esqs., Two of her Majesty's Justices of the Peace for the said county, this 11th day of Nov., 1712.

Cormock McGlone, of Carrowmore, in the parish of Killaspukbrone, in the Barony of Carbury, in the said county, yeoman, who being duly sworn upon the Holy Evangelists, and examined saith, that in his roade coming from Dublin homewards, about eight days ago he heard Mass said in a waste house at Kilcock, and that the persons there present were all strangers to him except Stephen Crane of Sligoe, and those of his company who were then coming from Dublin with him, and that he did not know the priest that did celebrate the said Mass, and further this examinant saith he heard Mass at *Drynaghan in the parish of Killaspukbrone*, aforesaid, from one McDonnah who was a young priest, and that it was about two months agoe, and that he believes he may be a young fryar because he did beg money, and that *he knows of no Popish Dignitary nor of any popish schoolmaster, tutor or usher,* and further this examinant saith not.

Paul Cunigham, of Drynaghan, in the parish of Killaspukbrone, in the said county, yeoman, being duly sworne upon the Holy Evangelists, and examined saith, that he heard Mass said in the fields at Drynahan aforesaid, about two months ago, from one who was a stranger, that said he was --------, and that he was a young priest, and this examinant was then told his name was McDonnah, and he also saith that he heard Mass about two months agoe in the said parish, from one John McDonnah, *non-juring Registered popish priest* of the parishes of KillMcOwen and Killaspukbrone, in this county, and this Deponent saith, that he knows of no Popish Bishop or Dignitary, nor of any popish schoolmasters, tutors, or ushers, in this county and further this examinant saith not.

William Ward, of Farrinacarny, in the barony of Carbury, in the said county, yeoman, being duly sworne upon the Holy Evangelists and examined, saith, that about three weeks agoe he heard Mass at Lysidyll, in the parish of Drumcliefe, in this county, from Cormock Feeny, who is Registered *non-juring Popish priest* of the said parish, and that there were no strangers present, but one Cassidy, who is no clergyman; and this examinant also saith that about June last he heard Mass in the said parish, from one that he is informed is Richard Doherty, a registered Popish Priest about Mullingar, and further the examinant saith not.

Hugh Gallagher, of Farrinacarny, in the said county, yeoman being duly sworne upon the Holy Evangelists and examined, saith, that he heard Mass about three weeks agoe at Lyssidyll, in the parish of Drumcliefe, in the said county from Cormock Feeny, *non-juring popish Registered priest* of the said parish, and that there were no strangers then there but one Cassidy, who was no clergyman, and this examinant also saith that he heard Mass as often as he could from the said Cormock Feeny, who is his *non-juring* parish priest, and this examinant also saith, that he did see one MacSwyne, in the parish of Aughamlish, in this county, who is said to be a fryar, and this examinant saith, that he is informed that there are young clergymen made, but not any more, and this examinant saith, that he has heard of one Manus O'Hara, a popish schoolmaster, but knows not now where he resides or dwells, and further this examinant saith not.

    PERCY GETHIN.
    ROBERT LINDSAY.
       Jur. co. nobis,
       11th Nov., 1712.

The country witnesses, it will be observed, are as ignorant about the residences of the incriminated persons as those of the town. Though Bryan McDonogh, of Behy, has heard that there are several friars in the country, he "neither knows them nor their places of abode;" and all William Bourke, of Doonamnrray, can tell of the whereabouts of Doctor O'Rorke and Doctor McDermot, respectively bishops of Killala and Elphin, is, that he saw the former travelling on the roads in the barony of Corran—a rather vague indication—and that he heard that the latter was some time ago in the upper part of the barony of Tirerrill—an information on which no sensible magistrate could think for a moment of taking action. If the same deponent appears to be somewhat more definite regarding the place of abode of Reverend Bryan Higgins, no doubt he took the precaution of putting the priest on his guard, in order that he would not be *at home* in case the agents of the law favoured Dunmore with a call.

Some facts worth noting may be gathered from these interesting depositions—first, that priests sometimes laid aside their real names and assumed others, in order the better to baffle their persecutors. Thus Reverend Bryan McDermot Roe dropped his suspicious Celtic patronymic, and took instead the simple sounding Saxon name of Smith. Second, that Mass used to be said in all sorts of places; in private houses, in waste houses, in the open fields, as at Drynaghan, and, at least before the Proclamation, in the ruins of the old Abbey. Third, that there was hardly any fixed time for the celebration of Mass—Thomas Corcoran and others hearing Mass "about fifteen days ago;" James Fahy, apothecary, "several times within the past six months;" William Ward and Hugh Gallagher, of Carney, "about three weeks ago". And the place was as unsettled as the time, the priest officiating now in one spot and again in another, the two spots being perhaps far distant from one another, as Kilshalvey and Carrickbanaghar, in which Reverend Teige Davy successively celebrated. The rule of these celebrations would seem to be that the priest selected a time and place when and where he expected to be secure, and communicated the selection through trusty messengers to the neighbouring Catholics, who at the appointed time proceeded as quietly as they could to the rendezvous. On this principle the people seldom continued to frequent the same place for any length of time, but moved about as considerations of safety and convenience required, like Bryan McDonogh of Behy, who heard Mass now at Tawnagh, and next time at Carrickbanaghar, in the parish of Ballysadare. By often shifting their stations in this way they eluded the plans of the local authorities, who kept constantly writing explanations and excuses to the Castle.

The same professions of zeal, the same apology for absence of results, the same application for military aid, made so often before, were renewed on the 29th October, 1714, on the part of the magistrates, by the High Sheriff, William Smith, who in reply to a communication from Dublin Castle inquiring "what Popish priests or other persons were under sentence of transportation in Sligo gaol", observes, "There never were any committed, nor under that sentence during my time; the magistrates here have been zealous and active in putting the law in execution against them, but the Papists are so numerous in this country that without the assistance of the army there is no good to be done". This letter, and the communication from the Castle, to which it is an answer, were written two months after the death of Anne, from which it appears that the persecution no way slackened in the county Sligo on her decease. Indeed, upon the accession of the House of Hanover there was rather an increase than a decline of persecution at Sligo, the cause or pretext being fear of the Pretender. John de Butte was provost of Sligo at that time, and consequently, the chief local authority; and a letter which he wrote to the Secretary of the Lords Justices, describing the measures he had taken in execution of their Lordships' instructions, contains so many interesting and authentic particulars of the treatment to which the Catholics of the town were subjected, that the reader will be glad to peruse the *ipsissima verba* for himself:—

"Sligo, August 4th, 1715.

"In obedience to their Excellencies, the Lords Justices, proclamation, which was delivered to me by the high sheriff of this county, for securing all horses, arms, armour, and ammunition in Papist, and disaffected hands, and for tendering the oath to them, I did immediately go with the high sheriff, Pierce Gethen, Esq., and George Ormsby, Esq., to search all suspected places within the borough, and found one caske of gunpowder in the hands of one Charles Ffallon, a Papist who refused to take the oath of abjuration as did three others of the beste sort of Papists of this town *for which I sent them to his Majesty's Gaole*, as I did also another Papist, who harboured two non-juring Popish Priests, and *had one of them in bed in his own house* when we went to search. I have ordered a good guard of thirty stanch Protestants to duty in this burough in order to assist the civil magistrates, and preserve the public peace if occasion be, and have secured all the Papists' horses in the burough. The Justices of the Peace are very active and diligent throughout the whole country, and particularly the High Sheriff, Pierce Gethen, Esq., George Ormsby, Esq., and Robert Lindsay, Esq., who went themselves in person to summon and seize all according to their Excellencies order, and am sure will give the Government a very satisfactory account of their proceedings. I thought it my indispencible duty to lett you know what is done in this Burrough in order to their Excellencies command.

"Your most humble servant,
JOHN DE BUTT, *Provost*".

The same real or pretended concern about the Pretender continued to trouble those in authority at Sligo; and, in 1729, Owen Wynne, Brigadier-General, now the foremost man in the borough, if not in the county, held an investigation on the subject, and examined several witnesses, much in the same way as suspected persons were recently examined in preliminary inquiries under the Crimes Act. With one exception, all the witnesses averred that they knew nothing of the matter; and the exception in question, one Edward Martin, while he "suspected a townsman named Thady Hart", of enlisting for the Pretender, was unable to prove any overt acts, though so eager to do so, that he communicated to the General a confidential letter he had received from Hart. It came out in these proceedings that "shipping goods" was the cant phrase for dispatching recruits to the Pretender. In Mr. Wynne's report to the Castle, he states his belief that Thady Hart, and any of his recruits, that had not been already shipped, might be found at the "Crown in Church-street".

We find the infamous Discovery clause of Anne's second Act, *To prevent the further growth of Popery*, in full operation in this district. It is often said that, though this and similar atrocious enactments may certainly be found on the Statute book, they were allowed to sleep or to remain a dead letter; but it is clear from what has been already said, and from the legal records of the country, that they were enforced as often as they safely could be.

The first discoverer under the act, in the county Sligo, was a wretch named Jeremiah Fury, a not inappropriate name for so malevolent a being. Finding Teige Reagh Kelly, a Catholic of Tireragh, holding, on lease, a valuable farm under William Griffith, Fury files a bill on the 28th August, 1754, against both Griffith and Kelly; and though the landlord, Griffith, who was a man of standing and influence in the county, used all the means, legal and other, which he could to defend the case, a decree for possession was granted on the 17th April, 1758, in the following terms:—"That the Plaintiff, as the first real Protestant discoverer under the acts to prevent the further growth of Popery, shall have the full benefit of the lease of the castle quarter of Bunina, being parcel of the lands of Ballinphull, in the county of Sligoe, and also the covenants for renewal for ever in said lease contained, executed by Humphrey Griffiths, and that an injunction shall forthwith issue directed to the sheriff of the county Sligo, to put the Plaintiff into the possession of said premises". *That property worth about £120 a year, is still in the possession of Jeremiah Fury's descendants.*

A few years later, in 1761, another villain received his decree for possession of various lands in and around Glaneask, in the barony of Leyney, the discoverer and his victim being each of the name of Fallen.

Another local instance of this iniquitous though legal spoliation of Catholics may be mentioned here. It was not precisely a case of discovery, though one of kindred, and perhaps, still deeper infamy. It was the violation of the sacred duties of trusteeship, for the purpose of robbing the innocent and confiding persons who delivered the trust. The sufferers in this case were Charles Hart and his brother, Right Reverend John Hart, bishop of Achonry. To save their estate of Cloonamahon, which they could not themselves retain without taking the oath of abjuration, they conveyed the property in due form, to Laurence Bettridge, a Protestant neighbour and intimate of theirs, who undertook and engaged to protect and administer it for them; but this vile hypocrite had hardly got formal possession, when he cast out the Harts on the highway, where they must have perished of cold and hunger, had not a good Samaritan, one of the Annaghmore O'Haras, given them a cottage and some land at Annaghbeg, where the bishop, whose hospitality at Cloonamahon had been celebrated in song by Carolan, was obliged to depend, through the remainder of his life, for his daily bread, on the charity of the neighbours.

Laurence Bettridge was the black sheep of the Protestant trustees of that period, for it is well known that those who undertook the trusteeship of the Catholic property performed the duties of the trust with singular fidelity and honour. On this subject Mr. Froude, writes: "Many Catholic families retained their properties without sacrificing their creed, by conveying them to a Protestant kinsman or neighbour. The terms of the statute were so stringent that they were obliged to trust entirely to honour and good faith; yet, in no known instance, was their confidence abused". The historian had not heard of the case of Laurence Bettridge and Charles Hart; and county Sligo people must regret that the disgrace of supplying the one "known instance" of violation of Protestant trusteeship, lies on their county.

The reader has, in this chapter, an authentic and suggestive specimen of the Penal Code, as enforced in the county, in the early years of the eighteenth century.

An anecdote connected with the Nugents of Westmeath, who had large possessions in the county Sligo, may he added, as it brings out well the demoralizing operations of the code. Owing to some after-dinner altercation between Christopher Nugent and his son Lewellyn, or Lally, the latter threatened to have his revenge; and mounting horse on the day after the quarrel, set off for Dublin' without letting anyone know what was bringing him there. The father, divining that the son's object was to conform to the State religion, and thus gain the family estate, took horse himself, and, travelling by a shorter road, reached the city before the son, and, having arrived in the capital, lost no time in proceeding to Christ Church, and going through the ceremony or process of abjuration. Having completed the act of apostasy he met, as he was leaving the church, the son coming in to conform, and to humiliate him for his defeat in the race of infamy, accosted him with the cynical jeer, "Lally, you are late!" Such was family virtue as developed by the anti-Catholic laws of the time.

CHAPTER XI

THE ABBEY

Resuming now, from a preceding page our account of the Abbey, or rather the convent, of Sligo—for convent is the correct designation of a Dominican monastery—the building was burned down in the year 1414.[1] Formidable as fire often proves even in this age of fire engines and fire brigades, it was incomparably more destructive in the past, when no such means of coping with the element existed, and when the materials of houses and other structures were much more combustible. The *Annals of the Four Masters*, in almost every page, records the burning of buildings, public and private, civil and ecclesiastical; the fire resulting sometimes from lightning, as happened at Lough Ce;[2] not infrequently from accident, as in the case under consideration, but chiefly from the deliberate act of man, who in former ages wrought almost as much mischief with the torch as with the sword. That this part of the country had no exemption from the visitation, we may infer from the facts that the Convent of Athleathan, built in 1252, the year in which Sligo was built, was burned down in 1254;[3] that the monastery of Church Island, in Lough Gill, was burned in 1416, two years after that of Sligo; that the church of Kilronan, erected in 1239, was reduced to ashes in 1240; and that the noble pile of Creevalea, constructed at enormous expense in 1508, succumbed to the flames in 1536, a few years after its erection.[4] And the evil was not confined to Ireland; for Fuller, in his Church History, states that there was scarcely a great abbey in England which had not been at least once burned down by lightning.

Though the town of Sligo was burned down at least five different times in 1257, 1270, 1383, 1396, and 1398 between the year 1252, when the convent was erected, and 1414 when it was destroyed by fire, it is no where

---

[1] The Monastery of Sligo was burned by a candle in the spring of this year. Four Masters, A.D. 1414.

[2] The Rock of Lough Key was burned by lightning. Duvesa, daughter of O'Heyne, and wife of Conor MacDermot, Lord of Moylung, with seven hundred (or seven score) others, or more, both men and women, were drowned or burned in it in the course of one hour. Four Masters, A.D. 1187.

[3] The Dominican Monastery of Ath-leathan was totally destroyed by fire, Four Masters, sub an.

[4] For a graphic history of Creevalea, and the other Franciscan Monasteries of Ireland, see Father Meehan's charming book, "The Franciscan Monasteries and the Irish Hierarchy in the 17th Century". And having mentioned Father Meehan's name, one cannot help adding that this gifted priest has shed more light on the civil and ecclesiastical history of Ireland in the seventeenth century than any other writer, living or dead, that could be named. It is hard to decide which we should admire more the exhaustive research, or the literary finish, of his numerous works.

stated that the religious house suffered on any of these occasions; and as it is very likely that there would have been special mention of the occurrence, had it happened, we may fairly infer that the monastery escaped the flames which destroyed the other structures of the place.

When it fell, in 1414, there was no time lost in restoring it. The Prior at the time was Bryan MacDonogh, son of Dermod MacDonogh, Tanist of Tirerrill, and member of the great family of that name, settled at Collooney. It was fortunate to have such a man in office then; for being connected by kindred or marriage with most of the great families of Lower Connaught—the MacDonoghs, the O'Connors, the O'Rorkes, the O'Dowds, he had more local influence than others could command. It is likely, too, he had private means, which, as he had given up his station in the world for the love of God, he would have been glad to devote from the same motive to the re-erection of the monastery. With such advantages he must have obtained much aid in the district towards the great work in hand; but as the undertaking was so weighty and expensive that he could not, with all his exertions and influence, secure means enough of himself in Ireland for its accomplishment, he solicited the co-operation of the Pope of the day, John XXIII.

It so happened that John was then at Constance, presiding over the Council assembled there, and though he was in a very critical situation at the moment, a situation from which he tried to free himself, two months later, by escaping from the city, disguised as a groom, he still found means to send the Prior the following apostolic letters:

"John, Bishop, servant of the servants of God, to all the faithful of Christ, who shall see these letters, health and apostolic benediction.

.   .   .   .

"Since then, as we have been informed, the church and convent of the Friars Preachers at Sligo, in the Diocese of Elphin, where, it is stated, twenty friars devoted themselves to the service of God, have been recently burned down, and the Prior and some friars of the Order desire to restore the same, in a style entailing great outlay, which they have no means themselves of meeting, we, who are anxious that the church itself be duly honoured, and that both church and convent be restored, confiding in the mercy of the Almighty God, and the authority of his apostles, Peter and Paul, do hereby grant, to such persons as shall devoutly visit the church on the festival of the Assumption of the Blessed Virgin Mary, and that of Saint Patrick, and contribute towards its restoration, an indulgence of ten years and as many quarantines (provided they be truly sorry for their sins, and have rightly confessed the same), in order that the faithful may be the more willing to betake themselves to the church, and have a hand in its restoration, when they know the grace and indulgence they may thus obtain.

We will, however, that these our letters have no effect if, mayhap, we should have already granted any indulgence, either in perpetuity or for a fixed time not yet fully expired, to persons visiting the church, or aiding it with their alms. Given at Constance on the sixteenth of the Kalends of February (17th January) and fifth of our Pontificate (1415)".

Notwithstanding the divisions which prevailed in Christendom at this period, for it was the time of the great schism of the West, there can be no doubt that the foregoing document procured abundant alms for the convent, and brought crowds of Pilgrims from all parts of Ireland, on the feasts of the Assumption and St. Patrick, to the church, in order to gain the indulgence.

There is nothing very definite known about local benefactors. The Four Masters mention none except the Prior, Bryan MacDonogh; but the names of one or two more are found in other writers. De Burgo informs us that the O'Connor of the day was the chief contributor, but he gives no authority for the statement, unless he refers, which is doubtful, to O'Heyne, who makes O'Connor the original founder of the abbey, and who, being wrong in this important point, is entitled to little credit in regard to the minor matter. Bryan, the son of Donnell O'Connor, was Lord of Sligo at this time. During his long rule of thirty-seven years he was constantly engaged in war; and though we have repeated mention in the *Annals of the Four Masters* of his military movements, there is no allusion to any benefaction of his to the convent. He may, however, notwithstanding this silence, have had a hand in the good work. In any case it is not from him but from his brother, Owen, the O'Connors Sligo descend.

The name of Pierce O'Timony is given as that of another special benefactor, in the *Hibernia Dominicana*, which also states, that he was a man of high family, great wealth, and singular virtue, and that his statue was set up by the Dominicans in the cloister of the convent, as a lasting memorial of their gratitude. Of this generous man there is nothing else handed down, either in writing, or tradition, nor are his descendants known, if he has left any. The statue too has disappeared, and has left no trace, or fragment behind, though De Burgo informs us, that it was to be seen in the cloister in his own day.

Between the Pope and local benefactors the convent was restored in a style of great magnificence. It was apparently the finest conventual building in Ireland; and the historian of the Irish Dominicans, while admitting, that the remains of Cashel and Ballindoon may have been more extensive and better preserved, maintains that for beauty, Sligo bears away the palm from them all.

To help us to a better idea of the building we should put out of mind their present surroundings. In former times the convent was the most easterly structure in Sligo; and even so late as the middle of the seventeenth century, it was spoken of as situated "near Sligo", which would prove that no streets or houses surrounded the site then, as they do now, to the great injury of its appearance. The establishment, too, was much more extensive than present appearances would lead one to think; for while it reached from the site of Abbey Street to the river, it stretched from the line of Thomas Street, to the old Distillery, the adjoining land being its gardens, parks, and pleasure grounds.

The church, which lay to the south of the conventual buildings, as usually happened in establishments of the Mendicant Orders in Ireland, was built of rubble limestone, the dressings of doors and windows being carved limestone. The present length of the ruin is, in interior measurement, 132 feet: that is, 43 feet 9 inches in chancel; 14 feet 3 inches in tower; and 74 feet in nave; but, as the western gable has long since disappeared, there is no means now of determining the exact original length of nave, which was probably longer than it now appears. There are in the eastern end of the south side wall, eight Early English lancet windows, fourteen feet high from lintel to soffit of arch, one of the windows, however, being blocked up by the tower wall, which, by the way, would show the tower to be an addition to the original building. At the western end of the same sidewall, there was a small aisle, having arches resting on octagon piers, and opening into the transept, a feature which is found also in the church of Kilcrea, county Cork, and other churches. The central tower rests on gothic arches, elaborately carved pendants descending from soffit,[1] and terminating in interlaced work. About 80 feet high, the tower is divided by two string courses into three stages, the two upper stages being lit by a two-light window, with a quatrefoil head. The roof of nave was very high pitched, for the water table, which protected it from the wet, at its junction with the tower wall, still projects from the wall, in the form of an acute angled triangle. A door leads from chancel to conventual buildings, and another, which is now blocked up, led from the tower to the ambulatory. The present level of the chancel and nave floor seems to be about two feet above the original level.

The high altar of cut stone, which was placed against the eastern gable, still remains *in situ*. The pendant, or front support of the slab, is richly decorated; ears of wheat and bunches of grapes, as emblems of the holy eucharist, being carved in relief upon it. It may be mentioned that the unsightly mass of bones, of which Gabriel Beranger[2] speaks, has been long since removed.

---

[1] Brash in Kilkenny Archaeological Journal, Vol. II., p. 88.
[2] This accomplished artist writes thus of Sligo convent, "The Abbey of Sligo is most pleasingly situated on the banks of the river Garrowoge, which originates in Lough Gill.

The eastern gable contains a fine pointed Gothic window, the head or arch being filled with graceful tracery, and the lower part divided into four lights by mullions. A slender staff or bead moulding of reddish sandstone, which rises from two exquisitely carved bases, and runs round the window, adds much to the beauty of its appearance.

While considerable portions of the conventual buildings remain, they are still incomplete and imperfect. A range of ruins, 137 feet long, stretches at right angles from the eastern end of the north side wall towards the river, and is terminated, on one side, by the side wall, and on the other by a spiral staircase, furnished still with many of the original stone steps. It was this staircase that led to the second floor, which contained the dormitories of the prior and community a large apartment, 27 feet wide, and well lighted by four square-headed windows. The floor of this range rested on vaults which are 13 feet 6 inches wide, clear of walls, and which are arched with sandstone flags, dropped endwise into the work. The basement under the arches contained the sacristy, the sacristan's laundry, and, probably, the cellar.

Parallel to the side wall of the church at the north side, and eastern end, is a structure which looks the oldest piece of masonry on the ground. It is terminated to the east by a gable, which is 20 feet 9 inches wide, and contains a small Gothic window with limestone mullions, but this window is plainly an insertion, as the jambs and mullions of a large original ope, with sandstone dressings, are still visible. The entrance to this apartment, at present, is through the east side of cloister, but this was not always so; and the interior too is so much changed by recent "restoration", as to afford no good idea of the details of the structure, as it stood in the past.

Though the plan of the whole establishment was, no doubt, a square, as was the plan of all similar structures in the Dominican and Franciscan Orders, there is little trace now of two sides of the square, the west and the north side. These must have been demolished when Thomas Street was forming; for it is known that the houses of that street were built, for the most part, with materials thus obtained; and only that Very Rev. Prior

---

It was a spacious and magnificent building, as well as one could judge by its remains of very good workmanship. The east window is beautiful. The altar under it was covered with bones and skulls in such quantity that they would serve to load a small vessel. The cloisters, of which three sides are extant, are magnificent. The arches and pillars being of excellent workmanship, and a few of these pillars adorned, as is seen in the drawing. The cloisters are still covered by an arched roof. In the corner to the right as one looks to the altar, and marked A in the plan, up several feet from the ground, are the tombs of the O'Connors, which was very exact in the drawing which Col. Burton gave us. The tower in the centre of the building is pretty entire except the battlements at the top. We could not discover any steps to get up, which must have been stopped up or destroyed by time. We were told that the building extended to the river side, but could not trace it". —Tour through Connaught in 1779.

Conlon succeeded in stopping this vandalism, much more of Holy Cross would have been ruined. The demolition of the northern side of the square, or of as much of it as is missing, dates apparently from the same time. Judging by the analogy of other religious houses, the west side contained the kitchen and the bake house, and, over these structures, apartments to serve for the library and for stranger's refectory and dormitories; while the chapter house, and some other adjuncts of the establishment stood to the north of the cloister, and formed the north side of the square. The people say that the convent extended formerly down to the river; but there are no remains or evidence now of such extension; and, with the exception of a mill and fish tank, which, there is reason to believe, were placed close to the water's edge, as usually happened in large monasteries similarly situated, it is doubtful whether any substantial structure stood between the north side of the square and the river.

The cloister must have been superior to anything of the kind in the country. All who visit the Abbey are filled with admiration in looking at it; and the greater the visitor's experience, culture, and taste, the greater his gratification. A gentleman, who was at once an architect and an artist, and whose studies made him intimately acquainted with all the ecclesiastical ruins of Ireland, having visited the convent in company with the writer, exhibited much feeling on coming before the cloister, and, after contemplating its beauties in silence for several minutes, threw up his hands in admiration, and exclaimed, nearly in the words already quoted from De Burgo:—"Oh, this beats out anything and everything we have in Ireland". It is told of the elder Pugin that, in his visits to Paris, it was almost impossible to tear him away from the *Sainte Chapelle*, which he always reckoned the most perfect piece of Gothic architecture in the world; and it was about as difficult a matter to get away this visitor from before the cloisters in which his professional and cultivated eye was constantly discovering new perfections.

Originally this cloister formed a square or great quadrangle, three sides of which still survive, and in fair preservation. All round the quadrangle ran a covered arcade. Each side is parted from the garth, or uncovered plat, by a series of Gothic arches which rest on piers; the height from base to apex of arch being 4 feet 2 inches; the width 1 foot 11½ inches; and 249 the perpendicular height from springing to soffit of arch, 15 inches. The piers consist each of two columns, one inside the other, and both connected together at top and bottom by means of common caps and bases. It is more especially in designing and executing these piers—columns, caps, and bases—the architect draws on his resources, and the artist shows his master hand. Though there are 14 piers in the north cloister,

18 in the east, and 13 in the south, hardly one in the three series resembles, in all respects, another.

While the size and proportions of the arches are all the same as they ought to be, to insure the necessary uniformity in the appearance of the ranges, the ornamentation is diverse, as well in the caps and bases, which are differently moulded, as in the columns, some of which are fluted, some diapered, some panelled, some twisted, the fluting, the diapering, the panelling, the twisting, being always varied in pattern if applied a second time or oftener to successive columns.

OLD ABBEY, AND SPECIMEN OF CLOISTERS, SLIGO, 1776.[1]

A buttress rose from the open square or garth against the centre of each side, and served, not only for strength, but for ornament, being beautifully designed and executed, and containing, probably, a small statue as one of its members; for this latter circumstance may fairly be inferred from the fact that the stone statue, which stands now on the high altar, fits exactly into the place of a missing member of one of these buttresses, to which, therefore, it must have belonged. The ambulatory, which ran round the four sides of the cloisters, was covered with a vaulted roof, most of which still remains, and was 6 feet 6 inches inside, so as to serve for exercise

---

[1] The convent church in this illustration is drawn on the wood by Mr. Wakeman from a sketch which was made in 1776, and which was kindly lent by the Honourable Evelyn Ashley to the writer.

The specimen columns are after Grose. It is right, however, to add, that the cloister arches are all, without exception, Gothic, though, through some unaccountable oversight, they are Norman, in Grose's "Antiquities of Ireland".

and recreation in wet or broken weather. The cloister square accommodated congregations, which assembled there, in the open air, to receive religious instruction; and the stone pulpit, from which the preacher addressed them, stood on the north side, and was built partly into the wall, at the height of about eight or ten feet from the ground, where some of it may still be seen. The approach from the pulpit was from the north wing of the conventual buildings, and was hid off from the congregation by a high wall, so that nothing could be seen of the preacher, till he emerged through the thickness of the wall, by a doorway that still remains, and appeared in the chair.

Though the sermons and discourses delivered from this pulpit were intended for congregations, assembled in fair weather under the sky, still, if it came on wet, there was no need to put off or interrupt the service, as the people could retire through the arches into the covered cloisters, where the speaker's voice easily followed and reached them. A visit, then, to this portion of the ruins, while it sets under the eye some beautiful works of art, for which we are indebted to the religious, brings also to mind a much higher sphere of their usefulness, in which they not only instructed the people habitually in the church, but assembled them in the open air, on special occasions, in numbers which the church could not contain, the better thus to stir up in them the energies of spiritual life, to strengthen them, perhaps, under the pressure of some great calamity, to nerve them, it may be, for the performance of some common duty, and, in any case, to train them to do and suffer everything for the "one thing necessary".

After a close examination of the building we find it impossible to discriminate confidently between the parts of the original foundation and those added in 1415, or since. Much of the Fitzgerald church still exists, though the walls have been, in all likelihood, somewhat lengthened at the western end, and the parts, breached by the fire, repaired. The south-eastern angle of the chancel bears, at present, unmistakable marks of burning, which goes far to show that this part of the house existed and suffered in 1414, though it is still quite possible that the injury may date from 1642, when Sir Frederick Hamilton gave the place to the flames. The lancet windows in the south side-wall are, most probably, co-eval with the original foundation; for we find a similar range of eight lancet windows in the Franciscan church of Buttevant, which was built in the thirteenth century, in 1251, within a year or two of the building of Sligo Convent. The small structure, parallel to the north sidewall of church, which, as has been said, appears to be the oldest bit of building on the premises, is certainly part of the work of Maurice Fitzgerald; while the walls to the back of the cloister ambulatory, at all events parts of them, are of more modern erection than the church, it is doubtful whether the same should be said of the cloister arches. The ornate and expensive style, in which this portion of the convent is finished, shows it to have been built at a time when architecture was flourishing, and by persons who had ample means to draw on; but this consideration is not enough to fix the time; for if the Apostolic Letters and the liberality of local benefactors placed such means at the disposal of Prior MacDonogh and his community, it is equally a fact that Maurice Fitzgerald, who was Lord Deputy, and probably, the wealthiest man of his day, had also abundant resources for the work. Nor does the state of architecture, at the period of the foundation, in 1253, militate against the earlier date; for we find that columns quite as finished and beautiful, which still exist, were put up in the church of Buttevant at that date. Some little argument, in favour of the later period, may perhaps be drawn from the appearance of the work, parts of which look as fresh and clean as if they had only come from under the chisel.

On the other hand, the central tower may be referred, with certainty, to the time of the restoration, as well, because it is not bonded into the side-walls, which it would be, had it formed part of the original design, as also because such towers are not found in churches anterior to the fourteenth century. If we except then this tower, some walls or parts of walls in the conventual buildings, and, of course, the roof, the whole establishment, such as it existed in its palmiest day, may have been the work of Maurice Fitzgerald, though some writers, without authority or reason to support them, date all the buildings from the time of the restoration after the fire.

The convent was dedicated from the beginning to God under the invocation of the Holy Cross; and, unlike some other religious establishments of Ireland, which have undergone several dedications, and received thus new names and new patrons, continued so dedicated to the end. The early Geraldines had a special devotion to the cross, which they showed not only by bearing a red cross on their coat of arms, as their descendants still do, but also by causing the three Dominican houses, which they founded in Ireland—Sligo, Tralee, and Youghal to be dedicated under the style and title of Holy Cross. It may be remarked here in passing, with De Burgo, that the Irish had always particular veneration for the cross, so that there was a custom among those of them who recited the divine office, to say always the antiphon, versicle, and collect of Holy Cross after the Salve Regina in Complin.

The church must have contained a large number of imposing tombs, judging by those which still exist, and, still more, by the numerous fragments that lie scattered about. To the left, as you enter, you see recessed into the north wall of the nave, an elaborate altar tomb, still in fair preservation, which from its proportions and sculpture one would be inclined to count the most interesting piece of art in the place. Petrie, it appears, made a detailed drawing of this beautiful monument, but the writer, who would gladly give an engraving of it, regrets that his many inquiries have not enabled him to learn where or with whom the drawing now is. This tomb belonged to the O'Creans or Creans who were the wealthiest people of Sligo, in the sixteenth and seventeenth centuries, and who expended no small share of their wealth on works of art, and, more especially, on works of art connected with religion. Several monuments of theirs which are now broken up, occupied the north and south sides of the tower. Inside the western arch of the tower are sculptured, on two small flags, two heraldic shields—one bearing the arms of the O'Creans, and the other the arms of the Jones of Banada; and under one of the shields may be deciphered, with some little trouble, the following curious lines:—

> *"Wee two are one by His decree*
> *That reigneth from eternity*
> *That first erected have these stones*
> *Wee Kobuck Crean and Alice Jones".*[1]

It would appear probable from these lines that one of the O'Creans was married to a daughter or niece of Sir Roger Jones, from whom the Joneses of Banada descend; he and a brother being the only Joneses then in Sligo; and we might be justified in inferring from the suggestive wording of the two first lines, coupled with the fact that Sir Roger's family was then Protestant, and the O'Crean's Catholic, that the marriage, while duly celebrated in *facie ecclesiae*, was not contracted before a Protestant minister, as the civil laws of the day required. At the top of the O'Crean shield is the date 1625.

The mural monument of Sir Donogh O'Connor and Lady Desmond, which stands seven or eighth feet above the ground, in the eastern end of the south side wall, has been often engraved from an admirable drawing of Mr. Grose, and is thus the best known object in the entire building. In this monument the knight and his wife are represented kneeling in prayer, under an alcove, with a *prie Dieu* between them, the lady wearing her coronet and the knight bare-headed, his helmet being laid on the floor behind him. The whole is divided into six stages by chamfered string courses; and on the lowest we see the emblems of death and the grave in four skulls, a spade, and a time glass; in the second, the effigies of two angels; in the third, which is the chiefest, the kneeling figures of Sir Donogh and Lady Desmond, as

---

[1] It is not likely that the above epitaph was composed on the principle of the following, which is found at Launceston in Tasmania:
"Beneath this rustic pile of stones
Lie the remains of Mary Jones
Her name was Lloyd; it was not Jones;
But Jones was put to rhyme with stones".

just described; in the fourth, three shields, one over the lady, another over the knight, and the third in the centre—the first bearing devices, which cannot be deciphered, the second bearing a tree, and the third, which is surmounted with a coronet, a swine; in the fifth, the effigies again of two angels; and in the sixth and last, Saint Peter on one side, Saint Paul on the other, and between them, but on a much higher level, the cross with the Redeemer fastene

The design is bold and effective; resembling much the great Earl of Boyle's famous monument in St. Patrick's Cathedral, Dublin,[1] and considering the hardness and untractableness of the material—native

---

[1] This monument, of which a beautiful engraving is given in Monk Mason's "Saint Patrick's Cathedral",—Notes, page 411, was erected by the Earl over "his most dear, virtuous, and religious wife, the Ladie Katherine", and is, says Mason, "an interesting object, as well from the grandeur of its appearance, as on account of the schisms and factions which it occasioned in the ecclesiastical and civil departments of the State". The object, however, of this reference to it, is not to notice the quarrel to the death which it bred between the Earl of Strafford, and the Earl of Cork, but to call attention to the great resemblance, which it bears in *outline and general appearance*, to the Sligo monument resemblance so striking as to lead to the conclusion that one must be a copy of the other. And, admitting the conclusion, the structure in St. Patrick's must be the copy, and that in Holy Cross, the original, as the latter was erected several years before the other. We thus get a good idea of the high estimation in which Sir Donogh's monument was held as a work of art, when we find the great Earl of Cork, the wealthiest man in Ireland, and the most magnificent in his tastes, come to Holy Cross for a model when about to erect, regardless of expense, as splendid a memorial as possible in honour of his wife.

limestone—the figures and other objects represented show a roundness, a softness, and a suppleness, which evince a considerable skill in the sculptor, as well as great fineness and delicacy of touch. The following epitaph appears on the lowest compartment:—"*Hic jacet famosissimus miles Donatus Cornelianus comitatus Sligiae dominus cum sua uxore illustrissima domina Elinora Butler comitissa Desmoniae, quae me fieri fecit A.D. 1624, post mortem sui mariti, qui obiit 11 Aug., 1609, item ejus filia et primi mariti, viz. Comitis Desmoniae nomine Elizabetha valde virtuosa domina Sepulta fuit hoc in tumulo 31 Novem. anno Domini, 1623".* Here lies the renowned knight Donogh O'Connor, Lord of the county Sligo, with his wife, the most noble Lady Eleanor Butler, Countess of Desmond, who caused me to be made in the year of our Lord, 1624, after the death of her husband, who died the 11th August, 1609. Also her daughter by her first husband, who was named Elizabeth, and was a most virtuous lady. She was buried in this tomb, the 31st November, AD. 1623.[1]

This monument was erected at the expense of Lady Eleanor, and apparently, during her lifetime; for though Lodge[2] implies the contrary, in using the word "bequeath "; the above epitaph, of which he appears to have known nothing, makes it clear that the structure was in existence in 1624, when the countess was alive. Lodge adds that the burial of Sir Donogh and his wife was to be "in a chapel which she directed to be built near the abbey of St. Dominick in Sligo;" but instead of such a chapel, apart from the convent, Lady Eleanor, no doubt, meant a crypt or subterranean chapel, in which the bodies should be laid, which, judging by a blocked up arch or doorway in the eastern gable, was actually built, and which, if searched for, may probably be found directly under the mural monument in the chancel part of the church.

Had this liberal lady her own way she would have left after her in Sligo an institution, which must have proved a great blessing. By her will she bequeathed £300—equal to ten times that sum now, towards the erection and support of an hospital for the poor,[3] the money to come out

---

[1] The original inscription is rapidly becoming illegible, and owing to its height from the ground, needs no little exertion in those who would decipher it. For his copy of it the writer is indebted to the kindness of Dr. Cox, St. Vincent's Hospital, Dublin.

[2] Lodge's Peerage of Ireland, Vol. I., p. 75.

[3] Lodge gives the following interesting particulars of her will:—By her will she appointed her sons-in-law, Sir Daniel O'Brien and Sir Robert Cressy, Knights, her executors, and willed them to pay all her debts, called her stated accounts, and her funeral expenses, out of her moveable goods and chattels; and after the discharge thereof, her legacies; she gave to her daughter Joan a silver ewer and basin, and to her daughter Ellen, all the rest of her plate, jewels and goods; she left to Daniel Cridegane, Clerk, £20; to her servant William Stanley, £20; to Mary ni-Meyleene, £10; to Ellen St. John, £20; to Donogh Gradie, £40; to Mary ni-Briene, 40s.; to Margaret Oge and to Margaret Geare, three young cows a-piece. She bequeathed towards the building of an hospital in Sligo £100, and £200 more (both out of her arrears in England), to be laid out in an annuity mortgage, or land, so as

of the arrears due her in England by the Government, in lieu, there is reason to think, of the jointure which she lost on the attainder of her first husband; but this benevolent provision of her will never received effect; and the cause of its nullity could hardly be any other than an objection, on the part of the public authorities, to co-operate, in any way, in what might seem to be the endowment of a religious establishment.

Though the three monuments mentioned are the only old ones now in the church, it is pretty certain that there existed others still older, though now effaced by time, or destroyed by man, considering the many persons of leading families buried in it. Before the erection of Ballindoon, Ballymote, and Creevalea or Drumahaire, it was the burying place of all the chief families of Lower Connaught, as well as of the O'Connors Sligo, as sufficiently appears from the following entries of the Four Masters:—

"1336. Aine, daughter of Teige MacDonough, and wife of Tiernan O'Rourke (Lord of Breifny), the most favoured of the women of Leth Chuinn, died at Tuaim Seancha, on Lough Finvoy, and was interred at Sligo".

1402. Farrell O'Rourke, heir to the lordship of Breifney, a powerful, energetic, comely, and truly hospitable man, was slain in his own house by the Clann Caba, and was interred in the monastery of Sligo.

1418. Tiernan More, the son of Ualgarg O'Rourke, Lord of Briefny, the bravest and most puissant man that had come of Hy-Bruin race, a man who had wrested his principality from his enemies by the strength of his arm, died at an advanced age, about the festival of Saint Bridget, and was interred in the monastery of Sligo.

1454. Brian MacDonough, Chief of Tirerrill, died on the Friday before the Calends of January, after Unction and due Penance, and was interred in the monastery of Sligo.

1581. The Calbhach, son of Domhnall, son of Tadgh, son of Cathal Oge O'Connor, the undisputed heir of Sligo and Lower Connaught, died the Friday between the two Easters of this year, and the last day of the month of March. He was interred in Sligo.—*Annals of Loch Ce.*

1586. O'Hart, that is, Felim, the son of William O'Hart, died on Easter night, and was buried in Sligo on Monday. -Id.

1587. Owen, son of Rory, son of Felim, son of Manus (O'Connor), died a fortnight before All-hallowtide, and was buried in Sligo.—Id.

---

to yield £20 a year towards the support of the poor residing in said hospital. She left to Andrew Creane, of Armagh, Esq., and to his son John, £100 of her said arrears; to her grandchild, Ellenor Browne (in lieu of the debt she owed her), eight score pounds sterling of her said arrears; to her grandchildren, Mary and Catherine Browne, towards their preferment, £200 a-piece of her said arrears; and the like sum to Ellenor Butler, daughters of the then Lord Dunboyne; leaves divers legacies to her servants out of the said arrears; and wills her executors (if they shall receive them), to take her servant Cormac McDonnell, his debts, into their consideration, and see them paid, being the sum of £210, as they shall think fit in their discretion. The will is dated 5th Sept., 1636. The Peerage of Ireland by John Lodge, &c., Vol. I., p. 75.

1588. O'Connor Sligo, that is, Domhnall, the son of Tadgh, son of Cathal Oge, the choice of the Gaeidhel of Erinn, died on Little Christmas night in Sligo, and was buried in it.—Id.

There is little known, in comparison of what ought to be, of those who passed through the convent as inmates, owing, first, to the notorious indolence[1] of the Irish in committing their transactions to writing, and, secondly, to the loss, partly by persecution and partly by accident, of such documents as did exist. The contrast between the English and Scotch, on the one side, and the Irish, on the other, in the matter of records, must be humiliating to every Irishman that examines the subject. There is hardly a monastery in England or Scotland which has not its separate history in local annals, registers, memoirs, or similar documents; but little of the kind is to be found in Ireland; and if such aids to history are met with in a few religious houses of Ireland, it is those that were Anglo-Norman rather than Celtic.

The convent of Sligo was as Celtic an establishment as any in Ireland; for its community was usually recruited from the families of local chiefs, so that De Burgo, quoting O'Heyne, says that its inmates were generally "nobles". And in confirmation of this remark it may be noted that whenever the name of a religious of Holy Cross, Sligo, occurs in history, it is sure to be O'Connor, McDonogh, O'Crean, O'Hart, O'Beolan, or that of some other distinguished family of the neighbourhood.

Meagre, however, as are the records of the convent, they suffice to show that it produced some men of note, and among them, five provincials of the Irish province of the order; a very large contribution to the Provincialate, considering that there were forty-three Dominican houses in Ireland, and that there are only thirty-two undoubted provincials in De Burgo's list of those officials. Though the order of Friars Preachers or Dominicans was introduced into Ireland, in the year 1224, the country was only a vicariate of the province of England up to the year 1484, when it appears to have been constituted an independent province, separate and distinct from England.

From 1484 to 1536 there were sometimes three separate provincials or quasi provincials; one of the Reformed convents, another of the unreformed, and the third of the convents of the Pale; but after 1536, when Henry VIII fell into schism, all three were united by Paul III. into one province.

---

[1] De Burgo complains bitterly and often of this indolence. In his preface (page viii.) to the *Hibernia Dominicana* he writes: "Nullam prorsus opem literiariam recepi, quod antiquae jam et heu! minium notae *Hibernigenarum*, hisce in rebus ignaviae (absit in injuria verbo) partim attribuendum videtur, partim vero quia coenobia omnia, eorumque proinde archiva adeoque et plurima preclarissima monumenta, ex quibus laudabilissima nunc historia conscribi posset, Acatholicorum rabie in haud interruptis bellorum, et persecutionum cladibus a lapsu in schisma Henrici VIII. destructa fuere". See also page 526.

1. Whether there were other provincials, properly so called, in office in the sixteenth century before Thaddeus O'Devany may perhaps admit of much doubt, but it is stated by the author of *Hibernia Dominicana* to be quite certain (*"certo certius"*) that O'Devany was provincial in the year 1563. This good man was an alumnus of the convent of Sligo, and a native of the neighbourhood, where the name is still common and respectable; and, during his long life, for he did not die till 1608, he reflected great honour on his convent, and conferred great benefit on the Order. He was twice Provincial, and whether in office or out of it, had the chief hand in promoting the interests of his Institute. A paper presented to the Sacred Congregation in 1627, and giving a list of the convents then in Ireland, says: "All these convents were occupied by members of the Order before Henry VIII., King of England, and his daughter Elizabeth usurped the title of Supreme Head of the Church, and suppressed all the convents of all the religious Orders both in England and Ireland, expelling all the inmates and appropriating the revenues; but they were never able to root out the Dominicans from Ireland. For, though driven from their monasteries, they did not leave the kingdom, but concealed themselves in the houses of lay Catholics, or betook themselves to some convent of the Order, situated in inaccessible places, and in the possession of Catholics; and there they held their chapters as best they could, and made regulations suited to the times, living all through in obedience to one provincial or one vicar-general, who, during the whole of that period, up to about the year 1612, was the Very Reverend Father Thaddeus Devany. At his death the friars were dispersed among the secular Catholics".[1]

According to the annals of the Order, Father O'Devany was a man of great zeal and successful labours for religion. He received a large number to the habit, and was the means of saving the Order from extinction in Ireland. He is said also to have possessed miraculous gifts; for when somebody was lamenting before him the ravages wrought throughout the country by George Bingham, the brother of Sir Richard, "Give yourself no trouble now on that score," says O'Devany, "for George Bingham can do no more harm either to church or country", a true saying, for Bingham was just then slain in the castle of Sligo by Ulick Burke, though O'Devany had no natural means of knowing the fact.

While rendering most important service to his Order by procuring numerous recruits for it in Ireland, he laid it under still greater obligation by securing a new convent in Louvain, which was to serve as a seminary and novitiate for the education and training of Dominicans destined for the Irish mission. To obtain this asylum he spared no effort, direct or indirect, bringing all the influence, he could, to bear on the Spanish and Belgian

---

[1] Spicilegium Ossoriense, Vol I., p. 156.

authorities, with such effect, that, though the house was not actually obtained for several years after his death, the credit of the foundation is given to him. "Thaddeus O'Devany", says De Burgo, "who was now the Provincial of the desolate province, foreseeing that our Order would very soon become extinct in Ireland, unless a suitable place for the education of Irish Dominicans were found in some Catholic kingdom, left no stone unturned to obtain such a place, and succeeded in his efforts, though our religious did not take possession of Louvain till after his death, which occurred in 1608".

Being such a benefactor, it was natural that he should be held in great esteem by his Order, and, accordingly, we find the following appreciation of his merits in the acts of a General Congregation held in Rome in 1656:

"Father Thaddeus O'Devany, being full of zeal for the interests of religion, and for those of his Order and Institute, having received a great number of young men from all quarters to the habit, thus prevented the extinction of the Order in those regions in which he filled twice the office of Provincial .... Broken down by labour and old age, when he had reached his last days, and while the Catholics, who surrounded him, were deploring his departure, and their own great loss in consequence, he calmly foretold that he would not quit life before the arrival of a religious of the Order, who would assist him in his agony, and then succeed him in the administration of the sacraments to the faithful. It occurred just as he foretold; for on the very day of his most happy decease, Father Daniel O'Creidegan arrived from Portugal (having completed his studies at Lisbon,) and in his hands Father Thaddeus, full of years and merit, breathed his last, and fell asleep sweetly in the Lord. He was buried in the church of his convent at Sligo in the year 1608".

It is right to add that the Dominican Convent of Louvain, which O'Devany had so large a share in founding, and which got the name of Convent of Holy Cross, was, most probably, so called after Holy Cross convent, Sligo.

2. The next provincial which the Sligo convent supplied, was Daniel O'Creidegan, or O'Crean (for the two names are the same,) but a different person from the Daniel O'Creidegan that assisted at the death-bed of Father O'Devany. The Daniel we now speak of, seems to have been a contemporary of Father O'Devany through life, and, like him, to have been twice Provincial of the Irish province; first, between 1570 and 1590, and second from 1600 to 1603. In this latter year he left the country for Spain. Of him Bernard De Jonghe thus writes in his *Dominican Belgium*:—

"Towards the close of the seventeenth century, Elizabeth, the illegitimate daughter of Henry VIII, usurping the kingdoms of England, Scotland, and Ireland, and assailing with fury, churches, monasteries, and everything belonging to religion, wrought such havoc on holy places, that in 1603, the year in which she died, she had not left one single house unprofaned in the three kingdoms. All the religious were either driven out of the country or put to death, except a few mendicants, who hid themselves in inaccessible places, to guard and strengthen the faith of the Catholics that survived the persecution. Among these was the venerable Father

Daniel O'Creidegain, then (1603,) Provincial, an office he had held for a long time, and the venerable Father Thaddeus O'Devany, of the Convent of the Holy Cross, Sligo, the latter succeeded the former in the rule of this desolate province".

It is worthy of remark that the convent of Sligo alone, of all the Dominican houses in Ireland, was in a condition to furnish the Provincials of this time of persecution; and the explanation would seem to be that given by Dr. Lynch in his manuscript *History of the Irish Church*, that, through the influence of Sir Donnell O'Connor, this house enjoyed a tranquillity unknown to the other religious houses of the country. This exceptional quiet and security dates from the earlier years of Elizabeth's reign.

3. The Daniel O'Creidegain, who administered the last rites to Father O'Devany, was elected Provincial in 1631, and continued in office beyond the usual term of four years. Having lost his sight and fallen into bad health, he was received into the convent of Athenry in 1641, and treated there with great kindness and respect, till the house was broken up under the pressure of persecution, when, at his own request, he was sent on to Ballymote. Very probably he selected this asylum because there were family relations between his family and that of the Taaffes, who then owned and held Ballymote castle. The castle, however, having been taken by the Parliamentary forces in 1652, Father O'Creidegain fell into their hands; and it is gratifying to be able to record, as it proves that no human heart, no matter how hardened, is always impervious to a feeling of compassion, that Sir Charles Coote not only spared his life, but, sympathizing with him in his misery, sent him on, under a safe conduct, to Sligo, and ordered every house in the town to contribute four pence a year towards his maintenance while he lived. The good man was so attached to his habit that nothing in the world could induce him to put it off. Clad in it he moved through the streets day after day; and, it is told, that those who differed from him in religion, instead of resenting the proceeding or molesting him in any way for it, only thought all the more of him for his consistency and constancy. Though disabled by blindness and poor health from doing much that he desired to do, he still managed to render valuable service to the cause of religion, by begging alms from the charitable throughout the country, and employing the large sums thus received, in supplying suitable food to persons imprisoned on account of their faith. He was the Daniel Creidegain, Clerk, mentioned in Lady Desmond's will for a legacy of £20, which, like the other sums that came into his hands, went, no doubt, to the relief of the imprisoned confessors. Father Creidegain died in 1655, and carried with him to his grave in the convent of Holy Cross, not only the love and veneration of Catholics, but the respect and admiration of all who knew him, whatever was their religion.

4. John O'Hart, of Holy Cross, Sligo, was instituted Provincial of the Irish Dominicans, in 1660, and was continued in that position by the Master

General of the Order to 1669, partly because it was hard to assemble a chapter for the election of a new Provincial at the end of Father O'Hart's first term of office, and, partly, because the Master General wished to mark, by re-appointing him for a second term, his appreciation of the Father's great personal worth. That this Provincial was a person of more than ordinary learning and culture, is sufficiently proved by his distinguished career. After completing with great applause his studies at Placentia, in Spain, he passed most of his time in teaching in colleges and other institutions of learning. He taught the Humanities in the Convent of Borrishoole, lectured on Philosophy for three years at Athenry, and was head professor of Theology for a long time in Kilkenny.

When the great Catholic Confederation was formed in that city, Father O'Hart gained the confidence, esteem, and admiration of the Confederates, both laymen and ecclesiastics, by the prudence of his counsels, as well as by the eloquence of his sermons, and the honour and integrity of his life, in the midst of the great trials, which he and others had to go through in these trying times. Nor did the close of the Cromwellian regime, and the restoration of the King, put an end to his troubles. Quite the reverse; for after escaping Cromwell, he fell in with Rev. Peter Walsh, who, though a priest and a friar like himself, proved to him, either wittingly or unwittingly, a deadlier enemy than either Cromwell or Cromwell's agents.

Father Walsh was a man of ability, learning, and energy, and with the confidence and friendship of Ormonde, which he certainly possessed, he became a conspicuous figure in the complicated religious movements of the period. His name is more particularly associated with a protestation, or, as it is commonly called, a "remonstrance" of loyalty—a kind of petition or memorial by which the subscribers declared and explained their duty towards the King and which, if he did not originally draw it up, he at least adopted, and had presented by the Duke of Ormonde to Charles II., after it was signed by "sixty nine of the clergy, secular and regular; five earls, six viscounts, two barons, twenty-four colonels and baronets, and sixty esquires and gentlemen".

The wording of this document which; to say the least, is open to weighty objection, gave offence to the majority of the bishops and priests; and when the Duke of Ormond set Walsh to work to induce the clergy to sign it, they refused, for the most part. In a short time the Remonstrance occasioned everywhere divisions and factions, so that both clergy and laity were divided into Remonstrants and Anti-Remonstrants. In the meantime Father O'Hart dispatched the document to Salamanca and Complutum (Alcala de Henares), and solicited the opinion of the eminent universities of these places on its orthodoxy—a proceeding which gave such offence to the Duke of Ormonde, that he had the Provincial forthwith arrested, and lodged, with two other priests, Fathers Christopher Farrell and Raymond Moore, in the gaol of Dublin, in which they were treated with such severity and cruelty, that they had to sleep without bed or bedding of any kind, on the hard earthen floor, where they had their feet often gnawed by rats, as one of them informed the historian O'Heyne. It was only after passing three years in this horrid prison, Father O'Hart was released, and not even then till he gave heavy bail to appear in court when called on. Walsh is commonly charged with being the prime cause of this treatment of the three religious; but it is only fair to remark, that those who make the charge adduce no direct proof of it, and base it always on the notoriously intimate relations between him and Ormonde.

In the earlier years of his provincialate, when he was at liberty, Father O'Hart occupied himself in repairing the evils done to religion by the Cromwellian persecutions. Finding, on entering office, not a single house of his Order surviving in Ulster, he sent Father Dominick O'Connor, of the Sligo Convent, to that province to labour for the re-introduction there of the Order; a mission in which this zealous Father was eminently successful, though he had arrayed against him, not only those who differed from him in religion, but some lay Catholics, and, more especially, certain Franciscans, who, having reached the North before Father O'Connor, resented his efforts to re-establish the Dominicans as an injury to themselves. The controversy continuing, it was carried eventually to Rome, and having been referred by the Holy See to the Primate, who was then Oliver Plunket, he decided in favour of the Dominicans.

Father O'Hart's zeal was as active in the other regions of the country as in the North. One instance of the good works he was everywhere promoting may be mentioned here to give an idea of their nature. Seeing popular education at a stand, in the neighbourhood of Athenry, for want of schoolmasters, he directed two Friars of his Order, Father Thomas Tully, and Father Cornelius McMahon, to open school in a secluded spot of that district. Both were men of great learning; one of them, Father McMahon, being said to know by heart a large part of St. Thomas's voluminous works; and yet, those highly cultivated men were happy to accept the duty assigned them, and to continue for ten years the lowly drudgery of teaching this school, surrounded, it is said, by three hundred pupils.

While Father O'Hart was so efficient and sedulous in the performance of his official duties, he employed such moments, as he had to himself, in private study. He had a special turn for Irish History and Antiquities, and left some writings on the subject, which O'Heyne calls, *Memorialia* (Memorials), and which, unfortunately, appear to have been lost. O'Heyne, in the *Epylogus Chronologicus*, says of him, "Father O'Hart was a most diligent student of the Antiquities of Ireland; and if I could lay my hand on his *Memorialia*, I should give more satisfaction to the readers of those short notes than I now can". And De Burgo, after citing those words of O'Heyne, says, on his own part, "Would that I at least had near me the productions of so eminent a student of our antiquities, whom, alas, so very few Irishmen try to imitate". Perhaps the writer of the present lines on the convent of Sligo may be allowed, in the interest of the convent, to add his regret to the regrets of O'Heyne and De Burgo; for if Father O'Hart's Memorials came down to our times, they would cast a light on the history of Holy Cross house, which nothing can now shed.

5. Father Ambrose O'Connor, a member of the O'Connor Sligo family, a child of the Sligo convent, and a Master in Theology, was instituted Provincial of Ireland, in 1700, by the Master General of the Order, and continued in office, for two terms, till 1709. Having joined the Order in Ireland, he made his studies in Spain, and exhibited such talents, learning, and aptitude for business, that he was appointed Procurator General to the court of Madrid for the Irish Dominicans, an office which he held for thirty years, and in which he gave the greatest satisfaction to his brethren, as well as to the Spanish authorities. On becoming Provincial he proceeded privately to Ireland, to visit the members of his Order, and found their number reduced to ninety Fathers, who were scattered in different hiding places through the country, from which they served the neighbouring districts, and five others who were in prison for the faith, all the rest having been banished from the country in 1698, under the Act of 7 and 9 William III.

Father O'Connor remained in Ireland for four years, which he passed not only in animating his own brethren to new labours and sacrifices for religion, but also in ministering to the people, and exhorting them to patience and perseverance amid their manifold afflictions. His duties calling him away, he left Ireland in 1704, after escaping countless attempts to capture him; for the agents of the government, knowing him to be in the country, were constantly in search of him while he remained. On returning to the Continent he drew up a description of the state of Ireland, which he first presented under the form of a petition, or *Memoriale*, to Pope Clement XI, and afterwards published, as a pamphlet, with the title: *"De praesenti Hiberniae sub Acatholico jugo statu, Anno 1704, in quo tria praesertim exponuntur; Primo, Fidem et Pacta Limericensia violari; Secundo, Orthodoxam extirpari Religionem; Tertio, S. Sedis Venerationem in nihilum redigi".* "The present condition of Ireland under the Heretics, in the year 1704; showing that they are violating the Articles of Limerick, extirpating the true religion, and destroying devotion to the Holy See". We are informed that Father O'Connor addressed some "Memorial" to Mary of Modena, the Queen of James II., but whether it was a copy of the preceding pamphlet, or a separate production, is not stated. For what he published, such as it is, he is classed by Echard and De Burgo among Dominican writers or authors, and is, unfortunately, the only Sligo Dominican so classed.

At his death, which took place at London about 1710, he was bishop designate of Ardagh. This is all that is recorded of Father O'Connor. It is not known whether he visited Sligo during his four years' stay in Ireland, but, if he did, it is extremely probable, he found the state of the Dominicans there more desperate than it had ever been before. As was mentioned above, the convent of Sligo, during the reign of Elizabeth, enjoyed exceptional security, so that while the Friars Preachers of other places had to quit the country, or go into hiding places, those of Sligo continued in tranquil possession of Holy Cross. Nor does it appear, that the Sligo religious were as much disturbed as others, even under James I., and Charles I., except perhaps for a short while after the death of Father O'Devany; for we learn from the Depositions regarding 1641, that they occupied the convent that year; and from the account of Sir Frederic Hamilton's raid in 1642, that they were in occupation at that date too. No doubt, they were dispersed in the terrible period of Cromwell and the Commonwealth, when, of 600 Dominicans, scarcely one remained; but, under the Restoration, they came back to Holy Cross; and that they were there in 1687, we learn from the Deed of Partition of the Sligo Estates, between Strafford, Leslie, and Wilson, in which there is mention of "the abbey in possession of the Fryars, paying thereout to his Majesty twelve shillings per annum". It may be said then that, with the exception of the time from 1653 to 1660, the Friars continued to occupy the convent all through up to the reign of William III.; though, as the persecution was of an intermittent character, and had its moments of paroxysm, as at the death of Father O'Devany, they may have been obliged more than once to disappear from view, and remain out of sight till the crisis had passed.

One of those paroxysms occurred during the Popish Plot, or, as it was more commonly called in Sligo, the Shaftesbury Plot, so named from the notorious Anthony Ashley Cooper, the first earl of Shaftesbury, the chief abettor, if not the author, of its worst impostures. In those dreadful days the Dominicans fled in panic from their convent; and the Prior, Father Felix O'Connor, whose great age left him little able to fly from the danger, even if he were inclined to do so, was arrested, and thrown into Sligo gaol, where, worn out with suffering, he died in 1679, secluded from all human society, the persecution being then "so cruel and vigorous that none of his brethren could come near him and assist him". The friars returned to the convent when the villainy of Oates and his confederates was discovered, but broke up house finally in the year 1698, under the operation of the 7th of William the Third, which enacts that "All Popish archbishops, bishops, vicars-general, deans, Jesuits, monks, friars, and all other regular popish clergy, and all papists exercising any ecclesiastical jurisdiction, shall depart this kingdom before the 1st of May, 1698. And if any of them shall be at any time after the said day within the kingdom, they shall be imprisoned, and remain there without bail till they be transported beyond the seas out of the king's dominions, wherever the king, his heirs, or successors, or chief governors of this kingdom shall think fit. And if any so transported, shall return again into this kingdom, then to be guilty of high treason, and to suffer accordingly. And from the 29th December, 1697, no popish archbishop, bishop, vicar-general, dean, Jesuit, monk, friar, or other regular popish clergy shall come into this kingdom from any parts beyond the seas, on pain of twelve months' imprisonment, and then to be transported in manner aforesaid; and if after such transportation, any of them return again into this kingdom, they shall be guilty of high treason and suffer accordingly".

The circumstances which immediately preceded the banishment or transportation of the Sligo Dominicans are described at length and with touching simplicity and earnestness in a paper, apparently a letter, drawn up at Bilbao, in Spain, in the year 1703, by Father Patrick McDonough, who was Prior of Sligo at the date of the dissolution or suppression. From this document, which is now in the possession of the Fathers of the Order in Sligo, we learn that the calamities of the times had brought the convent so low that its inmates were obliged to "live in a mean condition, and from hand to mouth, the country and their benefactors being reduced, and charity being very cold in the hearts of Christians". Having lost by the wars the only regular income belonging to them, a small annuity of £25 or £30, being the interest accruing on a sum of £300 bequeathed them in 1668, by one of their own brethren, the Rev. Terence or Theodoricus O'Connell, who, seeing the great need of priests in England, had served on the English mission, and there received this money for his services, they were so straitened in means when the Act of Parliament, which banished them, became law in 1697, that their whole effects would not pay their rent and other debts. "It is certain", says Father McDonogh, "that the friars of Sligo lost all their goods and effects by the unhappy wars of Ireland—only their chalices and ornaments—and were very poor, and, though they came to a head in the country, they lived in a mean condition, having but from the hand to the mouth, by reason we could benefit nothing by our mortgage, and the country and our benefactors were reduced, and charity was very cold in the hearts of Christians. And, when we were forced to break house and home by the Act of Parliament, our small effects could not pay our rent and debts".

Nothing better shows the depth of their misery than the means they were obliged to employ to relieve it, which was to sell their chalices. It is only in the last resort that such an act becomes lawful; but, that it is sometimes lawful, we learn both from the example of St. Laurence, who disposed thus of the sacred vessels of the altar, and from the teaching of Saint Ambrose, who, after referring to the case of Saint Laurence, and pointing out one or two similar instances, concludes thus:—"In these cases it is lawful to break to pieces, to melt down, or to sell, the vessels of the church, even after consecration". Having then no other resources, either in possession or prospect, the inmates of Holy Cross, after anxious deliberation, found themselves forced to the resolution of parting with their chalices; but they did not arrive at this resolution without the sanction of their superiors; for the Provincial of Ireland, in view of the hopeless condition of things, had authorized all the houses, under his jurisdiction, to dispose of the sacred vessels, if the prior and conventuals of each house, after taking counsel together, agreed that so extreme a proceeding was necessary. "There was a general licence", writes Father McDonogh, "given by the Provincial of Ireland, to every prior to dispose of all the goods and chalices of every convent, with the mutual consent of his conventuals, as he thought more expedient and convenient for the present necessity and for the future. The fathers of the convent of Sligo, having no other effects or worldly means but their chalices, they agreed unanimously to dispose of some of their chalices to redeem their present necessity, and found it more proper and lawful before God and the world to make use of them, than to perish in foreign countries, not knowing to what part of the universe would they be driven, nor what reception would they get amongst strangers". Nor did they take this step till they had tried in vain all other expedients. "It is certain", adds Father McDonogh, "before we agreed to dispose of our chalices, I took all the means possible to get a sum of money from our trustee, Mr. Coll. Keogh, upon the account of our mortgage, to put ourselves in a way to leave the kingdom".

But Mr. Coll. Keogh, being a dishonest man, and knowing that the friars had no legal remedy, as they could not show their faces in the law courts, resolved to rob them, since he could do so with impunity. It was in vain Father McDonogh, in an interview he had with this trustee, sought to get from him the legal instrument that proved the debt; for the moment the cheat saw the friar's object, he rushed out of his presence with the document, and never appeared there again. Despairing of being able by himself to bring Keogh to book, poor Father McDonogh, like other Catholics of the time, when in trouble, had recourse to the famous Counsellor, Terence McDonogh, for help; and to enable the Counsellor to prosecute the suit, the friar made over to him in due form the Convent's claims or interests, receiving some money as the consideration; but that nothing came of the proceeding, and that the defaulter got the better of the Counsellor, as he did of the friars, we may infer from the fact, that Father McDonogh returned the money given him for the consideration, as the good priest informs us in the following portion of his narrative:—"I gave Mr. Keogh a meeting in the County of Roscommon, in April '98, and another in the County of Galway, much about the same time, desiring him to bring the deed and our papers, for I did resolve to take the deed out of his hand by civil ways for fear of the worse; and though he appeared according to his promise, when he understood I did resolve to take the deed out of his hands, he run'd (ran) away with the deed, and never saw a sight of him since. By this deceitful and vile action he discovered his aims, and to hinder any design he might have for the future, after consulting and considering the matter seriously with the fathers, I sold all our interest to Councellor Terence McDonogh, in Galway, before we were confined, and gave him a deed of our interest in full form of law, signed, sealed, and delivered, by myself and the rest of the fathers, and received money, as it was agreed, for the same interest, in presence of good witnesses, both Roman Catholics and Protestants. All this was performed, for I paid the money back to prevent Mr. Keogh's proceedings".

We have, in the conduct of Keogh, an instance of an evil, which must have proved ruinous to several persons in the seventeenth and eighteenth centuries. When Catholics, whether secular or religious, were disabled by law from holding real estate, they often tried to evade the law by vesting their property in trustees, who were sometimes Catholics, as in this case, and sometimes Protestants. It would appear that these trustees were generally faithful to their trust; and O'Connell loved to tell of a Protestant tailor of Kerry, who was trustee for most of the Catholic estates of Munster, and who performed the duties of his position with fidelity and honour worthy of a prince. But that there was a reverse to the picture, this case of Keogh, and another, mentioned in the History of Ballysadare and Kilvarnet, abundantly prove. Had Keogh any just claim to be relieved from the obligation of payment, Father McDonogh would not have pressed him, as he did not press another gentleman, Mr. French, who was joined with Keogh in the transaction, and of whom he writes, "I did consider that it was not lawful, in conscience, to oblige the honest gentleman to pay us our interest during the time he was out of the possession of the estate". What a pity this Mr. Keogh did not take a lesson from Father McDonogh, who employed the first money he received on the chalices and other effects, in paying the debts of the convent. "When I had licence", says he, "to dispose of the effects of the convent for the friars use and necessity, I found it an obligation of conscience to pay our lawful debts". Those who desire to know more of the exodus of the friars from Sligo, in 1698, would do well to read for themselves the narrative of Father McDonogh, which they will find entire in the Appendix. It is little wonder that the paper has been carefully preserved by the Dominican fathers of Sligo, for it reflects great honour on their convent, as well by the facts which it records, as by the spirit which it breathes in every sentence. Calm resignation under the doom of perpetual banishment; forgetfulness of self; solicitude for "the common good and interest of the convent;" attachment to the "old walls" of Holy Cross; sensitiveness of conscience, that enforces the payment of debts even when undemanded and at the risk of starvation; sacrifice of all personal advantages to the honour and interests of the Order: these, and their kindred virtues, are proved by every line to have been the common possession of Prior McDonogh and his conventuals. In such circumstances the good fathers, as they were borne away in the transport ship, after having lost their country, their convent, and their worldly means, might well say with Francis I., and in a loftier sense, *"Tout est perdu fors l'honneur"*

Of course, as happens in other parts of Ireland where there are ruined churches or monasteries, the people have their legend about Holy Cross bell; and they tell you that it was made of silver, that it lies on the bottom of Loughgill, where it was deposited by Prior McDonogh to await better times, and that it still gives forth, on special occasions, its silvery notes, which, however, none but the perfect are privileged to hear. Some such legends, regarding church bells and royal crowns, are common in other countries as well as in Ireland; and in one of Uhland's songs we have the following reference to a sunken crown:

> *"Da drunten in dem grunde*
> *Da dämmert längst der Teich*
> *Es liegt in ihm vorsunken*
> *Eine Krone, stolz und reich;*
> *Sie lässt zu Nacht wohl spielen.*
> *Karfunkel und Saphir,*
> *Sie liegt seit grauen Jahren*
> *Und Niemand sucht nach ihr".*

It is to be regretted that there is no list extant of the Priors of Holy Cross, some of whom must have been men worth remembering. In the absence of any record, the writer thinks it may be of use to give here, in chronological order, the names of such Priors as he has come across, with a word or two of biography where he can, leaving to others to add new names, and to enlarge the biographical notices. The following are the names he has met with:—

1.—Manus, son of Baethghalach MacEgan, Prior of Sligo, died, according to the *Annals of Loch Ce*, in 1411. The name of this prior does not occur either in the Four Masters or the *Hibernia Dominicana*.

2.—Brian, the son of Dermot McDonogh, as we have seen, was Prior in 1416, when the convent was restored after the burning; His name is given in the Four Masters, the *Annals of Loch Ce*, and *Hibernia Dominicana*.

3.—The next Prior, we know of, is Andrew Crean, or O'Crean, who, from Prior of Sligo, became Bishop of Elphin. He was a native of Sligo, and a member of the most distinguished family then in the place, after that of the O'Connors. They appear to have settled in Sligo towards the close of the fifteenth century; and the first of this branch of whom we have any record, is Cormac, who is buried in the beautiful altar tomb which stands in the nave of the church, and which bears a Latin inscription, thus rendered by Mr. Langrishe, the distinguished architect and antiquary, in the "Kilkenny Journal" of October, 1884:—

> *"Hic . jacet . Cormacus. Ocraian .*
> *Et Ehon ac . Nanangasa . uxor .*
> *Eis . an° Do., M°CCCCC°VL"*

> Here lieth Cormac O'Craian,
> . . . . .and Nanangasa, his wife,
> The year of the Lord, 1506.

Originally of Tirconnell, where Donnell O'Crean, "a rich, humane merchant, died suddenly while hearing mass in the monastery of Donegal, in 1506", the O'Creans came, probably in the wake of O'Donnell, to Sligo, where they devoted themselves successfully to mercantile pursuits, as the *Annals of the Four Masters* record, under the year 1572, the death of Henry O'Crean, "a rich and affluent merchant of Lower Connaught".

It is to be feared that other members of the family were not always so honourably employed as these merchants, for we find "Baptist Crean, of Sleegaugh", granted in 1547, a fee of 12d. a day for life, by Henry the Eighth, which, considering the date of the gift and the character of the giver, is, to say the least, a suspicious transaction; while in 1593, another of the family, James O'Crean, appears to have acted as spy for the English authorities against some Irish bishops, including the Primate, Doctor Magauran. If these men were as guilty as they look, the infamy belongs to themselves, and should not be charged on the whole O'Crean family, which, indeed, produced men as honourable and virtuous as any of their day.

The O'Creans were not long in Sligo when they began to invest money in land; and before many years had passed, they held landed estate not only near the town, but in various other parts of the county. Andrew

O'Crean of Annagh, or Hazelwood, who was the head of the family, possessed not only Hazelwood and much of the parishes of Carbury and St. John, in the barony of Carbury, but also considerable stretches of land in Leyney, Tireragh, and Coolavin, as well as the abbey of Ballindoon, in the barony of Tirerrill. He appears to have died in 1641.

Bishop O'Crean, who was probably uncle of this Andrew, was Prior of Sligo convent in 1561, when Bernard O'Higgins, Bishop of Elphin, having resigned that see in his favour, he set out for Rome, bearing with him the resignation, and a letter of recommendation from the Very Rev. David Wolf, S.J., who, like Monsignor Persico at present, was then acting as Apostolic Delegate of the Holy See in Ireland, and whose word was decisive in everything that regarded the administration of the Irish church. This proceeding of the Prior, in going to Rome on such an errand, is in marked contrast with the conduct of a few others whom we read or hear of—of some, who, under the influence of genuine Christian humility, shrink, in reality as well as in seeming, from the responsibility of the episcopate; and of others, who, perhaps, from "the pride that apes humility", in dallying with offers of preferment, are only indulging personal vanity, or some equally unamiable constitutional idiosyncrasy; but Dr. O'Crean, when the call of duty came to him later on, proved his humility and other virtues by voluntarily laying down his dignity and becoming a simple friar—again a proof vastly more satisfactory than any amount of *"Nolo episcopari"* professions.

On reaching France, in the journey to Rome, Father O'Crean fell sick, and became unable to proceed further; but the Pope, on receiving his testimonials, and seeing his qualifications, issued the Brief for his consecration, which, apparently, took place in France, though this is not expressly mentioned. The appointment is thus recorded in the Consistorial Acts: *"Die 28º Januarii, 1562: referente Cardinali Morono, Sua Sanctitas providit ecclesiae, Elphinensi in Hibernia vacanti per resignationem Reverendi Domini O'Higgins (written O'Huyghiun,) ordinis Sancti Augustini professoris de persona Domini Andreae O'Crean, Hiberni, ordinis Praedicatorum Professoris, quem R. P. David, presbyter Societatis Jesu in Hibernia commorans per suas litteras commendavit".*

Unlike his predecessor, Dr. O'Higgins, whose self-will and untractableness of temper lost him the esteem of the people, Dr. O'Crean was a favourite with all classes in his diocese, but more particularly with the native inhabitants of Sligo, who were proud of him as one of themselves. The feeling was mutual, for the good bishop had a special love for his fellow townsmen; and among the benefits, conferred by him on his native town, may be mentioned, in particular, a cross, which he erected at the bottom of the present Market Street, from which that portion of the town is called, to this day, Market Cross, though people using the phrase now know nothing of its origin.

In thinking of market crosses, which were formerly very numerous in England, there being about 5,000 of them there before the Reformation, and not rare in Ireland, one must not conceive of them, as if they were mere naked pieces of stone or wood in the form of a cross; for they were often arched and elaborate stone structures, roomy enough to afford shelter to the market people upon the coming on of rain, so that, in erecting this Market Cross, Dr. O'Crean made a handsome and expensive present to the people of Sligo. And, the people must have been the more grateful, as it was the bishop's own money that paid for it.

A drinking fountain may have been combined with the market cross, for the combination was not unusual; and the discovery of a well, some time ago, at the foot of Market Street, on the spot where the cross stood, makes it probable, that the fountain was a part of the structure.

From 1562, the date of his appointment, to 1584, Dr. O'Crean seems to have been unmolested by the State in the performance of his episcopal functions, and even to have had the formal sanction of the authorities for the last two years of this period; but being summoned, in the year 1584, to take the oath of supremacy, and refusing, says Dr. Lynch, "to defile himself by such a sacrilegious act", the Government set him aside as far as they could, and put in his place John Lynch, to whom, of course, they gave the temporalities of the see. Lynch was an unprincipled hypocrite, and in such bad odour with the people, that they ascribed to his presence even the natural evils which befel the place of his residence, Grange in Magherow. "There was", says the *Annals of Loch Ce*, "a wicked, heretical bishop in Elphin, and God performed great miracles upon him. And his place of residence was the Grainsech of Magherow; and a shower of snow was shed for him, and a wild apple was not larger than each stone of it; and not a grain was left in his town; and it was with shovels the snow was removed from the houses; and it was in the middle month of Summer that shower fell". Even the Protestants came, in the course of time, to think as ill of him as the Catholics, and, as he was reconciled to the Church before his death, in 1611, Ware says of him, "He voluntarily resigned his See, on the 19th of August, 1611, having by alienations, fee farms, and other means, so wasted and destroyed it, that he left it not worth 200 marks a year. It is said, he lived a concealed, and died a public Papist".

"While this wretched man lived amid the execrations of his neighbours, Bishop O'Crean was surrounded by the love and respect of all, in the convent of Holy Cross, to which he retired, in 1584, and in which he lived, a model of every virtue, to 1594, when he went to his reward. He was buried, of course, in the convent, though this is not stated; and the small stone statue of a bishop, or abbot, with crozier in hand, which, after having been removed from, its proper place, now stands on the slab of the high altar, may have been intended to perpetuate his memory. The proper place of this statue was, no doubt, in the buttress of the east cloister, which at present lacks a part or member, for the statue exactly fills the space of the missing member. It is, perhaps, still more likely that the statue was intended to represent Saint Dominick, the founder of the Order of Friars Preachers, for a statue of Saint Francis, the patriarch of the Franciscans, occupies an analogous position in one of the cloister buttresses of Creevalea Abbey.

The writer is pained to have to add, that having just been to Holy Cross to test certain measurements, made some time ago, he found the buttress of the east cloister gone, though existing in fair preservation at the date of a preceding visit, a fact which shows the alarming rate at which the beauties of the structure are disappearing, and the need of taking prompt and vigorous action to stop or check the vandalism in progress.

It is recorded that Doctor O'Crean had a special devotion to St. Ursula, and her virgin companions.

4. Father Dominick O'Connor, of whom mention has been already made, was several times Prior of Holy Cross Convent. A native of Sligo, a member of the O'Connor family, an alumnus of Holy Cross, a man of singular zeal, prudence, and piety, and much esteemed for his family connections, by the leading men of the North, he was selected by the Provincial, as the fittest person to retrieve the interests of the Dominicans in Ulster, and the great success with which, as was seen above, he executed this difficult and delicate mission, amply justified the choice.

In the Provincial Chapter, held in Kilkenny, in 1643, Father O'Connor acted as Definitor for Ulster. It is told of him that, though he naturally stammered in his speech, the moment he ascended the pulpit, the defect completely disappeared, so that, he always spoke with ease and fluency, the subject of his sermons, being generally, the Rosary of the Blessed Virgin, to which devotion he was specially attached. Dear to his brethren for the great services he rendered the Order in Ulster, and still dearer to them for his saintly virtues, his death, which was of a piece with his holy life, was much regretted by all the Dominicans of Ireland. He died, in 1675, having lived to an extreme old age.

5. Father Felix O'Connor, who, like his namesake and relative, Father Dominick, was a native of Sligo, and an alumnus of Holy Cross, passed a very eventful life, and suffered severely for the faith. After completing his studies in Spain, he returned to Ireland, and was Prior, first of the Dominican Convent of Kilkenny, and next, on the break up of the Catholic Confederation, of Burrishoole Convent, on the east coast of Clew Bay. This establishment was repeatedly attacked by the Cromwellians, but the friars

and some soldiers of the Confederate army, who were stationed there, repelled successfully two of those attacks, but on a third assault, in which the Cromwellians exerted all their strength, they carried the place, put all the soldiers to the sword, and captured several friars, whom they had wounded, and who were, therefore, unable to escape, the others having fled to the mountains. Rather than fall into the hands of those rabid enemies, to whom he was personally obnoxious, and from whom he could expect no quarter, Father Felix, with one little boy, stepped on, or into, a small raft or skiff, made out of a single log of timber, and, commending himself and his companion to God, pushed away to sea, and, after a hundred miraculous escapes, succeeded in reaching an island, which lay sixteen miles from shore, and to which some Irish soldiers, and a few other ecclesiastics had already fled for safety. But he was not long here, when seven ships and twenty-two boats of the victorious enemy surrounded the island; and the ecclesiastics, after surrendering without resistance, and receiving the alternative offer of death or expatriation, electing to leave the country and live, were put on board ship and transported to Belgium.

In Belgium he settled down at Louvain, and was made Prior of the Dominican convent there. While in this office he devoted a great part of his time to the care of the Irish exiles who followed the fortunes of Charles the Second, and lived about the prince. These, it is said, amounted to more than 14,000 souls, so that Father O'Connor was overwhelmed with work in attending to the spiritual wants of so large a number. And he had to provide for the temporal wants, too, of a great many who depended on the convent for their support. To meet this charge he preached charity sermons, which were largely attended, as he was one of the most gifted preachers of the time; and the sums thus realized, which were considerable, he devoted entirely to the maintenance of his fellow exiles, whose hotel was the convent. It was thus he was occupied, all through, while abroad, with the exception of the time employed in two journeys, one from Louvain to Madrid, and the other from Madrid to Rome; the former undertaken for the purpose of obtaining from the King of Spain his sanction of an annual grant of 1,000 florins to the convent of Louvain, which the Belgian authorities had already agreed to give; and the other, having for its object, to induce the Congregation of Propaganda to provide an annual pension for the education, in the College of Louvain, of four students, to be bound by oath to devote themselves to the Irish mission. In both cases the good Father obtained what he sought.

Returning to Ireland, at the Restoration, Father Felix was repeatedly Prior of Holy Cross, and once Prior of Roscommon Convent. As on the Continent, so at home, he was assiduous in preaching; and the great pains he took to prepare himself for this all-important work, may be inferred from the fact, recorded of him, that he had by heart all the Homilies of the distinguished preacher and writer, Lanuza, who was called "the Dominick of his age". While Father O'Connor was equally solemn, and effective in the pulpit, he was lively and facetious in society; thus reminding one of a still greater Dominican, Father Tom Burke, who united those two qualities in larger proportions than any man of his Order, or of the century. Though O'Heyne and De Burgo relate that Father O'Connor died in Holy Cross about the year 1686, they are in error, for Father McDonogh, his contemporary and friend, in the narrative already quoted, but which neither O'Heyne nor De Burgo had an opportunity of seeing, states expressly that "Father Felix O'Connor died a prisoner in Sligoe in the heate of Shaftesberry's Plott the yeare 1679". In the good Father's life and death we have a strong illustration of the sufferings which priests had to endure in his day.

6. Father Patrick McDonogh, the author of the Narrative, succeeded as Prior on Father O'Connor's death, but as the persecution continued to rage, he and his conventuals had to keep out of the way for some time. "I was immediately elected Prior", says Father McDonogh, "on Father O'Connor's death, butt the rigour of the persecution was soe great that we cud not settle ourselves for some yeares after". Having settled again in the convent, they remained there during the reign of James II., sharing largely the trouble brought on the town by the conflict between that monarch and his son-in-law, William of Orange. They held on to the house, under the rule of William and Mary, for it was only in 1698, when William alone was on the throne, took place the final break-up of the establishment, as we learn from the touching account of that transaction left by him, of whom we are treating. From his banishment, in 1698, to his death, which happened in 1705, Father McDonogh lived in the Dominican Convent, of Bilbao, in Spain, in which he was Vicar.

Judging from what he has written himself, and from what has been written of him by others, he was a man of the rarest piety. Christian perfection appears in every word that dropped from the pen in his Narrative; and in writing of him in the *Epylogus Chronologicus*, Father O'Heyne regards him as a mirror of virtue, and a model to priest and people in everything. This estimate is not founded on hearsay, but on actual observation, for Heyne was a contemporary and intimate companion of Father McDonogh, so that when he writes of him, "I have never seen him under the influence of the slightest anger, and I do not remember, to have ever met a meeker man in religion", we have testimony beyond all exception. And that O'Heyne's estimate was the general one, we may infer from what he tells us, that in the great convent of Salamanca, both the novices and the fathers, spoke always of Father McDonogh as The Angel.

Such was the man whom the unnatural laws of the time treated as worse than a wild beast.

7. Father Michael O'Connor was Prior of Holy Cross in King James the Second's reign: but Father McDonogh's Narrative, to which we are indebted for this information, gives no further particulars.

8. On Father Michael O'Connor's death, Father Gregory Nellus became Prior. There is little known of the Dominicans from the time of Prior McDonogh till towards the close of the eighteenth century, though it is pretty certain that one or more of them might be always found in or near the town. From the depositions taken by Sligo magistrates in 1712, and quoted in the preceding chapter, we learn that Rev. James Feighney, a Regular, who in the words of the deponent, "is, or is to be Prior of the Dominican convent of Sligoe", said Mass on several occasions, that year, in the convent; and De Burgo, in *Hibernia Dominicana* (page 249) states that, in 1757, there were five fathers of the Order belonging to the convent of Sligo though hardly living there, whose names and ages he gives as follows: Rev. Edward Geraldine, Prior, aged 33; Rev. Ambrose Gilgan, aged 64; Rev. Michael Hart, aged 61; Rev. Patrick MacDonogh, aged 38; and Rev. Bartholomew Fergus, aged 43.

The names of the Priors, who intervened between 1757 and 1790, when Father Bernard Mullonay, S.T.L., was Prior, have not come down to us. Father Mullonay's successor was Father Dominick Conlon, after whom, according to a list kindly supplied by the present esteemed Prior, Father Boylan, came: between 1796 and 1820, Father Thomas Brennan, Father Gilgan, and Father Rochfort; between 1820 and 1834, Father MacDermot, Father Fallen, and Father Kane; in 1834, Father T. D. Hibbetts; in 1837, Father B. J. Goodman; in 1840, Father P. Kelly; in 1841, Father T. D. Hibbetts; and from that date to 1884, when the present Prior was elected, Father Goodman and Father Hibbetts filled the office alternately.

We may close this notice of the Priors of Holy Cross with a few words on Dr. Goodman, the last deceased Prior of the convent, as it might appear unbecoming to treat of living Priors, or ex-Priors, mindful of the fact, that Ecclesiasticus cautions us against praising any man before death, and of the other fact, that one could not speak either of Doctor Hibbetts or Father Boylan except in terms of the highest praise.

Dr. Goodman was born about the year 1810, in the county Galway, where he received his early education. Feeling a call to a religious life, and to the order of Saint Dominick, he set out in his sixteenth year for the Continent and made his noviciate there, giving, even then, abundant proof of the tender piety and distinguished talent for which he was noted through life. The noviciate over, his superiors employed him on the Irish mission, and after some little time sent him to Holy Cross, Sligo, where he passed the last forty years of his life.

Elected Provincial of the Irish province in 1864, he passed, while filling that high office, much of his time, in visiting the Dominican houses of the country, and left after him, wherever he sojourned, the reputation of a zealous, able, prudent, farseeing, and withal as gentle a superior as ever ruled the Dominican province of Ireland.

Those who enjoyed the intimacy of Dr. Goodman, and could appreciate him, were always struck by his great natural and acquired gifts. Deeply versed in the ecclesiastical sciences; a scripturist, a canonist, and a Master in Theology; a successful student of natural science; a brilliant conservationist, his voice being singularly sweet and sonorous; with a turn for the arts, both liberal and mechanical; and with a large acquaintance with the literature of the day: Dr. Goodman should be admired, for his qualities and culture, in any society in which he mixed. And to his other talents was joined a natural eloquence of a high order, which enabled him, if need were, to extemporize at his ease. Of this faculty, an instance, or illustration, may be mentioned.

Some time ago, on a Saint Dominick's day, the priest selected to preach the panegyric of the saint informed Dr. Goodman at the last moment, of his inability to perform the duty, owing to circumstances beyond his control. The communication was made to the good Prior almost at the very hour fixed for the sermon. What could he do in the situation thus sprung upon him? Would he announce that there could be no panegyric that day, and leave to somebody else the responsibility of the disappointment? Most other people in the circumstances, rather than encounter, without a moment's preparation, the immense, and, in large part, critical congregation, of both priests and laity assembled on such occasions, would dispense with the sermon altogether, even at the cost of marring the solemnity, and disappointing the pious expectations of numbers who had come great distances to hear the praises of Saint Dominick proclaimed; but the zealous and eloquent Prior, instead of doing what so many others would do, and would be justified in doing, threw himself into the breach, and taking, in a spirit of self-sacrifice, the place of the expected preacher, delivered as brilliant and effective a panegyric as was ever heard in Holy Cross convent on the Patron's day, though the pulpit on these occasions was sometimes occupied by such men as Father Tom Burke and Right Reverend Doctor Healy.

Dr. Goodman built the existing beautiful church of Holy Cross, in 1846, from a design of Sir John Benson, and, a few years ago, the conventual residence now attached to the church. Both structures were much needed. It was either Father Conlon or Father Thomas Brennan for there is some doubt on the subject that erected, in the closing decade of the last century, in Pound Street, the old church of which the walls still stand, though without the roof. The site, with a lease renewable forever, was granted by the then owner, Mr. Bruen, of Carlow. Before this church was built, the Dominican Fathers officiated in a stable, which still exists near the old walls, while, strange to say, nearly all the other houses of the same date have disappeared from the neighbourhood. The Pound Street Church, like most other places of Catholic worship in the last century, was placed some distance in off the street, and thus hidden away from public view, in order to avoid offence to the authorities, and to certain influential private persons, still more hostile to the Catholic religion than the authorities.

Though the Pound Street Church seems to have been sufficiently commodious and imposing in its day, it was no longer spacious enough in 1845 for the congregation frequenting it, or fit for the more imposing functions of public worship, when Dr. Goodman and his brethren decided to build a new church, and to build it on a conspicuous site, in the light of day, and abutting on the street. This site, if it has its advantages, is not without its disadvantages too, for the new temple loses greatly in effectiveness, from being jammed in between the shops, and other houses on either side. The tower, which is a very striking one, is built of the beautiful limestone of Ballysadare, elaborately carved. The roof is an open one of great beauty, as well as strength, while the altars, the furniture, and the decorations, are such as suit a first-class church. The tower terminates in eight pinnacles, one at each corner of the square, and one of lesser proportions on each of the four sides; and some might like the finish better if, instead of eight, there were only four pinnacles, as usually happens; for, looking from some parts of the town, the present arrangement of the summit reminds one of a chess-board, with its men, of unequal size, in different positions.

The eastern gable contains a noble stained-glass window, erected by his friends, to the memory of the lamented Dr. Goodman, and bearing the inscription: *"In memoriam, inclyti et venerandi Dei sacerdotis, Ad. R. P. Bern. Jos. Dom Goodman, Ord Praedicatorum qui ob praeclaras animi dotes diviti aeque ac pauperi nimis erat in desiderio clerus atque populus Sligoensis pie ponere curavere Kal. Januarii an. 1874".*

This "good man", in fact, as well as in name, died on the 11th May, 1874, and was buried in the nave of Holy Cross Church, where the remains of his old friend and brother, Father McEvoy, who went to his reward on the 9th July, 1876, were laid, in due time, by his side. Over their graves, Father Boylan and his brother, conventuals, in their affection, have placed a beautiful brass tablet, with the following inscription:—

Adm. Rev. P. Fr. B. J. D. GOODMAN, S.T.M.

Prudentia zelo et doctrina Claro
hujus conventus multoties Priori
Monasterium et Ecclesiam,
S. Crucis Sligoensis,
fratribus adjuvantibus a fundamentis erexit.
Ad gubernium totius Provinciae Hiberniae,
Anno 1864 vocatus
multa et praeclara gloriose fecit
et omnia boni pastoris munera
laudabiliter adimplevit
Vixit annos 64. Obiit die 11 Maii, anno 1874.

Rev. P. Fr. M. McEvoy, O.P.
Coenobii S. Crucis Sligoensis filio
"In omnibus exemplum bonorum operum
in doctrina in integritate in gravitate"
Vixit annos 92. Obiit die 9 Julii, anno 1876.
REQUIESCANT IN PACE.

It would hardly be in keeping with the role of a faithful chronicler, to omit all reference to a controversy which waxed warm, in the second decade of this century, and developed some little heat ever since, between the secular and regular clergy of Sligo, regarding their respective claims to the collections, accustomed to be made, on occasion of interments in the old abbey. At the first time referred to, Father Patrick Burke, afterwards Bishop of Elphin, was the administrator of St. John's parish, or union of parishes; and he not only advocated the claims of the secular clergy to the offerings, or a share of them, but he was in the habit of standing himself near the abbey, as funerals passed in, and of demanding, and receiving, offerings; while on the other hand, a Dominican father met the funerals about the same place, and claimed these contributions, as the exclusive right of himself and his brethren of Holy Cross convent. In the perplexity, occasioned by this conflict of claims, the people were at a loss to know what to do; and some gave to one side, some to the other, and many to both.

The arguments relied on by the disputants may not all have come down to us, but it is known that the Dominicans based their claim on their original rights, which, they maintained, continued always in existence, from the thirteenth century down to their own day, though the enforcement of these rights was interrupted, now and then, by the calamity of the times. The contention, on the other hand, of the seculars was, that the religious had lost their rights: first, by the royal transfer of the abbey, with its possessions, to Sir William Taaffe; second, by their own inaction, and the consequent consent of the Church to the status quo; and third, by the cemetery becoming, in some way not specified, parish property, after its transfer from the Dominicans. We shall leave it to others to appreciate the value of these arguments, which, if this were the place, might be discussed with advantage, from both the historical and the canonical point of view.

At the time of these troubles there was no access to the Pope, owing to the wars and confusion of the times; and Dr. Burke, on becoming bishop, took on himself the establishment of a *modus vivendi*, and decided, that the seculars should make the collections, but that the friars should receive a fourth part of all the proceeds, whether the burial took place in the abbey or in any other graveyard of the parish. Dr. Brown, in turn, sanctioned this arrangement.

It may be interesting to mention that, in the proceedings connected with the case, affidavits were made before Mayor McGowan, in 1857, by some of the oldest inhabitants of the town, including James Williams and Patrick Boland, from which we learn that, towards the close of the last century, the abbey grounds were without fence of any kind; that, later, a rough wall ran round them, with a gap in it for the passage of funerals; and that, later still, Mr. Martin Madden, who was a great friend of the friars, put up a fine entrance gate at his own expense.

The abbey is now in the possession of the Honourable Evelyn Ashley, who received it, with the rest of the Sligo property of the Temples, from Lord Palmerston and Lord Mount Temple. Lord Palmerston showed great interest in the ruin, and expended a substantial sum in strengthening the walls and repairing the breaches which were made in them by time, and not, as many, who should know better, suppose, by Oliver Cromwell, who never set foot in Sligo or any other county of Connaught.

It is to be hoped that the Abbey will be soon handed over to the Board of Works to be restored and preserved as a "National monument". The propriety of disposing of it in this way was talked of a good deal, a year or two ago, and was discussed at the time by the Board of Guardians, but the subject soon dropped, and has been allowed to rest since then.

Everybody, capable of forming an opinion on such a matter, was in favour of the transfer, and many would have exerted themselves to bring it about, only they fancied that there were two insuperable obstacles in the way: one, the determination of the landlord not to part with the ruin, and the other, the hostility of certain townspeople to the change.

Both these impediments were, in great part, imaginary—the first entirely so; for Mr. Ashley, as one would expect from a gentleman of his culture, is ready and willing to give up the place as soon as the two other parties, mainly concerned the persons having family graves, and the Board of Works—agree to the restoration. The opposition of the townspeople in question is no way formidable, for it is based on a misunderstanding, which would be easily removed. It arises from an impression that the restoration involves the disturbance of human remains in existing graves, and the prevention, in future, of any interment whatever in those graves; but, if the people were made aware that there would be no disturbance of the remains; that the few persons, who still bury in family graves, might, if they desired it, continue to do so; that the only thing not allowed would be the *taking up of new plots*, and, that, while the structural parts of the convent would be treated in a way to re-invest them with much of their pristine beauty, the grounds, both within and without the walls, would be cleared of the weeds, and rubbish, and nuisance that now lie about in such disgraceful higgledy piggledy—with this knowledge, the owners of family graves would, probably, be among the first to cry out for the restoration. For any one having such a family interest, would naturally desire, even more than others, to see the grounds become worthy of their destination, as the last resting-place of his relatives, as well as of some of the most exalted men and women that Ireland has produced.

To neglect the abbey, is to neglect the memory, not only of those buried in it, but of the other distinguished persons who were associated with it, and who deserve well to live in the remembrance of the people of Sligo. While it stood, all the men of note connected with the town, worshipped within its walls—the Fitzgeralds, for the sixty years, or thereabouts, during which they owned the town; Richard De Burgo, the Red Earl, the "most powerful subject of the Crown in Ireland", about the year 1310, when he rebuilt, or repaired the castle; the O'Connors Sligo, for the three hundred and fifty years of their rule, as Lords of Sligo, that is, from the early years of the 14th century, to the middle of the 17th; and the Taaffes, for though Sir William accepted the royal grant of the convent and its possessions, he and his descendants were Catholics, and so devoted that, as the present head of the family, Count Taaffe, the prime minister of Austria informs us, in his privately printed *Memoirs of the Taaffe Family*, they renounced their peerage, and other signal honours, with all their broad acres in the counties of Sligo and Louth, in order to preserve the faith.

Zeal, similar to that shown elsewhere, for the preservation of local monuments, should animate the people of Sligo. While the applications from other parts of Ireland to the Board of Works are so numerous that the Board cannot attend to a tithe of them, it would be a shame if Sligo men exhibited apathy or indifference regarding Holy Cross; and what would render their conduct more reprehensible, is the fact, that the abbey is the only structure in the town, which, either for its architectural qualities, or its historical associations, has any claim to be regarded as a National Monument. Now, that its twin establishment, the castle, has disappeared, it is the only building in the town of an historical character, no other structure dating so early, even as the era of the O'Connor Sligo; whereas, Holy Cross carries the mind back to the origin of the town, to the times when the site of Sligo was a wood, when its inhabitants were a few fishermen, living on the subsistence which they took daily out of the river with osier nets; and when their residences were a few fragile constructions, formed of willows, covered with the branches of trees, and set within the sod ramparts of the Green Fort, and one or two other earthen-work enclosures of the neighbourhood.

The advantages accruing to Creevalea, or Ballyrourke Abbey, from the renovation it underwent in 1884, under the enlightened direction of Mr. Scott, will give a good idea of the benefit sure to result to Holy Cross, from a similar process, under the same skilful hands. Those who remember the condition of Creevalea, before the Board of Works took it in charge, the walls decayed and crumbling, some of the tombstones out of place, and covered with accumulated rubbish, bits of coffins scattered about, bones of the dead sticking up here and there out of the earth, and skulls piled into heaps in the corners; and consider the state in which the restorers left it at the close of their labours—the walls secured and cleansed, the tombstones replaced in their respective positions, the skulls and bones re-interred, a cloister arcade, which was not even known to have existed, re-erected, and the whole place ordered with a neatness, that reminds one of a continental graveyard,—will be able to appreciate the value of a Board of Works restoration.

The discovery of lost or hidden portions of buildings, as in this case of the cloister arcade, is not an uncommon incident in restorations. Mr. Scott, with a sagacity, which resembles an instinct, will point out where missing parts of the structure may be found, and will get his men to turn up stone after stone, which he puts together, till he re-constructs a window, or niche, or other appendage, which had disappeared hundreds of years ago. In the same way, stones are sometimes found with inscriptions, which throw light on historical persons or things. A stone found at Creevalea, with an inscription regarding Bishop O'Rorke, is a case in point.

Holy Cross may not be now in quite as disordered a condition as Creevalea was, when taken in hand by Mr. Scott. Anyhow, it is no longer the Golgotha that it appears to have been in 1779, when the artists of the Honourable Mr. Conyngham visited it, and found a mass of skulls "sufficient to load a small vessel", heaped up over its high altar. Still, those who have been through it of late, had evidence enough before them, that the place, as well the ruin, as the grounds, is sadly in need of re-arrangement and renovation. As things stand, it is not only greatly behind the cemeteries of our cities and chief towns, but would suffer, by comparison, with some of our country churchyards. Owing to the strong language in which foreigners, after visiting Ireland, animadvert on the shameful neglect of our burying places, there set in, some years ago, a change for the better, which has removed many of the blots and evils complained of, but it is to be feared, that Sligo is still too open to reproach in the matter. Better, however, late than never; and there could hardly be a more appropriate time for an effort than the present, for it is particularly congruous, that the habitations of the dead should be looked after, when the habitations of the living are so improved and embellished, that, the Sligo of the present day, if compared with the Sligo of a century ago cannot be more aptly characterized, than by describing it as a transformation.

The interments in the abbey are daily becoming fewer, and are likely soon to cease altogether, as Sligo families prefer to lay their dead in the new cemetery. Nor is this surprising, for in all Ireland there is not a more beautiful burying ground. Lying, as it does, on the charming slope of Lough Gill, it realizes, in its position, as well as in its other circumstances, the ideal of poor Thomas Davis's wished-for place of rest:—

> "—*on an Irish green hill-side*
> *On an opening lawn—but not too wide*".

The ground is already largely occupied, though it is not as yet forty years opened. It was on the 23rd November, 1848, a trust deed of the place, which, as part of the old commons of the town, belonged to the Corporation, was executed by that body to the following trustees: Right Honorable John Wynne, Reverend Edward Day, Rector of St. John's, Rev. Owen Feeny, Parish Priest of Riverstown, Peter O'Connor, Esq., J.P., Andrew Walker, Esq., J.P., Robert McBride, Esq., J.P., the Mayor of Sligo, Alderman Lyons, Alderman Gallagher, Alderman Verdon, and the clergymen of all denominations resident in Sligo. Since that date the successive mayors, the successive aldermen, and the resident clergy of the town were members of the Cemetery Committee down to the 22nd September, 1885, when the Committee resigned their position and transferred their authority to the Sligo Corporation.

The Corporation was the most suitable body, in which to vest its management, as persons of different religious denominations are buried in it, though in different quarters. The charge for plots is moderate—the highest being five guineas, for a plot *à perpetuite* of nine feet square; a smaller plot in the same quarter costs much less; while a considerable stretch is provided, free of charge, for the interment of the poor.

Over the plots, that have been used, monuments are pretty general, many of which are costly and graceful. There is a goodly number of obelisks, some terminating in crosses and some in poppy heads. There is a variety of crosses—Greek crosses, Latin crosses, Irish crosses, one of the last named, that on the grave of the late Mr. Gayer, being elaborately and tastefully carved. There are two or three massive pyramids, which might, perhaps, be impressive enough, if elsewhere, but which seem out of keeping with the extent of the grounds and the size of the surrounding monuments. You see here and there the cremation urn, either as an independent memorial or as some subsidiary part or member of a group.

In general, the monuments afford evidence, not only of family affection, but of good taste and Christian feeling. The spacious plot of the lay brothers and sisters of the Order of St. Dominick; where they are all interred—the brothers in one aisle, and the sisters in the other—suggests their mutual charity, and that they, like Saul and Jonathan, united in life, even in death would not be separated. A small chapel of elegant design and highly artistic finish, erected over the remains of Miss O'Connor, is, from the standpoint, both of religion and art, a most effective memorial. The well-executed marble figure, which stands over the tomb of Mrs. Colleary, and which represents a weeping female looking down disconsolately on the grave, and in her agony clasping to the heart the cross, on which she leans for support, is very striking and suggestive. And the exquisite little Latin cross, in snow white marble, with its simple inscription, "In loving memory of Stella Wynne", is, perhaps, as appropriate and touching a memento of departed worth as the cemetery contains.

The run on monuments for this and other burying places of the county must increase employment, and diffuse a taste for art in the neighbourhood. But for this it will be necessary to give, as far as possible, a preference to local tradesmen and local material; and it is well to know, that in doing so, people giving orders would consult their own interests, for, however bright, marble, granite, or the different species of Scotch stone, may appear for a short time after being worked, they will soon lose colour and moulder away in the open air of our climate, while the limestone of Ballysadare or Cairns-hill would daily grow harder, and, with some care, look better. Let anyone who may have a doubt about the correctness of this assertion, visit the cloister of Holy Cross Abbey, where he will find the limestone of the columns nothing the worse for its four or five centuries' exposure to the injuries of the atmosphere.

The letters of the epitaphs in this and the other burying places of the county are incised. Raised characters were used occasionally in the first twenty years of the eighteenth century, specimens of which may be seen in Ballysadare and Killoran graveyards, but, as the century advanced, they were given up, owing, probably, to their expensiveness. The raised lettering, if more costly, is far more enduring than the other. Epitaphs in verse are not so common in Ireland as they are in England and other countries, and very few of them are to be met with in the county Sligo. In Ballysadare graveyard, over the grave of a sailor named Benson, we read:—

    Laborious blast on Neptune's waves has tossed me to and fro,
    But spite of all, by God's decree, I harbour here below;
    And now at anchor here I lie with many of our fleet,
    I hope to sail some day again our Saviour Christ to meet.

In the same place the inscription on the tomb of Father Walter Henery runs thus:—

    If generous merit, without pride or state,
    Or Heaven-born virtue could avert man's fate,
    If a God-like mind inclined to aid and give,
    Could furnish means to conquer death and live,
    The worthy pastor that entombed lies here,
    Would always live to give, instruct, and cheer
    The helpless poor, illume the church, and be
    God's faithful servant, Walter Henery.

We are indebted to the muse of our local bard, Father Casey, for this acrostic, on the monument of the Milmo family:—

    May Heaven rest the souls of those
    In peaceful bliss who here repose;
    Let angels come their souls to meet;
    May Heaven's Queen with welcome greet;
    On them may Jesus, God of love,
    Serenely smile in realms above.
    They fought the fight, they gained the prize
    On which on earth they kept their eyes;
    May we, like them, when life is o'er .
    Be crowned with bliss for evermore.

And the following epitaph on the monument of his parents, in the churchyard of Tawnagh, is by the same talented writer[1]:—

    Accept, fond parents, throned above
        Life's stormy ocean wild;
    This monument of filial love
        From your devoted child.
    You taught me young to worship God,
        And every sin to dread;
    Along the path the saints have trod
        Your children young you led.
    Faith, hope, love, and gifts beyond

---

[1] This able and hard-working missionary priest has given to the public various poems didactic, lyrical, etc., and has been most successful in all. While his verses, as to artistic form and finish, have received the high commendation of critics of plenary authority, like Cardinal Newman, they are regarded, in their moral aspect, by the bishops and priests of Ireland, as one of the most potent forces at work in resisting and abating the evils of intemperance.

All else between the poles;
I owe them to your teaching fond,
May heaven rest your souls.

The following, in Collooney churchyard, savours somewhat of the sectarian feeling very prevalent formerly in that neighbourhood:

Here lies the body of Thomas Stuart and his wife Jane,
A soldier in Flanders in all Queen Anne's reign,
He fought there with Marlborough in many a campaign,
Religion was the cause he strove to maintain.

This quaint production may be seen in Templeboy graveyard:

Here lie Tom and his wife Mary,
His Surname Burns, her's was Fary;
She modest was and to strangers good,
He Greek and Latin understood.
As they shared freely what was given
Pray that their souls may rest in heaven.

The effusion, that follows, is inscribed on the tomb of the Knott family, in the burying place of Emlaghfad:

Beneath the horrors of this tomb
In promiscuous ruins lye
The noblest charms that virtue gave
With all that nature could supply.

Miss Mary Knott, late of Battlefield, departed this life, on the 25th day of September, 1777 aged—23 years.

Ah! why dread tyrant was it given
To thee to sink (so young) such worth in dust?
Why, 'twas my great command from heaven
To crop the fairest flower first.

There are a few other inscriptions in verse, up and down the county, which are omitted here with regret for want of room.

CHAPTER XII

THE CHURCH OF ST. JOHN

THE church of St. John came much later than the neighbouring churches of Killaspugbrone and Kilmacowen; and, as far as the writer knows, there is no record, either in print or manuscript, to fix the time of the foundation. It is not mentioned in the *Annals of the Four Masters*; the *Annals of Loch Ce*, so full on the history of this part of Ireland; the *Annals of Boyle*, compiled in the neighbourhood; the *Annals of Clyn and Dowling*; or any of the other annals or histories to which Irish writers turn for information regarding the past of the country.

ST. JOHN'S CHURCH IN 1776[1]

Nor will the style of the building throw much light on the subject, for, with its jumble of semi-circular, pointed, and horizontal lines, it is a mixture of several styles, so that the work cannot be referred to any one definite period. And, when we recollect, that within the present century, the building has undergone substantial alterations, £3,500 having been expended on it in 1822, and about £1,000, a year or two ago, we may safely infer that, by the operations, which took place on these occasions, the original features of the church have been entirely altered, and that comparatively little of what now meets the eye formed part of the primitive

---

[1] This illustration was drawn on the wood by Mr. Wakeman, from a sketch made in 1776, which was kindly lent the writer by the Honourable Evelyn Ashley.

structure. No one would recognise in the church of to-day, the church of a hundred years back.

If the opinion, already expressed, that Maurice Fitzgerald was the true founder of Sligo, be, as it must be, admitted, it will follow that St. John's Church was not built before his day. And, in any case, an earlier date cannot be assigned, as Fitzgerald was, at all events, the first Anglo-Norman that acquired footing in Sligo, and, as the church is certainly a work of the Anglo-Normans, and not of the Celts. The invaders always showed a special devotion towards St. John the Baptist, and gave his name to their religious foundations. Strongbow founded the priory of Kilmainham in his honour; John de Courcy dedicated to him the church of Down; Walter de Eidelsford that of Castledermot; Walter de Lacy that of Kells; William Marshall, Earl of Pembroke, the Priory of St. John the Baptist, at Kilkenny; Maurice Fitzgerald himself founded the Preceptory of St. John the Baptist, at Kilteel, in county Kildare; and others manifested their devotion to this saint in the same way, in Dublin, in Cork, in Limerick, in Louth, in Roscommon, in Tuam, and in other places.

The Anglo-Normans being supreme in Sligo during the progress of this movement, would naturally exhibit their attachment to the Baptist at Sligo, in the same way as their fellow 300 countrymen were doing elsewhere though, no Celt of the time would dedicate a church to this favourite saint of the Foreigners. If, then, we suppose St. John's Church to be the work of the first invaders though it is not easy to reconcile the character of the building with so early an origin it must have been founded between the middle of the thirteenth century and the year 1315, as the Fitzgeralds first, and the De Burgos after, were masters of Sligo all this interval; but in 1315, owing to Bruce's invasion, the English lost authority in the place, and did not recover it till late in the reign of Elizabeth, so that St. John's could not be erected in. the intervening centuries, the O'Connors being then Lords of this place.

There is mention in official documents of a rectory, called the Rectory of Sligo, between the two bridges, to which, there is reason to think, the church of St. John belonged. The exact extent of this rectory is no where stated, but, as it is contradistinguished from the rectory and vicarage of Killaspugbrone, from the rectory and vicarage of Kilmacowen, and from the rectory and vicarage of Calry, it would appear to coincide with what is now called, the Parish of St. John, and to have extended from the bridge of Belladrehid, to the bridge of Sligo, these bridges being the two bridges in question. It appears from an Exchequer Inquisition, taken at Dublin, in the 38th year of Elizabeth, to inquire into the possessions of the Priory of St. John the Baptist, without the Newgate, Dublin, and from an Exchequer Inquisition, held in Ballymote, on the 12th January, 1593, before

Richard Boyle, that the Rectory of Sligo, between the two bridges, was appropriate to this establishment; a good reason why the church, built in the rectory, should be called the Church of St. John. No doubt, it was while the Fitzgeralds, or the Red Earl, ruled in Sligo, that the Dublin priory received this endowment.

At the dissolution, this rectory was granted to Robert Harrison, from whom it passed by purchase, to John Crofton, who possessed it in 1612, "with a half quarter of land, called Knappagh, and a half quarter called Tully". From Crofton it came into the hands of Sir Roger Jones, who was constantly adding to his possessions by purchase or mortgage.

Aware that Sir Roger Jones was the leading Anglo-Norman of Sligo in his day, the writer laid aside the pen at this point of the narrative, to try to find out, before proceeding further, the facts of Sir Roger's career. And the study was not without result, not merely as regards the Knight's biography, but, what will be more interesting to many, as regards the history of St. John's Church, about which nobody seemed to know anything definite, though it was taken as a settled matter, that it was a pre-Reformation structure; a conclusion in which the writer concurred, though with misgiving, and rather against his better judgment.

Notwithstanding, however, this general conviction, it would now appear to follow, from Sir Roger's will, that St. John's Church is a work of his, and, consequently, a building of the seventeenth century. The words of the will which seem to warrant this conclusion, are as follows:—"My body I committ to the earth, in my tombe in the chappel I lately erected in the parish of St. John's, in Sligo", which words, taken in their obvious sense, imply that he was the founder. This would be quite certain, only that the word "chappel", which signifies generally a small church, and frequently a parochial church, signifies, sometimes, a mortuary chapel in a church, or adjoining a church, such as honourable persons, not unfrequently, erect for their burying-place. But, if Sir Roger Jones meant a chapel in this sense, he would not say, "which I erected in St. John's parish", but, which I erected in St. John's Church, or adjoining St. John's Church, as the case might be. And another disposition of the will confirms the meaning now attached to his words, for he bequeaths to his wife "the parsonage of St. John's", the parsonage being, in those days, the advowson[1] acquired by the foundation of the church, and not, as the word now popularly signifies, the residence of the parson.

Lest it should be supposed, that the erection of the church was too weighty a work for one man, it should be stated, that Sir Roger was quite equal to the undertaking, being, probably, the richest man in the county in his day. His social standing was of the highest, for he was appointed

---

[1] The right of patronage of a church or ecclesiastical benefice, [Clachan ed.].

Governor of Sligo Castle, in 1606, in succession to Sir James Fullerton, and from that time, till his death, in 1637, he was daily acquiring lands in all the baronies of the county, and advancing money on mortgages, as freely as if he had a modern joint-stock bank to his back.

There is reason to believe, that he was engaged in trade, too; for among the bequests left to his second wife, was one which he describes, as "the house or tenement, called the shop". The mansion-house, which he built for himself, was a most sumptuous edifice, being the so-called castle in which Lady Jones lived after his death, and which, on her decease, came to be occupied by Percy Gethins, whom, the writers of the Ordnance Survey Letters, and others, credit erroneously with its erection. At his death he left several large bequests, and, among them, one towards the erection of a bridge over the Moy, at Banada, so that St. John's church would be a work well within his means, and just in keeping with his tastes and public spirit. In no way, indeed, could the outlay on this structure, considering its moderate size, its rubble masonry, its spireless tower, its single lights, and its plain roof, be regarded as formidable, for the first citizen of Sligo in his day; the whole cost, being, probably, a good deal less than the sum, which the leading citizen of Sligo, in our own day, Mr. Peter O'Connor, contributed, and only as one of his many benefactions, to the erection of the Cathedral.

At present the portions of Sir Roger's memorial, which remain, stand outside the walls of the church, in the angle between the south sidewall of the nave, and the south sidewall of the chancel; but this does not prove that it was originally so; for if, as is most likely, the sidewalls of the nave, at first extended further towards the east, they would include the Knight's monument, which, it is plain from the illustration, was a mural one, like that of Sir Donogh O'Connor in the abbey.[1] The chancel is plainly a modification of the original structure, and it was, no doubt, when the alteration was making, that this memento of Sir Roger was left out in the cold, a fate which it would probably have escaped, were his claims to the place better known.

It is certain that the east end of the building has been changed more than once. In 1884 the workmen engaged in the alterations, then in progress, came upon a semicircular foundation, which must have supported a wall of similar form at some time, and thus given to the eastern portion of the church an apse-like termination. It is right to add, that within the semicircle were found human bones which, it would now appear, were

---

[1] Mr. John Clarence, of Ballysadare, has made for the writer, a careful and very accurate drawing, in fac-simile, of the Knight's monument, or, rather, of as much of it as survives the rough handling it met with, at the restoration of the church. The illustration was copied on the wood, by Mr. Wakeman, from this drawing, and was engraved by Mrs. Millard.

those of Sir Roger Jones and his wife, and which the Rector took care to have decently reinterred. At the time of their discovery they were believed by the workmen, who found them, to be the remains of priests or bishops who lived in pre-Reformation times.

SIR ROGER JONES' MONUMENT.[1]

No doubt there had been churches in the district Between the Two Bridges before Sir Roger Jones built the chapel of which he speaks in his will. Maurice Fitzgerald himself would be likely to build one as a parish church for seculars, at the time he erected Holy Cross Convent for the Dominicans, and laid the foundations of Sligo. If such a fabric was not built by Maurice Fitzgerald, it may have been built by his son, or, still more probably, by the Red Earl De Burgo, who repaired or re-edified the castle of Sligo.

At all events, it may be taken for granted that the first church of the Rectory Between the Two Bridges, dates from the period when the English still retained rule in Sligo; for it is certain that the O'Connors, who came in as the English went out, would never consent that a church of their territory should be bestowed, as an endowment, on an English establishment like the Priory of St. John the Baptist without the New Gate, to which the Rectory Between the Two Bridges was appropriate.

1

The parish church once erected, a succession of fabrics would be kept up, either by new erections or by repairs; and, as a matter of fact, we read in the Royal Visitation Book, of 1615, that the then existing church of the place, like so many other churches of the county, was recently "repaired". In building the new church or chapel, Sir Roger Jones showed more zeal for the State religion than its ministers felt or exhibited in those days. That form of religion was at a very low ebb in Ireland towards the close of the sixteenth century, and in the earlier years of the seventeenth. It would serve no good purpose to repeat here the strong language of condemnation, and, indeed, of contempt, in which high English officials speak of the ministers of the new religion who were then in Ireland. It will be enough, at present, to say a word or two regarding some of those who were connected with the county Sligo.

By the admission of all, Protestants and Catholics, friends and foes alike, there lived not in those times a more unprincipled man than Milerus or Miler McGrath, Elizabeth and James's archbishop of Cashel; and it was he who had now the ecclesiastical administration of most of the county, having received, on the 17th September, 1606, a grant, *in commendam*, of Achonry and Killalla, with sundry rectories and prebends in these dioceses, as well as in the diocese of Elphin, including the Rectory of which we are now treating. The grant is thus entered on the Patent Roll of James I., page 106:— "Grant to Miller or (Miler,) Archbishop of Cashel, of the custody of the bishoprics of Killallagh and Aghaconry, and of their temporalities and spiritualities also, Castleconnor and Skreen rectories in Killallagh diocese, and Kilmacallan vicarage in Elphin Diocese, the prebend of Doughorne in Aghaconry diocese, *Inter Duos Pontes* rectory, that is, the rectory of St. John's, Sligo, in Elphin diocese, and the prebend and rectory of Killoshin (Killoran) in Aghaconry, diocese, to the use of the said archbishop, without accompt or payment of first fruits or twentieth parts, to hold the same for life in union with the archbishoprick of Cashel in like manner as the bishopricks of Lismore and Waterford are granted by other letters patent of Queen Elizabeth".

Once in authority over Killalla and Achonry, Miler swallowed up, by himself or his creatures, all the good things which the united dioceses contained. All through his simoniacal career, he never tired asking for preferments from Elizabeth and James; and so fascinated were these monarchs by him that they never refused him anything, being apparently as eager to give as he was to receive. It was only after his death that James seemed to discover his real character—a discovery which would never have been made, or, at all events, would never have been published, only that it became bruited abroad that the accomplished tergiversator, like Talleyrand in modern times,[1] died, at last, a Catholic; a report that derives no little probability from this mysterious epitaph, composed by himself, and conceived in the very spirit of the ambiguous oracle of Delphi:

MILERI MAGRATH,

Archiepiscopi Casheliensis ad viatorem Carmen.
Venerat in Dunum primo sanctissimus olim,
Patricius, nostri gloria magna soli.
Huic ego succedens, utinam tam sanctus ut ille,
Sic Duni primo tempore proesul eram.
Anglia, lustra decem sed post tua sceptra colebam,
Principibus placui, marte tonante, tuis.
Hic ubi sum positus, non sum, sum ubi non sum;
Sum nec in ambobus, sum sed utroque loco.
Dominus est qui me judicat
Qui stat timeat ne cadat.

TRANSLATION.

Patrick the glory of our isle and gown,
First sat a bishop in the see of Down.
I wish that I succeeding him in place,
As bishop, had an equal share of grace.
I served thee, England, fifty years in jars,
And pleased thy Princes in the midst of wars;
Here, where I'm placed, I'm not; and thus the case is,
I'm not in both, yet am in both the places.

Magrath's great object through life was to amass wealth, employing fair means if they were the most likely to succeed, but, if not, recurring, with equal facility, and without scruple, to the *"unde unde"*[2] of Horace. As is not surprising in the case of one who was so great a favourite with the monarchs of the day, and other people in high places, he was able to make the law serve his purposes often, and, in consequence, was generally engaged in litigation. In this way he came in conflict with the O'Haras of Templehouse, in regard to the Templehouse estate; with the O'Haras of Coolany, in regard to the possessions of Ballysadare Abbey; and with Mr. Perse, who had purchased, with other property, the rectories of some Tireragh churches, in regard to the rectories of Skreen and Castleconor. The royal visitors of 1615 summoned Mr. Perse before them, and, having examined him, left this minute on record:—"We sent for Mr. Henry Piers, and desired to be satisfied from him what title he had or pretended to the two rectories of Skreen and Castleconor, which have ever been reputed to be rectories institutive, wherein an incumbent hath lived. He came before me, the Chancellor, and answered me in this manner that those two parsonages

---

[1] The day after Talleyrand's death the Paris Charivari came out with the announcement: "Prince Talleyrand is dead. During life he deceived men; at his death he deceived the devil".

[2] By whatever means, 'by hook or crook', [Clachan ed.].

were found by office to be impropriate, and he purchased them; but yet, soon after the preferment of this archbishop to Killalla and Athconry, he was forced to give unto the archbishop, *to stop his mouth*, one hundred pounds".

It is no wonder that King James, on becoming acquainted with a long series of doings of this kind, should get incensed with his quondam favourite. Miler, however, being now beyond his reach, having passed before a higher tribunal to account for his stewardship, the king desired to exact retribution from the sons of the archbishop; and, with this object, he addressed a royal letter to the Lord Deputy (Patent Roll—22 James I.,) in which, after referring to "the late Milerus' robberies", his "dilapidations", and "ruinations" of church property of all kinds, he directed the Deputy to take order that the sons, "who had grown great by these robberies", should be compelled to make restitution.

Like master like man; and those who served under Miler Magrath always showed themselves worthy of such a patron. Take one or two instances: William Flanagan, who was his dean, had twenty-five livings in Killalla and Achonry, in a few of which he served a couple of times in the year, in some not at all, while in others he never set a foot in his life.

Dermot Ultagh, "one of the creatures and tools of Archbishop Miler Magrath" (Cotton's *Fasti*—The Province of Connaught p. 107), and who, as a tool, was all the more suitable for having been deprived of the office of Treasurer of Cashel, by the Royal Visitors, was his Archdeacon, and held, besides the lands of Kilturra, which formed the *corps* of the archdeaconry, at least two other livings, though it is recorded by the Royal visitors, that he could not read English, Irish, or Latin! And, Andrew Magrath, a relative, apparently a son of the Archbishop, had eleven or twelve livings in Achonry, Kilvarnet, Killoran, Kilmacteige, Killasser, Attymas, Strade, Killedan, Kilconduff, Kilbeagh, Mocholo (Bohola), Kilcoleman, and Templemurry as well as livings in other places, including one in Cashel. James Magrath, a son of Miler, but a layman, got from his father possession of the four quarters of Skreen, the half quarter of Dromard, and other lands, and held them till Archibald, Bishop of Killalla, obtained, on the 8th August, 1634, a decree of the Court of Exchequer for their recovery.

The Sligo portion of Elphin, though that diocese belonged to another bishop, was little better off than Killalla and Achonry. Hugh Brehoun held the vicarages of Kilmacallan, Coolea (Ballynakill), Drumduan (Ballysummaghan), and Drumcolumb; Erasmus Matthews had Tawnagh and Aghanagh; and Hugo O'Hohy held the rich vicarage of Drumcliff, and probably that of Ahamlish; and what an utter sham religious service or functions had become, we may learn from the case of this Hugo O'Hohy, of whom the Royal Visitors 1615 write:—"Hugo O'Hohy did not appear.

It is a certain fact, that he is unable to read English, Irish, or Latin!" Of another county Sligo incumbent, Nicholas Corcan, who held the vicarages of Templeboy, Dromard, and Kilmacshalgan, the same visitors say: "He did not appear, being a drunkard". Thomas Flanelly, Vicar of Kilcoman, was the only minister in those times, of whom the visitors had a good word to say. They describe him as "a man of good character, upright, a convert in religion; he understands and reads the Irish; he is diligent; he resides; and all his benefices are within three miles". They mention, however, one drawback—"*Uxor sua est Papista*"—his wife is a Papist. Were the truth known, the aforesaid Thomas Flanelly was, most probably, a Papist in heart, as well as his wife, though all these benefices, so conveniently situated, stopped his mouth for the time.

Such were the ministers of the State Church in the county Sligo, in the first half of the seventeenth century. Nobody can deny, that they would be a disgrace to any body of men to which they belonged. Hypocrites, drunkards, know-nothings, mammonists, simoniacs, they were the curse of religion, while pretending to be its ministers, so that no lover of Christianity, whatever may be his denomination, can look back without humiliation and pain on their sacrilegious doings.

It may, indeed, be retorted, that they were brought up Catholics, and that, in consequence, a large share of the reproach must be laid to the account of the Catholic Church for their bringing up. It is, no doubt, true, that numbers of them were originally Catholics; as Miler Magrath himself, who was Catholic Bishop of Down, before he became State Archbishop of Cashel; as Andrew Magrath, who was a Franciscan monk, before he became Protestant incumbent of over a dozen benefices; as Thomas Flanelly, who was a Catholic, before he figured as a *"conversus in religione"*. This cannot be gainsaid, so that Catholics have cause to exclaim:—

"Pudet et haec opprobria nobis
Et dici potuisse, et non potuisse refelli"[1].

But it may be urged in extenuation, that the Catholic Church in Ireland at that time, had little freedom of action; that, owing to persecution, it could not instruct its members either in the church or in the school; that its children had to grow up, to a great extent, in ignorance of their duties; and that, in consequence, some of them were little able to resist the temptations with which they were constantly beset by the proselytizer, who offered them riches, honours, and preferments, in return for conformity to the new religion. And, if a few units succumbed, the "seven thousand"

---

[1] It is shameful that such reproaches should be cast upon us and that we are unable to meet them with a refutation (Horace). [Clachan Ed.].

refused to bend the knee to Baal. Those, too, who went over, might be very well spared, being of the kind and class to which Dean Swift refers, in the facetious complaint, that the Pope, in his weeding operations, was in the habit of casting the weeds out of his own garden into that of the Protestants.

The Royal Visitors, of 1615, were greatly exercised over the rectories and prebends which they found in the possession of laymen, whom they, therefore, regarded as usurpers of the property of the church. Sir Roger Jones held the rectory Between the Two Bridges; Henry Piers, or Perse, as the name is more commonly written, possessed the rectories of Skreen, Castleconor, Easkey, Kilglass, and Dromard; and Edward Crofton had in hand the rectories of Kilvarnet and Killoran, in the barony of Leyney, as well as several other rectories and some vicarages in the baronies of Corran and Tirerrill, together with the prebends of Kilmorgan, Emlaghfad, Cloonoghill and Kilturrough. The visitors appealed to the King and Government against those "usurpations", but it would appear, that they appealed in vain, as most of the property in question, notably that of Edward Crofton, is still in the hands of the descendants of the so-called usurpers, or in the hands of their assignees.

If the Royal Visitors failed in their appeal, it was no fault of theirs, for they set forward, very strongly, the manifold evils that must result from leaving those ecclesiastical possessions in the hands of laymen; such as the loss of his rights of advowson by the bishop; the loss of his first fruits and twentieth parts by the king; and the loss of opportunities of promotion by the clergy. In their communication they call the attention of the government to a circumstance in connection with the usurpations, which, if things were as they alleged, would convict the powerful men of whom they complain, of shameful injustice and fraud. According to these allegations, the grantees of abbeys took to themselves far larger possessions than the royal grants included or covered; for when the king granted an abbey and its appurtenances, they found means to have their letters patent so manipulated and drawn as to convey not only the abbey and its temporal possessions, but, against the intention and will of the king, all the rectories, vicarages, and churches, which were connected in any way, directly or indirectly, with such abbey: *"Per istas usurpationes"*, say the Visitors, *"nonsolum episcopus jus suum deperdit, clerus promotionem, sed etiam Rex ipse primitias et vicesimam partem in his rectoriis et vicariis penitus amittit; et hunc morem minus juste continuatum observamus, quod si quis a regia Majestate literas obtinuerit alicujus abbatiae, monasterii, et prioratus, in temporalibus statim in literis patentibus omnes et singulas rectorias et vicarias, quae aliqua ratione vel spectabant vel dependebant ab illis abbatiis, monasteriis, et prioratibus (etiam non parcendo ecclesiis institutivis et taxatis contra intentionem principis) inserit".*

In conclusion they suggest to the king to issue a royal Commission with authority to summon before it the bishops of the dioceses concerned, and the "powerful usurpers" in question. It is only in this way, they aver, an end can be put to a state of things so injurious to the King, and so noxious, nay, so ruinous, to the church. The King wrote to the Lord Deputy on the subject, but with little immediate effect. The "powerful usurpers", no doubt, proved more than a match for both the Royal Visitors and the bishops, and found means to defeat their well meant and zealous suggestion or recommendation.

The lay "usurpers" soon found for themselves more congenial work than giving an account of their slippery proceedings before a royal Commission. And this work was the more acceptable, as it enabled them to forward at once their own interest, and the interest of the new religion; interests, indeed, inseparably connected; for if the religion failed, their new estates and worldly prospects necessarily failed with it. Their chief aim being henceforward to enforce the penal laws against Catholics, and, in the later language of the Statute Book, to prevent the further growth of Popery, they, in pursuance of this object, and in concert with the Government, succeeded in making the heirs of the different Irish families of the district wards of the reigning monarch, and thus had them brought up, as far as they could do it, members of the State church.

In acting thus they were influenced not more by zeal for the spread of Protestantism, than by a thirst for their own aggrandisement; for the guardianship, or wardship, as it was called, of these young gentlemen, which was always given to favourites, became a source of great profit to those who obtained it, and was generally secured by payment of a large fine to the king, and, sometimes, of a yearly rent in addition. In execution of this policy, the wardship of Sir Charles O'Connor was committed, first, to Sir Faithful Fortescue, and, next, to Sir Roger Jones; that of Brian O'Rorke, son of Sir Teige O'Rorke, to Richard, Earl of Clanrickarde, who was the ward's uncle (Patent Roll, James I., p. 71); that of Shane Oge O'Hara, son and heir of Shane O'Hara of Ballifennoge (Balliara), to Sir Roger Jones (Patent Roll, James I, p. 183); that of Thadeus O'Hara the younger, son of Thadeus O'Hara, to Sir Charles Coote, of Castlecoote in Roscommon (Patent Roll, James I., p. 339); that of Brian Oge McDermott, son and heir of Brian McDermott of Carrickmacdermott, to Talbot Dillon (Ibidem, p. 55,) and of Owen McDermott, son and heir of Cornelius McDermott, late of Carrickmacdermott, to Sir William Taaffe, Knight (Ibidem, p. 311); of Farall O'Gara, grandson and next heir of Iriell O'Gara, late of Moygara, in Sligo county, gentleman, deceased, to Sir Theobald Dillon, Knight (Ibidem, p. 311); of Owen McSwine (McSweeny), son and heir of Erevan McSwyne, of Longford, in Sligo county, gentleman, to William Crofton of Dublin city,

Esquire (Ibidem, p. 435); of David O'Dowde, son and heir of David O'Dowde, late of Killinglas (Kilglass), Sligo county, gentleman, deceased, to Captain Lionel Geste, or Ghest afterwards Sir Lionel Guest (Ibidem, p. 37); and of John, *alias* Shane McConnor McDonnogh, son and heir of Cornelius, *alias* Connor McDonnogh, lately of Ballendowne, in Sligo county, to Charles Brennan (Ibidem, p. 557).

These grants were made generally, *mutatis mutandis*, in the same words, so that the following formula concerning O'Gara, the ward of Sir Theobald Dillon, may be taken as a sample of all: "Grant to Sir Theobald Dillon, Knight, of the wardship of Farall O'Gara, grandson and next heir of Iriell O'Gara, late of Moygara, in Sligo county, gentleman, deceased, for a fine of £8 17s. 9½d., and an annual rent of £11 8s. 0d., retaining thereout £9 English, for his maintenance and education in the English religion and habits, and in Trinity College, Dublin, from the 12th to the 18th year of his age". With the wardship, control of the marriage of the ward was generally granted, which gave the grantee great additional opportunities of influencing the religion of his ward, as also of serving his own worldly interests by enabling him to marry his charge to some relative, friend, or favourite, of his own.

It may be remarked, that John O'Donovan indulges in a sneer against Farrell O'Gara, for his "Trinity College education" as if O'Gara alone lay open to the imputation, while the fact is, that all the heirs of the Celtic families of the county were, on becoming King's wards, subjected to the same condition. It is unfair then to the great patron of the Four Masters, to single him out for special reproach, while the O'Connors, O'Rorkes, McDermots, O'Dowds, etc., who are all in the same case, pass off unnoticed. If he is in fault, so are all these, and if they are free from blame, so also is Farrell O'Gara.

For, it appears from the foregoing, that the heirs of all the county Sligo chiefs, without exception—the O'Connors Sligo; the O'Haras, of Leyney; the O'Garas, of Coolavin; the McDonoghs, of Tirerrill and Corran; the O'Dowds and McSweenys, of Tireragh—were all gathered into the net; and it is a remarkable proof of their fidelity to the old religion, that, though the toils were so skilfully drawn around them, and so well guarded, they all, except, apparently, Thaddeus O'Hara, the ward of Sir Charles Coote, managed to break away from their captors, and to overcome the all-powerful worldly temptations employed to retain them. The Joneses and Croftons, and the rest, were powerful enough to keep a grip of their ill-gotten rectories and vicarages, in spite of the efforts of royal visitors to recover them, but they were powerless against the irresistible Catholic instincts of the young Celtic chiefs. And herein is witness enough, that these chiefs were little accountable for their royal wardships, and "Trinity College education". When the first use they make of their liberty of action and maturity of judgment, is to break through all their Anti-Catholic surroundings, we may well conclude, that whatever was amiss with them, in the period of their minority, was the outcome of no perversity of will, but of want of intelligence to understand, or want of liberty to regulate and control their actions.

St. John's Catholic parish, being a mensal parish, there are no Parish Priests to be named. Some information concerning a few of the Administrators may be found in other parts of the book.

There is no local record of the succession of Protestant incumbents in the parish of St. John's. The first we meet with is William Rycroft, who is mentioned in the Royal Visitation Book, of 1615, as holding the vicarage of Sligo. Judging by his preferments, Mr. Rycroft was a stirring and ambitious man. On the 22nd October, 17 James I, he was presented, by the King, to the *vicarage* of Drumcliff, in the diocese of Elphin, and to that of Rossinver, in the diocese of Kilmore; and on the 6th June, in the 20th year of this King, he was presented by him to the *prebend* of Drumcliff, with a voice in the chapter, and a stall in the choir. Mr. Rycroft enjoyed also the vicarage of Calry, and the *prebend* of Kilcooly. In the Visitation Book he is described as a preacher—"concionator".

William Newport is stated in the Visitation Book, of 1633, to be Vicar of St. John's, in Sligo, and of Killaspugbrone. John Wilkinson, prebendary of Oran, was rector of St. John's in 1666.

Coote Ormsby was presented by the Crown, in 1681, to the living of St. John's, which was then a rectory, as well as a vicarage. Upon the death of Sir Roger Jones, the rectory, no doubt, lapsed to the Crown. It was probably in the interest of Mr. Ormsby, that the four parishes of St. John's Sligo, Calry, Killaspugbrone, and Kilmacowen, were united by act of Council, in 1681, the year of his appointment.

John Fountanier, a Huguenot, was presented by the Crown, in 1695. This clergyman's name occurs in the records of the Provost's Court, in the case of "Rev. John Fountanier, plaintiff; William Flannery, defendant; James Rourk, bound for his appearance".

Rev. Eubule Ormsby succeeded Rev. John Fountanier as incumbent of St. John's. The first time we hear of Mr. Ormsby, is 172½ [sic], when he was appointed chaplain of the Prince of Wales' own regiment of horse, on the recommendation of Brigadier-General Wynne, who applied in the following letter to Secretary Hopkins, for the chaplain's commission:—

"Dublin, January 28th, 172½.

"SIR,—His Grace, my Lord Lieutenant, has been pleased to consent, that the Reverend Eubule Ormsby be made chaplain, in the room of Dr. Hallifax, deceased, to His Royal Highness, the Prince of Wales' own Royall

Regiment of Horse, now under my command, with which His Grace has commanded me to acquaint you, and that he desires a Commission may be drawn accordingly.—I am, Sir,

"Your most humble and obedient servant,
"OWEN WYNNE.

"*To* Mr. Secretary Hopkins".
"I desire the Commision may bear date, the first of this instant".

Mr. Ormsby's next preferment was the vicarage of Drumcliff, from which he was promoted to the rectory of St. John's. With the rectory, he acquired through time, the vicarages of Drumcliff and Ahamlish, and died about 1769, rector of St. John's, Calry, Kilmacowen, and Killaspugbrone, as well as vicar of Drumcliff and Ahamlish.

Mr. Ormsby was succeeded by Rev. Manly Gore, who held the rectory of St. John's, till 1774. In 1775 Rev. Wensley Bond became incumbent of St. John's, and continued in the position down to 1820. He was commonly spoken of as Dean Bond.

The next rector was Reverend Charles Hamilton, who died, April the 11th, 1844. After Mr. Hamilton, came Reverend Edward Day, who resigning, in 1876, died July the 23rd, 1886, and was buried on the 30th July, in the cemetery of St. John's Church, where his tomb hears the inscription—"Rev. Edward Day, died July 23, 1886; aged 83 years". On Mr. Day's resignation, the Venerable Archdeacon Kearney the actual rector, was instituted.

Some of the curates of St. John's have better claims to notice than some of the incumbents. The Reverend Edward Nicholson, who was curate of the Reverend John Fountanier, in the first quarter of the eighteenth century, was a man both of zeal and talents. We learn from the *Dublin Chronicle,* of 1788, that he established a free school for the maintenance, clothing, and instruction of thirty boys, increasing the number, with and with, till it had reached fifty, about the time of his death, at the age of eighty.

The writer in the *Chronicle* gives no information as to Mr. Nicholson's personal or family relations, so that one is at a loss to know whether he is the Mr. Nicholson mentioned in the report of the Commissioners of Endowed Schools, as leaving a lien of £120 a year on his estate, for a school at Knocknarea. This gentleman did not confine his benefactions to pupils of schools; for it is related of him, that he had peculiar pity for "wives linked to dissolute, careless, or inebriated husbands" and helped them as far as his means allowed.

His tongue and pen, as well as his purse, were devoted to the service of those around him. It is said, that he composed several pious and instructive tracts for the children of his school and others. His compositions were relished all the more, as they had a spice of quaintness about them, such as is found in the following lines, which he entitles, a *"Receipt to cure a plague*. With the sword of the Lord alarm the obstinate culprit, who may be subdued to repentance by fasting, solitary confinement, and the wholesome rod of correction, from the blossoms of which may be distilled, the elixir of contrition, with bitter herbs purging the whole body of sin; and with the due application of lenient balmy works, perfectly restore the foul offender to pardon and peace".[1] It appears he tried his hand at verse, and expounded the duty of a child in metre. Two lines of this piece remain:

"Your clothes keep neat, when worn and bare;
Be not so foul as slovens are,"

and they are hardly of such merit, as to cause one to regard the disappearance of the rest as a national loss.

The Reverend James Armstrong, who was curate of St. John's, as well as master of a classical school in the town, during the closing years of the eighteenth, and the opening years of the present century, is described by Charles Phillips, in a note to the Emerald Isle, as "a man of most extensive acquirements, great piety, and a cheerfulness of manner, which made every circle, in which he associated, happy". The body of the poem contains a very flattering portrait of Mr. Armstrong, which will be quoted later on, in connection with the facts of Charles Phillip's life.

The Reverend Mr. Montgomery, who held the curacy of St. John's, some years ago, was a man of great piety and considerable learning. In his ministrations, while in Sligo, he made the poor his special care, and did all he could, by word and example, to help them. Quitting his curacy, he joined the Catholic Church, where, after training in an ecclesiastical seminary and ordination, he was employed on the English mission. In his new sphere of duty, as in the old, he devoted himself in a special manner to the services

---

[1] It is likely Mr. Nicholson borrowed the idea of his "Receipt" from Italy, where, in the time of Savonarola, such pious prescriptions were common, both in prose and verse. The following sample was composed by a friend of Savonarola:—

"To tre once almen di speme
Tre di fede e sei d'amore
Due di pianto e poni insiema
Tutto al fuoco del timore.

Fa di bollir tre ore,
Premi in fine e aggiunge tanto
D'umiltade, e dolor quanto
Basta a far questa pazzia".

of the poor, who, in return, loved him through life, and mourned him as a father at his death.

We learn, from various advertisements and news paragraphs, which appeared in the *Sligo Journal*, in the year 1819, that St. John's Church was then too small to contain the number of Church Protestants in the benefice. To supply the accommodation wanted, the church of Calry was built in 1823; and its first incumbent was Reverend James Armstrong, who was succeeded by Rev. Messrs. Todd, Shone (the present bishop), Dowden, Heany, and Berry, the actual incumbent.

The pretty little church and parsonage of Strandhill are the outcome of private contributions. To collect money for the work, a "Knocknarea Endowment" fund was started in 1840, of which Messrs. Edward J. Cooper, William Phibbs, and Roger C. Walker, acted as Trustees; and these and other influential local gentlemen contributed liberally themselves, and obtained large subscriptions from their friends and the public. They were fortunate in securing the services of Sir John Benson as architect; for the church and clergyman's residence are not the least striking of the structures, on which the gifted Collooney man has left the trace of his master hand.

Strandhill Church is dedicated to God, in honour of St. Anne, as we learn from an inscription, which stands over the chief entrance, and which runs thus:—IN HONOREM B. ANNÆ DEO O.M. DEDICATA ÆRE PRIVATORUM COLLATO ÆDIFICATA, A.D. MDCCCXLIII.

The church, since its foundation in 1843, has been successively served by Rev. Messrs. Gully, Hamilton, Chambers, Day, Coulter, Hamilton, and Galbraith, the present incumbent.

CHAPTER XIII

THE BOROUGH OF SLIGO

OLD SEAL OF CORPORATION   **NEW SEAL OF CORPORATION**

SLIGO was one of the new boroughs created in 1613, the order "to draw forth a fiat of incorporation of the towne of Sligoe" being dispatched by Lord Deputy Chichester to the Attorney-General on the 20th of October, 1612, and the actual creation taking place on the 30th of March, 1613. On this occasion "the town and all hereditaments within the precinct thereof were created and incorporated the borough of Sligo, consisting of portriffe and twelve burgesses and commonalty; the portriffe and burgesses to return two members to Parliament; the portriffe to be chosen 24th June, and sworn 29th September, before his predecessor. Upon any vacancy within the year, a portriffe to be chosen within fifteen days, and a burgess within seven days, to supply such vacancy. To hold a court of record every Tuesday, and determine all actions of debt, etc., not exceeding the sum of five marks; to assemble and make bye-laws; to have a mercatory guild and a common seal; to appoint two sergeants-at-mace, and other inferior officers, during behaviour or pleasure. The portriffe to be clerk of the market".[1]

The names of the first burgesses were:—Provost, Roger Jones, Esq.; burgesses, Sir William Taaffe, John Gesbarbe, Edward Crofton, William Harrison, Hugh Jones, Edward Brackstone, Richard Robinson, Thomas Syngeie, John Hopkins, Thomas Reynolds, Robert Gymbel, and William Wilson.

---

[1] *Liber Munerum,* Vol. I., Part L, p. 35. The Sligo charters are not found, either in original or copy, among the Corporation records. It was intended to give them in the Appendix, but the idea had to be abandoned, as they would occupy too much space.

On the 9th December, 19th year of his reign, James I. created a guild of the staple for Sligo, to be a corporation, making Roger Jones, Mayor, and Edmond Carpenter, Andrew Crean, Edmond Braxton, Richard Robinson, John Hopkins, John Woodward, John O'Fewly, Robuccus Crean, William Crean, James French, and John French, merchants, to be a society, community, and incorporated body, with a perpetual succession. At first the Government had some doubt whether Sligo could be depended on to support their policy; for a letter of Sir Oliver St. John says, "Of the boroughs to be erected in Connaught, Roscommon, Carrick-Drumrusk, Sligo, and Castlebarre, all will send Protestants to the Parliament, unless some doubt be of Sligo; "but the authorities manipulated the business so skilfully, that Sligo, in the all-important election of 1613, returned, as its members, Henry Andrews, Clerk of the Crown, and Edward Southwell, another staunch Protestant partisan.

In 1687 James II. dissolved the corporation of Sligo as well as the other corporations of the country, substituting new charters for those abolished. His Sligo charter names Martin O'Connor, Esq., John Tafe, Esq., Willelm Gore, Baronet, Henrie Crofton, Esq., Pierce Gethin, Esq., James French, Esq., Philip Ormsby, Esq., George Crofton, Esq., Terence McDonnogh, Esq., Walter Phillips, Esq., Philip Cox, merchant, Jasper Bret, Esq., John Crean, gentleman, Andrew Lynch, farmacapol, Anthon Crean, merchant, Peter Darcy, merchant, John Delaps, merchant, Bartholomew Maly, merchant, Thomas Jones, Esq., Andrew Martin, merchant, and Charles Hart, gentleman, the first 24 free burgesses. This list of burgesses, including so many of the leading names of the county, tends to prove that the want of social standing, sometimes alleged against James the Second's corporations, is without foundation. It is known that James' new charters, including that of Sligo, received their death-blow at the Boyne and Aughrim, and that, with the triumph of William, the charter of 1613 revived.

Some of the records of the corporation, are, no doubt, lost, for the first entry in those now in the Town Hall is dated April 21, 1709. The existing records are contained in three volumes, all in paper, and in folio form—the first named "A Book of Record 1709", running from 1709 to 1754; the second from 1754 to 1842; and the third, the one now in use, beginning with 1842, and having for its first entry, "A list of Aldermen and Town Councillors of the Corporation of Sligo, as returned by the Revising Barrister on the 25th day of October, 1842". Imperfect though these books are, and badly kept, as they certainly were, they still acquaint us fairly with the objects of the Corporation meetings, which were: first, to elect provosts, burgesses, and parliamentary representatives; and, secondly, to provide for the peace and order of the town, the cleansing of the streets, and the regulation of the markets.

The "common seal", being prescribed in the Charter, must have been in use from the first, though it is duty in the middle of the eighteenth century we meet with impressions of it, in the Corporation records. While the device was always the same, the dies varied in form and size, one being oval, and two or three others circular, that most frequently employed having a diameter of 1⅞ inch. These seals are no longer in the Town Hall, though they were seen there less than twenty years ago. What has become of them?

We learn from the impressions left, that the device consisted of a tower in ruins; a tall tree near it, with, apparently, some brushwood around; a hare running across a river, and a strand studded with oysters, one of which is attached to a hind foot of the animal; and a rounded hill, or mountain, in the background. It is strange that the townspeople all misunderstand this device. According to them, the ruin, which is its chief feature, is the round tower of Drumcliff, while the hare, they say, is hastening from that tower to Sligo, to signify that Drumcliff had ceased to exist as a town, and that Sligo had sprung up in its stead. The Town Council, in a formal resolution of the 9th April, 1871, adopts and sanctions the popular opinion respecting the ruin, and orders, that in future, the official seal of the Corporation shall show the "round tower".[1] Of the tree, the brushwood, and the hill, the people seem to have formed no opinion.

It is unpleasant to have to note, that the archaeology of the Town Council is at fault, and that the round tower of Drumcliff, or any other "round tower", has as little to do with the genuine arms of Sligo, as the tower of Babel. A glance at the ruin, in the impressions of the seal, shows that, the tower in question is a square one, and no other than the tower of Sligo Abbey; and if an inspection and examination of the impression left any doubt on the mind, as to the meaning of the design, the doubt would be removed by a letter of Sir Francis Leycester, Gorst, England, which conveys his resignation of the office of burgess, in the Corporation of Sligo, and, which may be seen, in copy, in the Minute Book of the Town Council. In this letter, written in 1722, Sir Francis recites, that he was elected

---

[1] The resolution is dated, Sligo, April 3rd, 1871, and runs thus "Resolved: That the duplicate seals of the Corporation, hitherto used, be no longer used, and that, henceforth, until rescinded by resolution of the Town Council, the new seal which has been procured, with the words impressed, viz.: "Corporation of Sligo, 1612, J.R.,' and 'Sligo Borough Improvement Act, 1869,' bearing the device of a *round tower*, a tree, with a hare having its foot caught by an oyster, and which is impressed on this resolution, be adopted, and shall be the common seal of the Corporation of Sligo, for all acts necessary to be done by that body under their common seal.

"CHARLES ANDERSON, MAYOR.
9th April, 1871".

"burgess of the Abbey-ville of Sligo",[1] that is, of the town of the abbey of Sligo; thus, proving that the tower in the arms of the town, is the tower of the abbey. Sir Francis Leycester, at this time, was owner of the tolls and customs of Sligo,[2] which he inherited from his ancestor, Sir Robert Leycester, who, among other large grants, obtained from James I., in several counties of Ireland, received one, comprising "the site, etc., of the late Franciscan (should be Dominican) friary of Sligo, the buildings, orchard, and gardens thereof, and 1½ quarter of land adjoining, with two weirs near the said house, upon the river of Sligo, parcel of the estate of said monastery". Very probably it was Sir Francis himself that had the seal made, and the arms engraved; for his family had great taste for history and antiquities, one of them, Sir Peter Leycester, being described by Sir Bernard Burke (Landed Gentry—Article, Leycester) as the "well known historian of Cheshire". It may be mentioned, that Sligo was not the only town that had an ecclesiastical edifice in its arms; for the Corporation Seal of Irishtown, Kilkenny, bore a representation of the west end of St. Canice's Cathedral.[3]

As to the other objects figured in the device: the tree and brushwood represent the wood[4] which covered the site of the abbey in St. Patrick's time; the hare, with the oyster on its foot, and oysters strewn in its path, the noted shelliness from which the river got the name of Sligech, or the shelly river; and the hill, or mountain, in the back-ground, either Benbulben or Knocknarea. From this explanation, the reader will learn, that the device of the "common seal", gives a good idea of the origin of the town and its surroundings, and, that it is to Holy Cross Convent the county town is indebted for its armorial bearings.

The actual insignia of the Corporation are two silver maces—duplicates or facsimiles of each other—and a Mayor's gold chain. In a very

---

[1] Whereas, I was elected, and am a Burgess of the Abbeyvill or town of Sligo, and whereas, by distance I cannot discharge the duty of said office, I hereby resign, etc.
"F. LECESTER".
August 7th, 1722, Gorst.

[2] This appears from the following letter, addressed to Win. Smith, Esq., by Percy Gethins, who seems to have been agent of Sir F. Leycester:—
"Sligoe ye 2nd *of May,* 1709.
"Dr. Sir. Mr. Spranger, by Sir Fra. Lester's order, is to sett ye Tolls and Customs.
"PERCY GETHINS".

[3] *Kilkenny Archaeological Journal,* Vol. I., p. 486.
Since the above was written, a document has turned up, which confirms the view advocated in regard to the character of the tower, and leaves no room for doubt, that it stands for the tower of the abbey. The document in question, is the very important inquisition taken at Rosslee, in 1616, respecting the lands of the county, and their then possessors. In enumerating the possessions of Sir William Taaffe, the inquisition begins thus: "Sir William Taaffe, of Ballimota, is seized as of fee of the abbey-town of Sligo".

[4] Documenta de S. Patricio, etc.; E. Hogan, S. J., p. 85.

interesting account of these insignia, Mr. Francis Nelson writes of the maces:—"The maces are sterling silver, of antique design, bearing the Irish Hall Mark, 1702, measuring 18 inches long, and weighing 32 troy ounces each . . . On the side of the head of mace, are four medallions, embossed, representing the countries included in the Royal Title those on the dexter side, being the Rose and the Thistle, for England and Scotland, respectively, and on the sinister side, the Harp and the Fleur-de-lys for Ireland and France, each, and all four being surmounted by a Royal Crown. Beneath these medallions, around the head of mace, is engraved the following inscription:—"The Guift of Samuel Walton, Alderman, one of the representatives for the burrough of Sligoe, Anno Domini, 1703."

Of Alderman Walton there seems to be nothing known, except what is stated in the inscription, that he was representative of the borough of Sligo in 1703. If, as we may infer from the name Walton, the town is indebted to an Englishman, for one of its insignia, it is all the more gratifying that another of them, and that the more valuable, is the gift of an Irishman, and a townsman, Mr. Bernard Colleary. Feeling the want of such an ornament for the Mayor of Sligo, at a time when the mayors of other towns were in the habit, on solemn occasions, of wearing this badge of office, Mr. Colleary generously devoted to its purchase, the large addition to the mayor's salary voted by the town Council, in 1882, the year of his first mayoralty. This sacrifice was singularly creditable to Mr. Colleary; but it would be ungenerous not to record, that the mayors who had preceded him associated themselves with him in the generous proceeding, by contributing each a sum sufficient to add to the chain a separate link commemorative of his own year of office. The following full and graphic description of the chain, was drawn up by Mr. Francis Nelson, and kindly supplied to the writer by Messrs. Nelson Brothers, who, it may be here remarked, executed the order for the chain, and in a way which gave the Town Council a work of art as sterling as the gold of which it is made, and gave it at considerably less cost than that at which an inferior article could be procured elsewhere—these spirited Sligomen, not only declining to make any profit by the transaction, but taking on themselves sundry unforeseen incidental expenses incurred in the carrying out of the order:—
"The Mayoral chain is of modern design, 18 carat gold Hall-marked on every separate link and shield; it weighs $19\frac{1}{4}$ troy ounces, and is of singularly fine workmanship and finish; it is composed of eighteen shields, connected together by cable links, double, and the shield and centre links are each surmounted by a single shamrock, and bear on the obverse, the Crest, Motto, and Arms, and on the reverse, the name and date of year of office of each Mayor presenting it. The centre shield is rather larger than the others, and is backed by two Irish Harps ornamented with shamrocks,

and crowned with the Royal crown, finished and picked out with ermine and crimson green enamel. Pendant (and detachable) from the shield is the medallion bearing the arms of the Borough of Sligo, Incorporated by charter from King James I., 1612. It is circular in form, and surrounded by a wreath of shamrocks, rising from the top of which are a pair of Irish wolf-dogs at gaze, between which rises a spray of shamrocks. The well-known curious device of the Sligo arms is beautifully enamelled in Heraldic colours on the obverse of the medallion, ringed with the inscription, in black letters, "Corporation of Sligo 1612", and on the reverse, "Presented principally by Bernard Collery, Mayor of Sligo for 1882, and former Mayors". It may be added, that the Mayor, for the time being, is the custodian of those valuable insignia.

The first provost mentioned in the Book of Records is James Bennett, the town clerk and recorder being, then, George Bennett. John De Butts, who succeeded James Bennett as provost, was a man of some local importance, but had soon to give way to the Wynnes, who began to figure, at this time, in the public life of Sligo. The Wynnes were not long connected with the Corporation till they became its rulers. It was on the 20th March, 1711-12, the connection began, in the person of Captain Owen Wynne, who was then elected a free burgess of the borough of Sligo; and in the year 1722, they were already masters of the situation, the Honourable Major-General Owen Wynne, Captain John Wynne, and Major John Ffolliott, a connection of the family, being, that year, elected burgesses, which gave the Wynnes a dominant influence in the Corporation. This result was not brought about without some sharp practice, and a kind of *coup d'etat* on a small scale.

Before the new comers could become supreme, it was necessary to get rid of those who stood in the way, and, in particular, of the burgess and ex-provost, John De Butts, and the town clerk and recorder, George Bennett. The place was soon made rather hot for this pair; and when, with a view of having a pretext for expelling De Butts, the Corporation called on him to appear at a meeting of the Council, he excused himself by the following letter, which shows that, whatever temper may have been sometimes exhibited in debates of the present Town Council, things were carried much further in the good times of old:—

"The Worshipful Mitchelbourne Knox, Provost of Sligo.

"WORSHIPFUL SIR,—I received your summons requiring me to appear before you on Tuesday, the 23rd instant, to show cause why I should not be disfranchised for my manifest misbehaviour. I know no cause, if it be not for the conscientious discharge of my duty, and for fear of being turned out by the shoulders and sent to the stocks by you, as one of my brethren was ordered to be, and all this, and much more, is noe misbehaviour in these favourites of yours, and to avoid the like treatment, both I and my brother, had, in your presence, without the least resentment, is the cause I do not wait on you in person, that am, Worshipful Sir,

"Your most humble servant,
"JOHN DE BUTTS".

John De Butts' friend, or, as he calls him, his "brother", George Bennett, was disposed of in the same fashion; for, having been called on, says the Book of Record, "to show cause why he should not be disfranchised, he only endeavoured to provoke several of the members to use him ill", so that there was nothing for it but to expel him—the whole proceeding resembling, a good deal, the old affair of the fox and the lamb.

The Council being thus purged of these obnoxious members, the Wynnes might now manage it as they liked, the result being that the owner of Hazelwood, for the time being, had the Corporation of Sligo, as completely as his own household, under control; and when vacancies occurred in the body, by death or other cause, the persons elected were always members, connections, friends, or creatures, of the Wynne family.

The first and second class gentry of the county were generally represented in the Council. Arthur Cooper, who died in 1710, had been a burgess, as was also his son, Joshua, elected in 1738, and his grandson, another Joshua, who was elected in 1771, and who, in a letter written from Kevin Street, Dublin, resigned in 1790. The Council was hardly ever without one or more of the Ormsbys of Willowbrook. Ralph Gore was burgess in 1711, and complaisantly resigned to make room for Captain Owen Wynne, and thus introduce into the body the family that was soon to dominate it. Ralph was followed by Richard Gore and Arthur Gore. The late Colonel Perceval joined in 1817, but, getting tired of the position, resigned in 1827. The Knoxes of Bridge Street, who were always steady henchmen of the Wynnes, figure constantly in the Council all through the 18th century—Mitchelbourne Knox being elected to it in 1715, John, in 1727, George, in 1750, in the room of John, who died that year, and a second Mitchelburne in 1790, *vice* George, deceased. This George was treated with great distinction by his brother burgesses; and, on more than one occasion, when he was prevented by illness, or very advanced age, from coming to their place of assembly, they adjourned to his house, and held their meeting in his chamber. Arthur Martin was sworn freeman in 1738, and elected burgess in 1754, while Edward Martin became burgess the same year, and succeeded William Vernon as provost in 1759. The foregoing are the names one meets with most frequently among the members of the Council, but there was hardly a name of any note in the county, as Gethin, Booth, Parke, Hillas, Gibson, Phillips, Gilmor, Cox, Holmes, Soden, Fawcet, Slade, Bulteel, Betteridge, etc., that may not be found once, or oftener, on the burgess roll of the Corporation of Sligo. O'Hara, perhaps, is the only name conspicuous by its absence, and the absence, no doubt, has its significance. While the Wynnes surrounded themselves, in this way, with their Sligo friends, they took care also, to arm their relations living at a distance—the Coles, Farnhams, Sanders—with the franchises of the borough, in order that, if any hostile local combination threatened or showed itself, it might be crushed with the aid of this friendly family reserve.

The duties of the Town Council were few and easy. The municipal and parliamentary elections, which formed a large portion of these duties, were little else than matters of form, without any of the heat or stir, which, till very recently, used to accompany such, contests. The result was fixed beforehand at Hazelwood, and the burgesses assembled at Sligo only to register the decision, the proceedings occupying merely a few minutes, and the record, with the exception of names and dates, running always as in the following instance:—"Burrough de Sligoe—We, the Provost and free burgesses of the above Corporation, being assembled and met together, doe unanimously ellect and choose Owen Wynne, Esq., to be Provost of the above Burrough for one whole year, commencing the feast of St. Michael the Archangel next ensuing the date hereof, who is first to take the usual oaths, and then to enter into the office of Provost of the said Burrough, as witness our hands this 24th day of June, 1725. Owen Wynne, Provost; Richard Gore, William Smith, Mitchelburne Knox, John Jamieson, John Wynne, Thomas Jennings".

A parliamentary election was, if possible, a still tamer affair. For example: upon a vacancy occurring in the representation of the borough, by the death of Owen Wynne, in 1757, the Provost, and three or four other burgesses, assembled in a room; and while the burgesses were chatting about the weather, or some equally important topic, the Provost got through the work of the day, by inserting on the minutes this record:—"I, William Vernon, Provost, with the assent and consent of the rest of the burgesses, freemen, and electors, have elected William Ormsby, Willowbrook, to represent this burough in Parliament".

Even the first election to the Imperial Parliament after the Union, was disposed of in the same off-hand manner. The following is that election minute:—"We, the Provost and burgesses of the said burough, being assembled in the Town Office, in the said burough, pursuant to notice, have made choice of and elected Owen Wynne, Esq., to be a Burgess of our said burough of Sligo, to attend the Parliament to be held at Westminster, in that part of the United kingdom, of Great Britain and Ireland, called England, with all convenient speed, according to the tenor of the precept to the Provost, directed by James Crofton, Esq., High Sheriff of the County Sligo. Witness our hands, and the seal of the Corporation of Sligo, aforesaid, the 24th day of June, 1802. Thomas Soden, Provost; Wm. Gillmor, Robt. K. Manly, Saml. Bulteel, O. Wynne".

Nor did the cleansing of the streets give much trouble to the Council. Little more than a hundred years ago, Sligo was small in comparison of what it is at present; for it extended, east and west, only from Castle Street to John Street, and, north and south, only from Holborn Street to High Street, all the outlying portions being later additions. About that time, the Charter School was stated by John Howard, to stand "within a quarter of a mile of Sligo;" and somewhat earlier the abbey was spoken of as "near the town", a phrase which, considering the proximity of Castle Street, could only mean, that the building was detached from the town. In these days, turf was cut between John Street and Wine Street; what is now Pound Street, was the country road to Ballysadare and Collooney; the north side of Forthill was a first-rate covert for game and a favourite resort of sportsmen; while the southern slopes, since adorned with such striking structures, public and private—the showy, but well built Model School, the imposing Protestant Church of Calry, the twin institutions of fever hospital and infirmary, which for situation, proportions, and accommodation, are inferior to nothing of the kind in Ireland, and many private residences, such as Mr. Harper Campbell's, and others, superior, on the whole, to those in other parts of the town—were then without buildings of any kind, and formed, from the summit to the river's edge, the long, naked, talus of the Green Fort.

And the town was then shabby as well as small. Whatever Major Wood-Martin may say to the contrary, Sligo was never walled, though the project of surrounding it with a wall was more then once entertained. A letter of November 10, 1577, from Sir Nicholas Malbie to Walsingham, states that the merchants of Sligo desired to wall their town; and Sir Richard Bingham, writing, ten years later, to the treasurer, observes,—"if it shall please your lordship to procure warrant from her Majesty for the granting of a corporation to the town of Sligo, myself will find such means as the town shall be walled without any charge to Her Majesty". Nothing came of these or other efforts, so that Sligo remained and continued all through an open town.

Owing very much to this want of protection, costly houses were little built before the present century. Unlike the stately structures of Galway, and of the southern cities, the houses of Sligo were thatched cabins, with the exception, first, of two or three so-called castles or stone houses, erected in Castle Street, in the early years of the seventeenth century; and, second, of four or five stone-built and slated houses of the eighteenth century. Mr. Martin's, in Knox's Street; Mr. Debutt the wine merchant's, in the same street, now occupied by Messrs. Robinson and Kells, and lately re-roofed and repaired by them; Mr. Everard's, or Everett's house in Old Market Street, which was recently occupied by the late Mr. Tuite, and has been also re-roofed; the residence of Provost Soden, in Quay Street, on the site of the present college; the fine old Lungy House, and the Custom House. The shops had all a dingy look. Instead of the stately fronts, and the perches of plate glass, which are now to be seen in several large business establishments, nothing was then to be met with but little beggarly sashes of half-a dozen panes or so, each pane not more than five or six inches square, the whole window admitting so little light, that candles had to be used early in the day to enable people inside to see what they were doing.

Thomas Corkran was one of the first in modern time, that is, since the days of the O'Connors Sligo, to give an impulse to building in Sligo. Though, for some reason, now unknown, he was called, by his contemporaries, Thomas Gallda—Thomas the Anglicized—it is pretty certain he was a native of Sligo, and son or grandson of another Thomas Corkran, whose name occurs in the reports of the Provost's Court, under the date of July 5, 1720, in the case of "Thomas Corkran, plaintiff, and William Frizzell, defendant". After arranging terms with the Provost, who had received power from the Corporation, "to give up the slip at the Newbridge to Corkran, he to give up, in return, seven feet of his ground in breadth, and also to leave a water passage, with stone steps, in the new street he was about to make", Thomas Gallda built the fine houses known now as Corkran's Mall, and, at right angles with them, the street known as Thomas Street—the Mall getting its name from Corkran's surname, and the street from his Christian name, Thomas. The stones of the Abbey walls were employed in these erections.

Tom Gallda did not fare the better, in the end, for meddling with the Abbey. He was married to one of the Fitzgeralds of Turlough, a family of fire eaters, and Mrs. Corkran had her full share of the spirit of her kindred. Being at a fashionable ball, and her fan dropping, by some accident, on the floor, she called on her husband, who was present, to take it up, but he being in ill humour, at the moment, told her to stoop for it herself. This was more than a Fitzgerald could brook, so instead of taking up the fan she took up her slipper and struck Corkran with it on the cheek before all in the room. Whether this was the one solitary provocation received by Thomas Corkran, from his wife, during their marriage career, or was, on the contrary, the last drop that caused the already full cup of his mortifications to overflow, the result was very serious; for, in a day or two, he sold off his property, and went with his sons to the West Indies, leaving behind him his high-spirited wife, and, what was more blameworthy, two daughters, one of whom, it may be added, became the wife of Mr. Dolan, a small shopkeeper, of High Street, and died about forty years ago. Such was the end, in Sligo, of the builder of Corkran's Mall.

The streets were not in these days, half their present width, those who formed them, thinking only of the business of their own time, when there were no carts or cars, and when all the traffic was carried on by means of pack-horses, or asses. The consequence was, that when carts came into use, towards the close of the last century, and at the beginning of the present, there was hardly room for two of them abreast, so that even in Market Street, if two carts happened to enter it at the same time, one had to pull up till the other, that blocked it, got out of the way.

The scavenging staff of the Corporation could not be very effective, for it consisted of only one labourer, who was appointed in 1727, at £6 a year. Up to that, the streets were left very much to nature's care and mending. Being without pavement, without sidewalks, and with runnels of muddy water, which have been since covered, flowing over some streets, as Market Street, and Old Market Street, the passer-by had to pick his steps, when moving along; while, in Spring and Summer, he had to encounter dung heaps lying in his path, sometimes to get out of the way of ravenous pigs that crossed him, and again, to run the gauntlet with sturdy beggars who came from the country to ply their trade in the town. These nuisances gave the Corporation some trouble; and, in 1711, a beadle was appointed at £4 per annum, to "keep Sligo clear of strange beggars", who might be known by their not having the "badges" which town beggars were authorized and obliged to wear; in 1737, and again in 1760, the inhabitants were ordered, under penalty, to sweep before their doors, to keep the streets clear of dung, and to remove it on horses' backs; and in 1760, the sergeants of the mace and halberdiers were commanded "to take up any hog or swine of any sort, found within the streets, or by-lanes; 5s. to be levied for every hog so found, one half of such sum to be paid to the informer, the other half, to the rector or curate of the parish, for the poor of the parish". The rector could hardly like going half, in this way, with the informer.

These admonitions, then, to the inhabitants, to sweep before their doors, and the employment of one scavenger, seem to comprise all the Council did towards the cleansing of the streets, up to 1769, when, what was then regarded as a great effort to improve them took place. A public meeting of the Corporation, and of the leading inhabitants, being held that year, to take the state of the town into consideration, it was resolved to levy £77 8s. 9d., for the repairs of the streets and lanes; and as paid clerks of works were unknown in those days, the following inhabitants, whose names may have an interest for many, were deputed by the meeting to applot the money, and superintend the work in their respective districts:—Henry Thornton, Esq., and Mr. Arthur Martin, for High Street; W. O'Beirne, Esq., and Mr. Robert Stanley, for Castle Street; Mr. William Gibson, the elder, and Mr. John Gibson, for Radcliffe Street; the said Mr. William Gibson, and John Gibson, for John's Lane to the further church gate; George Knox, Esq., and Mr. Abraham Martin, for Bridge Street; Mr. Thomas Williamson, and Mr. James Gibson, for Stephen Street; and Mr. Robert Ormsby, and

Mr. Matthew Babington, from Mrs. Widdon's corner to Robert Stanley's, in the present Bridge Street.

In the minutes of the Council, there is mention, more than once, of the public passes to the river. As several of the houses, instead of being joined in a line, as all are now, were more or less detached, there were between some of them, private paths to the river; but in addition to these, there were, on the south side of the town, from Castle Street to the river, two public passes, which were kept in order, at the common expense; and of them we read the following resolution, passed at a public meeting of the provost, burgesses, freemen, and other, the inhabitants of the borough, held on the 5th October, 1754:—"We do find, that the water lane, leading from Castle Street to the river Garvogue, is very much out of repair, to the prejudice of the free burgesses, freemen, and others, the inhabitants, and that the same be repaired, and a slip made down to the water, for the benefit of the borough, to prevent carts and carrs from passing that way, and that the slip at the new bridge be repaired, for such as make use of carts and carrs, to draw water from said river, and that Mr. Joseph Davey, Mr. Abraham Martin, and Mr. Charles Martin, be overseers, to see the work done".

The river is much changed in appearance since the time of that resolution. Then, and a good while after, along the left bank, large stones rose here and there over the water, giving the stream a rugged, agitated look, very different from the broad, tranquil surface which it generally presents to the eye at present. It was these stones at the water's edge, and on the bank, that gave the adjoining townland the name of Garvagh, or rough place, a name, which in the course of time, passed to the river itself, under the forms of Garvagh and Garvogue, the rough river. Some writers, including Lewis, in his Topographical Dictionary of Ireland, take Garvogue to be the old and proper name of the river, but in this they are certainly mistaken, for all old authorities are unanimous in calling it *Sligeach*, or The Sligo; and it is so called in James the First's grants, as in that to Robert Leycester, where the phrase is "upon the river of Sligo;" and, as far as the writer has been able to make out, Garvagh was applied, for the first time, to the river, in the deed of partition of Sligo, between the Earl of Strafford, Joshua Wilson, and Reverend Doctor John Leslie.

To Mr. Abraham Martin we are indebted for the improvement of the *Sligeach*, as it was he that rooted up the rocks, and gave unimpeded passage to the water, forming with the stones, the first two islets you meet as you row up the lake from the river-side.

A narrow skew bridge, starting from the site of Mr. Whittaker's house, Stephen Street, and terminating in Bridgefoot Street, behind Mr. Maveety's, spanned the river at that time, and continued there, down to

1846, when the beautiful, commodious, and solid Victoria Bridge, was erected by Sir John Benson and Mr. St. Leger, the late County Surveyor. A "bridge of Sligo", is mentioned in the *Annals of the Four Masters*, so far back as the year 1188, the structure, of course, being of wood, like all the bridges of the period. It is not told, when a stone bridge took the place of the wooden one, but it was probably in the 14th century, about the time the stone and mortar bridge of Ballysadare was built, there being little opportunity, in the troublous times that preceded, of executing such a work. Cahal Og O'Connor was, as far as appears, the builder of the Sligo bridge, as well as that of Ballysadare.

There seems to be no record of the erection of the bridge at the end of Thomas Street. It did not exist in 1642, for, otherwise, Sir Frederick Hamilton would have passed by it to the Abbey, instead of crossing the river at Buckley's Ford; nor did it exist in 1673, as a description of the town, published that year, speaks only of one bridge; but, on the other hand, it was built before 1687, the date of the partition of the O'Connor Sligo estate, for, in the Indenture of Partition, a lane, running from Stephen Street to the river, is called "*Newbridge* Lane". As the parties to the Partition, were the owners of the town at the time, it was probably they that built the bridge. In any case there is nothing to show, that the Corporation had anything to do with the erection, there not being one word about it in their records.

If the "Regulation of the market", and the "peace and order" of the town involved numerous and onerous duties, there is no great trace of them in the Records. The Corporation took action once or twice—first, in 1711, and again in 1800—in adjusting the weights and measures of turf, hay, and straw. In 1732 the Council imposed quarterage, that is, a tax of 2s. 6d. a quarter on all Catholic inhabitants "exercising trades, art, or mastery, all sellers, or persons engaged in other occupations", those refusing payment to have their shops shut, and to be debarred from trade or occupation in the borough. This infamous exaction resembled that wrung from the Jews in some countries for leave to live in them.[1] Later, the Council took in hand the meat and butter markets; more, apparently, in the interests of their own members than in that of the community. Provost Thomas Soden, having erected shambles[2], in 1785, at the lower end of Knox's Street, between Quay Street and the Bridge, the Council ordered that all meat should be exposed for sale there, and there only, under a penalty of 10s. fine for every carcass found in any other part of the town. Soden was empowered to charge for every carcass of beef 1s. 1d.; of mutton 3d.; of veal 3d.; of swine 3d.; of lamb 2d.; and of kid 1d. The butchers, however, who, by the way,

---

[1] See an instructive note on Quarterage in Wyse's History of the Catholic Association. Vol. I., p. 85.
[2] Meat markets, [Clachan ed.].

have always approved themselves the most spirited portion of the population of Sligo, refused to comply with the order; but the friendly burgesses, in order to get their good brother Soden out of the lurch, and to procure him some return for his expenditure, commanded anew the butchers to make use of the place provided for them, informing them, by way of inducement to do as desired, that there would be no charge for the first half year, from November, 1785, to May, 1786. The records do not tell how the matter ended.

James Soden, like Thomas, wished to turn a penny on the markets. Leaving the butchers to his brother, James took the sellers of butter under his own wing, and provided, in 1787, a market for their accommodation near the shambles at the north end of Knox's Street. Of course the Council backed him, appointing him "public weighmaster of butter", with power to have a deputy, accountable to him for all moneys received. The issue of this job is not stated.

The burgesses, then, were always ready to help themselves and their friends, laying the burdens of the borough on others, and keeping the benefits to themselves, monopolizing its offices, emoluments, and other good things. The leases of the town parks having fallen in, the Council gave them to its favourites, William Vernon, William Boyd, James Boyd, and Robert Clarke, glazier; this Robert Clarke, glazier, not being a very reputable person, as a corporation minute, of 1761, directs that a "ball yard, kept in Stephen Street by Robert Clarke, glazier, be removed as a nuisance".

All this time Catholics were the helots of Sligo. Not only were they excluded from the Town Council and from the lands, of which the Town Council had the disposal, but a Catholic could not be a freeman of the corporation, an apprentice of the borough, or even a scavenger of the streets. Whatever else people were, or wherever they came from, the freedom or apprenticeship of the town was within their reach, provided only they abjured the Pope, and conformed to the Church of Ireland, as by law established. A minute of November 27, 1716, informs us that "Bryan Kelly, chandler and soap boiler, is promoted to be a Freeman of the Corporation, having taken the oath of freeman, and, by his certificate, having taken the oaths of abjuration and allegiance under the Mayor's hand and seal of the City of Londonderry;" and a minute of the 12th May, 1716, states, "This day Edward Scanlan received his indenture and his discharge thereon from his master, James Farrell of Sligo, Apothecary, bearing date 1st March, 1708, having served his time, honestly, for seven years, and, likewise, is a Protestant of the Church of Ireland as by law established".

The Council showed its orthodoxy, not only by insisting that its members should belong to the established church, which, of course, was only in conformity with the law, but also by selecting many of them from the clergymen of that church. Among the burgesses whose names are recorded, we find Rev. George Ormsby, Rev. Eubule Ormsby, the Bishop of Meath, Rev. Stephen Radcliffe, Dean Maxwell, Rev. Thomas Cuffe, Rev. W. C. Armstrong, Rev. John Yeates, Rev. Richard Wynne, Rev. B. Eyres, Rev. Henry Wynne, Rev. W. Willoughby Wynne, and Rev. C. Hamilton. Several of these clergymen served as Provosts. To another parson, the Rev. Doctor William Henery, the Council presented the freedom of the borough in a silver box; the silver box being a special, and so far as appears, a unique compliment on the part of the civic fathers. The record adds, that the favour was conferred on Dr. Henery "for his attachment and good service to the Corporation", but does not specify the exact nature of the "good service", which, probably, there was no desire to make known to the public.

The only person that has received the freedom of the borough under the Reformed Corporation, is Mr. Sexton, the member for West Belfast. The honour was voted to Mr. Edmund Dwyer Gray also, but, owing to that gentleman not signing the record, the legal act was not perfected, and the nomination fell through. It is to the credit of the Corporation that the freedom of the borough was conferred on Mr. Sexton unanimously. Unlike the Rev. Dr. William Henery, Mr. Sexton had claims, both of a public and private nature, to the distinction, which everyone recognised. The high place he occupied in the country as a public man, his brilliant eloquence, and the important services he rendered to the town and harbour, entitled him to any compliment the Corporation had it in its power to bestow. Still it was pleasant to find the Conservatives recognising his merits as freely as the Liberals, and joining as heartily in honouring him. It was on the 28th of October, 1885, the freedom was conferred; and the following is the minute of the proceedings, as it appears on the minute book of the Council:—

"Resolved: that the freedom of our ancient Borough be conferred on Thomas Sexton, Esq., M.P., pursuant to the provisions of the Municipal Privileges (Ireland) Act, 1876, that on and from this date his name be enrolled as Honorary Burgess of Sligo, as a mark of respect from this Council, and appreciation of his valuable services in the interests of our Town and Harbour since entering Parliament.

"That the following certificate be engrossed and signed by the Mayor and Town Clerk, and the Corporate Seal affixed thereto: 'This is to certify that, at a meeting of the Town Council held on the 28th day of October, 1885, Thomas Sexton, Esq., M.P., was elected an Honorary Burgess of the Borough of Sligo'.

"[Passed unanimously.]

"JAMES NELSON, Mayor;
"DANIEL MacGILL, Town Clerk
"Moved by EDWARD TIGHE, Alderman;
"Seconded by ROBERT CRAWFORD, T.C".

The Council of the old unreformed Corporation held its last meeting on the 29th of September, 1842; and it would appear from the subjoined minute, the only one entered, that the sole object, for which the meeting was convened, was to secure the offices of Town Clerk and Sergeant-at-mace for the persons named:—

"Borough of Sligo to wit } "We, the Provost and Free Burgesses of said borough, being duly assembled at the Town Office, within the said borough, Do unanimously elect and continue William Allen to be Town Clerk, and Robert Carey and Richard Merrick to be continued Sergeants-at-mace in and for said borough.

"Given under our hands and seal of the Corporation, this 29th day of September, one thousand eight hundred and forty-two.

W. FAUSSET, *Provost.*
JOHN WYNNE.
CHA. HAMILTON.
H. H. SLADE.
WM. WILLOUGHBY WYNNE.
R B. WYNNE.
HENRY FAUSSETT".

"Le roi est mart; vive le roi;" and the Council of the old Corporation having retired from the scene, the Council of the Reformed Corporation lost no time in making its bow. The first meeting of the new body was held on the 1st November, 1842, when the following Aldermen and Town Councillors attended: Aldermen Andrew Walker, Henry O'Connor, Michael Gallagher, and Robert Sherlock; Town Councillors Edward Kelly, Michael Gethin, James Boyle, Michael Gaffney, Martin Cogan, Roger Robinson, Jeremiah O'Donovan, James McLear, E. H. Verdon, William Fausset, James Beatty, James Madden, Henry Maudesley, Dominick Henry, Follis Clarke, Martin Madden, John Killilea, and James Townsend.

Alderman Walker having been called to the chair, it was moved by Alderman O'Connor, seconded by Alderman Sherlock, and resolved unanimously:—

"That Martin Madden, Esq., be elected Mayor for the Borough of Sligo for the ensuing year". With, the exception of naming law officers, this was the only business transacted at the first meeting of the new Council.

Narrow and dirty as the streets of Sligo were about the beginning of the century, the markets were held in them to a much greater extent than in the spacious streets of the present day. Then, as now, Saturday and Tuesday were the two market days: Saturday's market day being held in virtue of a grant made by James I, in 1604, to Sir James Fullerton "to hold a Saturday market and two fairs on 24th June and 29th September, to continue for those days only;" and the market on Tuesday in virtue of a patent granted in 1627 by Charles I; to Sir James Craig, Knight, "to hold a Tuesday market and two fairs on 17th March and 1st August, and the day after each, at the Bishop O'Crean's Cross, *alias* Laghtenaspicke, in the town of Sligo".

Saturday's market was the chief one in those times, as well as at present, but everything else was different. The streams of people that rolled down Gallows Hill North and Gallows Hill South—the two principal approaches—bore little resemblance to the crowds which now flock in on Saturdays by the Albert and the Victoria Road. Instead of the carts and other vehicles which create, nowadays, such movement, horses and asses, laden with sacks or panniers, ambled along. There being no footpaths or sidewalks, the people moved through the high-road in the same line with the horses and asses, and, like them, often carried loads of commodities to be disposed of in the market, such as flannels, drugget[1], linen, and yarn, though not the baskets of eggs and butter which one sees now so commonly in women's hands, as it was then counted a disgrace to sell either of these articles. So much did this silly shame prevail, that when small farmers or cotters began, through time, to take their butter to Sligo, they made it a point to remove it, privately, by night, in order not to leave it in the neighbours' power to upbraid them with the "meanness" at the next falling out.

The style of dress, for both men and women, was rather homely at the time. No one then dreamed of Chesterfields or Ulsters, flowing pantaloons or elastic boots, silk ties or nondescript hats. A blue frieze body-coat, corduroy small clothes, long stockings, a felt hat, "clouted brogues", and a shirt wide open round the chest and neck, formed the general outfit of men; and if some few had, in addition, a frieze overcoat, or *coathamore*, coming down to the feet, and worn both in summer and winter, there were others, particularly from the sea-side, who trudged to town in coarse, white flannel vests, without coat or overcoat, as well as without shoes and stockings, hat or cap: footless stockings, called "martyeens", often doing duty for coatsleeves.[2]

Females knew little then of the finery which makes it hard, at present, to distinguish mistress from maid. A kind of Spencer of home-made coarse cloth, falling, about the knee, over a skirt of drugget, was the general costume. A considerable number of the younger girls went without shoes or stockings; others carried those articles in their hands till they came near the town, when they put them on; and most of the middle-aged and elderly females wore caps as well as cloaks with hoods, which they turned over the head when rain came on. In the upper part of the county, as in the whole of the county Mayo, red or saffron was the common colour in skirts and

---

[1] Woollen fabric, [Clachan ed.].
[2] John Hill Burton, in his "History of Scotland from the Revolution to the extinction of the last Jacobite Insurrection",(Vol. II., p. 378,) speaks of the dress of the lower classes of Ireland as the "Concrete of glutinous rags now forming the national costume of the Irish peasant".

cloaks; but this was voted vulgar around Sligo, and blue tints were the fashion. Everything worn by either men or women was of domestic manufacture.

Most of the marketing came off in the streets, and comparatively little in the shops, more especially during the Christmas markets, which were supposed to last from. October to Easter. As it was at this time country people made the bulk of their purchases, tradesmen and other producers employed themselves for the month or two before Christmas, in providing their respective specialties for the season. To set the workers early to their task, a knot of boys called, popularly, "Waits" moved in the month of December, every morning, long before day, through the town, accompanied by a fiddler or two, and stopping in the chief business quarters, and directing the fiddler to ply the bow, woke up the sleepers. All this was taken in good part, and regarded as a valuable service, which it certainly was, at a time when there was no clock in the town to strike the time, so that any friend of industry that went round the streets an hour or two before day, could not fail to appreciate the good effect, when he heard the notes of labour sounded on all sides by the shuttle of the weaver and the hosier, the lathe of the turner, and the rhythmic strokes of the blacksmith's hammer, As a matter of course, the "Waits" received a handsome gratuity on Christmas Day for their pains.

The goods, thus produced, were exhibited on standings that lined the streets, during the Christmas markets. Each kind of goods had its own quarter. Frieze, flannel, and drugget were exposed for sale, on the west side of the top of High Street; wooden dishes, trenchers, noggins, "pygins", loy shafts, and other products of the turner's and the cooper's trade came next in line; shoes and brogues of all sizes and qualities followed; felt hats, manufactured, for the most part, in Hatters' Lane, now Waste Garden Lane, succeeded; articles of coarse pottery were ranged towards the bottom of Market Street; and lower down, usually stood several women, each behind a firkin of butter, and each tempting buyers, by proclaiming her own butter—the finest in the market. In the proper season, hogsheads of flax seed were ranged along the head of High Street; from a little before Christmas to Easter Sunday, tables on either side of Knox's Street, were covered with pork and beef; while in Pound Street, sally rods for scollops, and rushes for lights, were offered for sale, both articles being naturally in great demand at a time, when nearly all the houses of Sligo were thatched, and when rush candles were in common use. The hosier, the tailor, and the pedlar, generally dispensed with standings, and hawked their respective commodities through the crowded streets; the hosier his stockings, the tailor ready-made waistcoats, and the pedlar, pins, needles, brass buttons, and knickknacks.

While most of the market people returned home in due time, some few, instead of accompanying their neighbours, turned into the whiskey houses, of which the town was full, every second or third house being a *shebeen*. In several of these resorts, and particularly in those near the quays, the attraction of music and dancing was added to the liquors, and the carouse was sometimes kept up all night, with, unfortunately, the result, that an occasional straggler might be seen on Sunday morning, when the shebeen was closed, making for his home in the country, in much the same frame of mind, as the notorious Joe Adley, who never returned from the fair of Collooney, which he punctually attended, till the day after the fair, and who, if any one met him on such occasions, and asked, "Joe, is it now you are leaving the fair?" always replied, "Tut, man, it was not Joe left the fair, it was the fair left Joe". Convivialities were then carried much farther in the town of Sligo, than at present, and, as far as persons of the well-to-do class were concerned, came off, for the most part, in licensed houses of some kind; in inns, taverns, "holes in the wall", as some drinking places were called, and oyster saloons, one of which stood at the east end of the Old Bridge, another at the west, and a third, in Holborn Street; this last being kept by a Mrs. Bell, who managed to puff her commodities in the still well remembered couplet:—

"If you want Oysters, fresh and sweet,
Come to Molly Bell's of Holborn Street".

In spite of this state of things, more than one *laudator temporis acti avers*,[1] that there was little or no drunkenness or quarrelling among the lower classes in those days, an assertion—at least as far as drunkenness is concerned—which it is hard to credit, considering the cheapness of poteen at the time, and the frailty of our countrymen. The statement, however, that there was less quarrelling, seems better founded. From what has been handed down by persons who lived in those times, it may be inferred, that neighbours were more united then than now. One great cause of altercation, sectarian feeling, was, it is said, then unknown; and we are told, that Protestants and Catholics of the lower classes, met together in places of amusement and enjoyment, and passed the time as friends and brothers, without any of those bickerings on the score of religion or politics, which would be pretty sure to arise in such companies nowadays.

The friendly feelings subsisting between Catholics and Protestants, may be inferred from the fact that, at the building of the Catholic Chapel of Sligo, in the beginning of the century, not only did individual Protestants contribute generally and liberally in aid of the erection, but the Select Vestry of the parish of St. John's voted a considerable sum towards the completion

---

[1] one who praises past times, [Clachan ed.].

of the work (*Sligo Journal, January 9th,* 1819). This was the more remarkable, as, at that time controversies waxed warm between the different denominations of Nonconformists in the towns the Independents and Presbyterians championing their views on Election and Predestination, and the Methodists standing up for the tenet of Universal Redemption.

Having referred to the old chapel, one may take occasion to add, that in its day, it was regarded as a particularly imposing, and, what it certainly was, a very commodious structure. An altar-piece which it contained, and for which the painter one of the O'Donnells of Larkfield—received £50, was held by local aesthetes to be little, if at all inferior, as a work of art, to the *chef d'oeuvres* of Raphael and Michael Angelo. This house stood on a plot of ground, granted by a gentleman, named Le Grand, and on the site of a still older chapel, round which it was built up, and within which the congregation continued to assemble, till the new house was roofed in and completed, when only it was taken down.

A great change came over people's feelings and habits, between 1820 and 1830, in consequence of the agitation which preceded and accompanied the Emancipation Act of 1829. The controversies and discussions then so rife on religious subjects, tended to separate Catholics and Protestants into hostile parties; and, unfortunately, persons who should have tried to soften matters, and hinder divisions, exerted themselves only to widen the breach. On the passing of the Emancipation Act, a Reverend firebrand of the name of Seymour, taking on himself the role of missionary of mischief, came from the county Mayo to Sligo, and in public as well as in private, preached to the gentry of the county the necessity of keeping Catholics at an arm's length, and giving them neither land nor employment; an advice which was then largely taken, and has been since acted on pretty systematically by those to whom it was addressed. Up to that time Catholics served as domestics in the houses of the gentry; and as stewards, game-keepers, gate-keepers in their demesnes; but they were then got rid of, and thenceforward few of our county families admitted them to any employment, indoor or outdoor, except that of labourer, and few of our county landlords let them lands, except bits of bog or mountain, such as his own co-religionists would not accept. In acting on the advice of such fanatics or charlatans as Seymour, the shortsighted gentry fancied they were securing for themselves, and their sect, for all time, a monopoly of all the good things in the country; but, instead of that, they find now they were only depositing, in the minds and hearts of the public, the explosives of discontent, resentment, and longings for revenge; feelings which, when called into play, make as sad work of moral interests and institutions, as dynamite makes of material buildings.

It is only fair to add, that the fault was not altogether on one side. If there was action, there was also reaction and counteraction. When the cultivated and benevolent Dr. Petrie visited the county, in 1837, he was shocked by the divisions and quarrels he found among the inhabitants. In those days, the Petty Sessions Courts of the district were occupied mainly with those disorders; as, at Ballymote, where the Reverend Bernard Egan, C.C., had one case against Lewis and Robert Clarke, for discharging fire arms at him, and another against Dr. Lougheed and his apprentice, Charles Denning—the late Dr. Denning of Sligo—while in both instances, the parties concerned had cross cases against the priest.

Poor Petrie, while admiring the fine qualities, intellectual and moral, of the Sligo people, was so provoked by those miserable squabbles, that, in a letter to Sir Thomas Larcom, he describes them in the following rather queer sounding words, which would be omitted here, only that they may help us all to see ourselves as others see us: "They are all a civil, intelligent, and obliging people, but the demon of religious and political discord is playing the devil among them; the gentry and parsons are precious bigots on the one side, the priests and people on the other, and it is appalling to a benevolent and philosophical mind, 'to look forward to the probable' if not certain result of such a state of things".

CHAPTER XIV

THE HARBOUR OF SLIGO

SLIGO BAY is bounded, seaward, by a ledge of rock, stretching from Aughriss Head, in the barony of Tireragh to Roskeeragh point, at Knocklane, in the barony of Carbury, and proceeds eastward, in three separate inlets—one ending at Drumcliffe, another at Victoria Bridge, Sligo, and the third at the waterfall of Ballysadare. From observation of the coast, and more especially of Rosses Point, where the sea is visibly encroaching on the land, it appears that the water of the bay is deepening with time, Sligo being, in this respect, unlike some English and Continental places, which have been deserted by the sea: as Winchelsea in Sussex, once a fine port, and Adria, at the delta of the Po, in former times so famous a harbour, that it gave name to the Adriatic Sea, but now, left by the sea high and dry, fourteen miles inland.

There is reason to think, that in remote times, the Ballysadare inlet was more frequented by mariners than that of Sligo. Tradition represents Sligo as coming into note after Ballysadare; and in an old and curious account of the conflict between the Fomorians and Tuatha de Danaans, we are told that nine Fomorians, having been spared from the general massacre, and allowed to go back to their own people, they proceeded to Eas Dara, and embarked there, which they would hardly have done, had Sligo been then the chief port of the district.

But however, things may have been in the "pre-historic ages", Sligo has been, in more modern times, and particularly since the rise of the town, an incomparably more important harbour than Ballysadare. Hollinshead counts Sligo one of the chief towns in Connaught, and "its port, one of the chief havens there;" and a weighty State paper, of the year 1553, says of it, "The same Sliyggaghe, is the King's Majesty's, and it is the best haven town in all the country". In official documents it is classed with Galway. For instance, we read in a Close Roll, of the 2nd year of Henry VI, "It was agreed by James, Count of Ormond, that William De Burgo, Knight, and his brother, William de Burgo, should have payment for their services in the Irish wars, out of the Customs of the ports of Sligo and Galway". Once connected with the port, the De Burgos were slow to relinquish claims upon its revenues. In 1544, Lord Fitzwilliam Bourke, petitioned Sir Anthony Sentleger, and the Council, "to have in fee-farm the cockets of Sligo, Porterade (Portavade) and Leighborne, with all other creeks and havens, which his ancestors have had, and whereof, the King has never had profit, as they are kept from His Highness by usurpation; "and in 1606, an inquisition held at Sligo, by Jeoffry Osbaldston, William May, and Nicholas

Brady, to inquire into the possessions of the Earl of Clanrickarde, finds, that "anciently the Earls of Clanrickarde held and enjoyed the cocquetts of Sligo and Portavade, in the said county".

Lord Fitzwilliam Bourke's remark about "usurpation", refers to O'Donnell and O'Connor, Sligo, though Manus O'Donnell, about this time, made over to Henry VIII., a moiety of the cockets of Sligo, in the following terms:—"I, Magonius O'Donnell, captain of my nation, do give and grant to my King (in order that he shall be my protector), the moiety of the tribute due to me, in Ichdarconnachd (Lower Connaught). I also grant to him, the moiety of the cocket of all ships coming to Sligaghe to trade, from which I have had cocket; so that the King's bailiff or servant, called a marshal, accompanied by my bailiff, shall in like manner exact the tribute. ... If a multitude of herrings and other fish, called 'garbushe,' should resort to the country of Lord O'Donnell, or to his sea, such as now comes into Arayn or Ynisnycadryn, one-half thereof shall belong to the King, and the other to O'Donell". That O'Connor Sligo was also a party to the "usurpation", appears from the State paper of 1553, which adds to the extract, given above, the words, "And the same O'Connor, and certain his predecessors, keepeth the same by usurpation". Both the O'Donnells and the O'Connors lost the fishing in the beginning of the 17th century, as we find it in 1606, leased by the King to Sir Henry Folliott.

There was constant intercourse in these times between Sligo and the Continent, and particularly between Sligo and Spain. Spanish fishermen frequented the coast, and Spanish ships visited the harbour. In 1534, Lord Offaly sent his father, the Earl of Kildare's treasures, to Sligo, to be conveyed thence in a Spanish vessel to Spain; in 1599, Hugh Roe O'Donnell dispatched Reverend John Hewin from Sligo, with divers letters to Spain; in 1588, three ships of the Armada were lost in Sligo waters; in 1601, Sir George Carew wrote from Cork, to inform the Privy Council of a Spanish ship, which had put to sea, after having lain for a considerable time in the port of Sligo; and in various invasions of Ireland, contemplated by Spanish statesmen, Sligo was always regarded as one of the most suitable places for disembarkation. The Irish of the United States seem to count our harbour the fittest place for a landing in case of hostile invasion from that country, and accordingly, the Fenians, in 1867, ran the Jacknal into Sligo Bay.

It was only under an Act of Parliament, passed in 1729, the improvement of the channel began.[1] The Provost, Burgesses and Freemen, in virtue of the powers conferred by this Act, erected a Ballast Office in the Port of Sligo, and appointed Mr. Laurence Vernon, Ballast Master, an office

---

[1] An Act for cleansing the ports, harbours, and rivers, of the city of Cork, and of the towns of Galway, Sligoe, Drogheda, and Belfast, and for erecting a Ballast Office in the said city, and each of the said towns.

which he held till his death, in 1754, when he was succeeded by his son, Mr. William Vernon, who died in 1759, and was followed in office by Mr. Charles Martin. In 1765, on a petition from the Corporation, a grant was made by Parliament for the erection of a pier at Oyster Island, and with this money a substantial pier, 160 feet long, was erected on the side of the island facing Rosses Point; but having been injured by a storm, and never repaired or cared for, it broke up and disappeared, hardly a stone remaining now in situ. It is hard to understand why this pier was constructed on the island instead of Rosses Point shore.

The quay of Sligo was formed piecemeal, the narrow strip adjoining the old Custom House, coming first, having been constructed by the public authorities at the time they erected the Custom House and the Queen's Stores. The portion called Martin's Quay, owes its name to its builder, Mr. Charles Martin, and is still private property. The adjoining stretch was the work of Mr. James Cochrane, who built it on the site of a disused salt pan for the accommodation of his large store. Maintaining the quay to be his personal property, he charged dues, while he held it, on such vessels as moored there, and, on transferring it to the Harbour Commissioners, received compensation for the income thus parted with.

The Ballast Quay, so called from its facing the old ballast bank, is a later erection, and has been extended, from time to time, to such a length, that the whole structure is about two thousand feet long. From this quay proceeds a new pier, half a statute mile long, at which the Harbour Board of Sligo is constructing deep berths, capable of accommodating the largest vessels afloat. The berths, when finished, will be, at least, sixteen feet deep under low water mark. Though the works are at present suspended, for want of funds, a great deal is already done; for, of the eight hundred feet taken in hand, at first, by the engineer, as a commencement, four hundred, it is said, is already excavated to the proper depth. The pier is solidly built, as it needs to be, to resist the disturbing action of the waves, which rush in with great force at this point in stormy and unsettled weather. Till the work is completed the masonry must be protected, and, if any damage be sustained, repaired, that it may not fare, in any measure, like Oyster Island pier, which, as has been said, owing first, to want of care in protecting it, and, secondly, to want of repair, after having been injured, mouldered away, and has disappeared. It appears that about £20,000 was expended in 1883 and 1884 at the Ballast Quay, which, though a large sum, is not excessive, in view of the amount of work executed. But it is of great importance that the work should be resumed with the least possible delay, for, on the principle of "a stitch in time", a moderate sum, at present, would effect, what, in the future, would require a much larger outlay.

The pier, if finished, would afford one of the healthiest and finest promenades in the kingdom. In respect of sea air a stroll upon it would be attended with all the advantages which have made the pier of Kingstown so frequented and fashionable.

And, as to scenery, Kingstown would suffer in the comparison; for the Hill of Howth and the mountains of Wicklow, the chief scenic beauties in view from it, could not compete for a moment either in outline, in colour, or in historic and legendary associations, with the symmetrical Knocknarea, the stately Benbulben, the multiform Leitrim range, and the half-a-dozen other hills and mountains, each with surpassing characteristic beauties, which would meet the eye of the promenader wherever he or she might look.

But this advantage, whatever may be thought of it, would be a mere accident of the structure, and of very subordinate and small importance in comparison of the essential benefits which the pier, with deep water berths alongside, would confer. Indeed, one could hardly exaggerate the prosperity it would lead to in the town and neighbourhood. The leading cities and towns of England, Ireland, and Scotland, as well as of most other countries, owe their greatness and wealth chiefly to their seaports; and this is so well understood that the inhabitants of these places spend ungrudgingly on their ports, knowing well that the money thus employed is sure to bring them, in return, a hundred fold. Inexperienced people open their eyes in wonder when they hear of the fabulous sums that have been sunk in excavating the docks of London and Liverpool, or are told of the millions now being spent in cutting the Manchester Ship Canal, and of the hundreds of thousands devoted to the improvement of minor ports; but men of the world and merchants are aware that this is the most beneficial disposal of money that can be made, as well in regard to those who thus invest it, as in respect to the general community.

Remembering this, the people of Sligo should not grudge any outlay on their harbour; and they have, moreover, a strong special motive for such expenditure, in the fact that nature is working with them in a way that she is not doing elsewhere, by deepening, gradually, the waters of the bay. So far back as the year A.M. 3790, the increasing tides on the Sligo coast forced their way, for the first time, up the present estuary of Drumcliff, thus separating the district of the Rosses from the plain of Magherow, of which, to that time, it formed a connected part. Since then the waters of the bay have been rising somewhat, and, at such a rate, in recent times, that careful and competent observers set down the actual average level at or near two feet above what it was forty or fifty years ago. A great statesman, some time back, boasted that the "flowing" tide of politics was with him, and made use of the fact for an incitement to his followers to exert themselves; but whatever may be said in regard to the tide of which Mr. Gladstone spoke, there can be no doubt, that the tides on the Sligo coast are flowing fuller than ever into the harbour, so that the people of the town will be to blame if they withhold their co-operation from Nature in her beneficent work of improving their port, which is at present, and must remain in future, the ruling factor in their prosperity.

Hitherto, as is admitted on all hands, the Harbour Commissioners and the inhabitants of the town have done their duty to the port in a way that is highly to their credit. This has been proclaimed by more than one Royal Commission sent down to inquire into the state of the harbour. At the conclusion of an official inquiry on September 28, 1845, Captain Washington, the Tidal Harbour Commissioner, complimented the Harbour Board in these words: "You have set a good example of energy and public spirit. You have done the utmost with your funds, and you have raised funds by voluntary subscription;" and the late Royal Commissioners on Irish Public Works, in their Second Report, speak thus in terms of equal praise, "The commercial interests of Sligo are safe in the hands of its energetic inhabitants, who have already done so much for their port". Anyone who examines the subject for himself will find this praise richly deserved. It is not so long since no vessel of burden would venture up to the quays. The shallowness of the channel, the sharp bend in it near Stand-alone Point, the Flats, and the want of due depth at the quays, prevented masters of vessels from coming beyond Oyster Island or the Pool; but all this is now greatly, though not entirely, changed, the channel being deepened, the bend straightened out, the Flats left out of the way, and the berths along the quays so sunk that, some time ago, the "Cockermouth", an iron ship of more than 2,000 tons burden, which had carried 2,000 tons of flour from California, in 40,000 bags, got berthed at her ease alongside the inner jetty of the Ballast Quay.

Captain Washington's allusion to voluntary subscriptions refers to what occurred in connection with the Blennick. To rid the channel of this formidable obstruction, the Harbour Board got together £3,000 half being "voluntary subscriptions", and half a loan and with it they contracted for the removal of the impediment, with the late Mr. John Brett, of Tubbercurry, who executed his contract to the satisfaction of everyone. All these efforts and sacrifices are a subject of legitimate boast to the Harbour authorities and the inhabitants of Sligo, as well as a guarantee that what remains to be done shall be done in due time.

Sligo, no doubt, owes its *rise* and *early* importance to its strategic position. Not only Maurice Fitzgerald, who erected the castle of the town, but all the English officials, who held high military command in the country, regarded the place as the Key of Connaught. But its advantages, in this respect, are a very secondary consideration now, and, indeed, no longer exist, for, situated as it is, in a hollow, it could not resist, for an hour, cannon placed on any of the surrounding hills.

The chief, then, and abiding importance of the town comes from its port; which is so circumstanced that the trade of Lower Connaught must be carried on through it. The port has created the market, and the market, in return, sustains the port. Sligo is the great market for a large extent of country, there being no town, of any size, nearer to it, on the south, than Boyle; on the north, than Enniskillen; while on the east, there is no town at all within reasonable reach; so that the agricultural produce of this rich and extensive district must be disposed of in the town, and exported from it, by its merchants, who have generally thriven on the trade, and occupied a high place in the mercantile community of Ireland.

The most distinguished and prosperous merchants ever connected with Sligo were, probably, the Creans, or O'Creans. They came to the town from Tirconnell, or Donegal, early in the sixteenth century, and soon acquired great wealth and high station. At first they confined themselves to trade, and seem to have nearly monopolized the trade of the town, for, of the eleven merchants mentioned in King James' General Pardon, as belonging to Sligo, nine of them were O'Creans. They were very successful in business, and, after a time, taking to the purchase of land, they soon came to own a considerable part of the county, every foot of which, however, they lost through the Insurrection of 1641.

The Everards and Martins occupied, in a later day, the first place among the merchants of Sligo; and, judging by what Mr. Ignatius Everard once stated of his period, which covered the American and French wars, commerce was never so active and profitable in Sligo as during these wars. The Kellys, Maddens, and O'Connors came a little later than the Everards, and were held in like esteem. The Kellys and O'Connors were natives of Sligo or the neighbourhood; but the brothers Madden came, one of them, from Dublin, where he was a distiller, and the three others, from the Queen's County, where they were engaged in extensive business; and the enterprise, energy, and integrity which they exhibited, after settling in Sligo, added not a little to the respectability of the merchant body of the town.

The merchandise exported and imported through Sligo, varied in kind as well as in quantity with the times. Oats and oatmeal were among the earliest exports, as they have always continued to be among the largest. Linen, soon after the trade was introduced to this part of Ireland, became a leading export. The linen trade of the county grew up in the second half of the eighteenth century. Dr. McParlan states that, in 1755, there were not five pieces of linen sold in the county, but, that owing to the exertions of Mr. Wynne, Mr. O'Hara, Mr. Knox, and the Fitzmaurices of Ballymote, the business soon flourished. Its growth must have been quick; for Arthur Young, writing in 1778, says, "Upwards of 40,000 per annum, in yarn, is exported from Sligo to Manchester and Liverpool". From Appendix VIII. to Newenham's *View of Ireland*, we learn, that in 1808, 91,706 yards of plain linen were exported from Sligo, and 3,650 hogsheads of flax seed imported; while bleach-greens were in vigorous work at Colloony, Ballysadare, Thornhill, in the parish of Kilvarnet, Rathbroghan, Drumcliffe, and Springfield; the owner of the Springfield Bleach Mills, being Mr. John Tucker, the head of the highly respectable family of that name. The chief exports of that time may be taken to be oats, oatmeal, beef, butter, pork, linen, linen yarn, tallow, and hides; and the chief imports, timber, flax-seed, iron, coal, rum, tobacco, wine, potash, pitch, rosin, indigo, sugar, and hardware.

Wakefield, who published his *Account of Ireland*, in 1812, gives linen and butter as the "chief exports" of Sligo at that time. The butter trade received a strong impulse, about the beginning of the century, from the practice, which then set in, of packing it in well coopered casks, instead of crocks, as had been the case—this change of method increasing largely the demand for Sligo butter, and giving it a place second to none in the English and other markets. In 1801, twenty thousand pounds worth of it was exported.

If the system of making it up in small packages, instead of firkins, which is so strongly recommended at present by persons who can speak with authority on the subject, were generally adopted through the country, the result would probably be the same as that which followed the change from crocks to casks, that is, a marked rise in the price and character of Sligo butter. Were the people once persuaded that it is their interest to carry out the recommendation, they would be sure to do as desired, whatever additional trouble might be entailed. There never was a time when country women took such pains with their butter, and this, because they are convinced that their labour will not be lost, as they are sure that the present Inspector, in whom they have the fullest confidence, will act without fear or favour, and give them the exact "quality" they deserve.

It is no secret, however, that they look on the merchants in a different light from that in which they regard the Inspector. Anyone that goes much among them, is aware that they feel very sore in regard to certain alleged practices of the merchants, notably that of re-qualifying the butter, and altering, in private, the public and official qualification of the Inspector. This practice is not of to-day or yesterday's growth, for, in 1844, Mr. Christian, the weigh-master of the butter market, complained in his evidence before the Devon Commission, of the merchants in this respect. According to this witness, the merchants were in the habit of changing the market inspector's qualification, in order that they might be able to qualify, themselves, as they liked; and the witness swore that he knew merchants to often make the inspector's second quality first; sometimes the third quality first; and, extraordinary as it may seem, even the fourth quality first—so, that under the system in vogue, scarce a cask of butter left Sligo with the original mark or brand. If this state of things exist still, the sooner it is reformed the better.

It is said, that great improvements in the markets and market regulations of Sligo have been effected under the Sligo Borough Improvement Act of 1869. It was this Act that enabled the Town Council to become owners of the town markets, by purchasing them, in 1885, from Mr. Wynne. The purchase money amounted to £6,500. It is highly creditable to the Town Council, that Mr. Black, the member of the Royal Commission on Market Rights and Tolls, who visited Sligo, and took evidence concerning its markets, on the 21st August, of the current year (1888), gave it as his opinion, that the markets and market regulations of Sligo Borough were second to nothing he had met with in any of the forty-five towns of Ireland he had visited up to that date.

The fine fishery of Sligo Bay must count for something in the value of the port. The shell-fish of the estuary, and more especially its oysters, have been always so abundant, and of so prime a quality, that the river got the name of *Sligeach*—the shelly river—from the circumstance. The two other inlets of the bay, those of Ballysadare and Drumcliffe, are also noted habitats of the famous bivalve. At the Lower Rosses, where the soil has not been disturbed, you find still banks of oyster deposit, three or four feet deep; and the inlet of Ballysadare contains such evidence of the past extraordinary abundance of the fish, that a well informed and observant English traveller, who visited the place recently, wrote of it in the *Manchester News* on his return home:—"The shores of Ballysadare are unique in character, and at the risk of being charged with exaggeration, I may say, that they consist of one vast tract of oyster shell deposit". This was written of the right bank of the river, but it applies just as much to the left bank, of which the celebrated artists, Beranger and Bigari, write in their *Tour through Connaught*, in 1779:—"At Tanrego we were shown (when the tide was out) two islands, which, when the tide is in, are not accessible but by a boat, on which cattle were grazing; the foundation of which islands are oyster shells, with about six inches of earth over them. Walked round them and was amazed at the sight. The oysters are so plenty at Tanrego, that they are got by cars full, only paying the carriage". Mr. Verschoyle has at present a flourishing oyster bed at Tanrego.

The salmon fishery of the bay is remarkable for the number and quality of the fish, and for the fact, that they are in season throughout the whole year. Naturalists have not been able to account satisfactorily for this fact, but the authors of the old lives of St. Patrick, ascribe the valuable peculiarity to the blessing of the saint. The *Vita Tripartita* tells, that the saint, having in his missionary rounds reached the Sligo river in the winter season, and, being greatly fatigued, and in need of refreshment, having asked a salmon of fishermen whom he met at the river, was informed by them, that salmon were never taken there in the winter. They added, however, that as he desired it, they would cast the net, and having done so, they took a fine salmon, which they presented to the saint, when he, in return for the kindness, blessed the *Sligeach*, and imparted to it the privilege of yielding salmon all the year round.

This great privilege the *Sligeach* possesses still, and, in consequence, the Fishery Inspectors allow fishing to begin earlier here than elsewhere. Before according this privilege, the Inspectors laid on Mr. Petrie, the present lessee of the fishery, the onus of proving the justice of his claim to exceptional treatment, which he did, to their satisfaction, by actual experiment; for, sending his men to the river, on the 30th October, 1886, to try a haul, they netted one salmon, weighing 18lb., another 23lb., and some others, ranging from 10lb. to 16lb., all in excellent condition for the table. Other trials having been made later with similarly satisfactory results, the Inspectors directed the Sligo Fishery to open on the 1st January, though they keep the neighbouring fisheries of the Ballysadare, Drumcliffe, and Grange rivers closed up to the 4th February.

There is good ground for thinking, that the herring fishery might be rendered very beneficial to the port. In the fifteenth and sixteenth centuries, it attracted boats and men from Spain and other parts of the Continent; and Wakefield writes, that down to 1783, it was of "great importance to Sligo, and along the whole western coast of Ireland". Far from ceasing at the year mentioned, it continued to give fair employment, and to yield good profits, till thirty or forty years ago, when the boats used for fishing disappeared, and many of the fishermen emigrated or turned to other pursuits, though it is well known, that the herring are still in the bay.

If we add to the oysters, the salmon, and the herring, just mentioned, the various other kinds of fish which the Sligo waters yield, in almost equal abundance; notably, the turbot, of the three fine turbot banks of Milkhaven, Portavad, and Eniskrone; the cod, of the whole stretch from Aughris Head to Hawlboline, as well within as without the well-known ledge, which runs between these points; the lobsters, of the rocks along the coasts of Tireragh and Carbury, and round the island of Innismurry, so numerous, that 40,000 of them are taken annually, in the stretch running from Coney Island to Mullaghmore; and the shoals of mackerel and whiting which visit the bay in their respective seasons; we shall the better understand how valuable the fisheries of Sligo might be made, both to the town and port.

Neglect of these resources was little remarkable in the past, when oysters might be had for the asking, and salmon was sold for a couple of pence a pound, sometimes for one penny; but it would be very different now, when fish of all kinds have risen so enormously in price, when oysters fetch twenty shillings a hundred, and salmon average, for the year, about 2s. a pound, and have risen, on more than one occasion, to the fabulous price of 6s. 6d.

CHAPTER XV

STIRRING OCCURRENCES

SOME important occurrences took place in or near Sligo, in the closing years of the last century, and the earlier years of the present, which may be appropriately noticed here.

The Volunteer movement, which convulsed Ireland in 1782, was felt in Sligo as in the other parts of the country. The famous Dungannon Resolutions, of the 15th of February of that year stirred Ireland from end to end, and, for months, the great business of everybody was to endorse the Resolutions, and to engage in the course of conduct which they recommended. Parliamentary Independence was then the watchword that Home Rule is now, and created a similar agitation. The monster out-door meetings of the present day, were unknown then, and continued unknown down to O'Connell's Repeal agitation; but if the demonstrations of 1782 could not cope in numbers with those of Home Rule, they were even more formidable in some other respects, as in the thousands of uniformed troops that marched to them; in the defiant martial music that accompanied these troops; in the arms they had in their hands; and in the solemn resolution they put on record, never to lay down their arms till the object for which they had organized was gained.

The proceedings at these meetings were much the same as at those now held—the speeches as exciting, the resolutions as violent, and the spirit of all engaged as enthusiastic and unyielding. Even boycotting resolutions were employed. For instance, at a meeting of the *True Blue* Volunteers of Londonderry, held on the 11th March, 1782, Captain William Lecky in the chair, it was resolved unanimously, "That if any Irishman has been, or shall be, hardy enough to assert, that any body of men, other than the King, Lords, and Commons of Ireland, had, have, or ought to have, a right to make laws to bind this realm, in any case whatsoever, *every such man insults the majesty of the King of Ireland, the dignity of its Parliament, and the whole body of its people*, is AN ENEMY TO THIS KINGDOM, AND OUGHT TO BE REPROBATED AS SUCH BY EVERY FRIEND OF IRELAND".[1] The drama then was the same, the actors only were different—the Protestant nobility and gentry, Protestant parsons, and Protestant freeholders, playing in 1782, the parts now acted by the priests and the masses.

Several meetings were held in the county Sligo, or on the borders. The *Loyal Sligo Volunteers* assembled on parade at Sligo, on the 4th of March, 1782, under the presidency of Colonel John Ormsby, and passed the

---

[1] "Dungannon Resolutions". By C. H. Wilson, page 45.

following resolution:—That as citizens and soldiers, we do heartily approve of the Dungannon address to the minority of both houses of parliament, and do most cheerfully adopt their resolutions of the 15th of February last, for obtaining a redress of grievances; and that we will, to the utmost of our power, co-operate with them and the several volunteer corps of this kingdom, for so desirable a purpose".[1] On the 1st April, a meeting of the *"Gentlemen Freeholders"* of the county, convened by the High Sheriff, George Dodwell, and presided over by him, took place at Sligo, and passed several resolutions, including the following: "That the resolutions entered into by the Delegates, assembled at Dungannon and Ballinasloe, by the Volunteer associations, and since approved by the different meetings of several other corps and counties of this kingdom, are such as ought to be adopted by every friend to the liberties and commerce of Ireland".[2] At the same date— 1st April—there was a meeting at Collooney of the *"Tirerrill True Blues,"* the Rev. John Little in the chair, when several resolutions were passed, one of them containing this rather strong declaration, "And we also declare, that we will, in every capacity, *oppose the execution of all such statutes as the* (at present, to us, seemingly) *usurped authority of a British parliament has hitherto enacted, or may hereafter attempt to impose on a country, whose great wishes are to be FREE*".[3] Inhabitants of the county took part in the meeting of the *Loyal Ballina and Ardnaree Volunteers,* held on the 28th March, Lieutenant Robert Jones in the chair; and in a meeting of the Drumahaire Blues, of the 25th March, Lieutenant Armstrong in the chair while a deputation consisting of Colonel Charles O'Hara, Colonel Sir Booth Gore, Baronet, Colonel Lewis Francis Irwin, and Lieutenant Colonel John Ormsby, assisted at the great provincial meeting of Connaught Volunteers, held at Ballinasloe, under the chairmanship of Lord Clanrickarde, on 15th March, and attended by "Delegates from fifty-nine Volunteer Corps of the Province of Connaught."[4]

  The spirit of the Volunteers of the time was in the air, and penetrated into places where no one would expect it to enter. Boys' schools became as filled with it as officers' mess rooms, and the play-ground was turned into a place of parade. Athletic sports, as sometimes happens at present, took the form of mimic warfare, and the athletes practised their exercises with the view of acquiring dexterity in the use of arms, rather than of developing their physical powers.

  The lads attending Rev. Mr. Armstrong's school, catching the prevailing infection, donned military uniform, procured arms, formed

---

[1] Idem, p. 26.
[2] Idem, p. 147.
[3] Idem, p. 153.
[4] Idem, page 61.

themselves into a regiment, passed much of their time in going through military evolutions, and formed so high an opinion of their own effectiveness, that when the famous Henry Flood, in his role of General of Volunteers, reached Sligo on a tour of inspection, they asked him to review their regiment, which he not only did, but favoured them, besides, with a stirring speech.[1]

"Nothing under the sun is new", says Solomon, "neither is any man able to say, Behold this is new: for it hath already gone before, in the ages that were before us; "and whoever calls to mind the extraordinary doings of 1782, and compares them with those we have been witnessing for the last couple of years, will find, in the comparison, a striking illustration of the Wise Man's famous dictum.

In Sligo, as in other places, parliamentary elections were often a source of trouble and ill will to all classes. This observation does not apply to elections for the borough before the days of reform, which passed off quietly and almost unnoticed, as the nominees of Mr. Wynne, the patron of the borough, met, and could meet with no opposition. It was only in the borough election of 1833, which took place under the new law on the Municipal Corporations of Ireland, that a borough election first became a stirring affair. On that occasion, Mr. John Martin, whose father had a strife of some standing with the Wynnes of Hazelwood, opposed Mr. John Wynne, and ejected him from a position, which he, or some ancestor of his, had occupied for more than a hundred years.

Mr. Martin, in turn, lost the seat in 1837, chiefly through the interference of Dean Dunleavy, who, thinking that Mr. Martin had proved false to the promises and principles, which secured his election in 1833, ran Mr. Somers successfully against him, and sent him back to private life. The contests of 1847, between Mr. Somers and Mr. Townley; of 1852, between Mr. Sadlier and Mr. Townley; of 1857, between Mr. Somers and Mr. Wynne;

---

[1] Henry Flood, says Charles Phillips, "having come to my native town, Sligo, in his military capacity, the boys of the Rev. W. Armstrong's school appeared before him in martial uniform at a review; for, at that time, the spirit of arms alike animated the crutch and the nursery. Flood immediately addressed the schoolboy regiment in the following terms: '- 'It is related to the honour of a Spartan chief, that he was fond of superintending the sports of children: your sports are superior to those of the Spartan boys. But shall I call them sports? No, they are exertions which make youths men, and without which men are but children! Milton, in his treatise on Education, has set apart precepts for military exercises, which your worthy teacher has brought into example, and I behold your early, but auspicious exertions with the same pleasure the husbandman contemplates the pleasing promise of a benignant harvest. Go on and supply the succession of those fruitful labourers for the public good whom time may take away.' Such", continues Phillips, "was the impression of this beautiful address upon the youthful mind, that I had it verbatim from my father (who happened to be a member of the corps,) after a recollection of thirty years".—Emerald Isle. Sixth Edition.—page 210.

of 1865, between Sergeant Armstrong and Counsellor McDonogh; and of 1868, between Mr. Flanagan and Mr. Knox, were characterised by the evils of rioting, drunkenness, and corruption of various kinds, and issued not very unnaturally, in the disfranchisement of the borough, under circumstances which no friend of Sligo can look back on with pleasure.

County elections were sometimes the occasion of similar or still greater evils. From the beginning, the leading gentry of the county, who had come in under Cromwell and the Restoration, showed great ambition for a seat in Parliament, and, in general, were not over scrupulous as to the means they would employ to secure election, and defeat rival candidates. Judging from petitions lodged by defeated candidates, and praying for redress, it would appear, that sheriffs of the county, when acting as returning officers, decided in favour of their friends, irrespective of the votes of the constituents.

On the 4th September, 1695, Arthur Cooper, of Markrea, lodged a petition, complaining that "Adam Ormsby, Sheriff, returned Edward Wingfield and Hugh Morgan, as duly elected Knights of the shire, whereas, it was Edward Wingfield and the petitioner that were returned".

On the 30th September, 1703, William Ormsby presented a petition, alleging, "that Kane O'Hara, High Sheriff, refused the votes of the Reverend Mr. Bethall, and the Reverend Mr. Authenleck, who wished to vote for petitioner", and that O'Hara, when remonstrated with, and threatened with having his conduct brought under the notice of Parliament, said, "that the Committee of Elections, was a Committee of assertions", and that he "had interest enough, to continue sitting the man he returned, though he should have only three votes".

On the 31st July, 1719, Joshua Cooper lodged a petition, reciting, "that he was duly elected in the room of Chidley Coote, Esq.; that, notwithstanding, Francis Ormsby, Esq., procured himself to be returned by the management and partiality of Richard Gore, Esq., present Sheriff of the county, who is uncle to the said Mr. Ormsby; and praying the House to grant petitioner such relief, as to its great wisdom shall seem best".

A petition, of unusual interest in its circumstances, was presented on the 27th of October, 1777, by William Ormsby, stating, that "on the 1st May last, a writ issued for electing two Knights, to represent in Parliament the county Sligo; that the Honourable Owen Wynne and Joshua Cooper, declared themselves candidates, and publicly united their interest; that petitioner and Sir Booth Gore also declared themselves candidates; that the poll was carried on from the 23rd May to the 7th June, the booths being, sometimes, open from 6 o'clock in the morning to 10 o'clock at night; that several of Wynne's voters were influenced by bribery and corruption; that Henry Griffith, the Sheriff, acted all through with partiality; and, that petitioner would have had a majority, if Sheriff rejected wrong votes and admitted right ones". Another election and another petition soon followed, the contest lying between William Ormsby and Owen Wynne, junior.

The petition was presented to the House, on the 22nd July, 1778, by Mr. Charles O'Hara, member for the county, and, inextricably mixed with the petition of 1777, led to proceedings before two different committees of the House of Commons, which lasted for two years, and entailed, on the parties concerned, enormous expense, which is still felt by their descendants, after the lapse of more than a hundred years. This petition is also remarkable, for being the first great case in which Curran was employed; he, with Mr. Mee and Mr. Frazer, being counsel for Mr. Wynne; while Messrs. McCarthy and Finucane, acted for Ormsby. The record of the proceedings, including the examination of witnesses, is still extant, and may be found in the Public Record Office, Dublin, in a "bundle" of Parliamentary Papers, numbered "58". Though election contests often stir up bad blood, it is seldom they generate such bitter vindictiveness, as showed itself on this occasion. It would seem, as if each party were satisfied to ruin himself, provided, only he could ruin his opponent, which, of course, was the more remarkable, as they were brothers-in-law, and as the friendliest relations had hitherto prevailed between the two families. In the election of 1768, Mr. Ormsby was chosen one of the members for the borough of Sligo; and at the approach of the general election of 1776, Mr. Wynne informed him that he could have the seat no longer, as it was wanted for another: no doubt, Mr. Hutchinson, who afterwards obtained it. This incensed Mr. Ormsby, and he threatened, if the borough seat were taken from him, to oppose Mr. Wynne in the county. Both gentlemen were as good as their word, the result being one of the most bitter, protracted, and expensive election contests on record.

It is quite clear from the evidence, that the "bribery, corruption, and partiality of sheriff", complained of in the petition, actually took place. The bribery and corruption were practised very probably by both sides, in various shapes and ways, voters getting whatever they desired. Spirituous drinks, more especially in the form of "rum punch" and "claret", flowed about as freely as water; and, to use the words of an official document, "money, meat, drink, reward, entertainment, provisions, and gifts, as well as promises, and agreements, and engagements of such gifts and rewards", were the chief means employed to sway the electors. As to the partiality of the sheriff, it was abundantly established by the stealing of the Poll Book, which could hardly happen without, at least, his connivance; by the tearing out and burning of several pages of this book; and by the throwing across the battlement of Sligo bridge of sundry electoral lists, of which he was the legal custodian. Such were the doings of the gentry and public officials of the county Sligo, about a century ago.

The contest in 1822, between Colonel Percival, and Colonel afterwards General King, on occasion of the death of Mr. Charles O'Hara, if less expensive, was hardly less exciting while it lasted. The candidates, it is said, acted with great urbanity to each other, considerately leaving, though military men, all the fighting to their respective followers. Each had his mob; that of General King, being under the command of a notorious tinker, remarkable for his colossal size and his mastery of shilelagh practice, and that of Colonel Percival, being headed by a tenant of his own, the late Billy Healy, of Templehouse, one of the most powerful, active, and fearless men in the county. The mobs had their respective quarters in different districts of the town; and woe to the straggler, who, under the influence of bravado or drink, made his way to the quarters of the enemy. Collisions were constantly occurring between detached parties of each side, the belligerents being pretty evenly matched, till General King summoned to his aid a large contingent of reckless rascals from Coolcarney, who took Sligo, as it were by storm, and domineered in it while the polling lasted, and till the General had gained the victory, and was chaired. Still it was as much as the military could do to keep the mobs in order, and to quell the riots, which, notwithstanding all the efforts of the authorities, were constantly coming on; and on one occasion, a riot in front of the hustings became so formidable, that the soldiers had to fire in self-defence, it is said, on the rioters, but, as the report adds, "fortunately without doing injury to any one". As not unfrequently happens in Irish commotions, farce or comedy alternated with tragedy, so that those who loved a laugh might enjoy it while reading the squibs and pasquinades posted on the dead walls of the town. Though these effusions possessed only a very slender modicum of either rhyme or reason, a sample or two may be given, if for no other object, because they preserve the names and peculiarities, or fancied peculiarities of some of the *Dramatis personae* in the great King and Percival contest of 1822. The late Jeremiah Jones was often hit at by the poetasters, as in the following doggerel, regarding the bill of fare at a banquet of Colonel Percival's friends and supporters:—
Haunch of venison from Owen Wynne's park,

Brought specially to town by his man Percy Clarke.
There was also a dish of mutton ragout,
But how to dispense it put them in a stew.
Between fishing and fowling they fetched up some bones,
A delicate morsel for spruce Jerry Jones".

It appears that Mr. Jones was, at this time, confined for debt in Sligo jail, as was also a friend of his, Mr. Robert Ormsby, and, like others imprisoned for the same cause, they were let at large only on Sundays. Pasquin thus refers to the circumstance:—

> "Hallo, Bob, and Jerry you seem very merry,
> The Insolvency Act is a backing we know,
> One would suppose all Sligo was theirs,
> Though they never get out but on Sunday for prayers".

A reference to Mr. Abraham Martin is more spirited and pointed. To appreciate the following squib, it is well to remember that Mr. Martin had the reputation of being immensely rich and purse proud, and that he was willing to part with large sums, if he could thereby humble some of the magnates of the county. The formula of asseveration employed in the first line is in character; for it is well known that the interjection, or exclamation, or whatever else casuists may think it, was constantly coming up in his conversation, and that he regarded it as a clever device, which enabled him to indulge in the then fashionable luxury of an oath, and, at the same time, saved him, both here and hereafter, from any penalty for the indulgence. He was a sturdy supporter of King:—

> "By Clix, you beggar band, we'll pinch you tight and tighter,
> We've shining cash in hand, enough to fill a lighter.
> Money is the thing—it makes the mare go harder,
> I'll pump it out to King, and baffle all your ardour".

King, who was the popular favourite, gained the day, but numbers in Sligo and elsewhere had cause to rue the triumph, as it cost them dear. The General was liberal in his entertainments, but at other people's expense, for, though he had "open houses" everywhere, he was very chary of paying his bills; the result being that sundry owners of groceries and spirit stores became so impoverished, by executing his orders during the election, that they were soon driven from house and home, and had, in some instances, to take to hawking apples and cadging herrings.

Whatever other crimes may have been occasioned by this election of 1822, it appears that, long as it lasted, it was free from the guilt of murder. In this respect it had the advantage over some other contests, which, though of shorter duration, and in general, of a quieter character, led to loss of life. In the election of 1847, in which Mr. Somers and Mr. Townley were candidates, a man named Harte was killed in Knox's Street; in 1837, when the late Father Daniel Jones, then, of course, a layman, Mr. Cooper, and Colonel Percival, were candidates, Michael McDonogh, a highly respectable inhabitant of Collooney, was shot dead, on the high road, near

Townyfortes, as he was on his way home; and in 1868, in the contest of Mr. Denis O'Conor, with Colonel Cooper and Sir Robert Gore Booth, Captain King was shot in a scuffle, and, as far as appears, with his own pistol, and by his own nephew, who interfered only with the object of saving his uncle.

This election of 1822 is memorable for one noteworthy circumstance—it was the first County Sligo election in which priests took any active part. Up to that the Catholic clergy of the neighbourhood regarded themselves as outside the pale of the constitution, and wanted only to be let alone, leaving it to others to practise and manage politics as they liked. The new departure excited at the time much attention, and the more so, of course, as it was a success in the event. Reference was made to the matter more than once in the proceedings of the Select Committees of the Houses of Lords and Commons, appointed in 1824 to inquire into the State of Ireland. For example, O'Connell being under examination, and asked, "Are you able to specify any particular instance in which the interference of the clergy prevailed?" replied, "I understand it was successfully, and, I think, usefully exerted in Sligo".

It is remarkable that the priests were so successful on this occasion, considering that they had no experience in election proceedings. No doubt, it was owing to the great number of Catholic forty-shilling freeholders, that had votes at the time, most of whom would listen with deference to the advice or opinion of the priest in respect to their duty. In 1727 Catholics were deprived of the electoral franchise; in 1793 it was restored to them; and immediately the landlords of the county set themselves to making forty-shilling voters of the newly enfranchised as extensively as they could. The election of Wynne and Ormsby, in 1777, was fought with exclusively Protestant votes, and, much as it agitated the county, the priests had nothing to do with it, no name of a priest occurring in the voluminous account of the contest which has come down to us. It is told, in the report of the proceedings in connection with the petitions, which followed this election, that Holborn Street contained more forty-shilling freeholders than the rest of the town. The abolition of the forty-shilling vote in 1829 greatly simplified and curtailed election proceedings in the county, as may be inferred from the fact that, on the 1st of January, 1829, when the vote existed, there were 5,036 electors in the county, whereas on the 1st of January, 1830, after the abolition of the vote, there were only 610.

But the abolition led to an evil which far more than countervailed any advantage accruing from it. This was the Clearance System, which, more than anything else, has served to land the country in the political deadlock and *impasse* of the present time. So long as cottiers and small tenants brought the landlord consequence by their vote, they were encouraged and courted, but the moment the vote ceased, the landlord began to regard them as a nuisance, and employed all means, fair and foul, to get rid of them. The worm, when trodden on, turned on its aggressor, the result being the dreadful cry, Exterminate the Landlords, which is echoing at the moment through Ireland and America, and which proceeds, for the most part, from the evicted, and the descendants of the evicted. *Abyssus abyssum invocat*.[1]

In the year 1798, took place the latest of the many battles which have been fought, from time to time, within the limits of the county, that of Carricknagat, as it is locally called, or Collooney, as it is usually named by persons living at a distance. The French landed at Killalla, on the 22nd of August, under the command of Humbert, and from that day, till after their surrender to Lord Cornwallis, at Ballinamuck, on the 9th of September, nothing was talked of, or thought of, through the country, except their movements and designs. From their arrival they kept calling on the people to join them, but the people, at least those of the county Sligo, were loath to respond to the call, being held back by the advice of the clergy, who expected no good from the intervention of men whose hands were still reeking with the blood of the holiest priests and purest patriots of France. If left to themselves, our young men would have rallied at once to the French eagles, as one fact, out of many, which might be quoted, sufficiently shows. A night or two after the landing at Killalla, about three hundred young fellows of the parishes of Ballysadare and Kilvarnet, assembled at Killasser, near Annaghmore, and entered into an engagement to proceed in a few days to the French camp; but, after they took the advice of their priests, and thought better of the matter, the three hundred dwindled down to three individuals, who, of all that were assembled at Killasser, were the only persons to carry out the engagement.

Having completed his arrangements, Humbert set out, on the 26th August, with his countrymen, and a large Irish contingent, for the interior of the country. His first meeting with the English took place the following morning, at Castlebar, when their army, though three or four times as numerous as the French, and sustained by fourteen cannon, yielded to some unaccountable panic, and fled from their position so shamefully and precipitately, that the movement has been called, in sarcasm, the Castlebar Races.

The French met with no other obstacle worth mention, till they had crossed the bridge of Collooney, to the Leyney side, where they thought themselves so secure, that they halted for breakfast; but they had hardly begun the meal, when a cannon ball, from the direction of Carricknagat, fell in the midst of them, and proved they were already in the presence of the enemy.

---

[1] One hell summons another, [Clachan ed.].

The shot came from some British troops, under the command of Colonel Vereker, who, happening to be in garrison at Sligo, and learning that the French were marching in great numbers on the town, went out like a brave man to meet them, instead of falling back on Enniskillen, as advised by all, and ordered, it is said, by his superiors in command. So effective and secret were his movements, that before Humbert was aware of his presence, he had all his dispositions for a battle made—had posted his main body near the present railway signal station, where they were concealed and protected by the inequalities of the ground;—had placed a detachment under Major Ormsby, on the hill, at the railway bridge, so as to be able to sweep the road by which the French had to advance; and had secured his left by a few picked men, under Lieutenant-Colonel Gough—this wing being protected also by the river.

Though unprepared for the encounter, Humbert had his troops so well in hand, that he was ready for advance, in a few minutes, with all his force, which was 900 French and somewhat more than a thousand Irish recruits. The action, which began at two o'clock, lasted an hour and a half, and was fought with great spirit on both sides. The French opened the attack, which they made in two columns—one, the main body, moving straight down through Rinn on Yereker; and the other, after making a detour, crossing the river at Knockbeg ford,—passing up the Ardcotton glebe, and proceeding through the valley which separates the hill on which Major Ormsby was posted, from the cliffs of the Ox mountains. It was this column that decided the contest; for Major Ormsby, finding they were surrounding his own men, and on the point of taking the main body of the British in flank, withdrew towards the centre, when Vereker, realizing the danger, ordered a retreat across the river, which was executed in excellent order, though the French followed for a mile or two.

While all acquitted themselves creditably in this engagement, it is admitted that Colonel Vereker on the one side, and Bartholomew Teeling on the other, carried off the chief honours of the day. Vereker is praised for his spirit in measuring swords with the French, whose army was three or four times as numerous as his own, and flushed too with the great victory of Castlebar; for his consummate skill in choosing the site of the engagement—the best in the county for his purpose and in arranging his troops, so as to turn all the advantages of the situation to the best account; for the readiness of resource, with which, during the battle he met and defeated for an hour and a half, the measures of the experienced French tacticians; for the opportuneness with which he timed the retreat, and the coolness with which he superintended it, being himself among the last to cross the river; and, in fine and in sum, for his undoubted success in destroying the prestige of the French, counteracting their designs on Sligo, and forcing them to the route which led to their surrender, a few days later, at Ballinamuck.

On the other side, Bartholomew Teeling bore off the palm from all, both French and Irish. He was a young man of rare endowments, both of mind and body; and betaking himself to France, when the expedition for Ireland was organising, he offered his valuable services to Humbert, and cast in his lot with men whom he believed to be engaged in an effort to benefit his country. The French gave him all their confidence, which he justified by serving as interpreter and negotiator, by managing the Irish, over whom he acquired unbounded influence, and by being always foremost to encounter every danger which presented itself, as at Castlebar, where he greatly distinguished himself.

From the beginning of the conflict at Carricknagat, he was the soul of the movement, and eclipsed all his comrades; but towards the close, he eclipsed even himself by a feat which might appear incredible, if the evidence of its performance was not overwhelming. Finding the French advance arrested by a cannon, which was placed on Park's Hill, under an able gunner, named Whitters, and which had already struck down several men in the front of the column, he called again and again on those about him to advance, but meeting no response, he set spurs to a noble grey charger, on which he rode, galloped down a long stretch of level grass land, which still separated the contending forces, and pulling up at Park's Hill, and drawing coolly a pistol from its holster, shot dead the formidable Whitters behind his cannon; moving back, next moment, amid a shower of bullets, as unconcerned and as safe as one of Homer's heroes in the hands of a tutelary goddess. This episode decided the battle; for, when Teeling now called on the men in the column to follow him, they sprang forward to a man, and swept everything before them. Teeling's disposal of Whitters is almost the only incident of the engagement now remembered in the neighbourhood. Even the names of Vereker and Humbert have slipped from the people's memories, but Teeling and his famous grey, are still as vivid in the traditions of the Ox mountains, as they were on the morrow of Carricknagat. Honours of all kinds were now showered on Colonel Vereker.

Parliament voted him its thanks; George III. granted him the privilege of having supporters in his arms, and adopting the motto, "Coloony;" the Corporation of Dublin conferred on him the freedom of the city; while the Corporation of Limerick named the street leading to his residence Coloony Street, voted him a sword of honour, and passed the following resolution of thanks to him and his regiment: Resolved:—"That the steady, loyal, and gallant conduct of our fellow citizens of the Limerick City Regiment of Militia, on the 5th September last, under the command of Colonel Vereker, so intrepidly engaged and successfully opposed the progress of the whole French and rebel army at Coloony, merits our sincerest thanks and warmest applause; a conduct which has not only covered them as a regiment with eternal honour, but has also cast an additional lustre on this their native city, already so eminently distinguished for its loyalty and zeal for our happy constitution". Among other compliments that he received on this occasion, was an address from the High Sheriff and Grand Jury of the county Sligo, which may be found in the *Dublin Evening Post*, of the 28th October, 1798.

About twelve months after the battle, when things had settled down, magistrates were appointed by royal warrant to investigate the claims for compensation preferred by those who alleged that they had suffered from the French or Insurgents, and who got, in consequence, the name of "suffering loyalists". The magistrates entrusted with this delicate office were:—

> WILLIAM HARLOE PHIBBS, ESQ.
> ARTHUR IRWIN, ESQ.
> REV. CHARLES WEST.
> REV. CARNECROSS CULLEN.
> REV. W. DUKE.

And they held their first meeting on the 30th September, 1799. The routine was to read the claim, to examine the claimant or his witness on oath, and to admit, reject, or modify, the application as they judged fit. If they admitted the claim, either in whole or in part, they gave a certificate for the amount; and if they rejected it, they gave their reason for doing so, such as, that the claimant was not a loyalist, that they did not believe he had suffered for his loyalty, or that he was not furnished with a certificate of good conduct from the "resident clergyman" or parson. For instance, in the case of the second name on the list, which was that of James Dunleavy, of Ballygauley, who was, apparently, the grandfather of Dean Dunleavy, of Sligo, their memorandum is, "After examining James Dunleavy and his son, Morgan Dunleavy on oath, claim rejected, himself being a disaffected person, and not having proved his claim". As might be expected, the applications came from the more disturbed districts of the county, which lay in the baronies of Tirerrill, Leyney, and Tireragh. There was no claim from Coolavin, and only one from Carbury, that of Roger Smith, Sligo, for £96 17s. 9d., probably for losses sustained in one of the disturbed baronies. Naturally Collooney, so close to Carricknagat, must have suffered more, in proportion to population, than other places; and the following nine names of Collooney people, with the amount of compensation awarded to each, may serve as a sample of the list:

MARY FARRELL,	Collooney	£18	0	9
ROBERT KIVLEGHAN,	"	£ 4	1	0
ROBERT McKIM,		£72	19	10
JOHN LOWE,	"	£31	12	0

JAMES CONELLY,	"	£20	0	6	
JOHN CONELLY,	"	£7	7	6	
WILLIAM HOPS,		"£30	0	0	
WINIFRED DOHERTY,		"£3	19	1½	
WILLIAM FOSTER,	"	£39	0	0	

It need hardly be added, that some claimants exaggerated their losses. Take the case of James Wood, Esq., of Leekfield, who claimed £98 19s. 7d., but received only £26 19s. 7d., though it is clear, from the following minute of the magistrates, that they were disposed to deal tenderly with him: "Upon examining the claim of James Wood, we are of opinion that he has fully proved his claim to the amount of £26 19s. 7d., after deducting for cows £72". The whole list, which comprises 197 claims, with awards to the amount of £3,887 5s. 3d., throws considerable light on the state of the county ninety years ago, and is therefore given in the Appendix, being printed now for the first time.

In 1820 a PUBLIC INQUIRY was held in Sligo, which deserves some notice, as it created great excitement in the town at the time, and is not devoid of interest in other respects as well. It arose from a quarrel between the merchants of Sligo and the Collector of the Port, Mr. Robert Holmes, who had a low opinion of each other, the Collector charging the merchants with smuggling, and the merchants retorting on the Collector with the four following charges:—

First—Procuring his situation by purchase contrary to the express provisions of an Act of Parliament.

Second—Tampering with a superior officer to induce him to dispense with the oath required by the law to secure against the corrupt procurement of office.

Third—The abuse of power in office, both as it regards the subject and the Crown.

Fourth—Unprovoked attacks on the character of the merchants.

The public authorities acceded to the application of the merchants for an investigation of these charges, and deputed Paul Dawson, Esq., Surveyor-General of Customs, to preside at the inquiry, which, after an arrangement of preliminaries, was opened at the Custom House, on the 21st of April, and lasted to the 26th of June. The merchants appointed five of their number William Hume, Alexander Cochrane, William Kelly, Martin Madden, and John Black—a committee of management to prosecute the case, and Mr. Holmes conducted his own defence: Most of the merchants sided with the prosecution; some stood by Holmes; and a few held aloof from both sides notably Mr. Abraham Martin and Mr. Ignatius Everard, the two most respected traders of the town. The managers acquitted themselves of their part with great distinction, and the defence was maintained with conspicuous spirit and ability by Mr. Holmes, who was powerfully aided in his contentions by the evidence of one of his witnesses, Mr. William Middleton, merchant and ship-broker, the only one of all the merchants of that day that is now represented in the mercantile community of Sligo by descendants.

A report of the proceedings at the inquiry was printed under the title: "A Report of the Proceedings at a Public Investigation before a Surveyor-General of Customs, into certain charges preferred by the merchants of Sligo against Richard Holmes, Esq., then Collector of that port, as taken from the notes of a shorthand writer, with Extracts of the Original Correspondence on the subject of those charges. Printed for the Committee by Edward Duffy, Enniskillen, 1821".

Those who read this report attentively can hardly fail to come to the conclusion that there were faults on both sides—that Holmes, in his proceedings, had often his own interests more in view than those either of the public or the Crown, and that the merchants, on their side, were far from being as immaculate as they would have others believe.

The Lords of the Treasury must have taken the charges against the Collector to be proved, as, on the reception of Mr. Dawson's report, they issued an order for his suspension, and called on him to show cause why he should not he dismissed; at the same time they dismissed his son, who was pro-collector, and a Mr. Caithness, who was his clerk; and after a short delay they appointed Mr. Owen Wynne Collector of the Port in his stead.

It was well for the merchants that they were not on their trial, for, judging by facts which came casually to light during the investigation, some of them would have come ill through the ordeal. It was clear there was extensive smuggling; for it transpired that trading vessels, on entering the bay, sometimes despatched boats, on mysterious errands, to the shores of Tireragh or Carbury; that tobacco was landed at Raghly and the Rosses; that several bales of the commodity were discovered at a place called Lugadoon in Tireragh; and that large quantities of it were found made up in rosin casks, on board the *Juno*.

While three or four of the merchants were suspected of having a hand in those contraband proceedings, Mr. John Black got credit for being engaged in the business on an exceptionally large scale. His neighbours of the Rosses believed that the limestone caves on the brink of the sea at Bomore served as a depot for the ill-gotten goods; and some imaginative persons convinced themselves that a tunnel ran, under the hills, all the way from the caves to Elsinore Lodge, through which Black usually moved his dangerous wares.

Sligo suffered more than any other town in the kingdom from the first visitation of CHOLERA, which occurred in the year 1832. The inhabitants, knowing that the disease had been ravaging Dublin and other places from the month of April, and finding it month after month keeping away from themselves, were hoping they would escape it altogether, when unmistakeable cases occurred on the eleventh of August, which fell on a Saturday, and was a fair, as well as a market, day. In the morning there was a frightful thunderstorm, which the people regarded as a forerunner of the dreadful cholera, and as the day advanced, they learned that the cholera was already in their midst.

It was an unfortunate circumstance, that when the pestilence set in, the lower classes had lost confidence in the doctors of the town. From the arrival of the cholera in Ireland, the Sligo doctors employed themselves in studying its character, and in preparing for it; and, with this object, they sent up kites in search of some indication, whether it was or was not of atmospheric origin; they analysed the waters of the wells; they examined the sanitary state of private houses and their surroundings; and they pointed out the regimen to be followed, in order, if possible, to avert the threatened calamity. These proceedings were viewed with suspicion by many ignorant people, who when the disease appeared, persuaded themselves that it was all the work of the doctors who had brought the contagion down from the sky by their kites; who had started it by poisoning the wells; who had spread it by the drugs and nostrums which the people were recommended to use as a preventive. Absurd as these notions were, they held their ground for a time, and were not relinquished by many, even after the doctors had fallen victims to their martyr-like devotion to duty.

From the first, the disease raged with great violence in Sligo. In the *Daily Report of Cholera*, published by the Central Board of Health, in Dublin Castle, Sligo appears, for the first time, on the 18th of August, the return, then given, being sixty-three new cases, twenty-two deaths, and no recovery. From this date it went on increasing through the whole of August, and at such a rate that, on an average, fifty a day were dying, as many, it is said, as a hundred dying on one particular day. In giving the figures for all Ireland at this time, the *Daily Report*, while noting that the disease was stationary, or on the decline in other places, had always to add the words, "with the exception of Sligo", or, as the *Dublin Evening Post* of the date phrased it, "with the horrible exception of Sligo".

Medical Inspectors who had been to other cholera centres, were astonished at what they found before them in Sligo. The closed shops and doors; the complete suspension of business; the entire absence of people from the streets, except where an individual might be hastening silently for a doctor or a priest; the death-like silence that prevailed, broken only by the rumbling of the ponderous vehicle which conveyed the infected to the hospital, or by the ominous noise caused by twenty carpenters hammering at the making of coffins in the courthouse, then converted into a workshop—diffused such terror around, that people seldom felt able, or inclined, even to speak.[1] The twenty carpenters soon proving unable to supply the demand for coffins, most of the dead were rolled into pitched sheets, and thus dropped into the grave; and it is a noteworthy fact, that the prospect of the "pitched sheet" had as much horror almost for the dying as death itself, and that the last words of several were, "Oh! the horrible pitched sheet".

Stories are handed down of buryings alive, but they are not sufficiently authenticated for detailed mention here, though it is certain there must have been such cases. There was such haste to hurry away the dead, that the moment it went abroad that a person was taken ill, a hearse or dray hastened to the place to carry off the corpse. "I was sent for specially", writes a Government doctor, "to see a person who laboured only under the premonitory symptoms. On my arrival the hearse was at the door, waiting to carry him to interment". It is told, that a countryman who had caught the infection, as he was mounting his horse at the foot of Knox's Street, fell down dead on reaching the head of Market Street. Everybody, that could quit the town, left. The population, which at the beginning is set down as 15,000, fell soon so far away, that a letter from Sligo, which appears in the *Evening Post* of the 26th August, states "the present population does not exceed 2,000".

Nothing proves better the extent of the panic and of the ensuing demoralization, than the callousness which it developed, to the strongest and most sacred feelings which sway the human breast. Parental affection seemed gone, as children deserted by terror stricken parents mingled in large numbers, with the widows and orphans left by husbands and fathers who had perished in the pestilence. So great a sensation did this state of things create, wherever it became known, that the charitable of Dublin, in the midst of all their local calls and necessities, had a collection made for the relief of the widows and orphans and deserted children of unfortunate Sligo.

Though hard drinkers and the very poor suffered most, no class of the inhabitants escaped. The temperate and well-to-do succumbed as well as others; and the death of Mr. Patrick O'Connor, a leading merchant, and a gentleman of most regular and exemplary life, proved that neither position nor regularity of conduct could ensure exemption from attack. No class, in proportion to numbers, suffered so much as the doctors, which must be ascribed to their constant contact with the plague-stricken. Surgeon Bell,

---

[1] To illustrate the personal eccentricities which great crises sometimes develop, it may be mentioned that a blacksmith of the town, named Hatley, passed much of his time, night and day, in roaming through the streets, singing joyfully at the top of his voice.

Doctors Coyne, Beatty, and Anderson, as well as a medical man from Dublin, fell one after another in the heroic performance of their duty.

The Catholic clergy alone seemed to have a charmed life, and to be proof against the contagion, for, though as often with the sick as the doctors themselves, not one of them caught the infection. Father Gilleran's case was still more remarkable than that of his brethren; for while they lived in their private houses or lodgings, he passed most of his time, night and day, in the hospital among the sick, performing the offices both of a nurse and of a priest. A curate in Sooey, when the cholera broke out in Sligo, he offered himself to the bishop as a volunteer for Sligo, and the offer being accepted, he flew to the post of duty and danger, and all through the crisis, turned up always wherever and whenever he was wanted, as regularly as if he had the faculty of being in several places at the same time, and as intrepidly as if he had had a revelation from heaven that the cholera could do him no hurt.

This satisfactory state of things, in regard to the clergy, was owing very much to the benevolent and noble hearted bishop of Elphin of that day, the Right Reverend Patrick Burke. This good man remained throughout at his house in Finisklin, that he might be always at hand to sustain and cheer both priests and people. While panic fear confined the inhabitants of the town to their houses, he rode occasionally through the streets in order to inspire the timid with courage by his example; he visited from time to time, both in private houses and in the hospital, those who were struck down by the pestilence; and, above all, he took care to make the priests of the town pass the evening with him as often as they could, when he thanked them and blessed them for their heroic labours, and urged them on to continued exertions in the God-like cause in which they were engaged.

Nor was it the Sligo priests alone whom he thus tempered for the dread ordeal of the moment. Knowing Ballysadare to be tried by the visitation as severely as Sligo itself, and the priests of that parish to be overwhelmed with work, he induced them by friendly pressure, to come now and again to Finisklin, and join there himself and his priests in unbending the mind; and the writer is glad to have this opportunity of recording, what he often heard from Right Reverend Doctor Durcan and Father Michael Flynn, the then parish priest and curate of Ballysadare, that they derived the greatest comfort and strength from these meetings, and were moved by the words of the genial bishop, much in the same way as the disciples of our Lord felt "the heart burning within them" while He spoke to them on the road to Emmaus.

The total number of *recorded* cases for Sligo is 1,234, and of deaths 643; but it is certain, that many cases and deaths occurred of which there is no record. We read in the Evening Post, of September the 4th, "Sligo, out of a population of not more than 4,000, which remained in the town, has lost 600;" and the evil lasted for more than a month from this date; nor was Sligo dropped from the *Daily Cholera Report* of Dublin Castle, till the 16th of October, which shows that the disease had not quite disappeared earlier from the town, however much it may have diminished.

The virus must have been more malignant during the first three or four weeks than afterwards, as the recoveries were fewer, and the fatal termination more rapid. In the first official record, as we have seen, there was not a single recovery, though the cases were 63, and the deaths 22; while, at this early period, the catastrophe always followed fast on the attack. Mr. O'Connor was well when he went, in the morning, to the funeral of a clerk of his, a Mr. Garvey, and, being attacked while assisting at the interment, was dead that evening. It was said, that fear was the chief predisposing cause of the disease, but courageous people were struck down as well as the timid. Mr. William Middleton visited Mr. Peter O'Connor, on Mr. Pat O'Connor's death, and said to him, "Have no fear, Peter, for fear is cholera;" and the next thing Mr. O'Connor heard of his bold-spirited friend, was that he too had been attacked, and was already dead and buried.

CHAPTER XVI

STREETS AND HOUSES

Having been informed in the preceding pages of the shabbiness of the town in the last century, this may be the best place to take a view of it in its present state.

To one looking from the higher parts of the Albert Road, Sligo seems a mere congeries of houses, or rather of house roofs, with here and there a tower, spire, or tall factory chimney shaft, rising high above the surrounding structures. While the town itself, from the point of view indicated, appears an undistinguishable mass, there are on either side of it—to the right and left—a few detached, imposing structures, which look like wings opening from it, and add greatly to its appearance. The Mercy convent, the jail, the infirmary, the fever hospital, and the lunatic asylum, on the right, form one wing; while the cathedral, St. Mary's, and one or two houses more on the left, form the other. The convent, infirmary, fever hospital, and lunatic asylum, have one fine feature in common—a long, extended, symmetrical, southern facade, so constructed in each case as to realize in the best manner all the benefits of sun and air, thus showing that the builders proceeded on hygienic as well as on artistic lines. The jail, as intended for criminals, stands, in accordance with the fitness of things, on a much lower level than the institutions designed for relieving the sufferings of the well-behaved, and, surrounded as it is with a high, heavy, dead wall, shutting in the inmates, and shutting out much of the light of heaven, suggests the dreary fate which the unfortunates inside have brought upon themselves.

Viewed from the Albert Road, the left wing hardly shows to such advantage as the right. The cathedral, when viewed from John Street, or the railway station, is a stately, well-finished edifice, but looked at from the Albert Road, where the chief features visible are the campanile, the upper part of the tower, and the south transept, it strikes one as somewhat plain and heavy. St. Mary's is so massive a building that it looks not unlike a public institution of some kind. Considering its destination, it needed of course, to be spacious, but one can hardly help thinking that if it were constructed on less crowded and more varied lines, diminished somewhat in height, extended over a larger area, and lightened in feature, it would gain not a little in grace, without losing anything in roominess, wholesomeness, or any other of the more essential qualities of a residence. Mrs. Tighe's house, which shows in the left wing, is a neat, comfortable residence, and when first erected by its worthy owner, was a conspicuous object in the scene, but the big building now near it greatly overshadows it, like the man in Horace *qui praegravat artes infra se positas*[1].

On entering and examining the town it is found to be divided by the river into two parts, one on the right or northern bank, and the other and larger part, on the left bank, each portion containing good streets. It is well to bear in mind that the nomenclature of the streets is comparatively modern. When Henry Vaughan and Mr. Brett, in 1662 and 1663, made a "survey" of the town of Sligo, in virtue of a commission under the Great Seal, the streets had no distinctive names: the district of the town lying to the north of the river being called the Fort-hill Quarter, and that lying to the south, the Castle Quarter, and sometimes the New Fort Quarter. Things seem to have been in the same state in 1666, when Charles II. granted the great O'Connor estate to Lord William Strafford and Thomas Radcliffe, Esq., as no streets are named in the grant; but the new nomenclature was introduced on or before the year 1687, for in the Deed of Partition, executed that year by the Right Honourable William Earl of Strafford, Rev. John Leslie, and Joshua Wilson, the then owners of the estate, the following streets are mentioned:—Castle Street, Old Market Street, High Street, Radcliffe Street, Key Street, Bridge Street, Holborn Street, Stephen Street, St. John's Lane, and Church Lane; the other existing streets of the town coming later. It will be interesting to know whence the different streets derive their names.

Castle Street has its name from Fitzgerald's Castle, which stood where Mr. Tallant's hotel now stands, and from the two so-called castles of Sir Roger Jones and Andrew Crean, in the same neighbourhood; Old Market Street, which ran at first between High Street and Radcliffe Street, was so called from the market which was anciently held there round Bishop O'Crean's Cross, and which, later, was removed to the rear of Pat O'Brien's house in High Street; High Street, from its elevated situation in regard to the rest of the town; Radcliffe Street, from Sir George Radcliffe, and his son Thomas Radcliffe, successively owners of a great part of Sligo; Key Street, which ran behind Mr. Maveety's house, from its proximity to the quay; Bridge Street, or the present Knox's Street, from its leading to the bridge, the change of name being effected about 1784, in honour of the Knox family who lived there, and more especially of George Knox, chief favourite in his day of the Town Council; Holborn Street, from its namesake in London, which it resembles in its incline; Stephen Street, from Edmund Stephens, who owned in his day much house property in Sligo, as well as some town parks, including a park in Fort-hill quarter, which took in the area of Stephen Street, and brought the owner the honour of leaving the street his name; St. John's Lane, now John Street, from its leading to St.

---

[1] 'Who diminished the skills of those beneath him', Latin. [Clachan ed.].

John's Church; and Church Lane, from leading, higher up, from Market Street and High Street to the same church.

As to the other streets: Temple Street was so called in compliment to the Temple family, who owned much of the town; Burton Street, from Benjamin Burton, who purchased, in 1697, Lord Stafford's Sligo estate; Gore Street, from Lady Anne Gore, who was married, first, to Sir Francis Gore, and subsequently to Percy Gethin, Esq., and who was the daughter of Captain William Parke, and niece of Sir Roger Jones; Corkran's Mall, from Thomas Corkran, its builder; Thomas Street, from Thomas, the Christian name of this Mr. Corkran; Gallows Hill North, and Gallows Hill South, from the executions which took place in these quarters; Ropewalks, from the manufacture of ropes carried on there formerly; Wine Street, from the wine vaults kept there by the Bulteels, who lived in the premises now occupied by Messrs. Robertson and Kells; William Street, George's Street, Adelaide Street, Charles Street, Albert Street, Albert Road, Victoria Road, from members, for the most part, of the royal family of England; Vernon Street, Gethin Street, Armstrong Row, Walker's Row, Lynn's Place, from well-known local families.

The public buildings of the town are not unworthy of its beautiful environs. To begin with, the cathedral is a massive structure, and, thanks to the builder, Mr. Joseph Clarence, of Ballysadare, as solid a piece of masonry as there is in the kingdom. It is in the Romanesque style, and presents, externally, a lofty tower with a plain campanile (little liked by either connoisseurs or the public), a bold nave and transepts, and a rounded east-end or apse. Internally there is a vestibule which leads by a lofty door into the body of the church; a nave with a single aisle on either side; a semicircular chancel; and a Lady chapel covered with a vaulted roof. The high altar with its surmounting gilt canopy is an imposing object, and, striking as it is, would be still more effective, as well as still more in keeping with the Romanesque style, if, like the canopy of Corinthian brass which towers over the high altar of St. Peter's, it stood under a dome instead of standing, as it does, under a groin. The profusion of stained glass which meets the eye in all directions around, exhibits the decorations and furniture of the church in a very pleasing light, and, in a light not less pleasing, the charity of the diocese of Elphin, as each window in the large collection is the personal gift of some devout and generous diocesan.

Like the cathedral, the court-house is a well-built structure, as one would expect from the high character of the builder, Mr. Morris. The front facade, almost the only part of the edifice visible to the public, is so broken up with opes[1] of various kinds and sizes, as to leave hardly any continuous wall for the eye to rest on. It is a pity the architect did not treat his chimney

---

[1] An archaic word for open, [Clachan Ed.].

shaft in a different way from that adopted, and conceal it, as mediaeval architects knew so well how to do, in some ornamental finial or other feature; for, at present, the curious juxtaposition of the spire and shaft reminds one very much of a man with his back to a fire-place after a wetting. The design is more successful in the accommodation afforded—the hall in front of the courts being spacious, and well adapted for the interviews between clients and lawyers which so often take place there; the courts themselves, while well aired and well lighted and ordered in accordance with the principles of acoustics, being conveniently arranged for the bench, the bar, the jury, and the public; the grand jury rooms being equal to anything to be found elsewhere; and the apartments for the accommodation of the various county officials the county surveyor, the secretary of the grand jury, and the sub-sheriff—being ample and commodious.

Sligo seems to have been always well off in respect to its court-houses. In 1778 John Wesley preached in what he calls the "old court-house", which he describes as "an exceedingly spacious building;" and in 1785 he preached in what was then known as the "new court-house", with the proportions and style of which the reader is well acquainted, as it is the one that lasted to our own day and was taken down to make room for the existing structure.

The Sligo court-house suggests a word or two regarding certain other courts of the county. Except the judges of assize, who were accompanied in the olden time, both out of court and in court, with greater ceremonial than at present, the official dispensers of justice got through their functions in a rather rough and ready fashion. Previously to the establishment of Petty Sessions, which occurred about 1822, and in which proceedings took place in special court-houses, magistrates heard and decided cases at their private residences, generally in front of their hall doors, where the parties, witnesses and friends, attended, and acted their respective parts with a volubility of tongue and energy of action so stirring as to render the scene sometimes as exciting as a row at a fair. In some cases proceedings were sufficiently decorous. Of Mr. Wynne, of Hazelwood, for instance, Wakefield writes (Vol. II., p. 750):—

> "The litigants, many of whom come from the mountains, and cannot speak a word of English, make known their case, which is often some trifling quarrel, through the medium of an interpreter. In general, Mr. Wynne obliges them to present a written narrative, which they employ some schoolmaster to draw up. So numerous are the suitors sometimes, and so eager to be heard, that it is difficult to preserve order, and make them attend to their turn. Were it not established as an invariable rule, that no more than one shall speak at a time, so unaccustomed are these uncivilized mountaineers to regularity and decorum, that the accuser and the accused, with the whole train of witnesses, would be haranguing together, in their wild and uncouth jargon, intelligible to none but themselves and their interpreter".

In many instances, it is to be feared, that magistrates were swayed by interest or other unworthy motives, and that the merits of the case had little to do with their decision; for there were, in those days, what were called "trading magistrates", that is, magistrates who made a livelihood by the money or money's worth which they received as bribes for their decision. In the evidence on the State of Ireland given before the Houses of Parliament in 1824 (pages 50-51,) it came out that there were Justices of the Peace who had no other visible mode of support but the trade they carried on as magistrates, "receiving presents to a large amount, having their work done for them, getting presents of potatoes, corn, and cattle, and presents of money too".

The Manor courts of the closing years of the last century, and the first twenty or thirty years of the present, were often scenes of disorder, little better, indeed, in some places, than drunken orgies. The Manor court was generally held in public-houses, where spirituous drinks were always produced by the litigants for both the seneschal and the jurors; an entertainment so indispensable that there could be little hope of a verdict without it; and, as at the present day, one party to a trial always tries to have an attorney on his side if the other party has one employed, so, in the days of the Manor courts, one side took care to supply the court with as much whiskey as the other, in order not to be taken at a disadvantage.

The Coroner's court, too, was held as often as possible in the whiskey shop. Whether, however, held there or elsewhere, drinking formed the most characteristic incident of the proceedings. No doubt there are persons still living in Sligo who witnessed some of those disgraceful scenes, and, having witnessed them, must always remember them; for the huge, burly coroner, Abraham Fenton, and his jury of boon companions, sitting around a table covered with bottles, jugs, and glasses, and enveloped in an atmosphere reeking with the vapours of whiskey punch or *scalteen*[1], and the fumes of tobacco, formed a picture which, once seen, could hardly ever be forgotten. And if anything were needed to fix the picture indelibly in the memory, it was abundantly supplied by a torrent of abuse, mixed with imprecations, which this ill-mannered public officer was in the habit of pouring out on any witnesses who gave evidence which he did not like, and on any jurors who scrupled for an instant to adopt the verdict which he dictated.

It was about a score of years ago the commodious barrack on the Albert Road, was built for the Constabulary. Since the inauguration of the force in 1822, by the Act of Geo. IV., cap. 103, members of it have been stationed in various parts of the town. On their first introduction, they were located in three or four cabins, and one thatched house, two storied, which lay between the present gaol and the river, and from which the occupants

---

[1] Whiskey punch, often with honey, [Clachan ed.].

had been removed to make room for the peace preservers. Sixteen men, the number allowed by the Act of Parliament for each barony of a county, settled in the three or four cabins, and their officer, or Head Constable, as he was technically styled, a gentleman named Bulfin, took the two storied house to himself. In a few years the sixteen men and a new officer, named Tracy, got lodging or barrack accommodation in a house on the site of the college, in Quay Street.

Prior to the creation of the Constabulary by the Act of 1822, the minor executive officers of the law were called Baronial Constables, and popularly, Old Barneys; and being without uniform, without arms, without discipline, they presented a contrast to the new force, who were regularly trained, were armed with carbines, and were clad in a neat uniform. The Old Barneys were charged with many of the duties now performed by the Royal Irish Constabulary, but were so mercenary and so crapulous, that a few ten-pennies or a glass or two of whiskey would render them insensible to every obligation. If they were directed to arrest a law breaker, a moderate *douceur* prevented them from finding the man "wanted;" if they were conveying a prisoner to gaol, a friend had only to use his good offices, and they would let off their charge, and hasten back to the magistrate to say they had been waylaid on the road, and their prisoner rescued; and if they received a warrant to search for stolen goods, they would do with it just as they liked, "one of them", says Mr. Curtis, in his History of the Royal Irish Constabulary, "lending a search warrant to a comrade in an adjoining district to search for stolen turnips, which had originally been issued to himself to search for timber".

Drinking was their besetting weakness. Even those of them who were counted models of propriety, were addicted to this habit. If we are to rely on Mr. Curtis' *History of the Irish Constabulary*, the Baronial Constables were commonly called Old Barneys, "from Barny McKeon, undoubtedly the most celebrated man of his class".

Poor Barney! Peace to your manes! It is little your old neighbours in Collooney imagined that you would one day figure thus in history. How well do the elderly people of the village still remember your tall, angular figure, your mock gravity, and that facetious salutation of yours to all the young folk you met, "I'll break my arm across your face". Cross as you tried to look, the juveniles knew it was all make-believe, and far from feeling frightened themselves by your queer sounding greeting, or desiring, in consequence, any hurt to your precious "arm", or any other of your belongings, only wished you all the better for your pleasantries, as they answered, in a spirit like your own, "more power to your elbow".

Barney, like his comrades, had a weakness for toddy, and cultivated its acquaintance as diligently as he could. After the suppression of the

Baronials, he was sometimes hard put to in gratifying his tastes; but the good natured Orangemen of the neighbourhood appointed him doorkeeper of their Collooney lodge; and, as their meetings in those days were more frequent, and much more convivial than at present, Barney McKeon had a good time of it often enough, in drinking deep to the glorious, pious, and immortal memory of the great patron of the brotherhood.

Talking of Barney and his propensities, one is reminded of a certain comrade of his, Tom M ----. Tom too was not over well off after the collapse of the Baronials; but, as he passed for a "convert" from Popery, he had troops of friends among those who had all the patronage of the day in their hands, and was appointed by them to the office of assistant sexton to the Protestant church of Collooney. The habits acquired, while Barony Constable, had more influence on the sexton, than the solemn surroundings of his new position; and the unfortunate man, on receiving once into the vestry a quantity of wine, invited a poor half natural of the village to join him in a glass of it, when both, having tasted the beverage, liked it so well, that they continued their potations till they fell helpless on the floor, where they were found the following day more dead than alive.

This specimen of the Old Barneys, which is hardly an exaggerated one, shows the difference between them and their successors of the Irish Constabulary. The difference is sufficiently marked, even taking the constabulary as they proceeded from the hands of Peel, and were called Peelers, and were described, for their one-sidedness, "as an Orange yeomanry in green uniform;" but the contrast is much more striking, considering the force as reformed, and new moulded in 1836, by the incomparable Thomas Drummond, who left it, what it has since remained, the most respectable and most efficient police force in the world.

It is only persons who know the police and military of other countries that can duly appreciate the Royal Irish Constabulary. Compared, for instance, with the *gendarmerie* of France, or with the crack regiments of her army, the Constabulary have a decided superiority, both in *physique* and *morale*. The tall stalwart form, the handsome person, the manly bearing, the firm but elastic step of our countrymen, are physical qualities in which they easily carry off the palm from the choicest troops of that country. And their superiority in the most valuable moral qualities is hardly less marked. Loyal observance of the engagements of honour and conscience which they contracted on joining the force, ready obedience to those who are set in command over them, courage that knows no fear in the performance of duty, no matter how perilous; these are the highest virtues of men under command, and they are precisely the virtues for which the Irish Constabulary have been distinguished all through since their formation.

Nor are their private virtues less deserving of commendation; for there is no body of men, perhaps, in Ireland of any class or profession, that has a better record in this respect, which is all the more creditable for them as they are away, at least the younger men among them, from those family and local influences which have so much to do in keeping others in the right path. As to their charity and patriotism, they are so well known, that appeals for charitable or patriotic objects are addressed as confidently, and always as successfully, to the police barracks, as to the presbyteries and religious houses of the country, or to the residences of the most spirited and open-handed of our gentry and merchants.

Others might imitate advantageously much of their conduct, and more especially their concord and brotherhood, though they come from different regions of the country, and profess different creeds. The silly antipathies often felt, and often too manifested, by the inhabitants of one province in regard to the inhabitants of other provinces, is never heard of, or thought of, in the Constabulary barrack, where Connaughtmen and Munstermen, Leinstermen and Ulstermen, all regard one another alike as friends and comrades. And that other great cause of social estrangement, difference of creed, which operates so strongly and extensively in other places, seems, like typhus fever in certain favoured climates, to lose most of its malignity in those peaceful abodes; for episcopal Protestants, Presbyterians, and Catholics forget there their mutual religious differences, and remember only their common religious obligation of loving the neighbour—taking the definition of neighbour from the beautiful parable propounded expressly for the purpose of answering the weighty question, "And who is my neighbour?" In employing this language, it is by no means intended to justify various transactions in which the Constabulary have been engaged; for some of these occurrences are notoriously indefensible; but whatever was amiss or evil in them, should be imputed to the officers or other superiors, and not to the rank and file of the body—the portion of the force to which reference is here made.

The town-hall, which is in the modern Italian style, is probably the most faultless building in Sligo. Tourists of taste say it throws the town-halls of Cork, and Limerick, and, perhaps, that of Dublin, into the shade. While its exterior is striking and beautiful, the accommodation which the interior affords is, considering its proportions, extraordinary. The ground floor contains a Free Library and Reading Room, a Newsroom and Exchange, a Chamber of Commerce, a Borough Court, a Council Chamber, and other offices, as well as apartments for caretakers. The upper floor, which is reached by a fine broad stone staircase, comprises a noble Assembly room, the Town Clerk's office, probably the best lighted apartment in the town, rooms for the Harbour Commissioners, and a room for the Mayor, all lofty, well aired, well lighted, and admirably fitted for their several ends. A well proportioned tower crowns the fabric, and contains a fine clock, presented by the late Mr. Charles Anderson, who was a native of the town, an extensive merchant, and a gentleman of much public spirit. The whole building cost something more than £12,000.

The site of this edifice is historical, being that on which the Cromwellians built a fortress during their tenure of the townometim. In the year 1700, Alderman Benjamin Burton, the then owner, made over the plot to William III. for a barrack, in consideration of the sum of £50, and of a reserved yearly rent of one shilling. As the barrack was no lomeonger needed towards the close of the eighteenth century, the Ordnance Department, in the year 1792, leased the plot to Mr. Owen Wynne, Hazelwood, by the description of "all that piece of ground at Sligo, called the Old Fort, and the tenement and premises within the walls of the said Fort, containing, theretofore, the magazine storehouse, the house then occupied by the surveyor of excise, the ruins of the artillery barracks, and all other houses, buildings, and improvements, erected or made thereon", at the yearly rent of £16 12s. 4d., British currency. By deed of assignment, Lord Baron Panmure, Secretary of State for the War Department, sold the Government interest in 1856, to the trustees of Mr. John Arthur Wynne, for four hundred pounds; and on the 27th May, 1864, Mr. Wynne made a lease of the plot for a town-hall, to the mayor, aldermen, and burgesses of Sligo, for the term of 834 years, at the clear yearly rent of £50, the lease containing a covenant, that the lessees should expend on the proposed work at least £3,500 within three years.

Together with being a source of revenue to the Corporation, the Assembly Room serves as a centre for the mental and moral improvement of the townspeople, being largely used for lectures, dramatic performances, concerts, exhibitions, bazaars, and other refining and moralizing purposes.

One of the most effective agencies for the intellectual and moral improvement of Sligo is the Free Library and Reading Room. It is greatly to the credit of the Town Council, that they set apart the largest and best room in the town-hall for this purpose; and it must be gratifying to them, that the opportunity of self culture thus afforded to the people is turned into excellent account. Mr. Saultry, the intelligent and zealous superintendent, states that the room is open from 10 o'clock, a.m., to 10 o'clock, p.m., on weekdays, and from 2. o'clock to 7 o'clock on Sundays; that the attendances average 150 a day; that many of the readers confine themselves to the newspapers, but that a good number occupy themselves with the books, of which there are 1,600 volumes in the library; and that, though at first there was some little trouble in keeping order, everything at present passes as decorously as it does in the City Library, Dublin, or in the British Museum.

All this, as has been said, is highly creditable to the Town Council, and to no member of it more than to Mr. James Sedley, who was exceptionally active in bringing it about; and as the name of Mr. Sedley has occurred, it is only fair to add, that apart from politics, on which no opinion is offered here, he and his brother, Alderman Sedley, have, all through life, shown themselves thorough Sligo men, ever ready and willing to make efforts and sacrifices to benefit their native town and their fellow-townsmen.

The banking house of the Provincial Bank, built in 1884, and that of the Ulster Bank, erected in 1880, are a striking addition to the street in which they stand, and even to the town. The state of things in Sligo in the early years of the century showed the need of some solvent banking concerns. Coin was so scarce, that much of the traffic carried on resembled the contract of barter rather than that of sale, people usually giving yarn in exchange for other commodities. This was sometimes the case even in large transactions; and in Arthur Young's time, the rent of the Honourable Mr. Fitzmaurice's great estate, in and round Ballymote, was paid in hanks of yarn (Young's Tour). It was in the same way country people settled their accounts in the shops, handing hanks of yarn across the counter in exchange for groceries or colouring stuffs; and not unfrequently, priests at Station-houses received their dues in the same shape.

Tradesmen's tokens, common enough in the towns of the south, do not seem to have circulated much in Sligo. The only Sligo token, that has come under the writer's notice, is one of Walter Lynch, which bears the date of 1669; and, though other dealers may have done as Lynch did, this is not probable, seeing that none of their tokens have come down to us.

In the absence of regular banks, individuals, or firms, took on themselves to issue notes, containing promises to pay on demand. A clerk named Ballantyne, having been taken into partnership by Mr. McCreery, a Sligo merchant, the firm forthwith began to issue notes, and on so large a scale that their paper was in circulation all through the county, when the inevitable collapse came, on the 17th June, 1808, to the loss of many, and to the utter ruin of not a few.[1] A year or two earlier, a gentleman named

---

[1] The feelings spread through the country by the failure of Ballantyne and McCreery, may be gathered from a popular street ballad of the day, of which the following is a sample:—
"Bad luck to McCreery wherever he goes,
He's the author of all my privations and woes,
I swear by the Bank that while ever I live
My curse to the Ballantyne notes I will give,
From Cartorn to Keash, and all round Ballymote,
You won't get a straw for a Ballantyne note".

Mullen, who lived on the Green Fort, took to the business of private banker; but his notes were soon "called down", as the phrase was, though not before many of them had found their way into the pockets of tradesmen and farmers. Mr. John Black, a leading merchant of the town, appeared next on the scene, and did a large business, as the agent of Benjamin Ball, Dublin, but failed in the end with liabilities to the extent of £20,000. Mr. Black, it may be remarked, had a turn for building as well as for banking, and built at Rosses' Point, the handsome sea-side lodge of Elsinore, outside of which he had several cannon set, as if to command the Sligo river, as Kronborg Castle commands the Elsinore Sound. In this way he managed to dispose of a good share of Benjamin Ball's twenty thousand pounds.

The doings of these and other would-be-bankers attracted the notice of the Government, who sent down a commission to Sligo to inquire on the spot into what had been going on; and the inquiry makes us acquainted with another of the Sligo bankers, a small grocer of Stephen Street, named Thomas McGowan, who, thinking he had as good a right as others to issue notes payable on demand, settled some of his accounts in this way. Tom's trade lay largely in dyeing substances, which were then in great demand for colouring the home-made friezes and druggets of the farmers; and being summoned suddenly by the Commissioners to appear before them, he proceeded in haste from behind his counter to their court, his hands and face as black as if they were dyed all over with his own indigo. When in this plight he got into the witness chair, the Commissioners, after looking at him for some time, did not know well what to make of him, and asked him, "What are you?" and when Tom, full of his own dignity, replied with great gravity, "I am a Banker", the Commissioners, half afraid that they were being hoaxed, told him to go home and wash his face, that they might see what he looked like.

It was a case, however, for the application of the old admonition, *"Ne nimium crede colori"*[1]. Poor Tom may may not have been as particular as he might have been about the outside of the platter, but he took care to keep the inside all right; and it must be recorded to his honour that, while the other bankers mentioned beggared many of those who had dealings with them, Tom McGowan, like the honest man he was, paid everybody twenty shillings in the pound.

These proceedings having shown the need of regular financial agencies in Sligo, the Provincial Bank opened a branch there in 1826, and the Bank of Ireland another in 1830, the Ulster Bank following in 1860. The National Bank opened a branch in the town in 1836,[2] but it was soon

---

[1] Do not judge by the colour (or complexion), [Clachan ed.].
[2] The following list of the Sligo Shareholders of the National Bank, appears in the *Sligo Journal*, of December 2nd, 1836:—

given up, owing, it is said, to want of business, which local opinion laid to the account of the manager's unaccommodating method of dealing.

A similar fate overtook a branch of the Agricultural Bank, about 1841, the collapse in this case too being laid, and not without reason, at the door of the manager. Since 1820 there has been a Trustees Savings' Bank in Sligo, which is said to have brought much benefit to the poorer classes; and at present the Post Office Savings' Banks of the county are turned to good account, as a recent official return shows, that £44,678 lies there to the credit of county Sligo depositors.

The Infirmary building is admirably suited to its destination, both in itself, and in its situation. While the wards and other apartments are spacious, well-aired, and well-lighted, the views which they afford of the Sligo river, Lough Gill, Hazelwood, Cairns' Hill, and the mountains in the distance are so charming, that it would be almost worth a man's while to fall ill, and become an inmate, to have an opportunity of enjoying them. Even when the structure was much smaller than it is now, it was greatly admired, and a seal, with a view of the building, was executed by the distinguished medallist, William Stephen Mossop. It is matter of regret that this seal is no longer to be had; nor do there seem to be any impressions of

---

Martin Madden, Sligo.
James O'Donnell, Sligo.
James Madden, Sligo.
Richard Anderson, Sligo.
Thomas Boland, Sligo.
John Anderson, Sligo.
William Kelly, J.P., Camphill.
Thomas Kelly, Sligo.
Michael Gallagher, Sligo.
Rev. James Donleavy, P.P., Sligo.
J. P. S. Hadaway, Sligo.
William Aikman, Sligo.
Thomas Brady, Sligo.
Owen Foley, Sligo.
William Donnellan, Sligo.
James Boyle, Sligo.
Francis M'Gloin, Sligo.
Godfrey O'Rorke, Sligo.
Hugh Rooney, Sligo.
Michael Higgins, Sligo.
Owen O'Connor, Castlegal.
H. M'Loghlin, Highwood.
Charles Gardner, Glen-house.
Isaac Cordukes, Sligo.
Darby M'Morrey, Urlar.
Patrick Kelly, Sligo.
James Foley, Sligo.

John Durkan, Gurterslin.
Bernard M'Manus, Sligo.
B. M'Getrick, Ballymote.
James Crofton Dodwell, J.P., Knockrany.
John Gallagher, Carney.
John Keighran, Sligo.
John Hagarty, Sligo.
Patrick M'Manus, Sligo.
Matthew Walsh, sen., Glen-house.
John Gilhooley, Collooney.
Patrick O'Brien, Rathlee.
Philip Gomley, Ballymote.
John Byrne, Revenue Service, Manorhamilton.
Matt. Leonard.
Rev. P. Dowdican, P.P., Drumard.
John Parke, Castlegal.
John Cawley, Riverstown.
Rev. Bart. Costello, P.P., Screen.
Mark Cooke, Tubercorry.
Rev. Paul Henry, P.P., Carinacliagh.
Martin O'Brien, Carrotmachryun.
John Killilea, Sligo.
Peter Cunningham, Sligo.
James Henry, Sligo.

it left in the existing papers and books of the establishment. About fifty years ago were added the two wings, which make the infirmary a very graceful and well-proportioned edifice, while they nearly double the accommodation which was previously afforded.

The institution has been always under the care of medical men of eminence: Doctor Burnside, Doctor Overden, Doctor Biliar, Surgeon Bell, Doctor Coyne, Doctors Little (father and son); and it is well known that the actual occupant of the office, Doctor MacDowel, is fully equal to the most distinguished of his predecessors in professional ability, as well as in friendly feelings for his patients. As a physician and as a surgeon he has been equally successful; and those who take an interest in the institution are aware that surgical operations of the most difficult and delicate character are performed there, and with results which would do credit to the leading hospital of the metropolis.

Dr. MacDowel's staff consists of an apothecary; a treasurer, a matron, a house steward, three nurses, two ward maids, two laundry maids, a cook, and a night nurse. Some time ago one might hear, now and again, murmurings, as if one or other of the then nurses took special care of patients who could afford to give *douceurs*, and rather neglected, at least comparatively, others whose poverty left them unable to act in this way. There may have been no ground for such complaints, even in the past, but whether or not, there is nothing of the kind heard at present, which is very gratifying, as an impression or suspicion of that kind, whether well or ill-founded, could hardly fail to discredit in the eyes of the poor, an establishment of which the town and county have good reason to be proud.

The Fever Hospital enjoys all the advantages of situation which the Infirmary possesses. It stands on the same hill, at a somewhat higher elevation, where the supply of air, which is so necessary for such an institution, is pure and perfect to a degree very rarely met with. It was built between 1817 and 1822, and is for the most part a work of private munificence. A visitation of famine followed by fever, which afflicted the town and county in 1817, led to its erection. The famine was occasioned by the failure of the potato and oats crops, caused by continuous heavy rains, lasting from July to the end of October. Provisions, in consequence, rated so high in 1817 that oatmeal sold for sixpence a pound, or five shillings a peck, and Mr. Peter O'Connor states that he himself saw a small cargo of meal, which came from Drogheda, retailed at that price.

As always happens in Ireland, the famine was followed by fever, which grew so general and malignant in the town and county, that several hundred died of it. For want of due care, and particularly for want of an hospital, or other suitable place in which that care might be exercised, a great many preventable deaths occurred; and it was to guard against the recurrence of such a state of things that Mr. Edward Synge Cooper, one of the members of Parliament for the county, set, single-handed, about the erection of an hospital to be devoted to fever patients exclusively. In gratitude to this public benefactor, the Grand Jury wished to name the new structure The Cooper Hospital, but Mr. Cooper, who acted from motives of benevolence and charity, would not hear of such a thing, and insisted on the house being called simply the Sligo Fever Hospital. To avoid offending his friends of the Grand Jury, he allowed his name to be inscribed on a stone over the front entrance, but only on condition that he should not figure as the founder, but merely as a helper. In accordance with his desire, the stone bears this inscription:—

SLIGO FEVER HOSPITAL,
ERECTED AT THE JOINT EXPENSE OF THE COUNTY,
AND
EDWARD SYNGE COOPER, ESQ., M.P.,
1822.

The Hospital, which was finished and fitted for patients in 1822, was sadly needed that year, for famine raged then more fiercely than in 1817. To answer the cries for relief rising from all parts of the west of Ireland, the English people, with their characteristic humanity, organized a great Relief Committee in London, which was commonly called the Irish Distress Committee, and which collected funds to the amount of £304,180. Applications for relief were addressed to this body by the gentry and clergy of the county in letters which give a saddening picture of the state of things prevailing through the district at the time. Communications of this kind were forwarded by Colonel Percival, on the 6th of June, by Mr. Edward Synge Cooper, on the 8th of June, by Mr. Charles King O'Hara, M.P., on the 17th of June, by Mr. Owen Wynne, on the 1st of July, and at different dates by the clergy of all denominations, including the Right Reverend Doctor McNicholas, Bishop of Achonry, Rev. James Neligan, Protestant Rector of Kilmacteige, and Rev. William Urwick, Independent minister of Sligo.

All these letters are well worth studying for the light which they throw on that dismal period, but extracts from one or two, which derive a special interest from the lofty character of their writers, are all there is room for here. In one of his letters, the amiable and able Doctor McNicholas writes, under the date 23rd August, "This country owes an eternal debt of gratitude to England, whose prompt and noble generosity rescued our peasantry from the horrors of famine and pestilence. May Providence always enable the humane and liberal English nation to continue the benefactors of mankind." Mr. Cooper's letter is written from Mullingar, and is dated the 8th June; and in it the builder of the Fever Hospital is found doing his part in the crisis with characteristic humanity and generosity: "I am at present," says he, "employing persons to the amount of 150 per week in the county of Sligo and here, which will be continued during the pressure, besides 200 remitted to the Sligo Central Committee in cash, and half as much laid out in seed potatoes, and a weekly sum to the parish of Ballysadare". If landlords and country gentlemen generally evinced the sympathy with the people which was shown on this occasion by Mr. Cooper, they would never have incurred the odium with which too many of them have come to be popularly regarded.

During the terrible fever epidemic which followed the famine of 1846, the hospital was crowded as it had never been before, and as it has never been since. Though intended originally for only fifty patients, the doctors managed in 1846 and 1847 to make room for 165 in the hospital itself and the temporary sheds which were put up around it. The following are the statistics of the admissions in these years, as supplied by Mr. Morris, the obliging steward of the establishment:—

From September,	1846 to September,	1847	—1,231
" "	1847 to "	1848	—1,340
" "	1848 to January,	1849	— 97
		Total	2,668

Besides the Fever Hospital and its surrounding sheds, the building now serving for the Diocesan School received considerable numbers of the infected, but there seems to be no record of the admissions. While all these places, the Hospital, the Sheds, the Diocesan School, or Charter School, as it was commonly called at the time, were crowded to their utmost capacity, still scores of unfortunate fever stricken men and women might be seen lying on wads of straw along the road from the Calry church to Ballinode, waiting their turn to be received into one of the roofed structures. Persons who witnessed those scenes shudder still at the thought when telling of them, and rarely omit a prayer to be preserved from ever seeing such harrowing sights again—a prayer in which everyone must heartily join.

The ravages of the fever had hardly ceased when the still more dreaded cholera invaded the town in 1849. The recollection of 1832, as might be expected, filled the inhabitants with alarm, but the visitation of 1849 was much less destructive, though still sufficiently trying. The admissions that year to the Fever Hospital, turned for the occasion into a cholera hospital, were 166; of whom 98 died and 68 recovered. The first case came from Ballysadare, a woman named Ellen Gallagher, who was admitted into the hospital on the 29th May, and died that evening. There was no sign of epidemic at the time, and this was the only case that occurred till the following August.

The chief victim of the 1849 cholera was Doctor Little. As became the brave and good man he was known to be, he fell in the heroic performance of his duty. Having been engaged, the day before his death, till a late hour of the evening in attending sick calls at Ballincar, instead of going on his return to town to his own house, as he was urged to do, he drove to the Hospital and remained there till he had examined and prescribed for every patient in the house. This devotedness cost him his life, for he contracted the disease before leaving the place, and went home only to die.

The most extensive edifice in the town, or connected with it, is the District Lunatic Asylum, the building of which was begun in 1848, and finished in 1852, the house being opened for patients in 1855. The architect was Mr. Deane Butler, the builder Mr. Caldwell, Sligo, and the clerk of works Mr. John Battle, Collooney, by no means the least able of the many men of mark whom that little town has produced. The structure consists of two parts—a central range which cost £35,199, and two wings erected at a cost of £18,000 in 1877, when experience had shown the necessity of additional accommodation to that extent. The house, including the wings, is intended to accommodate 470 patients, and seems amply sufficient for its purpose. The actual annual number of patients up to the present ranging from 400 to 424, the latter being the highest figure yet reached. The institution is called the "Sligo Lunatic Asylum for the counties of Sligo and Leitrim", the proportion of inmates in 1886 being 217 for Sligo, and 187 for Leitrim. The expenditure for the year 1886 was £7,756 10s. 2d., which may be taken as the average annual expenditure. The administration of the establishment was carried on in 1886 by the following officers:—Resident Medical Superintendent, Dr. Joseph Petit; assistant to do., Dr. G. R. Lawless; matron, Mrs. Armstrong; Protestant chaplain, Rev. Thomas Heany; Roman Catholic chaplain, Rev. James Fallon; clerk and storekeeper, Mr. Robert Browne.

Mrs. Armstrong has lately resigned the office of matron, and her resignation has elicited from everybody connected with the place expressions of deep regret for losing the services of so kind, so able, and so accomplished a lady.

The only Superintendents connected with the institution since its opening have been Dr. McMunn, who held the office from 1855 to 1883, and Dr. Petit, who succeeded at that date, and still occupies the position. The leading feature of Dr. Petit's treatment of the insane is, as far as possible, the abolition of all those outward restraints, which some time ago were regarded as indispensable and a matter of course in the asylums of the country. In pursuance of this system he has done away with so called "airing courts"—spacious areas, which were surrounded with high stone walls, and into which the patients were turned at certain fixed hours to take there what exercise they could. Instead of caging in this way those under his charge,

Dr. Petit leaves them, during recreation time, free to move about through the extensive grounds of the place, and to take their exercise and recreation just as they think fit themselves. A large number of the male patients are employed on the farm, and with excellent results, both in regard to themselves and to the farm produce.

As another step in the direction of liberty he has discontinued, unless in exceptional cases, the use of single rooms appropriated to individuals, and has substituted spacious sleeping apartments or dormitories in which large numbers pass the night together; and he carries the principle of doing away with restraint so far that he has removed the doors of the dormitories and some other apartments, leaving the places quite open in order to impress the sense of freedom still deeper on the minds of all. One would think, considering the impulsive and wayward feelings of the insane, that those changes would lead to attempts at escape and other inconveniences, but the result has justified Dr. Petit's prevision and judgment, for the inmates were never so amenable to rule or so attached to the place as since the new system was put in force, in proof of which it may be noticed, that some who were taken out by their friends to be cared at home have returned of their own accord to the asylum, and put themselves again into the doctor's hands.

The Sligo asylum is conducted on very liberal principles as far as payment for patients is concerned. When a patient is sent in, there are no questions asked as to the ability or inability of relatives to contribute towards his maintenance—so that practically the matter of paying, or not paying, is left entirely to themselves. In these circumstances, friends or relatives seldom pay, though there may be a few who, either from regard for the patient, or from dread of being charged with shabbiness themselves, elect to pay less or more.

The private houses of Sligo, as well shop houses as simple residences, are in style and finish sufficiently in keeping with the public buildings. There are shop-houses in Market Street, Castle Street, Radcliffe Street, Knox's Street, and one or two other streets, as extensive and imposing as any that can be found in any other leading town or city in Ireland; and Mr. Campbell's ornate mansion on the Mall, the late Dr. Lynn's fine house, with its graceful portico in Stephen Street, the late Dr. Carter's stately residence in Wine Street, and some others of the town, can hardly be surpassed in the province for correctness of proportion, and suitableness of accommodation; while the suburbs are studded all round with handsome seats and villas, both those built some years ago—Merville, belonging to Mr. Tighe; Farmhill, to Mr. Peyton; Kevinsfort, to Mr. Lestrange; Thornhill, to Mr. Cullen; Rathedmond, to Mr. Middleton; Woodville, to Colonel Wood Martin; Cairns Hill, to Mr. O'Connor; Hermitage, to Major

Campbell; Ardowen, to Mr. Wynne; Marymount, to Mr. Woods and those just erected, Eden Hill, the fine villa of Mr. Walsh; Fern Bank, the commodious cottage of Mr. Michael O'Connor; and the boldly and salubriously situated Charlemont House, built by the late Mr. Charles Anderson, and called *Charlemont* from his Christian name, Charles.

The picturesque *Rus in Urbe* villas just erected by Mr. Morris marks a very desirable innovation in the architecture of the town. While pre-existing houses were substantial and imposing, they lacked in some measure the elegance and ornament which are found in similar structures in England and Scotland, as well as in other parts of Ireland. It is creditable then to Mr. Morris to have initiated a new departure; and it is to be hoped that others will follow the example he has set, and will, like him, without sacrificing in any way the solidity and accommodation of their residences, take more pains in future with their adornment.

While so many of the houses of the town are both lofty and spacious, the streets are wide in proportion, the centre well paved, the sideways neatly flagged, and the whole well cared and kept. From being what it was at the time of the first invasion of cholera, in 1832, a rather dirty town, Sligo has become one of the cleanest in the kingdom, this result being very much due to the system of sewerage lately perfected, with skilfully designed and well made drains running through all the streets, and conveying their contents to a main intercepting sewer, which in turn discharges itself into the sea.

The abundant water supply furnished to Sligo through the waterworks flushes thoroughly these drains, and thus contributes largely to the cleanliness and salubrity of the place. Before the execution of these works, the only water available for drinking, or other purposes, was that of the river, and of three or four *wells*. The river water was unfit for drinking and most other purposes; for the river, lying under the sloping streets, was a kind of *cloaca maxima*,[1] into which everything drained; and as the town was then full of tan-yards, slaughter houses, and breweries, the liquid refuse of these establishments, mixed with the nuisances coming from the inhabited houses, flowed into and poisoned the water of the river.

The chief, if not the only, wells from which people obtained spring water, were Tubber-an-shelmide, near Marymount, Mullowney's well close to the Green Fort, and those of Tubber-Gal, in Knox's Street, and the Lungy. Whatever may be said of the waters of *Tubber-na-Shelmide* and Mullowney's well, which were little used, being inconveniently situated, it is clear that Tubber-Gal and the Lungy could not escape gross pollution, lying, as they did, in populous districts, at the bottom of deep hollows, and in a porous soil.

---

1 An early drainage/sewerage system designed by the Romans, [Clachan Ed.].

By-the-bye, it was next to impossible to find any explanation of the strange word Lungy, the people being all in the dark on the subject, except one gentleman of rare intelligence, and with a larger knowledge of the Sligo of sixty or seventy years ago, than any other person living, who states that the name comes from *long*—pronounced lung—a ship, the motion of the morass, which formerly surrounded the well, and which, when stepped on by little boys in play, rose and fell in a swinging manner, thus resembling the rolling of a ship on sea, and suggesting the curious appellation.

The water taken from these polluted sources, was very different from that conveyed now by pipes direct from the fresh mountain springs into the streets and houses of Sligo, which is so pure and abundant, that it has contributed already very sensibly to the health and longevity of the population. Whatever difference of opinion may have formerly existed as to the merits of the Kilsellagh Water Scheme, all seem agreed, now that it is in operation, that it is, as well in regard to the quality, as to the abundance of the supply, the very best that could be devised in the circumstances.

Mr. Baptist Kernaghan, solicitor, who was the originator and principal promoter of the measure, and his partner, Mr. Saunders, had a Bill laid before the House of Commons on the subject in 1867, but the Bill being lost, and Mr. Kernaghan dying soon after, the matter was taken up energetically by a section of the Town Council, who carried it through in the face of great opposition, encountered both in the Corporation and in Parliament. It was during the mayoralty of Mr. Colleary, and with his energetic and influential assistance, the works were completed, and on the 13th November, 1884, the water was turned on for the first time, and sent on its beneficent mission to the town by his amiable and accomplished daughter, Miss Mary Rose Colleary, whose name must continue associated with this, perhaps the greatest temporal blessing Sligo has ever received.

The celebrated engineer, Mr. Hassard, designed the waterworks. Messrs. Sweeny and McLarnon were the contractors, and Mr. McCreery, C.E., the clerk of works. The works were begun in 1881. The cost, in round numbers, was £20,000 (in exact figures £19,457 16s. 6d.), this sum, including £1,231 17s. 8d., spent in repairing a slip or breach in the embankment, which was of so serious a character, that it took seventy thousand carts of stones to fill up the gap. It is said, that the reservoir which feeds the pipes contains, when full, 50,000,000 gallons, and that the supply would meet the requirements of a population twice as large as that which the town contains at present. The capabilities of the source were well tested in the long continued drought of the past summer, the result proving that the supply is, under present circumstances, practically inexhaustible.

From all this it is clear that Sligo is a handsome town. It is said to have the air of a business town too, more than any other in Connaught.

Tourists after travelling through the rest of the province, are struck with the trade and bustle they find in the place, notably on market days. Galway, the only town of Connaught that can be compared to it, is, it would appear, going to the bad, its exports and imports diminishing, its squares and streets neglected and deserted, its quondam "castles" turned into tenements for the very poor; while Sligo with its wide, clean, and well paved streets, its extensive and striking shops, its numerous new or renovated private houses, its noble public buildings, and its magnificent water works, exhibits most of the attributes of a prosperous, as well as a progressive town.

And tourists are as well pleased with the hotels, as with the sights of the town and neighbourhood. While they complain, often enough nor—probably without good cause—of the hotels of other places, both as to fare and charges, they have nothing but praise for the hotels and hotel keepers of Sligo. It is well known that the meat and fish markets of Sligo cannot be surpassed in Ireland; and it is equally admitted, that the cooks of the Victoria and Imperial can turn out their dishes in as appetizing a style as the *chef de cuisine* even of the Dublin Shelburne, so that those who patronise these establishments, are always as agreeably surprised at the excellence of the creature comforts provided, as at the extreme moderation of the bill that follows.

While the town has then gained greatly in appearance, elegance and healthiness, it has lost not a little in the matter of employments and industries, as, for instance, those connected with Messrs. Alexander Stewart and Co.'s distillery; with Mr. Martin's distillery and flour mills, where hundreds were kept at work, some indoors, some out of door; with several breweries—Jamieson's brewery, quite close to the spot on which Cleveragh gate now stands; Anderson's brewery in Brewery Lane, now Water Lane; Madden's brewery at the foot of Market Street; Holmes' brewery at Farmhill, taken over or purchased in 1819 by Messrs. Anderson and Co., from Thomas Holmes; and Love Lane brewery, apparently the first established in Sligo; with soap boiling and candle making establishments—Miller's in Old Market Street, Richard Anderson's in Market Street, John Street's, in Hadcliffe Street; with several tanneries, notably Corkran's in Corkran's Mall, and Corriston's at the Market Cross; with paper mills at Ballincar; and with the linen trade, the most extensive and remunerative industry which has ever existed in either town or county, which is utterly gone without leaving after it the slightest memorial of its existence—the Linen Hall, built in 1764 as its headquarters, being now incorporated with the Imperial hotel.

Of various handicrafts employing a great number of hands, both in the town and county, many have disappeared, or almost disappeared; such as those of potters, who manufactured crocks, basins, milk vessels, and other articles of coarse pottery; turners, who made wooden dishes, platters, and sundry domestic vessels or utensils; brogue makers, the most numerous trade fraternity in the county, though now without a single representative, perhaps; shoemakers and bootmakers who, so late as the O'Connell Centenary, mustered eighty-four in the town, but count now only sixteen or so, the reduction being due to machine work and gutta percha[1] boots and shoes; tailors reduced to a tenth of their former numbers, by the importation of ready-made goods; leather breeches makers, who turned out leather breeches for hunters and other hard riders, at a period when people passed much more of their time in the saddle than they do at present; hatters so numerous that they filled all Hatters' Lane, now Back Lane or Church Lane, and who made felt hats so staunch and solid, that, to use the illustration of one who wore the article, you might bale a boat with them; and—to say nothing now of others—coopers, who must have been very numerous, as they were connected in dozens with the breweries, distilleries, and slaughter houses of the town.

Mention of the slaughter houses reminds one of the benefit they brought the town in connection with the meat supply to the army and navy. The contract for the supply was generally taken by some prince merchant of London, who sublet it in parts to others, Sligo coming in for a good share. Those who usually got a part in the town were Mr. Edward Kelly, Knox's Street, Mr. Harry O'Connor, Wine Street, Mr. Hugh Rooney, Pound Street, Mr. John Beatty, John Street, and Messrs. Scott and Patrickson, Key Street. The slaughtering season for beef opened in October and lasted till Christmas, when the pork season began, which continued till March; and during all this time the business afforded extensive employment to several classes of persons—to buyers and drivers in connection with the fairs in which cattle and pigs were purchased, the purchases being on a large scale, as many as eight hundred bullocks changing owners at the Croghan fair, and only slightly fewer at others; to butchers and their helps in the slaughter houses; to cutters and salters and packers in the curing places; and to carters and labourers in putting the packed casks aboard ship. An indirect benefit to the poor of the town and county, and one of great value, was the large supply of wholesome meat put on the local market, at a moderate price, in the heads and certain other parts of the carcass not comprehended in the general contract.

In the first half of the century there was a good deal of emigration from the port of Sligo to America. The trade began about the year 1804, when the merchants most extensively engaged in it were the Messrs. Everard, and Messrs. Andrew and Alexander Hume. In the year 1825, Mr.

---

[1] Pliable substance made from latex, introduced to the west in 1843, probable origin of term 'guttes', [Clachan ed.].

Pat O'Connor having got from America a cargo of flax seed by a vessel called the Belsay Castle, of Sunderland, and having nothing else to load her with for the return voyage, fitted her up for emigrants, many of whom were taken on board and landed safe in St. John's, Newfoundland. Of the passengers brought out on this occasion by the Belsay Castle, seventy had their passage money paid by the noted Thady Conlon. While engaged in his biblical labours and speculations, Thady found means to collect money in England for this purpose, and in selecting persons to be sent out, he gave the preference, first, to members of his own family and, next, to inhabitants of Tireragh generally, so that the Conlon and Tireragh element must still be pretty considerable in the population of St. John's, The cost per head of emigration was £2 for others, but thirty shillings for Thady Conlon's seventy, Thady having bargained for this reduction in consideration of the numbers he was putting on board. At this passage money Mr. O'Connor supplied water and fuel, the passengers procuring their own food, which consisted for the most part of potatoes and salt herrings, each passenger taking with him a sack of potatoes and a few dozen of the fish.

In 1830, Mr. O'Connor sent out the Argo, a vessel of his own, which though only of 164 tons, took out 156 souls, including Mr. Peter O'Connor who made the voyage in order to secure humane treatment for the passengers. The abolition of the Corn Laws in 1846 gave an impulse to emigration from Sligo and from other ports, the vessels which came from America freighted with bread stuffs taking out emigrants in return. While the business lasted, it occasioned the circulation of money in the town; for straitened as were most of the emigrants for means, they had something to pay for lodging and necessary purchases; and the conveyance of themselves and their provisions to the Pool where the vessels were moored and the passengers embarked, gave employment to boatmen, carters, and labourers.

The following extract from a report of a meeting of the old Enniskillen and Sligo Railway Company, held in Dublin, on the 10th October, 1845, under the chairmanship of Lord Palmerston, will be interesting to many:—

> It will be seen by the Commissioners' Report on Railways in Ireland, that the imports and exports of Sligo are greater than any other on the North Western Coast of Ireland. In the year 1835 they amounted in value to £494,182, since which period the trade has been gradually increasing the value of the exports alone for the past year (1844) being £758,400, as appears by the following table, with a proportionate increase on the imports:
> AVERAGE TRADE OF SLIGO FOR SEASON 1844.

Quantity.	Description.	Average Value.	Total Value.
70,000	pigs slaughtered and shipped	£3	£210,000
10,000	" exported alive	.2	20,000
7,000	fat cattle, slaughtered and shippe	10	70,000
12,000	" shipped alive	12	14,400

70,000	firkins butter	.	3	210,000
20,000	tons oats .	.	3	110,000
12,000	tons oatmeal .	.	10 per ton	120,000
4,000	barrels wheat . .	.	1 per barrel	<u>4,000</u>
			Total value	

£758,400

[This is exclusive of sheep, eggs, fowl, and several other articles, the valuation of which has not yet been obtained.]—*Sligo Journal,* Oct. 24th, 1845.

The chief centre of employment at present in Sligo, is Messrs. McNeil and Sons' establishment, in Lynn's Place. What was, a century ago, a portion of the sea shore, washed regularly by the tides, is now the busiest hive of human industry in either town or county. The numbers employed have fallen off somewhat of late, but there are still near 300 hands in the concern receiving wages, which range from 3s. 6d. a week to 1 or more, the work hours being from 7 o'clock, a.m., to 6½ p.m., with two intervals of three-quarters of an hour each for meals.

Though punctuality is not generally supposed to be a leading quality of Irishmen, nothing can exceed the regularity with which the men keep up to time, as well in the morning as at their meal hours; and the ease and precision with which they fall into their respective places on getting inside the factory, is highly creditable to them, so that a visitor is at a loss to know which most to admire—the complex movements of vast ranges of machinery, or the dexterity of the men and boys who regulate and control all this mechanical action. The curious are not less interested in examining the admirable processes by which the manufactured objects are produced, than in considering the diversity of these objects—bobbins, of various sorts and sizes, for linen and woollen factories; handles for all implements, of the pick, hammer, sledge, hatchet, and edge kinds; articles for the dock yards and ships of the navy, and tools for the pioneers, as well as poles and staffs for the engineers of the army. One cannot fail to admire the economy as well as skill with which the concern is managed, every sound piece of timber, large and small, being manufactured, while the rejected or refuse pieces are used instead of coal, for heating the two steam engines, which work the machinery, or are put aside and sold for fuel to the poor, who run upon them, as making the cheapest and pleasantest fire they can have.

It is only by visiting the place and observing the large quantities of timber constantly coming in from all quarters, one can realize what an amount of employment the factory supplies, as it keeps going not only the army of mechanics and labourers on the spot, but numbers through the country who are engaged in cutting down the timber, moving it through the woods to the roadway, and conveying it to Sligo. Nor is it from Sligo and the adjoining counties alone the Messrs. McNeil obtain their supply, for they import largely from Norway and America, as they also export to suitable markets in England and Scotland, what is known as "green" timber, that is, the trees just as they come from the forest. It will be seen then, that the Messrs. McNeil give large employment elsewhere as well as in Sligo, and on sea as well as on land; for, to say nothing of the other vessels that they charter, they have a steamer of 1,500 tons, constantly afloat bringing them birch from the Baltic.

The old established firm of O'Connor and Cullen are large employers. Their saw mill in Union Street, is said to be one of the most extensive in the three Kingdoms, and to be fitted up with the most modern and best machinery and appliances for cutting, planing, and moulding timber. In this concern, which covers three acres, and their two other yards, where building materials of all kinds are stored and sold, Messrs. O'Connor and Cullen give constant employment to mechanics and labourers; and the extent of their transactions may be inferred from the fact, that nearly all the houses erected within the last forty or fifty years in the county Sligo, and not a few in the neighbouring counties, have been built with materials purchased from these merchants.

Within the last few years two considerable concerns in the same line of business have been opened in Sligo, and are now in active work—one in Bridge Street, belonging to Messrs. O'Connor, Walsh, and Company; and the other in Knox's Street, the property of the Sligo Wood and Iron Company.

CHAPTER XVII

COOLERRA

The district of Coolerra, including the two parishes of Killaspugbrone and Kilmacowen, belongs now to the ecclesiastical union of St. John's.

The peninsula of Coolerra (*rect*e Cuil Irra) is bounded on the west by the sea, on the east by Lough Gill, on the north, by the Sligo river, and on the south, partly by Ballysadare river, and partly by the heights of Glenagoola and Slieve da En. John O'Donovan in one place[1] adopts these boundaries, which make Coolerra co-extensive with the parishes of St. John, Kilmacowen, and Killaspugbrone; but in another place,[2] forgetting, apparently, what he had said, he confines the district to the two parishes of Killaspugbrone and Kilmacowen. The latter would seem to be the popular idea at the present time, but two centuries ago, when the deed for the Partition of Sligo was drawn up, Coolerra was regarded as comprising the whole of the three parishes mentioned.[3]

On examining the district you find that, with the exception of the immediate neighbourhood of Knocknarea, where the fall is rapid and shelving, the ground descends gradually on the one side from Knocknarea towards Cairns, and on the other from Cairns towards Knocknarea, thus forming a graceful curve; while, taking the tract north and south, you see the northern parts sloping gently to the bay of Sligo, but the southern region, as well along Ballysadare bay, as along the heights of Glenagoola, terminating steeply, more especially about the Curragh, which is a marsh not infrequently covered with water, except where it is traversed by the high-road between Belladrehid and Sligo. The interior of the southern half of the peninsula, and more particularly Carrick Henry and Carrowgobbodagh, is broken up into hillocks covered with scant grass, and sometimes with furze and whitethorn, but with so thin a coat of soil as to remind one of Virgil's lines:

Difficiles primum terrae, collesque maligni
Tenuis ubi argilla, et dumosis calculus arvis.[4]

These hillocks generally surround bowl-shaped hollows, many of which contain water, one of the best known of them going by the name of

---

[1] "Cuil Irra is a district bounded on the N East and East by the river Sligo and Lough Gill, and on the "West and S West, by the river and strand of Ballysadare".—Letter of John O'Donovan to Thomas O'Connor in Ordnance Survey Letter Book for County Sligo.
[2] Note to the year 511 in his edition of the Four Masters.
[3] "The parishes of St. John, Kilmacowen, and Killaspugbrone, called Culluren".—Tripartite Indenture, etc.
[4] "First, truculane earth and grudging hills, Where's meagre clay and and scree across the scrubby ground", from *The Georgics: A Poem of the Land, by* Virgil, [Clachan ed.].

the Punch-bowl. The surface of Coolerra is still largely covered with drift boulders detached, in the ice age, from the Ox Mountains, though great numbers of those rocks have, in the course of time, been sunk in the earth, many used for road metal, and many employed in the erection of stone houses and fences. It is these fences, ranging from three to six feet in height, which have made the district one of the best frequented and most fashionable hunting fields in Ireland. Any day in the season you may see on the ground scores of riders, including a good number of ladies; while equipages of all kinds range the roads, and crowds of men and boys flit from hill to hill after the sport, the whole scene begetting an exhilaration, felt alike by hounds, horses, sportsmen, and spectators.

The district of Coolerra—even leaving Sligo out of the account—is more than ordinarily populous, containing the villages of Strandhill, Culleenamore, Breeogue, Drumiskibbole; a goodly sprinkling of detached farm-houses—some perched on the hill tops, some nestling in the hollows, and others reposing on the declivities, all well whitewashed, and most of them girt with whitethorn and other bushes; and a considerable number of imposing residences, Mr. Walker's, at Rathcarrick, Mr, Barrett's, at Culleenamore, Mr. Phibbs's, at Seafield, Mr. Cochrane's, at Grange, the Misses Cochrane's, at Glen Lodge, Mr. Walsh's, at Breeogue, Mr. Chambers's, at Cloverhill, and some others.

A good view of most of Coolerra may be had from the north side of Sligo bay. Taking your stand on the Upper Rosses you have under the eye the best part of the district—at the north-east declivity of Knocknarea, several beautiful concave sweeps of well-planted and variously tinted ground, on one of which lies embosomed Mr. Walker's neat and cheerful residence amid trim little groves of various forms—crescents, circles, and ovals; further east the fine fields of Scardan sloping down symmetrically to the shore; next to them Cumen Head, looking out to sea, like a vigilant water-guard on duty; and between Cumen and Sligo, a rich, cultivated, picturesque tract, adorned with several elegant suburban villas, set off with lawns, paddocks, plantations, and pleasure grounds.

A considerable part of the peninsula is in tillage. Cereal and root crops are grown on about half of the land that adjoins, on either side, the high road from Ballydrehid to Sligo, including the fine farm of Tawnefortis, which a Scotchman, Mr. Petrie, has laid out and cultivated in accordance with the principles of high Scotch farming. About the same proportion of the stretch along the sea from Strandhill to Sligo is tilled; and some of this tract, more especially the portion belonging to Mr. Walker, could compete successfully with any equal area of the Scotch Lowlands for the neatness and symmetry of the fields and fences, the processes of the cultivation, and the richness of the crops.

Still larger scopes of the south and south-western sides are under crops; but the fields are small, averaging hardly an acre, excepting those of the late Mr. Walsh of Breeogue, who farmed on a large scale. More, however, than two-thirds of Coolerra, even excluding the rough lands of Knocknarea and Cairns, are permanently under grass, more particularly about the centre, where Cloverhill, Graigue, Carrowmore, and other large sweeps are nearly all green.

Knocknarea—Hill of the Moon, according to the Venerable Charles O'Connor;[1] Hill of the Executions, according to John O'Donovan;[2] Hill of the King, according to many of the inhabitants of Coolerra; and Hill of the smooth flat top, in the opinion of the present writer,[3] is as picturesque an elevation as Ireland contains. Its solitary situation renders it conspicuous for a great distance, and from all sides. With its back to the sea, and its right and left sides respectively to the Ballysadare and Sligo estuaries; and with all the mountains of Sligo and Leitrim converging in marshalled order around, it looks like a general officer, occupying a detached position, and reviewing his battalions.

Observing it in itself, you find the west side a sheer, naked precipice, and the north side a succession of retiring terraces, covered partly with grass, and partly with rich purple heath. Looking from a distance at the south and east sides, which are quite like one another, you are struck with the extreme regularity, smoothness, and polish of the contour, causing you to regard the hill as a work of art, rather than a rough and ready production of Nature. With its smooth summit, dipping slightly at either end, its overhanging brow, and its swelling sides, it reminds one of a Titanic dish-cover, Misgan Meave occupying the place, and serving the purpose, of the handle.

The Misgan is a much larger structure than one would take it to be at a first view. In 1761 Venerable Charles O'Connor reported it to be "thirty paces in conic height, and twenty-six paces in diameter at the top;" in 1799 Beranger and Bigari, the artists employed by Right Hon. W. Burton, speak of it as "a huge cairn of small stones, 60 feet high;"[4] about the same time Mr. Roger Walker, Q.C., of Rathcarrick, describes it in detail as "an enormous heap of small stones of oval figure, 630 feet circumference at the base, 79 feet slope on one side, 67 at the other, and the area at the top 100 feet in its longest diameter, and 85 in its shortest;"[5] in 1837 Dr. Petrie found the cairn to be but 590 feet in circumference at the base, and 80 feet in its

---

[1] Letter from Strandhill, dated 27th August, 1761.
[2] Letter of John O'Donovan, dated Sligo July 2nd, 1836, 2nd given in Ordnance Survey Letter Book for County Sligo.
[3] See *ante*, p. 54, [p. 46 this edition, Clachan ed.].
[4] Kilkenny Archaeological Journal, Vol. XL, p. 131.
[5] Ibidem.

largest diameter at the summit;[1] and on a recent visit, the writer ascertained by measurement that Mr. Walker's figures still represent, with sufficient accuracy, the present dimensions of the monument. It may be mentioned that, while small stones belonging, for the most part, to the limestone of the hill, compose the cairn, a few whin stone boulders, like those of Carrowmore, stand on points of the circumference at the base, thus suggesting that a circle of such stones originally enclosed and defined the whole base of the structure.

To the south and north of the Misgan are some remains of antiquity which call for a word of notice. To the south, and within a hundred yards or so of the great cairn, are three clusters of large Ox Mountain stones, each of which must have once formed a circle like those of Carrowmore— one, as far as can be judged now, having been about six yards in diameter, another eight, and the third eleven.

About eighty yards to the north of Misgan Meave, are the remains of a small rath or cashel, seventeen yards in diameter; and thirty yards further on, in the same direction, the remains of another, thirty-two yards in diameter. The surrounding fence of the latter was formed of the local limestone, which has been reduced by the weather to shingle. In the centre are a few white stone boulders, and a large limestone flag, of six feet by four, which, there is reason to believe, rested originally on the boulders, from which it was removed, very probably, with the object of excavating and exploring the ground under it. Judging by the extent of this latter fort, and the large quantity of debris within and around it, it must have been an important structure in its day, and was, not improbably, the Rath Righhairt said by the Four Masters to have been built by Fulman, *anno mundi,* 3,501.

As Knocknarea is conspicuous from all quarters, so in turn it commands a singularly extensive and varied prospect—earth and ocean, still lake and rapid river, level plain and lofty mountain, regions rich with the cultivation of centuries, and tracts as wild as nature first formed them. If it costs some effort to reach the summit, the fatigue is forgotten the moment you arrive there and look at the wonderful panorama around you. "From the platform of Meava's carn", writes the Venerable Charles O'Connor, "I took a prospect on which I feasted for more than half an hour. The counties of Donegal, Derry, Fermanagh, Leitrim, and Longford, bounded my view to the North and East; that northward was terminated by the prodigious cliffs above Killibegs, divided from the mountains of

---

[1] Stokes' Life of Petrie p. 255 Petrie accounts for the diminution of Misgan Meave by its having been "the common resort of the people of Cuil Irra for stones for building purposes, though the quarries of limestone at hand might be considered inexhaustible". There is no foundation for this account. Stones were never brought down from Misgan Meave, either for building or any other purpose.

Boylagh Barnsmore, stretching in a chain of pointed hills westward; nearer me were the vast cliffs Ben Golban, Ben Basgny, Ben Boe, and Collooney. These spiry and rugged hills exhibit numberless wild irregularities, and yet collect most of the waters, which fall from their sides into one noble basin, which they surround, called Lough Gill . . . Turning my eyes southward, my view extended beyond the Curlew mountains, and took in the great plain of Connaught, called Maghery, which ran out of sight like the immense ocean west of me". It says little for the tastes of some Sligo people, that, though living within a couple of miles of Knocknarea, few of them ever think of enjoying the glorious prospect on which the refined O'Connor feasted with such exquisite delight.

A most remarkable spot on Knocknarea, is that called The Glen, on the southern slope of the hill. At a distance it appears to be only a line of brushwood, running quite straight from west to east, but on reaching the place you find it a cut or cleft in the mountain, about three-quarters of a mile long, and of pretty uniform depth and width the whole way. Having entered the cut from the west by a short avenue of hazel, you see the sides of solid rock rise, right and left of you, as perpendicularly as if they were formed by rule and plummet, and the horizontal strata of limestone superimposed regularly one over the other like courses of masonry; the side to the left, that next the hill, rising to a height of about 60 feet, and that to the right, to a height of about 40 feet, while the distance between the sides is 40 feet or so. And these figures would serve for any other section of the glen, as the dimensions are nearly uniform all through. So striking indeed is this uniformity as to suggest the idea, that some monster mysterious grooving machine, directed by superhuman power and skill, must have been employed to cut clean out the masses of rock which lay once between the sides. Geologists will find it difficult to account for the phenomenon, though the matter lies within their province. One may date the fissure from the first cooling of the earth's crust, and say, that owing to some local disturbance, the sides parted asunder, when the earth was near cooled, and never since closed; others may ascribe it to an earthquake of later date; while a third may set it down with much greater probability, to the solvent action of water, which rolling down the slopes of the hill, through geological ages, sank here into the soft limestone rock, formed for itself a passage to the neighbouring sea, and carried away with it, time after time, in chemical solution, the portions of the mountain that have been displaced. To each of these theories there are special objections, as well as the one common to all three, that arises from the extreme regularity of form which appears all through the trench, and which it is hard to reconcile with one or other of the hypotheses mentioned.

Notwithstanding the depth of the glen, vegetation is luxuriant in it. What seemed at a distance a row of bushes, turns out to be the tops of lofty trees, some sycamore, a few beech, but by far the greater number ash, most of the last named springing out of crevices at different heights in the rocky sides; several of them, however, starting from the floor and shooting up so vigorously as to overtop the others. The floor itself is covered with a growth of rank grass and weeds, the latter attaining an abnormal size, as, for example, a nettle which lay across the path, and which measured more than eight feet in length, the leaf being eight inches broad. Much larger specimens of the weed might be found by searching for them. If the floor were bored here and there, and the deposits examined, light would probably he thrown on the history and character of this curious *lusus naturae*,[1] which seems to deserve more attention than it has hitherto received.

Near the Glen lies the district of Grange, divided now into four Granges,—Primrose Grange, Grange West, Grange East, and Grange North—corresponding with the four quarters of which the district formerly consisted. In each of three of the baronies into which the county is divided—Corran, Tireragh, and Carbury we find a spot called Grange:—in Corran, in the parish of Emlagfad, a little to the west of Ballymote, though the name has nearly died out there; in Tireragh, in the parish of Templeboy, where we have Grangemor and Grangebeg, not far from Aughris Head; and in Carbury, two of those denominations, one the well known village of Grange, in the parish of Ahamlish, and the other, this Grange of Coolerra, All those places belonged to the great Cistercian Abbey of Boyle,[2] and had their common name from their common destination. In medieval Latin *grangia*—from which we have the English word *grange*, and the Irish *grainseach*, signifies a barn or corn farm belonging to religious;[3] and the

---

[1] Unusual thing, [Clachan ed.].

[2] In a Chancery Inquisition of James I., taken at Sligo, 8th April 1606, before Nicholas Brady, the jurors find that Tomultagh McDermot, late Abbot of the Monastery of Boyle, was seized of one quarter, called the Graung of Sleight Brian (in Coolerra), ... of another grangia with appurtenances, called the grandge of Sleight Teigh O'Hart, ... of the town of Grainge, in the barony of Corran, ... of another grange called Grangemor, in Tireragh ... and of one other grange, called Grangebeg, in the same barony.

And in an Inquisition concerning the possessions of Boyle Abbey, taken on the 12th May, 1604, the jurors find among the possessions, "Grangenamanagh and Templenamanagh, in McDonogh's country of Corran, Great and Little Grange in Dowd's country of Tireragh; a castle and eight cottages, with the appurtenances, in the town of Grange, of Coulkirrie (Coolerra); and a new castle built by Hugh O'Harte; and seven cottages in the town of Grange, in O'Connor Sligo's country". Inishmore or Church Island, Lough Gill, belonged to Grange Sleight Brian.

[3] "Originally a place where the rents and tithes, paid in grain to religions houses were deposited; from granum, grain".—Imperial Dictionary. Grangia.—Area seu locus ubi bladum, teritur; *aire tout lieu ou l'on bat le ble*. Praedium, villa rustica; *ferme metairie*. L. *Abbe Mignet*. Lexicon Mediae et Infimae Latinitatis.

granges of the county Sligo, as well as those of Roscommon and Leitrim, got the name from being places in which the monks of Boyle grew and collected and stored their grain. Other religious houses had similar places in the county, but it would appear that the term "grange" was confined to those of Boyle Abbey.

Carns-hill or Carns, which terminates the eastern extremity of Coolerra, though only 392 feet high, is a very picturesque elevation and not devoid of boldness when looked at from north, east, or south, on which sides the gradients are sharp; while, on the west side, the incline is so long and gentle, that the spectator hardly realizes the full height of the hill. Unlike Knocknarea, which is in great part naked rock, Carns is covered all round with verdure from the base to the summit—the slopes over the river and lake being equal in freshness and vividness to the richest stretches in the county.

A good part of the hill on the east and south sides is wooded, and the timber is fine and flourishing, owing, much more to the proximity of water than to the character of the soil, which is rather shallow and poor. Some time ago the trees, here and there, were so crowded that they hardly afforded one a passage between them, but the storm of October, 1883, which wrought such havoc in the woods and plantations of the county, raged so violently in spots around the hill, as to level everything before it, to tear away and toss about the heaviest trees—trunks, roots, and branches—with the fragments of rock in which they grew, and to leave nothing standing over considerable spaces. In hearing persons, who witnessed the scene, relate their impressions, one would think that no such convulsion visited the locality since that which shot the hill itself above the surrounding land.

The most interesting objects on the hill are the two carns, which have given it its name, and which rest like crowns on the two peaks into which it is divided by a deep hollow that runs from the direction of Sligo. These carns, when viewed from a distance, look somewhat like cones truncated near the base, and are composed of rather small stones which, as they are of the same gneiss formation as those that lie scattered over the rest of the peninsula, must have been gathered off the surrounding land, and not quarried from the underlying strata, which are limestone. History gives no information of the origin or object of the carns, but the Dinsenchus[1] tells that they mark the graves of Omra and Romra, two chiefs that ruled over the plain now submerged by Lough Gill, before that traditionally fair and

---

Grangia.—A grange, a farm-house.—Stubbs' Documents illustrative of English History.
[1] An ancient text related to Irish places, [Clachan ed.].

fertile region was covered by the lake.[1] "Whether the builders of the piles had so vulgar an object in view, as the clearance of the land for the benefit of their cattle, is not stated, but it is certain that the removal of the stones from the surface increased immensely the feeding powers of the tract. At all events the ground was swept so clear that hardly a pebble was left, so that while the farm fences of the rest of the peninsula are built with surface stones, not one of such can be seen in the miles of high walls with which the Ormsbys, about 150 years ago, surrounded and intersected Carns, nor in those which enclose, on either side, the noble avenue that leads down to Belvoir, the material employed being invariably quarried limestone.

Here, too, as in so many other places, the writer cannot accept present popular views. Though it seems to be just now the general opinion that the two circles of stone on the so-called Cairns-hill are sepulchral carns, it would appear to be far more probable, if not entirely certain, that they are the remains of cashels or stone forts. For, in the first place, they have not the usual conical shape of carns. Second, they are never called carns in our old writings. And, thirdly, there is no tradition of their origin, which, considering their conspicuous position, and the notice they must have always attracted, could hardly be the case if they were of a monumental character; for as the people have their opinions regarding the person buried under the neighbouring carn of Knocknarea, they would hardly fail to have a view, be it right or wrong, respecting those interred in these structures, if the erections were supposed, in times past, to be carns.

The writer's opinion is, that they were cashels or stone forts, erected for the protection of men and cattle, like the hundred similar enclosures of the neighbourhood, with ramparts, in some few cases, of stone, though generally of earth; and this opinion is pretty satisfactorily established by the names the structures receive in documents a couple of centuries old, as, for example, the inquisition taken at Roslee, in 1616, where the hill now named Cairns-hill, is called "Corlis", *i.e.*, the Hill of Forts; in the Book of Distribution, connected with the Acts of Settlement and Explanation,

---

[1] John O'Donovan, quoting the Dinsenchus in a letter to Thomas O'Connor, given in the Ordnance Survey Letter Book for County Sligo, and dated September 10th, 1836, says, "Romra and Omra lived on the plains which Lough Gill now covers", etc., etc.; but there is no need to trouble the reader with the details of this or other legends and myths connected with our lake. Legends and myths are very well in a way in their proper time and place, but they are *de trop* in regular history.

These carns stand due east and west of one another, and are about equal in size at the base, the circumference of the western one being 152 yards. The diameter at the top of the same pile is 30 yards. Owing to the trees that surround and close in the eastern carn, it is not easy to make out its exact dimensions. At the summit it is a little less in diameter than the other, but it appears somewhat higher owing to the unevenness of the ground on which it rests.

where, too, it gets the name "Corlish;" and in the Deed of Partition of the O'Connor Sligo estate, in which they are described as "Carnes, alias Badhuns", the latter word signifying cow forts. It is fair, then, to conclude that in 1616, and previously, as well as long subsequently, they were regarded simply as forts or lisses; and that, in 1687, the lawyers who drew up the Deed of Partition took them to be cow forts or *Badhuns*, "Carnes" being added as an alias name to indicate that the forts were constructed of stone and not of earth.

Independently of these historical reasons, which seem conclusive, simple inspection of the objects in question would show their nature. The eastern circle is so dilapidated, and so closed in by the surrounding trees, that it is impossible to get a correct idea of its dimensions, and one cannot be so sure about it; but the western one, with its rampart, ten or twelve feet high, its circumference at base of 456 feet, its diameter at top of ninety feet, and its well defined passage to the interior of the area, has still all the features of a fort or cashel, and can be nothing else, whatever new-fangled name it may please people to give it.

It is worthy of remark, too, that they are the only structures, on or round the hill, which could have served for *lisses* or forts; for, while the neighbouring tracts are studded with raths, there is not one on Cairns-hill, a fact which proves that those so-called carns served as raths, as there must have been enclosures for the cattle of the district here as in all the adjoining townlands.

Coming now to ecclesiastical arrangements, the peninsula was divided into the three parishes of St. John's, Kilmacowen, and Killaspugbrone. In the order of time Killaspugbrone came first; for the church, which developed later into a parish, was founded by St. Patrick, and was the first church built in Carbury. The saint gave it in charge to his disciple Bronus, from whom it took the name, it has borne since, of Killaspugbrone, that is, the church of Bishop Bronus.

This Bronus, who is one of the best known of St. Patrick's disciples, and who received marks of special affection from the saint, contributed largely to the propagation of the faith in the county Sligo, not only by making Killaspugbrone a centre of religion for the neighbourhood, but also by consecrating Carellus bishop of Tawnagh, and Maneus bishop of Tirerrill.[1] From the Annotations of Tirechan, it appears that Bronus was a native of Coolerra, being the son of Icnus, chief of the district.[2] Colgau

---

[1] Carellum quem in episcopum ordinarunt Patricius, Bronus, et Bitaeus.—Colgan Trias Thaumaturga, p. 135. Maneum quem ordinavit episcopus Bronus, filius ignis, qui est in Caissel-irra, servus Dei, socius Sancti Patricii.—Id., p. 134.

[2] Venit in Muiriscsain apud Bronum filium Icni. . . Et venerunt trans littus Authuili in fines Icni.- *Irish Antiquarian Researches*, Vol. II., p. xxxi.

supposes the father of the saint to have been called Ignis (fire), and is at a loss to account for the name; but as Icnus, not Ignis, is the true reading, the difficulty disappears.

As Coolerra as well as the rest of Lower Sligo belonged at that time to Tireragh, Saint Patrick found it easy to get a site and endowment for the church, being then on the friendliest terms with the sons of Awley, whom he had just converted, and who, as the chief rulers of the whole territory of Tireragh, had the disposal of Coolerra; and it was all the easier for him to obtain what he wanted in this instance, as he intended to set the son of the local chief over the new foundation.

It is important to recollect the dependence of Lower Sligo on the chiefs of Tireragh, as modern writers, whether from ignorance or inadvertence, are all silent upon the subject. And this dependence related to ecclesiastical as well as to temporal affairs. Such is the want of knowledge on this matter that the reader will be probably surprised to be told, that the great district of Carbury, which is now, and has been for centuries so important a part of the diocese of Elphin, belonged at first, and for a considerable time, to the diocese of Killala. According to the synod of Rathbreasail, which was held in 1118, and which fixed or sanctioned the limits of the dioceses of Ireland, Killala extended from Nephin to Easroe, and from Cill-Ard-Bile to Srah-an-Fearainn. Nephin and Easroe or Assaroe, at Ballyshannon, being well known, there can be no doubt about the intermediate stretch, including Carbury, as well as the remainder of the sea coast, lying between the mouths of the Moy and the Erne. Cill-Ard-Bile and Srah-an-Fearainn have not been identified, but the writer is satisfied that Cill-Ard-Bile stood on the promontory of Ardelly in Erris, and that Srah-an-Fearainn is the Shramore of Union Wood, which lies in the Tirerrill portion of the parish of Ballysadare.[1]

There is no proof that any of Bronus' successors was a bishop, but it is not unlikely that such was the case, as before the synod of Rathbreasail, which effected a large reduction in the number of Irish bishops, "almost every distinguished church in Ireland had its bishop".[2] Though St. Biteus, who was a bishop, is spoken of as of Caissel-Irra,[3] it is much more probable that he lived there in community with Bronus, than that he was, as some would have it, his successor; for Bronus reached a very advanced old age, having lived long with Saint Patrick, and, after surviving him, having been much with Saint Brigid.[4] When writers speak of the "diocese" of

---

[1] See ... [*sic* - original footnote?, Clachan ed.].
[2] Rev. Matthew Kelly, in *Cambrensis Eversus*, Vol. 11, p. 385.
[3] Colgan Trias Thaum,, p. 136.
[4] Idem, Septima Vita, par. 2, c. 42, 43, 52, 96. And Ultan's Life of St. Bridget, c. 39, 40, 41, etc.

Killaspugbrone, they contemplate a state of diocesan jurisdiction, which probably had no existence at the time, nor for some centuries later. Two references to Killaspugbrone are found in the Four Masters:—one under the year 511, which states that "St. Bron, bishop of Cuil-Irra, in Connaught, died on the eighth day of the month of June", and another under 1306, telling that Peter O'Tuathalain, Vicar of Killaspugbrone, died; and if we add to those entries what we learn from the list of Parish Priests, registered at Sligo in 1704, namely, that John Dugan was then Parish Priest of Killaspugbrone, we have, perhaps, all the information that history affords regarding the succession of rulers in that church.

A relic, or alleged relic of this church claims a word of notice. We read in the Vita Tripartita,[1] that one of St. Patrick's teeth having fallen out of his mouth at Caissel Irra, the saint gave it to Bronus as a mark of special affection. In after time this object, not unnaturally, was held in esteem at Killaspugbrone; and in the fourteenth century, one of the Berminghams, Lords of Athenry, whose family was then connected by property with Ballysadare and Tireragh,[2] had made for it a brass case, elaborately ornamented with gold and silver relievo work.[3] Through time, the case with its contents fell into lay hands, and after having been "the most venerated relic in Connaught",[4] was often degraded, for lucre sake, by its new keepers to the vilest uses. These abuses continued, till a zealous priest, the abbot of Cong, found a way to obtain the relic, and put an end to the scandal.

Without agreeing with Dr. Petrie, who thinks, apparently on insufficient grounds, that the present ruin "may be well supposed to be the original structure erected for Bishop Bronus, by St. Patrick, in the fifth century",[5] one may go so far as to refer it to about the eleventh century, but hardly to an earlier date. It was built, it is said, in a cashel called Caissel Irra, the western cashel, because it stood on the most western part of the spit of land, which runs away from Knocknarea westward into the sea. From the particular mention of the cashel, this structure must have been anterior to the church, for if it were erected at the same time as the church, or subsequently, there would be nothing unusual in the circumstance, as "each

---

[1] "He gave a tooth out of his mouth to Bishop Bronus, because he was dear to Patrick".—Colgan, Vit. Trip., 142.
[2] Ballysadare and Kilvarnet, p. 255.
[3] "The Thomas de Bramingham, at whose expense this case was ornamented, was either sixth baron of Athenry, who flourished in the early part of the fourteenth century, or Thomas, the eighth baron, who died in 1374, or 1376".—Life of Petrie, p. 289.
[4] "In an ancient account of Connaught in my possession, the Fiachal Phadruigh is spoken of as the most venerated relic in the province".—Dr. Petrie, in Stokes' *Life of George Petrie*, LL. D., p. 290.
[5] Inquiry into the Origin and Uses of the Round Towers of Ireland, p. 178.

of the most celebrated churches of Ireland was surrounded by a wall in the eleventh century".[1]

No remains of the cashel are now visible; but Mr. O'Connor, in the Ordnance Survey Letter Book for the county Sligo, quotes Father Conolly, a former curate of the parish, as saying that "the cashel was visible the last time he attended funerals there". The structure, however, may be still *in situ*, though no longer visible, as from twenty to thirty feet of drifted sand are now accumulated over the place on which it lay. Only for the pains taken in recent years to keep away the sand by planting bent along the shore, the walls of the church, as well as the cashel, would have long since disappeared from view. A characteristic feature of this church is an open in the western gable, which stands several feet from the ground, and which must have served for an entrance, at a time when there was no other door in the edifice. A similar open is found in Ballysadare old church, and also in a church at Dungiven, in the county Derry,[2] but in no other church in Ireland, as far as the writer knows.

Kilmacowen—the church of the sons of Owen—is so called from the sons of Owen or Eugenius, a Munster chieftain. This Eugenius had six sons, whose names were Becanus, Culenus, Eminus, Diermitius, Cormac, and Broedan; and the whole six devoted themselves to the religious life in different parts of Ireland, Two of them remained in Munster, one passed to Leinster, another to Ulster, and two came to Connaught, Cormac and Diermitius, or Diarmaid. While Cormac fixed his abode near the mouth of the Moy, Diarmaid settled in Coolerra. And, here again, we meet with the dependence of Carbury on Tireragh, for it was one of the Tireragh chiefs, named Dubh Flann, or Flann Dubh, who granted Diarmaid a site and endowment for a religious house. No doubt, Dunflin, in the parish of Skreen, has its name from this chief.

The endowment was a noble one, as it took in the whole of the present parish of Kilmacowen, the limits of the grant, as detailed in Colgan's Life of St. Cormac, coinciding exactly with the existing limits of that parish. For it stretched, we are told,[3] from Droiched Martra (bridge of Ballydrehid) to Brugh Chinnslebhe (Seafield), and from Murbhuch de Rosbirn (marsh of Kelly's Town) to Aill-choidhin (mearing stone or flag at Barnasrahy). Diarmaid's church was at first called the church of Rosredheadh, but from Diarmaid's inhabiting it, and having with him, for a time, some of his brothers, it came, after a little, to be called the Church of the Sons of Owen.

---

[1] Fragment of old writing quoted in Miss Stokes' Early Christian Architecture in Ireland, p. 108.
[2] *Ulster Journal of Archaeology*, Vol. I., p. 306—Ballysadare and Kilvarnet, p. 22.
[3] Consecravit namque illi ecclesiae dotantae totum tractum, qui inter *Droiche-l Martra, et Brugh-chinnslebhe* versus occidentem et a Murbhuch de Rosbirne usque ad *Aill choidhin* interjacet.

How long the religious retained the endowment there is no means now of knowing; but they must have lost the whole, or a large part of it, before the middle of the thirteenth century; for, in 1239, we find Lasarina, the daughter of Cathal Crovderg O'Conor, and the wife of Donnell More O'Donnell, in possession of Rosbirn, or Rosborn, as a part of her dowry, and giving it, as an offering in honour of the Holy Trinity and the Virgin Mary, to Clarus MacMailin and the Canons of Lough Ce.[1] Whether the religious of Boyle retained in the sixteenth century any beneficial interest in the lands they formerly owned in the peninsula does not appear, but it is certain they did not occupy those lands at that period. As O'Donnell ousted the religious of Kilmacowen, so the O'Connors, in turn, took away, either in whole, or in part, from the monks of Trinity Abbey, what the O'Donnells had given; for we find the family of Brian O'Connor in possession of the district in the sixteenth century.

And this may be a suitable place to notice a rather important error or two into which O'Donovan and other writers have fallen, with regard to this family of Brian O'Connor and their peculiar patrimony. These writers take *sliocht Brian* to signify the descendants of Brian *Luignech* O'Connor, and, consequently, to include all the branches into which the entire O'Connor Sligo family divided. And they take the patrimony or territory of *sliocht Brian* to be Grange, in the parish of Ahamlish: "a small village", to use the words of O'Donovan,[2] "in the barony of Carbury, eight miles to the north of the town of Sligo".

In both suppositions they are in error, The *sliocht Brian* means, not the descendants of *Brian Luighnech*, the head of all the O'Connors Sligo, but the descendants of *Brian, the son of Donnell*. This Donnell, who died in 1395, came to be regarded as a second founder of the O'Connor Sligo family; and the Four Masters tell us[3] that, from his time to 1536, the chief of the family was styled MacDonnell Mic Murtough.

Donnell had four sons—Murtough Baccagh, Brian, Owen, and Turlough Carragh—each of whom ruled in succession over O'Connor Sligo's country, and left descendants who constituted four great branches of the O'Connor Sligo family, and were distinguished from one another by the name of their respective ancestor, as *Sliocht Murtough Baccagh, Sliocht Brian, Sliocht Owen, and Sliocht Turlough Carragh*. And this was not only their popular style and title, but their official designation as well, for Perrot's indenture of composition with the Sligo chiefs mentions them as "Sleight

---

[1] Lasarina, daughter of Cathal Crovderg O'Conor and the wife of O'Donnell, gave half a townland of her marriage dowry, viz., Rosbirn, to Clarus MacMailin and the Canons of Trinity Island, in honour of the Trinity and the Virgin Mary.—*Four Masters*.
[2] Annals of the Four Masters, 1526.
[3] Sub anno 1536.

Owyne O'Connor", "Sleight *Moryertaghe backaghe* O'Connor", "*Sleight Briene* O'Connor", and "Sleight *Tirrellagh Carraghe* O'Connor". It is clear then that O'Donovan and his copyists were napping when they confounded the Brian of *Sleicht Brian* with Brian Luighnech.

And they were equally mistaken with regard to the Grange in question, which was not that of Lower Carbury, as they supposed, but the Grange of Coolerra, or Knocknarea; for the Grange of Lower Carbury is called in the Inquisitions,[1] Grange Muinter Hart, or Grange Teige O'Hart, while the other is styled Grange Sliocht Brian of Coulirrie (Coolerra). Even O'Donovan's own Four Masters would have enabled him to avoid the mistake; for they show, under the year 1536, that it was only after O'Donnell, when coming from the north, had passed the *fearsat* of Sligo, "he proceeded into the country of the descendants of Brian O'Connor;" from which it follows that the district below the fearsat, or in Lower Carbury, was no part of that country. The "Owyne O'Connor of the Grawndge", then, who is given as one of the signatories of Perrot's indenture, belonged to the *Sliocht Brian* branch of the O'Connors, and lived "in the castle of the town of Grange of Coulirrie", and not in the Grange of Lower Carbury, as has been supposed. This correction is important in regard not only to the topography, but also to the history, both of Kilmacowen and Ahamlish.

If the O'Connors dispossessed the religious, they were dispossessed in due time themselves. Owen O'Connor's sons and others of the family having risen against the Government, and having been slain in rebellion, their lands fell at once to the disposal of the monarch; for the finding, by an inquisition, of "slain in rebellion", was itself an attainder in law in Ireland, dispensing with the tedious processes of formal outlawry. The lands in question were granted in the eleventh year of James I. to Captain John Baxter, who had been repeatedly recommended by Chichester to Salisbury for some such favour. In answer to those recommendations Salisbury directed that Baxter should receive a grant out of such "concealed" lands as he should himself "discover".

Set thus to work, the Captain soon found what he wanted, and after some formal proceedings, received a grant of many of his "discoveries", others of them being reserved for other favourites, though the modest Baxter applied for all, namely, "The rectories of Skreen and Castleconnor; the lands of Callo McOwen O'Connor; Kilmacteige; Aghenagh; the lands

---

[1] See the inquisitions regarding the possessions of Boyle Abbey, taken in 1604, and 1606, already quoted.
See also the inquisition taken at Roslee, on the 29th December, 1616, before Brian McDougH of Collooney, and other jurors, which finds that Sir John King, Knight, is seized as of fee, in right of the late dissolved monastery of Boile, of Grangagh Muinter Hart, 1 quarter, and Grangenamanagh, *alias* Grangagh Sliocht Brien, 4 quarters.

of Callo McCaher O'Connor; the two Rosses McKenertyne, Killaspugbrone; Ballybeolan; Ballyconnell; Ballygilgan; and the quarter of Drumcliffe; all in the county of Sligo", with other possessions situated elsewhere. Soon got, soon gone; and we find that no Baxter inherited, at the Restoration, any of the various lands which Captain John received from King James, and which his heir, Gerald Baxter, owned in 1641, the lands going to different new owners:—Bruy, to Cornet Cooper; Drynaglan and the Granges, to Anthony Ormsby and Henry Nicholson; and Bunsruhan, Oyster Island, Coney Island, etc., to Earl of Strafford.

The Carns end of Cuil Irra, having previously passed by mortgage from the O'Connors to the Crean family, passed away from the latter at the Restoration, and was granted, for the most part, to the Ormsbys. This fortunate family are said to have possessed a wide belt of land, stretching the whole length of the peninsula, from the sea to the lake, so that the avenue that still passes over Carns Hill on to the ruins of their mansion at Belvoir, would have then extended westward all the way to the Granges, and have been for extent, and the noble prospect it commanded, one of the finest avenues in Ireland.

As in the case of nearly all the ancient churches of Ireland, so also in the case of Kilmacowen, those who selected the site showed an appreciation of the picturesque, for the spot commands a good view of the sea, of the Ox mountains, and of much of the country lying beyond them. Nor was the church as much exposed to the storm as one might think, considering its situation on the side of a hill, for it reposes in the centre of little hillocks, which, though of no great elevation, are sufficiently high to protect it from the winds. As it stands at present, in the midst of those elevations, and encircled by the lines of trees, which the taste and zeal of Father Quinn, when curate in the parish, planted round it, it has the look of a bird's nest, placed by the instinct of its builder as far as possible out of harm's way.

It may be taken for certain, that the church, of which the walls remain, was not built so early as the time of the sons of Owen, who lived in the sixth century; and, judging by the size and style, it was probably erected between the twelfth and fifteenth centuries. The eastern gable, a considerable fragment of the south sidewall, and a lesser fragment of the north one, are all that survive of the work. The sidewalls were sixty-eight feet long, and two feet ten inches thick; and the gables were of the same thickness, and twenty-seven feet wide, exterior measurement. The sanctuary window is of the lancet kind, is formed of ten sand stones, five each side, and is five feet high, and four inches wide, splaying on the interior face of wall, to six feet. In the south sidewall, within three feet of eastern gable, there is a small window splaying to four feet ten inches on the inside.

Under this window there is a *piscina* nineteen inches square, and in the gable, on the epistle side, another recess of about the same size. A fragment, that still remains, shows there was a large arch in the south sidewall, from which we may infer, that a transept was attached on that side to the church, something like the transept of Sligo Abbey.

It is likely that this church is a later erection than Temple Bree (*recte, Tempul na brugh*), or *Cillen na Brugh*, as it is sometimes called. Misled by the word Temple, some think that this house belonged to the Templars, but there is no probability in the opinion, for Temple or Tempul, from the Latin *templum*, signifies merely a church, without any reference to the Templars. As this very old church, of which only a few feet of a gable remains, stood on the ground, which was given as an endowment by the Tireragh chief to the sons of Owen, there is reason to think that it was the first church built by them; and, very probably, it was only after it was disused or became inconvenient to the people, the church of Kilmacowen was erected. It may be in this way we should understand what is stated in the life of St. Cormac, that the name of the church founded by the sons of Owen, which at first was called the church of *Rosredheadh*, was changed in the course of time to Kilmacowen—a change intelligible enough if there were two churches, but not so easy to understand, if there was question of only one and the same structure.

Kilmacowen is the principal burying place for the people of Coolerra, Catholic and Protestant; and for a country churchyard, the monuments show considerable taste: The chief names on them are:— Brown, Atkinson, Allen, Boland, Connolly, Tighe, Hargadon, Killawee, and Walsh.

There are several holy wells in Coolerra—one, within about a hundred feet of the church of Kilmacowen, named after St. Patrick, and having over it a large stone, which, according to the country people, bears the print of the Saint's knee, and is still coloured with the blood drawn from the bare knee by the hard stone; a second, Tubber Padraig, in the townland of Scardan-beg; a third, our Lady's Well in the same townland; and a fourth, in Scardan-more, called St. Brigid's "Well. There is reason to think that St. Brigid, in her travels through Connaught, visited this district, for Colgan tells us, that she is the patron Saint of the parish of Kilmacowen, a circumstance which the well just mentioned goes to confirm.

The last Parish Priests of Kilmacowen, of whom there is any record, were Rev. John Dugan, who resided at Kilmacowen, and was Parish Priest both of Kilmacowen and Killaspugbrone; and Rev. John McDonnah, living in 1712, who was Parish Priest of the same parishes, after Father Dugan. Those two churches were no doubt in ruins in the days of Father Dugan and Father McDonnah, who were obliged, like nearly all the priests of the time, to officiate in the open air. As far as appears, they used to say Mass at a rock which stood on or near the site of the present chapel of Ransborough, and which was the ordinary meeting place of the priest and congregation in those evil days selected, no doubt, because it commanded an extensive view all round, and enabled those who were on the watch to descry the priest-catchers while they were still miles away. This spot is referred to in the Depositions taken by Sligo magistrates in 1711-'12, and given in a preceding page.

Old people tell that the place got the name of Ransborough from a wren (*Hibernica drean*) which had its nest in a hole of the, rock, and which flew in and out occasionally, even while the priest and people were at their devotions.

On this spot, as soon as the state of the country allowed it, the Catholics ran up a little chapel, and covered it with thatch, which rested on a roof constructed of the ribs of a whale, instead of timbers; and it was in this wretched hut, which was patched and stayed from time to time to keep it from falling, and in which, under the ribs of the whale, the persecuted worshippers must have felt themselves almost as straitened as Jonas in the whale's belly, that the inhabitants of Kilmacowen and Killaspugbrone heard Mass on Sundays and holidays, down to about sixty years ago, when Father O'Callaghan built the present church which was greatly improved by Father Andrew Quinn, when curate of St. John's.

CHAPTER XVIII

PARISH OF CALRY

CALRY parish, which stretches, partly, along, the north shore of Lough Gill, and, partly, along the right bank of the Sligo river, has its name from the old district of Calrigia, though it is less extensive than that district, which took in Drumlias and some other portions of the county Leitrim.[1] The parish has been sometime called Callgach, and is so-called in the county Sligo Survey of 1633, but the popular designation seems to have been always, as it now is, Calry, the English form of Calraidhe,—composed of *Cal*, a man's name, and *raidhe*, descendants[2]—the term signifying the descendants of Cal, who was grand-uncle of Maccon, though in the course of time, it came to express as well the districts occupied by those descendants.

There were several places of the name in Ireland, as Calry-an-Chala in Westmeath; Calry-Moy-Heleog in Mayo; and the county Sligo Calry. The name, when applied to the Sligo district, was qualified with additions at different times; being called in the Book of Armagh,[3] Calry-Tremaige; in the Topographical poem of Giolla Iosa Mor Mac Firbis,[4] Calry Laithim; and, in the Four Masters, Calry, Lough Gill, at one time,[5] and Calry Drumcliff at another.[6] There is good reason also for taking it to be the Calry de Culechernadan of the *Vita Tripartita*;[7] and the Calry Aelmhaighe of the Four Masters,[8] though the authority of O'Donovan may be adduced against the identity in both cases. Of Calry de Culechernadan he writes, "This is now Coolcarney, a district in the barony of Gallen, and county of Mayo, comprising the parishes of Attymass and Kilgarvan;[9] and of Calry

---

[1] Reversus est denuo Patricius ad jam memoratam *Calrigice*, regionem, et in loco, tunc *Druimdaire* vocato, baptizavit Mac-caerthanum, et in eo excitavit Monasterium *Druzm-lias*.—Patrick came back again to the aforesaid region of Calry, and, in a spot then called Drumdare, he baptized Maccarthan, and erected the monastery of Drumlias. Colgan.—Trias Thaumaturga, p. 143.

[2] Dr. Joyce's Irish Names of Places. First Series, p. 115.

[3] Et exiit ad regiones *Callrigi Tremaige* et fecit ecclesiam juxta Drumlias. He went out to the districts of *Callrigi Tremaige*, and constructed a church at Drumlias.—Betham's Irish Antiquarian Researches. Part II., p. xxxiii.

[4] Tribes and Customs of Hy Fiachrach, p. 277.

[5] Four Masters, A.D. 1251.

[6] Four Masters, 1252.

[7] Patricio Connacuae circuitum ad exitum prope ducenti et transeunti occurrerunt viri Calregiae de Culechernadan.—As Patrick was bringing his tour through Connaught to a close, some men of Calry de Culechernadan came before him.—Trias Thaum., p. 143.

[8] A.M. 3790; A.D. 781.

[9] Tribes and Customs of Hy Fiachrach, 471.

Aelmhaighe he says, "This sept of the Calraighe was probably that otherwise called Calraighe-an-Chala, and seated in the barony of Clonlonan, and county of Westmeath".

The writer's reasons for differing from O'Donovan, and identifying those two places with the Calry of Sligo, are:—with regard to Calry de Culechernadan: first, that it is mentioned in connection with the saint's last acts in Connaught, which acts certainly occurred in the district of Sligo; second, the authority of Colgan, who describes the place as a *"regiuncula prope Sligeach"*, a little tract near Sligo; and third, the authority of Dr. Lanigan, who observes of it, "This district must, besides a part of Sligo, have comprehended some part of the present county Leitrim".[1] These authorities are decisive.

And as to Calry Aelmagh, the writer would rest his contention on the passage from the Book of Armagh, of which a portion has been already quoted, and which runs thus in its completeness: "Et exiit ad regiones de Callrigi Tremaige et fecit ecclesiam juxta Drumleas, et baptizavit multos et erexit ad campum *Ailmaige* et fundavit ecclesiam ibi, id est, *Domnach Ailmaige* quia Patricius illic mansit tribus diebus et tribus noctibus".—And he went out to the districts Callrigi Tremaige, and constructed a church at Drumlias, and baptized many, and erected and founded a church at the plain of Ailmaige, that is, *Domnach Ailmaige*, for Patrick remained there three days and three nights. The Ailmaige of this passage, and the Aelmagh of the Four Masters, are plainly one and the same place, and consequently Aelmagh must be somewhere in Calry-Sligo, and not, as 'Donovan would have it, in Calry-an-Chala.

Calry is at least equal in beauty to any of the other environs of Sligo. Coologeoboy and Cashelgal mountains in the back ground; Lough Gill full in front; the whole space between the mountains and the lake parted into green sward, cultivated fields, and wooded tracts, varied with the little lakes of Colgach and Lougheneltin; the fine mansions of Hazelwood, Cloghereva, and Holywell; the handsome residences of Ballyglass and Rosslare; the neat gate lodges and labourers' cottages of Mr. Wynne; and the several comfortable farm-houses which stand out in prominent and picturesque positions over the district; with all these advantages, Calry lacks hardly a single element of the beautiful and the striking in landscape scenery. The ground slopes all the way from the mountains to Lough Gill, the gradients, however, increasing sharply as you near the mountain, so that within a mile or so of the base, the roads are in places so steep and abrupt, as to make it no easy matter for vehicles to ascend or descend.

The views from Calry are very fine, expanding as you mount, but losing in distinctness of object and vividness of colouring, what they gain

---

[1] Ecclesiastical History of Ireland, Vol. I., p. 257.

in extent. About half way up the slope you get the most satisfying prospect; for while you have then under the eye,—a large extent of country stretching from the sea to the Leitrim mountains, and from your stand-point to the Slieve-da-En, and Slieve Gamh ranges—you are still near enough to escape all sense of confusion or crowding in the objects, to realize the undulations of the surface, the outlines and extent of groves and lands, and the well rounded contours of Knocknarea and Carns, and to perceive and appreciate the various and ever varying shades of the landscape from the bare rock and purple heath of Knocknarea, to the rich, soft, and shining green of Belvoir and Tawnaphubble.

The most charming, as well as the most historical spot in Calry, is Hazel wood. It is only about 160 years ago it began to be so called, the old name being Annagh; but it is plain, that Annagh comprised a larger area than Hazelwood now does, and that it took in Willowbrook; for we find Francis Ormsby of that place, who was High Sheriff of the county in 1715, calling his residence Annagh. Indeed there is good proof that the whole parish of Calry went occasionally by the name of Annagh, for, in the Commonwealth Census of 1659, it is so designated.

It is the common opinion, shared too by O'Donovan, and, apparently, by the Four Masters, that Annagh had its name from being "boggy" land; but this would seem to be a mistaken opinion, without any foundation in the qualities of the soil, which is less boggy, and more sandy, than most of the county. In the Irish language there are two words of much the same sound—*eanaigh*, a marsh or bog, and *aenagh* or *aonagh*, a meeting or place of meeting; and it was, no doubt, by confounding one word with the other, that the old name of Hazelwood was supposed to be *eanaigh*; though the following stanza, in the celebrated poem of Giolla Iosa Mor Mac Firbis, who, as living in the neighbourhood, must be accepted as a decisive authority, proves clearly enough the old name to be *aenach*, a meeting or place of meeting:—

> *Callraidi Laithim na lann*
> *O'Nuadhan fuair afearrann,*
> *Fonn braenac gainmidi glan*
> *Aenac ainglidi, idan.*

> *Of Callraidhe Laithim of the swords*
> *O'Nuadhan obtained the land*
> *A droppy, sandy, fine land*
> *An angelic pure place of meetings.*

If confirmation of this proof were needed, it would be found in the old Irish life of Saint Ceallach, bishop of Kilmore Moy, where our Annagh is mentioned as Aenach Locha Gile.

Tourists of taste, after visiting the most picturesque places in Ireland declare that Hazel wood is, at least, fully equal in beauty to the most charming spots found in other parts of the country. While it is at present, as it stretches away from the suburbs of Sligo to beyond Holywell, one of the largest demesnes we have, it is still more remarkable for its beauty of outline, of colour, and of cultivation, than for its extent. The prevailing contour lines are gentle curves, with here and there some bold concave sweeps and level stretches; the colour of everything that meets the eye is exceptionally soft and rich, owing to the waters of the lake and river; and the cultivation, first, in laying out the landscape, and, next, in filling it in, or furnishing it, is plainly the outcome of unstinted outlay and exquisite taste.

Though the residence may not be equal in massiveness to some more modern mansions, it is still a very stately and graceful structure. It is built of cut and polished limestone, in the Italian style, with a bold four-story front façade, and two lateral curving wings, after the manner of a peristyle, reminding those who have seen prints of Edmund Burke's house at Beaconsfield, of that fine building. The hall door is reached by a noble flight of stone steps landing on a spacious platform, which commands a good view of the Leitrim and north Sligo mountains. A secondary front, rising from a fine terrace, looks to the south; and the area, running from the terrace to the lake, is divided between an open lawn and shady groves, in which are provided charming retreats for saunterers, including a cane house, a rock house, a shell house, and a curious chair of state, constructed of materials rarely found in these latitudes, the bones of the whale.

The part of the demesne on which this mansion stands is a cape which runs well into Lough Gill, and which is covered with trees and shrubs of a fresher and livelier hue than may be seen in any other part of Carbury. The arbutus lives and thrives in this favoured spot, and so flourishes as to attract the notice and admiration of the spectator, even amid the great variety of laurels, hollys, bays, and other evergreens, as well indigenous as exotic, in which the place abounds. This plant may be seen not only from the walks of the grounds, but to, perhaps, still greater advantage, from the water, where the curious, who frequent the lake at different seasons, may observe in the specimens that rise from the water's edge, the successive stages of vegetation through which the arbutus passes; first, the blossoms of clustering little white bells, and then the strawberry fruit, changing from green to yellow, and, about November, from yellow to scarlet, thus imparting to winter the warm colouring of spring.

The south front of the house commands the finest views of Lough Gill. With the exception of one or two small patches, the whole sheet of water, with all its islands and islets, and with almost every perch of its shores, falls at once under the eye of the spectator. In shape an oval or oblong, five or six miles long, and two or three broad, studded with islands varying in size from 41 acres to hardly a perch; closed in by shores that combine all the elements of the picturesque and the beautiful:—the towering, naked, rugged, rocks of *Slieve da En*; the timbered heights of Doonee, Rockwood, and Slishwood; the more gentle elevations of Shriff, rising up with all the regularity of an amphitheatre over the "smiling valley" which Moore has made famous; the shining verdant slopes of Holywell; the groves and lawns, the parterres and pleasure grounds of Hazelwood; the stately hill of Carns, with its two mysterious mounds, looking like watch towers for the guardians of the lake with these features and surroundings, Lough Gill is second in beauty to no lake in the three kingdoms, not excepting even our own Killarney. There are some, however, who think the prospect would be improved by more and higher mountains, but this, instead of a perfection, would be a fatal blemish, and would mar all the beauty of the scene by changing the Bright Lake (the literal meaning of Lough Gill,) into a second Avernus, or, to take the illustration from our own country, into that

— *"lake whose gloomy shore*
Skylark never warbles o'er"[1].

Without being crowded, Lough Gill is fully furnished with islands, most of them circular in form and covered with strong timber or brushwood. The two largest are Church Island and Cottage Island, each containing remains of ecclesiastical buildings. A Chancery inquisition of James I., taken at Sligo on the 3rd of September, 1612, before Geoffrey Osbaldeston and Nicholas Brady, informs us that Cottage Island, which was then called O'Gilleghan's Island, as it is now often called Gallagher's Island, was parcel of the church of Killross, which belonged itself to Trinity Abbey in Lough Ce, and passed, by royal grant, with the other possessions of that abbey, to Robert Harrison, and some years later, by purchase, to John Crofton. Church Island, *Hibernice* Inis Mor, must have belonged formerly to the O'Rorkes, as their annalists and followers, the O'Curnins, were in possession of it in 1416, when "The church of Inis Mor, in Lough

---

[1] From, *'Glendalough, By That Lake Whose Gloomy Shore'*, Thomas Moore (1779–1852), [Clachan ed.].

Gill was burned; and Screaptra O'Cumin, and the Leabhar Gearr of the O'Curnins, as well as many other precious articles were burned also".[1]

This occurrence was a great loss to the whole country, but to Sligo and the neighbourhood it was an irreparable disaster, as much of the materials for local history must have perished in the fire. O'Donovan declares himself unable "to determine what this book—the *leabhar ghear*—was", taking it to be some individual book, so named. But may not *leabhar ghear* have been a generic name for the journal in which current events were set down, while awaiting their final committal by the scribe of the monastery to the permanent record of the establishment? This conjecture derives some probability from the fact that we meet in the Four Masters, with another *leabhar ghear*, which could not be the book of the O'Curnins, that having been lost in the fire. The other, "precious articles" consumed, comprised "goblets, a tympanum, and a harp".

The lake and its surroundings are hardly less interesting for the historian than for the lover of natural scenery, as containing distinctive memorials of the different stages through which the country has passed. The pre-historic ages are, according to many, represented by the monuments of Carns Hill and of the Deer Park; the pre-Norman period, by a considerable fragment of the castle from which Dervorgilla, the wife of O'Rorke, was taken away by Dermod McMurrough; the English Ascendancy by the strong places of the Villiers at Dromahair, the Parkes at Newtown, and the Ormsbys at Willowbrook and Belvoir; and later times by the mansions of the Whites, the Gethins, and the Wynnes.

Nor are the ecclesiastical memorials of the region less suggestive than the secular. The ruins of religious edifices on the islands remind us of those days of fervour, when our forefathers left all things, even the mainland, to follow Christ. The abbey of Sligo, at one end of the lake, and of Creevalea, at the other, are monuments of the cultivated taste as well as of the ardent piety of the men that built them. The rectory of St. John, Sligo, now, and for three hundred years, in the possession of those who appropriated it by force, is itself a standing witness of the spoliation; while the secluded wells of Tubberconnell, and of Tubbernailt, with their rude altars, are always there to tell how the robbed and banned Catholics, after turning away from the desecrated temple which they could not now enter without sacrificing faith, elected, as became the followers of Him who had not a place whereon to lay His head, to betake themselves to the desert and the mountain, and there expose themselves, like the divine Master, to the rage of the elements as well as to the vengeance of man. But, thank Heaven, these dreadful days are gone; and the houses of worship, which now occupy

---

[1] These particulars are added by O'Flaherty and O'Mulconny, who are both quoted by O'Donovan in his note under the year 1416.

and adorn the town of Sligo—the massive Cathedral, the elegant Dominican convent, the imposing Protestant church of Calry, and the neat and commodious churches or Meetinghouses of the Methodists, the Independents, and the Presbyterians, testify to the better times in which our lot is cast, and in which every man is free to believe and worship according to his conscience.

Tranquil as the lake looks ordinarily, it is very dangerous to those who move upon it in windy weather. Judging by the casualties of the last few years, the loss of life on the lake must have been heavy in the past. In 1876, at a regatta, a sailing boat, the Glana, engaged in the contest, went down with her crew of four men, when three of them, named respectively, Kilgallen, Gallagher, and Conway, lost their lives; in 1882, at a rowing match, two highly esteemed young men, Messrs. Reynolds and Patterson, were drowned by the swamping of their boat; and a third, Mr. Hudson, the only son of a widowed mother, would have been lost but for Mr. Wynne, who saved him, gallantly, at the risk of his own life; and on the 9th August, 1883, Thomas H. Corry, Esq., Lecturer on Botany in King's College, Cambridge, and Charles Dixon, Esq., Solicitor, both natives of Belfast, and both men of promise, more especially Mr. Corry, were drowned a little off Goat Island, under circumstances which entitle them to be regarded as martyrs of science, they being engaged at the moment in an endeavour to secure certain rare botanical specimens for the Royal Irish Academy.

And in times past, when the lake was more frequented, from the fact of two, at least, of the islands being then occupied by religious, and from Church Island, being, as is said, a burying place for the parish of Calry, those casualties must have been still more numerous, though they would not be recorded, unless in exceptional circumstances, as in the case mentioned in The *Annals of Loch Ce*, under the year 1561, where we read, "Naisse, the son of Cithruadh, the most eminent musician that was in Erin, was drowned on Loch-Gile; and his wife, the daughter of MacDonogh, and Athairne, the son of Matthew Glas; and the son of O'Duigenan, was a great loss".

As Naisse and his party were musical people the accident may have occurred at a regatta, or on some such pleasurable occasion. It is likely that those entertainments were discontinued soon after this time, owing to the disturbances of the times, and that they were not resumed for near three centuries later, when, according to the *Sligo Journal* of the day, a boat race came off on the 14th August, 1827, which, as the same paper states, was the first entertainment of the kind instituted in this part of Ireland. The journal records that the day passed off most agreeably, that vast crowds attended, that no accident whatever happened, and that every one was highly gratified. It is pleasant to be able to note, that the regattas of 1887 and 1888, like that held just half a century previous, were red letter days in respect to the presence of crowds, the absence of accidents, and the gratification of everybody.

There are great and frequent variations of depth in Lough Gill. From a report of the late Mr. E. Hardman, who received a grant of £15 from the Royal Irish Academy for making soundings in the lake, we learn, that a difference of thirty feet in depth is not uncommon in a distance of four hundred feet, and that the principal depths in the section sounded by him, are: "Between Cottage Island and Church Island, 65 feet; one mile from the latter, 96.8 feet; a little further on eastward, 97.6 and 99 feet, then 105 and 116 feet". This depth of 116 feet, which was the greatest found, lay more than a mile to the east end of Church Island, and one and three quarters mile from the east or Shriff end of lake. Anyone who passes from the Carrowroe direction, and observes the abrupt and deep breaks constantly recurring in the surface of the land, must be struck with the similarity of form there is in that surface and in the bottom of the lake, as this is ascertained by Mr. Hardman's soundings.

Under Celtic rule, which lasted in this part of the country down to Sir John Perrott's Composition with the Sligo chiefs in 1584, Annagh, or Hazelwood, belonged to the O'Connors Sligo, and to that branch of the family whose head-quarters was at Dunally. Murtough O'Connor, who was grandson of Turlough Carragh, and owner of the castle of Annagh, in 1533, being at war with O'Donnell, and falling into his hands, the northern chief offered to spare his life on condition of receiving surrender of the castle; but Murtough's sons, who held the fortress, refused to comply with the condition, even to save their father's life, and their father, in consequence, was hanged on the *faitche*, or green, before the castle.

The O'Connors still owned the place in the early years of the seventeenth century, for in the third year of James I., we find that monarch granting a general pardon to "Donnell McTeige Oge McTurlough Connor of Annagh", in the county Sligo. There are now no remains of the castle of Annagh, nor is its exact site known, but it stood somewhere on the slender peninsula which lies to the east of Hazelwood House, and which is still called Castle Point; as the adjoining inlet is still called Annagh Bay, in memory of the old name of Hazelwood.

From the O'Connors, Annagh passed, in the second decade of the seventeenth century, to Andrew Crean, first by mortgage, and later by royal grant. Together with Annagh, Crean obtained from the king other large possessions in the parishes of Calry and St. John; but his son John, who inherited them, lost all in the hurly-burly of 1641. At the Restoration, Annagh, with the rest of the O'Connor Sligo estate, was granted to Lord William Strafford and Thomas Radcliffe; in the Tripartite division of that estate, in the year 1687, most of the Strafford and Radcliffe grant in the parish of Calry fell to the lot of Thomas Wilson; and from Wilson, through an intermediary or two, it came to Mr. Owen Wynne, of Lurganboy, in the county Leitrim, the ancestor of the present owner.

The Wynne family is one of the most distinguished in the country. Omitting their history in Wales, where they always occupied a foremost place, they have been connected either by kindred or affinity, with the first names in Great Britain and Ireland. Owen Wynne, who was the first of the family that settled in the country, married Catherine, relict of Sir James Hamilton, and daughter of Claud Hamilton, second Baron of Strabane, by his wife, the Lady Sarah Gordon, a lady who got into great trouble by her marriage, after the death of her first husband, with the ill-fated Sir Phelim O'Neil.

The Hazelwood family have played an important part in public affairs, more especially in connection with the army. Captain James Wynne came over with Major-General Kirk, in that general's expedition to raise the siege of Derry, and was sent by him to Enniskillen as colonel of dragoons. The colonel distinguished himself at the battle of Newtown Butler, rose through time to the rank of Brigadier-General, and was killed at the battle of Malplaquet. Lieutenant-General Owen Wynne, brother to James, after rising to the first place in the army in Ireland, was sent by the Government in 1719 to Galway, to defend that city against an apprehended attack of the Spaniards. It was the Lieutenant-General that built Hazelwood house. He died in 1736, and was Commander-in-Chief in Ireland at the time of his death. In 1743 another member of the family, Colonel Wynne, was Governor of Galway. While thus distinguished in the army, they were hardly less conspicuous in civil life, several of them being members of the Privy Council, some filling the office of Custos Rotulorum[1], and some that of Governor of the county Sligo.

In their capacity of landlords and country gentlemen, they have been differently judged by different writers. Mr. Wakefield's estimate, for instance, of the present Mr. Wynne's grandfather, Mr. Owen Wynne, is very different from that of Mr. Inglis'. If Wakefield had a brief for praising that gentleman, he could hardly have been more eulogistic than he actually is, holding him forth as a model for general imitation under every respect as a landlord, as a lover of his country, as a man of business, as a magistrate, as a friend of the people. The following may be taken as a fair specimen of this writer's references to Mr. Owen Wynne:—"If a high and dignified sense of honour; inflexible integrity; close application to business; an ardent zeal for the interest of one's native country, displayed in cultivating its soil, and improving its inhabitants, can create esteem and respect, then ought this gentleman have a seat in Parliament, where the assistance of his talents

---

[1] Keeper of the Rolls, [Clachan ed.].

and experience, at this perilous time, might be of essential service, As a great landed proprietor, he spreads civilization around him by residing on his estate, and spending a princely income among his tenants; as a father in the bosom of a numerous and happy family, who respect and adore him, he sets an example which cannot fail of having a beneficial influence on his servants, neighbours, and dependents; as a magistrate, discharging the duties of that important office, with strict attention to impartial justice, he is enabled to repress disorder, and to maintain peace and tranquility".

So far so good; but now, on the fair dealing old principle of, *Audi alteram partem*,[1] let us hear what Mr. Inglis has got to say regarding the same Mr. Wynne. Far from endorsing Wakefield's character of him, he singles him out from the landlords of the county for special censure as a rack-renting and anti-Catholic proprietor. This is Inglis's delineation of Mr. Owen Wynne, and it is a curious pendant to the picture of Wakefield:—

"The land in the barony of Carbury, especially Mr. Wynne's, is let extremely high. Mr. Wynne's tenants are, with very few exceptions, in arrear; but he is one of those short-sighted landlords who is resolved at all costs to keep up the nominal amount of his rent-roll. His rents are taken in dribbles, in shillings and copper; and agents have been known to accompany tenants to market with their produce, lest any part of its value should escape the landlord's pocket. This gentleman has been at great pains to establish a Protestant tenantry on his estate; and in the appearance of their houses, etc., there is some neatness and some show of comfort; but these are not, in reality, in any better condition than the other tenantry. None of them are able to do more than barely to subsist; and they, as well as the Catholic tenantry, are generally in arrear, indeed I found no one exception".

These are weighty charges; and whatever may be said of the allegation of rack-renting, it will hardly be denied, by any one acquainted with the composition of the Hazel wood tenantry, that the owners of the estate, or those who served them as agents, have been exceptionally sectarian in the selection of tenants.

Apart from this one-sidedness, for which, probably, he is little accountable, the present owner of Hazelwood is a fair-minded and high-minded gentleman, able and willing, if occasion required, to make sacrifices for the neighbour, as his conduct at the Lough Gill regatta, of 1881, sufficiently proves. On that occasion, when John Patterson and J. Reynolds were drowned, Mr. Wynne, though alone in a slight punt, seeing Richard Hudson, the companion of the drowned men, fainting and sinking, paddled bravely to him, and, at the imminent risk of his own life, saved that of the drowning youth. What enhanced Mr. Wynne's conduct on the occasion, is, that the crew of a pair-oared boat, to whom he called to join him in saving Hudson, instead of responding to his appeal, and doing their duty, skulked cowardly away with their boat in another direction. The public were proud

---

[1] To hear the other side. [Latin,] a concept in Criminal Law that no person should be condemned unheard; it is akin to due process, [Clachan ed.].

of Mr. Wynne's heroic act, and the Jury, in the inquest on poor Patterson and Reynolds, added the following rider to their verdict:—"We unanimously return our most cordial thanks to Mr. Wynne for the manliness and courage he displayed in having, at the risk of his own life, rescued Mr. Hudson".

It is agreed, on all hands, that the ladies of the Hazelwood family have been conspicuous for the faithful and exemplary discharge of the duties incumbent on the high social station which they held in the neighbourhood. Though Lady Sarah, the wife of Mr. Owen Wynne, died so far back as 1833, the memory of her almsgiving and other charities is still fresh all round the parish of Calry; Lady Anne Wynne, her daughterin-law, and wife of the Right Honourable John Wynne, was equally devoted to the poor and miserable; and it was the Good Samaritan virtues, and the exquisite womanly sensibilities and sympathies, in regard to the suffering classes, of the late Mrs. Wynne—much more than any other circumstance connected with her beautiful life, or singularly sad death—which, on the day of her decease, 5th March, 1887, sent a thrill of sorrow through every household, high and low, in the county, and on the day of her funeral attracted after her honoured remains such crowds of rich and poor, Protestants and Catholics, as, up to that, were unparalleled in the county of Sligo for numbers and the feelings that swayed them, and are little likely to be paralleled there again, in these respects, for a long time to come.

The ORMSBYS are second to no family of the county in social standing. They came over from Lincolnshire. According to a pedigree of the Ormsby family, lately compiled by G. J. F. Fuller, Esq., F.S.A., the first of them that settled in Ireland was Thomas, who was a younger son of John, and who, passing to this country, in the time of Elizabeth, married a granddaughter of Sir Nicholas Malby. The eldest son of this marriage was Edmond, who was twice married: first, to Susanna Kelke, by whom he had Edward Ormsby, of Tobervadda in county Roscommon, Anthony Ormsby, of Pusgallen in county Roscommon, and Malby Ormsby, of Cloghan, county Mayo; and, second, to Elizabeth Newman, by whom he had issue John Ormsby, Moyvola, county Galway; Philip Ormsby, Annagh or Willowbrook, county Sligo; and Thomas Ormsby, Cummin, county Sligo. In this pedigree the son of Thomas Ormsby of Cummin, was Anthony, who figured, under the Commonwealth, as one of the Tituladoes of the county, and, at the Restoration, as a grantee under the Acts of Settlement and Explanation. According to others, Philip and Anthony were brothers; but, according to the late Mrs. Ormsby Gore, who was an accomplished genealogist, they were not blood relations at all—an opinion, however, which it is not easy to reconcile with their arriving in Ireland about the same time, and bearing the same, or nearly the same, arms.

Be this matter of genealogy as it may, Philip and Anthony fared pretty equally in the county Sligo under the Acts of Settlement and Explanation. Philip received, in the barony of Carbury, the lands of Bunluiny, Tawnaphubble, Leagh Carrowcrane, Faughts, Lismarkrea, Kilbride, Lisduff, Gowlane, and the island of Inismore, or Church Island; and, in the barony of Leyney, Carrownaworane, Cungell, Tober Tillehy, Tober Scardan, Cashel Loyne, Carrowkeale, and Carrownagarkefree, in all 2,629 statute acres, receiving, by the same grant, 10,238 statute acres in Leitrim and Longford. And by letters patent of the Court of Grace, he got Shriff and other denominations in the half barony of Coolavin.

Quarter Master Anthony Ormsby, after having been Titulado of Cargin under the Cromwellian regime, received from Charles II. Corlis and Cavan, part of Aghamore, Common, the two quarters of Scardan, called Lissanally and Rathanury, Drinahane, seven cartrons in Grange, some in Loughineltine, Coolsoder, Grogah, and Carrignagragh, Tullagbe, and Corbullige, part of Clogherbeg, and part of Cloghermore—in all 3,040 acres plantation measure.

Willowbrook House, the seat of Philip Ormsby's descendants, was built in or about 1730, from a design by the same architect that drew for Hazelwood and Hollybrook, and was in its day a striking mansion in itself, as well as picturesquely situated—commanding fine views of Lough Gill and the Sligo and Leitrim mountains. Owing to the great election contest between William Ormsby and Right Honourable Owen Wynne, which is described in another page, Willowbrook House was abandoned by its owners, and has not been since occupied by them, except for some short time that William Ormsby, Collector of Sligo, sojourned in it. Early in this century the place was let to a Mr. -------, who was supposed to be not only a solvent tenant, but, what was much more important in the circumstances, a careful one, in whose hands the valuable house would be as safe as in those of its immediate owners. Mr.------- , however, did not prove the faithful custodian that was expected, for he was no sooner installed in his sumptuous quarters than he put up a private still in the house, and took to the manufacture of poteen whiskey. It is not known how long he was engaged in the contraband business, which, no doubt, he would have continued much longer, only that one day the liquid, in some process it was passing through, got aflame and communicated the fire to the surrounding woodwork, with the result, that the whole house—fixtures, floors, and roof—was soon a pile of ashes, the fire leaving nothing standing but the bare walls, which are still there, and in their weird condition, serve to remind the passer-by of Mr. ------- and his doings in the family mansion of the Ormsbys.

This was not the first time that Willowbrook gained notoriety in connection with strong drinks. So early as 1809 a great stir was occasioned through the town of Sligo and the neighbourhood, by a burglary committed on the cellar there, which was known to be well stocked with wines and whiskeys. At that time Mr. Owen Phibbs, who was then sojourning for the winter on the Continent, tenanted the mansion; and as it was known that, before leaving, he had replenished his cellar, in order to have the contents well matured upon his return, some of the reckless characters, so common at the time, broke into and robbed the place. As might be expected, Mr. Phibbs felt strongly this injury to his purse and his palate, and, on coming home, published, in the *Sligo Journal*, the following advertisement:—

> "Whereas, during my late absence from home, the windows of my cellar at Willowbrook were broken open and a quantity of spirits stolen from there; I hereby offer a reward of £50 to any person who will prosecute to conviction the perpetrators of said offence.
> "Willowbrook, December 29th, 1809.
> "OWEN PHIBBS".

It is not likely that the guilty parties were discovered, for, if they were, we should probably have heard more of the case, it being, at the time, a hanging matter.

It is to be hoped that others had not as unpleasant experience of outrages as Mr. Owen Phibbs. Three years or so before this burglary, he was obliged to offer a reward of 50 guineas for the conviction of the perpetrator of the outrage mentioned in the following advertisement, which appeared in the Sligo Journal of November 21st, 1806:—

> "50 GUINEAS REWARD!
> "Whereas, on the night of Tuesday last, the 4th instant, a part of the wall of my Deer-Park, on the lands of Ardcumber in this county was levelled, and two of the Deer in the said Park shot. The above reward will be paid by me on prosecuting to conviction the Perpetrator or Perpetrators of so wanting (*sic*) an outrage.
> "Willowbrook, November 6th, 1806.
> "OWEN PHIBBS".

This may be a convenient place to mention that Sligo was one of the first counties in which illicit distillation came to be practised. Private stills were very numerous in the early part of this century throughout the north-west of Ireland. Wakefield tells that they were set up in places where they would be least expected, as in the kitchens of baronets and the stables of clergymen; and he might have added, in the stores of merchants, as happened in the case of Messrs. Scott and Patrickson, Sligo. An instance is given in the History of Ballysadare and Kilvarnet (page 244,) of the patronage the still received from clergymen of the county.

The means sometimes employed by the authorities to stop the practice only served to stimulate it. The fine of £50, levied on places in which a still was found, led to collusion between revenue officers and private distillers; the latter, by concert, leaving a still where the officers would find it, and the officers, paying over, in due time, half the £50 to their obliging accomplices. In many instances the revenue officer connived at private distillation, and his usual charge for doing so being well known, was paid more regularly than the taxes of the State or the rent of the landlord. In some districts poteen whiskey was sold as openly as if the dealer had a formal licence for the sale. The consequence of all this was, that the country was inundated with the beverage to such an extent that, if a traveller, going the road, called to a way-side house for a drink of water, he was pretty sure to receive it strongly fortified with *usquebaugh*.

Coming back from this little digression: The Willowbrook Ormsbys intermarried with the first families of the country; the Croftons of Moate, the Kings of Rockingham, the Gores of Lissadell and Mayo, the Frenchs of Frenchpark, and the Wynnes of Hazelwood. With the Wynnes they lived on terms of exceptional intimacy till the election contest of 1776 rendered them as hostile to each other as they had been before friendly—an hostility which lasted down to 1841, when the present Lord Harlech came forward, for the first time, as a candidate for the representation of the county Sligo, on which occasion, Mr. Owen Wynne, forgetting the embittered family feud, proved himself a warm private as well as political friend. As this election contest has been already referred to, there is no need to dwell further on it here except to note that, as it made the Ormsbys and Wynnes bitter enemies of one another, so it divided the whole county into two hostile camps, each ranged behind its favourite candidate, and sharing to the full all his resentments and animosities.

The Willowbrook family gained an important accession of wealth by the marriage of Owen Ormsby to Margaret, eldest daughter, and, ultimately, heiress of William Owen, of Porkington, Shropshire. The issue of this marriage, Mary Jane, an only child, and heiress both of the Ormsby and Owen estates, became the wife of William Gore, who assumed, on his marriage, the additional name of Ormsby. The late Lord Harlech was son of Mr. and Mrs. Ormsby Gore, as is also the present Lord Harlech, who is himself married to Lady Emily Charlotte Seymour, eldest surviving daughter of Rear-Admiral Sir George Francis Seymour, and sister to Francis, present Marquis of Hertford. His lordship's children are William Seymour Ormsby Gore, George Ralph Charles Ormsby Gore, Henry Arthur Ormsby Gore, Seymour Fitzroy Ormsby Gore, and Emily, married to Viscount Ebrington, eldest son of Earl of Fortescue.

The late Mrs. Ormsby Gore, who survived her husband ten or twelve years, and died in 1869, was a singularly kind-hearted lady. Her tenants respected and loved her so much for her goodness, that they were preparing to erect a costly memorial in her honour, when her family, hearing of their intention, and taking the will for the deed, intimated a wish that the matter should proceed no further. The tenants, acquiescing in the suggestion, proceeded no further with their preparations; but, the memorial which their gratitude for her kindness preserves in their hearts, is much more honourable to the good lady than any of marble or stone could be.

It is due to Lord Harlech to record, that he inherits the benevolent dispositions of his mother. Those who know most about his dealings with his tenants, are loudest in praise of his treatment of them. To the old followers of his family he is equally kind, of which, an instance that occurred in our own neighbourhood may be quoted in illustration: Visiting, near forty years ago, the Sligo Workhouse, and finding among the inmates an old man named John Mullane, who had been in his early years a runner or kitchen-boy at Willowbrook, his Lordship had the poor man removed to suitable private lodgings, where he was able to pass the remainder of his days in comfort. Many would admire Lord Harlech more for this "touch of nature", than for all his broad acres or his Family and personal honours.

While speaking of the Willowbrook Ormsbys, we may notice a rather eccentric and sensational occurrence in which a *cadet* of the family figured, something less than a century ago. Being at Paris in the full swing of the French Revolution, when the white flag was detested and in the dust, and the *drapeau rouge* was an object almost of adoration, he appeared one night in a leading theatre, wearing a white cockade. The moment the hated object was observed, the occupants of the pit and gallery sprang to their feet, and yelled in a rage—*A bas la cockarde blanche.* Young Ormsby seemed the only person unmoved in the house; and when he rose quietly in his box, and stated in the best French he could muster, that he was an Irishman, and wore the emblem in honour of his own king and country, and that he would part with it only with his life, his explanation and intrepidity pleased everybody, admiration succeeded indignation, and instead of *A bas la cockarde blanche*, the theatre resounded with repeated cries of *Vive, vive l'Irlandais.*

The Cummen and Belvoir Ormsbys have long abandoned their handsome seats, Belvoir being now an utter ruin, and Cummen little better. George Ormsby, the last of the family who occupied Belvoir, died on December 29th, 1809. Thomas Ormsby, of Cummen, married a daughter of Teige O'Hara, of Leyney, and dying in 1662, was buried in St. John's, Sligo, as appears from a record in Sir Bernard Burke's office, being probably one of the first, if not the first, buried there after Sir Roger Jones. It would appear from Lady Morgan's *Patriotic Sketches*, that Cummen was still occupied by its owners in the first decade of this century, when her Ladyship, as Sydney Owenson, was a guest there.

The first of the Ormsbys that occupied Castle Dargan, was Stephen Ormsby, grandson of Malby. This Stephen is always spoken of in the neighbourhood as Stephen *Na Gliggagh*, from some peculiarly constructed vehicle that he drove. The present representative of this branch, John Robert Ormsby, resides now in America, where he is very popular, as he always was in Ireland before his emigration. He is married to Mary Middleton, daughter of the extensive and enterprising merchant of Sligo, the late William Middleton, Esq., J.P., by whom he has issue, Nicholson Ormsby, born 5th September, 1875; Eliza Middleton Ormsby, 16th October, 1876; William Middleton Ormsby, 22nd January, 1878; John Robert Ormsby, 17th February, 1879; Alexander Irwin Ormsby, 25th February, 1880; Amy Frances, 25th April, 1881; and Frances Mary, 14th October, 1882.

It is not quite ascertained to which branch of the county Sligo Ormsbys, a gentleman named William Ormsby belonged, who was tried at Sligo for wilful murder, at the March Assizes of 1731. Such particulars as are known of this sensational trial, will be stated in a future page. For the present it may be enough to give the following reference to the proceedings, which occurs in *Pue's Occurrences*, for March 23rd, 1731: "The tryal of William Ormsby, Esq., for the murder of Catherine Conaghane, in July, 1727, came on last Friday at the Assizes, before Mr. Baron St. Leger, and Mr. Attorney General; The tryal lasted from ten o'clock in the morning, till four in the afternoon, when the Jury received their charge and went in, where they continued till nine o'clock next morning, and then brought in their verdict, not guilty".

The PARKES of Dunally are one of the oldest Anglo-Irish families in the county. They came to this country with Sir Roger Jones, who was in Sligo in the first years of the seventeenth century, and probably earlier, as he succeeded Sir James Fullerton, in 1606, as constable of the castle of Sligo. Sir Roger was married twice. By his first wife he had issue, Thomas Jones, of Banada, and, at least, one daughter, Mary Jones, who was married, first, to John Ridge, Esq., a gentleman of high public office in the province, as also of large landed estate; and secondly, to Sir James Dillon, who took a leading part on the Irish side, in the ten years' war started by the insurrection of 1641. It is probable that Alice Jones, the wife of Robuck Crean, was a daughter of Sir Roger, though it is, perhaps, as likely that she was the daughter of a brother of his who lived in Sligo at the same time.

Sir Roger Jones' second wife was Mary, daughter of Roger Smith, of Crasmarsh, in Staffordshire, of whom there was no issue. Sir Roger's sister was married to Roger Parke, to whom she bore two sons, Robert Parke and William Parke, from the latter of whom the Parkes of Dunally descend; this William Parke being set down, in the Rental of 1692, as tenant of Dunally, by letters patent of Court of Grace. The elder son, Robert Parke, married Anne Povey, of county Roscommon, by whom he had one child, a daughter and heiress, Anne Parke, married successively to Sir Francis Gore, Knight, and Percy Gethins, Esq. In the documents of the period, as well before as after her second marriage, she is styled, after her first husband, Dame Anne Gore.

Robert Parke, or Captain Robert Parke, as he was commonly called, occupied as high a position in the county as any man of his day. He was member of Parliament in 1661, for the county Leitrim, and resided in the castellated mansion of Newtown, in that county, which must have been built by himself, his father, or his uncle, Sir Roger Jones, and which is well situated at the head of Lough Gill, within a few hundred yards of the O'Rorke's old castle of Newtown. Though he kept on good terms with the Commonwealth authorities, from whom he rented, in 1656, the tithes of several parishes through the county, he received from Charles II., at the Restoration, under the Acts of Settlement and Explanation, grants of large estates both in Sligo and Leitrim. At the marriage of his daughter to Sir Francis Gore, Newtown and other lands were passed to the Gores; and at her subsequent marriage to Percy Gethin, several parcels of land in the parishes of St. John and Calry, were passed to that gentleman. Sir Francis had issue, nine sons and three daughters by Anne Parke; one of the daughters, Isabella, marrying Adam O'Hara, of Annaghmore, and being the person whose name is thus recorded on a curious monument in the Annaghmore demesne:—"Erected by M. Isabella O'Hara, alias Gore, daughter to Francis Gore, Knight, of Sligoe, in May 1709". Anne Park is the ancestress of the Gores Booth of Lissadel.

The Parkes have been always popular in the neighbourhood; and the late Sir William, who was knighted by Lord Mulgrave, took a prominent part in his Lordship's reception in 1837, went with Right Reverend Dr. Burke, Sir James Crofton, and others, to Camphill to meet him, accompanied his triumphal procession to Sligo, and presided at the banquet given in his honour, in the town on that occasion. His Excellency's admirers wished to present an address to him in the court-house; and on Mr. James Knott, of Battlefield, who was high sheriff for the year, refusing the use of the court-house, Mr. Parke, as a member of the court-house committee, got the key and opened it in defiance of the sheriff and the sheriffs partisans. This spirited act pleased Earl Mulgrave, who, on entering the place, directed Mr. Parke to kneel, and then accosted him in the usual formula, "Arise, Sir William".

It was a pity that a previous engagement prevented Lord Mulgrave from waiting for the banquet of the evening, at which the new knight presided—for he would enjoy an incident or two of the proceedings. Sir

William, it is said, abounded in humour, and rather lacked eloquence; and people seemed at a loss to know, whether they should refer the incidents in question to his surplus humour or his defective command of language One of those little ambiguities occurred when at the close of his preface to Right Rev. Dr. Burke's health, he wound up with the remark, "His Lordship is a very nice gentleman, especially on horseback;" and the other, when passing to the next toast, he observed, "Gentlemen, or whatever else you are, fill your glasses". Everybody enjoyed those curious sallies, and nobody more than Sir William himself.

Dunally, which is a fertile, well-timbered, and pleasant tract, lies on the right bank of the Kilsellagh river. The Four Masters, under the year 1602, state:—"The place at which Caffar O'Donnell had his residence and fortress at this time was Dun Aille, to the west of Sligo;" and O'Donovan, in a note to this entry, identifies the place with that which Mr. Roger Parke now owns and occupies, though the identification is by no means clear. It is, on the contrary, pretty certain that the Dun Aille of the annalists lies in Coolerra, as it is said to be to the west of Sligo, while the Parke or Calry Dunally is situated to the north or north-east of the town.

And, in any case, the authority to which O'Donovan refers the Partition Deed of the O'Connor Sligo estate, so far from hearing him out, upsets his theory. The full statement in the Deed, of which O'Donovan quotes only a part, is as follows:—"Also half the castle of Downally and the lands of Lecarrowcrin, being half a quarter and containing 153 acres, 1 rood, perches of profitable land, and 3 acres, 32 perches unprofitable, mering and bordering on Carrownabrew, and situate in Collary in the barony of Carbery, and county of Sligo aforesaid". Now, even if the Dun Aille of the Four Masters were that of Calry, it would follow clearly from the juxtaposition, in the above extract, of Downally with Carrowcrin and Carrownabree, places certainly in Coolerra, that the Downally of the Partition Deed must belong to Coolerra. The denomination "Collary" is not decisive one way or the other, for there is nothing in the word itself to show whether it stands for Calry or Coolerra.

Dun Aille signifies the fort of the cliff or rock, and the Calry Dunally has the name, it is said, from a whitish boulder which lies beside a rath near Mr. Parke's house.

In a letter of Mr. Roger Parke, the present proprietor of Dunally, which is found in the new edition of O'Hart's Irish Pedigrees (p. 675,) the writer supposes that the Parke family were "followers of the great Earl of Strafford;" but, in this, he does an injustice to his family, for Roger Parke, their ancestor, was in Sligo with his brother-in-law, Sir Roger Jones, in the first years of the 17th century, if not earlier, and, therefore, near half a century before Strafford came to Ireland. And this Roger's son, Captain

Robert Parke, appears to have lived at Newtown, at the head of Lough Gill, since 1609, and certainly occupied the place in 1635; for in the Repertory to Decrees of Charles I., we find, under date of 17th June, 1635, the case of "Sir William Irwin, Knight, Sir John Spottiswood, Knight, Sir Roger Jones, Knight, and *Robert Parke, of Newtown, in the County Leitrim*, Gent., plaintiffs; Sir James Areskin, Knight, of Her Majesty's Privy Council, defendant". Captain Parke held Newtown in 1642 also; for Sir Frederick Hamilton, on the night of his raid on Sligo, in 1642, made him a prisoner, and placed a creature of his own over the Newtown garrison.

No doubt, at the surrender of the Connaught fortresses, in 1652, to the Parliamentary forces, Donogh Hart occupied the place, but it was only as military governor, just as Sir Teague O'Regan, at the same time, was in occupation of Sligo, Major Bryan O'Rorke, of Ballyshannon, and Colonel William Taaffe, of Ballinafad; though these military officers had no claim of private ownership to those places.

Of late a new-fangled origin has been assigned for the name of Newtown, but without a particle of reason or authority to support it. From time immemorial the place has been known by English-speaking people as Newtown, which is the exact equivalent of its old Irish name *Baile nua*. It has been even asserted, in the face of notorious facts, that the place was never called *Baile nua*, though it is thus designated in so well-known an authority as the *Annals of Loch Ce*, where it is mentioned under the year 1581, as *Baile nua Hi Ruairc*, (i.e.) Newtown O'Rorke. Like the rest of Leitrim, it belonged, under Celtic rule, to the O'Rorkes, and the O'Rorkes alone.

There is no spot in the county that has stronger claims on the attention of the antiquary than the townland of Deerpark, an enclosure of about three miles in circuit for Mr. Wynne's deer. The surface of this tract, and of the surrounding district, consists, for the most part, of steep upland hillocks, and deep bowl-shaped hollows, The highest of the hillocks rises in Deerpark, reaching an altitude of about 500 feet above sea level, standing between the little lakes of Calgach and Loughaneltin, and commanding the finest views of Lough Gill, of Sligo river and harbour, and of the Leitrim, Slieve-da-En, and Slieve Gamh mountains. It is this particular elevation that invests the townland of Deerpark with so much antiquarian interest.

At the base of the hill is the site of the old religious establishment of Clogher, now and from time immemorial, used as a burying place. The graveyard being neatly walled, and lined in part with trees, looks well from a distance, but a near view shows the interior overrun with weeds, which cover and conceal the tombs, and give the place a neglected and disordered look. Some remains of an oblong building that ran from east to west, and measured 52 feet long and 21 wide, interior measurement, are still in their place, though the eastern gable and south sidewall are levelled to the ground, while only about 12 feet high of the west gable and north sidewall continue standing. A very fine Irish cross, set over the grave of the late much-lamented Mrs. James O'Connor, is the most striking object in the place. It bears the inscription:—

IN AFFECTIONATE REMEMBRANCE OF
EMILY KATE,
THE BELOVED AND DEVOTED WIFE OF
JAMES CHARLES O'CONNOR,
OF BALLYGLASS.
BORN 21ST JULY, 1844; DIED 1ST MAY, 1872.
MAY SHE REST IN PEACE.

More than half-way up the slope is one of the most remarkable cashels of the country, unique, as far as the writer is aware, in its plan and mode of construction. It consists of three concentric circles of stones, each divided from the other by a three feet ring of clear ground, the outside circle of stones being eight feet thick, the middle, which is the chief one, thirteen feet, and the inside one eight feet. Within the inmost circle an L shaped cave or trench, now unroofed, but formerly covered with huge stones or flags, slopes from the surface to a depth of four feet, the sides being lined with uncemented masonry, the stones of which are of moderate size and put neatly together.

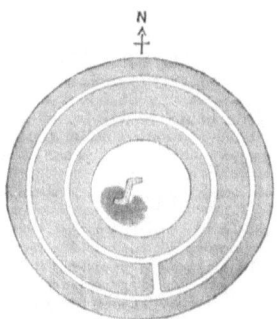

PLAN ON THE DEARPARK CASHEL[1].

Remarkable as is this piece of antiquity, it is thrown into the shade by another relic of the past, which crowns the hill, and which is called by some the Giant's Grave, and by others, the Druid's Altar. In its plan it is admittedly unique. As a glance at the illustration will give a better idea of it than any verbal description, it will be enough to note here that the structure is an oblong of something more than 100 feet in length, outlined by large stones, three to six feet high, and set on edge; that it consists of three divisions, a centre, and two wings or aisles—the centre being 49 feet long

---

[1] Drawn on the wood by Mr. Wakeman, from a sketch by Mr. James O'Connor, Ballyglass

and 25 wide—the west wing which is of an apse shape, 23 feet long and 12 wide, and the B east wing, which is divided longitudinally into three narrow compartments, 23 feet long and about the same wide; and that the wings communicate with the centre by three trilithon opes or doors, A.B.C., each trilithon formed by two jamb stones and one capstone—one trilithon, A., standing between the west end and centre, and two, B. and C., between east end and centre, that is, one for each of two of the three compartments into which that wing is divided; the third compartment, which is the middle one of the three, and which has no open into the centre, serving, apparently,

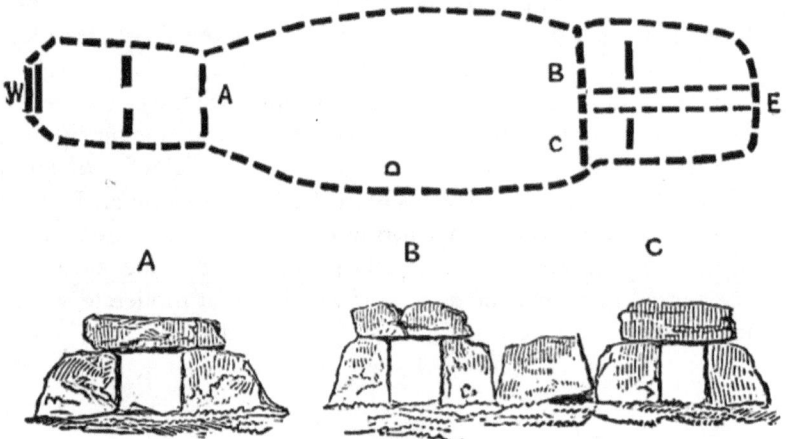

PLAN OF DRUID'S ALTAR WITH ITS TRILITHON OPES, A. B. C.[1]

only as a passage between the other two. It should be mentioned that an open of four feet in the south sidewall of the centre was the entrance from the outside to this part of the structure, while entrance from the wings into it was afforded by the trilithon opes; and, when it is added, that two flags, which, run across the western wing, with, however, a passage between them, divide that wing into two parts, and fit it, probably, for the purpose which the longitudinal divisions serve in the east wing, all is said that need be in the way of description.

    It is not much to the credit of Irishmen that they have shown so little interest in the Druid's Altar, which is the most singular monument of antiquity in the country, and which is sometimes compared with Stonehenge. Englishmen have acted very differently in regard to Stonehenge, for they have spared no pains, though hitherto without much result, to discover its nature and object. All sorts of conjectures and theories have been started by them as to its character: —It was a temple; it was a

---

[1] Drawn on the wood by Mr. Wakeman from a sketch by Mr. James O'Connor, Ballyglass.

planisphere[1]; it was an orrery;[2] it was a place of political assemblies; it was a stand-like centre of public games; it was a monument of 450 British nobles, murdered at a conference between Hengist and Yortigern; it was an antediluvian temple, erected under the immediate superintendence of Adam. All these theories and a dozen others, equally probable or improbable, have had their advocates, who have written volumes which count by the hundred in support of their respective views. It must be admitted that the problem is still unsolved; but it must also be admitted, that the efforts made to master it, are as creditable to all concerned, as the neglect of the Druid's Altar is the reverse to those who might throw light on it, but who are too incurious or too indolent to make the attempt.

In the absence of opinions or conjectures from more competent quarters, the writer ventures to think, that it is one of three objects, two of which are mentioned by old writers in connection with Calry. One of these two is a religious establishment, in which Saints Osnata, Muadhnata, and Talulla,[3] sisters of St. Molaisse, of Devenish, were honoured with a joint festival; the place to which this establishment belonged, being called Enach-ard or High Annagh; and as there is no spot in the whole parish of Calry or Annagh that answers so well to this description as the Deerpark hill, inasmuch as it rises higher than the rest of the parish, excepting the mere mountain, so it is probable enough, that the mysterious Druid's Altar is what remains of the religious establishment in question, the centre being the chapel, and the wings the cells of the religious. Looking at the Druid's

---

[1] Representation of the night sky, [Clachan ed.].
[2] Mechanical model of solar system, [Clachan ed.].
[3] They are thus commemorated in the Martyrology of Tallaght, at the 6th January, "Inghen Natfraoich in *Eanach Ard*", that is, the daughters of Natfraich, in *Eanach Ard*.
In the *Martyrology of Donegal*, they are separately mentioned thus:—"Muadhnat, Virgin. Caille is the name of her place in Carbery, of Drumcliffe. Talulla, Abbess of Kildare. Osnat, Virgin. These three were the three sisters of Mollaise of Devenish".
Archdall's *Monasticon*, page 633, states,—"The saints and sisters Odnata, Talulla, and Muadhnata, lived about the year 580, and are honored in *Enachaird*, which is now unknown, but was probably in Carbury". On this statement of Archdall, Dr. Lanigan, who is always fond of tripping up the author of the *Monasticon*, observes in a note: "Archdall thinks Enachaird might have been in Carbury, but there is no Annagh in that barony". (Ecclesiastical History, Vol. II., p. 328). Here it is Lanigan, and not Archdall, that is wrong. In his text, the learned author of the Ecclesiastical History says, "Three sisters of Molaisse of Devenish, Osnata, Muadhnata, and Talulla, are mentioned in the calendars at 6th January. A joint festival of these three holy sisters was kept at Enachaird, probably the place now called Annagh, in the county of Leitrim, and barony of Drumahaire".
To complete these references, the following note of Colgan (Acta Sanctorum, p. 339) is added "Osnata fuit filia Nadfraici, et soror S. Molassii Damhinisensis et sanctarum, Talullae et Muadhnatae, juxta Marian: ad 6 Januarii, quo die, ait, harum trium sororum festum celebrari. Eodem die de eis agit Aengussius auct: et Martyrologium Tamlachtense addens quod colantur in *Enac-ard*. Addit et Marian S. Muadhnatam coli in loco regionis Cairbre, qui Caille appellatur, et S. Talullam, Kildairae, ubi fiut Abbatissa".

Altar at present—with modern ideas of a monastery of monks or nuns in the mind—it would need no small effort to realise a monastery on this bleak hill, within those uncouth stones, with no covering, apparently, but the canopy of heaven; but if we carry back our thoughts to the sixth or seventh century; if we suppose that the interstices of those rude blocks were filled up and staunched, so as to exclude rain and wind; that a roof of sods or branches, and thatch, or some similar material, rose, by some rude appliance, above them; and that the whole place was sheltered by the hazel bushes which then covered the hill, as they still cover some of the neighbouring eminences; even thus, the structure would look extremely unlike a religious house of the present day, but still, would be not less habitable, perhaps, than many other places in which the monks and nuns of that time passed their lives.

An alternative object with which the Druid's Altar may be identified, is the sepulchre in which the remains of Eoghan Bel were interred, after their removal from Rath O'bh-Fiachrach. This sepulchre, as the life of St. Ceallach states, lay on the north side of the river Sligo, at Aonach Loch Gile, the exact position of the monument in question. We shall get a better idea of the circumstances of this singular interment, or re-interment, by recalling the words of the saint's life, which are as follows:—"Eoghan told them to bury himself with his red javelin in his hand in the grave. 'Place my face towards the north, on the side of the hill by which the northerns pass when flying before the army of Connaught; let my grave face them, and place me in it after this manner.' And this order was strictly complied with; and in every place where the Clanna Neil and the Connacians met in conflict, the Clanna Neil and the northerns were routed, being panic-stricken by the countenances of their foes; so that the Clanna Neil and the people of the north of Ireland therefore resolved to come with a numerous host to Rath O'bh-Fiachrach, and raise the body of Eoghan from the grave, and carry it northwards across the Sligo. This was done, and the body was buried at the other side of the river, at Aenach, Locha Gile, with the mouth down, that it might not be the means of causing them to fly before the Connacians".[1]

This little history proves, that there was a public cemetery in some part of Armagh or Calry; and while there is no trace of such a thing in any other part of the parish, the burying place of Clogher, which dates from time immemorial, and "the several round tumuli on a neighbouring eminence, looking like the burying place of the castellani",[2] would go to

---

[1] Life of St. Ceallach of Kilmore Moy, as quoted and translated by O'Donovan in Tribes and Customs of Hy-Fiachracb, p. 472.
[2] Rude Stone Monuments—By Sir James Ferguson, p. 235.

show that this was the sepulchral district in question—and therefore, the place in which the remains of Eoghan Bel were deposited, if they ever were removed, as is asserted, from their first resting place in Coolerra.

As games or sports of various kinds must have had a large place at the fairs or meetings of Annagh, as they had at other similar meetings elsewhere, it is probable that the Druid's Altar, assuming it to be the burying place of Eoghan Bel, had some connection with these games. Nor would its sepulchral character be any obstacle to this, but quite the contrary, for cemeteries were the chief scenes of such sports. "Aenachs or fairs", says Mr. Sullivan, in his learned introduction to O'Curry's Manners and Customs of the Ancient Irish (p. cclv.), "appear to have originated in funeral games, celebrated in honour of some distinguished chief or warrior, and in pagan, and even in early Christian times, were always celebrated in cemeteries".

If it be asked which of the two objects mentioned—the church of the Saints and the sepulchre of Eoghan Bel—has the stronger claim to be identified with the Druid's Altar, there need be little hesitation in regard to the answer to be given. The site of the Druid's Altar is all a solid limestone quarry, and bears no trace of a grave, and especially no trace of a grave deep enough for Eoghan Bel, whom those who are said to have removed him would wish to place as far beyond reach as possible. If the Connaught King, then, were ever removed from Knocknarea, and reinterred in any part of the Deerpark, it would be in the L shaped trench of the cashel, which was an exceptionally strong structure of the kind.

But one cannot help thinking that all this talk about removal was mere pretence, made use of for the purpose of disheartening the Connaughtmen, by making them believe that their palladium was gone, though it continued all the time undisturbed within its colossal cairn on the top of Knocknarea. Dr. Petrie, in his day, was anxious to explore this cairn; and it is a pity that he, or somebody else, did not do so; for there can hardly be a doubt, that if the centre of the pile were reached, light would be shed on the fate of Eoghan Bel, and on other interesting points of Sligo history. It is not still too late to carry out Petrie's project if the requisite spirit be forthcoming.

As to the church or nunnery theory, it is not a little striking that the ablest of the antiquaries, who visit the Druid's Altar, find a strong resemblance between its parts and those of a Christian temple. The late Mr. Hardman, in a paper read in 1879, before the Royal Historical and Archaeological Association of Ireland, observes on this point:—"It is curious to observe the general resemblance of the plan of this structure to that of a modern church or cathedral. The eastern end represents the chancel. The central space, the portion under the dome, while the eastern extremity is not without analogy to the nave, with side aisles. The bearing also, is nearly east and west". And Sir James Ferguson, in *"Rude Stone Monuments"* (p. 235), remarks:—"What, then, is this edifice? It can hardly be a tomb, it is so unlike any other tomb which we know of. In plan it looks like a temple; indeed, it is not unlike the arrangement of some Christian churches". Joining these opinions with the fact that Muadhnata and her sisters had a joint religious establishment of some kind on the hill, it must be admitted that the church theory is not without some probability. Still it is hard to understand how the saints could have lived there, and, particularly, how they could have passed through the trilithon opes from one apartment to the other, as they must have done habitually, if they occupied the place.

Even admitting then that Muadhnata, Osnata, and Tallula, had an establishment on Deerpark hill, it is doubtful whether it should be identified with the Druid's Altar. This may have been an entirely new erection, put up after the sisters or their successors had moved their house down the hill to the spot where the ruined church of Clogher now stands. Or, if not an entirely new erection, it may have undergone substantial alterations to fit it for the purposes of the games which used to come off in the district, which, *the writer ventures to think, was its real destination.*

For there can be no doubt that the place was famous for its public meetings and games. This appears, first, from the name Aonagh or Annagh a place of meeting; second, from the stanza of Giolla Iosa Mor Mac Firbis's poem already quoted; and, thirdly, from the following lines of Shane O'Dugan's Topographical Poem:—

> *"Clar cluithe, raon na radare,*
> *O'Maolcluiche a ceann adart".*
> *"Plain of the game, tract of the prospects,*
> *O'Maolcluiche is their head leader".*

By-the-bye, the name, O'Maolcluiche, must have come from these games, for it signifies *juvenis ludi*, that is, the youth of the game.

But what *special* purpose did the structure serve? Most probably as an arena for the combat of animals, such as dogs and wild boars, dogs and wolves, or dogs and badgers the so-called nave being the arena proper, and the aisles enclosures for the dogs and the animals with which they were to contend.

The details of the structure would harmonize with this destination—the aisles at one end, being for the dogs, that at the other for the wild beasts, and the central space for the actual conflict of which the spectators, massed round the exterior of the building, would have a good view. In this supposition, the trilithon opes, which, from their lowness, could hardly be meant for the passage of men or women, would answer perfectly for the passage of the dogs and other animals, while the narrow pass between the two little apartments of the east end, would be intended for the use of the caretaker of these animals. Some confirmation of the view now advanced may be drawn from the old Irish name of the place, which is Maghereconrosse, and which signifies the Plain of the Dog of the wood, a designation that points unmistakably to some peculiar connection of dogs with the spot.

There is nothing that would enable us to tell the exact time at which this structure was erected, or adapted to the sports of the place, though the quarried flags used in its construction, and the squared and dressed stones of the trilithons, would show it to be of comparatively modern origin. There is reason to believe that the sports were practised as early as the eleventh century, and probably earlier; and it is pretty certain that some of them came off on Lough Calgach at the foot of the hill; for one cannot help thinking that it was on the occasion of a regatta the fatality occurred, which is thus mentioned by the Four Masters at the year 1067:—"Muireadhach Ua Carthaigh was drowned in Loch Calgaich; he was the chief poet and chief ollamh of Connaught". As Ua Carthaigh was not a local name, Muireadhach must have come from some other region of the province, and there could hardly be anything else to attract him to the little out-of-the-way lake of Calgach except the public games celebrated on its waters and on its banks. It may be noticed, in passing, that O'Donovan, in a note in his edition of the Four Masters, marks Lough Calgach as "not identified;" a new proof of the little attention he paid to the history of the county Sligo; for all the inhabitants of the county are familiar with the name and situation of Lough Calgach.

Nor is it known when the public games of Annagh ceased. They were practised when Shane Mor O'Dugan, who died in 1372, wrote his poem; and as Giolla Iosa Mor Mac Firbis mentions them in his "Tribes and Customs of Hy Fiachrach", written about 1417, we may fairly conclude that they continued down to the close of the fifteenth century, or thereabouts.

Though this solution of the Deerpark "riddle" as the Druid's Altar is styled by Sir James Ferguson, may not please antiquaries of the antediluvian or pre-historic school, it seems to be the only one that has a particle of proof in its support. Indeed, no solution at all has been hitherto offered by those who have written about this mysterious object, if we except Major Wood Martin, who, in his History of Sligo, pronounces it a "fine example of a pagan sepulchre"—a dictum that counts for nothing, as it is not backed up by an iota of evidence, and is, besides, contradicted by archaeologists of authority, like Sir James Ferguson, and Mr. Hardman, who maintain that, *whatever else the Druid's Altar may be*, it is not a sepulchre, pagan or other. "It can hardly be a tomb", says Sir James Ferguson, "it is so unlike any other tomb which we know of;" and Mr. Hardman is still more positive, his words being: "It is *clearly not* a monumental or sepulchral structure, seeing that the solid rock occurs within a foot or so of the surface". It was hardly fair of Major Wood Martin, when quoting Mr. Hardman's description, to omit this important statement, even though it militated against his own peculiar opinion.

Whether the *special* function of the Druid's Altar was, as conjectured above, that of a rude amphitheatre for the combats of dogs and other animals, or not, it is, anyhow, highly probable, if not quite certain, that, instead of the structure being a nondescript relic of pre-historic times, it is all that remains of a *fixture of rather modern origin, connected in one way or another, if not in the exact way suggested, with the far-famed sports of Annagh or Calry.*

One of the most beautiful spots in the county or in Ireland, is said to lie in Calry, and to have been named in olden time Grianan Calry. Of this spot, Thomas O'Connor, one of the Ordnance Survey letter writers, says, in a letter written from Ballina, and dated September 20th, 1836:— "There is an old saying among the people, which runs thus –

> *"Connaught is the grianan of Ireland;*
> *Carbury the grianan of Connaught.*
> *Calry is the grianan of Carbury;*
> *And the Hill is the grianan of Calgaich".*

It would be strange if so picturesque a place should fail to be recognised, and yet there is reason to believe, that at present it "sleeps in the shade", though Thomas O'Connor, and Major Wood Martin, agree in identifying it with a little hill which rises a couple of hundred yards to the south of the chapel of Calry. In the letter just referred to, O'Connor places it "on the right of the road leading from Sligo to Manorhamilton", the position of the hill in question; and in the History of Sligo,[1] Major Wood Martin, borrowing O'Connor's words as well as his geography, situates it to "the right of the road leading from Sligo to Manorhamilton".

Thomas O'Connor tries to bolster up his identification in this wise:—"Grianan is interpreted by the people, a place possessed of some property superior to other places. Others say the hill was so-called, because it is so beautifully green, etc.;" and here again Major Wood Martin, borrowing O'Connor's reasons and words, as before he had borrowed his geography and words, writes, "Grianan is interpreted by the country people, as signifying a place possessed of some quality or property superior to other localities. Some say that the hill was so-called because it is so beautifully green", etc. Well, all that need be observed, in reference to these proofs, is,

---

[1] Page 75 this edition [Clachan ed.].

that the man himself must be "beautifully *green*" who would regard them as proving anything.

No doubt, O'Connor's error, if it was not wilful, arose from the fact, that a small patch of land at the south-western base of the little hill, is called Lionan or Leenaun, the diminutive of Lin (Dr. Joyce's Irish Names of Places, 2nd Series, pp. 383-4), because in winter it is submerged by water flowing over it from Calgach lake. Leenaun and Greenaun must have been confounded by him; and when, in his peregrinations through Calry, he was asking everybody he met for Grianan Calry, and somebody, struck by the partial resemblance in sound of Leenaun and Greenaun, pointed out the hill over Leenaun as the object of his search, the inquirer, thankful for small mercies, and glad to have something to tell O'Donovan, who had written to him, "Ascertain situation and present state of Grianan Cairbre Calraigh", opened his note book, and without more ado, dotted down *Eureka*.

Whether this is the correct explanation of the matter or not, it seems certain that he was mistaken about Grianan Calry. A stone-mason of the neighbourhood, named McDonogh, who possesses an intimate knowledge of the district, and who is somewhat of an archaeologist besides, affirms, that he always heard the place spoken of as Leenaun, but never as Greenaun, And other inhabitants, including an intelligent shopkeeper named Hargadon, who was born and bred near the spot, makes the same statement. Indeed, such authority is quite unnecessary; for no one with the slightest sense of the beautiful in scenery, would think for a moment, of identifying the far famed Grianan Cairbre Calry, with this despicable little hill, inferior in outline, in colour, in every element of beauty, to a hundred other places scattered up and down the parish of Calry.

What then has become of Grianan Calry? Has this delightful spot, like the garden of Eden, disappeared from mortal vision? This would be a great pity indeed, if it has any just claim to the superlative praise which has been bestowed upon it; and it is therefore pleasant to be able to re-assure the lovers of the picturesque on the point, and to certify them, that the incomparable Grianan, is still to be seen, and is still as bright and charming as ever.

Turning the back on Leenaun, and searching elsewhere for this Connaught Paradise, we come upon a region at the head of Lough Gill, which is certainly the place in question, as it possesses all the conditions assigned to it. First, part of it has always borne the name of "Grianan", and still bears it, though at present without the addition of "Calry", faring in this respect, as compound Irish names usually fare, in losing some of the appellation in the course of time. Second, though it may not belong to the present parish of Calry, it lies in *the old district of Calry or Calregia*, which, as is well known,[1] took in Drumlias and Dromahair, with the intervening stretch, including Grianan, Shriff and the Hill. And third, it is of such surpassing loveliness, both in itself and its surroundings, as to fully justify the extraordinary eulogy contained in the old Irish lines quoted and translated by O'Connor.

Greenan Hill stands like a section of some vast earthen amphitheatre, of nature's own formation, rising in graceful gradation, tier over tier, every perch of the surface being of as brilliant a green, as the finest emerald of Peru. What gives the hill its superiority, as a point of view, is the fact, that just as in our great National Exhibitions, the most striking objects of the collection are placed round the principal standpoint, so also the chief scenic beauties of the county are ranged in their very best aspects, round Greenan—to the right the beautiful Benbulben; to the left, the boldest elevation of Slieveda-En, shooting up majestically from the water's edge; in the front, the smooth and finely outlined Knocknarea; and further on, the Ox mountains, carrying away the thoughts and the eye to the western ocean; nearer, the sylvan glades of Holywell, Hazelwood, and Belvoir; and, at its foot, Lough Gill, unrolled before the eye in all its length and breadth—its bright islands shining like so many spangles, set by nature on its surface for its adornment, and its waters rippling over its beach of shingle with cadenced sound, as if to make its perfections audible as well as visible.

It is creditable to the taste of our ancestors, to have singled out this charming spot for their special admiration.

---

[1] See page 344, this edition [Clachan ed. adjustment].

CHAPTER XIX

PARISH OF DRUMCLIFF

THE ROSSES, DRUMCLIFF, AND CASTLETOWN

To the north of St. John's and Calry parishes, lies the extensive, populous, and rich parish of Drumcliff, stretching from the sea to the county Leitrim, with an area of 26,598 acres, a population of 6,898 souls in 1881, and a valuation of £15,937 12s.

The ROSSES in this district, are a strip of land, about three miles long and one wide, lying between the Sligo and Drumcliff estuaries, and running westwards on to the sea. At their western end they have the form of a horse-shoe, the toe turned inland, the sides projecting into the sea, and the space within the sides, which is a much lower level, forming the famous and commodious race-course of Bomore, where the horses are under the eye of the spectator, from the start to the finish. They are divided into the Lower or Northern Rosses, and the Upper or Southern; the latter being a beautiful and fashionable sea-side resort.

Though this watering-place is popular at present, it is sure to be much more frequented when better known, as its attractions are superior to those of most places of the kind in Ireland. Lying along the sunny southern slope of a gently rising ridge of green land; looking down on the picturesque and historical Oyster and Coney islands, swimming at its feet; commanding a clear view of almost every perch of the curving, converging, well defined, richly cultivated, and highly varied shores of Sligo harbour, as well as of the extensive crescent of striking buildings—stretching from the Lunatic Asylum, in the east, to the Cathedral, in the west—which the town forms, when looked at from this point; in full view of some of the finest mountain scenery of Leitrim, Mayo, and Sligo, ranging round from Slieve-an-Ierin, in the east, to Kilcummin Head, in the west; surrounded on all sides with beautiful walks the esplanade between the village and the Pool; the beaches of Bomore and Lower Rosses, long enough to satisfy the most indefatigable pedestrian; and the extensive *Green*, as the summit of the plateau is called—where the dryness at all times, and springiness, of the turf under the foot, the balminess of the air, and the lively and varied movements of the promenaders and saunterers, child and adult, cannot fail to interest and entertain, while the eye feasts on the beauty of the landscape, and the lungs are invigorated with the ozone of the Atlantic; these and a hundred other advantages, which might be named, when coupled with the safest and pleasantest sea-bathing in Ireland, must always commend the Rosses Point, alike to the lover of the picturesque and the votary of health.

Should drives be desired, there is no neighbourhood in the county which supplies more, or more beautiful ones, such as the valley of Glencar, superior to anything in Wicklow or Kerry; the romantic region near the Heels—as they are locally called—of Benbulben, and Benweeskin; and the noble demesne of Lissadell, with its magnificent mansion, its charming glen, and its stirring historical associations. If a trip on water be fancied, a row or a sail to Knocknarea, Ardtermon, Innismurray, or the coast of Tireragh, cannot fail to gratify; while those who wish to enjoy sea air and society together, have only to take a seat in the river steamer, or the road *char a banes*, in any of the several trips, which each of those gay conveyances makes every day, when they will find themselves in the midst of the fashionables of Sligo.

And every new day brings some fresh novelty to sojourners at Rosses Point. One day it is a contest at cricket, in which the leading athletes of the county, with, occasionally, some from the neighbouring counties, exhibit all their agility, dexterity, nerve, and prowess; next day it is a match of lawn tennis, when the great object of those engaged in this *Dolce far niente*[397] pastime, is to outshine others in gracefulness of movement, and fashionableness of costume. Here, it is the Sligo Militia, at cannon practice, and apparently at war with the incoming waves, on which they fire, but with little success, as to making the enemy fall back; and there, it is a body of the Royal Irish police, going through military evolutions, and displaying in their movements, as well as in their handsome, manly, and martial forms, those qualities and attributes which have earned for them the reputation of being the finest body of military, or quasi-military men in Europe; while on the summit of the Green, may often be seen the coast-guards of Rosses Point, signalling by mirrors to the coast-guards of Raghly, who flash back in turn, question and answer—this strange correspondence often drawing from some of the gaping simpletons, who witness it, remarks and exclamations hardly less entertaining, than the manipulation of the mirrors.

Each of these attractions brings numbers of the curious from Sligo and elsewhere; and if other inducements in the form of regattas, horse races, fire-works, or band music, were provided on as liberal a scale, as they are provided in other quarters, the Point would soon become as fashionable, as it is a healthful watering place.

The interior of this tract, with the exception of Bomore, is uneven and rugged, broken up into small rath-like mounds or hillocks, from twenty to thirty feet high; the surface of the sides and summits being, in great part, naked rock. Taking advantage of the configuration of the land, people in remote times turned the mounds into formidable fortifications, by rearing round them, and on them circles of large stones, many of which still remain

---

[397] Pleasant idleness, literally: sweet doing nothing, Italian, [Clachan ed.].

in situ. One of these elevations, which is called Liscorrach, and is twenty-three yards in diameter, had a cave excavated in the centre, and a ring of sand stones round the top; while another, which goes by the name of Doonemeelin, owes much more to art than the rest, as it is coated all round, and on the top, with earth and sods, and is surrounded at the base with a deep ditch, as well as surmounted with a parapet, which served as an enclosure and defence for the summit. In the southern half of the space within the parapet, are the remains of another enclosure, which was of an oblong form, and which manifestly encompassed two or three small structures of some kind, the foundation stones of which may still he seen. The whole was probably an ecclesiastical establishment, and the small buildings may have been those beehive shaped cells, that are sometimes found in such places; though local gossip connects Doonemeelin with the Danes, and tells a long story about how it was once given with an Irish maiden, as a marriage portion, to a sea rover from Denmark.

Frequent mention of the Rosses occurs in the annals of Ireland. Under the year 3790, the Four Masters record the eruption of the sea, between Eabha and Ros-Cette, from which we may infer, that previously to that date, the Rosses formed part of Magherow, or the Plain of Eabha. Geologists will be inclined to demur to the statement of the Four Masters, and to refer the "eruption", or, speaking more correctly, the irruption, to geological, rather than to historical time; but the changes which have taken place on this coast, even within the last century, lend great probability to the assertions of the Annalists.

About a hundred years ago, the village in which the inhabitants of Lower Rosses lived, stood on the strand which is now regularly covered with, the sea, at the flow of the tide; much later still, the channel in front of Lissadell was so narrow, that, to use the quaint expression of an old inhabitant of the neighbourhood, a man might throw a riddle across it; and, twenty or thirty years back, boats bringing in rack to Lower Rosses, had to wait near Raghley for the rise of the tide, to get over a ridge or *fearsat* that ran from there to John's Port, where now sailing boats of considerable draught can move freely about at all times. Whoever, bearing these facts in mind, and looking seaward, when the tide is well out, observes the scene before him—to the left a low ledge of rock, running from Coney Island to the lighthouse, and to the right, a ridge of sand, no doubt, covering rock, stretching almost the whole way from Lower Rosses to Raghley, will get a good idea of the rapid inroads which the sea is making on this coast, and will find it easier to accept, than to reject, the account of the Four Masters.

In the *Vita Tripartita* of St. Patrick, by Colgan, we read that the saint visited the Rosses, when removing from Connaught to Ulster, passing through them on his way from Killaspugbrone to Magh Cedne.[398] It is not recorded that he erected a church in the district, but it is not unlikely that he did so, as there are some traditions in the place of a primitive church, which St. Columba frequented when a little boy, and which may fairly be supposed to have been built by Saint Patrick. Nor is there any proof that Columba himself built any of his churches in the Rosses, for, though his name is mingled largely with the gossiping traditions of the inhabitants, the stories told, from their nature, must be of modern origin, and arose, apparently, from the saint's well known connection with the neighbouring district of Drumcliff.

One of these stories is, that he lived in the place as a poor scholar; and that while others turned the back upon him, a lad named Killerlean took him home, and treated him hospitably. To repay the kindness, Columba, when quitting the school, left Killerlean an old shoe, with a promise, that while the Killerleans kept it, they would never want money, and would, besides, be able to cure several specified diseases of cattle. The shoe, it is said, remained for long an heir-loom in the family, bringing them all sorts of good luck; but having been lent to a "man of the North", who had cattle sick, it was never returned, thus, unfortunately, leaving the Killerleans of the Rosses, as poor as their neighbours. How this story arose, it is left to others to investigate; but, most probably it was concocted to popularize some alleged cattle cure.

Cattle cures, however, did not cease in the Rosses with the disappearance of the shoe. What this talisman did in the past is now affected by the Elf-stones. A *nomme* A ------ of Lower Rosses is the owner or guardian of these, to him, precious stones, which are warranted to cure all elf-shot cattle; and elf-shot cattle, according to the large local interpretation, are cattle suffering from any disease whatever.

Happening one day to be on the hill of Upper Rosses, and seeing a lad with a bottle in one hand, and a small parcel in the other, coming in haste from the Lower Rosses, the writer asked him what he had with him, and was told it was the Elf-stones. Asking to see them, the lad, half reluctantly, handed over the parcel which, being opened, was found to contain eight small stones—one of quartz, of about five ounces weight; another of quartz, of about three ounces; one of silica, of an ounce and a half; and five more, which seemed chips of different kinds of sandstone—all tied up in a rag. The bottle, the lad said, contained water of three mearings, that is, water taken out of a pool, where the mearings of three tenants' holdings meet. Before application, the stones with sixpence in

---

[398] Trias Thaumaturga, Vita Tripartita, S. Patricii, page 143 -".Patrick went afterwards past Drumcliffe, from Caisel-Irra, by the Rosses eastwards along Magh-Enni, and founded Domhnach-mor of Magh-Enni".—Hennessy's Translation of the Tripartite Life of St. Patrick, p. 432.

silver, and two pence in copper, were to be thrown into a jug and covered with the water of the bottle; and after this mysterious operation, three drops of the liquid were to be administered internally to the sick animal, when the rest should be applied with friction externally, beginning at the tail, traversing both sides of the back bone, and finishing with the roots of the horns. It is well to add, though it may serve as a testimonial for the crafty owner of the Elf-stones, that the simple boy, that carried them on this occasion to the sick beast, boasted afterwards, and firmly believed, that the cure proved efficacious the moment it was applied.

Church structures however stood in the Rosses, whoever were the builders; for one is shown on the Down Survey maps in the Upper Rosses, on a spot belonging at present to Captain Gillen; while two, now disused, burying grounds in the Lower Rosses—one called *Lisheen na paiste*, and another, to the west of the *Lisheen*, were, no doubt, in the past attached to churches.

From time immemorial, down to the recent disestablishment of the church in Ireland, the Rosses were church land, belonged first, to the religious of Drumcliff, but later, to the bishop of Elphin, and were held under him by tenants at an annual rent, as we learn from an exchequer inquisition, sped at Sligo, on the 7th July, 1612, under John Kinge,[399] in which inquisition the Upper Rosses is called Rossibeolain, from the Drumcliff ecclesiastical family, named Beolan, and the Lower Rosses, Rosse McAnerleyne, the original, probably, of the name Killerlean, common still in the place.

The "striping", as it is called, of the Rosses, including Gregg, which divided the district into the existing holdings, took place about 1860, and against the will of nearly all the tenants. Two men, named Barber and Yeates, were the chief instruments employed in the operation, Barber taking the lion's share of the work, and incurring most of the odium of the transaction. Up to that time the people held in rundale, and were spoken of as One-cow tenants, Two-cow tenants, etc., according to their right to graze one, two, or more cows. It was pretended by the "stripers" that the new holdings would be made out on the principle of giving to each tenant a quantity of land proportionable to his former grazing right; but, instead of acting on this equitable principle, the managers, if we are to believe what everyone in the Rosses says, so handled the matter as to help their favourites at the expense of all others. The stripes being arranged, the poor people had to take what they got; and to add to the evil, while the land they received was less than it ought to be, their rents were enormously increased.

Nor was this the only injustice they had to put up with. Before the striping, Bomore, and what is now known as the Green, were a common,

---

[399] Sligo Inquisitions. —Inquisitio 15a.

on which all the tenants had a prescriptive right to pasture cattle free; but they were now tricked out of this; for Barber and Co., professing a desire to serve them by planting bent along the sea to keep off the blowing sand, and pretending they could not do this without receiving possession of the land from the tenants, asked the possession, giving at the same time an assurance that the people would get the grass again at a nominal rent. The simpletons gave what was asked, but found, when too late, that they were juggled out of their rights, and that the new charges for grazing were up to the full value of the land.

The Rosses were purchased in 1867 by the late Mr. William Middleton, from the Misses Cooper, the purchase money being £17,500. Under its new owners the place has greatly prospered, about £2,500 having been expended by Mr. Middleton and his family in improvements. Between the substantial and commodious lodges built by Mr. Middleton himself, those put up by others, to whom he granted building leases, the hotels and shops that have been erected, and the many houses that have been recently enlarged and otherwise improved, Rosses Point has now ample and suitable accommodation for all classes of sea-side visitors.

The place is daily extending; and remembering that, in the early years of the century, there was not a single house on the site of the village, there is good ground for thinking that it is destined to be soon much larger and more important than it is, so as to hold, in regard to Sligo, the same relation that Kingstown does in regard to Dublin. In the past the absence of places of worship and schools interfered very much with its progress, but this want is now well supplied by the neat little Gothic church and schools of the Protestants, and the beautiful church and schools erected, in 1878-9, by the indefatigable Father Moraghan, for the Catholic inhabitants and visitors. With all these advantages—natural, social, and religious—the future of Rosses Point is assured.

The Rosses property comprises 642 acres, 2 roods, 6 perches, Irish measure, and was, every foot of it, church land. The details are given in what is called "A Map of the twelve cartrons of the Upper and Lower Rosses and Creggiconnell, in the barony of Carbury, and county of Sligo, being part of the See lands of Elphin, in lease to Mrs. Cooper, surveyed anno 1721, per Garrett Hogan", and are as follows:—

		A.	R.	P.
Upper	and Lower Rosses and Creggiconnell—arable	456	0	0
"	Island—arable	4	0	
"	Rocky Pasture	45	0	0
"	Land overblown with sand	93	0	0
"	Sand Banks	19	2	0

"   Doonierin ½ Cartron—arable   25   0   0
                                        Total   642   2   6
            [Exclusive of 9 acres of bog.]

There is a difference of opinion as to the origin of the name, DRUMCLIFF. Some will have it, that it means the ridge of the mountain, not because it is mountainous in itself, but because it is at the back of the mountain—an explanation which savours too much of the "lucus a non lucendo"[400] school of etymology. Drumcliff, ridge of the chest, as others say, from some resemblance between its physical outline and that of the human trunk. The Dinnseanchus derives it from a fleet of 150 wicker work curraghs *(cliabh cureich)* prepared there in pre-historic times for the siege of Dunbare, a fortress which Thomas O'Connor, in one of the Ordnance Survey Letters,[401] locates in the Rosses, though, on inquiry, we find it has neither a "local habitation, nor a name", in that district; but the Dinnseanchus is as fanciful in this as it is in many other of its derivations. "While still taking *cliabh* (basket, cage, hamper,) for the root of the name, others make other applications—one, that the place was so called from its abounding in hazel, the material of wicker-work; another, from its being strewed with specimens of the manufactured work, such as fishing baskets, hampers, panniers for beasts of burden; and a third, from its being covered, after the erection of the monastery, with wicker-work cells for the monks: an account of the matter which gains considerable probability from the analogy of the neighbouring Drumlias, so called, as expressly stated in the Vita Tripartita,[402] from being studded with the huts of the religious.

Lying between Glencar and the bay, and flanked on either side with noble mountains, the surroundings of Drumcliff are picturesque. It would be impossible to find, in Ireland, a more charming spot than GLENCAR, of which Drumcliff may be regarded as a kind of prolongation. This valley, which runs from east to west, between the parallel mountain ranges of Slieve Carbury to the north, and Castlegal, or *Slieve-gan-baistead* to the south, is about three miles in length, and about one mile in breadth, being straight and symmetrical from end to end. Receiving the rays of the morning and of the evening sun in their direct flow, and those of the hot and glaring

---

[400] *[it is] a grove by not being light,* From late 4th-century grammarian Honoratus Maurus, mocking an example of an etymological contradiction, [Clachan ed.].
[401] In his letter Mr. O'Connor writes, "Drumcliff took its name, it is stated in the Dinnseanchus, from 150 wicker boats (cliabh curach,) which Curnan Cos dubh fitted out there for the purpose of plundering Dun-bare, then in the possession of Ainnle, the son of Luighaid of the Long Hands. He continued the siege for a year and a half, at the expiration of which time he succeeded in razing the fort. Dunbarc is still in existence, at least, as to name, it lies in the Rosses in Carbury". —Letter Book of Ordnance Survey for county Sligo, p. 394.
[402] Trias Thaumaturga, 143. Drumlias "nuncupatum a multitudine casarum et œoedicularum".

noonday, after having been agreeably mellowed by their passage over the depressions and through the peaks of the southern range, Glencar is admirably lighted and heated throughout the entire day, unlike too many glens, which, from having bends or projections that obstruct the light, and from having too much depth for their width, are at once sombre and cold, so as, at the same time, to depress the mind and chill the body. As the setting sun of the summer and autumn months floods, with its gorgeous beams, this charming valley—lighting up its sides and bringing out the varied vegetation with which they are clothed—the singularly green grasses near the base; the stately ferns that lift their graceful forms on every ledge and in every recess; the many indigenous shrubs adorned with variously tinted blossoms that gladden the eye; the rich, glowing, purple of the heath, which covers, as with a canopy, the summits of the sides; and the luxuriant young plantations, with which skilled hands have supplemented the work of Nature, wherever there was room for such an addition; with such surroundings, you forget that you are near the "melancholy ocean", and fancy yourself away in some southern clime, with, however, this important difference, that there you would have to guard yourself from insects and reptiles, while here you may give yourself up to the tranquil enjoyment of the scene, untroubled by the thought of annoyance or danger:—

> "*At rabidae tigres absunt, et saeva leonum*
> *Semina; nec miseros fallunt aconita legentes;*
> *Nec rapit immensos orbes per humum, neque tanto*
> *Squameus in spiram tractu se colligit anguis*".[403]

Nor is this favoured spot without its peculiar advantages in winter. Protected by Slieve Carbury from the most piercing of the winds, the temperature is sufficiently genial, even at times when the weather is insufferably cold elsewhere. And, assuredly, the motions of that man's spirit must be "dull as night", who is not moved with the "concord of sweet sounds" that issue from the thousand streams, streamlets, rills, and rivulets, which, like the strings of a harp, run down from the mountain tops to the river, each current, from the largest stream to the tiniest rillet, contributing its own distinct and separate note to the full diapason, that thrills upon the ear, and fills the whole valley with harmony.

The Glencar waterfall affords as much gratification to the eye as to the ear. At any time through the year, but especially in the winter, it is a striking sight as its body of water leaps from ledge to ledge, down precipices of some hundred feet high.

As to the mysterious *Sruth-an-ail-an-ard*: when the wind blows strongly from the west, the spectacle is nothing short of the sublime, as the

---

[403] Virgil. Georgica. Lib. II., Lin. 151-4.

rushing rivulet, having reached the edge of the precipice, instead of rolling down, in accordance with the laws of gravitation, gets caught, as it were, in some great chemical laboratory, which resolves it into its original elements, and then projects and dissipates these elements, in clouds of glittering spray, through the higher regions of the atmosphere.

The river into which all these streamlets discharge themselves is, of itself, and apart from its incomparable surroundings, of considerable beauty, and great historical interest. It is the scene of one of the most startling events, that have ever occurred in Carbury, though our most learned antiquarians, after repeated attempts to fix the exact locality of the occurrence, have all failed to do so. The event in question is recorded in the *Annals of the Four Masters*, under the year 1029, and is contained in the following entry:—"Hugh O'Ruairc, Lord of Dartry; and the Lord of Carbury; and Aengus O'Hennessy, airinech of Drumcliff; and three score persons along with them, were burned in Innis-na-lainne, in Carbury Mor".[404]

Under this entry, O'Donovan, in his edition of the Four Masters, writes in a note, "Inis-na-lainne, i.e., the Sword Island. This was the name of an island off the coast of the barony of Carbury, and county of Sligo, but it is now obsolete". In this location our great topographer is in error, as he not infrequently is, in his fancied identification of other localities in the county Sligo.

Inis-na-lainne is certainly the eastern crannoge, which, still exists, though somewhat diminished in size, in that expansion of Glencar river, which is now called Glencar Lake, or Lough-na-Glena; and this is proved by the words of the Four Masters; by the peculiar situation of the crannoge; and by a decisive passage of the Book of Fenagh.

---

[404] Annals of the Four Masters, A.D. 1029. In the Annals of Tighernach the entry is, "Great mortality in the island of Lana in Carbria Magna". The event is recorded in the Chronicon Scotorum under the year 1027, and runs thus: "A great loss of life in Inis-na-lainne in Cairbre-mor, in which were burned twelve score men of the nobles of Cairbre, and the King of Dartraighe, and the King of Cairbre, and the airchinnech of Drumcliff". It will be seen that the Four Masters and the Chronicon Scotorum differ as to the number lost—the former making it three score, and the latter twelve score.

It is not said whether it was by accident or design this calamity was brought about. A similar conflagration was caused in the following century by lightning in Rock Island, Loch Ce: "The Rock of Loch Ce was burned by lightning. Duvesa, daughter of O'Heyne, and wife of Conor Mac Dermot, Lord of Moylurg, with seven hundred (or seven score) others or more, both men and women, were drowned or burned in it in the course of one hour".—Annals of the Four Masters, A.D. 1187.

From the smallness of Rock Island it was impossible to escape once the place was on fire; and it was, no doubt, from a similar cause—the crannage being immediately surrounded on all sides with water—that the conflagration of Inis-na-lainne proved so fatal. And this consideration shows that the occurrence of 1029 could not have happened in any of the islands off the coast, as there would have been ample room to fly to for safety even in the smallest of them.

And, first, as the words of the annalists are not "*Near* Carbury Mor", or "off the coast of Carbury Mor", but "*In* Carbury Mor", they indicate an island in the inland and not in the sea, as O'Donovan and his copyists would have it.

Secondly, the situation of the crannoge, lying partly in Dartry, O'Rorke's territory, partly in Carbury, the territory of the Lord of Carbury, and quite close to Drumcliff, the abode of the erenagh O'Hennessy, is just the central situation which would be selected for the conference of the two chiefs and the erenagh. This consideration struck the writer so forcibly, that he concluded the crannoge to be the scene of the tragedy, even before he fell in with the statement of the Book of Fenagh, which seems quite decretorial on the subject.

Lastly then, and chiefly, our river is expressly called the Lainne in the Book of Fenagh, where we read of one of the O'Rorkes:—

> *"That Cu will be an erector of churches.*
> *I will tell you his territory:*
> *The mild belted Cu will possess*
> *From Bun-Lainne to Lemain".* [405]

In the last line the author lays down the limits of Breffney, or O'Rorke's country; and, as the Four Masters themselves, when describing the territorial jurisdiction of the Archdeacon of Breffney, fix these limits as Drumcliff, on the one side, and Kells on the other,[406] it follows that Bun-Lainne, the mouth of the Lainne[407], J stands for Drumcliff, and Lemhain for Kells; Lemhain being, apparently, the Blackwater of Meath, which rises in Lough Ramor, passes through Kells, and mingles at Navan with the Boyne.

This river was called Sele in St. Patrick's time.[408] Colgan has the following note on the passage in which it is so called: "Hodie fluvius hic Abhan-dhubh, id est, fluvius niger appellatur"[409]. It is not hard to conjecture how Sele became Lemhain. By adding the word abhain, we get Sele-abhain, the river Sele, which, from the general tendency of time to shorten words, would soon change, first, into Slemhain (Sele-abhain,) and, then, into Lemhain.

Major Wood Martin would identify Inis-na-Lainne with Inismurray, and seems to think he has made an important discovery in connection with

---

[405] The Book of Fenagh. By W. M. Hennessy, M.R.I.A., and D. H. Kelly, M.R.I.A. Pages 77-78.

[406] Annals of the Four Masters, 1296. Maelpeter O'Duigenan, Archdeacon of Breifny, from Drumcliff to Kells.

[407] The mouths of all the smaller rivers in this part of the country are called Bun—as Bunduff, Bundrowes, Bunbreunoge, Bunina, Bunlainne, etc.

[408] Trias Thaumaturga, p. 129 —Wilde's *Boyne and Blackwater,* p. 137.

[409] "Today this river, Abhan-dhubh, is the river called black", [Clachan ed.].

the subject; for, in a note to the fourth Chapter of his History, page 168, he writes:—"Since this chapter has gone through the press, a closer examination of the map, made in 1609, of the Sligo and Donegal coasts, disclosed the interesting fact that Inismurray was therein described as Enish Humae, or Murrie. The former name may be a corruption of Inis-na-Lainne, where in A.D. 1209" (should be 1029,) "the Erenagh of Drumcliff and sixty other persons were burned to death". This is all he says in support of his peculiar view; and how it goes to show the identity of the two islands mentioned, others, perhaps, may be able to make out, but the present writer "gives it up". It may be that Major Wood Martin meant his suggestion as a joke, for the purpose of "sending the fool further", for Inismurray is absolutely the last spot in the neighbourhood that could be selected for the conference in question. The difficulty of getting into the island, even in the fine sailing or rowing craft of our own time, and the danger of being weather-bound when got in, prevent tourists, and most other people, from venturing across the sound at present; but the transport of the Lord of Dartry, the Lord of Carbury, and the Erenagh of Drumcliff, with their suite of sixty, or two hundred and forty, attendants, in the tiny *currachs* of the eleventh century, would have been, in those times, an operation quite as extraordinary and sensational as Professor Baldwin's journey, *per parachute*, in our own days, from his balloon to *terra firma*.

And supposing, *per impossible,* this host of people assembled in Inismurray, and a fire broken out among them, they would surely have room enough in the three hundred acres around them to get out of harm's way. The conjecture, then, under consideration, whether meant in jest or in earnest, is nothing short of fantastic in all its parts.

Coming back, now, to the writer's contention, it is confirmed by the name, Lough Dolan, given in the Down Survey maps, to Glencar lake. At first view it would look as if Lough Dolan was so called from some person or family named Dolan; but, as no such person or family is known to have ever had any connection with the district, another explanation must be searched for; and the most probable, indeed, the only probable, explanation, that suggests itself, is to regard the second syllable, *lan*, in Dolan, as the essential part of the name, the "Do" being, probably, an English corruption of Dubh (whose most usual English forms, according to Dr. Joyce, are *duff, doo*, and *du*), the compound word thus signifying, the black or dark Lan, or Lainne, or Lana, for the name appears under each of these forms. Nor would black or dark be an inappropriate epithet, as the lake proper, owing to the towering mountain on either side, wears occasionally a somewhat gloomy look.

From all this, it is abundantly clear that Inis-na-Lainne is the crannoge referred to above; and this fact, once ascertained, it is easy enough to understand the loss of life that ensued, and was inevitable, in so confined and crowded an area.

Further on, a conjecture will be offered, as to the origin of the name Lan, Lana, or Lainne, of which nobody seems to know anything.

The tragedy of 1029 was near being repeated in 1541, the actors, at the latter date, being, probably, moved to act by the example of 1029. At both times, the eastern crannoge of the island belonged to the O'Rorkes; and one branch of the family having taken it by force from another, two sons of the dispossessed chief came stealthily by night, and set fire to it. The fire, fortunately, was immediately discovered, and got under; while the incendiaries having been pursued on the lake, one of them was drowned, and the other captured and hanged.[410]

The part of Glencar which is contained in the county Sligo, belonged to the O'Connors Sligo, and was held in 1606 by Phelim O'Connor; and we learn from the Book of Distributions that the O'Connors lost it after 1641, and that Glendallan and Lislahely were reserved for Pious Uses, with the exception of 9 acres, not specified, which were granted to Roger Parke.[411]

As to the meaning of the word Glendallan, John O'Donovan and others derive it from a man named Dalian, Glendallan being according to them, "Dalian's Glen;"[412] but it is not less likely that it means the "glen of the pillar stone". O'Donovan himself explains the *alias* name of Glendallan, namely Glencar, in Irish *gleann a chairthe*, as signifying the glen of the pillar stone; and as *dallan* as well as *cairthe* means a monumental stone,[413] it is reasonable to give the word that sense here, thus allowing two words which designate the same object, to have the same signification. This, perhaps, is

---

[410] The eastern crannoge on the Lough of Glenn Dallain was taken by the sons of Donnell, son of Donnell O'Rourke, from Donough, the son of Donough O'Rourke. In some time after this, the sons of Donogh O'Rourke, i.e. Donnell and Fergannain, made an attack upon the crannog, and privately set fire to the town; but that thing being discovered and perceived, they were pursued upon the lake, and overtaken by the sons of Donnell. Fergannain, the son of Donough, was slain and drowned; and Donnell was taken and afterwards hanged by the sons of Donnell, son of Donough O'Rourke. Annals of the Four Masters, 1541.

[411] In an Inquisition taken at Rosslee, on the 29th December, 1616, concerning the lands of the county Sligo, the jury find "that Phelim O'Connor is seized in demesne as of fee, and in full possession of the town and lands of Glendallan, the quarter of Glendallan, the town and lands of Lislahely, the quarter of Lislahely, with their appurtenances, in the barony of Carbury". And the Book of Distributions tells us, that "Lislahely, consisting of six different parcels, being respectively 213 acres, 54 acres, 16 acres, 68 acres, 17 acres, and 322 acres, having belonged to Cahall O'Connor, was reserved for pious uses, as was also (excepting 9 acres granted to Roger Park) the whole of Glencarbry (Glendallan), consisting of 106 acres, 9 acres, 154 acres, 155 acres, 37 acres, 38 acres, and 68 acres, belonging also to Cahall O'Connor.

[412] Note under A.D. 1541 in O'Donovan's Four Masters.

[413] Ulster Journal of Archaeology. Vol. VIII., p. 115.

more natural than to conjure up the unknown Dalian, who may seem, to some, to be invented for the occasion.

The term, however, may, under the circumstances, have either sense the glen of the pillar stone, or the Glen of Dalian for we learn from the *Genealogia Sanctorum* (cap. 18), that a man named Dalian, father of St. Loman of Lough Gill, lived in this neighbourhood, after whom the valley may have been called.

And this suggests a word or two on the saints or holy persons, whose names are associated with Glendallan. They are three—Talulla, Osnata, and Muadhnata, daughters of Nadfraich, and sisters of one another, as well as of St. Molaisse of Devenish; and their joint festival is set down in the Martyrologies for the 6th January. Talulla travelled south, and became abbess of Kildare; Osnata lived at the eastern end of Glencar, leaving her name to the parish of Killasnet, *Cille Osnat*; and Muadhnata had her residence in a part of Carbury called Caille, which has not been identified, but which the writer believes to be Ballynagalliagh. For Ballynagalliagh is only a corruption of Bally-na-Caillech, the town of the nuns; and as caillech, a nun, comes from *caille*, the veil that nuns take on becoming religious, it is not hard to understand how this word, in combination or composition with some other, which it lost in the course of time, came to designate a habitation of nuns. In his interesting notice of St. Osnata, Father O'Hanlon observes, "There was a tradition among the people that the old church of Killasnat was first built in Castletown townland; but that it was afterwards removed and built in one night, where the old churchyard, called Killasnat, is now situated . . . This, however, is a worthless tradition, although Irish local traditions are, in the main, highly valuable". This, after all, may not be so meaningless a tradition as it looks; for, very probably, it signifies that the religious establishment of Killasnat is a daughter of that of Ballynagalliagh, which lies near Castletown, and that Muadhnata's community having become numerous, she sent some of the nuns, under her sister Osnata, to found a new house at the eastern side of the glen.

Ballynagalliagh itself depended on, and belonged to, the Benedictine nunnery of Kilcreunat, in Galway. This we learn from a chancery inquisition of James I. sped at Sligo, under Geoffry Osbaldston, on the 26th April, 1606, in which the jurors find "that there belonged to the late nunnery of Kilcrenat, in the county Galway, 1½ qr. called Ballenagallagh, and certain other small spots of land in the town of Dromclive, in the barony of Carbury". It is nowhere stated when or how, Ballynagalliagh became connected with Kilcreunat, but, probably, it was very soon after the foundation of the latter by Cathal Crovderg O'Conor (A.D. 1200); for the descendants of Cathal's uncle, Brian Luignech, were then at Castletown, and would naturally like to have near them an offshoot of their great relative's establishment. By this time, too, the spiritual family of Muadhnata may have died out, or may have needed an infusion of new blood, as sometimes happened in those times with other religious establishments; and, in either case, it would have been easy for the nuns of Kilcreunat to effect a settlement at Ballynagalliagh. At the suppression, Kilcreunat, with its dependencies, including Ballynagalliagh, was granted to Richard, Earl of Clanrickarde.

Coming back, now, to Drumcliff, we find that the place was once called *Cnoc na teagh*, though we are not informed why it was so called. The only name of the place, however, which we meet with, in the annals of the country, is that by which it is known at the present day, Drumcliff. Lying far out of the former highway between Connaught and Ulster, the district was little known, and less frequented, till St. Columba founded there one of his many churches—an event which Dr. Reeves, who has taken special pains to elucidate the acts of the saint, fixes at 574,[414] immediately after the close of the famous convention at Drumceat, and immediately before the saint's visit to Ballysadare, where, as we read in Colgan's Life of St. Farannan,[415] he was met by the "chief saints" of Ireland.

Even apart from its picturesque surroundings, there is something striking in the immediate location of Drumcliff. Stretched between the western end of Glencar valley and the sea, a man of travel or reading, in looking at it, would almost fancy it to be the dried up delta of some great river, which once rolled on between Castlegal and Slieve Mor, and discharged its waters into the sea at the mouth of the valley.

It is admitted, on all hands, that Drumcliff was a place of some importance in times long past. Some writers affecting to give particulars, for which they have neither authority nor data, would have us believe that, exclusive of stone structures, it counted fifteen hundred wooden houses.[416] But this is only ridiculous exaggeration, there being hardly fifteen hundred houses or huts of any kind, in the times referred to, throughout the entire district comprised in the present county Sligo. It is bounce like this, that has brought discredit on much of our early history.

As far as we know now, whatever importance Drumcliff could boast of, was of a purely ecclesiastical character, and it fared with it as with most other religious houses in Ireland. When a monastery prospered, population flowed towards it:—consisting, first, of young persons who came to join the community as novices; secondly, of such lay persons as were wanted for agricultural or other works, always in progress about the place; thirdly,

---

[414] Reeve's *Adamnan*, p. 37
[415] Acta Sanctorum.—Vita S. Farannani, pp. 339, 340.
[416] *Dublin Penny Journal*, Vol. I., p. 64. This article gives "several magnificent stone churches and fifteen hundred houses of oak;" but it refers only to the "village tradition", as its authority. Dr. Petrie seems to be the writer of the article. Certain other writers, however, set the statement down as fact without any qualification.

of the poor and sick, who were fed, and clothed, and cared, by the religious; and fourthly, as in the case of Armagh, Bangor, Clonfert, Lismore, and other large establishments, famed for their schools, by students whom love of learning attracted from other parts of the country, and even from other countries. Considering that Drumcliff was the only religious house of note in Carbury, in early times, large numbers of the first three classes must have flocked to it; and it is said, though the evidence on the point is by no means conclusive, that it imparted "a higher kind of education", something analogous to what is now called a college education, and thus became the centre of flocks of students. In any case the abodes of the lay people did not form a town in the modern sense of the word, with its shops, and business, and commerce, but were rather an extension of the monastery, as the inhabitants depended altogether on the religious establishment for employment and subsistence.

There is nothing known of the monastery during the two or three centuries which followed its foundation. It is this absence of knowledge that makes Dr. Lanigan lean to the belief, that Columba is not to be accounted its founder;[417] but the arguments, on the other side, are so strong, as to leave hardly any room for doubt on the subject.

In the first place, the Life of St. Farannan informs us expressly, that Saint Columba, after the convention of Drumceat, founded a religious house in Carbury; while all writers seem agreed, that this house can be no other than that of Drumcliff.

Secondly, the tradition of the locality, and of the whole country, counts Columba to be the founder.

Thirdly, abbots of Drumcliff are styled in our annals, "comarbs of Columba", which seems decisive on the matter, as in Irish writings, the comarb of an abbot or of a bishop, always means the formal successor in office of that abbot or bishop.

Fourthly, it is represented by old writers as a favourite resort of the saint.[418]

And some probability may be drawn from the very situation of Drumcliff; for it must have formed part of the great battlefield of Cooldruman; and nothing is more natural, or more in accordance with the ideas of religious men at all times, than that Columba, on revisiting those blood-stained scenes, in which, unfortunately, he had been a chief actor, and thinking, like Judas Machahaeus, well and religiously of the resurrection,[419] should desire to leave for ever on the spot a place of prayer,

---

[417] Ecclesiastical History of Ireland, Vol. II., p. 132.
[418]   "Beloved to my heart also in the west,
Drumcliff at Culcinne's strand".
—Adamnan's Life of St. Columba. By Dr. Reeves, p. 289.
[419] Second Book of Machabees, c. xii., v. 43.

where petitions should be constantly put up for the souls of those who had fallen in that ill-starred engagement. Putting all those arguments together, and without dwelling on others, which might be adduced, such as the authority of ancient and modern biographers, the man must be abnormally prone to doubt—as Dr. Lanigan sometimes shows himself—who does not admit their conclusiveness. To insist on further proof for primitive facts, like that under consideration, would be only to unsettle nine-tenths of our early Irish history.

Nor is the silence, regarding Drumcliff, for the first three centuries of its existence a matter of surprise. The place being then singularly secluded, and remote from thoroughfares, it was almost a matter of course that it should remain long unnoticed and unknown, unlike other monasteries of Saint Columba, which stood in the most frequented parts of Ireland, and thus attracted attention from the outset. And only for the accident, that a local chief of distinction was buried there in 871, the monastery might have continued much longer without mention; the connection of Dunadhach's burial with Drumcliff, thus suggesting how the place had escaped notice for the two preceding centuries, for want of some similar occurrence. Even after Dunadhach's burial, fifty years more elapsed before mention is again made of Drumcliff; but after that time, references are sufficiently frequent and regular in old authorities, as will appear from the list given below, which the writer has taken pains to make as complete as possible.

The following appeared here as a lengthy footnote in the original, [Clachan ed.]
574. Mothorianus, first abbot O'Donnell's Life of St. Columba; lib. 1, cap. 60.
871. Dunadhach, son of Raghallach, lord of Cinel-Cairbre-Mor, died; of his death was said:—"Dunadhach, a noble protection, a famous man by whom hostages were held,
A pious soldier of the race of Conn (lies interred), under hazel crosses at Drumcliff". —Annals of the Four Masters.
921. Maelpadraig, son of Moran, abbot of Drumcliff and Ardstraw, died.—Four Masters.
930. Maengal, son of Becan, abbot of Drumcliff, died,—Four Masters.
950. Flann O'Becan, arinech of Drumcliff; Scribe of Ireland, died.—Four Masters.
1029. Aengus O'Hennessy, airinech of Drumcliff, burned in Inis-na-lainne.—Four Masters.
1053. Murchadh O'Beollain, airinech of Drumcliff, died.—Four Masters.
1177. Died, Murroh O'Bollan, comarb of Drumcliff and St. Columb.—Archdall's *Monasticon Hiberntcum*, p. 631.
1187. Drumcliff was plundered by the son of Melaghlin O'Rorke, Lord of Hy Briuin and Conmaicne.—Four Masters.
And St. Columbkille wrought a remarkable miracle; for the son of Melaghlin O'Rorke was killed in Conmaicne a fortnight afterwards, and the eyes of the son of Cathal O'Rorke were put out by O'Muldory in revenge of Columbkille. One hundred and twenty of the sons of Melaghlin's retainers were also killed, throughout Conmaicne and Carbury of Drumcliff.—Four Masters.
1188. Rory O'Cannanain was slain by O'Muldory, after having been enticed out from the middle of Drumcliff.—Annals of Loch Ce.

1201. Great numbers of Northerns slain between Ballysadare and Drumcliff.—Annals of Loch Ce.

1213. Finn O'Brolloghan went to Carbury of Drumcliff to collect O'Donnell's tribute.—Four Masters.

1225. Awley O'Beollain, principal upholder of the hospitality and guest houses of Erinn, died in this year.—Annals of Loch Ce.

1252. Malachy O'Beollain, comarb of Columbkille in Drumcliff, i.e., the man of greatest prosperity, wealth, and esteem, of greatest charity, hospitality, and honour, in his own time in Erinn, died after the triumph of devotion and penitence.—Annals of Loch Ce.

1254. Maelfinnen O'Beollain, coarb of Drumcliff, died.—Four Masters.

1258. Hostages of all the Hy-Briun from Kells to Drumcliff, delivered up to Hugh O'Neil.—Four Masters.

1267. A depredation by the English of West Connaught in Carbury of Drumcliff.—Four Masters.

1296. Maelpeter O'Duigenan, archdeacon of Breffny, from Drumcliff to Kells, died.—Four Masters.

1306. Nicholas O'Donaghy (i.e., who was a priest and pure virgin in Drumcliff) was killed without cause or offence, by the Gerran-dubh of the Barretts, who subjected him to a martyr's death.—Annals of Loch Ce.

To this entry is added, in Annals of Ulster, "and whosoever saieth a Pater Noster for his soule, he hath 26 dayes forgiveness of his sins as often as he sayth it".—Note in O'Donovan's edition of Four Masters, sub anno.

1315. The daughter of Manus O'Conor, wife of O'Donnell, attacked the churches of Drumcliff, where several of the clerics and comarbs of Drumcliff were plundered by her.—Annals of Loch Ce.

1317. A battle on the brink of the Methenagh (i.e., a river) of Drumcliff.—Four Masters.

1330. Maelisa O'Ooinel, coarb of Drumcliff, died.—Four Masters.

1355. Conor Mac Consnava, Bishop of Breifny, from Drumcliff to Kells, died.—Four Masters.

1362. O'Beollain, coarb of Drumcliff, died.—Four Masters.

1416. Maurice O'Coineoil, coarb of Drumcliff, was burned in his own house by robbers.—Four Masters.

1503. O'Beollain, coarb of St. Columbkille at Drumcliff, died.—Four Masters.

The chief authority in the monastery, as well temporal as spiritual, seems to have become, very early, hereditary in two families; for, with the exception of "Maelpadraig, son of Moran, abbot of Drumcliff;" "Flann, grandson of Becan, erenagh[420] of Drumcliff;" and "Aengus O'Hennessy, erenagh of Drumcliff;" the other rulers of the establishment belonged to one or other of the two families, O'Beollain and O'Coineil, and are called at one time "abbots", at another, "coarbs of Drumcliff and Columbkille;"[421] and again, "erenaghs and biatachs[422]" of Drumcliff. It is plain that the two

---

[420] A medieval Irish office—erenagh (from old Irish *érenach*) was responsible for receiving parish revenue from tithes and rents, building and maintaining church property and overseeing the termon lands that generated parish income, [Clachan ed.].

[421] Annals of Four Masters. 1252, 1254, 1330, 1362, 1416, 1503.

[422] A Biatach was responsible for the welfare of the poor and homeless and for the provision of food and shelter to travellers, [Clachan ed.].

families of O'Beollain and O'Coineoil were of great note in Carbury in their day; and we have a lasting proof of their consequence in the many places of the neighbourhood to which they have left their names, as Ballyconnell, near Lissadell; Gregg Connell, to the east of Lower Rosses; Rossbeolain, one of the old names of Upper Rosses; Ballybeolain and Templebeolain, near Raghly; and Inisbeolain—*insula Beolain*—now known as Horse Island.

With the exception of the outrage of the O'Rorkes, in 1187, which was so signally avenged, and a depredation by the English in 1267, Drumcliff appears to have had a rather exceptional career of peace and prosperity from its foundation, in 574, to the fourteenth century. This will appear the more extraordinary, when we consider the melancholy record of burned and plundered churches which one meets with in almost every page of the annals of that period. For this comparative exemption from outrage, the monastery was indebted mainly to its then outlying and unfrequented position.

After the fourteenth century, when it had become a place of great resort, Drumcliff had its share of the calamities, which were going; as in 1315, when Dervorgilla, the wife of O'Donnell, who belonged herself to the turbulent family of Murtough Muimnech O'Conor, attacked its churches, and plundered its monks; and in 1416, when its abbot, Maurice O'Coineoil, was burned in his house by robbers, probably with the object of destroying the witness of their crime.

We may, perhaps, infer from these facts, that Drumcliff had attained its zenith in the thirteenth century. And the inference derives no small probability from the entries in our annals; for, from one, under 1213, we learn that the place had then become so famous, as to change the name of Carbury Mor, into Carbury of Drumcliff; and of Calry of Lough Gill, into Calry of Drumcliff; and from another, under 1252, that its abbot, in the middle of the thirteenth century, was "a man of great esteem and wealth, the most illustrious for hospitality, and the most honoured and venerated by the English and Irish in his time". Indeed, the wealth of Drumcliff was so well known, that the fact is recorded in song[423] and story.

The decline of the place must have set in soon after the death of Malachy O'Beollain; for there is nothing in the references of the *Annals of the Four Masters*, between this time and 1503, to show a continuance of the prosperity of his day; and, as there is no mention at all of the monastery in

---

[423]   "On Derry's plains—in rich Drumcliff
Throughout Armagh the Great, renowned
In olden years,
No day could pass, but woman's grief
Would rain upon the burial ground,
Fresh floods of tears!"
—Lament for the Princes, in Rev. C. P. Meehan's
Fate and Fortunes of the Earls, p. 513.

the native annalists, after 1503, it is likely that it ceased to exist, or had become of little note soon after that date which is the more probable, as, in a list of the abbeys in the county Sligo, which contained monks in 1574, Drumcliff is not included.[424]

The frustum of a round tower, a stone cross, and the shaft of a stone cross, which still exist on the grounds, date, apparently, from before the thirteenth century. As to the tower, this seems certain, for the rude style of the building, the round lumpish stones used, and the absence of all ornament in the way of cornice or carving, would indicate the tenth century, or thereabouts, as the date of the erection.

There is nothing about this structure in our annalists, except, that it was struck by lightning in 1396 ("Campanile, *i.e.*, *Cloightech Drumcliabh*, fulmine destructum"—Mac Firbis—in O'Donovan's Four Masters, A.D. 1396); but there is reason to believe, that it suffered more from man than from the electric fluid; for it is said in the neighbourhood, that the walls were ripped down to find stones for the bridge of Drumcliff.

And the cross may be referred to the same time, for though it is well finished, being decorated with sculptured ornaments and groups of figures—of considerable merit both in design and workmanship—this is not incompatible with the age assigned; for the crosses of Monasterboice, which contain still finer carving, come, according to antiquaries, from the middle of the ninth or the first quarter of the tenth century.[425] The shaft of the other cross, which is devoid of ornament of any kind, and was never touched with chisel, appears to be of a still earlier origin.[426] As Drumcliff was so famous for its crosses, that it got the name of *Drumcliabh na g cros*—Drumcliff of the crosses[427]—we may presume, that it began early to practise the art of carving stone crosses, and acquired early a proficiency in the art.

These three objects are all that remain to attest the ancient importance of Drumcliff. The wood that covered the whole region, has perished, root and branch; the considerable number of oak houses—not to say with the village tradition, the "fifteen hundred"—have not left a trace on the spot; and the "several magnificent stone churches", are as invisible, both in themselves and in remains of any kind, as if they lay buried in the bottom of the neighbouring sea—not a single stone or morsel of mortar surviving to witness their past existence. Indeed, the ground looks so unlike ground which had served for building purposes, that it would be hard to think it ever supported stone and mortar structures, only that the

---

[424] Calendar of Carew MSS., Vol. IV., p. 146.
[425] Ulster Journal of Archaeology, Vol. I., p. 56.
[426] This seems natural, though there is no proof of it.
[427] Letter of Thomas O'Connor, in the Ordnance Survey Letters of the county Sligo, dated, Sligo, Sept. 8th, 1836.

inquisition, already quoted,[428] supplies proof of the fact, the only direct proof, perhaps, adducible; for this authority avers, that at the time of the inquisition,[429] there stood at Drumcliff, "a certain vaulted stone house, called Tagh O'Chonneil", and also, "a church and a house, belonging to the parson of Drumcliff, to the west end of the church".

In the whole barony of Carbury there is not a more interesting spot, excepting, perhaps, Sligo and Drumcliff, than the townland of CASTLETOWN, though this assertion is sure to come by surprise on most readers, so little known, or rather so utterly unknown, at the present day, is the history of the place, even in the immediate neighbourhood. Leaning against the slope of Benbulben, some hundred feet above the level of the sea, Castletown is exceptionally picturesque and salubrious. The view from it is at once extended, varied, and of rare beauty—taking in sea, mountain ranges, several stretches of undulating ground diversified with plantations, crop land, green sward, and near the coast, round sandy dunes; while the bracing air of the lofty mountain slopes, impregnated with the ozone of the sea, is specially fitted to foster health and vigour, to give energy to the brain, action to the heart and lungs, and bloom to the cheek.

If inhabitants of mountain districts have been always remarkable for high spirit and deeds of daring, one would expect Castletown to produce men of superior stamp, in regard both to thought and action; and in this expectation one would not be disappointed, as even an outline of the history of the spot, when now set under the eye, will amply prove.

This place may be called the cradle of the O'Connors Sligo. Rocked in its invigorating atmosphere, and reared amid the stirring associations, in which it abounded, of the renowned Conal Gulban and the Fenians, that family produced men as hardy and soaring as the falcon, which continued in the congenial heights of the adjoining Benbulben, long after eagles had disappeared from most of their other haunts throughout the country. Cathal O'Connor, Rory O'Connor, Cathal Og O'Connor, and other members of the Sligo branch of the Sil-Murray, second to no men in Ireland in their day, for enterprise and heroic conduct, were all born and bred in Castletown.

It was to this eligible spot the survivors of the vanquished O'Conors retired after the battle of Crich-Carbury. In this secluded angle of the country they settled down, in order to increase their flocks and herds, with the view of being one day powerful enough to assert that claim to the territory of Carbury which they had just failed to make good.

And for their purpose, the region of Castletown was the most desirable they could select. There they were beyond the reach of those hostile movements, which were constantly going on in the more open parts

---

[428] Chancery Inquisition, sped at Sligo. By Geoffry Osbaldston, 26th April, 1606.
[429] A.D. 1606.

of the country. There too, in the midst of a vast wood, with several clear spaces of sweet and abundant pasture, they had an inexhaustible supply of food for their cattle, as well as shade in summer, and shelter in winter. And there too, from the elevated position of their residence, they might easily descry the approach of raiders or robbers—but too common at the time— and thus be able to protect their stock, whether the marauders came from the east, through the valley of Glencar, or from some other direction, by the plain of Magherow. In such a situation and with such surroundings, it is little wonder that their flocks and herds soon multiplied to numbers almost beyond counting.

The first name by which the Castletown district was called, is Fassa-coille, which signifies the waste or unoccupied place of the wood. This name it must have retained for centuries, for it is only in 1536 it appears for the first time in the Annals, as Braghaid-coille, a word which means the neck of the wood, and which is a most appropriate designation, as Braghaid-coille holds, in regard to the low-land on one side, and Benbulben mountain on the other, the exact position which the neck occupies in relation to the human body and head. Braghaid-coille soon changed into Bradhiliy, and it is so-called, and marked with a castle, in the map of Norden, who places it under the south-west brow of Benbulben, its exact position. Bradhiliy gave way in a short time to Bradcullen, which, in its turn, was modified to Bradcullium, the form under which the name appears in the Down Survey. It is strange that there is no memory of those names now in the locality, nor any trace of them, except in a small rath-like enclosure, which is commonly called Kilty, *i.e.*, Coillte or Coille—the wood—this part of the name surviving all the changes the original Fassa-coille has undergone in its passage down to the present time.

The name, Castletown, has still to be accounted for, as the Ordnance Survey writers have left us in the dark, in which they found themselves. The writer believes that light may be derived in this matter from an entry in the *Annals of Loch Ce*, under the year 1316, an entry which hitherto has been misunderstood; it runs as follows:—"Hugh O'Donnell and all the Cinel Connell mustered a large army, and they came again into Carbury, and went to Caislen-Conor on this occasion; and Rory, son of Donnell O'Conor, separated from his own brothers, and made peace with O'Donnell, and gave him the lordship of Carbury". The Caislen-Conor here mentioned, is certainly the original of Castletown; though other writers, and among them Mr. Hennessy himself, with his superior knowledge and great ability, but lacking that personal acquaintance with the district, without which errors in descriptive topography are inevitable, suppose the place here referred to, to be Caislen-Conor, or rather Caislen-mic-Conor,[430] of Tireragh.

---

[430] In the works of the Mac Firbises this castle is always called Caislen-mic-Conor, or Dun-mic-Conor, as also in the Four Masters, a fact which, of itself, would show the place to be

But a little reflection would show the error of this supposition. On other occasions, when any chief of the O'Donnells went to Tireragh, it is told how he went there, what he did in it, and how he got back, but here, except the mention of Caislen-Conor, there is not a single circumstance to indicate that he set foot in that district. On the contrary, every word in the entry "he came again into Carbury", and "went to Caislen-Conor", and "Rory gave him the lordship of Carbury "goes to prove, that the expedition was limited to Carbury, that it was undertaken for the sake of Carbury, and that its object was accomplished, when Rory, the eldest of the O'Conors, conceded the lordship of Carbury. The remark, "he went to Caislen-Conor on this occasion", merely tells us that O'Donnell, instead of keeping, as in former expeditions, to the beaten route, described elsewhere,[431] along the sea coast and across the strand, turned aside from it, and passed to the fortress of the O'Conors—Caislen-Conor—on the slopes of Benbulben. We may then conclude with certainty, that the castle of Castletown existed in 1316, and, with great probability, that it was erected in the latter half of that century, when the example of the FitzGeralds, at Sligo, could hardly fail to induce the O'Conors to build; and the qualities of the small fragment which still remains of the original structure, with its grouting, its shell mortar, and other indications of great antiquity, go far to establish this early date, or perhaps, a still earlier one.

The O'Connors had ample means at the time to build such a structure, as also intelligence and spirit enough to see and feel its utility, or, rather, its necessity. The funeral of Donnell supplies abundant proof of their means; for it proves them to be inferior in possessions of all kinds to no family in the country; and as to their intelligence and spirit, their constant contact with the monastery of Drumcliff, which stood at their door, and which was one of the most flourishing establishments of the period, could hardly fail to bring them correct ideas of what was alike due to their own dignity, and needed for their security.

Their own conduct, too, proves them to have been men who could appreciate the requirements of their position, Though they were willing, and even anxious to live at peace with all the world, they were not the less able or inclined to punish whoever should molest them, as they proved on one memorable occasion, when, after hurling back the combined attack of all their enemies, they chased the assailants through Connaught, dethroned the leader of them, who was the king of the province, and put on the throne, in his room, one of themselves, Cathal, as energetic a prince as ever bore rule in this part of Ireland. Even if there were no other proof of the existence of a stone and mortar castle at Fassa-Coille in those early times,

---

different from the Caislen-Conor of the entry under consideration.—O'Donovan's Hy Fiachrach, p. 282.
[431] See Four Masters, 1536.

this character of the O'Connors of the day, would supply a strong one, for such men could not be content to pass their lives in the huts and dens which were the common habitations of the time. While the heads of the family occupied the castle, the rest of the clan had to put up with such frail and humble dwellings as cabins of clay, or booths of wattles. It was in this way the population of the district was lodged; and that population must have been exceptionally large, considering the well-manned expeditions which sometimes set out from Castletown. While other parts of the country were far less populous then than now, there is good reason to believe that Fassa-Coille was more populous in these times than it has ever been since, though the district has been at all times, at least till very recently, the most thickly peopled region in Carbury, excluding the town of Sligo. A strong proof of this populousness is the number of raths or forts, which the neighbourhood still contains, a larger number than any other spot of equal size in this part of the country, though some of those that formerly existed must have been levelled.

These raths, and their surroundings, must always awaken stirring thoughts in the minds of persons acquainted with the history of the place, for it was on them were formed the most successful captains that North Connaught has produced, as it was on the adjoining slopes, and amid the surrounding woods, were trained those intrepid and dashing youths, who swept through all the regions of Connaught in many an irresistible foray, and were known, from the Erne to the mouth of the Shannon, as "the young soldiers of Carbury".

It is pretty certain that Caislen Conor continued to be occupied by the O'Connors as long as it remained habitable. Some people in the district, including the farmer who holds the site of the castle, say they heard that the last occupant of the building was a person named Hart Gormley, but this statement, however it may have originated, has no support in the authentic annals of the country, which always represent the O'Connors as holding the place. They held it up to the beginning of the 17th century; for, in an inquisition taken at Rosslee, on the 29th December, 1616, the jury find "the castle, town, and lands" of Bradcullen, and the quarter called Carrowbradcullen, to be "part of the inheritance of Callough O'Connor, now his Majesty's ward, by descent from his father, Daniel O'Connor, and his uncle, Sir Donough O'Connor". They held it in the middle of that century, at the time of Sir Frederick Hamilton's raid. Sir Frederick having heard, from his spies, that two bodies of Ulster troops had joined Captain Teige Mac Phelim O'Connor at Bradcullen, sent a force of horse and foot to assail them. The attack, as generally happened with Sir Frederick, was successful, and the Manorhamilton men slew about 60 of the Irish, "with all their captains", this latter circumstance proving that the native leaders were brave, if unfortunate, and preferred death to flight.

As a matter of course, the victors practised their accustomed barbarity, and, not satisfied with the 60 men and all the captains, "killed also Captain Teige O'Connor's wife". After despatching the birds, they destroyed the nest "by burning the town of Bradcullen, *belonging to O'Connor*, with divers other small villages neere it". It is a striking proof of the vitality of Bradcullen or Castletown, that even the breath of Hamilton could not blast it; for, in the Cromwellian Census of 1659, it is still set down as the most populous place in the barony of Carbury, after the town of Sligo, the population being fifty-five—four English and fifty-one Irish—the next highest population in the barony being twenty-eight in the Rosses, twenty-seven in Grange, twenty-four in Bunduff, and so on, in diminishing numbers, through the rest of the district. Though it is abundantly clear, from the Rosslee inquisition, and from the account of the Hamilton raid, that the O'Connors retained possession of Castletown, as long as they were left their other estates in the county, additional evidence of the fact, if required, might be had in the Book of Distributions belonging to the Down Survey, where it is recorded, that "Bradcullen, Cloonengeere, Cartron Comyn, *alias* Sleavany, Coyle, and Lisdnff, Urlare, and Cullaghmore, Carrowcurragh, Carrowclogh, Barnaribben, and Cartron William Oge", were granted away, at the Restoration, from O'Connor Sligo to Robert Parke.

These fine lands passed, at the close of the 17th century, by marriage, from the Parkes to the Gores, in the person of Sir Francis Gore, of Ardtermon and Sligo, who married Anne, daughter and heiress of Robert Parke, and thus came into her father's estate. By this means Sir Francis obtained the property in an easier, pleasanter, and, probably, honester way, than some other landlords of the county obtained their land; for the marriage ring did for him, what the sword or chicane did for them; so that the following distich, addressed to an Austrian monarch, who was indebted to marriage for most of his kingdom, might, *mutatis mutandis*, have been applied to the lucky bridegroom:—

"*Bella gerant alii; tu, Felix Austria, nube;*
Quae dat Mars aliis, dat tibi regna Venus".

The side and foot of Benbulben, comprising much of these lands, though of no very great extent, varies much in qualities and appearance. Ascending from the mouth of the river to the summit of the mountain, one seems to pass, in respect to herbage and plant forms, through different latitudes, as one passes through the three or four zones or belts, into which the elevation may be divided.

Near the water's edge, the texture of the sod is spongy, the herbage coarse, and the colour rather russet; though even in this belt the fertility of the region shows itself, as the grasses, though of an inferior kind, are fresher and richer than those found in similar situations elsewhere.

The second and principal belt, stretching along the foot of the mountain, and rising up a good way on its side, is a rich, cultivated, and beautiful region. The soil is good for tillage, but so excellent for meadow, that it produces twice as much hay as ordinary land. The exceptional fertility of this zone, is due to the limestone of the mountain, which, after being disintegrated by the weather, is carried down in considerable quantities by the descending streamlets, and incorporated with the low lying lands, thus reminding one of Virgil's lines:

> "*At quae pinguis humus, dulcique uligine laeta,*
> *Quique frequens herbis, et fertilis ubere campus,*
> *Qualem saepe cava montis convalle solemus*
> *Despicere; hue summis liquuntur rupibus amnes,*
> *Felicemque trahunt limum*".[432]—*Georgica, Lib. II., 184-8.*

The advantages bestowed by nature on this favoured district, have been duly appreciated by man, as is proved by its having been always the most thickly peopled spot, for its extent, in Carbury. Now, too, the population, relatively to that of other places, is large, but not to such an extent as to prevent the holdings from being ample enough to enable the inhabitants "to live and thrive". In this beautiful spot—*il va sans dire*[433]—there is no village of the kind described by Carleton, "with its series of dunghills, each with its concomitant sink of green rotten water", nor indeed any village at all; for the houses, which are substantial, roomy, and tastefully covered with straw, are not connected, but stand on detached and picturesque sites, all the way from Rathcormick to Barnaribben. What adds to the beauty of the landscape, as well as to the comfort of the inmates, is, that each house is retired somewhat from the road, and surrounded with at least enough planting, to serve for shade in summer, and shelter in winter, thus recalling the picture of the Scripture scene, when "Juda and Israel dwelt, every one under his vine, and under his fig tree".

It is gratifying to be able to state, that these external indications of well-being, are realized in the interiors of the cottages—the furniture being commodious, the food wholesome and abundant, and the dress, both of males and females, neat and becoming. It would not be hard to meet, here

---

[432] "But the ground which is fat and rich with sweet moisture, and the field which is full of grass, and abounding with fertility, such as we are often wont to look down on the valley of some hill, where rivers are melted down, from the tops of the rocks, and carry a rich ooze along with them." As in *Publii Virgilii Maronis Georgicorum Libri Quatuor.* the Georgicks of Virgil, with an English Translation and Notes. by John Martyn, . the Third Edition – Virgil, [Clachan ed.].

[433] "it goes without saying'" {Fr}, [Clachan ed.].

and there, in other places, individual farmers of far greater means than any one in this district, but it would not be easy to find elsewhere, on an equal area, so large a number of well-to-do landholders; and as the state of agricultural tenants, in a great part of Ireland, is very much the reverse of all this, it would be a great national benefit to multiply, through the country, districts with the same social conditions as the region of Castletown. It is to this region Giolla Iosa Mor Mac Firbis[434] refers in the lines:—

> *"A small land of most extensive tillage,*
> *Of the green land of Ben Gulban".*

The third belt, comprising all the area between the zone we have been considering and the naked rock, contains no houses, and very little tillage, but runs up in long, well marked, quadrangular stripes of pasture ground. The grass of these stripes is of a vivid green, and of a quality greatly relished by sheep, these animals having it all to themselves, with the exception of what grows low down on the slopes, which is shared by light-footed cattle, though one or more of them, now and then, lose their balance and their footing in the attempt to reach a dainty mouthful. A sheep, too, occasionally tumbles down.

The fourth and last belt is perpendicular naked rock, with, here and there, a patch of heath. Even in this zone streaks of green grass occur; for a kind of contest for possession seems to be going on in spots between it and the heath; and the genial temperature of Benbulben, even at this high elevation, is shown by the fact, that in some fissures where grasses have earth to germinate in, lines of green diversify and dominate the dark-coloured plants.

The summit of Benbulben range is a table land of considerable extent, the highest point of Benbulben proper being 1,721 feet above sea level, of Benweeskin, 1,963, and of Truskmore, 2,115. The botany of the range is singularly rich in rare Irish plants; and in ferns, both as to number and varieties, it is said to surpass every other district in Ireland.

It is a great loss to science—a loss naturally more felt in Sligo than elsewhere—that Mr. Corry was prevented by his tragic and much lamented death on Lough-gill, from completing his exploration of the botany of Benbulben, a service for which he had received a money grant from the Royal Irish Academy, and which he was engaged in executing, at the time he met his sad end. The curious will find in the Proceedings of the Royal

---

[434] Dubhaltach MacFhirbhisigh, also known as Dubhaltach Óg mac Giolla Íosa Mór mac Dubhaltach Mór Mac Fhirbhisigh, Duald Mac Firbis, Dudly Ferbisie, and Dualdus Firbissius (1643 – January 1671) was an Irish scribe, translator, historian and genealogist. A traditionally trained Irish Gaelic scholar, his best-known work is the *Leabhar na nGenealach,—The Great Book of Irish Genealogies*, [Clachan ed.].

Irish Academy, for July 1884, a list of 136 plants of different species which he gathered on the range, and which include the following Alpine species:—

Sedum Rhodiola.	Oxyna reniformis.	Asplenium Viride.
Polygonum viviparum.	Arabia petraea.	Salix herbacea.
Draba incana.	Aspiduim lonchitis.	Arenaria ciliata.
Canex rigida.	Saxifraga nivalis.	Hieracium anglicum.
Poa Alpina.	Juniperus nana.	Silenae acaulis.
Hieracuim iricum.	Saxifraga aizoides.	Hieracuim gibsoni.
Dryas octopetala.	Selaginella selaginoidas.	

The surface of the summit is broken in some places by holes, against which it behoves one to be on one's guard, as, from their being covered by the rich vegetation around the edges, more than one unwary person has fallen into them. The country people are at a loss to account for these borings, but it is plain that they have been produced by the action of water. The rain percolating through crevices, and between strata, wears away and hollows the mountain limestone. It takes time to do this, but, as "*gutta cavat lapidem non vi sed saepe cadendo*"[435], it is easy to conceive how, time enough being given, the rain, falling for ages on the same area, scoops out the rock by means of the carbonic acid gas which the water contains. Geologists trace to the same cause effects of much greater magnitude, such as the channelling of underground rivers, the sinking of lake beds, and the formation of caverns.

Of the last named effect we have a remarkable example, on this very range, in the great cavern that looks down on the valley of Gleniffe, at the north-east side of Benbulben. The entrance of this huge grotto is thirty or forty feet wide, by, at least, fifty high; and, with the spacious apartments to the right and left as you enter, the lofty gallery in front, and the corridors or passages here and there, the interior has the features of some lordly mansion; or, if the great opens to the right and left were removed further back, so as to resemble transepts, the gallery would then take the place of a nave, and the whole would rise up before you, like some great cathedral of the Middle Ages, picturesquely vaulted and groined in genuine, solid stone, and not, like the degenerate edifices of our own days, in what Pugin styles the "abomination of lath and plaster". Such is the actual present appearance of the place; but as the work of erosion is going constantly on; as stalactites, without number, are, after the manner of gigantic leeches, always swallowing down the substance of the roof, while immense stalagmites are eating away the sides and floor, he must be a very bold man that would undertake to forecast the appearance of the cavern at the end of, let us say, a hundred thousand years to come.

Benbulben and its surroundings have given rise to more than one romantic legend. Like many other places, Drumcliff had, in the olden time,

---

[435] A drop of water hollows a stone—not by force, but by falling often, [Clachan ed.].

its local Piast or spectre, and was freed from the monster by Finn Mc Cumhall (pronounced Mc Coole), the Irish Hercules; and it was on the slopes of Benbulben that Diarmuid O'Duibhne, after a thousand hair-breadth 'scapes, north, south, east, and west, at last lost his charmed life in an encounter with the enchanted boar of the mountain. The conflict is described at great length in the Fenian tale, styled "The Pursuit of Diarmuid and Grainne", of which the following extract, containing the catastrophe of the tragedy, will sufficiently acquaint the reader with the grotesque exhibition of which Benbulben is taken to have been the scene about sixteen hundred years ago:—"The wild boar then came up the face of the mountain with the Fenians after him; Diarmuid struck a heavy stroke upon the wild boar's back, stoutly and full bravely, yet he cut not a single bristle upon him, but made two pieces of his sword. Then the wild boar made a fearless spring upon Diarmuid, so that he tripped over him and made him fall headlong; and when he was risen up again, it happened that one of his legs was on either side of the wild boar, and his face backward toward the hinder part of the wild boar. The wild boar fled down the fall of the hill, and was unable to put Diarmuid off during that space. After that he fled away until he reached Assaroe, and, having reached the red stream, he gave three nimble leaps across the fall, hither and thither, yet he could not put off Diarmuid during that space; and he came back by the same path until he reached up to the height of the mountain again. And when he had reached the top of the hill he put Diarmuid off his back; and when he was fallen to the earth the wild boar made an eager—exceeding mighty—spring upon him, and ripped out his bowels and his entrails, so that they fell about his legs. Howbeit, as the boar was leaving the *tulach*, Diarmuid made a triumphant cast of the hilt of the sword, that chanced to be still in his hand, so that he dashed out his brains and left him dead without life. Therefore, *Rath na h-Amhrann* is the name of the place that is on the top of the mountain from that time to this".

Many will learn with surprise that this group, or range of mountains lay, for ages, at the bottom of the ocean, and that, vast as it is, it is composed, in great measure, like the coral islands of the South Sea, of fossil fish, as well shells as animal matter. And yet there is little or no room for doubt on the subject; for specimens of the stone, when examined under the microscope, by competent judges, exhibit, unmistakably, this formation. Professor Hull, an authority, second to none, on the geology of Ireland, bears witness, after careful examination and study, that the remains of marine animals form the chief constituents of Benbulben

END OF VOL. I.

Originally Printed by EDMUND BURKE & Co., 61 & 62 Great Strand Street, Dublin.

INDEX

Abbeytown, 11, 12
Account of Ireland, 264
Act of Uniformity, 109
Acta Sanctorum,, 23, 41
Acts of Settlement and Explanation, 319, 338, 339, 344
Aghamore, 16
Aghaphreghan, 7
Ahamlish, 16, 94, 110, 126, 316, 323, 324
Ainmire, son of Sedna, 32
Ainnidh, son of Duach, 32
Airghialla, 62
An Aphorismical Discovery, 122, 130
Annaghmore, 2, 13, 17
Annals of Boyle, 63
Annals of Clonmacnoise, 67, 69, 71, 73, 75, 77
Annals of Clyn and Dowling, 221
Annals of Dudley Firbis, 81
Annals of Loch Ce, 49, 52, -54, 57, 58, 59, 61-72, 334, 346
Annals of the Four Masters, xxi, 5, 22, 23, 30, 33, 52, 55, 58, 60, 61-68, 71, 74, 75, 76, 79, 80, 81, 84, 85, 86, 108, 140, 179, 181, 204, 221, 249, 323, 365, 366, 368, 372, 374
Annals of Ulster, 21, 56, 71
Aongus Bronbachall, i, 21
Aphorismical Discovery, 122, 127
Archbishops of Tuam, iii, 1, 94, 121, 122

Archdall's *Monasticon*, 349, 372
Ardcotton, 18
Ardnaree Abbey, 109
Ardtermon, 358, 380
Arigna Collieries and Iron Works, 10
Arigna mining, i
Arigna River, 10
Armstrong, Reverend James, 235, 236
Arrow River, the, or Uncion, 17
Articles of Limerick, 167, 199
Ath Angaile, xiv
Ath-chinn-locha, 86, 87
Aughriss, 7, 20, 94

Baccagh, Murtough, 76, 77, 79, 96
Ballantyne & McCreery currency notes, 296
Ballifernan, 7
Ballike, 6
Ballina, 17, 28
Ballinacarrow, 17
Ballintogher, 10, 90, 159
Ballisodare,, 12
Ballybeg, 7
Ballydrehid, 312. 322
Ballygawley, 13, 16
Ballygawley Wood, 13
Ballyglass, 329, 347, 348
Ballylahan, 3
Ballymote, 70, 97, 102, 109, 132, 133
Ballynagalliagh, 369
Ballyrourke Abbey, 216
Ballysadare, ii, xx, 5, 7, 8, 11, 12, 17, 18, 30-35, 39, 44, 48, 57, 60, 68, 73, 75, 77, 92, 101
Ballyshannon, 71, 76, 80, 103, 114, 132
Banks, 296, 297, 298
Barnesrahy, 39, 40

Baronial Constables, 292
Barracks, 291, 292, 294, 295
Battle of Athenry, 69
Battle of Aughrim, 109
Battle of Cuil-dreimhne, 46
Battle of Sligeach, 32
Battle of Sligo, i, 31, 32, 44, 45
Bawns, 53, 60, 61, 81
Baxter, Captain John, 324
Baxter, John, 109
Beggars, 247
Belladrehid, ii, 5, 83, 85, 86, 110
Bellaghy, 7
Belleek, 33, 66
Beltra, 5, 7, 41, 75
Beltra Strand, 5, 75
Belturbet, 160
Belvoir, 318, 325, 330, 333, 342, 356
Benada Convent, 16
Benbo, 26
Benbulben, i, viii, 8, 9, 14, 27, 28, 36, 48, 64, 85, 240, 261, 356, 358, 376-383
Benson, Sir John, 211, 236, 249
Benweeskin, 358, 382
Berminghams, 60, 67
Betham's Irish Antiquarian Researches, 328
Biatachs, 373
Bingham, Sir Richard, 98, 99
Bishop Bronus, i, 21
Bishops of Achonry, 4, 177, 300
Bishops of Elphin, 171, 172, 173, 204, 205, 213, 285, 361
Bishops of Leyney, 4
Black Death, ii, 73
Boate's, *'Natural History of Ireland'*, 11
Bobbin Mill, 13
Bodkin, Christopher, 1
Bomore, 7, 282, 357, 358, 361
Book of Armagh, xiv, 30, 45, 328, 329
Book of Ballymote, xxi
Book of Distributions, 368, 380

Book of Fenagh, 24, 63, 365, 366
Booth Gore, Sir, 272
Borough election of 1833, 271
Boyds, 250
Boyle, iii, vii, xvi, 65, 88, 89, 107, 109, 112, 123, 127, 137, 142, 160, 161, 165, 189, 221, 223, 252, 263, 298, 317, 323, 324
Boyle Abbey, 64, 316, 317
Bradcullen, 377, 379, 380
Bradcullen/Castletown, 152
Braghaid-coille, 377
Braulieve, 7, 8
Breffney, 33, 60, 69, 108
Breweries, 304, 306, 307
Brian Luighnech, 62, 63, 64, 65, 66, 76, 92
Bronus, 319
Bucks, The, xvii
Bun Lainne, xiv
Bunduff Strand, 7
Buninadden, 17
Bunluiny, 339
Burke, Reverend Patrick, 285
Burkes, 18, 55, 74, 88, 100
Burton, Benjamin, 149
Butler, Lady Eleanor, 103
Butler, Theobald, 55, 60
Butlers, 88
Butter, 249, 250, 253, 254, 264, 265

Cael Uisge, 66
Cairbre, 5, 20, 21, 22, 23, 24, 63
Cairbre Mor, 22, 23
Cairbre Teffia, 23
Cairnsfoot, 152, 154
Calry, viii, xiii, xiv, 16, 70, 115, 137, 170, 172, 222, 233, 234, 236, 245
Calry Deerpark, xiii
Calvach Caecb, 83
Carbrians, i, 20, 23, 24
Carbury, i, ii, iv, xiv, xvii, xx, 2, 5-8, 15, 16, 19, 20, 22-25, 29, 40, 55, 59, 62-70, 74, 75, 76, 79,

80-83, 86, 88, 90, 94, 96, 109, 110, 126, 134, 136, 137, 147, 153, 173, 174, 205, 258, 266, 280, 282, 316, 320-324, 331, 337, 339, 349, 354, 362-372, 373-381
Carbury Mor, 365, 366
Carbury Teffia, 22
Carew, 103, 104
Carlyle, i, 28
Carney, 7, 33
Carns, 317, 318, 325, 330, 332
Carns Hill, 325, 333
Carns-hill or Carns, 317
Carragh, Turlough, 323, 324, 335
Carrickadda, 7
Carricknagat, 277, 279, 280
Carrig-na-shouk, 14
Carrowcrin, 33, 35, 40, 44
Carrowmore, i, ii, xiii, xv, xvi, xxi, 31, 35, 38-46, 173, 313, 314
Carrowmore circles, xvii, 45, 46
Carrownabinna, 7
Carrownamodow, 85
Carrownrush, 7
Carrowroe, 153
Cashel Gal or Slieve-gan-baiste, 27
Cashelgal,, 28
Castlebar Races, 277
Castleconor, 7
Castlegal, 298, 363, 370
Castletown, 369, 376, 377, 378, 379, 380, 382
Cath Criche Carbury, 63
Cathal Oge O'Connor, ii, 72, 77, 82, 95, 99
Cath-Criche-Carbury, 66
Cathedral, 287, 289, 352
Cathmugh, son of Flaherty, 22
Catholic clergy, 276, 285
Catholic Confederation, 196, 208
Catholics, 136, 138, 143, 152, 157, 167, 168, 175, 176, 177, 193, 194, 195, 196, 197, 202, 206, 215, 226, 229, 231, 250, 255, 256
Cattle, 15, 46, 53, 59, 61, 65, 66, 68
Cattle cures, 360
Celebration of Mass, 175
Charles I, 145, 199, 253
Charles II, 144, 196, 288, 339, 344
Charter School, 245, 301
Chemical Works, 13
Chichester, 324
Chiefs of Tirconnell, 62, 68
Cholera, 283, 285, 286, 301, 302, 304
Chronicon Scotorum, 4, 6, 23, 31, 65
Church of Ireland, 250
Cillespuig-Brone, 21
Cinel Cairbre, 20, 21, 22, 23, 24
Cinel Conaill, 4, 32
Cinel Connell, 24, 53, 55, 56, 60, 62, 63, 71, 377
Cinel Owen, 24, 53, 55, 60, 62
Cistercian Abbey of Boyle, 316
Clanna Neil, 350
Clanrickard, Lord, 114
Clanrickarde, Earls of, 231, 259
Clarence, Mr. Joseph, 289
Clarkes, 166, 250, 252, 257
Clearance System, 276
Clement XI, Pope, 198
clergy, 276, 277, 285, 300
Cliffony, 16
Clifford, Sir Conyers, 100
Cloghagh, 7
Cloghereva, 329
Cloonacleigha, 16
Cloonacool, 13
Cloonoghill, 17
Cloonty, 16
Cloverhill, 35
Cluithe an Rigli, 72
Cluithe an Rigli (the King's Game), 73
Cnoc-Buidhe (Knockavoe), 85

Cod. Clarend., 23
Codnach, 4
Cogan, John, 55
Colgach, 329
Colgagh, 16
Colgan, 320-322, 326, 328, 329, 349, 366, 370
Colleary, Mr. Bernard, 241
Collearys, the, 305
Collections on Irish Church History, 168
Collooney, vii, xx, 13, 17, 18, 64, 70, 97, 100, 110, 132, 136, 140, 144, 159, 165, 180, 220, 236, 245, 255
Collooney, Lord, 139, 143, 150, 159
Coman or Coeman, 21
Comarbs, 371, 372, 373
Commissioners of Fisheries, 36
Commissioners of Plantation, 6
Commonwealth, the, 136, 140, 144, 150, 199
Conal Crimthan, 20
Conal Gulban, 20, 32, 376
Coney Island, 7, 11, 134, 325, 359
Cong, 45
Conlon, Thady, 308
Connacians, 24, 40, 63, 66, 76, 85, 350
Connaught, i, ii, xviii, xix, 1-3, 6, 8, 11, 20, 24, 25, 32, 33, 39, 40, 43, 44, 48, 52-56, 62, 63, 65-71, 74-75, 77-81, 84-86, 90-101, 104, 107, 110, 115, 119, 121, 122, 125, 127, 129, 132-135
Connaught Volunteers, 270
Connaught, Lower, 18, 24, 25, 55, 76, 82, 85, 86, 96
Constabulary Act of 1822, 292
Convent of Athleathan, 179
Convent of Borrishoole, 196
Convent of Holy Cross, 194
Convention of Dromceat, 30, 57
Conynghams, 150, 216

Coolany, 14
Coolavin, i, 2, 4, 7, 8, 17, 97, 134
Cooldruman, 371
Cooleageboy, 26
Coolerra, vii, viii, 7, 33, 41, 46, 96
Coologeoboy, 329
Cooper, Anthony Ashley, 199
Cooper, Colonel, xxii, 13, 15
Cooperhill, 17
Coopers, xvi, xx, 135, 137
Coote, Chidley, 159
Coote, Colonel Richard, 130, 132
Coote, Sir Charles, 114, 119, 121, 129, 130, 131, 139, 143, 195, 231, 232
Cootes, xvi, 135, 137, 143
Corann, 3, 22
Coranna, 3
Corkran, Thomas, 246
Corkran's Mall, 246
Cormac Galeng, 3
Corn Laws in 1846, 308
Cornwallis, Lord, 277
Coroner's courts, 291
Corran, i, xiv, xvi, 2-4, 8, 16, 17, 33, 68, 86, 90, 97, 109, 134, 136, 137, 147, 173, 175, 230, 232, 316
Corrann, 3
Corrownamodow, 16
Costellos, 67
Cottage Island, 332
Cottlestown, 159
Cotton's *Fasti*, 228
County elections, 272
Court Abbey, 109
Court-houses, 289-290, 344
crannoges, 365-368
Creans, 168, 188, 204, 205, 263, 288, 325, 335, 343
Creevalea, 179, 191, 207, 216
Creevalea Abbey, 207
Crich Carbury, ii, 62
Crich-Carbury, 376
Crich-Conaill, 5
Criche Carbury, 71

Crinder, 35
"Critical Essay on the Ancient Inhabitants of the Northern Parts of Britain or Scotland", xv
Crofton, Edward, 136, 230
Crofton, John, 99, 109
Crofton, William, 109
Croftons, 341
cromlechs, i, xiii, xv, xvii, 31, 35, 36, 38, 44, 45
Cromwellians, iii, iv, xxi, 18, 135, 136-140, 144, 159, 208, 295
Crossboy, 153
Cuil Irra, 31, 39
Culleen Grin, 35
Cumen Head, 312
Cummen, 342
Cunghill, 3
Curlews, 7, 9, 12, 62, 65, 76, 85, 101, 111, 127, 128, 132
Curtis' *History of the Irish Constabulary*, 292

Davis, Sir John, 15
De Burgos, 67, 79, 181, 184, 187, 192, 194, 198, 199, 209, 210, 215, 258
De Butts, John, 176, 242, 243
de Gray, John, 66
de Lacy, Hugh, 59
De Praesulibus Hiberniae, 98
de Vesci, William, 56
Deerpark hill, 349, 352
Delahide, Christopher, 109
Depositions as to non-juring Priests, 170
Derreens, 13
Devany, Thaddeus, Very Rev., 193
Dillon, Lord, 119, 121
Dillon, Sir James, 122
Dillon, Sir Theobald, 231, 232
Dillon, Talbot, 231
Diocesan School, 301

Discoverie of the True Causes why Ireland was never entirely subdued, 15
Distilleries, 306
Dodwell, Mr., 35
Dominican Belgium, 194
Dominicans, v, xviii, 3, 58, 59, 111, 179, 183, 187, 192, 194, 195, 199, 203, 207, 208-213, 240
Donagh, 7
Donnchadh, Lord of Cairbre, 22
Doonemeelin, 359
Down Survey, 16, 33, 144, 361, 367, 377, 380
Dress, 253
Dromahair, i, 10, 26, 27, 59, 110, 118, 130
Drowes, the, 1, 6, 7, 29, 33
Drumcliff, viii, xix, 4, 7, 22-24, 64, 68, 69, 82, 94, 110, 137, 139, 140, 228, 233, 234, 239, 261, 328, 357, 360-367, 370-378, 383
Drummond, Thomas, 293
Drumrat, 17
Dubhduin, 21
Duelling, xvii
Duff River, the, 5, 6, 7, 8, 33, 62
Dukes of Leinster, 52, 58
Dunadhach, son of Raghallach, 22, 23, 372
Dunally, 335, 344, 345
Dunamase, 55
Dunflin, 153
Dungannon Resolutions, 269
Dunmoran, 7
Dunneill, 7
Dwellings, xvii

Eabha, 359
Eagles, i, 14, 15
Earls of Clanrickarde, 370
Earls of Strafford, 143, 144, 145, 147, 148, 149, 189
Earls of Ulster, 55, 56, 59, 78

Easky, 7
Education, xvii, 145, 194, 197, 208, 232, 233, 271
Election of 1822, 276
Elections, 196, 238, 244
Elizabeth I, iii, xx, 2, 79, 88, 89, 92, 94, 96, 99, 102, 104, 109
Emancipation Act of 1829, 256
Emigration, 308, 343
Emlaghfad, 17
Enach-ard, 349
Eochy O'Flynn, 17
Eoghan Bel, i, viii, 32, 39, 40, 41, 44, 46, 350, 351
Eothuile the Artificer, 5
Epidemics, 301, 302
Epylogus Chronologicus, 198, 209
erenaghs, 373
Everards, 263

Fairs, 277, 283, 290, 296, 307, 336, 337
Famine, 299, 300, 301
Fasachoille (Castletown), 69
Fassa-Coille, 378
Fearghal, son of Foghartach, 22
Fenians, 259, 376, 384
Ferbis, Dudley, 81
Ferguson, Sir James, ii, xv, 45, 351-354
Fever Hospital, 299-301
Fiach, 20
Finaghty, Father, 123, 124, 125
Fined, 7, 33, 35
Finisklin, 33
Firbolgs, 31, 41
First burgesses, 237
Fisheries, 265, 266
Fitz Maurice, Gerald, 52
Fitzgerald, Maurice, ii, 18, 52, 54
Fitzgeralds, ii, 18, 67, 78, 88
FitzThomas, John, 56
Flaherty O'Muldory, 62, 63
Flood, Henry, 271
Fortescue, Sir Faithful, 231

Forty-shilling freeholders, 276
Fossa Riabairt, 45
Four Masters, the, viii, xiv, 3, 5, 20-24, 31, 32, 44, 45, 46, 51, 52, 54, 57, 63, 65, 67, 71-83, 86, 88, 89, 93, 96, 111
Foxford, 10
Franciscans, 58, 179, 183, 186, 197, 207, 229, 240
Frenches, 109, 341
Frenchpark, 341
Fullerton, Sir James, 102, 109, 224, 252

Gael Uisce, 54
Gailenga, 3
Galen, 3
Galenga, 3
Garavogue, 17
Garban, 21
Garvagh, River, 148
Gates, Titus, 140, 157
Genealogia Sanctorum, 369
Geraldines, 55, 56, 60, 62, 67, 78, 87, 187
Giant's Grave/Altar, 347
giants' graves, xiii
Gilleran, Father, 285
Ginkell, 164
Giolla Iosa Mor Mac Firbis, 328, 330
Giolla Iosa Mor McFirbis, 5
Giraldus Cambrensis' *Topography of Ireland*, 49
Glen, the - Knocknarea, 315
Glenagoola, 311
Glencar, viii, 16, 358, 363-370
Glendallan, 368, 369
Gleniffe, 383
Goodman, Dr., 210, 211
Gore Booth, Sir Henry, 15, 270
Gore Booths, 276
Gore, Sir Francis, 128
Gores, viii, xvi, 128, 129, 272, 289, 338, 341, 344, 380
Gores Booth of Lissadel, 344

Governors of Connaught, 92, 100
Governors of Sligo, 164
Grace's Annals, 52, 56
Granard, Lord, 5, 22, 23, 165, 166
Grange, 312, 316, 323, 324, 339, 380
Greagraidhe, 4
Green Fort, 159, 162, 163, 164, 166, 216, 245
Greene, Thomas, 109
Griffith, Sir Richard, 11

Hamilton, Sir Frederick, 114-118, 346, 379
Handicrafts, 307
Hardiman, 79, 97
Hardman, Mr., 335, 351, 354
Harlech, Lord, 341, 342
Hart, Right Reverend John, 177
Harts, 168, 177
Hazelwoods, 271, 290, 295, 298, 329, 330, 332, 335, 336, 337, 338, 341, 356
Hennessy, Mr., 377
Henry III, 53, 79
Henry VIII, 193, 194, 259
Hibernia Dominicana, 181, 192, 193, 204, 210
Hibernian Mining Company, 11
Hill Burton, John, xiii
Holborn Street, 245, 255
Holy Cross, xviii, 157, 184, 187, 189, 192, 218, 225, 240
Holy Wells, xvii
Holywell, 329, 331, 332, 356
Hotels, 306, 362
Housing, 245
Hugh Brefneach, 62
Hull, Professor, 384
Humbert, 277, 278, 279
Hy Fiachrach, 4, 5
Hy Many, 69, 94

Infirmary buildings, 298
Inis-na-Lainne, 366-367, 372
Innes, Rev. Father, xv

Innismurray, 358
Insignia of Sligo, 241
Ireton, 132
Irish Mining Company, 11

Jacobites, 160, 253
James I., 199, 226, 231, 238, 240, 242, 316, 324, 332, 335, 369
Jones, Jeremy, 137, 157, 158
Jones, Sir Roger, 109, 111, 188, 223, 225, 226, 230, 231, 233, 288, 289, 342, 343, 344, 346
Joneses, xvi, 140, 188, 232
Justices of the Peace, 291

Kernaghan, Mr. Baptist, 305
Kilcoleman, 4
Kilcoleman-Finn, 3
Kilcooly, 233
Kilcummin Head, 357
Kilfree, 17
Kilglass, 7
Killasnat, 369
Killaspickbrone,, 148
Killaspugbrone, vi, vii, 21, 25, 30, 45, 221, 222, 233, 234, 311, 319, 321, 325, 327, 360
Killasser, 277
Killross, 332
Kilmacley, 10
Kilmacowen, 148, 221, 222, 233, 234, 311, 319, 322-327
Kilmactrany, 7
Kilmoremoy, 7
Kilronan, 2, 64
Kilsellagh, 5, 7, 110
Kilshahy, 17
Kilvarnet, xxi, 18, 48, 56
King James, of Scotland, 83
King O'Hara, Mr. Charles, M.P, 300
King Roderick O'Conor, 53
King, Sir John, 109
Kings of Connaught, 32, 52, 62, 69, 70, 71, 74, 75

Kings of the West of Connaught, 63
Kingston, Lord, 141, 159, 160
Kinnasharnagh, 7
Kinsale, Battle of, 101, 109
Knockbeg, 165
Knocklane, i, 7, 15, 26, 27
Knocknarea, i, vii, 8, 9, 27-29, 36, 39, 40-44, 48, 311-324, 330, 351, 356, 358
Knoxes, 243

Lackaverna, 7
Lackmeeltaun, 7
Lakes, xiii, 15, 16, 59
Lanigan, Dr., 329, 349, 371, 372
leabhar ghear, 333
Leckacurry, 7
Lecky, Captain William, 269
Leitrim, xviii, 1, 2, 6, 7, 10, 12, 16, 36, 110, 115
Lenadoon, 7
Leny, 3, 4
Leslie, Doctor John, 147, 148, 248
Lewis, in his Topographical Dictionary of Ireland, 248
Ley Castle, 56
Leycester, Sir Peter, 240
Leyney, i, 2-4, 7, 8, 16-18, 27, 29, 56, 60, 68, 71, 86, 90, 94, 97, 109, 126, 134
Libraries, 294, 295, 296
Limerick, Siege of, 132
Linen trade, 263
Liscorrach, 359
Lismarkrea, 339
Lissadell, 13, 28, 33, 128, 341, 358, 359, 374
Little Sisters of the Poor, 153
Little, Doctor, 302
Lloyd, 161, 162, 163
Loch Ce, xvi, 6, 52, 54, 57, 64, 68, 69, 73, 80, 85-87, 92, 93, 96, 191, 204, 206, 221, 365, 372, 373, 377
Loegaire, 20

Loftus, Adam, 139
Lord Justices, 52, 55, 56, 57, 60, 66, 79, 88
Lord Mountrath (see also Sir Charles Coote), 143
Lord of Tirconnell, 63
Lords of Carbury, 22, 74, 76, 81, 82
Lords of Connaught, 59
Lords of Sligo, 80, 81, 105
Lords of Tirconnell, 72
Lords of Tirerrill, 69, 81
Lough Arrow, 16, 17
Lough Esk, 12, 13, 101
Lough Gara, 12, 16
Lough Gill, viii, 15, 16, 27, 126, 132, 298, 311, 315-318, 328, 329, 331, 332, 335, 337, 339, 344, 346, 355, 356, 369, 374
Lough Melvin, 5
Lough Techet, 16
Lougheneltin, 329, 346
Louvain Convent, 194, 208
Lower Connaught, 53, 180, 191, 204, 259, 263
Lower Rosses, 357, 359-362, 374
Loyal Ballina and Ardnaree Volunteers, 270
Loyal Sligo Volunteers, 269
Lsyney, 16
Lugnia, 3
Lugny, 3
Luigni of Connaught, 23
Lunatic Asylum, 302, 357
Lundy, Colonel, 160
Lungy, 305
Luttrell, Colonel Henry, 163
Lynches, 109

Mac Firbis, 21
Mac William Burke, 70, 74, 77, 82
MacDermot of Moylurg, 84
MacDermot, Mulrony, 69
MacDonogh, Brian, of Collooney, xvi
MacDonogh, Bryan, Prior, 180

MacDonogh, Dermod-Tanist, 180
MacDonogh, Tomultagh, xxi, 69
MacDonoghs, xvi, 74, 135, 168, 180
MacDonoughs, 81, 85
MacFeorais, 71
MacFirbises, xxi
MacSweeneys, xvi
MacWilliam, 71, 76, 77
MacWilliam Burke, 83, 84
MacWilliam of Clanrickard, 84
Maelduin, 21, 22
Magh-Diughbha, 62, 63
Magherow, viii, 28, 359, 377
Malbie, Sir Nicholas, 91, 92, 95
Manius, 20
Manor courts, 291
Manorhamilton, 298, 354, 379
Market crosses, 206
Market days, 252
Markrea, xx, 13, 17, 110, 111
Markree, 159
Martin, Abraham, 248
Martin, Major Wood, 141, 161, 163
Martin, Mr. John, 271
Martyrology of Tallaght, 57
Mayo, 1, 3, 4, 6, 7, 16, 17, 31, 43, 48, 74, 122, 132
Mayors of Sligo, 238
McConnor McDonnogh, Shane, 232
McDermot, Donogh Reagh, 71
McDermots, 232
McDermott, Brian, 231
McDermott, Cornelius, 231
McDonnell, Randal, Earl of Antrim, 107
McDonogh, Father Patrick, 157, 209
McDonogh's Castle, 18
McDonoghs, 232
McDonongh, Brian, 110
McDonough, Father Patrick, xviii, 200
McDonoughs, 100, 109

McGlanaghan, 35
McGowan, Thomas, 297
McGrath, Miler, (Milerius), 226
McMailin, Clarus, 57
McMurrough, Dermot, 52, 67
McNeil and Sons, 309
McNicholas, Rt. Rev. Dr., 300
McParlan, Dr, 263
McSweenys, 232
McSwine (McSweeny), Owen, 232
Meelick, 3
Melaghlin O'Donnell, 53
Melghe Molbhthach, 5
Memoirs of the Taaffe Family, 215
Memorialia - O'Hart, 198
Merchandise of Sligo, 263
Merchants of Sligo, 263
Methodists, 256
Meyler de Exeter, 69
Misgan Meave, vii, 39-41, 313-314
Mitchelburn, 166
Model School, 245
Moighmedhoin, 3
Momsen, Dr., xiii
Mongfmna, 3
Monk, 130
Moon worship, xiv
Moore, Sir Garret, 130, 131
Mountjoy, Lord, 67, 101
Moy, the, i, 4, 5, 6, 7, 8, 16, 29, 33, 54, 60
Moytura, xiii, 31, 33, 45
Muadhnata, 349, 352, 369
Muircheartach Mac Earca, 32
Muirghes, 22
Mullaghmore, 7
Munster, 52, 60, 84, 85, 100, 104
Munster chieftain, 322
Murchadh, son of Searrach, 22
Murtough Muimneach, 62

Nadfraich, 369
Neligan, Rev. James, 300
Nellus, Father Gregory, 210

Newspapers, xvii
Newtown,, 159
Niall of the Nine Hostages, 20
Nicholson, Reverend Edward, 234
Nolans of Galway, 109
Norden, map of, 377
Nunneries, 351, 369
Nymphsfield, 12

O'Briens, 55, 84, 88
O'Clery, Brother Michael, xxi
O'Connell's Repeal, 269
O'Connor and Cullen, 310
O'Connor Corcomroe, 98
O'Connor Don, 98
O'Connor of Offaley, 98
O'Connor Roe, 98, 104
O'Connor Sligo, iii, iv, xx, 25, 62, 74, 81, 86, 89-98, 101-107, 110, 113, 118, 119, 132
O'Connor Sligo estate, 143-144, 150, 151, 249
O'Connor, Cahal Og, 249
O'Connor, Cahall, 368
O'Connor, Captain Teige Mac Phelim, 379
O'Connor, Cathal, 376
O'Connor, Cathal Og, 376
O'Connor, Charles, 105, 106, 110, 113
O'Connor, Daniel, 379
O'Connor, Donnell, ii, iii, 65, 68, 83, 88, 93, 96, 97, 98, 103, 104, 105, 132
O'Connor, Donough, 379
O'Connor, Father Dominick, 197, 207
O'Connor, Father Felix, 157, 199, 207, 209
O'Connor, Hugh and Charles, 114
O'Connor, Mr. Peter, 152, 153, 154, 224
O'Connor, Murtough, 335
O'Connor, Owen, ii, iii, 81, 94, 95
O'Connor, Owen / Eugene, 93
O'Connor, Rory, 376
O'Connor, Teige, iii, 64, 107, 110, 111, 114, 115, 118
O'Connor, Teige Oge, ii, 85, 86
O'Connor, Walsh, and Company, 310
O'Connors, i, ii, iv, viii, xvi, xix, 24, 56, 58, 62-67, 72, 74, 77, 78, 80, 82-85, 88, 92, 96, 97, 99, 107-109, 113, 115, 129, 135, 144, 150, 152, 180, 181, 183, 191, 204, 215, 222, 225, 232, 246, 259, 263, 323-325, 335, 368, 376-380
O'Connors Sligo, xvi, 67, 74, 76, 81, 82, 108, 335
O'Conor Don, 84, 104
O'Conor Roe, 84, 85, 105
O'Conor, Cathal Crovderg, 323, 369
O'Conor, Charles, xiv, 41, 42, 43
O'Conor, Felim, 56, 60
O'Conor, Hugh, 3, 56, 60, 65, 70
O'Conor, Manus, 3, 65, 68, 69
O'Conor, Neal Gealbuy, 64
O'Conor, Rev. Dr., 48
O'Conor, Rory, 3, 64, 68, 70
O'Conor, Turlough, 62, 63, 69, 70
O'Conors, 52, 53, 66, 74, 76, 81, 87
O'Crean, Father, 205
O'Creidegan, Daniel, Vey rev., 194
O'Donnell, Balldearg, 165
O'Donnell, Con, 83
O'Donnell, Donnell Oge, 56, 60, 67, 72, 82
O'Donnell, Hugh, ii, 33, 68, 69, 72, 83, 96, 100
O'Donnell, Rory, 102, 103
O'Donnells, ii, 25, 52, 56, 60, 71, 72, 74, 82, 83, 84, 88, 93, 298, 323, 324, 335, 345, 372, 373, 374, 377, 378
O'Donovan, John, i, vii, viii, xii, xiv, xv, xx, 3, 4, 20-24, 29, 31,

32, 40-43, 54, 71, 75, 76, 80, 89, 95, 96, 104, 232, 311, 313, 318, 323, 324, 328, 329, 333, 345, 350, 353, 355, 365, 366, 368, 373, 375, 378
O'Donovans, 252
O'Dowde, David, 232
O'Dowds, 18, 24, 97, 135, 180, 232
O'Droma, Solomon, xxi
O'Dugan's Topographical Poem, 5
O'Duigenan, Manus, xxi
O'Gara, Farrell, xxi, 232
O'Gara, Iriell, 231, 232
O'Garas, 97, 109, 135, 232
O'Halloran, Sylvester, xv
O'Hanlon, Father, 369
O'Hara, Colonel Charles, 270
O'Hara, Donnell Duv, 60
O'Hara, Mr., 13, 15
O'Hara, Shane, 231
O'Hara, Thaddeus, 232
O'Hara, Thadeus, 231
O'Haras, xvi, 3, 18, 97, 109, 135, 137, 178, 227, 232
O'Hart, John, Very Rev., 196
O'Hart's Irish Pedigrees, 345
O'Heyne, Father, 209
O'Hohy, Hugo, 228, 229
O'Lochlan, Nial, 62, 63
O'Neil, Hugh Buy, 64
O'Regan, Sir Teague, 163, 164
O'Reillys, 10
O'Rorke, Brian Oge, 100
O'Rorke, Mor, 93
O'Rorke, Owen, 111, 113, 114
O'Rorke, Sir Teige, 231
O'Rorke, Ualgarg, 69, 70
O'Rorke's Table, 26
O'Rorkes, 5, 67, 74, 118, 180, 232, 298, 332, 333, 344, 346, 366, 368, 372, 374
O'Rourke, Brian Ballagh, 5
O'Dowds, xvi
O'Dugan, John, 5

Oilill, 2
Ordinance for the Satisfaction of the Adventurers for Lands in Ireland, and the Arrears due to the Soldiery, 134
Ormond, Duke of, 196
Ormonde, 118, 119, 121, 125, 127, 128, 129, 130, 131, 141, 157, 158, 196
Ormsby Gore, viii, 342
Ormsby, Colonel John, 270
Ormsby, Major, 130, 135
Ormsby, Philip, 339
Ormsby, Thomas, 338
Ormsby, William, 339, 343
Ormsbys, vii, viii, xvi, 135, 137, 168-172, 176, 233, 234, 238, 244, 248, 251, 272-278, 318, 325, 330, 333, 338, 340-343
Ormsbys of Willowbrook, 243
Orrery, Lord (see also Lord Broghill), 143
Osnata, 349, 352, 369
Owen O'Rorke, Owen, 110
Owen Roe, 119, 127, 128, 129, 130
Owenbeg, 17
Owenmore, i, 2, 7, 8, 15, 18, 92
Ox Mountains, 11, 12, 16, 29, 42, 278, 279, 325, 356
Oyster Island, 260, 262
Oysters, 239, 240, 255, 265

Pacata Hibernia, 103
Parish Priests, 321, 327
Parke, Captain Robert, 344, 346
Parkes, viii, xvi, 333, 344, 380
Parkes of Dunally, 343
Parliamentary elections, 271
Partholan, 17, 50
Penal Laws, the, 167
Perceval, Mr., 15
Percival, Sir John, 144
Perrot, Sir John, 92
Perrott, 97, 98, 100
Perrott's Compositions, iii, 2

Perse, Mr., 227
Petrie Dr., i, vi, xii, xix, 35, 46, 47, 188, 257, 266, 314, 321, 351, 370
Petty Sessions, 257, 290
Pheasants, 14
Phibbs, Mr. Owen, 340
Phillips, Charles, 235
Plantation, the, 6
Plunket, Oliver, 197
Pollnagat, 7
Popish Plot, 140, 157, 158, 199
Population, 280, 284, 286, 305, 308, 357, 370, 379, 380, 381
Portavad, 7
poteen, 339, 341
Premonstratensian Order, 57
Presbyterians, 256
Preston, General, 127
Priors of Holy Cross, 203
Priors of Sligo, 200, 204, 205
Protestant incumbents in the parish of St. John's, 233
Protestants, 136, 139, 176, 202, 206, 226, 230, 236, 238, 255, 256
Ptolemy, ii, 47, 48
Pue's Occurrences, 343
Puritans, 110
Pursuit of Diarmuid and Grainne, 384

Queely, Malachy, 121

Rabbits, 15, 46
Radcliffe, Esq., Thomas, 143, 144, 288
Radcliffs, xvi
Raghley, 7, 282, 359, 358, 374
Rath Ard Creeve, xiv
Rath O'Fiachrach, 40, 45
Rath Righbaird, 45
Rath Righhairt, 314
Rathavritoge, 59
Rathbreasail, Synod of, 320
Rathbroghan, 148, 264

Rathlee, 7
Rathmagurry, 17
Rathvritoge, 29
Red Earl De Burgo 56, 67, 78, 225
Red Hugh, 100, 101, 103
Remonstrants and Anti-Remonstrants, 196
Renehan, Dr., 168
Rerum Hibernicarum Scriptores, 48, 50
Restoration, the, 141-144, 199, 208
Richard de Burgo, the Red Earl, 55, 56, 79
Richard de Rupella, or Capella, 55
Ridge, John, 109
Rinnadoolish, 7
Rivers, i, xiii, 7, 15, 16, 17, 50, 54
Riverstown, 17
Roads, xvii
Roderic, of Cathal Croderg, 62
Rory O'Canannain, 53
Roscommon, i, 1, 2, 4, 6, 7, 10, 11, 16, 33, 49, 60, 80, 109, 113, 127, 133
Rosredheadh, 323, 326
Rosses Point, 357, 358, 362
Rossinver, 110, 233
Rosskeeragh, 7
Rosslare, 329
Rosslee, 368, 379, 380
Round Towers, xii, 375
Royal Irish Academy, 334, 335, 382, 383
Royal Irish Constabulary, 292, 293, 358
Rude Stone Monuments - Ferguson, 45, 351, 352
Rundale, 361
Russell, Colonel, 161, 162

Saint Farannan, 30
Salisbury, 324
Salmon, 265, 266, 267
Sarsfield, 160, 161, 162, 163

Saw Mills, 13
Schomberg, 161-163
Scott, Colonel Edward, 165
Seachnasach, 21
Seals of Sligo town, 237, 239, 240
Sedley, Mr. James, 296
Sessus, the, 13
Sewerage, 304
Sexton, Thomas, Esq., M.P, 251
Seymour, Rev., 256
Sgandal, 21
Shaftesbury Plot, 199
Shancoe, 7
shebeens, 255
Shriff, 332, 335, 339, 356
Siege of Derry, 336
Sir Albert Conyngham, 141, 165
Sir John Perrott Composition, 335
Skreen, 7, 8, 94
slaughter house, 307
Slieve Carbury, 363
Slieve da En, 7, 8, 10, 12, 13, 16, 29, 36, 311, 332
Slieve Gamh, 2, 16, 36, 68
Slieve-an-Ierin, 357
Slieveda-En, 356
Slieve-gan-baistead, 363
Sligeach, i, ii, 15, 17, 32, 35, 51, 75, 248, 265, 266, 329
Sligo Borough Improvement Act of 1869, 265
Sligo Council members, 243
Sligo Depositions, 327
Sligo Journal, 298, 309, 334, 340
Sligo Wood and Iron Company., 310
Sodens, 137, 243, 245, 246, 249, 250
Southern Hy-Nialls, 20
Spain, 164, 194, 196, 209, 259, 266
Springfield Bleach Mills, 264
Sruth-an-ail-an-ard, 364
St. Bernard's *Life of St. Malachy*, 49

St. Ceallach, 350
St. Columba, xvi, 21, 360, 370, 371, 372
St. Farannan, 370, 371
St. Finian of Clonard, xvi
St. John, Sir Oliver, 109
St. Leger, Sir Anthony, 2, 7
St. Molaisse, 349, 369
St. Patrick, v, xvi, 5, 20, 30, 45, 84, 94, 181, 189, 240, 266, 319, 321, 366
St. Patrick's Mountain, 2
St. Sauveur, Captain, 162, 163
Strabo, xv
Strafford, Lord William, 288, 335
Straffords, xvi 110, 126, 149
Streamstown, 7, 33, 35
Streedagh, 7
Street names, 288
striping land, 361
Strongbow, 67
Sweeneys, xvi
Synge Cooper, Edward, 300

Taafes, xvi, 195, 215
Taaffe, Jack, 10
Taaffe, John, 109
Taaffe, Lord, 123, 127
Taaffe, Major-General Lucas, 129, 132
Taaffe, Sir William, 102, 106, 109, 231, 240
Talulla, 349, 369
Taverns, 255
Teeling, Bartholomew, 278, 279
Teffia, i, 5, 23
Templehouse, 13, 16, 17, 109, 120
Thornhill, 17
Tillage, xvii
timber, 12, 13, 28, 61, 116
Tir Tuathail, 2
Tirconnell, 6, 69, 71, 72, 74, 80, 82, 84, 85, 86, 103
Tirechan, - Annotations in the Book of Armagh, 30

Tireragh, i, iv, vii, xvi, xxi, 2, 4, 5, 7, 8, 16, 18, 20, 21, 27, 33, 40, 60, 68, 71, 86, 90, 94, 97, 109, 111, 120, 136, 137, 140, 147, 153, 157, 159, 165, 177, 205, 227, 232, 258, 266, 280, 282, 308, 316, 320, 321, 322, 326, 358, 377, 378
Tirerril, 109, 134
Tirerrill, i, xvi, 2, 4, 7, 8, 16, 33, 69, 74, 80, 86, 90, 94, 97, 109, 110, 136, 137, 147, 153, 173, 175, 191, 205, 230, 232, 280, 320
Tirerrill True Blues, 270
Tituladoes, 136, 137, 138
Tituladoes - names and locations, 137
Townly, Charles, 146
Trappes, 145, 146, 147
Trawativa, 7
Trawnavannoge, 7
Trias Thaumaturga, 320, 328, 360, 363, 366
Trinity Abbey, 323, 332
Trinity College, Dublin, 232
Trout, 16
Truskmore, 382
Tuatha de Danaans, 31
Tuathal Maelgarb, 20
Tuathal Maolgarbh, 21
Tubberconnell, 333
Tubbernailt, 333
Tubberscanavan, 16
Turlough an Fhina O'Donnell, 74
Turlough More, 62, 63, 65, 76
Turlough More O'Conor, 63
Tyrconnell, 25, 52, 53, 54, 104

Ui Duibhduin, 21, 23
Ui Duibhne, 21
Ulster, 6, 12, 21-24, 32, 39, 52, 75, 83, 88, 100, 107, 110, 116, 121, 127

Ulster Journal of Archaeology, 61
Undertakers, 6
Upper Rosses, 312, 360, 361, 374

Vallancey, General, xv
Vereker, Colonel, 278, 279, 280
Vernons, 243, 244, 250, 260
Verschoyle, Mr, 265
Vita Tripartita of St. Patrick i, 5, 22, 30, 266, 359
Volunteer movement, 269

Wakefield, 264, 266
Wakefield's *Account of Ireland*, 12
Wakes, xvii
Walker, Mr of Rathcarrick, 312
Walsh, Rev. Peter, 196
Wandesford, Christopher, 145
Wardships, 231, 232
Water Scheme, 305
Wesley, Rev. John, xix
William III, 159, 160, 161, 162, 169, 198, 199, 209
Williamites, 159, 160, 161, 162, 164, 165
Willowbrook House, 339
Wilson, Joshua, 146, 147, 148, 248
Wood-Martin, viii, xxi, 51, 245, 'History of Sligo', 353
Wynne, Captain James, 336
Wynne, Mr., 15
Wynne, Mr. John, 271
Wynne, Owen, Brigadier-General, 176 336
Wynnes, 242, 243, 244, 271, 272, 273, 274, 276, 282, 290, 295, 300, 304, 329, 333, 334, 336, 337, 338, 339, 341, 346

Young, Arthur, *'Tour in Ireland'* Arthur, 12

Clachan's 'Historic Irish Journeys' series

Travels in Ireland - J.G. Kohl - This is a very readable account by a German visitor of his tour around Ireland immediately before the Great Famine.

Disturbed Ireland – 1881 - Bernard Becker

A series of letters written as the author travelled around the West of Ireland, visiting key places in the 'Land War'. We meet Captain Boycott and other members of the gentry, as well as a range of small farmers and peasants.

A Journey throughout Ireland, During the Spring, Summer and Autumn of 1834 - Henry D. Inglis

Inglis travels Ireland attempting to answer the question, 'is Ireland and improving country?' using discussion with landlords, manufacturers and tenants plus his own insightful observations.

The West Of Ireland: Its Existing Condition and Prospects - Henry Coulter

This is a collection of letters from *Saunders's News-Letter* relating to the condition and prospects of the people of the West of Ireland after the partial failure of the harvests of the early 1860s.

Highways and Byways in Donegal and Antrim - Stephen Gwynn

Take this book with you as you travel around Donegal and the Glens of Antrim and you will find that you journey not only over land, but also over time.

Clachan 'Local History' Series

The West Of Ireland: Its Existing Condition and Prospects - Henry Coulter has been sub-divided for the convenience of local and family historians.

The West of Ireland: Its Existing Condition and Prospects, Part 1, by Henry Coulter

This is an extract from the complete edition dealing with Athlone, Co. Clare and Co. Galway.

The West of Ireland: Its Existing Condition and Prospects, Part 2, by Henry Coulter

This is an extract from the complete edition dealing with Co. Mayo.

The West of Ireland: Its Existing Condition and Prospects, Part 3, by Henry Coulter

The final extract from the complete edition dealing with Counties Co Sligo, Donegal, Leitrim and Roscommon.

Travels in Ireland - J.G. Kohl, has been sub-divided for the convenience of local and family historians.

Travels in Ireland – Part 1, takes us through Edgeworthtown, The Shannon, Limerick, Edenvale, Kilrush and Father Mathew.

Travels in Ireland – Part 2, his journey continues through Tarbet, Tralee, Killarney, Bantry, Cork, Kilkenny and Waterford.

Travels in Ireland – Part 3, this section deals with Wexford, Enniscorthy, Avoca, Glendalough and Dublin.

Travels In Ireland - Part 4 – he goes north for the last part of his journey through Dundalk, Newry, Belfast, The Antrim Coast, Rathlin, The Giant's Causeway.

*   *   *   *   *

A Journey throughout Ireland, During the Spring, Summer and Autumn of 1834 - Henry D. Inglis has also been sub-divided for the convenience of local and family historians.

A Journey throughout Ireland, During the Spring, Summer and Autumn of 1834, Part 1 takes us from Dublin. Through Wexford, Waterford and Cork.

A Journey throughout Ireland, During the Spring, Summer and Autumn of 1834, Part 2 is an account of Kerry, Clare, Limerick and the Shannon and concludes in Athlone.

*   *   *   *   *

Highways and Byways in Donegal and Antrim - Stephen Gwynn, has also been sub-divided for the convenience of local and family historians.

Highways and Byways in Donegal and Antrim Part One: Donegal

Highways and Byways in Donegal and Antrim Part: Two - Derry & Co. Antrim

Aghaidh Achadh Mór, The Face of Aghamore – edited by Joe Byrne. This is a reproduction of a title originally published in 1991 and is of enduring interest to local historians and to those with ancestral roots in East Mayo. It covers such topics as Stone Age archaeology, family history, local hedge schools, O'Carolan's connection with the parish, the Civil War and townland surveys.

Lough Corrib, Its Shores and Islands: with Notices of Lough Mask - by William R. Wilde, first published in 1867. In the words of the author: 'A work intended to … rescue from oblivion, or preserve from desecration, some of the historic monuments of the country'.

A Statistical and Agricultural Survey of the County of Galway – by Hely Dutton

Dutton's survey has resulted in a detailed description of the agricultural conditions and practices of Galway in the early Nineteenth

Century. He has added a detailed chronologies of the leading officials of Galway town and its governance, as well as of the senior churchmen of the bishopric of Tuam and the abbeys, monasteries and convents, of the area.

* * * * *

Ballads and Songs
Songs of the Glens of Antrim, Moiré O'Neill
These Songs of the Glens of Antrim were written by a Glenswoman in the dialect of the Glens, and chiefly for the pleasure of other Glens-people.

The History of Sligo: Town and County Vol. I
By James Hardiman

Special Bicentenary Edition
of this 1819 classic Irish history.

Clachan Publishing
Clachan Publishing, Ballycastle, County Antrim.